The Sacred Books of the East

VEDIC HYMNS

TRANSLATED BY

F. MAX MULLER

PART - I

HYMNS TO THE MARUTS, RUDRA VAYU, AND VATA

Low Price Publications

Delhi-110052

Sales Office:
D.K. Publishers Distributors (P) Ltd.
1, Ansari Road, Darya Ganj,
New Delhi-110002
Phones: 3261465, 3278368
Fax: 091-011-3264368

First Published 1891
First LPP Reprint 1996

ISBN 81-7536-000-3 (Set)
81-7536-032-1 (Vol.XXXII)

Published By:
Low Price Publications
B-2, Vardhaman Palace
Nimri Commercial Centre
Ashok Vihar Phase IV,
Delhi-110052
Phone: 7401672
Fax: 091-011-7138265

Printed at:
D.K. Fine Art Press (P) Ltd.
Delhi-110052

PRINTED IN INDIA

SACRED BOOKS OF THE EAST

TRANSLATED

By VARIOUS ORIENTAL SCHOLARS

AND EDITED BY

F. MAX MÜLLER

VOL. 32

INTRODUCTION.

I finished the Preface to the first volume of my translation of the Hymns to the Maruts with the following words:

'The second volume, which I am now preparing for Press, will contain the remaining hymns addressed to the Maruts. The notes will necessarily have to be reduced to smaller dimensions, but they must always constitute the more important part in a translation or, more truly, in a deciphering of Vedic hymns.'

This was written more than twenty years ago, but though since that time Vedic scholarship has advanced with giant steps, I still hold exactly the same opinion which I held then with regard to the principles that ought to be followed by the first translators of the Veda. I hold that they ought to be decipherers, and that they are bound to justify every word of their translation in exactly the same manner in which the decipherers of hieroglyphic or cuneiform inscriptions justify every step they take. I therefore called my translation the first traduction raisonnée. I took as an example which I tried to follow, though well aware of my inability to reach its excellence, the Commentaire sur le Yasna by my friend and teacher, Eugène Burnouf. Burnouf considered a commentary of 940 pages quarto as by no means excessive for a thorough interpretation of the first chapter of the Zoroastrian Veda, and only those unacquainted with the real difficulties of the Rig-veda would venture to say that its ancient words and thoughts required a less painstaking elucidation than those of the Avesta. In spite of all that has been said and written to the contrary, and with every wish to learn from those who think that the difficulties of a translation of Vedic hymns have been unduly exaggerated by me, I cannot in the least modify what I said twenty, or rather forty years ago, that a mere translation of the Veda, however accurate, intelligible, poetical, and even beautiful, is of absolutely no value for the advancement of Vedic scholarship, unless it is followed by pièces justificatives, that is, unless the translator gives his reasons why he has translated every word about which there can be any doubt, in his own way, and not in any other.

It is well known that Professor von Roth, one of our most eminent Vedic scholars, holds the very opposite opinion. He declares that a metrical translation is the best commentary, and that if he could ever think of a translation of the Rig-veda, he would throw the chief weight, not on the notes, but on the translation of the text. 'A translation,' he writes, 'must speak for itself. As a rule, it only requires a commentary where it is not directly convincing, and where the translator does not feel secure.'

Between opinions so diametrically opposed, no compromise seems possible, and yet I feel convinced that when we come to discuss any controverted passage, Professor von Roth will have to adopt exactly the same principles of translation which I have followed.

On one point, however, I am quite willing to agree with my adversaries, namely, that a metrical rendering would convey a truer idea of the hymns of the Vedic *Ri*shis than a prose rendering. When I had to translate Vedic hymns into German, I have generally, if not always, endeavoured to clothe them in a metrical form. In English I feel unable to do so, but I have no doubt that future scholars will find it possible to add rhythm and even rhyme, after the true meaning of the ancient verses has once been determined. But even with regard to my German metrical translations, I feel in honesty bound to confess that a metrical translation is often an excuse only for an inaccurate translation. If we could make sure of a translator like Rückert, even the impossible might become possible. But as there are few, if any, who, like him, are great alike as scholars and poets, the mere scholar seems to me to be doing his duty better when he produces a correct translation, though in

SACRED BOOKS OF THE EAST

EDITOR: F. Max Müller

These volumes of the Sacred Books of the East Series include translations of all the most important works of the seven non-Christian religions. These have exercised a profound influence on the civilizations of the continent of Asia. The Vedic Brahmanic System claims 21 volumes, Buddhism 10, and Jainism 2; 8 volumes comprise Sacred Books of the Parsees; 2 volumes represent Islam; and 6 the two main indigenous systems of China, thus placing the historical and comparative study of religions on a solid foundation.

VOLUMES

1, 15. THE UPANISADS: in 2 Vols. *F. Max Müller*

2, 14. THE SACRED LAWS OF THE ARYAS: in 2 Vols. *Georg Bühler*

3, 16, 27, 28, 39, 40. THE SACRED BOOKS OF CHINA: in 6 Vols. *James Legge*

4, 23, 31 THE ZEND-AVESTA: in 3 Vols. *James Darmesteter & L. H. Mills*

5, 18, 24, 37, 47. PAHALVI TEXTS: in 5 Vols. *E. W. West*

6, 9. THE QUR'AN: in 2 Vols. *E. H. Palmer*

7. THE INSTITUTES OF VIṢṆU: *J. Jolly*

8. THE BHAGAVADGĪTĀ with the Sanatsujātiya and the Anugitā: *K. T. Telang*

10. THE DHAMMAPADA: *F. Max Müller*
SUTTA-NIPĀTA: *V. Fausböll*

11. BUDDHIST SUTTAS: *T. W. Rhys Davids*

12, 26, 41, 43, 44. THE ŚATAPATHA-BRĀHMAṆA: in 5 Vols. *J. Eggeling*

13, 17, 20. VINAYA TEXTS: in 3 Vols. *T. W. Rhys Davids & H. Oldenberg*

19. THE FO-SHO-HING-TSAN-KING: *Samuel Beal*

21. THE SADDHARMA-PUṆḌARĪKA or THE LOTUS OF THE TRUE LAWS: *H. Kern*

22, 45. JAINA SUTRAS: in 2 Vols. *Hermann Jacobi*

25. MANU: *Georg Bühler*

29, 30. THE GṚIHYA-SŪTRAS: in 2 Vols. *H. Oldenberg & F. Max Müller*

32, 46. VEDIC HYMNS: in 2 Vols. *F. Max Müller & H. Oldenberg*

33. THE MINOR LAW-BOOKS: *J. Jolly*

34, 38. THE VEDĀNTA SŪTRAS: in 2 Vols. with Śaṅkarācārya's Comm.: *G. Thibaut*

35, 36. THE QUESTIONS OF KING MILINDA: in 2 Vols.: *T. W. Rhys Davids*

42. HYMNS OF THE ATHARVA-VEDA: *M. Bloomfield*

48. THE VEDĀNTA-SŪTRAS with Rāmānuja's Śrībhāṣya: *G. Thibaut*

49. BUDDHIST MAHĀYĀNA TEXTS: *E. B. Cowell, F. Max Müller & J. Takakusu*

50. INDEX : *M. Winternitz*

CONTENTS.

SACRED BOOKS OF THE EAST

TRANSLATED

By VARIOUS ORIENTAL SCHOLARS

AND EDITED BY

F. MAX MÜLLER

VOL. 32

INTRODUCTION.

I finished the Preface to the first volume of my translation of the Hymns to the Maruts with the following words:

'The second volume, which I am now preparing for Press, will contain the remaining hymns addressed to the Maruts. The notes will necessarily have to be reduced to smaller dimensions, but they must always constitute the more important part in a translation or, more truly, in a deciphering of Vedic hymns.'

This was written more than twenty years ago, but though since that time Vedic scholarship has advanced with giant steps, I still hold exactly the same opinion which I held then with regard to the principles that ought to be followed by the first translators of the Veda. I hold that they ought to be decipherers, and that they are bound to justify every word of their translation in exactly the same manner in which the decipherers of hieroglyphic or cuneiform inscriptions justify every step they take. I therefore called my translation the first traduction raisonnée. I took as an example which I tried to follow, though well aware of my inability to reach its excellence, the Commentaire sur le Yasna by my friend and teacher, Eugène Burnouf. Burnouf considered a commentary of 940 pages quarto as by no means excessive for a thorough interpretation of the first chapter of the Zoroastrian Veda, and only those unacquainted with the real difficulties of the Rig-veda would venture to say that its ancient words and thoughts required a less painstaking elucidation than those of the Avesta. In spite of all that has been said and written to the contrary, and with every wish to learn from those who think that the difficulties of a translation of Vedic hymns have been unduly exaggerated by me, I cannot in the least modify what I said twenty, or rather forty years ago, that a mere translation of the Veda, however accurate, intelligible, poetical, and even beautiful, is of absolutely no value for the advancement of Vedic scholarship, unless it is followed by pièces justificatives, that is, unless the translator gives his reasons why he has translated every word about which there can be any doubt, in his own way, and not in any other.

It is well known that Professor von Roth, one of our most eminent Vedic scholars, holds the very opposite opinion. He declares that a metrical translation is the best commentary, and that if he could ever think of a translation of the Rig-veda, he would throw the chief weight, not on the notes, but on the translation of the text. 'A translation,' he writes, 'must speak for itself. As a rule, it only requires a commentary where it is not directly convincing, and where the translator does not feel secure.'

Between opinions so diametrically opposed, no compromise seems possible, and yet I feel convinced that when we come to discuss any controverted passage, Professor von Roth will have to adopt exactly the same principles of translation which I have followed.

On one point, however, I am quite willing to agree with my adversaries, namely, that a metrical rendering would convey a truer idea of the hymns of the Vedic *Ri*shis than a prose rendering. When I had to translate Vedic hymns into German, I have generally, if not always, endeavoured to clothe them in a metrical form. In English I feel unable to do so, but I have no doubt that future scholars will find it possible to add rhythm and even rhyme, after the true meaning of the ancient verses has once been determined. But even with regard to my German metrical translations, I feel in honesty bound to confess that a metrical translation is often an excuse only for an inaccurate translation. If we could make sure of a translator like Rückert, even the impossible might become possible. But as there are few, if any, who, like him, are great alike as scholars and poets, the mere scholar seems to me to be doing his duty better when he produces a correct translation, though in prose, than if he has to make any concessions, however small, on the side of faithfulness in favour of rhythm and rhyme.

If a metrical, an intelligible, and, generally speaking, a beautiful translation were all we wanted, why should so many scholars clamour for a new translation, when they have that by Grassmann? It rests on Böhtlingk and Roth's Dictionary, or represents, as we are told, even a more advanced stage of Vedic scholarship. Yet after the well-known contributors of certain critical Journals had repeated ever so many times all that could possibly be said in praise of Grassmann's, and in dispraise of Ludwig's translation, what is the result? Grassmann's metrical translation, the merits of which, considering the time when it was published, I have never been loth to acknowledge, is hardly ever appealed to, while Ludwig's prose rendering, with all its drawbacks, is universally considered as the only scholarlike translation of the Rig-veda now in existence. Time tries the troth in everything.

There is another point also on which I am quite willing to admit that my adversaries are right. 'No one who knows anything about the Veda,' they say, 'would think of attempting a translation of it at present. A translation of the Rig-veda is a task for the next century.' No one feels this more strongly than I do; no one has been more unwilling to make even a beginning in this arduous undertaking. Yet a beginning has to be made. We have to advance step by step, nay, inch by inch, if we ever hope to make a breach in that apparently impregnable fortress. If by translation we mean a complete, satisfactory, and final translation of the whole of the Rig-veda, I should feel inclined to go even further than Professor von Roth. Not only shall we have to wait till the next century for such a work, but I doubt whether we shall ever obtain it. In some cases the text is so corrupt that no conjectural criticism will restore, no power of divination interpret it. In other cases, verses and phrases seem to have been jumbled together by later writers in the most thoughtless manner. My principle therefore has always been, Let us translate what we can. and thus reduce the untranslateable portion to narrower and narrower limits. But in doing this we ought not to be too proud to take our friends, and even our adversaries, into our confidence. A translation on the sic volo sic jubeo principle does far more harm than good. It may be true that a judge, if he is wise, will deliver his judgment, but never propound his reasons. But a scholar is a pleader rather than a judge, and he is in duty bound to propound his reasons.

In order to make the difference between Professor von Roth's translations and my own quite clear, I readily accept the text which he has himself chosen. He took one of the hymns which I had translated with notes (the 165th hymn of the first Ma*nd*ala), and translated it himself metrically, in order to show us what, according to him, a really perfect translation ought to be[a]. Let us then compare the results.

On many points Professor von Roth adopts the same renderings which I had adopted, only that he gives no reasons, while I do so, at least for all debatable passages. First of all, I had tried to prove that the two verses in the beginning, which the Anukrama*n*î ascribes to Indra, should be ascribed to the poet. Professor von Roth takes the same view, but for the rest of the hymn adopts, like myself, that distribution of the verses among the singer, the Maruts, and Indra which the Anukrama*n*î suggests. I mention this because Ludwig has defended the view of the author of the Anukrama*n*î with very strong arguments. He quotes from the Taitt. Br. II, 7, 11, and from the Tâ*nd*ya Br. XXI, 14, 5, the old legend that Agastya made offerings to the Maruts, that, with or without Agastya's consent, Indra seized them, and that the Maruts then tried to frighten Indra away with lightning. Agastya and Indra, however, pacified the Maruts with this very hymn.

Verse 1.

The first verse von Roth translates as follows:

'Auf welcher Fahrt sind insgemein begriffen
Die altersgleichen mitgebornen Marut?
Was wollen sie? woher des Wegs? Das Pfeifen
Der Männer klingt: sie haben ein Begehren.'

[a] Z. D. M. G., 1870, XXIV, p. 301.

Von Roth here translates *s*ubh by Fahrt, journey. But does *s*ubh ever possess that meaning? Von Roth himself in the Dictionary translates *s*ubh by Schönheit, Schmuck, Bereitschaft. Grassmann, otherwise a strict adherent of von Roth, does not venture even to give Bereitschaft, but only endorses Glanz and Pracht. Ludwig, a higher authority than Grassmann, translates *s*ubh by Glanz. I say then that to translate *s*ubh by Fahrt, journey, may be poetical, but it is not scholarlike. On the meanings of *s*ubh I have treated I, 87, 3, note 2. See also Gaedicke, Accusativ, p. 163.

But there comes another consideration. That mimikshire is used in the sense of being joined with splendour, &c. we see from such passages as I, 87, 6, bhânú-bhi*h* sám mimikshire, i. e. 'they were joined with splendour,' and this is said, as in our passage, of the Maruts. Prof. von Roth brings forward no passage where mimikshire is used in the sense in which he uses it here, and therefore I say again, his rendering may be poetical, but it is not scholarlike.

To translate ar*k*anti *s*úshmam by 'das Pfeifen klingt,' is, to say the least, very free. *S*ushma comes, no doubt, from *s*vas, to breathe, and the transition of meaning from breath to strength is intelligible enough. In the Psalms we read (xviii. 15), 'At the blast of the breath of thy nostrils the channels of waters were seen, and the foundations of the earth were discovered.' Again (Job iv. 9), 'By the blast of God they perish, and by the breath of his nostrils are they consumed;' Isaiah xi. 4, 'And with the breath of his lips shall he slay the wicked.' Wrestlers know why breath or wind means strength, and even in the expression 'une œuvre de longue haleine,' the original intention of breath is still perceived. In most passages therefore in the Rig-veda where *s*ushma occurs, and where it means strength, prowess, vigour, we may, if we like, translate it by breath, though it is clear that the poet himself was not always aware of the etymological meaning of the word. Where the sound of *s*ushma is mentioned (IX, 50, 1; X, 3, 6, &c.), it means clearly breath. But when, as in VI, 19, 8, *s*ushma has the adjectives dhanaspr*i*t, sudáksha, we can hardly translate it by anything but strength. When, therefore, von Roth translates *s*ushma by whistling, and ar*k*anti by sounding, I must demur. Whistling is different from breathing, nor do I know of any passage where ar*k* with *s*ushma or with any similar word for sound means simply to sound a whistle. Why not translate, they sing their strength, i.e. the Maruts, by their breathing or howling. proclaim themselves their strength? We find a similar idea in I, 87, 3, 'the Maruts have themselves glorified their greatness.' Neither Grassmann nor Ludwig venture to take *s*ushma in the sense of whistle, or ar*k*anti in the sense of sounding. Bergaigne seems to take v*ri*sha*n*a*h* as a genitive, referring to Indra, 'ils chantent la force à Indra,' which may have been the original meaning, but seems hardly appropriate when the verse is placed in the mouth of Indra himself (Journ. Asiat. 1884, p. 199). *S*ushma never occurs as an adjective. The passages in which von Roth admits *s*ushma as an adjective are not adequate. Does mitgeboren in German convey the meaning of sánî*l*â*h*, 'of the same nest?'

Verse 2.

The second verse contains few difficulties, and is well rendered by von Roth:

'An wessen Sprüchen freuen sich die Jungen?
Wer lenkt die Marut her zu seinem Opfer?
Gleich Falken streichend durch den Raum der Lüfte—
Wie bringt man sie mit Wunscheskraft zum Stehen?'

Verse 3.

The third verse is rendered by von Roth:

'Wie kommt es, Indra, dass du sonst so munter,
Heut' ganz alleine fährst, sag an Gebieter!
Du pflegtest auf der Fahrt mit uns zu plaudern;
Was hast du wider uns, sprich, Rosselenker!'

Von Roth takes kúta*h* in a causal sense, why? I believe that kúta*h* never occurs in that sense in the Rig-veda. If it does, passages should be produced to prove it.

Mấhina*h* can never be translated by 'sonst so munter.' This imparts a modern idea which is not in the original.

*S*ubhânai*h* does not mean auf der Fahrt, and plaudern, adopted from Grassmann, instead of sám p*r*ikk*h*ase, introduces again quite a modern idea. Ludwig calls such an idea 'abgeschmackt,' insipid, which is rather strong, but not far wrong.

Verse 4.

Von Roth:

'Ich liebe Sprüche, Wünsche und die Tränke,
Der Duft steigt auf, die Presse ist gerüstet;
Sie flehen, locken mich mit ihrem Anruf,
Und meine Füchse führen mich zum Mahle.'

It is curious how quickly all difficulties which beset the first line seem to vanish in a metrical translation, but the scholar should face the difficulties, though the poet may evade them.

To translate *s*úshma*h* iyarti by 'der Duft steigt auf,' the flavour of the sacrifices rises up, is more than even Grassmann ventures on. It is simply impossible. Benfey (Entstehung der mit r anlautenden Personalendungen, p. 34) translates: 'My thunderbolt, when hurled by me, moves mightily.'

Again, prábh*r*ita*h* me ádri*h* does not mean die Presse ist gerüstet. Where does Indra ever speak of the stones used for pressing the Soma as my stone, and where does prábh*r*ita*h* ever mean gerüstet?

Verse 5.

Von Roth:

'So werden wir und mit uns unsre Freunde (Nachbarn),
Die freien Männer, unsre Rüstung nehmen,
Und lustig unsre Schecken alsbald schirren.
Du kommst uns eben ganz nach Wunsch, o Indra.'

The first lines are unnecessarily free, and the last decidedly wrong. How can svadhấm ánu hí na*h* babhûtha mean 'Du kommst uns eben ganz nach Wunsch?' Svadhâ does not mean wish, but nature, custom, wont (see I, 6, 4, note 2; and Bergaigne, Journ. Asiat. 1884, p. 207). Babhûtha means 'thou hast become,' not 'thou comest.'

Verse 6.

Von Roth:

'Da war's auch nicht so ganz nach Wunsch, o Maruts,
Als ihr allein mich gegen Ahi schicktet!
Ich aber kräftig, tapfer, unerschrocken,
Ich traf die Gegner alle mit Geschossen.'

The only doubtful line is the last. Von Roth's former translation of nam, to bend away from, to escape from (cf. φεύγω and bhug), seems to me still the right one. He now translates 'I directed my arrow on every enemy,' when the genitive, as ruled by ánamam, requires confirmation. As to sam ádhatta I certainly think von Roth's last interpretation better than his first. In the Dictionary he explained samdhâ in our passage by to implicate. Grassmann translated it by to leave or to desert, Ludwig by to employ. I took it formerly in the usual sense of joining, so that yát mâm ékam samádhatta should be the explanation of svadhâ, the old custom that you should join me when I am alone. But the construction is against this, and I have therefore altered my translation, so that the sense is, Where was that old custom you speak of, when you made me to be alone, i.e. when you left me alone, in the fight with Ahi? The udâtta of ánamam is not irregular, because it is preceded by hi.

Verse 7.

Von Roth:

'Gewaltiges hast du gethan im Bunde
Mit uns, o Held, wir mit vereinter Stärke,
Gewaltiges vermögen wir, du mächtiger
Indra, wenn es uns Ernst ist, ihr Gesellen.'

By this translation, the contrast between 'thou hast done great things with us,' and 'Now let us do great things once more,' is lost. K*rin*ávâma expresses an exhortation, not a simple fact, and on this point Grassmann's metrical translation is decidedly preferable.

Verse 8.

Von Roth:

'V*ri*tra schlug ich mit eigner Kraft, ihr Marut,
Und meine Wuth war's, die so kühn mich machte,

Ich war's, der—in der Faust den Blitz—dem Menschen
Den Zugang bahnte zu den blinkenden Gewässern.'

This is a very good translation, except that there are some syllables too much in the last line. What I miss is the accent on the I. Perhaps this might become stronger by translating:

'Ich schlug mit eigner Kraft den V*ri*tra nieder,
Ich, Maruts, stark durch meinen Zorn geworden;
Ich war's, der blitzbewaffnet für den Menschen
Dem lichten Wasser freie Bahn geschaffen.'

Verse 9.

Von Roth:

'Gewiss, nichts ist was je dir widerstünde,
Und so wie du gibts keinen zweiten Gott mehr,
Nicht jetzt, noch künftig, der was du vermöchte:
Thu' denn begeistert was zu thun dich lüstet.'

Here I doubt about begeistert being a true rendering of prav*ri*ddha, grown strong. As to karishyā́*h* instead of karishyā́, the reading of the MSS., Roth is inclined to adopt my conjecture, as supported by the analogous passage in IV, 30, 23. The form which Ludwig quotes as analogous to karishyam, namely, pravatsyam, I cannot find, unless it is meant for Âpast. *S*rauta S. VI, 27, 2, namo vo*-*stu prâvâtsyam iti Bahv*rikâh*, where however prâvâtsyam is probably meant for prâvâtsam.

Grassmann has understood devátâ rightly, while Roth's translation leaves it doubtful.

Verse 10.

Von Roth:

'So soll der Stärke Vorrang mir allein sein:
Was ich gewagt, vollführ' ich mit Verständniss.
Man kennt mich als den Starken wohl, ihr Marut,
An was ich rühre, Indra der bemeistert's.'

Von Roth has adopted the translation of the second line, which I suggested in a note; Ludwig prefers the more abrupt construction which I preferred in the translation. It is difficult to decide.

Verse 11.

Von Roth:

'Entzückt hat euer Rühmen, mich, ihr Marut,
Das lobenswerthe Wort, das ihr gesprochen,
Für mich—den Indra—für den freud'gen Helden,
Als Freunde für den Freund, für mich—von selbst ihr.'

The last words für mich—von selbst ihr are not very clear, but the same may be said of the original tanvẽ tanũbhi*h*. I still adhere to my remark that tanu, self, must refer to the same person, though I see that all other translators take an opposite view. Non liquet.

Verse 12.

Von Roth:

'Gefallen find ich, wie sie sind, an ihnen,
In Raschheit und in Frische unvergleichlich.
So oft ich euch, Marut, im Schmuck erblickte,
Erfreut' ich mich und freue jetzt an euch mich.'

This is again one of those verses which it is far easier to translate than to construe. Á*kkh*ânta me may mean, they pleased me, but then what is the meaning of *kh*adáyâtha *k*a nûnám, 'may you please me now,' instead of what we should expect, 'you do please me now.' In order to avoid this, I took the more frequent meaning of *kh*ad, to appear, and translated, 'you have appeared formerly, appear to me now.'

To translate ánedya*h* *s*ráva*h* ấ ísha*h* dádhânâ*h*, by 'in Raschheit und in Frische unvergleichlich,' is poetical, but how does it benefit the scholar? I take â dhâ in the sense of bringing or giving, as it is often used; cf. II, 38, 5. This is more compatible with ísha*h*, food, vigour. I am not certain that ănēdўā*h* can mean blameless. Roth s. v. derives ánedya from a-nedya, and nedya from nid. But how we get from nid to nedya, he does not say. He suggests anedyâ*h* or anedya*s*rava*h* as emendations. I suggested anedyam. But I suspect there is something else behind all this. Anedîya*h* may have been intended for 'having nothing coming nearer,' and like an-uttama, might express excellence. Or anedya*h* may have been an adverb, not nearly.

These are mere guesses, and they are rather contradicted by anedyâ*h*, used in the plural, with anavadyâ*h*. Still it is better to point out difficulties than to slur them over by translating 'in Raschheit und in Frische unvergleichlich.' It is possible that both Roth and Sâya*n*a thought that anedya*h* was connected with nedîya*h*; but what scholars want to know is the exact construction of a sentence.

Verse 13.

Von Roth:

'Ist irgendwo ein Fest für euch bereitet,
So fahrt doch her zu unsrer Schaar, ihr Schaaren!
Der Andacht Regungen in uns belebend,
Und werdet Zeugen unserer frommen Werke.'

In this verse there is no difficulty, except the exact meaning of apivâtáyanta*h*, on which I have spoken in note 1.

Verse 14.

Von Roth:

'Wo dankbar huldigend der Dichter lobsingt,
Hier wo uns Mânya's Kunst zusammenführte,
Da kehret ein, ihr Marut, bei den Frommen,
Euch gelten ja des Beters heil'ge Sprüche.'

Prof. von Roth admits that this is a difficult verse. He translates it, but again he does not help us to construe it. Grassmann also gives us a metrical translation, but it differs widely from von Roth's:

'Wenn wie zur Spende euch der Dichter herlockt,
Und der Gesang des Weisen uns herbeizog,' &c.;

and so does Geldner's version, unless we are to consider this as an improved rendering from von Roth's own pen:

'Wenn uns des Mânya Kunst zur Feier herzieht,
Wie Dichter ja zu Festen gerne rufen,' &c.

Here Geldner conjectures duvasyā́ for duvasyā́t, and takes duváse as an infinitive.

Verse 15.

Von Roth:

'Geweiht ist euch der Preis, Marut, die Lieder,
Des Mânya, des Mandârasohns, des Dichters,
Mit Labung kommt herbei, mir selbst zur Stärkung
[Gebt Labung uns und wasserreiche Fluren].'

How tanvẽ vayā́m is to mean 'mir selbst zur Stärkung' has not been explained by von Roth. No doubt tanvẽ may mean mir selbst, and vayâm zur Stärkung; but though this may satisfy a poet, scholars want to know how to construe. It seems to me that Roth and Lanman (Noun-inflection, p. 552) have made the same mistake which I made in taking ishám for an accusative of ish, which ought to be ísham, and in admitting the masculine gender for v*rig*ána in the sense of Flur.

I still take yâsîsh*t*a for the 3 p. sing. of the precative Âtmanepada, like *g*anishîsh*t*a and vanishîsh*t*a. With the preposition áva, yâsisîsh*th*â*h* in IV, 1, 4, means to turn away. With the preposition ā́ therefore yâsîsh*t*a may well mean to turn towards, to bring. If we took yâsîsh*t*a as a 2 p. plur. in the sense of come, we could not account for the long î, nor for the accusative vayâm. We thus get the meaning, 'May this your hymn of praise bring vayā́m,' i. e. a branch, an offshoot or offspring, tanvẽ, for ourselves, ishā́, together with food. We then begin a new sentence: 'May we find an invigorating autumn with quickening rain.' It is true that ishá, as a name of an autumn month, does not occur again in the Rig-veda, but it is found in the *S*atapatha-brâhma*n*a. V*rig*ána, possibly in the sense of people or enemies, we have in VII, 32, 27, á*gñ*âtâ*h* v*rig*ánâ*h*, where Roth reads wrongly á*gñ*âtâ v*rig*ánâ; V, 44, 1 (?); VI, 35, 5. *G*îrádânu also would be an appropriate epithet to ishá.

Professor Oldenberg has sent me the following notes on this difficult hymn. He thinks it is what he calls an Âkhyâna-hymn, consisting of verses which originally formed part of a story in prose. He has treated of this class of hymns in the Zeitschrift der D. M. G. XXXIX, 60 seq. He would prefer to ascribe verses 1 and 2 to Indra, who addresses the Maruts when he meets them as they return from a sacrifice. In this case, however, we should have to accept rîramâma as a pluralis majestaticus, and I doubt whether Indra ever speaks of himself in the plural, except it may be in using the pronoun na*h*.

In verse 4 Professor Oldenberg prefers to take prábh*ri*to me ádri*h* in the sense of 'the stone for pressing the Soma has been brought forth,' and he adds that me need not mean 'my stone,' but 'brought forward for me.' He would prefer to read *s*úshmam iyarti, as in IV, 17, 12; X, 75, 3, though he does not consider this alteration of the text necessary.

Professor Oldenberg would ascribe vv. 13 and 14 to Indra. The 14th verse would then mean, 'After Mânya has brought us (the gods) hither, turn, O Maruts, towards the sage.' Of this interpretation I should like to adopt at all events the last sentence, taking varta for vart-ta, the 2 p. plur. imperat. of v*ri*t, after the Ad class.

The text of the Maitrâya*n*î Sa*m*hitâ, lately published by Dr. L. von Schrœder, yields a few interesting various readings: v. 5, ekam instead of etâñ; v. 12, *s*ravâ instead of *s*rava; and v. 15, vayâ*m*si as a variant for vayâm, which looks like a conjectural emendation.

A comparison like the one we have here instituted between two translations of the same hymn, will serve to show how useless any rendering, whether in prose or poetry, would be without notes to justify the meanings of every doubtful word and sentence. It will, no doubt, disclose at the same time the unsettled state of Vedic scholarship, but the more fully this fact is acknowledged, the better, I believe, it will be for the progress of our studies. They have suffered more than from anything else from that baneful positivism which has done so much harm in hieroglyphic and cuneiform researches. That the same words and names should be interpreted differently from year to year, is perfectly intelligible to every one who is familiar with the nature of these decipherments. What has seriously injured the credit of these studies is that the latest decipherments have always been represented as final and unchangeable. Vedic hymns may seem more easy to decipher than Babylonian and Egyptian inscriptions, and in one sense they are. But when we come to really difficult passages, the Vedic hymns often require a far greater effort of divination than the hymns addressed to Egyptian or Babylonian deities. And there is this additional difficulty that when we deal with inscriptions, we have at all events the text as it was engraved from the first, and we are safe against later modifications and interpolations, while in the case of the Veda, even though the text as presupposed by the Prâti*s*âkhyas may be considered as authoritative for the fifth century B.C., how do we know what changes it may have undergone before that time? Nor can I help giving expression once more to misgivings I have so often expressed, whether the date of the Prâti*s*âkhyas is really beyond the reach of doubt, and whether, if it is, there is no other way of escaping from the conclusion that the whole collection of the hymns of the Rig-veda, including even the Vâlakhilya hymns, existed at that early time[a]. The more I study the hymns, the more I feel staggered at the conclusion at which all Sanskrit scholars seem to have arrived, touching their age. That many of them are old, older than anything else in Sanskrit, their grammar, if nothing else, proclaims in the clearest way. But that some of them are modern imitations is a conviction that forces itself even on the least sceptical minds. Here too we must guard against positivism, and suspend our judgment, and accept correction with a teachable spirit. No one would be more grateful for a way out of the maze of Vedic chronology than I should be, if a more modern date could be assigned to some of the Vedic hymns than the period of the rise of Buddhism. But how can we account for Buddhism without Vedic hymns? In the oldest Buddhist Suttas the hymns of three Vedas are constantly referred to, and warnings are uttered even against the fourth Veda, the Âthabbana[b]. The Upanishads also, the latest productions of the Brâhma*n*a period, must have been known to the founders of Buddhism. From all this there seems to be no escape, and yet I must confess that my conscience quivers in assigning such compositions as the Vâlakhilya hymns to a period preceding the rise of Buddhism in India.

[a] See Preface to the first edition, p. xxxii.

[b] Tuva*t*akasutta, ver. 927; Sacred Books of the East, vol. x, p. 176; Introduction, p. xiii.

I have often been asked why I began my translation of the Rig-veda with the hymns addressed to the Maruts or the Storm-gods, which are certainly not the most attractive of Vedic hymns. I had several reasons, though, as often happens, I could hardly say which of them determined my choice.

First of all, they are the most difficult hymns, and therefore they had a peculiar attraction in my eyes.

Secondly; as even when translated they required a considerable effort before they could be fully understood, I hoped they would prove attractive to serious students only, and frighten away the casual reader who has done so much harm by meddling with Vedic antiquities. Our grapes, I am glad to say, are still sour, and ought to remain so for some time longer.

Thirdly, there are few hymns which place the original character of the so-called deities to whom they are addressed in so clear a light as the hymns addressed to the Maruts or Storm-gods. There can be no doubt about the meaning of the name, whatever difference of opinion there may be about its etymology. Marut and maruta in ordinary Sanskrit mean wind, and more particularly a strong wind, differing by its violent character from vâyu or vâta[a]. Nor do the hymns themselves leave us in any doubt as to the natural phenomena with which the Maruts are identified. Storms which root up the trees of the forest, lightning, thunder, and showers of rain, are the background from which the Maruts in their personal and dramatic character rise before our eyes. In one verse the Maruts are the very phenomena of nature as convulsed by a thunderstorm; in the next, with the slightest change of expression, they are young men, driving on chariots, hurling the thunderbolt, and crushing the clouds in order to win the rain. Now they are the sons of Rudra and P*ri*sni, the friends and brothers of Indra, now they quarrel with Indra and claim their own rightful share of praise and sacrifice. Nay, after a time the storm-gods in India, like the storm-gods in other countries,

[a] The Vâyus are mentioned by the side of the Maruts, Rv. II, 11, 14.

obtain a kind of supremacy, and are invoked by themselves, as if there were no other gods beside them. In most of the later native dictionaries, in the Medinî, Visva, Hemakandra, Amara, and Anekârthadhvanimañgari, Marut is given as a synonym of deva, or god in general [a], and so is Maru in Pâli.

But while the hymns addressed to the Maruts enable us to watch the successive stages in the development of so-called deities more clearly than any other hymns, there is no doubt one drawback, namely, the uncertainty of the etymology of Marut. The etymology of the name is and always must be the best key to the original intention of a deity. Whatever Zeus became afterwards, he was originally conceived as Dyaus, the bright sky. Whatever changes came over Ceres in later times, her first name and her first conception was Sarad, harvest. With regard to Marut I have myself no doubt whatever that Mar-ut comes from the root MAR, in the sense of grinding, crushing, pounding (Sk. m*ri*n*âti, him*s*ayâm, part. mûr*n*a, crushed, like m*ri*dita ; âmúr and âmúri, destroyer). There is no objection to this etymology, either on the ground of phonetic rules, or on account of the meaning of Marut [b]. Professor Kuhn's idea that the name of the Maruts was derived from the root MAR, to die, and that the Maruts were originally conceived as the souls of the departed, and afterwards as ghosts, spirits, winds, and lastly as storms, derives no support from the Veda. Another etymology, proposed in Böhtlingk's Dictionary, which derives Marut from a root MAR, to shine, labours under two disadvantages; first, that there is no such root in Sanskrit [c]; secondly, that the lurid splendour of the lightning is but a subordinate feature in the character of the Maruts. No better etymology having been proposed, I still maintain that the derivation of Marut from MAR, to pound, to smash, is free from any objection, and that the original conception of the Maruts was that of the crushing, smashing, striking, tearing, destroying storms.

---

[a] Anundoram Borooah, Sanskrit Grammar, vol. iii, p. 323.

[b] See Lectures on the Science of Language, vol. ii, p. 357 seq.

[c] Marîki is a word of very doubtful origin.

It is true that we have only two words in Sanskrit formed by the suffix ut, marút and garút in garút-mat, but there are other suffixes which are equally restricted to one or two nouns only. This ut represents an old suffix vat, just as us presupposes vas, in vidus (vidushî, vidush-*t*ara) for vid-vas, nom. vid-vân, acc. vidvâ*m*sam. In a similar way we find side by side párus, knot, párvan, knot, and párvata, stone, cloud, presupposing such forms as *parvat and parut. If then by the side of *parut, we find Latin pars, partis, why should we object to Mars, Martis as a parallel form of Marut? I do not say the two words are identical, I only maintain that the root is the same, and the two suffixes are mere variants. No doubt Marut might have appeared in Latin as Marut, like the neuter cap-ut, capitis (cf. prae-ceps, prae-cipis, and prae-cipitis); but Mars, Martis is as good a derivation from MÆR as Fors, Fortis is from GHÆR[a]. Dr. von Bradke (Zeitschrift der D.M.G., vol. xl, p. 349), though identifying Marut with Mars, proposes a new derivation of Marut, as being originally *Mav*ri*t, which would correspond well with Mavors. But *Mav*ri*t has no meaning in Sanskrit, and seems grammatically an impossible formation.

If there could be any doubt as to the original identity of Marut and Mars, it is dispelled by the Umbrian name çerfo Martio, which, as Grassmann[b] has shown, corresponds exactly to the expression *s*árdha-s mãruta-s, the host of the Maruts. Such minute coincidences can hardly be accidental, though, as I have myself often remarked, the chapter of accidents in language is certainly larger than we suppose. Thus, in our case, I pointed out that we can observe the transition of the gods of storms into the gods of destruction and war, not only in the Veda, but likewise in the mythology of the Polynesians; and yet the similarity in the Polynesian name of Maru can only be accidental[c].

---

[a] Biographies of Words, p. 12.

[b] Kuhn's Zeitschrift, vol. xvi, p. 190; and note to Rv. I, 37, 1, p. 70.

[c] M. M., Science of Religion, p. 255.

And I may add that in Estonian also we find storm-gods called Marutu uled or maro, plural marud[a].

Fourthly, the hymns addressed to the Maruts seemed to me to possess an interest of their own, because, as it is difficult to doubt the identity of the two names, Marut and Mars, they offered an excellent opportunity for watching the peculiar changes which the same deity would undergo when transferred to India on one side and to Europe on the other. Whether the Greek Ares also was an offshoot of the same root must seem more doubtful, and I contented myself with giving the principal reasons for and against this theory[b].

Though these inducements which led me to select the hymns to the Maruts as the first instalment of a translation of the Rig-veda could hardly prevail with me now, yet I was obliged to place them once more in the foreground, because the volume containing the translation of these hymns with very full notes has been used for many years as a text book by those who were beginning the study of the Rig-veda, and was out of print. In order to meet the demand for a book which could serve as an easy introduction to Vedic studies, I decided to reprint the translation of the hymns to the Maruts, and most of the notes, though here and there somewhat abbreviated, and then to continue the same hymns, followed by others addressed to Rudra, Vâyu, and Vâta. My task would, of course, have been much easier, if I had been satisfied with making a selection, and translating those hymns, or those verses only, which afford no very great difficulties. As it is, I have grappled with every hymn and every verse addressed to the Maruts, so that my readers will find in this volume all that the Vedic poets had to say about the Storm-gods.

In order to show, however, that Vedic hymns, though they begin with a description of the most striking phenomena of nature, are by no means confined to that

[a] Bertram, Ilmatar, Dorpat, 1871, p. 98.

[b] Lectures on the Science of Language, vol. ii, p. 357.

narrow sphere, but rise in the end to the most sublime conception of a supreme Deity, I have placed one hymn, that addressed to the Unknown God, at the head of my collection. This will clear me, I hope, of the very unfair suspicion that, by beginning my translation of the Rig-veda with hymns celebrating the wild forces of nature only, I had wished to represent the Vedic religion as nature-worship and nothing else. It will give the thoughtful reader a foretaste of what he may expect in the end, and show how vast a sphere of religious thought is filled by what we call by a very promiscuous name, the Veda.

The MS. of this volume was ready, and the printing of it was actually begun in 1885. A succession of new calls on my time, which admitted of no refusal, have delayed the actual publication till now. This delay, however, has been compensated by one very great advantage. Beginning with hymn 167 of the first Ma*nd*ala, Professor Oldenberg has, in the most generous spirit, lent me his help in the final revision of my translation and notes. It is chiefly due to him that the results of the latest attempts at the interpretation of the Veda, which are scattered about in learned articles and monographs, have been utilised for this volume. His suggestions, I need hardly say, have proved most valuable; and though he should not be held responsible for any mistakes that may be discovered, whether in the translation or in the notes, my readers may at all events take it for granted that, where my translation seems unsatisfactory, Professor Oldenberg also had nothing better to suggest.

Considering my advancing years, I thought I should act in the true interest of Vedic scholarship, if for the future also I divided my work with him. While for this volume the chief responsibility rests with me, the second volume will contain the hymns to Agni, as translated and annotated by him, and revised by me. In places where we really differ, we shall say so. For the rest, we are willing to share both blame and praise. Our chief object is to help forward a critical study of the Veda, and we are well aware that much of what has been done and can be done in the present state of Vedic scholarship, is only a kind of reconnaissance, if not a forlorn hope, to be followed hereafter by a patient siege of the hitherto impregnable fortress of ancient Vedic literature.

F. MAX MÜLLER.

OXFORD:
6th Dec. 1891.

PREFACE

TO THE FIRST EDITION.

What a translation of the Rig-veda ought to be.

When some twenty years ago I decided on undertaking the first edition of the two texts and the commentary of the Rig-veda, I little expected that it would fall to my lot to publish also what may, without presumption, be called the first translation of the ancient sacred hymns of the Brahmans. Such is the charm of deciphering step by step the dark and helpless utterances of the early poets of India, and discovering from time to time behind words that for years seemed unintelligible, the simple though strange expressions of primitive thought and primitive faith, that it required no small amount of self-denial to decide in favour of devoting a life to the publishing of the materials rather than to the drawing of the results which those materials supply to the student of ancient language and ancient religion. Even five and twenty years ago, and without waiting for the publication of Sâya*n*a's commentary, much might have been achieved in the interpretation of the hymns of the Rig-veda. With the MSS. then accessible in the principal libraries of Europe, a tolerably correct text of the Sa*m*hitâ might have been published[1], and these ancient relics of a primitive religion might have been at least partially deciphered and translated in the same way in which ancient inscriptions are deciphered and translated, viz. by a careful collection of all grammatical forms, and by a complete intercomparison of all passages in which the same words and the same phrases occur. When I resolved to devote my leisure to a critical edition of the text and commentary of the Rig-veda rather than to an independent study of that text, it was chiefly from a conviction that the traditional interpretation of the Rig-veda, as embodied in the commentary of Sâya*n*a and other works of a similar character, could not be neglected with impunity, and that sooner or later a complete edition of these works would be recognised as a necessity. It was better therefore to begin with the beginning, though it seemed hard sometimes to spend forty years in the wilderness instead of rushing straight into the promised land.

It is well known to those who have followed my literary publications that I never entertained any exaggerated opinion as to the value of the traditional interpretation of the Veda, handed down in the theological schools of India, and preserved to us in the great commentary of Sâya*n*a. More than twenty years ago, when it required more courage to speak out than now, I expressed my opinion on that subject in no ambiguous language, and was blamed for it by some of those who now speak of Sâya*n*a as a mere drag in the progress of Vedic scholarship. Even a drag, however, is sometimes more conducive to the safe advancement of learning than a whip; and those who recollect the history of Vedic scholarship during the last five and twenty years, know best that, with all its faults and weaknesses, Sâya*n*a's commentary was a sine quâ non for a scholarlike study of the Rig-veda. I do not wonder that others who have more recently entered on that study are inclined to speak disparagingly of the scholastic interpretations of Sâya*n*a. They hardly know how much we all owe to his guidance in effecting our first entrance into this fortress of Vedic language and Vedic religion, and how much even they, without being aware of it, are indebted to that Indian Eustathius. I do not withdraw an opinion which I expressed many years ago, and for which I was much blamed at the time, that Sâya*n*a in many cases teaches us how the Veda ought not to be, rather than how it ought to be understood. But for all that, who does not know how much assistance may be derived from a first translation, even though it is imperfect, nay, how often the very mistakes of our predecessors help us in finding the right track? If now we can walk without Sâya*n*a, we ought to bear in mind that five and twenty years ago we could not have made even our first steps, we could never, at least, have gained a firm footing without his leading strings. If therefore we can now see further than he could, let us not forget that we are standing on his shoulders.

I do not regret in the least the time which I have devoted to the somewhat tedious work of editing the commentary of Sâya*n*a, and editing it according to the strictest rules of critical scholarship. The Veda, I feel convinced, will occupy scholars for centuries to come, and will take and maintain for ever its position as the most ancient of books in the library of mankind. Such a book, and the commentary of such a book, should be edited once for all; and unless some unexpected discovery is made of more ancient MSS., I do not anticipate that any future Bekker or Dindorf will find much to glean for a new edition of Sâya*n*a, or that the text, as restored by me from a collation of the best MSS. accessible in Europe, will ever be materially shaken[a]. It has taken a long time, I know; but those who find fault with me for the delay, should remember that few

[a] Since the publication of the first volume of the Rig-veda, many new MSS. have come before me, partly copied for me, partly lent to me for a time by scholars in India, but every one of them belonged clearly to one of the three families which I have described in my introduction to the first volume of the Rig-veda. In the beginning of the first Ash*t*aka, and occasionally at the beginning of other Ash*t*akas, likewise in the commentary on hymns which were studied by native scholars with particular interest, various readings occur in some MSS., which seem at first to betoken an independent source, but which are in reality mere marginal notes, due to more or less learned students of these MSS. Thus after verse 3 of the introduction one MS. reads: sa prâha n*ri*pati*m*, râ*g*an, sâya*n*âryo mamânu*g*a*h*, sarva*m* vetty esha vedânâ*m* vyâkhyât*ri*tvena, yu*g*yatâm. The same MS., after verse 4, adds: ityukto mâdhavâryе*n*a vîrabukkamahîpati*h*, anva*s*ât sâyâ*n*â*k*âryam vedârthasya prakâ*s*ane.

I had for a time some hope that MSS. written in Grantha or other South-Indian alphabets might have preserved an independent text of Sâya*n*a, but from some specimens of a Grantha MS. collated for me by Mr. Eggeling, I do not think that even this hope is meant to be realised. The MS. in question contains a few independent various readings, such as are found in all MSS., and owe their origin clearly to the jottings of individual students. When at the end of verse 6, I found the independent reading, vyutpannas tâvatâ sarvâ *rik*o vyâkhyâtum arhati, I expected that other various readings of the same character might follow. But after a few additions in the beginning, and those clearly taken from other parts of Sâya*n*a's commentary, nothing of real importance could be gleaned from that MS. I may mention as more important specimens of marginal notes that, before the first puna*h* kîd*ri*sam, on page 44, line 24 (1st ed.), this MS. reads: athavâ ya*gñ*asya devam iti sambandha*h*, ya*gñ*asya prakâ*s*akam ityartha*h*, purohitam iti p*ri*thagvi*s*esha*n*am. And again, page 44, line 26, scholars, if any, have worked for others more than I have done in copying and editing Sanskrit texts, and that after all one cannot give up the whole of one's life to the collation of Oriental MSS. and the correction of proof-sheets. The two concluding volumes have long been ready for Press, and as soon as I can find leisure, they too shall be printed and published *.

In now venturing to publish the first volume of my translation of the Rig-veda, I am fully aware that the fate which awaits it will be very different from that of my edition of the text and commentary. It is a mere contribution towards a better understanding of the Vedic hymns, and though I hope it may give in the main a right rendering of the sense of the Vedic poets, I feel convinced that on many points my translation is liable to correction, and will sooner or later be replaced by a more satisfactory one. It is difficult to explain to those who have not themselves worked at the Veda, how it is that, though we may understand almost every word, yet we find it so difficult to lay hold of a whole chain of connected thought, and to discover expressions that will not throw a wrong shade on the original features of the ancient words of the Veda. We have, on the one hand, to avoid giving to our translations too modern a character, or paraphrasing instead of translating; while, on the other, we cannot retain expressions which, if literally rendered in English or any modern tongue, would have an air of quaintness or absurdity totally foreign to the intention of the ancient poets. There are, as all Vedic scholars know, whole verses which, as yet, yield no sense whatever. There are words the meaning of

before puna*h* kîd*ri*s*am, this MS. adds: athavâ *ri*tvigam *ri*tvigvid (vad) yag*ñ*anirvâhaka*m* hotâra*m* devânâm âhvâtâram; tathâ ratnadhâtamam. In the same line, after ratnânâm, we read rama*n*îyadhanânâ*m* vâ, taken from page 46, line 2. Various readings like these, however, occur on the first sheets only, soon after the MS. follows the usual and recognised text. [This opinion has been considerably modified after a complete collation of this MS., made for me by Dr. Winternitz.] For the later Ash*t*akas, where all the MSS. are very deficient, and where an independent authority would be of real use, no Grantha MS. has as yet been discovered.

* They have since been printed, but the translation has in consequence been delayed.

which we can only guess. Here, no doubt, a continued study will remove some of our difficulties, and many a passage that is now dark, will receive light hereafter from a happy combination. Much has already been achieved by the efforts of European scholars, but much more remains to be done; and our only chance of seeing any rapid progress made lies, I believe, in communicating freely what every one has found out by himself, and not minding if others point out to us that we have overlooked the very passage that would at once have solved our difficulties, that our conjectures were unnecessary, and our emendations wrong. True and honest scholars whose conscience tells them that they have done their best, and who care for the subject on which they are engaged far more than for the praise of benevolent or the blame of malignant critics, ought not to take any notice of merely frivolous censure. There are mistakes, no doubt, of which we ought to be ashamed, and for which the only amende honorable we can make is to openly confess and retract them. But there are others, particularly in a subject like Vedic interpretation, which we should forgive, as we wish to be forgiven. This can be done without lowering the standard of true scholarship or vitiating the healthy tone of scientific morality. Kindness and gentleness are not incompatible with earnestness,—far from it!—and where these elements are wanting, not only is the joy embittered which is the inherent reward of all bonâ fide work, but selfishness, malignity, aye, even untruthfulness, gain the upper hand, and the healthy growth of science is stunted. While in my translation of the Veda and in the remarks that I have to make in the course of my commentary, I shall frequently differ from other scholars, I hope I shall never say an unkind word of men who have done their best, and who have done what they have done in a truly scholarlike, that is, in a humble spirit. It would be unpleasant, even were it possible within the limits assigned, to criticise every opinion that has been put forward on the meaning of certain words or on the construction of certain verses of the Veda. I prefer, as much as possible, to vindicate my own translation, instead of examining the translations of other scholars, whether Indian or European. Sâyaṇa's translation, as rendered into English by Professor Wilson, is before the world. Let those who take an interest in these matters compare it with the translation here proposed. In order to give readers who do not possess that translation, an opportunity of comparing it with my own, I have for a few hymns printed that as well as the translations of Langlois and Benfey[a] on the same page with my own. Everybody will thus be enabled to judge of the peculiar character of each of these translations. That of Sâya*n*a represents the tradition of India; that of Langlois is the ingenious, but thoroughly uncritical, guess-work of a man of taste; that of Benfey is the rendering of a scholar, who has carefully worked out the history of some words, but who assigns to other words either the traditional meaning recorded by Sâya*n*a, or a conjectural meaning which, however, would not always stand the test of an inter-comparison of all passages in which these words occur. I may say, in general, that Sâya*n*a's translation was of great use to me in the beginning, though it seldom afforded help for the really difficult passages. Langlois' translation has hardly ever yielded real assistance, while I sincerely regret that Benfey's rendering does not extend beyond the first Ma*nd*ala.

It may sound self-contradictory, if, after confessing the help which I derived from these translations, I venture to call my own the first translation of the Rig-veda. The word translation, however, has many meanings. I mean by translation, not a mere rendering of the hymns of the Rig-veda into English, French, or German, but a full account of the reasons which justify the translator in assigning such a power to such a word, and such a meaning to such a sentence. I mean by translation a real deciphering, a work like that which Burnouf performed in his first attempts at a translation of the Avesta,—a traduction raisonnée, if such an expression may be used. Without such a process,

The first traduction raisonnée.

[a] In the new edition, Langlois' translation has been omitted, and those of Ludwig and Grassmann have been inserted occasionally only.

without a running commentary, a mere translation of the ancient hymns of the Brahmans will never lead to any solid results. Even if the translator has discovered the right meaning of a word or of a whole sentence, his mere translation does not help us much, unless he shows us the process by which he has arrived at it, unless he places before us the pièces justificatives of his final judgment. The Veda teems with words that require a justification; not so much the words which occur but once or twice, though many of these are difficult enough, but rather the common words and particles, which occur again and again, which we understand to a certain point, and can render in a vague way, but which must be defined before they can be translated, and before they can convey to us any real and tangible meaning. It was out of the question in a translation of this character to attempt either an imitation of the original rhythm or metre, or to introduce the totally foreign element of rhyming. Such translations may follow by and by: at present a metrical translation would only be an excuse for an inaccurate translation.

While engaged in collecting the evidence on which the meaning of every word and every sentence must be founded, I have derived the most important assistance from the Sanskrit Dictionary of Professors Böhtlingk and Roth, which has been in course of publication during the last sixteen years. The Vedic portion of that Dictionary may, I believe, be taken as the almost exclusive work of Professor Roth, and as such, for the sake of brevity, I shall treat it in my notes. It would be ungrateful were I not to acknowledge most fully the real benefit which this publication has conferred on every student of Sanskrit, and my only regret is that its publication has not proceeded more rapidly, so that even now years will elapse before we can hope to see it finished. But my sincere admiration for the work performed by the compilers of that Dictionary does not prevent me from differing, in many cases, from the explanations of Vedic words given by Professor Roth. If I do not always criticise Professor Roth's explanations when I differ from him, the reason is obvious. A dictionary without a full translation of each passage, or without a justification of the meanings assigned to each word, is only a preliminary step to a translation. It represents a first classification of the meanings of the same word in different passages, but it gives us no means of judging how, according to the opinion of the compiler, the meaning of each single word should be made to fit the general sense of a whole sentence. I do not say this in disparagement, for, in a dictionary, it can hardly be otherwise; I only refer to it in order to explain the difficulty I felt whenever I differed from Professor Roth, and was yet unable to tell how the meaning assigned by him to certain words would be justified by the author of the Dictionary himself. On this ground I have throughout preferred to explain every step by which I arrived at my own renderings, rather than to write a running criticism of Professor Roth's Dictionary. My obligations to him I like to express thus once for all, by stating that whenever I found that I agreed with him, I felt greatly assured as to the soundness of my own rendering, while whenever I differed from him, I never did so without careful consideration.

The works, however, which I have hitherto mentioned, though the most important, are by no means the only ones that have been of use to me in preparing my translation of the Rig-veda. The numerous articles on certain hymns, verses, or single words occurring in the Rig-veda, published by Vedic scholars in Europe and India during the last thirty years, were read by me at the time of their publication, and have helped me to overcome difficulties, the very existence of which is now forgotten. If I go back still further, I feel that in grappling with the first and the greatest of difficulties in the study of the Veda, I and many others are more deeply indebted than it is possible to say, to one whose early loss has been one of the greatest misfortunes to Sanskrit scholarship. It was in Burnouf's lectures that we first learnt what the Veda was, and how it should form the foundation of all our studies. Not only did he most liberally communicate to his pupils his valuable MSS., and teach us how to use these tools, but the results of his own experience were freely placed at our service, we were warned against researches which he knew to be useless, we were encouraged in undertakings which he knew to be full of promise. His minute analysis of long passages of Sâya*n*a, his independent interpretations of the text of the hymns, his comparisons between the words and grammatical forms, the thoughts and legends of the Veda and Avesta, his brilliant divination checked by an inexorable sense of truth, and his dry logical method enlivened by sallies of humour and sparks of imaginative genius, though not easily forgotten, and always remembered with gratitude, are now beyond the reach of praise or blame. Were I to criticise what he or other scholars have said and written many years ago, they might justly complain of such criticism. It is no longer necessary to prove that Nâbhânedish*th*a cannot mean 'new relatives,' or that there never was a race of Etendhras, or that the angels of the Bible are in no way connected with the Angiras of the Vedic hymns; and it would, on the other hand, be a mere waste of time, were I to attempt to find out who first discovered that in the Veda deva does not always mean divine, but sometimes means brilliant. In fact, it could not be done.

In a new subject like that of the interpretation of the Veda, there are certain things which everybody discovers who has eyes to see. Their discovery requires so little research that it seems almost an insult to say that they were discovered by this or that scholar. Take, for instance, the peculiar pronunciation of certain words, rendered necessary by the requirements of Vedic metres. I believe that my learned friend Professor Kuhn was one of the first to call general attention to the fact that semivowels must frequently be changed into their corresponding vowels, and that long vowels must sometimes be pronounced as two syllables. It is clear, however, from Rosen's notes to the first Ash*t*aka (I, 1, 8), that he, too, was perfectly aware of this fact, and that he recognised the prevalence of this rule, not only with regard to semivowels (see his note to RV. I, 2, 9) and long vowels which are the result of Sandhi, but likewise with regard to others that occur in the body of a word. 'Animadverte,' he writes, 'tres syllabas postremas vocis adhvarâ*n*âm dipodiae iambicae munus sustinentes, penultima syllaba praeter iambi prioris arsin, thesin quoque sequentis pedis ferente. Satis frequentia sunt, in hac praesertim dipodiae iambicae sede, exempla syllabae natura longae in tres moras productae. De qua re nihil quidem memoratum invenio apud Pingalam aliosque qui de arte metrica scripserunt: sed numeros ita, ut modo dictum est, computandos esse, taciti agnoscere videntur, quum versus una syllaba mancus non eos offendat.'

Now this is exactly the case. The ancient grammarians, as we shall see, teach distinctly that where two vowels have coalesced into one according to the rules of Sandhi, they may be pronounced as two syllables; and though they do not teach the same with regard to semivowels and long vowels occurring in the body of the word, yet they tacitly recognise that rule, by frequently taking its effects for granted. Thus in Sûtra 950 of the Prâti*s*âkhya, verse IX, 111, 1, is called an Atyash*t*i, and the first pâda is said to consist of twelve syllables. In order to get this number, the author must have read,

ayâ ru*k*â hari*n*yâ punâna*h*.

Immediately after, verse IV, 1, 3, is called a Dh*ri*ti, and the first pâda must again have twelve syllables. Here therefore the author takes it for granted that we should read,

sakhe sakhâyam abhy â vav*ri*tsva[a].

No one, in fact, with any ear for rhythm, whether *S*aunaka and Pingala, or Rosen and Kuhn, could have helped observing these rules when reading the Veda. But it is quite a different case when we come to the question as to which words admit of such protracted pronunciation, and which do not. Here one scholar may differ from another according to the view he takes of the character of Vedic metres, and here one has to take careful account of the minute and

[a] See also Sûtra 937 seq. I cannot find any authority for the statement of Professor Kuhn (Beiträge, vol. iii, p. 114) that, according to the Rik-prâti*s*âkhya, it is the first semivowel that must be dissolved, unless he referred to the remarks of the commentator to Sûtra 973.

ingenious observations contained in numerous articles by Professors Kuhn, Bollensen, Grassmann, and others.

With regard to the interpretation of certain words and sentences too, it may happen that explanations which have taxed the ingenuity of some scholars to the utmost, seem to others so self-evident that they would hardly think of quoting anybody's name in support of them, to say nothing of the endless and useless work it would entail, were we obliged always to find out who was the first to propose this or that interpretation. It is impossible here to lay down general rules:—each scholar must be guided by his own sense of justice to others and by self-respect. Let us take one instance. From the first time that I read the fourth hymn of the Rig-veda, I translated the fifth and sixth verses:

> utá bruvantu na*h* nída*h* ní*h* anyáta*h* *k*it ârata,
> dádhânâ*h* índre ít dúva*h*,
> utá na*h* su-bhágân arí*h* vo*k*éyu*h* dasma k*r*ish*t*áya*h*,
> syấma ít índrasya *s*árma*n*i.

1. Whether our enemies say, 'Move away elsewhere, you who offer worship to Indra only,'—

2. Or whether, O mighty one, all people call us blessed: may we always remain in the keeping of Indra.

About the general sense of this passage I imagined there could be no doubt, although one word in it, viz. arí*h*, required an explanation. Yet the variety of interpretations proposed by different scholars is extraordinary. First, if we look to Sâya*n*a, he translates:

1. May our priests praise Indra! O enemies, go away from this place, and also from another place! Our priests (may praise Indra), they who are always performing worship for Indra.

2. O destroyer of enemies! may the enemy call us possessed of wealth; how much more, friendly people! May we be in the happiness of Indra!

Professor Wilson did not follow Sâya*n*a closely, but translated:

1. Let our ministers, earnestly performing his worship,

exclaim: Depart, ye revilers, from hence and every other place (where he is adored).

2. Destroyer of foes, let our enemies say we are prosperous: let men (congratulate us). May we ever abide in the felicity (derived from the favour) of Indra.

Langlois translated:

1. Que (ces amis), en fêtant Indra, puissent dire: Vous, qui êtes nos adversaires, retirez-vous loin d'ici.

2. Que nos ennemis nous appellent des hommes fortunés, placés que nous sommes sous la protection d'Indra.

Stevenson translated:

1. Let all men again join in praising Indra. Avaunt ye profane scoffers, remove from hence, and from every other place, while we perform the rites of Indra.

2. O foe-destroyer, (through thy favour) even our enemies speak peaceably to us, the possessors of wealth; what wonder then if other men do so. Let us ever enjoy the happiness which springs from Indra's blessing.

Professor Benfey translated:

1. And let the scoffers say, They are rejected by every one else, therefore they celebrate Indra alone.

2. And may the enemy and the country proclaim us as happy, O destroyer, if we are only in Indra's keeping[a].

Professor Roth, s.v. anyáta*h*, took this word rightly in the sense of 'to a different place,' and must therefore have taken that sentence 'move away elsewhere' in the same sense in which I take it. Later, however, s.v. ar, he corrected himself, and proposed to translate the same words by 'you neglect something else.'

Professor Bollensen (Orient und Occident, vol. ii, p. 462),

[a] I add Grassmann's and Ludwig's renderings:

Grassmann: Mag spottend sagen unser Feind:
'Kein Andrer kümmert sich um sie;
Drum feiern Indra sie allein.'
Und glücklich mögen, Mächtiger!
Die Freundesstämme nennen uns,
Nur wenn wir sind in Indra's Schutz.

Ludwig: Mögen unsere tadler sagen: sogar noch anderes entgeht euch (dabei), wenn ihr dienst dem Indra tut.

Oder möge uns glückselige nennen der fromme, so nennen, o wundertäter, die (fünf) völker, in Indra's schutze mögen wir sein.

adopting to a certain extent the second rendering of Professor Roth in preference to that of Professor Benfey, endeavoured to show that the 'something else which is neglected,' is not something indefinite, but the worship of all the other gods, except Indra.

It might, no doubt, be said that every one of these translations contains something that is right, though mixed up with a great deal that is wrong; but to attempt for every verse of the Veda to quote and to criticise every previous translation, would be an invidious and useless task. In the case just quoted, it might seem right to state that Professor Bollensen was the first to see that arí*h* should be joined with k*ri*sh*t*áya*h*, and that he therefore proposed to alter it to arî*h*, as a nom. plur. But on referring to Rosen, I find that, to a certain extent, he had anticipated Professor Bollensen's remark, for though, in his cautious way, he abstained from altering the text, yet he remarked: Possitne arí*h* pluralis esse, contracta terminatione, pro araya*h*?

After these preliminary remarks I have to say a few words on the general plan of my translation.

Plan of the work.

I do not attempt as yet a translation of the whole of the Rig-veda, and I therefore considered myself at liberty to group the hymns according to the deities to which they are addressed. By this process, I believe, a great advantage is gained. We see at one glance all that has been said of a certain god, and we gain a more complete insight into his nature and character. Something of the same kind had been attempted by the original collectors of the ten books, for it can hardly be by accident that each of them begins with hymns addressed to Agni, and that these are followed by hymns addressed to Indra. The only exception to this rule is the eighth Ma*nd*ala, for the ninth being devoted to one deity, to Soma, can hardly be accounted an exception. But if we take the Rig-veda as a whole, we find hymns, addressed to the same deities, not only scattered about in different books, but not even grouped together when they occur in one and the same book. Here, as we lose nothing by giving up the old arrangement, we are surely at liberty, for our own purposes, to put together such hymns as have a common object, and to place before the reader as much material as possible for an exhaustive study of each individual deity.

I give for each hymn the Sanskrit original[a] in what is known as the Pada text, i. e. the text in which all words (pada) stand by themselves, as they do in Greek or Latin, without being joined together according to the rules of Sandhi. The text in which the words are thus joined, as they are in all other Sanskrit texts, is called the Sa*m*hitâ text. Whether the Pada or the Sa*m*hitâ text be the more ancient, may seem difficult to settle. As far as I can judge, they seem to me, in their present form, the product of the same period of Vedic scholarship. The Prâti*s*âkhyas, it is true, start from the Pada text, take it, as it were, for granted, and devote their rules to the explanation of those changes which that text undergoes in being changed into the Sa*m*hitâ text. But, on the other hand, the Pada text in some cases clearly presupposes the Sa*m*hitâ text. It leaves out passages which are repeated more than once, while the Sa*m*hitâ text always repeats these passages; it abstains from dividing the termination of the locative plural su, whenever in the Sa*m*hitâ text, i e. according to the rules of Sandhi, it becomes shu; hence nadîshu, a*g*ishu, but ap-su; and it gives short vowels instead of the long ones of the Sa*m*hitâ, even in cases where the long vowels are justified by the rules of the Vedic language. It is certain, in fact, that neither the Pada nor the Sa*m*hitâ text, as we now possess them, represents the original text of the Veda. Both show clear traces of scholastic influences. But if we try to restore the original form of the Vedic hymns, we shall certainly arrive at some kind of Pada text rather than at a Sa*m*hitâ text; nay, even in their present form, the original metre and rhythm of the ancient hymns of the *Ri*shis are far more perceptible when the words are divided, than when we join them together throughout according to the rules of Sandhi. Lastly, for practical purposes, the Pada text is far superior to the Sa*m*hitâ text in which the final

[a] This is left out in the second edition.

and initial letters, that is, the most important letters of words, are constantly disguised, and liable therefore to different interpretations. Although in some passages we may differ from the interpretation adopted by the Pada text, and although certain Vedic words have, no doubt, been wrongly analysed and divided by *S*âkalya, yet such cases are comparatively few, and where they occur, they are interesting as carrying us back to the earliest attempts of Vedic scholarship. In the vast majority of cases the divided text, with a few such rules as we have to observe in reading Latin, nay, even in reading Pâli verses, brings us certainly much nearer to the original utterance of the ancient *Ri*shis than the amalgamated text.

Principles of criticism.

The critical principles by which I have been guided in editing for the first time the text of the Rig-veda, require a few words of explanation, as they have lately been challenged on grounds which, I think, rest on a complete misapprehension of my previous statements on this subject.

As far as we are able to judge at present, we can hardly speak of various readings in the Vedic hymns, in the usual sense of that word. Various readings to be gathered from a collation of different MSS., now accessible to us, there are none. After collating a considerable number of MSS., I have succeeded, I believe, in fixing on three representative MSS., as described in the preface to the first volume of my edition of the Rig-veda. Even these MSS. are not free from blunders,—for what MS. is?—but these blunders have no claim to the title of various readings. They are lapsus calami, and no more; and, what is important, they have not become traditional [a].

[a] Thus X, 101, 2, one of the Pada MSS. (P 2) reads distinctly ya*gñ*ám prá k*rin*uta sakhâya*h*, but all the other MSS. have nayata, and there can be little doubt that it was the frequent repetition of the verb k*ri* in this verse which led the writer to substitute k*rin*uta for nayata. No other MS., as far as I am aware, repeats this blunder. In IX, 86, 34, the writer of the same MS. puts ra*g*asi instead of dhâvasi, because his eye was caught by râ*g*â in the preceding line. X, 16, 5, the same MS. reads sá*m* ga*kkh*asva instead of ga*kkh*atâm, which is supported by S 1, S 2, P 1, while S 3 has a peculiar and more important reading, ga*kkh*atât. X, 67, 6, the same MS. P 2 has ví *k*akartha instead of ví *k*akarta.

A number of various readings which have been gleaned from Pandit Târâ-

The text, as deduced from the best MSS. of the Sa*m*hitâ text, can be controlled by four independent checks. The first is, of course, a collation of the best MSS. of the Sa*m*hitâ text.

The second check to be applied to the Sa*m*hitâ text is a comparison with the Pada text, of which, again, I possessed at least one excellent MS., and several more modern copies.

The third check was a comparison of this text with Sâya*n*a's commentary, or rather with the text which is presupposed by that commentary. In the few cases where the Pada text seemed to differ from the Sa*m*hitâ text, a note was added to that effect, in the various readings of my edition; and the same was done, at least in all important cases, where Sâya*n*a clearly followed a text at variance with our own.

The fourth check was a comparison of any doubtful passage with the numerous passages quoted in the Prâti*s*âkhya.

These were the principles by which I was guided in the critical restoration of the text of the Rig-veda, and I believe I may say that the text as printed by me is more correct than any MS. now accessible, more trustworthy than the text followed by Sâya*n*a, and in all important points identically the same with that text which the authors of the

---

nâtha's Tulâdânâdipaddhati (see Trübner's American and Oriental Literary Record, July 31, 1868) belong to the same class. They may be due either to the copyists of the MSS. which Pandit Târânâtha used while compiling his work, or they may by accident have crept into his own MS. Anyhow, not one of them is supported either by the best MSS. accessible in Europe, or by any passage in the Prâti*s*âkhya.

RV. IX, 11, 2,	read	devayu	instead of	devayu*h* [b].
IX, 11, 4,	,,	ar*k*ata	,,	ar*k*ate [b].
IX. 14, 2,	,,	yadî sabandhava*h*	,,	yaddîptabandhava*h* [b].
IX, 16, 3,	,,	anaptam	,,	anuptam [b].
IX, 17, 2,	,,	suvânâsa	,,	stuvânâsa [b].
IX, 21, 2,	,,	prav*rin*vanto	,,	prav*rin*vato [b].
IX, 48, 2,	,,	sa*m*v*ri*kta	,,	sa*m*yukta [b].
IX, 49, 1,	,,	no [x] pâm	,,	no yâm [b].
IX, 54, 3,	,,	sûrya*h*	,,	sûryam [b].
IX, 59, 3,	,,	sîda ni	,,	sîdati [b].

[b] As printed by Pandit Târânâtha.

Prâti*s*âkhya followed in their critical researches in the fifth or sixth century before our era. I believe that starting from that date our text of the Veda is better authenticated, and supported by a more perfect apparatus criticus, than the text of any Greek or Latin author, and I do not think that diplomatic criticism can ever go beyond what has been achieved in the constitution of the text of the Vedic hymns.

Aufrecht's Romanised Reprint of the Rig-veda.

Far be it from me to say that the editio princeps of the text thus constituted was printed without mistakes. But most of these mistakes are mistakes which no attentive reader could fail to detect. Cases like II, 35, 1, where *góg*ishat instead of *gó*shishat was printed three times, so as to perplex even Professor Roth, or II, 12, 14, where *s*asamânám occurs three times instead of *s*a*s*amânám, are, I believe, of rare occurrence. Nor do I think that, unless some quite unexpected discoveries are made, there ever will be a new critical edition, or, as we call it in Germany, a new recension of the hymns of the Rig-veda. If by collating new MSS., or by a careful study of the Prâti*s*âkhya, or by conjectural emendations, a more correct text could have been produced, we may be certain that a critical scholar like Professor Aufrecht would have given us such a text. But after carefully collating several MSS. of Professor Wilson's collection, and after enjoying the advantage of Professor Weber's assistance in collating the MSS. of the Royal Library at Berlin, and after a minute study of the Prâti*s*âkhya, he frankly states that in the text of the Rig-veda, transcribed in Roman letters, which he printed at Berlin, he followed my edition, and that he had to correct but a small number of misprints. For the two Ma*nd*alas which I had not yet published, I lent him the very MSS. on which my edition is founded; and there will be accordingly but few passages in these two concluding Ma*nd*alas, which I have still to publish, where the text will materially differ from that of his Romanised transcript.

No one, I should think, who is at all acquainted with the rules of diplomatic criticism, would easily bring himself to touch a text resting on such authorities as the text of the Rig-veda. What would a Greek scholar give, if he could say of Homer that his text was in every word, in every syllable, in every vowel, in every accent, the same as the text used by Peisistratos in the sixth century B.C.! A text thus preserved in its integrity for so many centuries, must remain for ever the authoritative text of the Veda.

To remove, for instance, the eleven hymns 49–59 in the eighth Ma*nd*ala from their proper place, or count them by

Vâlakhilya Hymns.

themselves as Vâlakhilya [a] hymns, seems to me, though no doubt perfectly harmless, little short of a critical sacrilege. Why Sâya*n*a does not explain these hymns, I confess I do not know [b]; but whatever the reason was, it was not because they did not exist at his time, or because he thought them spurious. They are regularly counted in Kâtyâyana's Sarvânukrama, though here the same accident has happened. One commentator, Sha*d*guru*s*ishya, the one most commonly used, does not explain them; but another commentator, *G*agannâtha, does explain them, exactly as they occur in the Sarvânukrama, only leaving out hymn 58. That these hymns had something peculiar in the eyes of native scholars, is clear enough. They may for a time have formed a separate collection, they

---

[a] The earliest interpretation of the name Vâlakhilya is found in the Taittirîya-âra*n*yaka, I, 23. We are told that Pra*g*âpati created the world, and in the process of creation the following interlude occurs:

sa tapo*s*tapyata. sa tapas taptvâ *s*arîram adhûnuta. tasya yan mâ*m*sam âsît tato*s*ru*n*â*h* ketavo vâtara*s*anâ *ri*shaya udatish*th*an. ye nakhâ*h*, te vaikhânasâ*h*. ye bâlâ*h*, te bâlakhilyâ*h*.

He burned with emotion. Having burnt with emotion, he shook his body. From what was his flesh, the *Ri*shis, called Aru*n*as, Ketus, and Vâtara*s*anas, sprang forth. His nails became the Vaikhânasas, his hairs the Bâlakhilyas.

The author of this allegory therefore took bâla or vâla in vâlakhilya, not in the sense of child, but identified it with bâla, hair.

The commentator remarks with regard to tapas: nâtra tapa upavâsâdirûpam, ki*m*tu srash*t*avya*m* vastu kîd*ri*sam iti paryâlo*k*anarûpam.

[b] A similar omission was pointed out by Professor Roth. Verses 21–24 of the 53rd hymn of the third Ma*nd*ala, which contain imprecations against Vasish*th*a, are left out by the writer of a Pada MS., and by a copyist of Sâya*n*a's commentary, probably because they both belonged to the family of Vasish*th*a. See my first edition of the Rig-veda, vol. ii, p. lvi, Notes.

may have been considered of more modern origin [a]. I shall go even further than those who remove these hymns from the place which they have occupied for more than two thousand years. I admit they disturb the regularity both of the Ma*nd*ala and the Ash*t*aka divisions, and I have pointed out myself that they are not counted in the ancient Anukrama*n*îs ascribed to *S*aunaka; (History of Ancient Sanskrit Literature, p. 220.) But, on the other hand, verses taken from these hymns occur in all the other Vedas [b]: they are mentioned by name in the Brâhma*n*as (Ait. Br. V, 15; VI, 24), the Âra*n*yakas (Ait. Âr. V, 10, p. 445), and the Sûtras (Â*s*v. *S*rauta Sûtras, VIII, 2, 3), while they are never included in the manuscripts of Pari*s*ish*t*as or Khilas or apocryphal hymns, nor mentioned by Kâtyâyana as mere Khilas in his Sarvânukrama. Eight [c] of them are mentioned in the B*ri*haddevatâ, without any allusion to their apocryphal character:

Parâ*n*y ash*t*au tu sûktâny *ri*shî*n*âm tigmate*g*asâm,
Aindrâ*n*y atra tu sha*d*vi*m*sa*h* pragâtho bahudaivata*h*.
*Ri*g antyâgner a*k*ety agni*h* sûryam antyapado *g*agau.
Praska*n*vas *k*a p*ri*shadhras *k*a prâdâd yad vastu ki*mk*ana
Bhûrîd iti tu sûktâbhyâm akhilam parikîrtitam.
Aindrâ*n*y ubhayam ity atra sha*l* âgneyât parâ*n*i tu.

'The next eight hymns belong to *Ri*shis of keen intellect [d]; they are addressed to Indra, but the 26th Pragâtha

[a] Sâya*n*a (RV. X, 88, 18) quotes these hymns as Vâlakhilya-sa*m*hitâ. In the Mahâbhârata XII, 59; 110 seq. the Vâlakhilyas are called the ministers of King Vainya, whose astrologer was Garga, and his domestic priest *S*ukra; see Kern, B*ri*hat-sa*m*hitâ, transl. p. 11.

[b] This is a criterion of some importance, and it might have been mentioned, for instance, by Professor Bollensen in his interesting article on the Dvipadâ Virâ*g* hymns ascribed to Parâ*s*ara (I, 65-70) that not a single verse of them occurs in any of the other Vedas.

[c] Sâya*n*a in his commentary (RV. X, 27, 15) speaks of eight, while in the Ait. Âr. V, 10, the first six are quoted (containing fifty-six verses, comm.), as being used together for certain sacrificial purposes.

[d] Lest *S*aunaka be suspected of having applied this epithet, tigmate*g*as, to the Vâlakhilyas in order to fill the verse (pâdapûra*n*ârtham), I may point out that the same epithet is applied to the Vâlakhilyas in the Maitry-upanishad 2, 3. The nom. plur. which occurs there is tigmate*g*asâ*h*, and the commentator remarks: tigmate*g*asas tîvrate*g*aso x tyûr*g*itaprabhâvâ*h*; te*g*asâ ityeva*m*vidha eta*kkh*âkhâsaṅketapâ*th*as *kh*ândasa*h* sarvatra. See also Maitr. Up. VI, 29.

(VIII, 54, 3–4, which verses form the 26th couplet, if counting from VIII, 49, 1) is addressed to many gods. The last verse (of these eight hymns), VIII, 56, 5, beginning with the words a*k*ety agni*h*, is addressed to Agni, and the last foot celebrates Sûrya. Whatsoever Praska*n*va and P*ri*shadhra gave (or, if we read p*ri*shadhrâya, whatever Praska*n*va gave to P*ri*shadhra), all that is celebrated in the two hymns beginning with bhûrît. After the hymn addressed to Agni (VIII, 60), there follow six hymns addressed to Indra, beginning with ubhayam.'

But the most important point of all is this, that these hymns, which exist both in the Pada and Sa*m*hitâ texts, are quoted by the Prâti*s*âkhya, not only for general purposes, but for special passages occurring in them, and nowhere else. Thus in Sûtra 154, hetáya*h* is quoted as one of the few words which do not require the elision of a following short a. In order to appreciate what is implied by this special quotation, it is necessary to have a clear insight into the mechanism of the Prâti*s*âkhya. Its chief object is to bring under general categories the changes which the separate words of the Pada text undergo when joined together in the Ârshî Sa*m*hitâ, and to do this with the utmost brevity possible. Now the Sandhi rules, as observed in the Sa*m*hitâ of the Rig-veda, are by no means so uniform and regular as they are in later Sanskrit, and hence it is sometimes extremely difficult to bring all the exceptional cases under more or less general rules. In our passage the author of the Prâti*s*âkhya endeavours to comprehend all the passages where an initial a in the Veda is not elided after a final e or o. In ordinary Sanskrit it would be always elided, in the Sa*m*hitâ it is sometimes elided, and sometimes not. Thus the Prâti*s*âkhya begins in Sûtra 138 by stating that if the short a stands at the beginning of a pâda or foot, it is always elided. Why it should be always elided in the very place where the metre most strongly requires that it should be pronounced, does not concern the author of the Prâti*s*âkhya. He is a statistician, not a grammarian, and he therefore simply adds in Sûtra 153 the only three exceptional passages where the a, under these very circumstances, happens to be not elided. He then proceeds in Sûtra 139 to state that a is elided even in the middle of a pâda, provided it be light, followed by y or v, and these y or v, again followed by a light vowel. Hence the Sa*m*hitâ writes te ˟vădan, so˟yăm, but not sîkshanto˟vratam, for here the a of avratam is heavy; nor mitramaho˟vadyât, for here the a following the v is heavy

Then follows again an extension of this rule, viz. in the case of words ending in âvo. After these, a short a, even if followed by other consonants besides y or v, may be elided, but the other conditions must be fulfilled, i. e. the short a must be light, and the vowel of the next syllable must again be light. Thus the Sa*m*hitâ writes indeed gâvo ˟bhĭta*h*, but not gâvo˟gman, because here the a is heavy, being followed by two consonants.

After this, a more general rule is given, or, more correctly, a more comprehensive observation is made, viz. that under all circumstances initial a is elided, if the preceding word ends in aye, aya*h*, ave, or ava*h*. As might be expected, however, so large a class must have numerous exceptions, and these can only be collected by quoting every word ending in these syllables, or every passage in which the exceptions occur. Before these exceptions are enumerated, some other more or less general observations are made, providing for the elision of initial a. Initial a, according to Sûtra 142, is to be elided if the preceding word is va*h*, and if this va*h* is preceded by â, na, pra, kva, *k*itra*h*, savitâ, eva, or ka*h*. There is, of course, no intelligible reason why, if these words precede va*h*, the next a should be elided. It is a mere statement of facts, and, generally speaking, these statements are minutely accurate. There is probably no verse in the whole of the Rig-veda where an initial a after va*h* is elided, unless these very words precede, or unless some other observation has been made to provide for the elision of the a. For instance, in V, 25, 1, we find va*h* preceded by a*kkh*a, which is not among the words just mentioned, and here the Sa*m*hitâ does not elide the a of agnim, which follows after va*h*. After all these more or less general observations as to the elision of an initial a are thus exhausted, the author of the Prâti*s*âkhya descends into particulars, and gives lists, first, of words the initial a of which is always elided; secondly, of words which, if preceding, require under all circumstances the elision of the initial a of the next word, whatever may have been said to the contrary in the preceding Sûtras. Afterwards, he gives a number of passages which defy all rules, and must be given on their own merits, and as they stand in the Sa*m*hitâ. Lastly, follow special exceptions to the more or less general rules given before. And here, among these special exceptions, we see that the author of the Prâti*s*âkhya finds it necessary to quote a passage from a Vâlakhilya hymn in which hetáya*h* occurs, i.e. a word ending in aya*h*, and where, in defiance of Sûtra 141, which required the elision of a following initial a under all circumstances (sarvathâ), the initial a of asya is not elided; VIII, 50, 2, Sa*m*hitâ, *s*atấnîkâ hetáyo asya. It might be objected that the Prâti*s*âkhya only quotes hetáya*h* as an exceptional word, and does not refer directly to the verse in the Vâlakhilya hymn. But fortunately hetáya*h* occurs but twice in the whole of the Rig-veda; and in the other passage where it occurs, I, 190, 4, neither the rule nor the exception as to the elision of an initial a, could apply. The author of the Prâti*s*âkhya therefore makes no distinction between the Vâlakhilya and any other hymns of the Rig-veda, and he would have considered his phonetic statistics equally at fault, if it had been possible to quote one single passage from the hymns VIII, 49 to 59, as contravening his observations, as if such passages had been alleged from the hymns of Vasish*th*a or Vi*s*vâmitra.

It would lead me too far, were I to enter here into similar cases in support of the fact that the Prâti*s*âkhya makes no distinction between the Vâlakhilya and any other hymns of the Rig-veda-sa*m*hitâ [a]. But I doubt whether the bearing of this fact has ever been fully realised. Here we see that the absence of the elision of a short a which follows after a word ending in aya*h*, was considered of sufficient importance

[a] The Prâti*s*âkhya takes into account both the *S*âkala and Bâshkala *s*âkhâs, as may be seen from Sûtra 1057.

to be recorded in a special rule, because in most cases the Sa*m*hitâ elides an initial a, if preceded by a word ending in aya*h*. What does this prove? It proves, unless all our views on the chronology of Vedic literature are wrong, that in the fifth century B.C. at least, or previously rather to the time when the Prâti*s*âkhya was composed, both the Pada and the Sa*m*hitâ texts were so firmly settled that it was impossible, for the sake of uniformity or regularity, to omit one single short a; and it proves à fortiori, that the hymn in which that irregular short a occurs, formed at that time part of the Vedic canon. I confess I feel sometimes frightened by the stringency of this argument, and I should like to see a possibility by which we could explain the addition, not of the Vâlakhilya hymns only, but of other much more modern sounding hymns, at a later time than the period of the Prâti*s*âkhyas. But until that possibility is shown, we must abide by our own conclusions; and then I ask, who is the critic who would dare to tamper with a canon of scripture of which every iota was settled before the time of Cyrus, and which we possess in exactly that form in which it is described to us by the authors of the Prâti*s*âkhyas? I say again, that I am not free from misgivings on the subject, and my critical conscience would be far better satisfied if we could ascribe the Prâti*s*âkhya and all it presupposes to a much later date. But until that is done, the fact remains that the two divergent texts, the Pada and Sa*m*hitâ, which we now possess, existed, as we now possess them, previous to the time of the Prâti*s*âkhya. They have not diverged nor varied since, and the vertex to which they point, starting from the distance of the two texts as measured by the Prâti*s*âkhya, carries us back far beyond the time of *S*aunaka, if we wish to determine the date of the first authorised collection of the hymns, both in their Pada and in their Sa*m*hitâ form.

Instances abound, if we compare the Pada and Sa*m*hitâ texts, where, if uniformity between the two texts had been the object of the scholars of the ancient Parishads, the lengthening or shortening of a vowel would at once have removed the apparent discordance between the two traditional texts. Nor should it be supposed that such minute discordances between the two, as the length or shortness of a vowel, were always rendered necessary by the requirements of the metre, and that for that reason the ancient students or the later copyists of the Veda abstained from altering the peculiar spelling of words, which seemed required by the exigencies of the metre in the Sa*m*hitâ text, but not in the Pada text. Though this may be true in some cases it is not so in all. There are short vowels in the Sa*m*hitâ where, according to grammar, we expect long vowels, and where, according to metre, there was no necessity for shortening them. Yet in these very places all the MSS. of the Sa*m*hitâ text give the irregular short, and all the MSS. of the Pada text the regular long vowel, and the authors of the Prâti*s*âkhyas bear witness that the same minute difference existed at their own time, nay, previous to their own time. In VII, 60, 12, the Sa*m*hitâ text gives:

iyá*m* deva puróhitir yuvábhyâ*m* yag*ñ*éshu mitrâvaru*n*âv akârî.

This primacy, O (two) gods, was made for you two, O Mitra and Varu*n*a, at the sacrifices!

Here it is quite clear that deva is meant for a dual, and ought to have been devâ or devau. The metre does not require a short syllable, and yet all the Sa*m*hitâ MSS. read devă, and all the Pada MSS. read devâ; and what is more important, the authors of the Prâti*s*âkhya had to register this small divergence of the two texts, which existed in their time as it exists in our own [a].

Nor let it be supposed, that the writers of our MSS. were so careful and so conscientious that they would, when copying MSS., regulate every consonant or vowel according to the rules of the Prâti*s*âkhya. This is by no means the case. The writers of Vedic MSS. are on the whole more accurate than the writers of other MSS., but their learning does not seem to extend to a knowledge of the minute rules of the Prâti*s*âkhya, and they will commit

[a] See Prâti*s*âkhya, Sûtra 309 seqq., where several more instances of the same kind are given. I should prefer to take devapurohiti as one word, but that was not the intention of the authors of the Sa*m*hitâ and Pada texts.

occasionally the very mistakes against which they are warned by the Prâti*s*âkhya. Thus the Prâti*s*âkhya (Sûtra 799) warns the students against a common mistake of changing vaiya*s*va into vayya*s*va, i. e. by changing ai to a, and doubling the semivowel y. But this very mistake occurs in S 2, and another MS. gives vaiyya*s*va. See p. lvi.

Aufrecht's mistakes.

If these arguments are sound, and if nothing can be said against the critical principles by which I have been guided in editing the text of the Rig-veda, if the fourfold check, described above, fulfils every requirement that could be made for restoring that text which was known to Sâya*n*a, and which was known, probably 2000 years earlier, to the authors of the Prâti*s*âkhyas, what can be the motives, it may fairly be asked, of those who clamour for a new and more critical edition, and who imagine that the editio princeps of the Rig-veda will share the fate of most of the editiones principes of the Greek and Roman classics, and be supplanted by new editions founded on the collation of other MSS.? No one could have rejoiced more sincerely than I did at the publication of the Romanised transliteration of the Rig-veda, carried out with so much patience and accuracy by Professor Aufrecht. It showed that there was a growing interest in this, the only true Veda; it showed that even those who could not read Sanskrit in the original Devanâgarî, wished to have access to the original text of these ancient hymns; it showed that the study of the Veda had a future before it like no other book of Sanskrit literature. My learned friend Professor Aufrecht has been most unfairly charged with having printed this Romanised text me insciente vel invito. My edition is publici juris, like any edition of Homer or Plato, and anybody might, with proper acknowledgment, have reprinted it, either in Roman or Devanâgarî letters. But far from keeping me in ignorance of his plan, Professor Aufrecht applied to me for the loan of the MSS. of the two Ma*nd*alas which I had not yet published, and I lent them to him most gladly, because, by seeing them printed at once, I felt far less guilty in delaying the publication of the last volumes of my edition of the text and commentary. Nor could anything have been more honourable than the way in which Professor Aufrecht speaks of the true relation of his Romanised text to my edition. That there are misprints, and I, speaking for myself, ought to say mistakes also, in my edition of the Rig-veda, I know but too well; and if Professor Aufrecht, after carefully transcribing every word, could honestly say that their number is small, I doubt whether other scholars will be able to prove that their number is large. I believe I may with the same honesty return Professor Aufrecht's compliment, and considering the great difficulty of avoiding misprints in Romanised transcripts, I have always thought and I have always said that his reprint of the hymns of the Veda is remarkably correct and accurate. What, however, I must protest against, and what, I feel sure, Professor Aufrecht himself would equally protest against, is the supposition, and more than supposition of certain scholars, that wherever this later Latin transcript differs from my own Devanâgarî text, Professor Aufrecht is right, and I am wrong; that his various readings rest on the authority of new MSS., and constitute in fact a new recension of the Vedic hymns. Against this supposition I must protest most strongly, not for my own sake, but for the sake of the old book, and, still more, for the sake of the truth. No doubt it is natural to suppose that where a later edition differs from a former edition, it does so intentionally; and I do not complain of those who, without being able to have recourse to MSS. in order to test the authority of various readings, concluded that wherever the new text differed from the old, it was because the old text was at fault. In order to satisfy my own conscience on this point, I have collated a number of passages where Professor Aufrecht's text differs from my own, and I feel satisfied that in the vast majority of cases, I am right and he is wrong, and that his variations do not rest on the authority of MSS. I must not shrink from the duty of making good this assertion, and I therefore proceed to an examination of such passages as have occurred to me on occasionally referring to his text, pointing out the readings both where he is right, and where he is wrong. The differences between the two texts may appear trifling, but I shall not avail myself of that plea. On the contrary, I quite agree with those scholars who hold that in truly critical scholarship there is nothing trifling. Besides, it is in the nature of the case that what may, by a stretch of the word, be called various readings in the Veda, must be confined to single letters or accents, and can but seldom extend to whole words, and never to whole sentences. I must therefore beg my readers to have patience while I endeavour to show that the text of the Rig-veda, as first published by me, though by no means faultless, was nevertheless not edited in so perfunctory a manner as some learned critics seem to suppose, and that it will not be easy to supplant it either by a collation of new MSS., such as are accessible at present, or by occasional references to the Prâti*s*âkhya.

I begin with some mistakes of my own, mistakes which I might have avoided, if I had always consulted the Prâti*s*âkhya, where single words or whole passages of the Veda are quoted. Some of these mistakes have been removed by Professor Aufrecht, others, however, appear in his transcript as they appear in my own edition.

I need hardly point out passages where palpable misprints in my edition have been repeated in Professor Aufrecht's text. I mean by palpable misprints, cases where a glance at the Pada text or at the Sa*m*hitâ text or a reference to Sâya*n*a's commentary would show at once what was intended. Thus, for instance, in VI, 15, 3, v*ri*dhé, as I had printed in the Sa*m*hitâ, was clearly a misprint for v*ri*dhó, as may be seen from the Pada, which gives v*ri*dhá*h*, and from Sâya*n*a. Here, though Professor Aufrecht repeats v*ri*dhé, I think it hardly necessary to show that the authority of the best MSS. (S 2 alone contains a correction of v*ri*dhó to v*ri*dhé) is in favour of v*ri*dhá*h*, whatever we may think of the relative value of these two readings. One must be careful, however, in a text like that of the Vedic hymns, where the presence or absence of a single letter or accent begins to become the object of the most learned and painstaking discussions, not to claim too large an indulgence for misprints. A misprint in the Sa*m*hitâ, if repeated in the Pada, or if admitted even in the commentary of Sâya*n*a, though it need not be put down to the editor's deplorable ignorance, becomes yet a serious matter, and I willingly take all the blame which is justly due for occasional accidents of this character. Such are, for instance, II, 12, 14, *s*asamânám instead of *s*a*s*amânám; I, 124, 4, *s*udhyúva*h*, in the Pada, instead of *s*undhyúva*h*; and the substitution in several places of a short u instead of a long û in such forms as *s*û*s*ávâma, when occurring in the Pada; cf. I, 166, 14; 167, 9.

It is clear from the Prâti*s*âkhya, Sûtra 819 and 163, 5, that the words ûtī́ índra in IV, 29, 1, should not be joined together, but that the hiatus should remain. Hence ûtī́ndra, as printed in my edition and repeated in Professor Aufrecht's, should be corrected, and the hiatus be preserved, as it is in the fourth verse of the same hymn, ûtī́ itthā́. MSS. S 1, S 3 are right; in S 2 the words are joined.

It follows from Sûtra 799 that to double the y in vaiya*s*va is a mistake, but a mistake which had to be pointed out and guarded against as early as the time of the Prâti*s*âkhya. In VIII, 26, 11, therefore, vaiyya*s*vásya, as printed in my edition and repeated in Professor Aufrecht's, should be changed to vaiya*s*vásya. MSS. S 1, S 3 are right, likewise P 1, P 2; but S 2 has the double mistake vayya*s*vásya, as described in the Prâti*s*âkhya; another MS. of Wilson's has vaiyy. The same applies to VIII, 23, 24, and VIII, 24, 23. P 1 admits the mistaken spelling vayya*s*va.

Some corrections that ought to be made in the Padapâ*th*a only, as printed in my edition, are pointed out in a note to Sûtra 738 of the Prâti*s*âkhya. Thus, according to Sûtra 583, 6, *s*rûyā́*h* in the Pada text of II, 10, 2, should be changed to *s*ruyā́*h*. MSS. P 1, P 2 have the short u.

In V, 7, 8, I had printed *s*ú*k*i*h* shma, leaving the a of shma short in accordance with the Prâti*s*âkhya, Sûtra 514, where a string of words is given before which sma must not be lengthened, and where under No. 11 we find yásmai. Professor Aufrecht has altered this, and gives the â as long, which is wrong. The MSS. S 1, S 2, S 3 have the short a.

Another word before which sma ought not to be lengthened is mấvate. Hence, according to Sûtra 514, 14, I ought not to have printed in VI, 65, 4, shmâ mấvate, but shma mấvate. Here Professor Aufrecht has retained the long â, which is wrong. MSS. S 1, S 2, S 3 have the short a.

It follows from Sûtra 499 that in I, 138, 4, we should not lengthen the vowel of sú. Hence, instead of asyấ û shû́ *n*a úpa sâtáye, as printed in my edition and repeated by Professor Aufrecht, we should read asyấ û shú *n*a úpa sâtáye. S 1, S 2, S 3 have short u[a].

In VII, 31, 4, I had by mistake printed viddhí instead of viddhī́. The same reading is adopted by Professor Aufrecht (II, p. 24), but the authority of the Prâti*s*âkhya, Sûtra 445, can hardly be overruled. S 1, S 2, S 3 have viddhī́.

While in cases like these, the Prâti*s*âkhya is an authority which, as far as I can judge, ought to overrule the authority of every MS., however ancient, we must in other cases depend either on the testimony of the best MSS. or be guided, in fixing on the right reading, by Sâya*n*a and the rules of grammar. I shall therefore, in cases where I cannot consider Professor Aufrecht's readings as authoritative improvements, have to give my reasons why I adhere to the readings which I had originally adopted.

In V, 9, 4, I had printed by mistake purú yó instead of purū́ yó. I had, however, corrected this misprint in my edition of the Prâti*s*âkhya, 393, 532. Professor Aufrecht decides in favour of purú with a short u, but against the authority of the MSS., S 1, S 2, S 3, which have purū́.

---

[a] In the same verse, I, 138, 4, the shu in ó shú tvâ should not be lengthened, for there is no rule, as far as I can see, in the Prâti*s*âkhya that would require the lengthening of sú before tvâ. See Prâti*s*âkhya, 491.

It was certainly a great mistake of mine, though it may seem more excusable in a Romanised transcript, that I did not follow the writers of the best MSS. in their use of the Avagraha, or, I should rather say, of that sign which, as far as the Veda is concerned, is very wrongly designated by the name of Avagraha. Avagraha, according to the Prâti*s*âkhya, never occurs in the Sa*m*hitâ text, but is the name given to that halt, stoppage, or pause which in the Pada text separates the component parts of compound words. That pause has the length of one short vowel, i.e. one mâtrâ. Of course, nothing is said by the Prâti*s*âkhya as to how the pause should be represented graphically, but it is several times alluded to as of importance in the recitation and accentuation of the Veda. What we have been in the habit of calling Avagraha is by the writers of certain MSS. of the Sa*m*hitâ text used as the sign of the Viv*ri*tti or hiatus. This hiatus, however, is very different from the Avagraha, for while the Avagraha has the length of one mâtrâ, the Viv*ri*tti or hiatus has the length of ¼ mâtrâ, if the two vowels are short; of ½ mâtrâ, if either vowel is long; of ¾ mâtrâ, if both vowels are long. Now I have several times called attention to the fact that though this hiatus is marked in certain MSS. by the sign ऽ, I have in my edition omitted it, because I thought that the hiatus spoke for itself and did not require a sign to attract the attention of European readers; while, on the contrary, I have inserted that sign where MSS. hardly ever use it, viz. when a short initial a is elided after a final e or o; (see my remarks on pp. 36, 39, of my edition of the Prâti*s*âkhya.) Although I thought, and still think, that this use of the sign ऽ is more useful for practical purposes, yet I regret that, in this one particular, I should have deviated from the authority of the best MSS., and caused some misunderstandings on the part of those who have made use of my edition. If, for instance, I had placed the sign of the Viv*ri*tti, the ऽ, in its proper place, or if, at least, I had not inserted it where, as we say, the initial a has been elided after e or o, Professor Bollensen would have seen at once that the authors of the Prâti*s*âkhyas fully agree with him in looking on this change, not as an elision, but as a contraction. If, as sometimes happens, final o or e remain unchanged before initial short a, this is called the Pa*ñk*âla and Prâ*k*ya padav*ri*tti (Sûtra 137). If, on the contrary, final o or e become one (ekîbhavati) with the initial short a, this is called the Abhinihita sandhi (Sûtra 138). While the former, the hiatus of the Pa*ñk*âla and Eastern schools, is marked by the writers of several MSS. by the sign ˣ, the Abhinihita sandhi, being a sandhi, is not marked by any sign[a].

I, 3, 12. rấ*g*ati (Aufr. p. 2) instead of râ*g*ati (M. M. vol. i, p. 75) is wrong.

I, 7, 9. ya éka*h* (Aufr. p. 5) should be yá éka*h* (M. M. vol. i, p. 110), because the relative pronoun is never without an accent. The relative particle yathâ may be without an accent, if it stands at the end of a pâda; and though there are exceptions to this rule, yet in VIII, 21, 5, where Professor Aufrecht gives yáthâ, the MSS. are unanimous in favour of yathâ (M. M. vol. iv, p. 480). See Phi*t*-sûtra, ed. Kielhorn, p. 54.

I, 10, 11. â tű (Aufr. p. 7) should be ấ tű (M. M. vol. i, p. 139), because â is never without the accent.

I, 10, 12. *g*úsh*t*â*h*, which Professor Aufrecht specially mentions as having no final Visarga in the Pada, has the Visarga in all the MSS., (Aufr. p. 7, M. M. vol. i, p. 140.)

I, 11, 4. kávir (Aufr. p. 7) should be kavír (M. M. vol. i, p. 143).

I, 22, 8, read rấdhâ*m*si.

I, 40, 1 and 6. There is no excuse for the accent either on tvémahe or on vó*k*ema, while sá*k*âñ in I, 51, 11, ought to have the accent on the first syllable.

I, 49, 3. Rosen was right in not eliding the a in divó ántebhya*h*. S 1, S 2, S 3 preserve the initial a, nor does the Prâti*s*âkhya anywhere provide for its suppression.

I, 54, 8. kshátram (Aufr. p. 46) is a mere misprint for kshatrám.

---

[a] As to the system or want of system, according to which the Abhinihita sandhi takes place in the Sa*m*hitâ, see p. xlviii seq.

I, 55, 7. vandana*s*rúd (Aufr. p. 47) instead of vandana*s*rud (M. M. vol. i, p. 514) is wrong.

I, 57, 2. samā́*s*îta instead of samá*s*îta had been corrected in my reprint of the first Ma*nd*ala, published at Leipzig. See Bollensen, Zeitschrift der D. M. G., vol. xxii, p. 626.

I, 61, 7, read víshnu*h*; I, 64, 2, read *s*ú*k*aya*h*; I, 64, 5, read dhū́taya*h*.

I, 61, 16. Rosen had rightly printed hâriyo*g*anâ with a long â both in the Sa*m*hitâ and Pada texts, and I ought not to have given the short a instead. All the MSS., S 1, S 2, S 3, P 1, and P 2, give the long â. Professor Aufrecht gives the short a in the Pada, which is wrong.

I, 67, 2 (4). vidántîm (M. M. vol. i, p. 595) is perfectly right, as far as the authority of the MSS. and of Sâya*n*a is concerned, and should not have been altered to vindántîm (Aufr. p. 57).

I, 72, 2, read vatsám; I, 72, 6, read pa*s*ū́n; I, 76, 3, read dhákshy; I, 82, 1, read yadā́.

I, 83, 3. Rosen was right in giving ása*m*yatta*h*. I gave ása*m*yata*h* on the authority of P 1, but all the other MSS. have tt.

I, 84, 1. indra (Aufr. p. 68) cannot have the accent on the first syllable, because it does not stand at the beginning of a pâda (M. M. vol. i, p. 677). The same applies to índra, VI, 41, 4, (Aufr. p. 429) instead of indra (M. M. vol. iii, p. 734); to ágne, I, 140, 12, (Aufr. p. 130) instead of agne (M. M. vol. ii, p. 133). In III, 36, 3, on the contrary, indra, being at the head of a pâda, ought to have the accent on the first syllable, índra (M. M. vol. ii, p. 855), not indra (Aufr. p. 249). The same mistake occurs again, III, 36, 10 (Aufr. p. 250); IV, 32, 7, (Aufr. p. 305); IV, 32, 12, (Aufr. p. 305); VIII, 3, 12, (Aufr. vol. ii, p. 86). In V, 61, 1, nara*h* should have no accent; whereas in VII, 91, 3, it should have the accent on the first syllable. In VIII, 8, 19, vipanyû should have no accent, and Professor Aufrecht gives it correctly in the notes, where he has likewise very properly removed the Avagraha which I had inserted.

I, 88, 1, read yâta (M. M. vol. i, p. 708), not yâtha (Aufr. p. 72).

I, 90, 1, read *rig*unîtí; I, 94, 11, read yavasấdo (M. M. vol. i, p. 766), not yayasấdo (Aufr. p. 80).

I, 118, 9. abhibhû́tim (Aufr. p. 105) instead of abhíbhûtim (M. M. vol. i, p. 957) cannot be right, considering that in all other passages abhíbhûti has the accent on the second syllable. S 1, S 2, S 3 have the accent on the i.

I, 128, 4. gh*ri*ta*s*rîr (Aufr. p. 117) instead of gh*ri*ta*s*rî́r (M. M. vol. ii, p. 52) is wrong.

I, 144, 2, read párîv*ri*tâ*h* (M. M. vol. ii, p. 155) instead of parî́v*ri*tâ*h* (Aufr. p. 133).

I, 145, 5. Professor Aufrecht (p. 134) gives upamasyấm, both in the Sa*m*hitâ and Pada texts, as having the accent on the last syllable. I had placed the accent on the penultimate, (Pada, upa-másyâm, vol. ii, p. 161,) and whatever may be the reading of other MSS., this is the only possible accentuation. S 1, S 2, S 3 have the right accent.

I, 148, 4. pûrû́*n*i (Aufr. p. 136) instead of purû́*n*i (M. M. vol. ii, p. 170) does not rest, as far as I know, on the authority of any MSS. S 1, S 2, S 3 have purû́*n*i.

I, 151, 7. ga*kkh*atho (Aufr. p. 137) should be gá*kkh*atho (M. M. vol. ii, p. 181).

I, 161, 12. All the Pada MSS. read prá ábravît, separating the two words and accentuating each. Though the accent is irregular, yet, considering the peculiar construction of the verse, in which prá and pró are used as adverbs rather than as prepositions, I should not venture with Professor Aufrecht (p. 144) to write prá abravît. The MSS. likewise have ấ á*g*agan, I, 161, 4; and prá ágâ*h*, VIII, 48, 2, not prá agâ*h*, as Aufrecht gives in his second edition.

I, 163, 11. dhrá*g*îman (Aufr. p. 147) instead of dhrá*g*îmân (M. M. vol. ii, p. 245) is wrong.

I, 163, 13. gamyâ (Aufr. p. 148) instead of gamyấ (M. M. vol. ii, p. 246) is wrong.

I, 164, 17, read páre*n*a (M. M. vol. ii, p. 259) instead of paré*n*a (Aufr. p. 149).

I, 164, 38. The first *k*ikyú*h* ought to have the accent, and has it in all the MSS., (Aufr. p. 151, M. M. vol. ii, p. 278.)

I, 165, 5. A mere change of accent may seem a small

matter, yet it is frequently of the highest importance in the interpretation of the Veda. Thus in I, 165, 5, I had, in accordance with the MSS. S 1, S 2, S 3, printed étân (vol. ii, p. 293) with the accent on the first syllable. Professor Aufrecht alters this into etấn (p. 153), which, no doubt, would be the right form, if it were intended for the accusative plural of the pronoun, but not if it is meant, as it is here, for the accusative plural of éta, the speckled deer of the Maruts.

I, 165, 15. yâsish*t*a (Aufr. p. 154) instead of yâsîsh*t*a (M. M. vol. ii, p. 298) is not supported by any MS.

I, 169, 7, instead of patayánta (Aufr. p. 158), read patáyanta (M. M. vol. ii, p. 322).

I, 174, 7. kúyâvâ*k*am (Aufr. p. 162) should be kúyavâ*k*am (M. M. vol. ii, p. 340).

I, 177, 1. yuktấ, which I had adopted from MS. S 3 (prima manu), is not supported by other MSS., though P 2 reads yuttkấ. Professor Aufrecht, who had retained yuktấ in the text, has afterwards corrected it to yuktvấ, and in this he was right. In I, 177, 2, gâhi for yâhi is wrong.

I, 188, 4. astri*n*an (Aufr. p. 171) instead of ast*ri*n*an (M. M. vol. ii, p. 395) can only be a misprint.

II, 29, 6. kártâd (Aufr. p. 203) instead of kartấd (M. M. vol. ii, p. 560) is wrong.

II, 40, 4. *k*akra (Aufr. p. 214) instead of *k*akrá (M. M. vol. ii, p. 614) is wrong.

III, 7, 7. gu*h* (Aufr. p. 226) instead of gú*h* (M. M. vol. ii, p. 666) is wrong; likewise III, 30, 10, gâ*h* (Aufr. p. 241) instead of gấ*h* (M. M. vol. ii, p. 792).

III, 17, 1. i*g*yate (Aufr. p. 232) instead of a*g*yate (M. M. vol. ii, p. 722) is impossible.

III, 47, 1. Professor Aufrecht (p. 256) puts the nominative índro instead of the vocative indra, which I had given (vol. ii, p. 902). I doubt whether any MSS. support that change (S 1, S 2, S 3 have indra), but it is clear that Sâya*n*a takes indra as a vocative, and likewise the Nirukta.

III, 50, 2. Professor Aufrecht (p. 258) gives asya, both in the Sa*m*hitâ and Pada, without the accent on the last syllable. But all the MSS. that I know (S 1, S 2, S 3, P 1,

P 2) give it with the accent on the last syllable (M. M. vol. ii, p. 912), and this no doubt is right. The same mistake occurs again in III, 51, 10, (Aufr. p. 259); IV, 5, 11, (Aufr. p. 281); IV, 36, 2, (Aufr. p. 309); V, 12, 3, (Aufr. p. 337); while in VIII, 103, 9, (Aufr. vol. ii, p. 195) the MSS. consistently give asya as unaccented, whereas Professor Aufrecht, in this very passage, places the accent on the last syllable. On the same page (p. 259) amandan, in the Pada, is a misprint for ámandan.

III, 53, 18. asi (Aufr. p. 262) instead of ási (M. M. vol. ii, p. 934) is wrong, because hí requires that the accent should remain on ási. S 1, S 2, S 3, P 1, P 2 have ási.

IV, 4, 7. svá ā́yushe (Aufr. p. 279) instead of svá ā́yushi (M. M. vol. iii, p. 37) is not supported by any good MSS., nor required by the sense of the passage. S 1, S 2, S 3, P 1, P 2 have ā́yushi.

IV, 5, 7. árupitam, in the Pada, (Aufr. p. 280) instead of ā́rupitam (M. M. vol. iii, p. 45) is right, as had been shown in the Prâti*s*âkhya, Sûtra 179, though by a misprint the long â of the Sa*m*hitâ had been put in the place of the short a of the Pada.

IV, 5, 9. read gaú*h* (M. M. vol. iii, p. 46) instead of gó*h* (Aufr. p. 281).

IV, 15, 2. yā́ti, with the accent on the first syllable, is supported by all MSS. against yâti (Aufr. p. 287). The same applies to yā́ti in IV, 29, 2, and to várante in IV, 31, 9.

IV, 18, 11. amî, without any accent (Aufr. p. 293), instead of amī́ (M. M. vol. iii, p. 105) is wrong, because amī́ is never unaccented.

IV, 21, 9. no, without an accent (Aufr. p. 296), instead of nó (M. M. vol. iii, p. 120) is wrong.

IV, 26, 3. átithigvam (Aufr. p. 300) instead of atithigvám (M. M. vol. iii, p. 140) and VI, 47, 22, átithigvasya (Aufr. p. 437) instead of atithigvásya (M. M. vol. iii, p. 776) are wrong, for atithigvá never occurs again except with the accent on the last syllable. The MSS. do not vary. Nor do they vary in the accentuation of kútsa: hence kutsám (Aufr. p. 300) should be kútsam (M. M. vol. iii p. 139).

IV, 36, 6. Professor Aufrecht (p. 309) has altered the accent of ávishu*h* into âvishú*h*, but the MSS. are unanimous in favour of ấvishu*h* (M. M. vol. iii, p. 181).

Again in IV, 41, 9, the MSS. support the accentuation of ágman (M. M. vol. iii, p. 200), while Professor Aufrecht (p. 313) has altered it to agman.

IV, 42, 9. ádâ*s*at, being preceded by hí, ought to have the accent; (Aufrecht, p. 314, has adâ*s*at without the accent.) For the same reason, V, 29, 3, ávindat (M. M. vol. iii, p. 342) ought not to have been altered to avindat (Aufr. p. 344).

IV, 50, 4. vyóman is a misprint for vyòman.

V, 15, 5. Professor Aufrecht (p. 338) writes dîrghám instead of dógham (M. M. vol. iii, p. 314). This, no doubt, was done intentionally, and not by accident, as we see from the change of accent. But dógham, though it occurs but once, is supported in this place by all the best MSS., and has been accepted by Professor Roth in his Dictionary.

V, 34, 4. práyato (Aufr. p. 351) instead of práyatâ (M. M. vol. iii, p. 371) is wrong.

V, 42, 9. visármâ*n*am (Aufr. p. 358) instead of visarmấ*n*am (M. M. vol. iii, p. 402) is wrong.

V, 44, 4. parva*n*é (Aufr. p. 360) instead of prava*n*é (M. M. vol. iii, p. 415) is wrong.

V, 83, 4. vânti (Aufr. p. 389) instead of vấnti (M. M. vol. iii, p. 554) is supported by no MSS.

V, 85, 6. âsí*ñk*antî*h* (Aufr. p. 391) instead of âsi*ñk*ántî*h* (M. M. vol. iii, p. 560) is not supported either by MSS. or by grammar, as si*ñk* belongs to the Tud-class. On the same grounds isháyanta*h*, VI, 16, 27 (M. M. vol. iii, p. 638), ought not to have been changed to ishayánta*h* (Aufr. p. 408), nor VI, 24, 7, avakar*s*áyanti (M. M. vol. iii, p. 687) into avakár*s*ayanti (Aufr. p. 418).

VI, 46, 10, read girva*n*as (M. M. vol. iii, p. 763) instead of gírva*n*as (Aufr. p. 435).

VI, 60, 10. k*rin*oti (Aufr. p. 450) instead of k*rin*óti (M. M. vol. iii, p. 839) is wrong.

VII, 40, 4. aryamấ ấpa*h* (Aufr. vol. ii, p. 35), in the Pada instead of aryamấ ápa*h* (M. M. vol. iv, p. 81) is wrong.

VII, 51, 1. âdityânấm (Aufr. vol. ii, p. 40) instead of âdityấnâm (M. M. vol. iv, p. 103) is wrong.

VII, 64, 2. i*l*ấm (Aufr. vol. ii, p. 50) instead of í*l*âm (M. M. vol. iv, p. 146) is wrong. In the same verse gopâ*h* in the Pada should be changed in my edition to gopâ.

VII, 66, 5. yó (Aufr. vol. ii, p. 51) instead of yé (M. M. vol. iv, p. 151) is indeed supported by S 3, but evidently untenable on account of atipíprati.

VII, 72, 3. In abudhran Professor Aufrecht has properly altered the wrong spelling abudhnan; and, as far as the authority of the best MSS. is concerned (S 1, S 2, S 3), he is also right in putting a final ñ, although Professor Bollensen prefers the dental n; (Zeitschrift der D. M. G., vol. xxii, p. 599.) The fact is that Vedic MSS. use the Anusvâra dot for final nasals before all class-letters, and leave it to us to interpret that dot according to the letter which follows. Before I felt quite certain on this point, I have in several cases retained the dot, as given by the MSS., instead of changing it, as I ought to have done according to my system of writing Devanâgarî, into the corresponding nasal, provided it represents an original n. In I, 71, 1, S 2, S 3 have the dot in a*g*ushran, but S 1 has dental n. In IX, 87, 5, as*ri*gran has the dot; i. e. S 1 has the dot, and n*kh*, dental n joined to *kh*; S 2 has n*kh* without the dot before the n; S 3 has the dot, and then *kh*. In IV, 24, 6, the spelling of the Sa*m*hitâ áviṿena*m* tám would leave it doubtful whether we ought to read ávivenan tám or ávivenam tám; S 1 and S 3 read ávivena*m* tá*m*, but S 2 has ávivenan tám; P 2 has ávi-venan tám, and P 1 had the same originally, though a later hand changed it to ávi-vena*m* tá*m*. In IV, 25, 3, on the contrary, S 1 and S 3 write ávivena*m*; S 2, ávivenam; P 1 and P 2, ávi-vena*m*. What is intended is clear enough, viz. ávivenan in IV, 24, 6; ávi-venam in IV, 25, 3. [In the new edition ávivenam has been left in both passages.]

VII, 73 1. a*s*vinâ (Aufr. vol. ii, p. 56) instead of a*s*vínâ (M. M. vol. iv, p. 176) is wrong. On the same page, dhísh*n*ye, VII, 72, 3, should have the accent on the first syllable.

VII, 77, 1. In this verse, which has been so often dis-

cussed (see Kuhn, Beiträge, vol. iii, p. 472; Böhtlingk and Roth, Dictionary, vol. ii, p. 968; Bollensen, Orient und Occident, vol. ii, p. 463), all the MSS. which I know, read *k*arấyai, and not either *k*arấthai nor *g*arấyai.

VIII, 2, 29. kîrí*n*am (Aufr. vol. ii, p. 84) instead of kârí*n*am (M. M. vol. iv, p. 308) does not rest on the authority of any MSS., nor is it supported by Sâya*n*a.

VIII, 9, 9. Professor Aufrecht has altered the very important form â*k*u*k*yuvîmáhi (M. M. vol. iv, p. 389) to â*k*u*k*yavîmáhi (vol. ii, p. 98). The question is whether this was done intentionally and on the authority of any MSS. My own MSS. support the form â*k*u*k*yuvîmáhi, and I see that Professor Roth accepts this form.

VIII, 32, 14. âyántâram (Aufr. vol. ii, p. 129) instead of âyantấram (M. M. vol. iv, p. 567) is wrong.

VIII, 47, 15. dushvápnyam (Aufr. vol. ii, p. 151) is not so correct as du*h*shvápnyam (M. M. vol. iv, p. 660), or, better, dushshvápnyam (Prâti*s*âkhya, Sûtras 255 and 364), though it is perfectly true that the MSS. write dushvápnyam.

[I ought to state that all these errata have been corrected by Professor Aufrecht in his second edition.]

In the ninth and tenth Ma*nd*alas I have not to defend myself, and I need not therefore give a list of the passages where I think that Professor Aufrecht's text is not supported by the best MSS. My own edition of these Ma*nd*alas will soon be published, and I need hardly say that where it differs from Professor Aufrecht's text, I am prepared to show that I had the best authorities on my side.

My own mistakes.

Professor Aufrecht writes in the second edition of his Romanised text of the Rig-veda (p. iv): 'Um den Herren, die diese Druckfehler in majorem gloriam suam mit so grosser Schonung hervorgehoben haben, einen Gegendienst zu erweisen, bemerke ich einige derselben.' Dieser Gegendienst, so gut er gemeint war, ist leider nicht sehr bedeutend ausgefallen, auch nicht immer in majorem gloriam Catonis.

In I, 161, 2, Professor Aufrecht objects to *k*aturas kri*n*otana. I felt doubtful about it, and in the commentary I printed *k*atura*h* kri*n*otana. In IV, 33, 5, the reading

*k*atus kara is sanctioned by the authority of the Prâti*s*âkhya, Sûtra 281, 4.

In I, 181, 5, Aufrecht prefers mathrâ; Sâya*n*a, Böhtlingk and Roth, and I prefer mathnâ.

In II, 11, 10, he has discovered that *g*ûrvît was meant for *g*ûrvât. Whitney still quotes *g*ûrvît.

In III, 9, 4, he has discovered that apsu should be ·psu; but this had been already corrected.

In III, 25, 2, the final a of vaha ought to be long in the Sa*m*hitâ.

In IV, 19, 4, instead of d*r*il*h*â ni read d*r*il*h*âni.

In VII, 33, 2, instead of av*r*i*n*îtâ read ·v*r*i*n*îtâ.

In VII, 35, 13, the Visarga in devagopâ*h* should be deleted.

In VII, 42, 2, the Anusvâra in yu*m*kshvâ should be deleted.

In VIII, 2, 30, the anudâttatara should be shifted from the ultimate to the penultimate, dadhiré, not dadhire.

In VIII, 51, 3, avishyanta was meant for arishyantam.

In VIII, 55, 5, for na read â. The MSS. vary in both cases.

In IX, 108, 7, in vanakraksha, the kra was printed as *ri*. Professor Aufrecht might have seen it correctly printed in the index. Sâya*n*a read vana*r*iksha.

In X, 28, 11, Professor Aufrecht thinks that the Pada should have godhâ*h* instead of godhâ. I think godhâ is right, in spite of Professor Aufrecht's appeal to the silence of the Prâti*s*âkhya. The fact is that godhâ*h* never occurs, while godhâ occurs in the preceding verse, and again VIII, 69, 9.

After such a flourish of trumpets, we expected more from Professor Aufrecht; still we must learn to be grateful even for small mercies.

Having said so much in vindication of the text of the Rig-veda as published by me, and in defence of my principles of criticism which seem to me so self-evident as hardly to deserve the name of canones critici, I feel bound at the same time both to acknowledge some inaccuracies that have occurred in the index at the end of each volume, and to defend some entries in that index which have been challenged without sufficient cause.

Sâyana's quotations from the Sarvânukramanî.

It has been supposed that in the index at the end of my fourth volume, the seventeenth verse of the 34th hymn in the seventh Mandala has been wrongly assigned to Ahi Budhnya, and that one half only of that verse should have been reserved for that deity. I do not deny that we should be justified in deriving that sense from the words of the Anukramanikâ, but I cannot admit that my own interpretation is untenable. As Sâyana does not speak authoritatively on the subject, I followed the authority of Shadgurusishya. This commentator of the Anukramanikâ says: atra ka abgâm ukthair ahim grinìsha ity ardharko-bganâmno[a] devasya stutih; mâ no-hir budhnya ity ardharko-hirbudhnyanâmno devasya[b]. Another commentator says: abgâm ukthair ardharko-hih; uttaro mâ no-hir ity ahir budhnyah. From this we learn that both commentators looked upon the Dvipadâs as ardharkas or half-verses, and ascribed the whole of verse 16 to Ahir abgâh, the whole of verse 17 to Ahir budhnyah. It will be seen from an accurate examination of Sâyana's commentary on verse 17, that in the second interpretation of the second half of verse 17, he labours to show that in this portion, too, Ahir budhnyah may be considered as the deity.

It is perfectly right to say that the words of the Anukramanikâ, abgâm aheh, signify that the verse beginning with abgâm, belongs to Ahi. But there was no misprint in my index. It will be seen that Shadgurusishya goes even beyond me, and calls that deity simply Abga, leaving out Ahi altogether, as understood. I was anxious to show the distinction between Abgâ Ahih and Ahir Budhnyah, as the deities of the two successive verses, and I did not expect that any reader could possibly misinterpret my entry[c].

With regard to hymns 91 and 92 of the seventh Mandala, it is true, that in the index I did not mention that certain verses in which two deities are mentioned (91, 2;

[a] I find that Mr. Macdonell in his edition of the Sarvânukramanî reads ardharko-hinâmno. If this is right, part of my argument would fall.

[b] MS. Wilson 379 has, ardharko nâmano daivatasya, and in the margin -hi. Ahirbudhnya seems to have been taken as one word.

[c] The editor of the Bombay edition of the text of the Rig-veda assigns verse 16 to Ahi, verse 17 to Ahirbudhnya.

4-7; 92, 2), must be considered as addressed not to Vâyu alone, but to Vâyu and Indra. It will be seen from Sâya*n*a's introduction to hymn 90, that he, too, wrongly limits the sentence of the Anukrama*n*ikâ, aindrya*s* *k*a yâ dvivaduktâ*h*, to the fifth and following verses of hymn 90, and that he never alludes to this proviso again in his introductory remarks to hymn 91 and 92, though, of course, he explains the verses, in which a dual occurs, as addressed to two deities, viz. Indra and Vâyu. The same omission, whether intentional or unintentional, occurs in Sha*d*guru*s*ishya's commentary. The other commentary, however, assigns the verses of the three hymns rightly. The subject has evidently been one that excited attention in very early days, for in the Aitareya-brâhma*n*a, V, 20, we actually find that the word vâm which occurs in hymn 90, 1, and which might be taken as a dual, though Sâya*n*a explains it as a singular, is changed into te[a].

In hymn VII, 104, rakshoha*n*au might certainly be added as an epithet of Indrâ-Somau, and Sha*d*guru*s*ishya clearly takes it in that sense. The Anukrama*n*ikâ says: indrâsomâ pa*ñk*âdhikaindrâsoma*m* râkshoghna*m* *s*âpâbhi*s*âpaprâyam.

In hymn VIII, 67, it has been supposed that the readings Samada and Sâmada instead of Sammada and Sâmmada were due to a misprint. This is not the case. That I was aware of the other spelling of this name, viz. Sammada and Sâmmada, I had shown in my History of Ancient Sanskrit Literature (2nd ed.), p. 39, where I had translated the passage of the *S*âṅkhâyana-sûtras in which Matsya Sâmmada occurs, and had also called attention to the Â*s*valâyana-sûtras X, 7, and the *S*atapatha-brâhma*n*a XIII, 3, 1, 1,

[a] The interpunction of Dr. Haug's edition (p. 128) should be after te. Sha*d*guru*s*ishya says:- ata eva brâhma*n*asûtrayo*h* praüge vâyavyatvâya pra vîrayâ *suk*ayo dadrire[b] vâm iti dviva*k*anasthâne ta ity ekava*k*anapâ*th*a*h* k*r*ita*h*, vâm ity ukta*m* *k*ed aindratva*m* *k*a syâd iti. Possibly the same change should be made in Â*s*valâyana's *S*rauta Sûtras, VIII, 11, and it has been made by Râma Nârâya*n*a Vidyâratna. The remark of the commentator, however, dadrire ta iti prayogapâ*th*a*h*, looks as if vâm might have been retained in the text. The MSS. I have collated are in favour of te.

[b] Mr. Macdonell (Sarvânukrama*n*î, p. 133) inserts ta iti after dadrire.

where the same passage is found. I there spelt the name Sâmmada, because the majority of the MSS. were in favour of that spelling. In the edition of the Â*s*valâyana-sûtras, which has since been published by Râma Nârâya*n*a Vidyâra*n*ya, the name is spelt Sâmada. My own opinion is that Sâmmada is the right spelling, but that does not prove that Sâya*n*a thought so; and unless I deviated from the principles which I had adopted for a critical restoration of Sâya*n*a's text, I could not but write Sâmada in our passage. B 1 and B 4 omit sâmada, but both give samadâkhyasya; Ca. gives likewise samadâkhyasya, and A. semadâkhyasya. This, I believe, was meant by the writer for sammadâkhyasya, for in the passage from the Anukrama*n*î both A. and Ca. give sâmmado. I then consulted the commentary of Sha*d*guru*s*ishya, and there again the same MS. gave twice sâmmada, once sâmada, which is explained by samadâkhyamahâmînarâ*g*aputra*h*. A better MS. of Sha*d*guru*s*ishya, MS. Wilson 379 gives the readings sâmmado, sâmmada, and sammadâkhyasya. The other commentary gives distinctly sâmanda. [I have adopted sammada in the new edition.]

In IX, 68, Professor Aufrecht adopts what he considers the bold reading Vatsaprî; I prefer to be timid and allow Sâya*n*a his own reading Vatsaprĭ; see Sarvânukrama*n*î, ed. Macdonell, pp. 34, 146.

It will be seen from these remarks that many things have to be considered before one can form an independent judgment as to the exact view adopted by Sâya*n*a in places where he differs from other authorities, or as to the exact words in which he clothed his meaning. Such cases occur again and again. Thus in IX, 86, I find that Professor Aufrecht ascribes the first ten verses to the Ak*r*ish*t*as, whereas Sâya*n*a calls them Âk*r*ish*t*as. It is perfectly true that the best MSS. of the Anukrama*n*ikâ have Ak*r*ish*t*a, it is equally true that the name of these Ak*r*ish*t*as is spelt with a short a in the Hariva*m*sa, 11,533, but an editor of Sâya*n*a's work is not to alter the occasional mistakes of that learned commentator, and Sâya*n*a certainly called these poets Âk*r*ish*t*as.

Verses 21–30 of the same hymn are ascribed by Professor Aufrecht to the P*ris*niya*h*. Here, again, several MSS. support that reading; and in Sha*d*guru*s*ishya's commentary, the correction of p*ris*niya*h* into *pris*naya*h* is made by a later hand. But Sâya*n*a clearly took p*ris*naya*h* for a nominative plural of p*ris*ni, and in this case he certainly was right. The Dictionary of Böhtlingk and Roth quotes the Mahâbhârata, VII, 8728, in support of the peculiar reading of p*ris*niya*h*, but the published text gives p*ris*naya*h*. Professor Benfey, in his list of poets (Ind. Stud. vol. iii, p. 223), gives p*ris*niyo*g*a as one word, not p*ris*niyogâ, as stated in the Dictionary of Böhtlingk and Roth, but this is evidently meant for two words, viz. p*ris*nayo*x*gâh. However, whether p*ris*niya*h* or p*ris*naya*h* be the real name of these poets, an editor of Sâya*n*a is bound to give that reading of the name which Sâya*n*a believed to be the right one, i. e. p*ris*naya*h*[a].

Again, in the same hymn, Professor Aufrecht ascribes verses 31–40 to the Atris. We should then have to read t*ri*tîye*x*traya*h*. But Sâya*n*a read t*ri*tîye traya*h*, and ascribes verses 31–40 to the three companies together of the *Ri*shis mentioned before. On this point the MSS. admit of no doubt, for we read: *k*aturthâsya *k*a dasar*k*asya âk*ri*sh*t*â mâshâ ityâdidvinâmânas trayo ga*n*â drash*t*âra*h*. I do not say that the other explanation is wrong; I only say that, whether right or wrong, Sâya*n*a certainly read traya*h*, not atraya*h*; and an editor of Sâya*n*a has no more right to correct the text, supported by the best MSS., in the first and second, than in the third of these passages, all taken from one and the same hymn.

Old mistakes in the text.

But though I insist so strongly on a strict observance of the rules of diplomatic criticism with regard to the text of the Rig-veda, nay, even of Sâya*n*a, I insist equally strongly on the right of independent criticism, which ought to begin where diplo-

[a] Professor Aufrecht in his new edition of the text (1877) adopts the more timid reading p*ris*naya*h*. See also B*ri*hat-Sa*m*hitâ, transl. by Kern, p. 2: Sikatâ*h* p*ris*nayo gargâ vâlakhilyâ marî*k*ipâ*h* bh*ri*gavo*x*ṅgirasas *k*aiva sûkshmâs *k*ânye maharshaya*h*.

matic criticism ends. Considering the startling antiquity which we can claim for every letter and accent of our MSS., so far as they are authenticated by the Prâti*s*âkhya, to say nothing of the passages of many hymns which are quoted verbatim in the Brâhma*n*as, the Kalpa-sûtras, the Nirukta, the B*ri*haddevatâ, and the Anukrama*n*îs, I should deem it reckless to alter one single letter or one single accent in an edition of the hymns of the Rig-veda. As the text has been handed down to us, so it should remain; and whatever alterations and corrections we, the critical Mle*kkh*as of the nineteenth century, have to propose, should be kept distinct from that time-hallowed inheritance. Unlikely as it may sound, it is true nevertheless that we, the scholars of the nineteenth century, are able to point out mistakes in the text of the Rig-veda which escaped the attention of the most learned among the native scholars of the sixth century B.C. No doubt, these scholars, even if they had perceived such mistakes, would hardly have ventured to correct the text of their sacred writings. The authors of the Prâti*s*âkhya had before their eyes or ears a text ready made, of which they registered every peculiarity, nay, in which they would note and preserve every single irregularity, even though it stood alone amidst hundreds of analogous cases. With us the case is different. Where we see a rule observed in 99 cases, we feel strongly tempted and sometimes justified in altering the 100th case in accordance with what we consider to be a general rule. Yet even then I feel convinced we ought not to do more than place our conjectural readings below the textus receptus of the Veda,—a text so ancient and venerable that no scholar of any historical tact or critical taste would venture to foist into it a conjectural reading, however plausible, nay, however undeniable.

Sthâtú*h k*ará-tham.

There can be no clearer case of corruption in the traditional text of the Rig-veda than, for instance, in I, 70, 4, where the Pada text reads:

várdhân yám pûrvî́*h* kshapá*h* ví-rûpâ*h* sthâtú*h k*a rátham *ri*tá-pravîtam.

All scholars who have touched on this verse, Professors Benfey, Bollensen, Roth, and others, have pointed out that instead of *k*a rátham, the original poet must have said *k*arátham. The phrase sthâtú*h* *k*arátham, what stands and moves, occurs several times. It is evidently an ancient phrase, and hence we can account for the preservation in it of the old termination of the nom. sing. of neuters in *ri*, which here, as in the Greek *μάρ-τυρ* or *μάρ-τυς*, masc., appears as ur or us, while in the ordinary Sanskrit we find *ri* only. This nom. sing. neut. in us, explains also the common genitives and ablatives, pitu*h*, mâtu*h*, &c., which stand for pitur-s, mâtur-s. This phrase sthâtú*h* *k*arátham occurs:

I, 58, 5. sthâtú*h* *k*arátham bhayate patatrí*nah*.

What stands and what moves is afraid of Agni.

I, 68, 1. sthâtú*h* *k*arátham aktū́n ví ûr*n*ot.

He lighted up what stands and what moves during every night.

I, 72, 6. pa*s*ū́n *k*a sthât*rī́*n *k*arátham *k*a pâhi.

Protect the cattle, and what stands and moves!

Here it has been proposed to read sthâtú*h* instead of sthât*rī́*n, and I confess that this emendation is very plausible. One does not see how pa*s*ú, cattle, could be called immobilia or fixtures, unless the poet wished to make a distinction between cattle that are kept fastened in stables, and cattle that are allowed to roam about freely in the homestead. This distinction is alluded to, for instance, in the *S*atapatha-brâhma*n*a, XI, 8, 3, 2. saurya evaisha pa*s*u*h* syâd iti, tasmâd etasminn astamite pa*s*avo badhyante; badhnanty ekân yathâgosh*th*am, eka upasamâyanti.

I, 70, 2. gárbha*h* *k*a sthâtā́m gárbha*h* *k*aráthâm, (read sthâtrā́m, and see Bollensen, Orient und Occident, vol. ii, p. 462.)

He who is within all that stands and all that moves.

The word *k*arátha, if it occurs by itself, means flock, movable property:

III, 31, 15. ā́t ít sákhi-bhya*h* *k*arátham sám airat.

He brought together, for his friends, the flocks.

VIII, 33, 8. puru-trā́ *k*arátham dadhe.

He bestowed flocks on many people.

X, 92, 13. prá na*h* pûshā́ *k*arátham—avatu.

May Pûshan protect our flock!

Another idiomatic phrase in which sthâtú*h* occurs is sthâtú*h* *g*ágata*h*, and here sthâtú*h* is really a genitive :

IV, 53, 6. *g*ágata*h* sthâtú*h* ubháyasya yá*h* vas*î*.

He who is lord of both, of what is movable and what is immovable.

VI, 50, 7. vís*v*asya sthâtú*h* *g*ágata*h* *g*ánitrî*h*.

They who created all that stands and moves.

VII, 60, 2. vís*v*asya sthâtú*h* *g*ágata*h* *k*a gopấ*h*.

The guardians of all that stands and moves. Cf. X, 63, 8.

I, 159, 3. sthâtú*h* *k*a satyám *g*ágata*h* *k*a dhárma*n*i putrásya pâtha*h* padám ádvayâvina*h*.

Truly while you uphold all that stands and moves, you protect the home of the guileless son. Cf. II, 31, 5.

But although I have no doubt that in I, 70, 4, the original poet said sthâtú*h* *k*arátham, I should be loath to suppress the evidence of the mistake and alter the Pada text from *k*a rátham to *k*arátham. The very mistake is instructive, as showing us the kind of misapprehension to which the collectors of the Vedic text were liable, and enabling us to judge how far the limits of conjectural criticism may safely be extended.

A still more extraordinary case of misunderstanding on the part of the original compilers of the Vedic texts, and likewise of the authors of the Prâtis*â*khyas, the Niruktas, and other Vedic treatises, has been pointed out by Professor Kuhn. In an article of his, 'Zur ältesten Geschichte der Indogermanischen Völker' (Indische Studien, vol. i, p. 351), he made the following observation: 'The Lithuanian laukas, Lett. lauks, Pruss. laukas, all meaning field, agree exactly with the Sk. lokas, world, Lat. locus, Low Germ. (in East-Frisia and Oldenburg) louch, lôch, village. All these words are to be traced back to the Sk. uru, Gr. εὐρύς, broad, wide. The initial u is lost, as in Goth. rûms, O. H. G. rûmi, rûmin (Low Germ. rûme, an open uncultivated field in a forest), and the r changed into l. In support of this derivation it should be observed that in the Veda loka is frequently preceded by the particle u, which probably was only separated from it by the Diaskeuastæ, and that the meaning is

Uloka.

that of open space.' Although this derivation has met with little favour, I confess that I look upon this remark, excepting only the Latin locus[a], i. e. stlocus, as one of the most ingenious of this eminent scholar. The fact is that this particle u before loka is one of the most puzzling occurrences in the Veda. Professor Bollensen says that loka never occurs without a preceding u in the first eight Ma*nd*alas, and this is perfectly true with the exception of one passage which he has overlooked, VIII, 100, 12, dyaú*h* dehí lokám vá*g*râya vi-skábhe, Dyu! give room for the lightning to step forth! Professor Bollensen (l. c. p. 603) reads v*ri*trấya instead of vá*g*râya, without authority. He objects to dyaú*h* as a vocative, which should be dyaŭ́*h*; but dyaú*h* may be dyó*h*, a genitive belonging to vá*g*râya, in which case we should translate, Make room for the lightning of Dyu to step forth!

But what is even more important is the fact that the occurrence of this unaccented u at the beginning of a pâda is against the very rules, or, at least, runs counter to the very observations which the authors of the Prâti*s*âkhya have made on the inadmissibility of an unaccented word in such a place, so that they had to insert a special provision, Prât. 978, exempting the unaccented u from this observation: anudâttam tu pâdâdau novar*g*am vidyate padam, 'no unaccented word is found at the beginning of a pâda except u!' Although I have frequently insisted on the fact that such statements of the Prâti*s*âkhya are not to be considered as rules, but simply as more or less general statistical accumulations of facts actually occurring in the Veda, I have also pointed out that we are at liberty to found on these collected facts inductive observations which may assume the character of real rules. Thus, in our case, we can well understand why there should be none, or, at least, very few instances, where an unaccented word begins a pâda. We should not begin a verse with an enclitic particle in any other language either; and as in Sanskrit a verb at the

[a] On locus, see Corssen, Krit. Beitr. p. 463, and Aussprache, 2nd ed., p. 810. Corssen does not derive it from a root stâ or sthâ, but identifies it with Goth. strik-s, Engl. stroke, strecke.

beginning of a pâda receives ipso facto the accent, and as the same applies to vocatives, no chance is left for an unaccented word in that place, except it be a particle. But the one particle that offends against this general observation is u, and the very word before which this u causes this metrical offence, is loka. Can any argument be more tempting in favour of admitting an old form uloka instead of u loka? Lokám is preceded by u in I, 93, 6; II, 30, 6; (asmín bhayá-sthe k*rin*utam u lokám, make room for us, grant an escape to us, in this danger!) IV, 17, 17; VI, 23, 3; 7 (with urúm); 47, 8 (urúm na*h* lokám, or ulokám?); 73, 2; VII, 20, 2; 33, 5 (with urúm); 60, 9 (with urúm); 84, 2 (with urúm); 99, 4 (with urúm); IX, 92, 5; X, 13, 2; 16, 4 (suk*rí*tâm u lokám); 30, 7; 104, 10; 180, 3 (with urúm). Loké is preceded by u in III, 29, 8; V, 1, 6; loka-k*rí*t, IX, 86, 21; X, 133, 1. In all remaining passages u loká is found at the beginning of a pâda: loká*h*, III, 37, 11; lokám, III, 2, 9 (u lokám u dvé (íti) úpa *g*âmím îyatu*h*); V, 4, 11; loka-k*ri*tnúm, VIII, 15, 4; IX, 2, 8. The only passages in which loka occurs without being preceded by u, are lokám, VI, 47, 8 (see above); VIII, 100, 12; X, 14, 9; 85, 20 (am*rí*tasya); lokấ*h*, IX, 113, 9; lokấn, X, 90, 14; loké, IX, 113, 7^2; X, 85, 24.

It should be remembered that in the Gâthâs the u of words beginning with urv° does not count metrically (Hübschmann, Ein Zoroastrisches Lied, p. 37), and that in Pâli also uru must be treated as monosyllabic, in such passages as Mahâv., p. 2, line 5. The same applies to passages in the Rig-veda, such as I, 138, 3; VII, 39, 3, where the metre requires uru to be treated as one syllable. In IX, 96, 15, the original reading may have been urur iva, instead of uru-iva.

Considering all this, I feel as convinced as it is possible to be in such matters, that in all the passages where u loká occurs and where it means space, carrière ouverte, freedom, we ought to read uloká; but in spite of this I could never bring myself to insert this word, of which neither the authors of the Brâhma*n*as nor the writers of the Prâti*s*âkhyas or even later grammarians had any idea, into the text. On the contrary, I should here, too, consider it most useful to leave the traditional reading, and to add the corrections in the margin, in order that, if these conjectural emendations are in time considered as beyond the reach of doubt, they may be used as evidence in support of conjectures which, without such evidence, might seem intolerable in the eyes of timid critics.

There remains one difficulty about this hypothetical word uloká, which it is but fair to mention. If it is derived from uru, or, as Professor Bollensen suggests, from urva*k* or urvak, the change of va into o would require further support. Neither maghon for maghavan, nor duro*n*a for dura-va*n*a are strictly analogous cases, because in each we have an a preceding the va or u. Strictly speaking, uroka presupposes uravaka, as *s*lóka presupposes *s*ravaka, or óka, house, avaka (from av, not from u*k*). It should also be mentioned that a compound such as RV. X, 128, 2, urúlokam (scil. antáriksham) is strange, and shows how completely the origin of loka was forgotten at the time when the hymns of the tenth Ma*nd*ala were composed. But all this does not persuade us to accept Ascoli's conjecture (Lezioni di Fonologia Comparata, p. 235), that as uloga (but not uloka) is a regular Tamil form of loka, uloka in the Veda might be due to a reaction of the aboriginal dialects on the Vedic Sanskrit. We want far more evidence before admitting such a reaction during the Vedic period.

The most powerful instrument that has hitherto been applied to the emendation of Vedic texts, is the metre.

Metrical criticism.

Metre means measure, and uniform measure, and hence its importance for critical purposes, as second only to that of grammar. If our knowledge of the metrical system of the Vedic poets rests on a sound basis, any deviations from the general rule are rightly objected to; and if by a slight alteration they can be removed, and the metre be restored, we naturally feel inclined to adopt such emendations. Two safeguards, however, are needed in this kind of conjectural criticism. We ought to be quite certain that the anomaly is impossible, and we ought to be able to explain to a certain extent how the deviation from the original correct text could have occurred. As this subject has of late years received considerable attention, and as emendations of the Vedic texts, supported by metrical arguments, have been carried on on a very large scale, it becomes absolutely necessary to re-examine the grounds on which these emendations are supposed to rest. There are, in fact, but few hymns in which some verses or some words have not been challenged for metrical reasons, and I feel bound, therefore, at the very beginning of my translation of the Rig-veda, to express my own opinion on this subject, and to give my reasons why in so many cases I allow metrical anomalies to remain which by some of the most learned and ingenious among Vedic scholars would be pronounced intolerable.

Even if the theory of the ancient metres had not been so carefully worked out by the authors of the Prâti*s*âkhyas and the Anukrama*n*îs, an independent study of the Veda would have enabled us to discover the general rules by which the Vedic poets were guided in the composition of their works. Nor would it have been difficult to show how constantly these general principles are violated by the introduction of phonetic changes which in the later Sanskrit are called the euphonic changes of Sandhi, and according to which final vowels must be joined with initial vowels, and final consonants adapted to initial consonants, until at last each sentence becomes a continuous chain of closely linked syllables.

It is far easier, as I remarked before, to discover the original and natural rhythm of the Vedic hymns by reading them in the Pada than in the Sa*m*hitâ text, and after some practice our ear becomes sufficiently schooled to tell us at once how each line ought to be pronounced. We find, on the one hand, that the rules of Sandhi, instead of being generally binding, were treated by the Vedic poets as poetical licences only; and, on the other, that a greater freedom of pronunciation was allowed even in the body of words than would be tolerated in the later Sanskrit. If a syllable was wanted to complete the metre, a semivowel might be pronounced as a vowel, many a long vowel might be protracted so as to count for two syllables, and short vowels might be inserted between certain consonants, of which no trace exists in the ordinary Sanskrit. If, on the contrary, there were too many syllables, then the rules of Sandhi were observed, or two short syllables contracted by rapid pronunciation into one ; nay, in a few cases, a final m or s, it seems, was omitted. It would be a mistake to suppose that the authors of the Prâti*s*âkhyas were not aware of this freedom allowed or required in the pronunciation of the Vedic hymns. Though they abstained from introducing into the text changes of pronunciation which even we ourselves would never tolerate, if inserted in the texts of Homer and Plautus, in the Pâli verses of Buddha, or even in modern English poetry, the authors of the Prâti*s*âkhya were clearly aware that in many places one syllable had to be pronounced as two, or two as one. They were clearly aware that certain vowels, generally considered as long, had to be pronounced as short, and that in order to satisfy the demands of the metre, certain changes of pronunciation were indispensable. They knew all this, but they did not change the text. And this shows that the text, as they describe it, enjoyed even in their time a high authority, that they did not make it, but that, such as it is, with all its incongruities, it had been made before their time. In many cases, no doubt, certain syllables in the hymns of the Veda had been actually lengthened or shortened in the Sa*m*hitâ text in accordance with the metre in which they are composed. But this was done by the poets themselves, or, at all events, it was not done by the authors of the Prâti*s*âkhya. They simply register such changes, but they do not enjoin them, and in this we, too, should follow their example. It is, therefore, a point of some importance in the critical restoration and proper pronunciation of Vedic texts, that in the rules which we have to follow in order to satisfy the demands of the metre, we should carefully distinguish between what is sanctioned by ancient authority, and what is the result of our own observations. This I shall now proceed to do.

First, then, the authors of the Prâti*s*âkhya distinctly admit that, in order to uphold the rules they have themselves laid down, certain syllables are to be pronounced as two syllables.

Vyûha.

We read in Sûtra 527: 'In a deficient pâda the right number is to be provided for by protraction of semivowels (which were originally vowels), and of contracted vowels (which were originally two independent vowels).' It is only by this process that the short syllable which has been lengthened in the Sa*m*hitâ, viz. the sixth, or the eighth, or the tenth, can be shown to have occupied and to occupy that place where alone, according to a former rule, a short syllable is liable to be lengthened. Thus we read:

I, 161, 11. udvatsvasmâ âk*ri*n*o*tanâ t*ri*n*am.

This would seem to be a verse of eleven syllables, in which the ninth syllable na has been lengthened. This, however, is against the system of the Prâti*s*âkhya. But if we protract the semivowel v in udvatsv, and change it back into u, which it was originally, then we gain one syllable, the whole verse has twelve syllables, na occupies the tenth place, and it now belongs to that class of cases which is included in a former Sûtra, 523.

The same applies to X, 103, 13, where we read:

pretâ *g*ayatâ nara*h*.

This is a verse of seven syllables, in which the fifth syllable is lengthened, without any authority. Let us protract pretâ by bringing it back to its original component elements pra itâ, and we get a verse of eight syllables, the sixth syllable now falls under the general observation, and is lengthened in the Sa*m*hitâ accordingly.

The same rules are repeated in a later portion of the Prâti*s*âkhya. Here rules had been given as to the number of syllables of which certain metres consist, and it is added (Sûtras 972, 973) that where that number is deficient, it should be completed by protracting contracted vowels, and by separating consonantal groups in which semivowels (originally vowels) occur, by means of their corresponding vowel.

The rules in both places are given in almost identically

the same words, and the only difference between the two passages is this, that, according to the former, semivowels are simply changed back into their vowels, while, according to the latter, the semivowel remains, but is separated from the preceding consonant by its corresponding vowel.

These rules therefore show clearly that the authors of the Prâti*s*âkhya, though they would have shrunk from altering one single letter of the authorised Sa*m*hitâ, recognised the fact that where two vowels had been contracted into one, they might yet be pronounced as two; and where a vowel before another vowel had been changed into a semivowel, it might either be pronounced as a vowel, or as a semivowel preceded by its corresponding vowel. More than these two modifications, however, the Prâti*s*âkhya does not allow, or, at least, does not distinctly sanction. The commentator indeed tries to show that by the wording of the Sûtras in both places, a third modification is sanctioned, viz. the vocalisation, in the body of a word, of semivowels which do not owe their origin to an original vowel. But in both places this interpretation is purely artificial. Some such rule ought to have been given, but it was not given by the authors of the Prâti*s*âkhya. It ought to have been given, for it is only by observing such a rule that in I, 61, 12, gor na parva vi radâ tiras*k*â, we get a verse of eleven syllables, and thus secure for dâ in rađâ the eighth place, where alone the short a could be lengthened. Yet we look in vain for a rule sanctioning the change of semivowels into vowels, except where the semivowels can rightly be called kshaipra-var*n*a (Sûtra 974), i.e. semivowels that were originally vowels. The independent (svâbhâvika) semivowels, as e.g. the v in parva, are not included; and to suppose that in Sûtra 527 these semivowels were indicated by var*n*a is impossible, particularly if we compare the similar wording of Sûtra 974[a].

[a] It will be seen from my edition of the Prâti*s*âkhya, particularly from the extracts from Uva*t*a, given after Sûtra 974, that the idea of making two syllables out of go*h*, never entered Uva*t*a's mind. M. Regnier was right, Professor Kuhn (Beiträge, vol. iv, p. 187) was wrong. Uva*t*a, no doubt, wishes to show that original (svâbhâvika) semivowels are liable to vyûha, or at least

We look in vain, too, in the Prâtisâkhya for another rule according to which long vowels, even if they do not owe their origin to the coalescence of two vowels, are liable to be protracted. However, this rule, too, though never distinctly sanctioned, is observed in the Prâtisâkhya, for unless its author observed it, he could not have obtained in the verses quoted by the Prâtisâkhya the number of syllables which he ascribes to them. According to Sûtra 937, the verse, RV. X, 134, 1, is a Mahâpankti, and consists of six pâdas, of eight syllables each. In order to obtain that number, we must read:

samrâgam karshaninâm.

We may therefore say that, without allowing any actual change in the received text of the Samhitâ, the Prâtisâkhya distinctly allows a lengthened pronunciation of certain syllables, which in the Pada text form two syllables; and we may add that, by implication, it allows the same even in cases where the Pada text also gives but one instead of two syllables. Having this authority in our favour, I do not think that we use too much liberty if we extend this modified pronunciation, recognised in so many cases by the ancient scholars of India themselves, to other cases where it seems to us required as well, in order to satisfy the metrical rules of the Veda.

Shortening of long vowels.

Secondly, I believe it can be proved that, if not the authors of the Prâtisâkhya, those at least who constituted the Vedic text which was current in the ancient schools and which we now have before us, were fully aware that certain long vowels and diphthongs could be used as short. The authors of the Prâtisâkhya remark that certain changes which can take place before a short syllable only, take place likewise before the word no, although the vowel of this 'no' is by them supposed to be long. After having stated in Sûtra 523 that the eighth syllable of hendecasyllabics and dodecasyllabics, if short, is lengthened, provided a short syllable

to vyavâya; but though this is true in fact, Uvata does not succeed in his attempt to prove that the rules of the Prâtisâkhya sanction it.

follows, they remark that for this purpose na*h* or no is treated as a short syllable:

X, 59, 4. dyŭ-bhī*h* hĭtā*h* *g*ărĭmā sŭ nâ*h* āstū, (Sa*m*h. sû nŏ āstū.)

Again, in stating that the tenth syllable of hendecasyllabics and dodecasyllabics, if short, is lengthened, provided a short syllable follows, the same exception is understood to be made in favour of na*h* or no, as a short syllable:

VII, 48, 4. nŭ dēvâsā*h* vărĭvā*h* kārtănā nā*h*, (Sa*m*h. kārtănâ nŏ, bhûta no, &c.)

With regard to e being shortened before a short a where, according to rule, the a should be elided, we actually find that the Sa*m*hitâ gives a instead of e in RV. VIII, 72, 5. véti stótave ambyām, Sa*m*h. véti stótava ambyām. (Prâti*s*. 177, 5.)

I do not ascribe very much weight to the authority which we may derive from these observations with regard to our own treatment of the diphthongs e and o as either long or short in the Veda, yet in answer to those who are incredulous as to the fact that the vowels e and o could ever be short in Sanskrit, an appeal to the authority of those who constituted our text, and in constituting it clearly treated o as a short vowel, may not be without weight. We may also appeal to the fact that in Pâli and Prâk*ri*t every final o and e can be treated as either long or short[a]. Starting from this we may certainly extend this observation, as it has been extended by Professor Kuhn, but we must not extend it too far. It is quite clear that in the same verse e and o can be used both as long and short. I give the Sa*m*hitâ text:

I, 84, 17. ka îshate | tu*g*yate kō bĭbhâyā
ko ma*m*sate | santam indrā*m* kŏ āntī,
kas tokâya | ka ibhâyōtă rāyē
adhi bravat | tanve kō *g*ănâyā.

[a] See Lassen, Inst. Linguæ Pracriticæ, pp. 145, 147, 151; Cowell, Vararu*k*i, Introduction, p. xvii. Kedârabha*tt*a says: Pâ*n*inir bhagavân prâk*ri*talaksha*n*am api vakti sa*m*sk*ri*tâd anyat, dîrghâkshara*m* *k*a kutra*k*id ekâm mâtrâm upaitîti. Secundum d'Alwisium commentator docet sermonem esse de litteris Sanscriticis *e* et *o*. Cf. Pischel, De Grammaticis prakriticis, 1874.

But although there can be no doubt that e and o, when final, or at the end of the first member of a compound, may be treated in the Veda as anceps, there is no evidence, I believe, to show that the same licence applies to a medial or initial e or o. In IV, 45, 5, we must scan

usrâ*h* *g*arante prati vasto*h* a*s*vinâ,

ending the verse with an epitritus tertius instead of the usual dijambus[a].

Thirdly, the fact that the initial short a, if following upon a word ending in o or e, is frequently not to be elided, is clearly recognised by the authors of the Prâti*s*âkhya (see p. xlviii). Nay, that they wished it to be pronounced even in passages where, in accordance with the requirements of the Prâti*s*âkhya, it had to disappear in the Sa*m*hitâ text, we may conclude from Sûtra 978. It is there stated that no pâda should ever begin with a word that has no accent. The exceptions to this rule are few, and they are discussed in Sûtras 978–987. But if the initial a were not pronounced in I, 1, 9, sá*h* na*h* pitā́-iva sûnáve ágne su-upâyaná*h* bhava, the second pâda would begin with gne, a word which, after the elision of the initial a, would be a word without an accent[b].

Fourthly, the fact that other long vowels, besides e and o, may under certain circumstances be used as short in the Veda, is not merely a modern theory, but rests on no less an authority than Pâ*n*ini himself.

---

[a] See Professor Weber's pertinent remarks in Kuhn's Beiträge, vol. iii, p. 394. I do not think that in the verses adduced by Professor Kuhn, in which final o is considered by him as an iambus or trochee, this scanning is inevitable. Thus we may scan the Sa*m*hitâ text:

I, 88, 2. rukmo na *k*itra*h* svadhitîvân.

I, 141, 8. ratho na yâta*h* *s*ikvabhi*h* kr*i*to.

I, 174, 3. si*m*ho na dame apâ*m*si vasto*h*.

VI, 24, 3. aksho na *k*akryo*h* *s*ûra br*i*han

X, 3, 1. ino râgann arati*h* samiddho.

This leaves but one of Professor Kuhn's examples (Beiträge, vol. iv, p. 192) unexplained: I, 191, 1. kaṅkato na kaṅkato, where iva for na would remove the difficulty.

[b] This subject, the shortness of e and o in the Veda, has been admirably treated by Mr. Maurice Bloomfield, 'Final as before Sonants,' Baltimore, 1882. Reprinted from the American Journal of Philology, vol. iii, No. 1.

Pâ*n*ini says, VI, 1, 127, that i, u, *ri* (see RV. Bh. IV, 1, 12) at the end of a pada (but not in a compound[a]) may remain unchanged, if a different vowel follows, and that, if long, they may be shortened. He ascribes this rule, or, more correctly, the first portion of it only, to *S*âkalya, Prâti*s*âkhya 155 seq.[b] Thus *k*akrî atra may become *k*akrĭ atra or *k*akry atra. Madhû atra may become madhŭ atra or madhv atra. In VI, 1, 128, Pâ*n*ini adds that a, i, u, *ri* may remain unchanged before *ri*, and, if long, may be shortened, and this again according to the teaching of *S*âkalya, i.e. Prâti*s*âkhya 136[c]. Hence brahmâ *ri*shi*h* becomes brahmă *ri*shi*h* or brahmarshi*h*; kumârî *ris*ya*h* becomes kumârĭ *ris*ya*h* or kumâry *ris*ya*h*. This rule enables us to explain a number of passages in which the Sa*m*hitâ text either changes the final long vowel into a semivowel, or leaves it unchanged, when the vowel is a prag*ri*hya vowel. To the first class belong such passages as I, 163, 12; IV, 38, 10, vâ*g*ī́ árvâ, Sa*m*h. vâ*g*yárvâ; VI, 7, 3, vâ*g*ī́ agne, Sa*m*h. vâ*g*yăgne; VI, 20, 13, pakthī́ arkaí*h*, Sa*m*h. pakthyărkaí*h*; IV, 22, 4, *s*ushmī́ ấ gó*h*, Sa*m*h. *s*ushmyấ gó*h*. In these passages î is the termination of a nom. masc. of a stem ending in in. Secondly, IV, 24, 8, pátnî á*kkh*a, Sa*m*h. pátnyá*kkh*a; IV, 34, 1, devī́ áhnâm, Sa*m*h. devyáhnâm; V, 75, 4, vấ*n*î*k*î ấ-hitâ, Sa*m*h. vấ*n*î*k*yấhitâ; VI, 61, 4, avitrī́ avatu, Sa*m*h. avitryăvatu. In these passages the î is the termination of feminines. In X, 15, 4, ûtī́ arvấk, Sa*m*h. ûtyărvấk, the final î of the instrumental ûtî ought not to have been changed into a semivowel, for, though not followed by íti, it is to be treated as prag*ri*hya; (Prâti*s*. 163, 5.) It is, however,

[a] There are certain compounds in which, according to Professor Kuhn, two vowels have been contracted into one short vowel. This is certainly the opinion of Hindu grammarians, also of the compiler of the Pada text. But most of them would admit of another explanation. Thus dhánvar*n*asa*h*, which is divided into dhánva-ar*n*asa*h*, may be dhánu-ar*n*asa*h* (RV. V, 45, 2). Dhánar*k*am, divided into dhána-ar*k*am, may have been dhána-*rik*am (RV. X, 46, 5). *S*atár*k*asam (RV. VII, 100, 3) may be taken as *s*atá-*rik*asam instead of *s*atá-ar*k*asam.

[b] In the Prâti*s*âkhya the rule which allows vowel before vowel to remain unchanged, is restricted to special passages, and in some of them the two vowels are savar*n*a; cf. Sûtra 163.

[c] Cf. Vâ*g*asan. Prâti*s*âkhya, IV, 48; Indische Studien, vol. ix, 309; vol. x, 406.

mentioned as an exception in Sûtra 174, 9. The same applies to II, 3, 4, védî íti asyā́m, Sa*m*h. védyasyā́m. The prag*ri*hya î ought not to have been changed into a semivowel, but the fact that it had been changed irregularly, was again duly registered in Sûtra 174, 5. These two prag*ri*hya î therefore, which have really to be pronounced short, were irregularly changed in the Sa*m*hitâ into the semivowel; and as this semivowel, like all semivowels, may take vyavâya, the same object was attained as if it had been written by a short vowel. With regard to prag*ri*hya û, no such indication is given by the Sa*m*hitâ text; but in such passages as I, 46, 13, *s*ambhû íti *s*am-bhû ā́ gatam, Sa*m*h. *s*ambhû ā́ gatam; V, 43, 4, bâhū́ íti ádrim, Sa*m*h. bâhū́ ádrim, the prag*ri*hya û of the dual can be used as short, like the û of madhû atra, given as an example by the commentators of Pâ*n*ini.

To Professor Kuhn, I believe, belongs the merit of having extended this rule to final â. That the â of the dual may become short, was mentioned in the Prâti*s*âkhya, Sûtra 309, though in none of the passages there mentioned is there any metrical necessity for this shortening (see p. lii). This being the case, it is impossible to deny that where this â is followed by a vowel, and where Sandhi between the two vowels is impossible, the final â may be treated as short. Whether it must be so treated, depends on the view which we take of the Vedic metres, and will have to be discussed hereafter. I agree with Professor Kuhn when he scans:

VI, 63, 1. kvă tyâ valgû puru-hûtâ adya, (Sa*m*h. puruhûtâdya); and not kvă tyâ valgû puruhûtâdya, although we might quote other verses as ending with an epitritus primus.

IV, 3, 13. mâ ve*s*asya pra-minata*h* mâ âpe*h*, (Sa*m*h. mâpe*h*,) although the dispondeus is possible.

I, 77, 1. kathâ dā́*s*ema agnaye kâ asmai, (Sa*m*h. kâsmai.)

VI, 24, 5. arya*h* va*s*asya pari-etâ asti.

Even in a compound like tvâ-ûta, I should shorten the first vowel, e. g.

X, 148, 1. tmanâ tanâ sanuyâma tvă-ûtâ*h*,

although the passage is not mentioned by the Prâti*s*âkhya

among those where a short final vowel in the eighth place is not lengthened when a short syllable follows[a].

But when we come to the second pâda of a Gâyatrî, and find there a long â, and that long â not followed by a vowel, I cannot agree with Professor Kuhn, that the long â, even under such circumstances, ought to be shortened. We may scan:

V, 5, 7. vâtasya patman î*l*itâ daivyâ hotârâ manusha*h*.

The same choriambic ending occurs even in the last pâda of a Gâyatrî, and is perfectly free from objection at the end of the other pâdas.

So, again, we may admit the shortening of au to o in sâno avye and sâno avyaye, as quoted in the Prâti*s*âkhya, 174 and 177, but this would not justify the shortening of au to av in Anush*t*ubh verses, such as

V, 86, 5. martâya devâu adabhâ,
a*ms*â-iva devâu arvate,

while, with regard to the Trish*t*ubh and *G*agatî verses, our views on these metres must naturally depend on the difficulties we meet with in carrying them out systematically.

There is no reason for shortening â in

V, 5, 10. devânâm guhyâ nâmâni.

It is the second pâda of a Gâyatrî here; and we shall see that, even in the third pâda, four long syllables occur again and again.

For the same reason I cannot follow Dr. Kuhn in a number of other passages where, for the sake of the metre, he proposes to change a long â into a short one. Such passages are in the Pada text:

VI, 46, 11. dîdyava*h* tigma-mûrdhâna*h*, not mûrdhăna*h*.

I, 15, 6. *ri*tunâ ya*gñ*am â*s*âthe, not â*s*ăthe.

V, 66, 2. samyak asuryam â*s*âte, not â*s*ăte.

V, 67, 1. varshish*th*am kshatram â*s*âthe, not â*s*ăthe. See Beiträge, vol. iii, p. 122.

I, 46, 6. tâm asme râsâthâm isham, not râsăthâm isham.

---

[a] I see that Professor Kuhn, vol. iv, p. 186, has anticipated this observation in esh*t*au, to be read ă-ish*t*au.

IV, 32, 23. babhrû yâmeshu *s*obhete, not *s*obhete.

IV, 45, 3. uta priyam madhune yu*ñg*âthâm ratham, not yu*ñg*âthâm ratham.

V. 74, 3. kam a*kkh*a yu*ñg*âthe ratham, not yu*ñg*âthe ratham.

IV, 55, 1. dyâvâbhûmî (íti) adite trâsîthâm na*h*, not trâsîthâm na*h*.

V, 41, 1. *ri*tasya vâ sadasi trâsîthâm na*h*, not trâsîthâm na*h*.

I must enter the same protest against shortening other long vowels in the following verses which Professor Kuhn proposes to make metrically correct by this remedy:

I, 42, 6. hira*n*yavâ*s*îmat-tama, not vâ*s*imat-tâma.

Here the short syllable of ga*n*a*s*ri-bhi*h* in V, 60, 8, cannot be quoted as a precedent, for the i in ga*n*a*s*ri, walking in companies, was never long, and could therefore not be shortened. Still less can we quote nâri-bhya*h* as an instance of a long î being shortened, for nâri-bhya*h* is derived from nâri*h*, not from nârî, and occurs with a short i even when the metre requires a long syllable; I, 43, 6. n*ri*-bhya*h* nâri-bhya*h* gave. The fact is, that in the Rig-veda the forms nârîshu and nârî-bhya*h* never occur, but always nârishu, nâri-bhya*h*; while from vâ*s*î we never find any forms with short i, but always vâ*s*îshu, vâ*s*î-bhi*h*.

Nor is there any justification for change in I, 25, 16. gâva*h* na gavyûtî*h* anu, the second pâda of a Gâyatrî. Nor in V, 56, 3. *ri*ksha*h* na va*h* maruta*h* *s*imî-vân ama*h*. In most of the passages mentioned by Professor Kuhn on p. 122, this peculiarity may be observed, that the eighth syllable is short, or, at all events, may be short, when the ninth is long:

VI, 44, 21. v*ri*sh*n*e te indu*h* v*ri*shabha pîpâya.

I, 73, 1. syona-*s*î*h* atithi*h* na prî*n*âna*h*.

VII, 13, 1. bhare havi*h* na barhishi prî*n*âna*h*.

II, 28, 7. ena*h* k*ri**n*vantam asura bhrî*n*anti.

Before, however, we can settle the question whether in

these and other places certain vowels should be pronounced as either long or short, we must settle the more general question, what authority we have for requiring a long or a short syllable in certain places of the Vedic metres.

Metre and Grammar.

If we declare ourselves free from all authority, either grammatical or metrical, we may either sacrifice all grammar to metre, or all metre to grammar. We may introduce the strictest rules of metre, determining the length or shortness of every syllable, and then ignore all rules of grammar and quantity, treat short syllables as long, or long ones as short, and thus secure the triumph of metre. Or, we may allow great latitude in Vedic metres, particularly in certain pâdas, and thus retain all the rules of grammar which determine the quantity of syllables. It may be said even that the result would really be the same in either case, and that the policy of 'thorough' might perhaps prove most useful in the end. It may be so hereafter, but in the present state of Vedic scholarship it seems more expedient to be guided by native tradition, and to study the compromise which the ancient students of the Veda have tried to effect between grammar on one side and metre on the other.

Now it has generally been supposed that the Prâti*s*âkhya teaches that there must be a long syllable in the eighth or tenth place of Traish*t*ubha and *G*âgata, and in the sixth place of Ânush*t*ubha pâdas. This is not the case. The Prâti*s*âkhya, no doubt, says, that a short final vowel, but not any short syllable, occupying the eighth or tenth place in a Traish*t*ubha and *G*âgata pâda, or the sixth place in a Gâyatra pâda, is lengthened, but it never says that it must be lengthened; on the contrary, it gives a number of cases where it is not so lengthened. But, what is even more important, the Prâti*s*âkhya distinctly adds a proviso which shows that the ancient critics of the Veda did not consider the trochee as the only possible foot for the sixth and seventh syllables of Gâyatra, or for the eighth and ninth, or tenth and eleventh syllables of Traish*t*ubha and *G*âgata pâdas. They distinctly admit that the seventh and the ninth and the eleventh syllables in such pâdas may be long, and that in that case the preceding short vowel is not lengthened. We thus get the iambus in the very place which is generally occupied by the trochee. According to the Prâti*s*âkhya, the general scheme for the Gâyatra would be, not only

6 7
+ + + + | + – ⏑ +,

but also

6 7
+ + + + | + ⏑ – +;

and for the Traish*t*ubha and *G*âgata, not only

8 9
+ + + + | + + + – | ⏑ + + (+),

but also

8 9
+ + + + | + + + ⏑ | – + + (+).

And again, for the same pâdas, not only

10 11
+ + + + | + + + + | + – ⏑ (+),

but also

10 11
+ + + + | + + + + | + ⏑ – (+).

Before appealing, however, to the Prâti*s*âkhya for the establishment of such a rule as that the sixth syllable of Ânush*t*ubha and the eighth or tenth syllable of Traish*t*ubha and *G*âgata pâdas must be lengthened, provided a short syllable follows, it is indispensable that we should have a clear appreciation of the real character of the Prâti*s*âkhya. If we carefully follow the thread which runs through these books, we shall soon perceive that, even with the proviso that a short syllable follows, the Prâti*s*âkhya never teaches that certain final vowels m u s t be lengthened. The object of the Prâti*s*âkhya, as I pointed out on a former occasion, is to register all the facts which possess a phonetic interest. In doing this, all kinds of plans are adopted in order to bring as large a number of cases as possible under general categories. These categories are purely technical and external, and they never assume, with the authors of the Prâti*s*âkhya, the character of general rules. Let us now, after these preliminary remarks, return to the Sûtras 523 to 535, which we discussed before. The Prâti*s*âkhya simply says that certain syllables which are short in the

Pada, if occupying a certain place in a verse, are lengthened in the Sa*m*hitâ, provided a short syllable follows. This looks, no doubt, like a general rule which should be carried out under all circumstances. But this idea never entered the minds of the authors of the Prâti*s*âkhya. They only give this rule as the most convenient way of registering the lengthening of certain syllables which have actually been lengthened in the text of the Sa*m*hitâ, while they remain short in the Pada; and after having done this, they proceed to give a number of verses where the same rule might be supposed to apply, but where in the text of the Sa*m*hitâ the short syllable has not been lengthened. After having given a long string of words which are short in the Pada and long in the Sa*m*hitâ, and where no intelligible reason of their lengthening can be given, at least not by the authors of the Prâti*s*âkhya, the Prâti*s*âkhya adds in Sûtra 523, 'The final vowel of the eighth syllable is lengthened in pâdas of eleven and twelve syllables, provided a syllable follows which is short in the Sa*m*hitâ.' As instances the commentator gives (Sa*m*hitâ text):

I, 32, 4. tâdī́tnâ *s*ā́trum nắ kīlă vĭvītse.

I, 94, 1. ā́gne sākhyé mā́ rīshâmă văyám tắva.

Then follows another rule (Sûtra 525) that 'The final vowel of the tenth syllable in pâdas of eleven and twelve syllables is lengthened, provided a syllable follows which is short in the Sa*m*hitâ.' As instances the commentator gives:

III, 54, 22. ắhâ vī́*s*vâ sŭmă̄nâ dī́dihi na*h*.

II, 34, 9. ắvă rudrâ ā*s*ắso hăntană vắdha*h*.

Lastly, a rule is given (Sûtra 526) that 'The final vowel of the sixth syllable is lengthened in a pâda of eight syllables, provided a syllable follows which is short:'

I, 5, 10. ī́*s*âno yăvăyă vădhám.

If the seventh syllable is long no change takes place:

IX, 67, 30. ā́ pavăsvă devă soma.

While we ourselves should look upon these rules as

founded in the very nature of the metre, which, no doubt, to a certain extent they are, the authors of the Prâti*s*âkhya use them simply as convenient nets for catching as many cases as possible of lengthened syllables actually occurring in the text of the Sa*m*hitâ. For this purpose, and in order to avoid giving a number of special rules, they add in this place an observation, very important to us as throwing light on the real pronunciation of the Vedic hymns at the time when our Sa*m*hitâ text was finally settled, but with them again a mere expedient for enlarging the preceding rules, and thus catching more cases of lengthening at one haul. They say in Sûtra 527, that in order to get the right number of syllables in such verses, we must pronounce sometimes one syllable as two. Thus only can the lengthened syllable be got into one of the places required by the preceding Sûtra, viz. the sixth, the eighth, or the tenth place, and thus only can a large number of lengthened syllables be comprehended under the same general rule of the Prâti*s*âkhya. In all this we ourselves can easily recognise a principle which guided the compilers of the Sa*m*hitâ text, or the very authors of the hymns, in lengthening syllables which in the Pada text are short, and which were liable to be lengthened because they occupied certain places on which the stress of the metre would naturally fall. We also see quite clearly that these compilers, or those whose pronunciation they tried to perpetuate, must have pronounced certain syllables as two syllables, and we naturally consider that we have a right to try the same expedient in other cases where to us, though not to them, the metre seems deficient, and where it could be rendered perfect by pronouncing one syllable as two. Such thoughts, however, never entered the minds of the authors of the Prâti*s*âkhyas, who are satisfied with explaining what is, according to the authority of the Sa*m*hitâ, and who never attempt to say what ought to be, even against the authority of the Sa*m*hitâ. While in some cases they have ears to hear and to appreciate the natural flow of the poetical language of the *Ri*shis, they seem at other times as deaf as the adder to the voice of the charmer.

A general rule, therefore, in our sense of the word, that the eighth syllable in hendecasyllabics and dodecasyllabics, the tenth syllable in hendecasyllabics and dodecasyllabics, and the sixth syllable in octosyllabics should be lengthened, rests in no sense on the authority of ancient grammarians. Even as a mere observation, they restrict it by the condition that the next syllable must be short, in order to provoke the lengthening of the preceding syllable, thereby sanctioning, of course, many exceptions; and they then proceed to quote a number of cases where, in spite of all, the short syllable remains short[a]. In some of these quotations they are no doubt wrong, but in most of them their statement cannot be disputed.

As to the eighth syllable being short in hendecasyllabics and dodecasyllabics, they quote such verses as,

VI, 66, 4. āntār (íti) sāntă*h* āvădyānĭ pūnānā*h*.

Thus we see that in VI, 44, 9, vārshîyă*h* văyă*h* k*ri*n*uhĭ să*k*îbhī*h*, hi remains short; while in VI, 25, 3, *g*ahī v*ri*sh*n*yăni k*ri*n*uhî părā*k*ā*h*, it is lengthened in the Sa*m*hitâ, the only difference being that in the second passage the accent is on hí.

As to the tenth syllable being short in a dodecasyllabic, they quote

II, 27, 14. ădĭtē mītră văru*n*ă ŭtā m*ri*lă.

As to the tenth syllable being short in a hendecasyllabic, they quote

II, 20, 1. văyām tē văyă*h* īndră vīddhĭ sŭ nā*h*.

As to the sixth syllable being short in an octosyllabic, they quote

VIII, 23, 26. mahā*h* vī*s*vân ăbhĭ sătā*h*.

A large number of similar exceptions are collected from

---

[a] 'Wo die achtsilbigen Reihen mit herbeigezogen sind, ist es in der Regel bei solchen Liedern geschehen, die im Ganzen von der regelmässigen Form weniger abweichen, und für solche Fälle, wo auch das Prâti*s*âkhya die Längung der sechsten Silbe in achtsilbigen Reihen vorschreibt, nämlich wo die siebente von Natur kurz ist. Die achtsilbigen Reihen bedürfen einer erneuten Durchforschung, da es mehrfach schwer fällt, den Sa*m*hitâtext mit der Vorschrift der Prâti*s*âkhya in Übereinstimmung zu bringen.' Kuhn, Beiträge, vol. iii, p. 450: and still more strongly, p. 458.

528, 3 to 534, 94, and this does not include any cases where the ninth, the eleventh, or the seventh syllable is long, instead of being short, while it does include cases where the eighth syllable is long, though the ninth is not short, or, at least, is not short according to the views of the collectors of these passages. See Sûtra 522, 6.

Besides the cases mentioned by the Prâtisâkhya itself, where a short syllable, though occupying a place which would seem to require lengthening, remains short, there are many others which the Prâtisâkhya does not mention, because, from its point of view, there was no necessity for doing so. The Prâtisâkhya has been blamed[a] for omitting such cases as I, 93, 6, urum yagñâya kakrathŭr u lokam; or I, 96, 1, devâ agnim dhârayan drăvinodâm. But though occupying the eighth place, and though followed by a short syllable, these syllables could never fall under the general observation of the Prâtisâkhya, because that general observation refers to final vowels only, but not to short syllables in general. Similar cases are I, 107, 1[a]; 122, 9; 130, 10; 152, 6; 154, 1; 158, 5[a]; 163, 2; 167, 10[a]; 171, 4; 173, 6; 179, 1[a]; 182, 8[a]; 186, 6, &c.

If, therefore, we say that, happen what may, these metrical rules must be observed, and the text of the Veda altered in order to satisfy the requirements of these rules, we ought to know at all events that we do this on our own responsibility, and that we cannot shield ourselves behind the authority of Saunaka or Kâtyâyana. Now it is well known that Professor Kuhn[b] has laid down the rule that the Traishtubha pâdas must end in a bacchius or amphibrachys ◡ – ⏓, and the Gâgata pâdas in a dijambus or pæon secundus ◡ – ◡ ⏓. With regard to Ânushtubha pâdas, he requires the dijambus or pæon secundus ◡ – ◡ ⏓ at the end of a whole verse only, allowing greater freedom in the formation of the preceding pâdas. In a later article,

[a] 'Dazu kommt, dass der uns vorliegende Samhitâtext vielfältig gar nicht mit Saunaka's allgemeiner Regel übereinstimmt, indem die Verlängerung kurzer Silben nicht unter den Bedingungen eingetreten ist, die er vorschreibt.' Kuhn, Beiträge, vol. iii, p. 459.

[b] Beiträge zur Vergleichenden Sprachforschung, vol. iii, p. 118.

however, the final pâda, too, in Ânush*t*ubha metre is allowed greater freedom, and the rule, as above given, is strictly maintained with regard to the Traish*t*ubha and *G*âgata pâdas only.

This subject is so important, and affects so large a number of passages in the Veda, that it requires the most careful examination. The Vedic metres, though at first sight very perplexing, are very simple, if reduced to their primary elements. The authors of the Prâti*s*âkhyas have elaborated a most complicated system. Counting the syllables in the most mechanical manner, they have assigned nearly a hundred names to every variety which they discovered in the hymns of the Rig-veda[a]. But they also observed that the constituent elements of all these metres were really but four, (Sûtras 988, 989):

The four principal Pâdas.

1. The Gâyatra pâda, of eight syllables, ending in ◡ –.
2. The Vairâ*g*a pâda, of ten syllables, ending in – –.
3. The Traish*t*ubha pâda, of eleven syllables, ending in – –.
4. The *G*âgata pâda, of twelve syllables, ending in ◡ –.

Then follows an important rule, Sûtra 990: 'The penultimate syllable,' he says, 'in a Gâyatra and *G*âgata pâda is light (laghu), in a Vairâ*g*a and Traish*t*ubha pâda heavy (guru).' This is called their v*ri*tta.

This word v*ri*tta, which is generally translated by metre, had evidently originally a more special meaning. It meant the final rhythm, or if we take it literally, the turn of a line, for it is derived from v*ri*t, to turn. Hence v*ri*tta is the same word as the Latin versus, verse; but I do not wish to decide whether the connection between the two words is historical, or simply etymological. In Latin, versus is always supposed to have meant originally a furrow, then a line, then a verse. In Sanskrit the metaphor that led to the formation of v*ri*tta, in the sense of final rhythm, has nothing to do with ploughing. If, as I have tried to prove (Chips from a German Workshop,

V*ri*tta = versus.

[a] See Appendix to my edition of the Prâti*s*âkhya, p. cclvi.

vol. i, p. 84), the names assigned to metres and metrical language were derived from words originally referring to choregic movements, *vri*tta must have meant the turn, i. e. the last step of any given movement; and this turn, as determining the general character of the whole movement, would naturally be regulated by more severe rules, while greater freedom would be allowed for the rest.

Having touched on this subject, I may add another fact in support of my view. The words Trish*t*ubh and Anush*t*ubh, names for the most common metres, are generally derived from a root stubh, to praise. I believe they should be derived from a root stubh, which is preserved in Greek, not only in στυφελός, hard, στυφελίζω, to strike hard, but in the root στεμφ, from which στέμφυλον, stamped or pressed olives or grapes, and ἀστεμφής, untrodden (grapes), then unshaken; and in στέμβω, to shake, to ram, στοβέω, to scold, &c. In Sanskrit this root is mentioned in the Dhâtupâ*th*a X, 34, shtubhu stambhe, and it exists in a parallel form as stambh, lit. to stamp down, then to fix, to make firm, with which Bopp has compared the German stampfen, to stamp; (Glossarium, s. v. stambh.) I therefore look upon Trish*t*ubh as meaning originally tripudium, (supposing this word to be derived from tri and pes, according to the expression in Horace, pepulisse ter pede terram, Hor. Od. iii. 18,) and I explain its name 'Three-step,' by the fact that the three last syllables ⏑ – ⏑, which form the characteristic feature of that metre, and may be called its real *vri*tta or turn, were audibly stamped at the end of each turn or strophe. I explain Anush*t*ubh, which consists of four equal pâdas, each of eight syllables, as the 'After-step,' because each line was stamped regularly after the other, possibly by two choruses, each side taking its turn. There is one passage in the Veda where Ânush*t*ubh seems to have preserved this meaning:

X, 124, 9. anu-stúbham ánu *k*arkûryámâ*n*am índram ní *k*ikyu*h* kaváya*h* manîshấ.

Poets by their wisdom discovered Indra dancing to an Anush*t*ubh.

In V, 52, 12, *kh*anda*h*-stúbha*h* kubhanyáva*h* útsam ấ

kîrí*nah* n*r*ituh, in measured steps (i.e. stepping the metre) and wildly shouting the gleemen have danced toward the spring.

Other names of metres which point to a similar origin, i.e. to their original connection with dances, are Padapaṅkti, 'Step-row;' Nyaṅku-sâri*n*î, 'Roe-step;' Abhisâri*n*î, 'Contre-danse,' &c.

If now we return to the statement of the Prâti*s*âkhya in reference to the v*r*ittas, we should observe how careful its author is in his language. He does not say that the penultimate is long or short, but he simply states, that, from a metrical point of view, it must be considered as light or heavy, which need not mean more than that it must be pronounced with or without stress. The fact that the author of the Prâti*s*âkhya uses these terms, laghu and guru, instead of hrasva, short, and dîrgha, long, shows in fact that he was aware that the penultimate in these pâdas is not invariably long or short, though, from a metrical point of view, it is always heavy or light.

It is perfectly true that if we keep to these four pâdas, (to which one more pâda, viz. the half Vairâ*g*a, consisting of five syllables, might be added,) we can reduce nearly all the hymns of the Rig-veda to their simple elements which the ancient poets combined together, in general in a very simple way, but occasionally with greater freedom. The most important strophes, formed out of these pâdas, are,

1. Three Gâyatra pâdas = the Gâyatrî, (24 syllables.)
2. Four Gâyatra pâdas = the Anush*t*ubh, (32 syllables.)
3. Four Vairâ*g*a pâdas = the Virâ*g*, (40 syllables.)
4. Four Traish*t*ubha pâdas = the Trish*t*ubh, (44 syllables.)
5. Four *G*âgata pâdas = the *G*agatî, (48 syllables.)

Between the Gâyatrî and Anush*t*ubh strophes, another strophe may be formed, by mixture of Gâyatra and *G*âgata pâdas, consisting of 28 syllables, and commonly called Ush*n*ih; likewise between the Anush*t*ubh and the Virâ*g*, a strophe may be formed, consisting of 36 syllables, and commonly called B*r*ihatî.

In a collection of hymns, however, like that of the Rig-veda, where poems of different ages, different places, and different families have been put together, we must be prepared for exceptions to many rules. Thus, although the final turn of the hendecasyllabic Traish*t*ubha is, as a rule, the bacchius, ⏑ – –, yet if we take, for instance, the 77th hymn of the tenth Ma*n*d*ala, we clearly perceive another hendecasyllabic pâda of a totally different structure, and worked up into one of the most beautiful strophes by an ancient poet. Each line is divided into two halves, the first consisting of seven syllables, being an exact counterpart of the first member of a Saturnian verse (fato Romae Metelli); the second a dijambus, answering boldly to the broken rhythm of the first member[a]. We have, in fact, a Trish*t*ubh where the turn or the three-step, ⏑ – –, instead of being at the end, stands in the middle of the line.

X, 77, 1–5, in the Pada text:

1. ābhrā-prūshă*h* nă vā*k*â̆ prūshă̄ vāsŭ,

 hăvīshmāntă*h* nă yăg*ñ*â*h* vĭ-gânŭshă*h* | &c.

Another strophe, the nature of which has been totally misapprehended by native metricians, occurs in IV, 10. It is there called Padapaṅkti and Mahâpadapaṅkti; nay, attempts have been made to treat it even as an Ush*n*ih, or as a kind of Gâyatrî. The real character of that strophe is so palpable that it is difficult to understand how it could have been mistaken. It consists of two lines, the first embracing three or four feet of five syllables each, having the ictus on the first and the fourth syllables, and resembling the last line of a Sapphic verse. The second line is simply

[a] Professor Kuhn (vol. iii, p. 450) is inclined to admit the same metre as varying in certain hymns with ordinary Traish*t*ubha pâdas, but the evidence he brings forward is hardly sufficient. Even if we object to the endings ⏑ – ⏑ – and – – ⏑ –, V, 33, 4, may be a *G*âgata, with vyûha of dâsa, the remark quoted from the Prâti*s*âkhya being of no consequence on such points; and the same remedy would apply to V, 41, 5, with vyûha of eshe. In VI, 47, 31, vyûha of a*s*vapar*n*ai*h*; in I, 33, 9, vyûha of indra and rodasî; in II, 24, 5, vyûha of mâdbhi*h* would produce the same effect; while in I, 121, 8, we must either admit the Traish*t*ubha v*ri*tta – ⏑ – or scan dhūkshăn. In III, 58, 6, I should admit vyûha for nărâ̆; in IV, 26, 6, for māndrăm; in I, 100, 8, for *g*yŏti*h*, always supposing that we consider the ending – – ⏑ – incompatible with a Trish*t*ubh verse.

a Trish*t*ubh. It is what we should call an asynartete strophe, and the contrast of the rhythm in the first and second lines is very effective. I am not certain whether Professor Bollensen, who has touched on this metre in an article just published (Zeitschrift der D. M. G., vol. xxii, p. 572), shares this opinion. He has clearly seen that the division of the lines, as given in the MSS. of the Sa*m*hitâ text, is wrong; but he seems inclined to admit the same rhythm throughout, and to treat the strophe as consisting of four lines of five syllables each, and one of six syllables, which last line is to submit to the prevailing rhythm of the preceding lines. If we differ, however, as to the internal architecture of this strophe, we agree in condemning the interpretation proposed by the Prâti*s*âkhya; and I should, in connection with this, like to call attention to two important facts: first, that the Sa*m*hitâ text, in not changing, for instance, the final t of martât, betrays itself as clearly later than the elaboration of the ancient theory of metres, later than the invention of such a metre as the Padapaṅkti; and secondly, that the accentuation, too, of the Sa*m*hitâ is thus proved to be posterior to the establishment of these fanciful metrical divisions, and hence cannot throughout claim so irrefragable an authority as certainly belongs to it in many cases. I give the Sa*m*hitâ text:

1. Āgnē tām ādyă | ă*s*vă*m* nă stōmai*h* | krătu*m* nă bhādrăm,
   h*rĭ*dīsp*rĭs*am *rĭ*dhyâmâ ta ōhai*h*.
2. Ădhâ hy āgnē | krătōr bhādrăsyă | dākshăsyă sâdhō*h*,
   răthīr *rĭ*tăsyă b*rĭ*hătō băbhûthă, &c.

Now it is perfectly true that, as a general rule, the syllables composing the v*ri*tta or turn of the different metres, and described by the Prâti*s*âkhya as heavy or light, are in reality long or short. The question, however, is this, have we a right, or are we obliged, in cases where that syllable is not either long or short, as it ought to be, so to alter the text, or so to change the rules of pronunciation, that the penultimate may again be what we wish it to be?

If we begin with the Gâyatra pâda, we have not to read

long before we find that it would be hopeless to try to crush the Gâyatrî verses of the Vedic *Ri*shis on this Procrustean bed. Even Professor Kuhn very soon perceived that this was impossible. He had to admit that in the Gâyatrî the two first pâdas, at all events, were free from this rule, and though he tried to retain it for the third or final pâda, he was obliged after a time to give it up even there. Again, it is perfectly true, that in the third pâda of the Gâyatrî, and in the second and fourth pâdas of the Anush*t*ubh strophe, greater care is taken by the poets to secure a short syllable for the penultimate, but here, too, exceptions cannot be entirely removed. We have only to take such a single hymn as I, 27, and we shall see that it would be impossible to reduce it to the uniform standard of Gâyatrî pâdas, all ending in a dijambus.

Gâyatra Pâdas.

But what confirms me even more in my view that such strict uniformity must not be looked for in the ancient hymns of the *Ri*shis, is the fact that in many cases it would be so very easy to replace the irregular by a regular dipodia. Supposing that the original poets had restricted themselves to the dijambus, who could have put in the place of that regular dijambus an irregular dipodia? Certainly not the authors of the Prâti*s*âkhya, for their ears had clearly discovered the general rhythm of the ancient metres; nor their predecessors, for they had in many instances preserved the tradition of syllables lengthened in accordance with the requirements of the metre. I do not mean to insist too strongly on this argument, or to represent those who handed down the tradition of the Veda as endowed with anything like apaurusheyatva. Strange accidents have happened in the text of the Veda, but they have generally happened when the sense of the hymns had ceased to be understood; and if anything helped to preserve the Veda from greater accidents, it was due, I believe, to the very fact that the metre continued to be understood, and that oral tradition, however much it might fail in other respects, had at all events to satisfy the ears of the hearers. I should

Conjectural emendations.

have been much less surprised if all irregularities in the metre had been smoothed down by the flux and reflux of oral tradition, a fact which is so apparent in the text of Homer, where the gaps occasioned by the loss of the digamma, were made good by the insertion of unmeaning particles; but I find it difficult to imagine by what class of men, who must have lived between the original poets and the age of the Prâti*s*âkhyas, the simple rhythm of the Vedic metres should have been disregarded, and the sense of rhythm, which ancient people possess in a far higher degree than we ourselves, been violated through crude and purposeless alterations. I shall give a few specimens only. What but a regard for real antiquity could have induced people in VIII, 2, 8, to preserve the defective foot of a Gâyatrî verse, samâne adhi bhârman? Any one acquainted with Sanskrit would naturally read samâne adhi bhârma*n*i. But who would have changed bhârma*n*i, if that had been there originally, to bhârman? I believe we must scan samâne adhi bhârman, or samane adhi bhârman, the pæon tertius being a perfectly legitimate foot at the end of a Gâyatrî verse. In X, 158, 1, we can understand how an accident happened. The original poet may have said: Sûryo no divas pâtu pâtu vâto antarikshât, agnir na*h* pârthivebhya*h*. Here one of the two pâtu was lost. But if in the same hymn we find in the second verse two feet of nine instead of eight syllables each, I should not venture to alter this except in pronunciation, because no reason can be imagined why any one should have put these irregular lines in the place of regular ones.

In V, 41, 10, g*rin*îte agnir etarî na *s*ûshai*h*, *sok*ishke*s*o ni ri*n*âti vanâ, every modern Pandit would naturally read vanâni instead of vanâ, in order to get the regular Trish*t*ubh metre. But this being the case, how can we imagine that even the most ignorant member of an ancient Parishad should wilfully have altered vanâni into vanâ? What surprises one is, that vanâ should have been spared, in spite of every temptation to change it into vanâni: for I cannot doubt for one moment that vanâ is the right reading, only that the ancient poets pronounced it vanâ. Wherever we alter the text of the Rig-veda by conjecture, we ought to be able, if possible, to give some explanation how the mistake which we wish to remove came to be committed. If a passage is obscure, difficult to construe, if it contains words which occur in no other place, then we can understand how, during a long process of oral tradition, accidents may have happened. But when everything is smooth and easy, when the intention of the poet is not to be mistaken, when the same phrase has occurred many times before, then to suppose that a simple and perspicuous sentence was changed into a complicated and obscure string of words, is more difficult to understand. I know there are passages where we cannot as yet account for the manner in which an evidently faulty reading found its way into both the Pada and Sa*m*hitâ texts, but in those very passages we cannot be too circumspect. If we read VIII, 40, 9, pûrvîsh *t*a indropamâtaya*h* pûrvîr uta pra*s*astaya*h*, nothing seems more tempting than to omit indra, and to read pûrvîsh *t*a upamâtaya*h*. Nor would it be difficult to account for the insertion of indra; for though one would hardly venture to call it a marginal gloss that crept into the text—a case which, as far as I can see, has never happened in the hymns of the Rig-veda—it might be taken for an explanation given by an Â*k*ârya to his pupils, in order to inform them that the ninth verse, different from the eighth, was addressed to Indra. But however plausible this may sound, the question remains whether the traditional reading could not be maintained, by admitting synizesis of opa, and reading pûrvîsh *t*a indropamâtaya*h*. For a similar synizesis of – ◡, see III, 6, 10. prâ*k*î adhvareva tasthatu*h*, unless we read prâ*k*y adhvareva.

Another and more difficult case of synizesis occurs in

VII, 86, 4. ava tvânenâ namasâ tura(*h*) iyâm.

It would be easy to conjecture tvareyâm instead of tura iyâm, but tvareyâm, in the sense of 'let me hasten,' is not Vedic. The choriambic ending, however, of a Trish*t*ubh can be proved to be legitimate, and if that is the case, then even the synizesis of tura, though hard, ought not to be regarded as impossible.

In II, 18, 5, â vi*ms*atyâ tri*ms*atâ yâhy arvâṅ,
â *k*atvâri*ms*atâ haribhir yugâna*h*,
â pa*ñk*â*s*atâ surathebhir indra,
â shash*t*yâ saptatyâ somapeyam,
Professor Kuhn proposes to omit the â at the beginning of the second line, in order to have eleven instead of twelve syllables. By doing so he loses the uniformity of the four pâdas, which all begin with â, while by admitting synizesis of haribhi*h* all necessity for conjectural emendation disappears.

If the poets of the Veda had objected to a pæon quartus (◡◡◡–) at the end of a Gâyatrî, what could have been easier than to change IV, 52, 1, divo adar*s*i duhitâ, into adar*s*i duhitâ diva*h*? or X, 118, 6, adâbhya*m* g*ri*hapatim, into g*ri*hapatim adâbhyam?

If an epitritus secundus (–◡––) had been objectionable in the same place, why not say VI, 61, 10, stomyâ bhût sarasvatî, instead of sarasvatî stomyâ bhût? Why not VIII, 2, 11, revanta*m* hi *sri*n*o*mi tvâ, instead of revanta*m* hi tvâ *sri*n*o*mi?

If an ionicus a minore (◡◡––) had been excluded from that place, why not say I, 30, 10, *g*arit*ri*bhya*h* sakhe vaso, instead of sakhe vaso *g*arit*ri*bhya*h*? or I, 41, 7, varu*n*asya mahi psara*h*, instead of mahi psaro varu*n*asya?

If a dispondeus (––––) was to be avoided, then V, 68, 3, mahi vâ*m* kshatra*m* deveshu, might easily have been replaced by deveshu vâ*m* kshatram mahi, and VIII, 2, 10, *s*ukrâ â*s*ira*m* yâ*k*ante, by *s*ukrâ yâ*k*anta â*s*iram.

If no epitritus primus (◡–––) was allowed, why not say VI, 61, 11, nidas pâtu sarasvatî, instead of sarasvatî nidas pâtu, or VIII, 79, 4, dvesho yâvîr aghasya *k*it, instead of yâvîr aghasya *k*id dvesha*h*?

Even the epitritus tertius (– – ⏑ –) might easily have been avoided by dropping the augment of apâm in X, 119, 1–13, kuvit somasyâpâm iti. It is, in fact, a variety of less frequent occurrence than the rest, and might possibly be eliminated with some chance of success.

Lastly, the choriambus (– ⏑ ⏑ –) could have been removed in III, 24, 5, *s*i*s*îhi na*h* sûnumata*h*, by reading sûnumata*h* *s*i*s*îhi na*h*, and in VIII, 2, 31, sanâd am*ri*kto dayate, by reading am*ri*kto dayate sanât.

But I am afraid the idea that regularity is better than irregularity, and that in the Veda, where there is a possibility, the regular metre is to be restored by means of conjectural emendations, has been so ably advocated by some of the most eminent scholars, that a merely general argument would now be of no avail. I must therefore give as much evidence as I can bring together in support of the contrary opinion; and though the process is a tedious one, the importance of the consequences with regard to Vedic criticism leaves me no alternative. With regard, then, to the final dipodia of Gâyatrî verses, I still hold and maintain, that, although the dijambus is by far the most general metre, the following seven varieties have to be recognised in the poetry of the Veda[a]:

Seven Gâyatra V*ri*ttas.

1. ⏑ – ⏑ –, 2. ⏑ ⏑ ⏑ –, 3. – ⏑ – –, 4. ⏑ ⏑ – –, 5. – – – –, 6. ⏑ – – –, 7. – – ⏑ –, 8. – ⏑ ⏑ –.

I do not pretend to give every passage in which these varieties occur, but I hope I shall give a sufficient number in support of every one of them. I have confined myself almost entirely to the final dipodia of Gâyatrî verses, as the Ânush*t*ubha verses would have swelled the lists too much.

§ 2. ⏑ ⏑ ⏑ –.

I, 12, 9. tasmai pâvaka m*ril*aya. (Instead of m*ril*aya, it has been proposed to read mar*d*aya.)

I, 18, 9. divo na sadmamakhasam.

I, 42, 4; 46, 2; 97, 1–8; III, 11, 3; 27, 10; IV, 15, 7;

[a] See some important remarks on these varieties in Mr. J. Boxwell's article 'On the Trish*t*ubh Metre,' Journal Asiat. Soc. Beng., 1885, p. 79.

32, 4; 52, 1; V, 5, 9; 7, 4; 7, 5; 7, 7; 9, 4; 53, 12; 61, 3; 61, 11; 64, 5; 65, 4; 82, 9; VI, 16, 17; 16, 18; 16, 45; 45, 17; 61, 4; VII, 15, 14; 66, 2; VIII, 6, 35; 6, 42; 32, 10; 44, 28; 45, 31; 72, 6; 72, 13; 80, 1; 83, 3; 93, 27; IX, 61, 5; 64, 1; X, 118, 6.

§ 3. – ⏑ – –.

I, 22, 11. a*kkh*innapatrâ*h* sa*k*ântâm.

I, 30, 13. kshumanto yâbhir madema.

I, 41, 8; 90, 1; 90, 4; 120, 1; V, 19, 1; 70, 3; VI, 61, 10; VIII, 2, 2; 2, 4; 2, 5; 2, 11; 2, 12; 2, 13; 2, 14; 2, 15; 2, 16; 2, 17; 2, 29; 2, 30; 2, 32; 2, 33; 2, 36; 2, 37; 7, 30; 7, 33; 11, 2; 11, 3; 11, 4; 16, 3; 16, 4; 16, 5; 16, 7; 46, 2; 71, 2; 81, 1; 81, 3; 81, 4; 81, 7; 81, 9; 94, 2; IX, 62, 5; X, 20, 4; 20, 7.

§ 4. ⏑ ⏑ – –.

I, 3, 8. usrâ iva svasarâ*n*i.

I, 27, 4. agne deveshu pra vo*k*a*h*.

I, 30, 10; 30, 15; 38, 7; 38, 8; 41, 7; 43, 7; II, 6, 2; III, 27, 3; V, 82, 7; VI, 16, 25; 16, 26; 61, 12; VIII, 2, 1; 2, 3; 2, 8; 2, 18; 2, 19; 2, 21; 2, 22; 2, 23; 2, 26; 2, 35; 16, 2; 16, 6; 16, 8; 71, 9; 79, 3; IX, 21, 5; 62, 6; 66, 21; X, 20, 5; 185, 1; 185, 2; 185, 3.

§ 5. – – – –.

I, 2, 7. dhiya*m* gh*ri*tâ*k*î*m* sâdhantâ.

I, 3, 4. a*n*vîbhis tanâ pûtâsa*h*.

I, 27, 3; 90, 2; II, 6, 4; III, 41, 8; V, 68, 3; 68, 4; VIII, 2, 10; 2, 24; 16, 1; 16, 12; 79, 2; IX, 66, 17; X, 20, 6; 20, 8.

§ 6. ⏑ – – –.

I, 15, 6. *ri*tunâ yag*ñ*am â*s*âthe.

I, 38, 2. kva vo gâvo na ra*n*yanti (see note to I, 38, 2).

I, 38, 9; 86, 9; III, 27, 2; 41, 3; IV, 32, 23; V, 68, 5; 70, 2; VI, 61, 11; VIII, 2, 20; 2, 25; 7, 32; 26, 19; 79, 4; 79, 5; 81, 6; X, 158, 4.

§ 7. – – ᴗ –.

I, 10, 8. sa*m* gâ asmabhya*m* dhûnuhi.

I, 12, 5. agne tva*m* rakshasvina*h*.

I, 37, 15; 43, 8; 46, 6; III, 62, 7; IV, 30, 21; V, 86, 5; VIII, 5, 32; 5, 35; X, 119, 1–13; 144, 4.

§ 8. – ᴗ ᴗ –.

I, 2, 9. daksha*m* dadhâte apasam (or § 2).

I, 6, 10. indra*m* maho vâ ra*g*asa*h*.

I, 27, 6; 30, 21; 41, 9; 90, 5; III, 24, 5; V, 19, 2; 70, 1; 70, 4; 82, 8; VIII, 2, 27; 2, 31; 16, 9; 55, 4; 67, 19; 81, 5; 81, 8; IX, 47, 2.

Traish*t*ubha and *G*âgata Pâdas.

But although with regard to the Gâyatra, and I may add, the Ânush*t*ubha pâdas, the evidence as to the variety of their v*ri*ttas is such that it can hardly be resisted, a much more determined stand has been made in defence of the v*ri*tta of the Traish*t*ubha and *G*âgata pâdas. Here Professor Kuhn and those who follow him maintain that the rule is absolute, that the former must end in ᴗ – ᴗ, the latter in ᴗ – ᴗ –, and that the eighth syllable, immediately preceding these syllables, ought, if possible, to be long. Nor can I deny that Professor Kuhn has brought forward powerful arguments in support of his theory, and that his emendations of the Vedic text recommend themselves by their great ingenuity and simplicity. If his theory could be carried out, I should readily admit that we should gain something. We should have throughout the Veda a perfectly uniform metre, and wherever we found any violation of it, we should be justified in resorting to conjectural criticism.

The only question is at what price this strict uniformity can be obtained. If, for instance, in order to have the regular v*ri*ttas at the end of Traish*t*ubha and *G*âgata lines, we were obliged to repeal all rules of prosody, to allow almost every short vowel to be used as long, and every long vowel to be used as short, whether long by nature or by position, we should have gained very little, we should have robbed Peter to pay Paul, we should have removed no difficulty, but only ignored the causes which created it. Now, if we examine the process by which Professor Kuhn establishes the regularity of the v*ri*ttas or final syllables of Traish*t*ubha and *G*âgata pâdas, we find, in addition to the rules laid down before, and in which he is supported, as we saw, to a great extent by the Prâti*s*âkhya and Pâ*n*ini, viz. the anceps nature of e and o, and of a long final vowel before a vowel, the following exceptions or metrical licences, without which that metrical uniformity at which he aims, could not be obtained:

Prosodial Licences.

1. The vowel o in the body of a word is to be treated as optionally short:

II, 39, 3. prati vastor usrâ (see Trish*t*. § 5).

Here the o of vasto*h* is supposed to be short, although it is the Gu*n*a of u, and therefore very different from the final e of sarve or âste, or the final o of sarvo for sarvas or mano for manas[a]. It should be remarked that in Greek, too, the final diphthongs corresponding to the e of sarve and âste are treated as short, as far as the accent is concerned. Hence ἄποικοι, τύπτεται, and even γνῶμαι, nom. plur. In Latin, too, the old terminations of the nom. sing. o and u, instead of the later us, are short. (Neue, Formenlehre, § 23 seq.)

VI, 51, 15. gopâ amâ.

Here the o of gopâ is treated as short, in order to get ⏑–⏑– instead of ––⏑–, which is perfectly legitimate at the end of an Ush*n*ih.

2. The long î and û are treated as short, not only before vowels, which is legitimate, but also before consonants.

VII, 62, 4. dyâvâbhûmî adite trâsîthâ*m* na*h* (see Trish*t*. § 5).

The forms î*s*îya and râsîya in VII, 32, 18, occur at the end of octosyllabic or Gâyatra pâdas, and are therefore

[a] A very strong divergence of opinion is expressed on this point by Professor Bollensen. He says: 'O und E erst später in die Schrifttafel aufgenommen, bewahren ihre Länge durch das ganze indische Schriftenthum bis ins Apabhra*m*sa hinab. Selbstverständlich kann kurz o und e im Veda erst recht nicht zugelassen werden.' Zeitschrift der D. M. G., vol. xxii, p. 574.

perfectly legitimate, yet Professor Kuhn would change them too, into îsîya and râsîya. In VII, 28, 4, even mâyî is treated as mâyî (see Trish*t*. § 5); and in VII, 68, 1, vîtam as vîtam. If, in explanation of this shortening of vîtam, vîhi is quoted, which is identified with vĭhi, this can hardly be considered as an argument, for vĭhĭ occurs where no short syllable is required, IV, 48, 1; II, 26, 2; and where, therefore, the shortening of the vowel cannot be attributed to metrical reasons.

3. Final m followed by an initial consonant is allowed to make no position, and even in the middle of a word a nasal followed by a liquid is supposed to make positio debilis. Several of the instances, however, given in support, are from Gâyatra pâdas, where Professor Kuhn, in some of his later articles, has himself allowed greater latitude; others admit of different scanning, as for instance,

I, 117, 8. mahah kshonasya asvinâ kanvâya.

Here, even if we considered the dispondeus as illegitimate, we might scan ka*n*vâya, for this scanning occurs in other places, while to treat the first a as short before *n*v seems tantamount to surrendering all rules of prosody.

4. Final n before semivowels, mutes, and double n before vowels make no position[a]. Ex. III, 49, 1. yasmin vi*s*vâ (Trish*t*. § 5);. I, 174, 5. yasmiñ *k*âkan; I, 186, 4. sasmin(n) ûdhan[b].

5. Final Visarga before sibilants makes no position[c]. Ex. IV, 21, 10. satya*h* samrâ*t* (Trish*t*. § 5). Even in I, 63, 4.

[a] Professor Kuhn has afterwards (Beiträge, vol. iv, p. 207) modified this view, and instead of allowing a final nasal vowel followed by a mute to make positio debilis, he thinks that the nasal should in most cases be omitted altogether.

[b] Here a distinction should be made, I think, between an n before a consonant, and a final n following a short vowel, which, according to the rules of Sandhi, is doubled, if a vowel follows. In the latter case, the vowel before the n remains, no doubt, short in many cases, or, more correctly, the doubling of the n does not take place, e.g. I, 63, 4; 186, 4. In other places, the doubling seems preferable, e.g. I, 33, 11, though Professor Kuhn would remove it altogether. Kuhn, Beiträge, vol. iii, p. 125.

[c] Here, too, according to later researches, Professor Kuhn would rather omit the final sibilant altogether, loc. cit. vol. iv, p. 207.

*k*odî*h* sakhâ (probably a *G*âgata), and V, 82, 4. sâvî*h* saubhagam (a Gây. § 7), the long î is treated as short, and the short a of sakhâ is lengthened, because an aspirate follows.

6. S before mutes makes no position. Ex. VI, 66, 11. ugrâ aspr*i*dhran (Trish*t*. § 3).

7. *S* before *k* makes no position. Ex. vi*s*va*sk*andrâ*h*, &c.

8. Mutes before s make no position. Ex. rakshas, according to Professor Kuhn, in the seventh Ma*nd*ala only, but see I, 12, 5; kutsa, &c.

9. Mutes before r or v make no position. Ex. su*s*ipra, dîrgha*s*rut.

10. Sibilants before y make no position. Ex. dasyûn.

11. R followed by mutes or sibilants makes no position. Ex. âyur *g*îvase, *kh*ardi*h*, varshish*th*am.

12. Words like smaddish*t*in, &c. retain their vowel short before two following consonants.

We now proceed to consider a number of prosodial rules which Professor Kuhn proposes to repeal in order to have a long syllable where the MSS. supply a short:

1. The vowel *ri* is to be pronounced as long, or rather as ar. Ex. I, 12, 9. tasmai pâvaka m*ri*laya is to be read mardaya; V, 33, 10. sa*m*vara*n*asya *ri*she*h* is to be read arshe*h*. But why not sa*m*vara*n*asya *ri*she*h* (i. e. siarshe*h*)?

2. The a privativum may be lengthened. Ex. a*g*ara*h*, am*ri*ta*h*.

3. Short vowels before liquids may be long. Ex. nara*h*, tarutâ, tarati, marutâm, hariva*h*, arushi, dadhur iha, suvitâ (p. 471).

4. Short vowels before nasals may be lengthened. Ex. *g*anân, sanitar, tanû*h*, upa na*h*.

5. Short vowels before the ma of the superlative may be lengthened. Ex. n*ri*tama.

6. The short a in the roots *s*am and yam, and in am (the termination of the accusative) may be lengthened.

7. The group ăvă is to be pronounced āuă. Ex. ăvăsē becomes āuăsē; săvĭtâ becomes săuĭtâ; năvă becomes nāuă.

8. The group ăyă is to be changed into aīă or eă. Ex. năyasĭ becomes naiasĭ.

9. The group vă is to be changed into ua, and this ua to be treated as a kind of diphthong and therefore long. Ex. kā*n*vătămă*h* becomes kā*n*uatamā*h*; văru*n*ā*h* becomes uăru*n*ah.

10. The short vowel in the reduplicated syllable of perfects is to be lengthened. Ex. tātanā*h*, dādhīre.

11. Short vowels before all aspirates may be lengthened. Ex. răthâ*h* becomes rāthâ*h*; săkhâ becomes sākhâ.

12. Short vowels before h and all sibilants may be lengthened. Ex. măhĭnĭ becomes māhĭnĭ; ŭsĭgâm becomes ūsĭgâm; rĭshătē becomes rīshătē; dăsat becomes dāsat.

13. The short vowel before t may be lengthened. Ex. vâgavăta*h* becomes vâgavāta*h*; ătithi*h* becomes ātithi*h*.

14. The short vowel before d may be lengthened. Ex. ŭdaram becomes ūdaram; ŭd ava becomes ūd ava.

15. The short vowel before p may be lengthened. Ex. ăpâm becomes āpâm; tăpushim becomes tāpushim; *gri*hăpatim becomes *gri*hāpatim.

16. The short vowel before g and *g* may be lengthened. Ex. sânushăg asat becomes sânushāg asat; yună*g*an becomes yunā*g*an.

Let us now turn back for one moment to look at the slaughter which has been committed! Is there one single rule of prosody that has been spared? Is there one single short syllable that must always remain short, or a long syllable that must always remain long? If all restrictions of prosody are thus removed, our metres, no doubt, become perfectly regular. But it should be remembered that these metrical rules, for which all this carnage has been committed, are not founded upon any a priori principles, but deduced by ancient or modern metricians from those very hymns which seem so constantly to violate them. Neither ancient nor modern metricians had, as far as we know, any evidence to go upon besides the hymns of the Rig-veda; and the philosophical speculations as to the origin of metres in which some of them indulge, and from which they would fain derive some of their unbending rules, are, as need hardly be said, of no consequence whatever. I cannot understand what definite idea even modern writers connect with such statements as that, for instance, the Trish*t*ubh metre sprang from the *G*agatî metre, that the eleven syllables of the former are an abbreviation of the twelve syllables of the latter. Surely, metres are not made artificially, and by addition or subtraction. Metres have a natural origin in the rhythmic sentiment of different people, and they become artificial and arithmetical in the same way as language with its innate principles of law and analogy becomes in course of time grammatical and artificial. To derive one metre from another is like deriving a genitive from a nominative, which we may do indeed for grammatical purposes, but which no one would venture to do who is at all acquainted with the natural and independent production of grammatical forms. Were we to arrange the Trish*t*ubh and *G*agatî metres in chronological order, I should decidedly place the Trish*t*ubh first, for we see, as it were before our eyes, how sometimes one foot, sometimes two and three feet in a Trish*t*ubh verse admit an additional syllable at the end, particularly in set phrases which would not submit to a Trish*t*ubh ending. The phrase *sam* no bhava dvipade *sam* *k*atushpade is evidently a solemn phrase, and we see it brought in without hesitation, even though every other line of the same strophe or hymn is Trish*t*ubh, i.e. hendecasyllabic, not dodecasyllabic. See, for instance, VI, 74, 1; VII, 54, 1; X, 85, 44; 165, 1. However, I maintain by no means that this was the actual origin of *G*agatî metres; I only refer to it in order to show the groundlessness of metrical theories which represent the component elements, a foot of one or two or four syllables as given first, and as afterwards compounded into systems of two, three or four such feet, and who therefore would wish us to look upon the hendecasyllabic Trish*t*ubh as originally a dodecasyllabic *G*agatî, only deprived of its tail. If my explanation of the name of Trishtubh, i. e. Three-step, is right, its origin must be ascribed to a far more natural process than that of artificial amputation. It was to accompany a choros, i.e. a dance, which after advancing freely for eight steps in one direction, turned back (*vri*tta) with three steps, the second of which was strongly marked, and would therefore, whether in song or recitation, be naturally accompanied by a long syllable. It certainly is so in the vast majority of Trish*t*ubhs which have been handed down to us. But if among these verses we find a small number in which this simple and palpable rhythm is violated, and which nevertheless were preserved from the first in that imperfect form, although the temptation to set them right must have been as great to the ancient as it has proved to be to the modern students of the Veda, are we to say that nearly all, if not all, the rules that determine the length and shortness of syllables, and which alone give character to every verse, are to be suspended? Or, ought we not rather to consider, whether the ancient choregic poets may not have indulged occasionally in an irregular movement? We see that this was so with regard to Gâyatrî verses. We see the greater freedom of the first and second pâdas occasionally extend to the third; and it will be impossible, without intolerable violence, to remove all the varieties of the last pâda of a Gâyatrî of which I have given examples above, pages civ seqq.

Traish*t*ubha Vr*i*tta.

It is, of course, impossible to give here all the evidence that might be brought forward in support of similar freedom in Trish*t*ubh verses, and I admit that the number of real varieties with them is smaller than with the Gâyatrîs. In order to make the evidence which I have to bring forward in support of these varieties as unassailable as possible, I have excluded nearly every pâda that occurs only in the first, second, or third line of a strophe, and have restricted myself, with few exceptions, and those chiefly referring to pâdas that had been quoted by other scholars in support of their own theories, to the final pâdas of Trish*t*ubh verses. Yet even with this limited evidence, I think I shall be able to establish at least three varieties of Trish*t*ubh. Preserving the same classification which I adopted before for the Gâyatrîs, so as to include the important eighth syllable of the Trish*t*ubh, which does not properly belong to the *vri*tta, I maintain that class 4. ⏑ ⏑ – –, class 5. – – – –, and class 8. – ⏑ ⏑ – must be recognised as legimate endings in the hymns of the Veda, and that by recognising them we are relieved from nearly all, if not all, the more violent prosodial licences which Professor Kuhn felt himself obliged to admit in his theory of Vedic metres.

§ 4. ⏑ ⏑ – –.

The verses which fall under § 4 are so numerous that after those of the first Ma*nd*ala, mentioned above, they need not be given here in full. They are simply cases where the eighth syllable is not lengthened, and they cannot be supposed to run counter to any rule of the Prâti*s*âkhya, for the simple reason that the Prâti*s*âkhya never gave such a rule as that the eighth syllable must be lengthened, if the ninth is short. Examples will be found in the final pâda of Trish*t*ubhs: II, 30, 6; III, 36, 4; 53, 15; 54, 12; IV, 1, 16; 2, 7; 9; 11; 4, 12; 6, 1; 2; 4; 7, 7; 11, 5; 17, 3; 23, 6; 24, 2; 27, 1; 28, 5; 55, 5; 57, 2; V, 1, 2; VI, 17, 10; 21, 8; 23, 7; 25, 5; 29, 6; 33, 1; 62, 1; 63, 7; VII, 21, 5; 28, 3; 42, 4; 56, 15; 60, 10; 84, 2; 92, 4; VIII, 1, 33; 96, 9; IX, 92, 5; X, 61, 12; 13; 74, 3; 117, 7.

In support of § 5. – – – –, the number of cases is smaller, but it should be remembered that it might be considerably increased if I had not restricted myself to the final pâda of each Trish*t*ubh, while the first, second, and third pâdas would have yielded a much larger harvest:

§ 5. – – – –.

I, 89, 9. mâ no madhyâ rîrishatâ̄yur gā̆nto*h*.

I, 92, 6. supratîkâ saumanasā̂yā̂*g*ī̂ga*h*.

I, 114, 5; 117, 2; 122, 1; 122, 8; 186, 3; II, 4, 2; III, 49, 2; IV, 3, 9; 26, 6; V, 41, 14; VI, 25, 2; 66, 11; VII, 8, 6; 28 4; 68, 1; 71, 2; 78, 1; 93, 7[b]; IX, 90, 4; X, 11, 8.

I do not wish to deny that in several of these lines it would be possible to remove the long syllable from the ninth place by conjectural emendation. Instead of ấyur in I, 89, 9, we might read ấyu; in I, 92, 6, we might drop the augment of a*g*îgar; in II, 4, 2, we might admit synizesis in aratir, and then read *g*îra-asvā*h*, as in I, 141, 12. In VI, 25, 2, after eliding the a of ava, we might read dâsî*h*. But even if, in addition to all this, we were to admit the possible suppression of final m in asmabhyam, mahyam, and in the accusative singular, or the suppression of s in the nominative singular, both of which would be extreme measures, we should still have a number of cases which could not be righted without even more violent remedies. Why then should we not rather admit the occasional appearance of a metrical variation which certainly has a powerful precedent in the dispondeus of Gâyatrîs? I am not now acquainted with the last results of metrical criticism in Virgil, but, unless some new theories now prevail, I well recollect that spondaic hexameters, though small in number, much smaller than in the Veda, were recognised by the best scholars, and no emendations attempted to remove them. If then in Virgil we read,

'Cum patribus populoque, penatibusque et magnis dis,'

why not follow the authority of the best MSS. and the tradition of the Prâti*s*âkhyas and admit a dispondeus at the end of a Trish*t*ubh rather than suspend, in order to meet this single difficulty, some of the most fundamental rules of prosody?

I now proceed to give a more numerous list of Traish*t*ubha pâdas ending in a choriambus, – ◡ ◡ –, again confining myself, with few exceptions, to final pâdas:

§ 8. – ◡ ◡ –.

I, 62, 3. sam usriyâbhir vâva*s*antă nără*h*.

I, 103, 4. yad dha sûnu*h* *s*ravase nâmă dădhe.

I, 121, 9; 122, 10[b]; 173, 8; 186, 2; II, 4, 3; 19, 1; 33, 14; IV, 1, 19[c a]; 25, 4; 39, 2; V, 30, 12; 41, 4; 41, 15;

[a] 'Nur eine Stelle habe ich mir angemerkt, wo das Metrum âam verlangt.'

VI, 4, 7; 10, 5; 11, 4; 13, 1^{b}; 13, 1^{d}; 20, 1^{b}; 20, 1^{d}; 29, 4; 33, 3; 33, 5; 44, 11; 49, 12; 68, 5; 68, 7; VII, 19, 10; 62, 4; IX, 97, 26; X, 55, 8; 99, 9; 108, 6; 169, 1.

It is perfectly true that this sudden change in the rhythm of Trish*t*ubh verses, making their ending iambic instead of trochaic, grates on our ears. But, I believe, that if we admit a short stop after the seventh syllable, the intended rhythm of these verses will become intelligible. We remarked a similar break in the verses of hymn X, 77, where the sudden transition to an iambic metre was used with great effect, and the choriambic ending, though less effective, is by no means offensive. It should be remarked also, that in many, though not in all cases, a cæsura takes place after the seventh syllable, and this is, no doubt, a great help towards a better delivery of these choriambic Trish*t*ubhs.

While, however, I contend for the recognition of these three varieties of the normal Trish*t*ubh metre, I am quite willing to admit that other variations besides these, which occur from time to time in the Veda, form a legitimate subject of critical discussion.

§ 2. ⏑ ⏑ ⏑ –.

Trish*t*ubh verses, the final pâda of which ends in ⏑ ⏑ ⏑ –, I should generally prefer to treat as ending in a *G*âgata pâda, in which this ending is more legitimate. Thus I should propose to scan:

I, 122, 11. pras*a*staye mahinâ rathavate.

III, 20, 5. vasûn rudrâñ âdityâñ iha huve.

V, 2, 1. pura*h* pas*y*anti nihitam (tam) aratau.

VI, 13, 5. vayo v*ri*kâyâraye *g*asuraye.

§ 1. ⏑ – ⏑ –.

I should propose the same medela for some final pâdas of Trish*t*ubhs apparently ending in ⏑ – ⏑ –. We might indeed, as has been suggested, treat these verses as single instances of that peculiar metre which we saw carried out in the whole of hymn X, 77, but at the end of a verse the ad-

Kuhn, Beiträge, vol. iv, p. 180; Bollensen, Zeitschrift der D. M. G., vol. xxii, p. 587.

mission of an occasional *G*âgata pâda is more in accordance with the habit of the Vedic poets. Thus I should scan:

V, 33, 4. v*ri*shâ samatsu dâsasya nâma *k*it[a]

V, 41, 5[b]. râya eshe ʼvase dadhîta dhî*h*.

After what I have said before on the real character of the teaching of the Prâti*s*âkhya, I need not show again that the fact of Uva*t*a's counting ta of dadhîta as the tenth syllable is of no importance in determining the real nature of these hymns, though it is of importance, as Professor Kuhn remarks (Beiträge, vol. iii, p. 451), in showing that Uva*t*a considered himself at perfect liberty in counting or not counting, for his own purposes, the elided syllable of avase.

VII, 4, 6. mâpsava*h* pari shadâma mâduva*h*.

§ 6. ⏑ – – –.

Final pâdas of Trish*t*ubhs ending in ⏑ – – – are very scarce. In VI, 1, 4,

bhadrâyâ*m* te ra*n*ayanta sa*m*d*ri*sh*t*au,

it would be very easy to read bhadrâyâ*m* te sa*m*d*ri*sh*t*au ra*n*ayanta; and in X, 74, 2,

dyaur na vârebhi*h* k*ri*navanta svai*h*,

we may either recognise a *G*âgata pâda, or read

dyaur na vârebhi*h* k*ri*navanta svai*h*,

which would agree with the metre of hymn X, 77.

§ 7. – – ⏑ –.

Pâdas ending in – – ⏑ – do not occur as final in any Traish*t*ubha hymn, but as many *G*âgata pâdas occur in the body of Traish*t*ubha hymns, we have to scan them as dodecasyllabic:

I, 63, 4[a]. tva*m* ha tyad indra *k*odî*h* sakhâ.

IV, 26, 6[b]. parâvata*h* *s*akuno mandram madam.

The adjective pâvaka which frequently occurs at the end of final and internal pâdas of Trish*t*ubh hymns has always

[a] Professor Kuhn has finally adopted the same scanning, Beiträge, vol. iv, p. 184.

to be scanned pâvakā. Cf. IV, 51, 2; VI, 5, 2; 10, 4; 51, 3; VII, 3, 1; 9; 9, 1^b; 56, 12; X, 46, 7^b.

I must reserve what I have to say about other metres of the Veda for another opportunity, but I cannot leave this subject without referring once more to a metrical licence which has been strongly advocated by Professor Kuhn and others, and by the admission of which there is no doubt that many difficulties might be removed, I mean the occasional omission of a final m and s, and the subsequent contraction of the final and initial vowels. The arguments that have been brought forward in support of this are very powerful. There is the general argument that final s and m are liable to be dropt in other Aryan languages, and particularly for metrical purposes. There is the stronger argument that in some cases final s and m in Sanskrit may or may not be omitted, even apart from any metrical stress. In Sanskrit we find that the demonstrative pronoun sas appears most frequently as sa (sa dadâti), and if followed by liquid vowels, it may coalesce with them even in later Sanskrit. Thus we see saisha for sa esha, sendra*h* for sa indra*h* sanctioned for metrical purposes even by Pâ*n*ini, VI, 1, 134. We might refer also to feminines which have s in the nominative singular after bases in û, but drop it after bases in î. We find in the Sa*m*hitâ text, V, 7, 8, svádhitîva, instead of svádhiti*h*-iva in the Pada text, sanctioned by the Prâti*s*âkhya 259; likewise IX, 61, 10, Sa*m*hitâ, bhū́my ā́ dade, instead of Pada, bhū́mi*h* ā́ dade. But before we draw any general conclusions from such instances, we should consider whether they do not admit of a grammatical instead of a metrical explanation. The nominative singular of the demonstrative pronoun was sa before it was sas; by the side of bhū́mi*h* we have a secondary form bhū́mî; and we may conclude from svádhitî-vân, I, 88, 2, that the Vedic poets knew of a form svádhitî, by the side of svádhiti*h*.

Omission of final m and s.

As to the suppression of final m, however, we see it admitted by the best authorities, or we see at least alternate forms with or without m, in túbhya, which occurs frequently instead of túbhyam[a], and twice, at least, without apparently any metrical reason[b]. We find asmâka instead of asmâkam (I, 173, 10), yushmâka instead of yushmâkam (VII, 59, 9-10), yágadhva instead of yágadhvam (VIII, 2, 37) sanctioned both by the Sa*m*hitâ and Pada texts[c].

If then we have such precedents, it may well be asked why we should hesitate to adopt the same expedient, the omission of final m and s, whenever the Vedic metres seem to require it. Professor Bollensen's remark, that Vedic verses cannot be treated to all the licences of Latin scanning[d], is hardly a sufficient answer; and he himself, though under a slightly different form, would admit as much, if not more, than has been admitted on this point by Professors Kuhn and Roth. On a priori grounds I should by no means feel opposed to the admission of a possible elision of final s or m, or even n; and my only doubt is whether it is really necessary for the proper scanning of Vedic metres.

Synizesis.

My own opinion has always been, that if we admit on a larger scale what in single words can hardly be doubted by anybody, viz. the pronunciation of two syllables as one, we need not fall back on the elision of final consonants in order to arrive at a proper scanning of Vedic metres. On this point I shall have to say a few words in conclusion, because I shall frequently avail myself of this licence, for the purpose of righting apparently corrupt verses in the hymns of the Rig-veda; and I feel bound to explain, once for all, why I avail myself of it in preference to other emendations which have been proposed by scholars such as Professors Benfey, Kuhn, Roth, Bollensen, and others.

The merit of having first pointed out some cases where

---

[a] I, 54, 9; 135, 2; III, 42, 8; V, 11, 5; VII, 22, 7; VIII, 51, 9; 76, 8; 82, 5; IX, 62, 27; 86, 30; X, 167, 1.

[b] II, 11, 3; V, 30, 6.

[c] See Bollensen, Orient und Occident, vol. iii, p. 459; Kuhn, Beiträge, vol. iv, p. 199.

[d] Orient und Occident, vol. iv, p. 449.

two syllables must be treated as one, belongs, I believe, to Professor Bollensen in his article, 'Zur Herstellung des Veda,' published in Benfey's Orient und Occident, vol. ii, p. 461. He proposed, for instance, to write hyânấ instead of hiyânấ, IX, 13, 6; dhyânó instead of dhiyânó, VIII, 49, 5; sáhyase instead of sáhîyase, I, 71, 4; yânó instead of iyânó, VIII, 50, 5, &c. The actual alteration of these words seems to me unnecessary; nor should we think of resorting to such violent measures in Greek where, as far as metrical purposes are concerned, two vowels have not unfrequently to be treated as one.

That iva counts in many passages as one syllable is admitted by everybody. The only point on which I differ is that I do not see why iva, when monosyllabic, should be changed to va, instead of being pronounced quickly, or, to adopt the terminology of Greek grammarians, by synizesis [a]. Synizesis is well explained by Greek scholars as a quick pronunciation of two vowels so that neither should be lost, and as different thereby from synalœphe, which means the contraction of two vowels into one [b]. This synizesis is by no means restricted to iva and a few other words, but seems to me a very frequent expedient resorted to by the ancient *Ri*shis.

Originally it may have arisen from the fact that language allows in many cases alternate forms of one or two syllables. As in Greek we have double forms like ἀλεγεινός and ἀλγεινός, γαλακτοφάγος and γλακτοφάγος, πετηνός and πτηνός, πυκινός and πυκνός [c], and as in Latin we have the shortening

[a] Synizesis in Greek applies only to the quick pronunciation of two vowels, if in immediate contact; and not, if separated by consonants. Samprasâra*n*a might seem a more appropriate term, but though the grammatical process designated in Sanskrit by Samprasâra*n*a offers some analogies, it could only by a new definition be applied to the metrical process here intended.

[b] A. B. p. 835, 30. ἐστὶ δὲ ἐν τοῖς κοινοῖς μέτροις καὶ ἡ καλουμένη συνεκφώνησις ἡ καὶ συνίζησις λέγεται. Ὅταν γὰρ φωνηέντων ἐπάλληλος γένηται ἡ προφορά, τότε γίνεται ἡ συνίζησις εἰς μίαν συλλαβήν. Διαφέρει δὲ συναλοιφῆς· ἡ μὲν γὰρ γραμμάτων ἐστὶ κλοπή, ἡ δὲ χρόνων· καὶ ἡ μὲν συναλοιφή, ὡς λέγεται, φαίνεται, ἡ δὲ οὔ. Mehlhorn, Griechische Grammatik, § 101. Thus in Νεοπτόλεμος we have synizesis, in Νουπτόλεμος synæresis.

[c] Cf. Mehlhorn, Griechische Grammatik, § 57.

or suppression of vowels carried out on the largest scale[a]; we find in Sanskrit, too, such double forms as p*ri*thvî or p*ri*thivî, adhi and dhi, api and pi, ava and va. The occurrence of such forms which have nothing to do with metrical considerations, but are perfectly legitimate from a grammatical point of view, would encourage a tendency to treat two syllables—and particularly two short syllables—as one, whenever an occasion arose. There are, besides, in the Vedic Sanskrit a number of forms where, as we saw, a long syllable has to be pronounced as two. In some of these cases this pronunciation is legitimate, i. e. it preserves an original dissyllabic form which in course of time had become monosyllabic. In other cases the same process takes place through a mistaken sense of analogy, where we cannot prove that an original dissyllabic form had any existence even in a prehistoric state of language. The occurrence of a number of such alternate forms would naturally leave a general impression in the minds of poets that two short syllables and one long syllable were under certain circumstances interchangeable. So considerable a number of words in which a long syllable has to be pronounced as two syllables has been collected by Professors Kuhn, Bollensen, and others, that no doubt can remain on this subject. Vedic poets, being allowed to change a semivowel into a vowel, were free to say nâsatyâ and nâsatyâ, VIII, 5, 32; p*ri*thivyâs and p*ri*thivyâ*h*; pitro*h* and pitro*h*, I, 31, 4. They could separate compound words, and pronounce gh*ri*tânna*h* or gh*ri*ta-anna*h*, VII, 3, 1. They could insert a kind of shewa or svarabhakti in words like sâmne or sâmne, VIII, 6, 47; dhâmne or dhâmne, VIII, 92, 25; arâv*n*a*h* and arâv*n*a*h*, IX, 63, 5. They might vary between pânti and pânti, I, 41, 2; yâthana and yâthana, I, 39, 3; nidhâto*h* and nidhâto*h*, I, 41, 9; tredhâ and tredhâ, I, 34, 8; devâ*h* and devâ*h* (besides devâsa*h*), I, 23, 24; rodasî and rodasî, I, 33, 9; 59, 4; 64, 9; and rodasyo*h*, I, 33, 5; 59, 2; 117, 10;

[a] See the important chapters on 'Kürzung der Vokale' and 'Tilgung der Vokale' in Corssen's 'Aussprache des Lateinischen;' and more especially his remarks on the so-called irrational vowels in Plautus, ibid. vol. ii, p. 70.

VI, 24, 3; VII, 6, 2; X, 74, 1[a]. Need we wonder then if we find that, on the other hand, they allowed themselves to pronounce prithivî as prithivî, I, 191, 6; VII, 34, 7; 99, 3; dhrishnâva as dhrishnava, V, 52, 14; suvâna as suvâna? There is no reason why we should change the spelling of suvâna into svâna. The metre itself tells us at once where suvâna is to be pronounced as two or as three syllables. Nor is it possible to believe that those who first handed down and afterwards wrote down the text of the Vedic hymns, should have been ignorant of that freedom of pronunciation. Why, there is not one single passage in the whole of the ninth Mandala, where, as far as I know, suvâna should not be pronounced as dissyllabic, i.e. as suvâna; and to suppose that the scholars of India did not know how that superfluous syllable should be removed, is really taking too low an estimate of men like Vyâli or Saunaka.

But if we once admit that in these cases two syllables separated by a single consonant were pronounced as one and were metrically counted as one, we can hardly resist the evidence in favour of a similar pronunciation in a large number of other words, and we shall find that by the admission of this rapid pronunciation, or of what in Plautus we should call irrational vowels, many verses assume at once their regular form without the necessity of admitting the suppression of final s, m, n, or the introduction of other prosodial licences. To my mind the most convincing passages are those where, as in the Atyashti and similar hymns, a poet repeats the same phrase twice, altering only one or two words, but without endeavouring to avoid an excess of syllables which, to our mind, unless we resort to synizesis, would completely destroy the uniformity of the metre. Thus we read:

I, 133, 6. apûrushaghno pratîta sûra satvabhih,
trisaptaih sûra satvabhih.

[a] Professor Bollensen in some of these passages proposes to read rodasios. In I, 96, 4, no change is necessary if we read visâm. Zeitschrift der D. M. G., vol. xxii, p. 587.

Here no pra must be pronounced with one ictus only, in order to get a complete agreement between the two iambic diameters.

I, 134, 5. ugrâ isha*n*anta bhurva*n*i,
apâm ishanta bhurva*n*i.

As ishanta never occurs again, I suspect that the original reading was isha*n*anta in both lines, and that in the second line isha*n*anta, pronounced rapidly, was mistaken for ishanta. Is not bhurvá*n*i a locative, corresponding to the datives in váne which are so frequently used in the sense of infinitives? See note to I, 6, 8, page 47 seq. In I, 138, 3, we must read:

ahe*l*amâna uru*s*a*m*sa sarî bhava,
vâ*g*e-vâ*g*e sarî bhava.

In I, 129, 11,

adhâ hi tvâ *g*anitâ *g*i*g*anad vaso,
rakshoha*n*am tvâ *g*i*g*anad vaso,

we might try to remove the difficulty by omitting vaso at the end of the refrain, but this would be against the general character of these hymns. We want the last word vaso, if possible, at the end of both lines. But, if so, we must admit two cases of synizesis, or, if this seems too clumsy, we must omit tvâ.

I shall now proceed to give a number of other examples in which the same consonantal synizesis seems necessary in order to make the rhythm of the verses perceptible to our ears as it was to the ears of the ancient *Ri*shis.

The preposition anu takes synizesis in

I, 127, 1. gh*ri*tasya vibhrâsh*t*im anu vash*t*i *s*o*k*ishâ. Cf. X, 14, 1.

The preposition abhi:

I, 91, 23. râyo bhâga*m* sahasâvann abhi yudhya.

Here Professor Kuhn changes sahasâvan into sahasva*h*, which, no doubt, is a very simple and very plausible emendation. But in altering the text of the Veda many things have to be considered, and in our case it might be objected that sahasva*h* never occurs again as an epithet of Soma.

As an invocation sahasva*h* refers to no deity but Agni, and even in its other cases it is applied to Agni and Indra only. However, I do not by any means maintain that sahasva*h* could not be applied to Soma, for nearly the same arguments could be used against sahasâvan, if conjecturally put in the place of sahasva*h*; I only wish to point out how everything ought to be tried first, before we resort in the Veda to conjectural emendations. Therefore, if in our passage there should be any objection to admitting the synizesis in abhi, I should much rather propose synizesis of sahasâvan, than change it into sahasva*h*. There is synizesis in maha, e.g. I, 133, 6. avar maha indra dâd*ri*hi *s*rudhî na*h*. Although this verse is quoted by the Prâti*s*âkhya, Sûtra 522, as one in which the lengthened syllable dhî of *s*rudhî does not occupy the tenth place, and which therefore required special mention, the original poet evidently thought otherwise, and lengthened the syllable, being a syllable liable to be lengthened, because it really occupied the tenth place, and therefore received a peculiar stress.

The preposition pari:

VI, 52, 14. mâ vo va*k*â*m*si pari*k*akshyâ*n*i vo*k*am,
sumneshv id vo antamâ madema.

Here Professor Kuhn (Beiträge, vol. iv, p. 197) begins the last pâda with vo*k*am, but this is impossible, unless we change the accent of vo*k*am, though even then the separation of the verb from mâ and the accumulation of two verbs in the last line would be objectionable.

Hari is pronounced as hari:

VII, 32, 12. ya indro harivân na dabhanti ta*m* ripa*h*.

II, 18, 5. â *k*atvâri*ms*atâ haribhir yu*g*âna*h*.

Hence I propose to scan the difficult verse I, 167, 1, as follows:

sahasra*m* ta indra-ûtayo na*h*,
sahasram isho harivo gûrtatamâ*h*[a],

[a] As to the scanning of the second line see p. cxiv.

sahasra*m* râyo mâdayadhyai,

sahasri*n*a upa no yantu vâ*g*â*h*.

That the final o instead of as is treated as a short syllable we saw before, and in I, 133, 6, we observed that it was liable to synizesis. We see the same in

I, 175, 6. maya ivâpo na t*ri*shyate babhûtha.

V, 61, 16. â ya*gñ*iyâso vav*ri*ttana.

The prag*ri*hya î of the dual is known in the Veda to be liable in certain cases to Sandhi. If we extend this licence beyond the limits recognised by the Prâti*s*âkhya, we might scan

VI, 52, 14. ubhe rodasy apâ*m* napâ*k* *k*a manma, or we might shorten the î before the a, and admitting synizesis, scan:

ubhe rodasî apâ*m* napâ*k* *k*a manma.

In III, 6, 10, we must either admit Sandhi between prấ*k*î and adhvaréva, or contract the first two syllables of adhvaréva.

The o and e of vocatives before vowels, when changed into av or a(y), are liable to synizesis:

IV, 48, 1. vâyav â *k*andre*n*a rathena (Anush*t*ubh, c.)

IV, 1, 2. sa bhrâtara*m* varu*n*am agna â vav*ri*tsva.

The termination ava*h* also, before vowels, seems to count as one syllable in V, 52, 14, divo vâ dh*ri*sh*n*ava o*g*asâ, which would render Professor Bollensen's correction (Orient und Occident, vol. ii, p. 480), dh*ri*sh*n*úo*g*asâ, unnecessary.

Like ava and iva, we find aya and iya, too, in several words liable to be contracted in pronunciation; e.g. vayam, VI, 23, 5; ayam, I, 177, 4; iyam, VII, 66, 8[2]; I, 186, 11 (unless we read vo·sme); X, 129, 6. Professor Bollensen's proposal to change iyam to îm, and ayam to âm (Orient und Occident, vol. ii, p. 461), would only cause obscurity, without any adequate gain, while other words would by a similar suppression of vowels or consonants become simply irrecognisable. In I, 169, 6, for instance, ádha has to be pronounced with one ictus; in VI, 26, 7, sadhavîra is trisyllabic. In VI, 10, 1, we must admit synizesis in adhvaré; in I, 161, 8, either in udakám or in abravîtana; I, 110, 9, in *ri*bhumân; VIII, 79, 4, in divá*h*; V, 4, 6, in n*ri*tama (unless we read so *s*gne); I, 164, 17, in pará*h*; VI, 15, 14, in pâvaka; I, 191, 6; VII, 34, 7; 99, 3, in p*ri*thivî; II, 20, 8, in púra*h*; VI, 10, 1, in prayatí; VI, 17, 7, in b*ri*hát; IX, 19, 6, in bhiyásam; I, 133, 6, in mahá*h*; II, 28, 6; IV, 1, 2; VI, 75, 18, in varu*n*a; III, 30, 21, in v*ri*shabha; VII, 41, 6, in vâgína*h*; II, 43, 2, in *s*í*s*umatî*h*; VI, 51, 2, in sanutár; VI, 18, 12, in sthávirasya, &c.

These remarks will, I hope, suffice in order to justify the principles by which I have been guided in my treatment of the text and in my translation of the Rig-veda. I know I shall seem to some to have been too timid in retaining whatever can possibly be retained in the traditional text of these ancient hymns, while others will look upon the emendations which I have suggested as unpardonable temerity. Let everything be weighed in the just scales of argument. Those who argue for victory, and not for truth, can have no hearing in our court. There is too much serious work to be done to allow time for wrangling or abuse. Any dictionary will supply strong words to those who condescend to such warfare, but strong arguments require honest labour, sound judgment, and, above all, a genuine love of truth.

The second volume, which I am now preparing for Press, will contain the remaining hymns addressed to the Maruts. The notes will necessarily have to be reduced to smaller dimensions, but they must always constitute the more important part in a translation or, more truly, in a deciphering of Vedic hymns.

F. MAX MÜLLER.

PARKS END, OXFORD:
March, 1869.

VEDIC HYMNS.

VEDIC HYMNS.

MANDALA X, HYMN 121.

ASHTAKA VIII, ADHYÂYA 7, VARGA 3-4.

To the Unknown God.

1. In the beginning there arose the Golden Child (Hiranya-garbha[1]); as soon as born, he alone was the lord of all that is. He stablished the earth and this heaven:—Who is the God to whom we shall offer sacrifice?

2. He who gives breath, he who gives strength, whose[1] command all the bright gods revere, whose shadow[2] is immortality, whose shadow is death:—Who is the God to whom we shall offer sacrifice?

3. He who through his might became the sole king of the breathing and twinkling[1] world, who governs all this, man and beast:—Who is the God to whom we shall offer sacrifice?

4. He through whose might[1] these snowy mountains are, and the sea, they say, with the distant river (the Rasâ[2]), he of whom these regions are indeed the two arms:—Who is the God to whom we shall offer sacrifice?

5. He through whom the awful heaven and the earth were made fast[1], he through whom the ether was stablished, and the firmament; he who measured the air in the sky[2]:—Who is the God to whom we shall offer sacrifice?

6. He to whom heaven and earth[1], standing firm by his will, look up, trembling in their mind; he over whom the risen sun shines forth:—Who is the God to whom we shall offer sacrifice?

7. When the great waters[1] went everywhere, holding the germ (Hira*n*ya-garbha), and generating light, then there arose from them the (sole[2]) breath of the gods:—Who is the God to whom we shall offer sacrifice?

8. He who by his might looked even over the waters which held power (the germ) and generated the sacrifice (light[1]), he who alone is God above all gods[2]:—Who is the God to whom we shall offer sacrifice?

9. May he not hurt us, he who is the begetter of the earth, or he, the righteous, who begat the heaven; he who also begat the bright and mighty waters:—Who is the God to whom we shall offer sacrifice?

[10. Pra*g*âpati, no other than thou embraces all these created things. May that be ours which we desire when sacrificing to thee: may we be lords of wealth!]

NOTES.

This hymn is ascribed to Hira*n*yagarbha Prâ*g*âpatya, and is supposed to be addressed to Ka, Who, i.e. the Unknown God.

First translated in my History of Ancient Sanskrit Literature, 1859, p. 569; see also Hibbert Lectures, 1882, p. 301; Muir, Original Sanskrit Texts, IV, p. 15.

Verse 1=VS. XIII, 4; XXIII, 1; XXV, 10; TS. IV, 1, 8, 3; 2, 8, 2; AV. IV, 2, 7.

Verse 2=VS. XXV, 13; TS. IV, 1, 8, 4; VII, 5, 17, 1; AV. IV, 2, 1; XIII, 3, 24.

Verse 3=VS. XXIII, 3; XXV, 11; TS. IV, 1, 8, 4; VII, 5, 16, 1; AV. IV, 2, 2.

Verse 4=VS. XXV, 12; TS. IV, 1, 8, 4; AV. IV, 2, 5.

Verse 5=VS. XXXII, 6; TS. IV, 1, 8, 5; AV. IV, 2, 4.

Verse 6=VS. XXXII, 7; TS. IV, 1, 8, 5; AV. IV, 2, 3.

Verse 7=VS. XXVII, 25; XXXII, 7; TS. II, 2, 12, 1; IV, 1, 8, 5; TA. I, 23, 8; AV. IV, 2, 6.

Verse 8=VS. XXVII, 26; XXXII. 7; TS. IV, 1, 8, 6.

Verse 9=VS. XII, 102; TS. IV, 2, 7, 1.

Verse 10=VS. X, 20; XXIII, 65; TS. I, 8, 14, 2; III, 2, 5, 6; TB. II, 8, 1, 2; III, 5, 7, 1; AV. VII, 79, 4; 80, 3.

This is one of the hymns which has always been suspected as modern by European interpreters. The reason is clear. To us the conception of one God, which pervades the whole of this hymn, seems later than the conception of many individual gods, as recognised in various aspects of nature, such as the gods of the sky, the sun, the storms, or the fire. And in a certain sense we may be right, and language also confirms our sentiment. In our hymn there are several words which do not occur again in the Rig-veda, or which occur in places only which have likewise been suspected to be of more modern date. Hira*n*yagarbhá itself is an ἅπαξ λεγόμενον. Sám avartata is found only in the last Ma*nd*ala, X, 90, 14; 129, 4. Bhûtá also, in the sense of what is, occurs in the tenth Ma*nd*ala only. It is used three times (X, 55, 2; 58, 12; 90, 2) as opposed to bhávya, i. e. what is and what will be; and once more in the sense of all that is (X, 85, 17). Âtmadā́*h*, in the sense of giving life, is another ἅπαξ λεγόμενον. Pra*s*ísh is restricted to Ma*nd*alas I (I, 145, 1), IX (IX, 66, 6; 86, 32), and our passage. Himávat, ἅπαξ λεγόμενον. The repetition of the relative pronoun in verses 2 and 4 is unusual. In the tenth verse the compound yat-kâma*h* is modern, and the insertion of etā́ni between tvat and anyá*h* is at all events exceptional. The passage V, 31, 2 is not parallel, because in tvát indra vásya*h* anyát, the ablative tvát is governed by vásya*h*. In VI, 21, 10, ná tvā́vân anyá*h* am*ri*ta tvat asti, anyá*h* is separated from tvát by a vocative only, as in VIII, 24, 11.

But when we say that a certain hymn is modern, we must carefully consider what we mean. Our hymn, for instance, must have existed not only previous to the Brâhma*n*a period, for many Brâhma*n*as presuppose it, but previous to the Mantra period also. It is true that no verse of it occurs in the Sâma-veda, but in the Sâma-veda-brâhma*n*a IX, 9, 12, verse 1 at least is mentioned[a]. Most of its verses, however, occur in the Vâ*g*asaneyi-sa*m*hitâ, in the Taittirîya-sa*m*hitâ, and in the Atharva-veda-sa*m*hitâ, nay, the last verse, to my mind the most suspicious of all, occurs most frequently in the other Sa*m*hitâs and Brâhma*n*as.

But though most of the verses of our hymn occur in other Sa*m*hitâs, they do not always occur in the same order.

In the Vâ*g*. Sa*m*h. we have the first verse in XIII, 4, but no other verse of our hymn follows. We have the first verse again in XXIII, 1, but not followed by verse 2, but by verse 3 (XXIII, 3)[b]. Then we have verse 1 once more

[a] The last line is here, tasmai ta indo havishâ vidhema, let us sacrifice to him with thy oblation, O Soma!

[b] Var. lect. nimeshatá*h*.

in XXV, 10, followed by verse 3 (XXV, 11), by verse 4 (XXV, 12), and then by verse 2 (XXV, 13).

We have verses 5, 6, 7, 8 in VS. XXXII, 6 and 7, and verses 7 and 8 in VS. XXVII, 25 and 26, while verse 9 is found in XII, 102 only[a], and the last verse in X, 20[b], and XXIII, 65. In the Taitt. Sa*m*hitâ the verses follow more regularly, still never quite in the same order as in the Rig-veda. In TS. IV, 1, 8, 3[c], we have verses 1 to 8, but verse 3 before verse 2, and verse 6 before verse 5, while verse 9 follows in IV, 2, 7, 1.

In TS. v. 3 stands before v. 2, in VII, 5, 16, 1, and VII, 5, 17, 1.

In TS. II, 2, 12, the pratîkas of verses 1, 7, 10 are quoted in succession.

Verse 7 occurs with important various readings in TA. I, 23, 8, ā́po ha yád b*ri*hatī́r gá*r*bham ā́yan dáksha*m* dádhânâ *g*anáyantî*h* svayambhúm, táta imé*s*dhyás*rig*y*a*nta sárgâ*h*.

Lastly in the AV. we find verses 1 to 7 from IV, 2, 1, to IV, 2, 7, but arranged in a different order, viz. as 2, 3, 6, 5, 4, 7, 1, and with important various readings.

Verse 2, yṓ 3 syé*s*e dvipádo yá*s k*átushpada*h*, as third pâda; also in XIII, 3, 24.

Verse 3, ekó rā́*g*â; yásya *kh*âyā́m*rí*ta*m* yásya m*ri*tyú*h*, as third pâda.

Verse 4, yásya ví*s*ve; samudré yásya rasā́m íd âhú*h*; imā́*s k*a.

Verse 5, yásya dyaúr urvī́ p*ri*thivī́ *k*a mahī́ yásyâdá urvá-ntáriksham, yásyâsaú sū́ro vítato mahitvā́.

Verse 6, ávata*s k*askabhâné bhiyásâne ródasî áhvayethâm (sic), yásyâsaú panthā́ rá*g*aso vimâna*h*.

Verse 7, ā́po ágre ví*s*vam âván gárbha*m* dádhânâ am*rí*tâ *ri*ta*g*ñā́*h*, yā́su devī́shv ádhi devá âsît.

Verse 10, vī́*s*vâ rûpā́*n*i paribhūr *g*a*g*âna, see VII, 79, 4, and 80, 3.

We are justified, therefore, in looking upon the verses, composing this h mn, as existing before the

[a] Var. lect. mā́ mâ, satyádharmâ vyā́na*t*, prathamó for b*ri*hatī́*h*.

[b] Var. lect. rûpā́*n*i for bhûtā́ni.

[c] Var. lect., ver. 5, d*ridh*é, dual for d*rilh*ā́; ver. 6, úditau vyéti for údito vibhā́ti; ver. 8, agním for ya*g*ñā́m.

final arrangement of the four Sa*m*hitâs, and if we persist in calling a hymn, dating from that period, a modern hymn, we must make it quite clear that, according to the present state of our knowledge, such a hymn cannot well be more modern than 1000 B.C. Besides the variations in the arrangement of the verses of our hymn, the very considerable various readings which we find in the VS., TS., and AV. are highly instructive, as showing the frequent employment of our hymn for sacrificial purposes. In several cases these various readings are of great importance, as we shall see.

Verse 1.

MUIR: Hira*n*yagarbha arose in the beginning; born, he was the one lord of things existing. He established the earth and this sky: to what god shall we offer our oblation?

LUDWIG: Hira*n*yagarbha hat zuerst sich gebildet, er ward geboren als einziger herr alles gewordenen, dise erde und disen himel hält er; Ka, dem gotte, möchten wir mit havis aufwarten.

Note 1. Hira*n*yagarbha[a] has been translated in different ways, and it would perhaps be best to keep it as a proper name, which it is in later times. It means literally the golden embryo, the golden germ or child, or born of a golden womb, and was no doubt an attempt at naming the sun. Soon, however, that name became mythological. The golden child was supposed to have been so called because it was Pra*g*âpati, the lord of creation, when dwelling as yet in the golden egg, and Hira*n*yagarbha became in the end a recognised name of Pra*g*âpati, see Sây. on X, 121, 1. All this is fully explained by Sâya*n*a, TS. IV, 1, 8, 3; IV, 2, 8, 2; by Mahîdhara, VS. XIII, 4.

Verse 2.

MUIR: He who gives breath, who gives strength, whose command all, [even] the gods, reverence, whose shadow is immortality, whose shadow is death: to what god shall we offer our oblation?

[a] M. M., India, What can it teach us? pp. 144, 162.

LUDWIG: Geber des lebendigen hauches, geber der kraft, zu des unterweisung alle götter sich einfinden, des glanz die unsterblichkeit, dessen der tod ist, Ka, dem gotte, möchten wir mit havis aufwarten.

Note 1. In order to account for the repetition of yasya, Sâya*n*a and Mahîdhara take vi*s*ve for men, and devâ*h* for gods.

Note 2. It is difficult to say what is meant by *kh*âyâ, shadow. I take it in the sense of what belongs to the god, as the shadow belongs to a man, what follows him, or is determined by him. In that sense Sâya*n*a also takes it, TS. IV, 1, 8, 4, yasya pra*g*âpate*s* *kh*âyâvat svâdhînam am*ri*tam, moksharûpam, m*ri*tyu*h*, prâ*n*inâm mara*n*am api, yasya *kh*âyeva svâdhîna*h*; and, though not quite so clearly, in RV. X, 121, 2. Mahîdhara on the contrary takes *kh*âyâ in the sense of refuge, and says, whose shadow, i.e. whose worship, preceded by knowledge, is am*ri*ta, immortality, a means of deliverance[a], while ignorance of him is death, or leads to sa*m*sâra.

Verse 3.

MUIR: Who by his might became the sole king of the breathing and winking world, who is the lord of this two-footed and four-footed [creation]: to what god shall we offer our oblation?

LUDWIG: Der des atmenden, augenbewegenden lebendigen durch seine grösze der einzige könig geworden; der verfügt über disz zwei- und vier-füszige, Ka, dem gotte, möchten wir mit havis aufwarten.

Note 1. It is difficult to say whether nimishata*h* means twinkling or sleeping. It has both meanings as to wink has in English. Sâya*n*a (X, 121, 3; TS. IV, 1, 8, 4) and Mahîdhara (VS. XXIII, 3[b]) explain it by winking. This may be right as expressing sensuous perception, in addition to mere breathing. In X, 190, 2, ví*s*vasya mishatό va*s*î́ means, lord of all that winks, i.e.

---

[a] muktihetu, not yuktihetu, as Weber prints.

[b] Is nimesháto in XXIII, 3, a varia lectio, or an a*s*uddha? In XXV, 13, we read nimishato.

lives. The later idea, that the gods do not wink, has nothing to do with our passage.

Verse 4.

MUIR: Whose greatness these snowy mountains, and the sea with the Rasâ (river), declare,—of whom these regions, of whom they are the arms: to what god shall we offer our oblation?

LUDWIG: Dessen die schneebedeckten (berge, die Himavân) vermöge seiner grösze, als des eigentum man ocean und Rasâ nennt, des dise himelsgegenden, des arme sie, Ka, dem gotte, möchten wir mit havis aufwarten.

Note 1. Muir's translation, which suggests itself very naturally to a European mind, is impossible, because mahitvấ cannot be either mahitvám (as Sâya*n*a also and Mahîdhara suggest), or mahitvấni; and because âhú*h* does not mean declare. Otherwise nothing could be better than his rendering: 'Whose greatness these snowy mountains, and the sea with the Rasâ (river), declare.'

Mahitvấ, as Sâya*n*a also rightly perceives, TS. IV, 1, 8, 4, is a very common instrumental (see Lanman, Noun-inflection, pp. 335–6), and the same mahitvấ must be supplied for samudrám. We might make the whole sentence dependent on âhu*h* without much change of meaning. The Atharva-veda text supplies a lectio facilior, but not therefore melior.

Note 2. The Rasâ is a distant river, in some respects like the Greek Okeanos. Dr. Aufrecht takes it as a name of the milky way, Z. D. M. G. XIII, 498: see Muir, S. T. II, p. 373, n. 19.

Verse 5.

MUIR: By whom the sky is fiery, and the earth fixed, by whom the firmament and the heaven were established, who in the atmosphere is the measurer of the aerial space: to what god shall we offer our oblation?

LUDWIG: Durch den gewaltig der himel und fest die erde, durch den gestützt Svar, und das gewölbe, der die räume im mittelgebiete ausgemeszen, Ka, dem gotte, möchten wir mit havis aufwarten.

Note 1. In this verse I decidedly prefer the reading of the Atharva-veda, yena dyaur ugrâ p*ri*thivî *k*a d*rilh*e. It seems not a lectio facilior, and we avoid the statement that the heaven has been made ugrâ. Ugrâ, as applied to dyaus, means awful and grand, as an inherent quality rather, and not simply strong. See Ludwig, Notes, p. 441.

Note 2. Rá*g*aso vimâna*h* has been fully discussed by Muir, S. T. IV, p. 71, but it is difficult to find a right translation for it, because the cosmography of the Veda is so different from our own (see I, 6, 9, note 1, and I, 19, 3, note 1). I think we may translate it here by the air, or even by space, particularly the bright air in the sky, the sky (antariksha or nabhas) being between heaven (dyu) and earth (p*ri*thivî), while sva*h* and nâka are still higher than the heaven (dyu), sva*h* being sometimes explained as the abode of the sun, the ether, or empyrean, nâka, the firmament, as svarga (Mahîdhara); or sva*h* as svarga, and nâka as âditya (Sâya*n*a). Vimâna is here simply the measurer, though vimâ, from meaning to measure, is apt to take the meaning of to make, which is an excuse for Sâya*n*a's rendering, 'who makes the rain in the sky.'

The Atharva-veda rendering is very free, and certainly no improvement.

Verse 6.

MUIR: To whom two contending armies, sustained by his succour, looked up, trembling in mind; over whom the risen sun shines: to what god shall we offer our oblation?

LUDWIG: Auf den die beiden schlachtreihen durch (ihre) begirde aufgestellt in ordnung ihren blick richten, zitternd, im geiste, wo darüber hin aufgegangen Sûra ausstralt, Ka, dem gotte, möchten wir mit havis aufwarten.

Note 1. It would be well to read ródasî for krándasî (which B. R. explain by 'two armies'), and the various reading in AV. IV, 2, 3 decidedly points in that direction. But even if krándasî stands, it must be taken in the same sense as ródasî. Uditau vyeti in TS. IV, 1, 8, 5 is explained by udayavishaye vividha*m* ga*kkh*ati.

Verse 7.

MUIR: When the great waters pervaded the universe containing an embryo, and generating fire, thence arose the one spirit (asu) of the gods: to what god shall we offer our oblation?

LUDWIG: Als die groszen waszer kamen, die allen keim in sich faszten, zeugend den Agni, da kam zu stande der götter einziger lebensgeist; Ka, dem gotte, möchten wir mit havis aufwarten.

Note 1. The waters here referred to have to be understood as the waters in the beginning of the creation, where, as we read (RV. X, 129, 3), 'everything was like a sea without a light,' or, as the *S*atapatha-brâhma*n*a (XI, 1, 6, 1) says, 'everything was water and sea.' These waters held the germ[a], and produced the golden light, the sun[b], whence arose the life of all the gods, viz. Pra*g*âpati. The Atharvaveda adds a verse which repeats the same idea more clearly: ā́po vatsá*m* *g*anáyantîr gárbham ágre sámairayan, tásyotá *g*ā́yamânasyólba âsîd dhira*n*yáya*h*, 'In the beginning the waters, producing a young, brought forth an embryo, and when it was being born, it had a golden covering.' The sunrise serves here as elsewhere as an image of the creation.

Note 2. Grassmann proposes to omit eka, because it is absent in the Maitrâya*n*î *S*âkhâ. The metre shows the same.

Verse 8.

MUIR: He who through his greatness beheld the waters which contained power, and generated sacrifice, who was the one god above the gods: to what god shall we offer our oblation?

LUDWIG: Der in seiner grösze sogar die waszer überschaute, wie sie die fähigkeit besitzend erzeugten das opfer, der der einzige gott war über den göttern, Ka, dem gotte, möchten wir mit havis aufwarten.

Note 1. In dáksha*m* dádhânâ *g*anáyantîr ya*gñ*ám, we have a repetition of what was said in the preceding verse,

---

[a] See RV. X, 82, 5–6. [b] See RV. X, 72, 7.

dáksham standing for gárbham, *yagñam* for agním, which is actually the reading of TS. The Atharva-veda does not contain this verse, which is used as an anyâ vikalpitâ yâ*g*yâ in TS.

Note 2. It is curious that one of the most important sentences in the Rig-veda, yo deveshv adhi deva eka âsît, should have been changed in the Atharva-veda IV, 2, 6 into yâsu devîshv adhi deva âsît, 'over which divine waters there was the god.' See Ludwig, Notes, p. 441.

Verse 9.

MUIR: May he not injure us, he who is the generator of the earth, who, ruling by fixed ordinances, produced the heavens, who produced the great and brilliant waters: to what god shall we offer our oblation?

LUDWIG: Nicht schädige uns, der der erde erzeuger, oder der den himel bereitet mit warhafter satzung, der auch die wasser, die hellen, die mächtigen erzeugt hat, Ka, dem gotte, mochten wir mit havis aufwarten.

Verse 10.

MUIR: Pra*g*âpati, no other than thou is lord over all these created things: may we obtain that, through desire of which we have invoked thee: may we become masters of riches.

LUDWIG: Pra*g*âpati, kein anderer als du hat umfasst die wesen alle, der wunsch, um deswillen wir dir opfern, der werde uns zu teil, besitzer von reichtümern mögen wir sein.

Note 1. This verse is certainly extremely weak after all that preceded, still, to judge from its frequent occurrence, we cannot well discard it. All we can say is that nowhere, except in the Rig-veda, does it form the final verse of our hymn, and thus spoil its whole character.

That character consists chiefly in the burden of the nine verses, Kasmai devâya havishâ vidhema, 'To what god shall we offer sacrifice?' This is clearly meant to express a desire of finding out the true, but unknown god, and to do so, even after all has been said that can be said of a supreme god. To finish such a hymn with a statement that Pragâpati is the god who deserves our sacrifice, may be very natural theologically, but it is entirely uncalled for poetically. The very phrase Kasmai devâya havishâ vidhema must have been a familiar phrase, for we find in a hymn addressed to the wind, X, 168, 4, after all has been said that can be said of him, the concluding line: ghóshâ*h* ít asya *srin*vire ná rûpám tásmai vấtâya havíshâ vidhema, 'his sound indeed is heard, but he is not seen—to that Vâta let us offer sacrifice.'

But more than this, on the strength of hymns like our own in which the interrogative pronoun ka, 'who,' occurs, the Brâhmans actually invented a god of the name of Ka. I pointed this out many years ago in my History of Ancient Sanskrit Literature (1860, p. 433), where I said: 'In accordance with the same system, we find that the authors of the Brâhma*n*as had so completely broken with the past that, forgetful of the poetical character of the hymns, and the yearning of the poets after the unknown god, they exalted the interrogative pronoun into a deity, and acknowledged a god 'Ka, or Who.' In the Taittirîya-sa*m*hitâ (I, 7, 6, 6), in the Kaushîtaki-brâhma*n*a (XXIV, 4), in the Tâ*nd*ya-brâhma*n*a (XV, 10), and in the *S*atapatha-brâhma*n*a [a], whenever interrogative verses occur, the author states, that Ka is Pragâpati, or 'the Lord of Creatures' (Pragâpatir vai Ka*h*). Nor did they stop there. Some of the hymns in which the interrogative pronoun occurred were called Kadvat, i.e. having kad or quid. But soon a new adjective was formed, and not only the hymns, but the sacrifices also, offered to the god, were called Kâya, or who-ish [b]. This word, which is not to be identified with the Latin cujus, cuja, cujum, but is merely the artificial product of an effete mind, is found in the Taittirîya-sa*m*hitâ (I, 8, 3, 1), and in the Vâ*g*asaneyi-sa*m*hitâ (XXIV, 15). At the time of Pâ*n*ini

[a] *S*atap. Brâhm. I, 1, 1, 13; II, 5, 2, 13; IV, 5, 6, 4; also Aitar. Brâhm. III, 21.

[b] Âsv. *S*r. Sûtra II, 17, 14; Kâty. *S*r. Sûtra V, 4, 23; Vait. Sûtra VIII, 22, ed. Garbe.

this word had acquired such legitimacy as to call for a separate rule explaining its formation (Pâ*n*. IV, 2, 25). The commentator there explains Ka by Brahman. After this we can hardly wonder that in the later Sanskrit literature of the Purâ*n*as, Ka appears as a recognised god, as the supreme god, with a genealogy of his own, perhaps even with a wife; and that in the Laws of Manu, one of the recognised forms of marriage, generally known by the name of Pra*g*âpati-marriage, occurs under the monstrous title of 'Kâya.' Stranger still, grammarians who know that ka forms the dative kasmai only if it is an interrogative pronoun, consider kasmai in our hymn as irregular, because, as a proper name, Ka ought to form the dative Kâya.

MA*ND*ALA I, HYMN 6.

ASH*T*AKA I, ADHYÂYA 1, VARGA 11-12.

TO INDRA AND THE MARUTS (THE STORM-GODS).

1. Those who stand around[2] him while he moves on, harness the bright red (steed)[1]; the lights in heaven shine forth[3].

2. They harness to the chariot on each side his (Indra's)[1] two favourite bays, the brown, the bold, who can carry the hero.

3. Thou who createst light where there was no light, and form, O men[1]! where there was no form, hast been born together with the dawns[2].

4. Thereupon[1] they (the Maruts), according to their wont[2], assumed again the form of new-born babes[3], taking their sacred name.

5. Thou, O Indra, with the swift Maruts[1], who break even through the stronghold[2], hast found even in their hiding-place the bright ones[3] (days or clouds).

6. The pious singers[1] (the Maruts) have, after their own mind[2], shouted towards the giver of wealth, the great, the glorious (Indra).

7. Mayest thou[1] (host of the Maruts) be verily seen[2] coming together with Indra, the fearless: you are both happy-making, and of equal splendour.

8. With the beloved hosts of Indra, with the blameless, hasting[2] (Maruts), the sacrificer[1] cries aloud.

9. From yonder, O traveller (Indra), come hither, or from the light of heaven[1]; the singers all yearn for it;—

10. Or we ask Indra for help from here, or from heaven, or from above the earth, or from the great sky.

NOTES.

This hymn is ascribed to Ka*n*va, the son of Ghora. The metre is Gâyatrî throughout.

Verse 1 = SV. II, 818; VS. XXIII, 5; AV. XX, 26, 4; 47, 10; 69, 9; TS. VII, 4, 20, 1; TB. III, 9, 4, 1.

Verse 2 = SV. II, 819; VS. XXIII, 6; AV. XX, 26, 5; 47, 11; 69, 10; TS. VII, 4, 20, 1.

Verse 3 = SV. II, 820; VS. XXIX, 37; AV. XX, 26, 6; 47, 12; 69, 11; TS. VII, 4, 20, 1; TB. III, 9, 4, 3.

Verse 4 = SV. II, 101; AV. XX, 40, 3; 69, 12.

Verse 5 = SV. II, 202; AV. XX, 70, 1.

Verse 6 = AV. XX, 70, 2.

Verse 7 = SV. II, 200; AV. XX, 40, 1; 70, 3.

Verse 8 = AV. XX, 40, 2; 70, 4.

Verse 9 = AV. XX, 70, 5.

Verse 10 = AV. XX, 70, 6.

Verse 1.

WILSON: The circumstationed (inhabitants of the three worlds) associate with (Indra), the mighty (Sun), the indestructive (fire), the moving (wind), and the lights that shine in the sky.

BENFEY: Die rothe Sonne schirr'n sie an, die wandelt um die stehenden, Strahlen strahlen am Himmel auf.

LUDWIG: Sie spannen an den hellen, den roten, den vom feststehenden hinwegwandelnden; heller glanz erstralt am Himmel.

Note 1. The poet begins with a somewhat abrupt description of a sunrise. Indra is taken as the god of the bright day, whose steed is the sun, and whose companions the Maruts, or the storm-gods. Arushá, meaning originally red, is used as a proper name of the horse or of the rising sun, though it occurs more frequently as the name of the red horses or flames of Agni, the god of fire, and also of the morning light. In our passage, Arushá, a substantive, meaning the red of the morning, has taken bradhná as an adjective,—bradhná meaning, as far as can be made out, bright in general, though, as it is especially applied to the Soma-juice, perhaps bright-brown or yellow. Names of colour are difficult to translate from one language into another, for their shades vary, and withdraw themselves from sharp definition. We shall meet with this difficulty again and again in the Veda; see RV. X, 20, 9.

As it has actually been doubted whether bradhná arushá can be meant for the sun, and whether the Vedic poets ever looked upon the sun as a horse, I may quote Vâg. Sa*m*h. XXIII, 4, where the same verse occurs and is declared to be addressed to the sun; and *S*atap. Br. XIII, 2, 6, 1, where we read, yu*ñg*anti bradhnam arusha*m* *k*arantam iti, asau vâ âdityo bradhno*rusho*mum evâsmâ âditya*m* yunakti svargasya lokasya samash*t*yai. Ludwig remarks justly that the sun has been conceived as a chariot also, and that bradhná arushá may have been thus understood here. Delbrück translates quite boldly: Sie schirren die rothe Sonne an. See also Tait. Br. III, 7, 7, 4; Tâ*nd*ya Br. XXIII, 3, 5; *S*âṅkh. Br. II, 17, 3; Ludwig, Comm. ii. p. 173. M. Bergaigne (Rél. Ved. iii. p. 324) remarks very truly: 'Le soleil est tantôt une roue, tantôt un char, tantôt un cheval, trainant le char, tantôt un héros monté sur le char et dirigeant les chevaux.'

The following passages will illustrate the principal meaning of arushá, and justify the translation here adopted.

ARUSHÁ, AS AN ADJECTIVE.

Arushá is used as an adjective in the sense of red:

VII, 97, 6. tám *s*agmẫsa*h* arushẫsa*h* á*s*vâ*h* b*ri*haspátim saha-vẫha*h* vahanti,—nábha*h* ná rûpám arushám vásânâ*h*.

Powerful red horses, drawing together draw him, B*ri*haspati: horses clothed in red colour, like the sky.

III, 1, 4. *s*vetám *g*a*ñ*ânám arushám mahi-tvẫ.

Agni, the white, when born; the red, by growth.

III, 15, 3. k*ri*sh*n*ẫsu agne arushá*h* ví bhâhi.

Shine, O Agni, red among the dark ones.

III, 31, 21; VI, 27, 7.

VII, 75, 6. práti dyutânấm arushấsa*h* ásvâ*h* *k*itrấ*h* ad*ri*sran ushásam váhanta*h*.

The red horses, the beautiful, were seen bringing to us the bright dawn.

V, 43, 12; I, 118, 5; IV, 43, 6; V, 73, 5; I, 36, 9; VII, 3, 3; 16, 3; X, 45, 7; I, 141, 8.

II, 2, 8. sá*h* idhâná*h* ushása*h* rấmyâ*h* ánu svấ*h* ná dîdet arushé*n*a bhânúnâ.

He (Agni), lit after the lovely dawns, shone like the sky with his red splendour.

III, 29, 6; IV, 58, 7; I, 114, 5; V, 59, 5; 12, 2; 12, 6; VI, 8, 1.

VI, 48, 6. syâvấsu arushá*h* v*rí*shâ.

In the dark (nights) the red hero (Agni). Cf. III, 7, 5.

In one passage v*rí*shan arushá is intended for fire in the shape of lightning.

X, 89, 9. ní amítreshu vadhám indra túmram v*rí*shan v*rí*shâ*n*am arushám sisîhi.

Whet, O strong Indra, the heavy strong red weapon, against the enemies.

X, 43, 9. út *g*âyatâm parasú*h* *g*yótishâ sahá—ví ro*k*atâm arushá*h* bhânúnâ sú*k*i*h*.

May the axe (the thunderbolt) appear with the light—may the red one blaze forth, bright with splendour.

X, 1, 6; VI, 3, 6.

X, 20, 9. k*ri*sh*n*á*h* svetá*h* arushá*h* yấma*h* asya bradhná*h* *ri*grá*h* utá só*n*a*h*.

His (Agni's) path is black, white, red, bright, reddish, and yellow.

Here it is extremely difficult to keep all the colours distinct.

Arushá is frequently applied to Soma, particularly in the 9th Ma*nd*ala. There we read:

IX, 8, 6. arushá*h* hári*h*. IX, 71, 7. arushá*h* divá*h* kaví*h* v*rí*shâ. IX, 74, 1. vấ*g*î arushá*h*. IX, 82, 1. arushá*h* v*rí*shâ hári*h*. IX, 89, 3. hárim arushám.

IX, 111, 1. arushá*h* hári*h*. See also IX, 25, 5; 61, 21. In IX, 72, 1, arushá seems used as a substantive in the sense of red-horse.

Professor Spiegel, in his important review of my translation (Heidelberger Jahrbücher, 1870, p. 104), points out that aurusha in Zend means white, so that it would seem as if the original meaning of arusha had been bright, bright like fire, and thus red.

Arushá, as an Appellative.

Arushá is used as an appellative, and in the following senses:

1. The one red-horse of the Sun, the two or more red-horses of Agni.

I, 6, 1. yu*ñg*ánti bradhnám arushám.

They yoke the bright red-horse (the Sun).

I, 94, 10. yát áyukthâ*h* arushā́ róhitâ ráthe.

When thou (Agni) hadst yoked the two red-horses and the two ruddy horses to the chariot. I, 146, 2.

II, 10, 2. *s*ruyā́*h* agní*h*—hávam me—*s*yâvā́ rátham vahata*h* róhitâ vâ utá arushā́.

Mayest thou, Agni, hear my call, whether the two black, or the two ruddy, or the two red-horses carry you.

Here three kinds of colours are clearly distinguished, and an intentional difference is made between róhita and arushá. IV, 2, 3.

IV, 6, 9. táva tyé agne haríta*h*—róhitâsa*h*—arushā́sa*h* vrí*s*ha*n*a*h*.

To thee (Agni) belong these bays, these ruddy, these red-horses, the stallions.

Here, again, three kinds of horses are distinguished—Haríts, Róhitas, and Arushás.

VIII, 34, 17. yé *r*i*g*rā́*h* vā́ta-ra*m*hasa*h* arushā́sa*h* raghusyáda*h*.

Here arushá may be the subject, and the rest adjectives; but it is also possible to take all the words as adjectives, referring them to â*s*ú in the next verse. The fact that *r*i*g*rá likewise expresses a peculiar red colour, is no objection, as may be seen from I, 6, 1; 94, 10.

VII, 42, 2. yuṅkshvá—haríta*h* rohíta*h* *k*a yé vâ sádman arushā́*h*.

Yoke (O Agni) the bays, and the ruddy horses, or the red-horses which are in thy stable. VII, 16, 2.

2. The cloud, represented as one of the horses of the Maruts.

I, 85, 5. utá arushásya ví syanti dhấrâ*h*.

(When you go to the battle, O Maruts), the streams of the red (horse) flow off.

V, 56, 7. utá syá*h* vấgî arushá*h*.

This strong red-horse,—meant for one of the horses of the Maruts, but, at the same time, as sending rain.

Arushá, as the Proper Name of a Solar Deity.

Besides the passages in which arushá is used either as an adjective, in the sense of red, or as an appellative, meaning some kind of horse, there are others in which, as I pointed out in my Essay on Comparative Mythology[a], Arushá occurs as a proper name, as the name of a solar deity, as the bright deity of the morning (Morgenroth). My interpretation of some of these passages has been contested, nor shall I deny that in some of them a different interpretation is possible, and that in looking for traces of Arushá, as a Vedic deity, representing the morning or the rising sun, and containing, as I endeavoured to show, the first germs of the Greek name of Eros, I may have seen more indications of the presence of that deity in the Veda than others would feel inclined to acknowledge. Yet in going over the same ground again, I think that even verses which for a time I felt inclined to surrender, yield a better sense, if we take the word arushá, which occurs in them as a substantive, as the name of a matutinal deity, than if we look upon it as an adjective or a mere appellative. It might be said that wherever this arushá occurs, apparently as the name of a deity, we ought to supply Agni or Indra or Sûrya. This is true to a certain extent, for the sun, or the light of the morning, or the bright sky form no doubt the substance and

[a] Chips from a German Workshop, 2nd ed., vol. ii, p. 137 seq. Selected Essays, vol. i, p. 444.

subject-matter of this deity. But the same applies to many other names originally intended for these conceptions, but which, nevertheless, in the course of time, became independent names of independent deities. In our passage I, 6, 1, yu*ñg*ánti bradhnám arushám, we may retain for arushá the appellative power of steed or red-steed, but if we could ask the poet what he meant by this red-steed, or if we ask ourselves what we can possibly understand by it, the answer would be, the morning sun, or the light of the morning. In other passages, however, this meaning of red-steed is really no longer applicable, and we can only translate Arushá by the Red, understanding by this name the deity of the morning or of the morning sun, the later Aru*n*a.

VII, 71, 1. ápa svásu*h* ushása*h* nák*g*ihîte *rin*ákti k*ri*sh*n*ı̂́*h* arushā́ya pánthâm.

The Night retires from her sister, the Dawn; the Dark one yields the path to the Red one, i. e. the red morning.

Here Arushá shares the same half-mythological character as Ushas. Where we should speak of dawn and morning as mere periods of time, the Vedic poet speaks of them as living and intelligent beings, half human, half divine, as powers of nature capable of understanding his prayers, and powerful enough to reward his praises. I do not think therefore that we need hesitate to take Arushá in this passage as a proper name of the morning, or of the morning sun, to whom the dark goddess, the Night, yields the path when he rises in the East.

VI, 49, 2. divá*h* *s*í*s*um sáhasa*h* sûnúm agním ya*gñ*ásya ketúm arushám yá*g*adhyai.

To worship the child of Dyu, the son of strength, Agni, the light of the sacrifice, the Red one (Arushá).

In this verse, where the name of Agni actually occurs, it would be easier than in the preceding verse to translate arushá as an adjective, referring it either to Agni, the god of fire, or to ya*gñ*ásya ketúm, the light of the sacrifice. I had myself yielded[a] so far to these considerations that I

---

[a] Chips from a German Workshop, vol. ii, p. 139.

gave up my former translation, and rendered this verse by 'to worship Agni, the child of the sky, the son of strength, the red light of the sacrifice[a].' But I return to my original translation, and I prefer to see in Arushá an independent name, intended, no doubt, for Agni, as the representative of the rising sun and, at the same time, of the sacrificial fire of the morning, but nevertheless as having in the mind of the poet a personality of his own. He is the child of Dyu, originally the offspring of heaven. He is the son of strength, originally generated by the strong rubbing of the ara*n*is, i. e. the wood for kindling fire. He is the light of the sacrifice, whether as reminding man that the time for the morning sacrifice has come, or as himself lighting the sacrifice on the Eastern altar of the sky. He is Arushá, originally as clothed in bright red colour, but gradually changed into the representative of the morning. We see at once, if examining these various expressions, how some of them, like the child of Dyu, are easily carried away into mythology, while others, such as the son of strength, or the light of the sacrifice, resist that unconscious metamorphosis. That Arushá was infected by mythology, that it had approached at least that point where nomina become changed into numina, we see by the verse immediately following:

VI, 49, 3. arushásya duhitárâ vírûpe (íti ví-rûpe) st*ri*bhi*h* anyấ pipi*s*é sû́ra*h* anyấ.

There are two different daughters of Arushá; the one is clad in stars, the other belongs to the sun, or is the wife of Svar.

Here Arushá is clearly a mythological being, like Agni or Savitar or Vai*s*vânara; and if Day and Night are called his daughters, he, too, can hardly have been conceived otherwise than as endowed with human attributes, as the child of Dyu, as the father of Day and Night, and not as a mere period of time, not as a mere cause or effect.

IV, 15, 6. tám árvantam ná sânasím arushám ná divá*h* *s*í*s*um marm*ri*g*yánte divé-dive.

[a] Journal of the Royal Asiatic Society, 1867, p. 204.

They trim the fire day by day, like a strong horse, like Arushá, the child of Dyu.

Here, too, Arushá, the child of Dyu, has to be taken as a personal character, and, if the ná after arushám is right, a distinction is clearly made between Agni, the sacrificial fire, to whom the hymn is addressed, and Arushá, the child of heaven, the pure and bright morning, here used as a simile for the cleaning or trimming of the fire on the altar.

V, 47, 3. arushá*h* su-par*n*á*h*.

Arushá, the morning sun, with beautiful wings.

The Feminine Árushî, as an Adjective.

Árushî, like arushá, is used as an adjective, in the same sense as arushá, i. e. red :

III, 55, 11. *s*yẫvî *k*a yát árushî *k*a svásârau.

As the dark and the red are sisters.

I, 92, 1 and 2. gẫva*h* árushî*h* and árushî*h* gẫ*h*.

The red cows of the dawn.

I, 92, 2. rú*s*antam bhânúm árushî*h* a*s*i*s*rayu*h*.

The red dawns obtained bright splendour.

Here ushása*h*, the dawns, occur in the same line, so that we may take árushî*h* either as an adjective, referring to the dawns, or as a substantive, as a name of the dawn or of her cows.

I, 30, 21. á*s*ve ná *k*itre arushi.

Thou beautiful red dawn, thou, like a mare.

Here, too, the vocative arushi is probably to be taken as an adjective, particularly if we consider the next following verse:

IV, 52, 2. á*s*vâ-iva *k*itrẫ árushî mâtẫ gávâm *ri*tá-varî sákhâ abhût a*s*víno*h* ushẫ*h*.

The dawn, beautiful and red, like a mare, the mother of the cows (days), the never-failing, she became the friend of the A*s*vins.

X, 5, 5. saptá svás*rî*h árushî*h*.

The seven red sisters.

The Feminine Árushî, as a Substantive.

If used as a substantive, árushî seems to mean the dawn. It is likewise used as a name of the horses of Agni, Indra, and Soma; also as a name for mare in general.

It means dawn in X, 8, 3, though the text points here so clearly to the dawn, and the very name of dawn is mentioned so immediately after, that this one passage seems hardly sufficient to establish the use of árushî as a recognised name of the dawn. Other passages, however, would likewise gain in perspicuity, if we took árushî by itself as a name of the dawn, just as we had to admit in several passages arushá by itself as a name of the morning. Cf. I, 71, 1.

Árushî means the horses of Agni, in I, 14, 12:

yukshvá hí árushî*h* ráthe haríta*h* deva rohíta*h*.

Yoke, O god (Agni), the red-horses to the chariot, the bays, the ruddy.

I, 72, 10. prá nî*k*î*h* agne árushî*h* a*g*ânan.

They knew the red-horses, Agni, coming down. VIII, 69, 5.

Soma, as we saw, was frequently spoken of as arushá*h* hári*h*.

In IX, 111, 2, tridhấtubhi*h* árushîbhi*h* seems to refer to the same red-horses of Soma, though this is not quite clear.

The passages where árushî means simply a mare, without any reference to colour, are VIII, 68, 18, and VIII, 55, 3.

It is curious that Arushá, which in the Veda means red, should, as pointed out before, in its Zend form aurusha, mean white. That in the Veda it means red, and not white, is shown, for instance, by X, 20, 9, where *s*vetá, the name for white, is mentioned by the side of arushá. Most likely arushá meant originally brilliant, and became fixed with different shades of brilliancy in Sanskrit and Persian. Arushá presupposes a form ar-vas, and is derived from a root ar in the sense of running or rushing. See Chips from a German Workshop, vol. ii, pp. 135, 137.

Having thus explained the different meanings of arushá and árushî in the Rig-veda, I feel it incumbent, at least for once, to explain the reasons why I differ from the classification of Vedic passages as given in the Dictionary published by Boehtlingk and Roth. Here, too, the passages in which arushá is used as an adjective are very properly separated from those in which it appears as a substantive. To begin with the first, it is said that 'arushá means ruddy, the colour of Agni and his horses; he (Agni) himself appears as a red-horse.' In support of this, the following passages are quoted:

III, 1, 4. ávardhayan su-bhágam saptá yahvî*h* *s*vetám *g*a*g*ñânám arushám mahi-tvấ, *s*í*s*um ná *g*âtám abhí âru*h* á*s*vâ*h*. Here, however, it is only said that Agni was born brilliant-white[a], and grew red, that the horses came to him as they come to a new-born foal. Agni himself is not called a red-horse.

III, 7, 5. Here, again, v*r*í*sh*n*ah* arushásya is no doubt meant for Agni. But v*r*íshan by itself does not mean horse, though it is added to different names of horses to qualify them as male horses; cf. VII, 69, 1, ấ vâm rátha*h* v*r*íshabhi*h* yâtu á*s*vai*h*, may your chariot come near with powerful horses, i. e. with stallions. See note to I, 85, 12. We are therefore not justified in translating arushá v*r*íshan by red-horse, but only by the red male, or the red hero.

In III, 31, 3, agní*h* *g*a*g*ñe *g*uhvấ ré*g*amâna*h* mahá*h* putrấn arushásya pra-yákshe, I do not venture to say who is meant by the mahá*h* putrấn arushásya, whether Âdityas or Maruts, but hardly the sons of Agni, as Agni himself is mentioned as only born. But, even if it were so, the father of these sons (putra) could hardly be intended here for a horse.

IV, 6, 9. táva tyé agne harítа*h* gh*r*ita-snấ*h* róhitâsa*h* *r*i*g*u-áñ*k*a*h* su-áñ*k*a*h*, arushấsa*h* v*r*ísha*n*a*h* *r*i*g*u-mushkấ*h*. Here, so far from Agni being represented as a red-horse, his different horses, the Haríts or bays, the Róhitas or

[a] See V, 1, 4. *s*vetá*h* vâ*g*î́ *g*âyate ágre áhnâm. X, 1, 6. arushá*h* *g*âtá*h* padé *l*/âyâ*h*.

ruddy, and the arushâsa*h* v*ri*sha*n*a*h*, the red stallions, are distinctly mentioned. Here v*ri*shan may be translated by stallion, instead of simply by male, because arushá is here a substantive, the name of a horse.

V, 1, 5. *g*ánish*t*a hí *g*énya*h* ágre áhnâm hitá*h* hitéshu arushá*h* váneshu. Here arushá*h* is simply an adjective, red, referring to Agni, who is understood throughout the hymn to be the object of praise. He is said to be kind to those who are kind to him, and to be red in the woods, i. e. brilliant in the wood which he consumes; cf. III, 29, 6. Nothing is said about his equine nature.

In V, 12, 2 and 6, VI, 48, 6, we have again simply arushá v*ri*shan, which does not mean the red-horse, but the red male, the red hero, i. e. Agni.

In VI, 49, 2, divá*h* s*i*sum sáhasa*h* sûnúm agním ya*gñ*ásya ketúm arushám yá*g*adhyai, there is no trace of Agni being conceived as a horse. He is called the child of the sky or of Dyu, the son of strength (who is produced by strong rubbing of wood), the light or the beacon of the sacrifice, and lastly Arushá, which, for reasons stated above, I take to be used here as a name.

Next follow the passages in which, according to Professor Roth, arushá, as an adjective, is said to be applied to the horses, cows, and other teams of the gods, particularly of the dawn, the A*s*vins, and B*ri*haspati.

I, 118, 5. pári vâm á*s*vâ*h* vápusha*h* patañgâ*h* váya*h* vahantu arushâ*h* abhîke. Here we find the váya*h* arushâ*h* of the A*s*vins, which it is better to translate by red birds, as immediately before the winged horses are mentioned. In fact, whenever arushá is applied to the vehicle of the A*s*vins, it is to be understood of these red birds, IV, 43, 6.

In I, 92, 1 and 2 (not 20), árushî occurs three times, referring twice to the cows of the dawn, once to the dawn herself.

In IV, 15, 6, tám árvantam ná sânasím arushám ná divá*h* s*i*sum marm*ri*gyánte divé-dive, arushá does not refer to the horse or any other animal of Agni. The verse speaks of a horse by way of comparison only, and says that the sacrificers clean or trim Agni, the fire, as people clean a horse. We cannot join arushám in the next pâda with árvantam in the preceding pâda, for the second ná would then be without any construction. The construction is certainly not easy, but I think it is safer to translate: they trim him (Agni), day by day, as they clean a strong horse, as they clean Arushá, the child of Dyu. In fact, as far as I know, arushá is never used as the name of the one single horse belonging to Agni, but always of two or more.

In III, 31, 21, antár (íti) k*ri*sh*n*ā̃n arushai*h* dhā̃ma bhi*h* gât, dhā̃ma bhi*h* is said to mean flames of lightning. But dhā̃man in the Rig-veda does not mean flames, and it seems better to translate, with thy red companies, scil. the Maruts.

That arushá in one or two passages means the red cloud, is true. But in X, 43, 9, arushá refers to the thunderbolt mentioned in the same verse; and in I, 114, 5, everything refers to Rudra, and not to a red cloud, in the proper sense of the word.

Further on, where the meanings attributable to árushî in the Veda are collected, it is said that árushî means a red mare, also the teams of Agni and Ushas. Now, here, surely, a distinction should have been made between those passages in which árushî means a real horse, and those where it expresses the imaginary steeds of Agni. The former, it should be observed, occur in one Ma*n*d*a*la only, and in places of somewhat doubtful authority, in VIII, 55, 3, a Vâlakhilya hymn, and in VIII, 68, 18, a dânastuti or panegyric. Besides, no passage is given where árushî means the horses of the dawn, and I doubt whether such a passage exists, while the one verse where árushî is really used for the horses of Indra, is not mentioned at all. Lastly, two passages are set apart where árushî is supposed to mean flames. Now, it may be perfectly true that the red-horses of Agni are meant for flames, just as the red-horses of Indra may be the rays of the sun. But, in that case, the red-horses of Agni should always have been thus translated, or rather interpreted, and not in one passage only. In IX, 111, 2, árushî is said to mean flames, but no further light is thrown upon that very difficult passage.

Note 2. Pári tasthúsha*h*. I take this form as a nominative plural like ábibhyusha*h*, I, 11, 5, tvā́m devā́*h* ábibhyusha*h* tu*g*yámânâsa*h* âvishu*h*, 'the gods, stirred up, came to thee, not fearing;' and like dadúsha*h*, I, 54, 8, yé te indra dadúsha*h* vardháyanti máhi kshatrám, 'who giving or by their gifts increase thy great power, O Indra.' Here we might possibly take it as a gen. sing. referring to te, but dadivân is far more appropriate as an epithet of the sacrificer than of the god. (See Benfey, Vocativ, p. 24; and Hermes, p. 16.) It is well known among Sanskrit scholars that Professor Whitney, in reviewing my translation, declared that the participial form tasthusha*h* had no right to be anything but an accusative plural or a genitive or ablative singular. (See Chips from a German Workshop, vol. iv, p. 508.) Dr. Kern, however, in his translation of the B*ri*hat-Sa*m*hitâ had shown long before that nom. plur. such as vidusha*h* are by no means rare, even in the Mahâbhârata and kindred works. Dr. Lanman (Journ. Americ. Or. Soc. X, p. 513) has now entered abibhyusha*h* as a nom. plur., but he prefers to take tasthusha*h* as an acc. plural, so that we should have to translate *k*árantam pári tasthúsha*h* by 'walking round those who stand.' This may be grammatically possible; but who could be meant by tasthusha*h*, standing ones? And, secondly, is it usual in Vedic Sanskrit to say *k*arati pári tam, 'he walks round him?' We find pari ta*m* yâti, or tam pari yâti, but hardly yâti pari tam, 'he goes round him,' except when pari stands independent of the verb and means 'around,' e.g. IX, 72, 8, pavasva pári pā́rthivam rá*g*a*h*. It is more difficult to decide whether we should adopt Ludwig's interpretation, who takes pari tasthusha*h* in the sense of 'away from what is firm.' This is correct grammatically, and tasthivat, as opposed to *g*ágat, is often used in the sense of what is immovable. But is it ever used in that sense by itself? I doubt it, though I may add in support of it such a passage as I, 191, 9, út apaptat asaú sū́rya*h* . . . . âdityá*h* párvatebhya*h*, a verse where the expression vi*s*vád*ri*sh*t*a*h* ad*rī*sh*t*ahā́ is analogous to our ketúm k*ri*n*v*án aketáve. I therefore retain pari tasthusha*h* as a nom. plural in the sense of standing around, circumstantes, possibly of pari*k*ara, attendants. Parish*th*âna or sthâna comes to mean an abode, and paritasthivantas would be bystanders, attendants, the people, in fact, who are supposed to harness the horse.

Though I do not assign great weight to interpretations of hymns, as given by the Brâhma*n*as, I may mention that in the Taitt. Br. III, 9, 4, 1, paritasthusha*h* is explained as a nom. plur., ime vai lokâ*h* paritasthusha*h*, while Sâya*n*a in his commentary (Sâma-veda II, 6, 3, 12, 1) has parito-vasthitâ lokatrayavartina*h* prâ*n*ina*h*.

Note 3. Ró*k*ante ro*k*anấ. A similar expression occurs III, 61, 5, where it is said of Ushas, the dawn, that she lighted the lights in the sky, prá ro*k*anấ ruru*k*e ra*n*vásand*ri*k.

Verse 2.

WILSON: They (the charioteers) harness to his car his two desirable coursers, placed on either hand, bay-coloured, high-spirited, chief-bearing.

BENFEY: Die lieben Falben schirren sie zu beiden Seiten des Wagens an, braune, kühne, held-tragende.

LUDWIG: Sie spannen seine lieblichen falben an den wagen mit auseinandergehenden seiten, die blutroten, mutigen, helden-bringenden.

Note 1. Although no name is given, the pronoun asya clearly refers to Indra, for it is he to whom the two bays belong. The next verse, therefore, must likewise be taken as addressed to Indra, and not to the sun or the morning-red, spoken of as a horse or a chariot in the first verse.

Vipakshasâ is well explained by Sâya*n*a, vividhe pakshasî rathasya pâr*s*vau yayos tau vipakshasau, rathasya dvayo*h* pâr*s*vayor yogitâv ity artha*h*. The only doubt is whether it refers to the two sides of the chariot, or of the principal horse. That horses were sometimes yoked so that one should act as leader, and two should be harnessed on each side, we see in I, 39, 6, note.

Verse 3.

Wilson: Mortals, you owe your (daily) birth (to such an Indra), who, with the rays of the morning, gives sense to the senseless, and to the formless, form.

Benfey: Licht machend—Männer!—das Dunkele und kenntlich das Unkenntliche, entsprangst du mit dem Morgenroth.

Ludwig: Sichtbarkeit schaffend dem unsichtbaren, gestalt o schmuckreiche (Marut) dem gestaltlosen, wurdet ihr mit den Ushas zusammen geboren.

Note 1. In the TB. III, 9, 4, several of these mantras are enjoined for the A*s*vamedha. When the banner (dhva*g*a) is fastened, this verse is to be used, because ketu was supposed to mean a banner. The vocative maryâ*h*, which I have translated by O men, had evidently become a mere exclamation at a very early time. Even in our passage it is clear that the poet does not address any men in particular, for he addresses Indra, nor is marya used in the general sense of men. It means males, or male offspring. It sounds more like some kind of asseveration or oath, like the Latin mehercle, or like the English O ye powers, and it is therefore quoted as a nipâta or particle in the Vâ*g*. Prâti*s*. II, 16. It can hardly be taken here as addressed to the Maruts, though the Maruts are the subject of the next verse. Kluge in Kuhn's Zeitschrift, vol. xxv, p. 309, points out that maryâ*h* as an interjection does not occur again in the Rig-veda. But the Rig-veda contains many words which occur once only, and the author of Vâ*g*. Prâti*s*âkhya is no mean authority. See also Tâ*nd*ya Brâhm. VII, 6, 5. If Dr. Kluge proposes to read mâryâi as a dative (like λύκῳ) he knows, of course, that such a form does not only never occur again in the Rig-veda, but never in the whole of Sanskrit literature. Grassmann and Lanman (N. I., p. 339) both seem to imagine that the Pada text has marya, but it has maryâ*h*, and no accent. If maryâ*h* had the accent, we might possibly translate, 'the youths, i. e. the Maruts, made,' taking k*rin*van for ak*rin*van, or the more usual akurvan; but in that case the transition to a*g*âyathâ*h* would be very sudden. See, however, I, 6, 7.

Sâya*n*a explains it maryâ*h*, manushyâ*h*! idam â*sk*aryam pa*s*yata. Another explanation of this verse, which evidently troubled the ancient commentators as much as us, is, 'O mortal, i.e. O sun (dying daily), thou hast been born with the dawn.'

Note 2. Ushádbhi*h*, an instrumental plural which attracted the attention of the author of the Vârttika to Pâ*n*. VII, 4, 48. It occurs but once, but the regular form, ushobhi*h*, does not occur at all in the Rig-veda. The same grammarian mentions mâs, month, as changing the final s of its base into d before bhis. This, too, is confirmed by RV. II, 24, 5, where mâdbhi*h* occurs. Two other words, svavas, offering good protection, and svatavas, of independent strength, mentioned together as liable to the same change, do not occur with bhi*h* in the Rig-veda, but the forms svavadbhi*h* and svatavadbhi*h* probably occurred in some other Vedic writings. Svatavadbhya*h* has been pointed out by Professor Aufrecht in the Vâ*g*asan. Sa*m*hitâ XXIV, 16, and svatavobhya*h* in *S*atap. Br. II, 5, 1, 14. That the nom. svavân, which is always trisyllabic, is not to be divided into sva-vân, as proposed by *S*âkalya, but into su-avân, is implied by Vârttika to Pâ*n*. VIII, 4, 48, and distinctly stated in the Siddhânta-Kaumudî. That the final n of the nom. su-avân disappeared before semi-vowels is confirmed by the *S*âkalaprâti*s*âkhya, Sûtra 287; see also Vâ*g*asan. Prâti*s*. III, Sûtra 135 (Weber, Ind. Stud. vol. iv, p. 206). On the proper division of su-avas, see Aufrecht, Zeitschrift der Deutschen Morgenländischen Gesellschaft, vol. xiii, p. 499.

Verse 4.

WILSON: Thereafter, verily, those who bear names invoked in holy rites (the Maruts), having seen the rain about to be engendered, instigated him to resume his embryo condition (in the clouds).

BENFEY: Sodann von freien Stücken gleich erregen wieder Schwangerschaft die heilgen Namen tragenden.

LUDWIG: Da haben nämlich in ihrer göttlichen weise dise der P*ris*ni leibesfrucht gebracht, opfer verdienenden namen erwerbend.

Note 1. Ât must here take vyûha and be pronounced as an iambus. This is exceptional with ât, but there are at least two other passages where the same pronunciation is necessary. I, 148, 4, ā́t ro*k*ate váne ā́ vi-bhā́-vâ, though in the line immediately following it is monosyllabic. Also in V, 7, 10, ā́t agne ápri*n*ata*h*.

Note 2. Svadhā́, literally one's own place, afterwards, one's own nature. It was a great triumph for the science of Comparative Philology that, long before the existence of such a word as svadhâ in Sanskrit was known, it should have been postulated by Professor Benfey in his Griechisches Wurzellexicon, published in 1839, and in the appendix of 1842. Svadhā́ was known, it is true, in the ordinary Sanskrit, but there it only occurred as an exclamation used on presenting an oblation to the manes. It was also explained to mean food offered to deceased ancestors, or to be the name of a personification of Mâyâ or worldly illusion, or of a nymph. But Professor Benfey, with great ingenuity, postulated for Sanskrit a noun svadhā́, as corresponding to the Greek ἔθος and the German sitte, O. H. G. sit-u, Gothic sid-u. The noun svadhā́ has since been discovered in the Veda, where it occurs very frequently; and its true meaning in many passages where native tradition had entirely misunderstood it, has really been restored by means of its etymological identification with the Greek ἔθος or ἦθος. See Kuhn's Zeitschrift, vol. ii, p. 134; vol. xii, p. 158.

The expressions ánu svadhā́m and svadhā́m ánu are of frequent occurrence. They mean, according to the nature or character of the persons spoken of, and may be translated by as usual, or according to a person's wont. Thus in our passage we may translate, The Maruts are born again, i. e. as soon as Indra appeared with the dawn, according to their wont; they are always born as soon as Indra appears, for such is their nature.

I, 165, 5. índra svadhā́m ánu hí na*h* babhū́tha.

For, Indra, according to thy wont, thou art with us.

VIII, 20, 7. svadhā́m ánu *s*ríyam nára*h*—váhante.

According to their wont, the men (the Maruts) carry splendour.

Thou hast grown (Indra) according to thy nature.

IV, 33, 6. ánu svadhấm *ri*bhávа*h* *g*agmu*h* etấm.

According to their nature, the *Ri*bhus went to her, scil. the cow; or, according to this their nature, they came.

IV, 52, 6; I, 33, 11; I, 88, 6; VII, 56, 13; III, 51, 11.

In all these passages svadhấ may be rendered by manner, habit, usage, and ánu svadhấm would seem to correspond to the Greek ἐξ ἔθους. Yet the history of these words in Sanskrit and Greek has not been exactly the same. First of all we observe in Greek a division between ἔθος and ἦθος, and whereas the former comes very near in meaning to the Sanskrit svadhấ, the latter shows in Homer a much more primitive and material sense. It means in Homer, not a person's own nature, but the own place, for instance, of animals, the haunts of horses, lions, fish; in Hesiod, also of men. Hom. Il. XV, 268, μετά τ' ἤθεα καὶ νομὸν ἵππων, loca consueta et pascua. Svadhấ in the Veda does not occur in that sense, although etymologically it might take the meaning of one's own place: cf. dhâ-man, familia, &c. Whether in Greek ἦθος, from meaning lair, haunt, home, came, like νομός and νόμος, to mean habit, manner, character, which would be quite possible, or whether ἦθος in that meaning represents a second start from the same point, which in Sanskrit was fixed in svadhấ, is impossible to determine. In Sanskrit svadhấ clearly shows the meaning of one's own nature, power, disposition. It does not mean power or nature in general, but always the power of some one, the peculiarity, the individuality of a person. This will appear from the following passages:

II, 3, 8. tisrá*h* devî́*h* svadháyâ barhí*h* ấ idám á*kkh*idram pântu.

May the three goddesses protect by their power the sacred pile unbroken.

IV, 13, 5. káyâ yâti svadháyâ.

By what inherent power does he (the Sun) move on?

IV, 26, 4. a*k*akráyâ svadháyâ.

By a power which requires no chariot, i.e. by himself without a chariot.

The same expression occurs again X, 27, 19.

In some places the verb mad, to delight, joined with svadháyâ, seems to mean to revel in his strength, to be proud of his might.

V, 32, 4. svadháyâ mádantam.

V*ri*tra who delights in his strength.

VII, 47, 3. svadháyâ mádantî*h*.

The waters who delight in their strength. See X, 124, 8.

In other passages, however, as we shall see, the same phrase (and this is rather unusual) requires to be taken in a different sense, so as to mean to rejoice in food.

I, 164, 38; III, 17, 5.

III, 35, 10. índra píba svadháyâ *k*it sutásya agné*h* vâ pâhi *g*ihváyâ ya*g*atra.

Indra drink of the libation by thyself (by thy own power), or with the tongue of Agni, O worshipful.

To drink with the tongue of Agni is a bold but not unusual expression. V, 51, 2. agné*h* pibata *g*ihváyâ. X, 15, 3.

I, 165, 6. kvã syã va*h* maruta*h* svadhã âsît yát mãm ékam sam-ádhatta ahi-hátye.

Where was that custom of yours, O Maruts, when you left me alone in the killing of Ahi?

VII, 8, 3. káyâ na*h* agne ví vasa*h* su-v*ri*ktím kãm ûm (íti) svadhãm *rin*ava*h* *s*asyámâna*h*.

In what character dost thou light up our work, and what character dost thou assume, when thou art praised?

IV, 58, 4; IV, 45, 6.

I, 64, 4. sâkám *g*a*gñ*ire svadháyâ.

They (the Maruts) were born together, according to their nature; very much like ánu svadhãm, I, 6, 4. One can hardly render it here by 'they were born by their own strength,' or 'by spontaneous generation.'

In other passages, however, svadháyâ, meaning originally by its own power, or nature, comes to mean, by itself, sponte suâ.

VII, 78, 4. ã asthât rátham svadháyâ yu*g*yámânam.

She, the dawn, mounted the chariot which was harnessed by itself, by its own power, without requiring the assistance of people to put the horses to.

X, 129, 2. ā́nît avâtám svadháyâ tát ékam.

That only One breathed breathlessly (or freely) by its own strength, i.e. by itself.

In the same sense svadhā́bhi*h* is used in several passages: I, 113, 13. am*ri*tâ *k*arati svadhā́bhi*h*.

The immortal Dawn moves along by her own strength, i.e. by herself.

VIII, 10, 6. yát vâ svadhā́bhi*h* adhi-tísh*th*atha*h* rátham.

Or whether ye mount your chariot by your own strength, ye Asvins.

I, 164, 30. *g*îvá*h* m*ri*tásya *k*arati svadhā́bhi*h* ámartya*h* mártyena sá-yoni*h*.

The living moves by the powers of the dead, the immortal is the brother of the mortal. III, 26, 8; V, 60, 4.

There are doubtful passages, such as I, 180, 6, in which the meaning of svadhā́bhi*h*, too, is doubtful. In VI, 2, 8, svadhā́ looks like an adverb, instead of svadháyâ, and would then refer to pári*g*mâ. The same applies to VIII, 32, 6.

But svadhā́ means also food, lit. one's own portion, the sacrificial offering due to each god, and lastly, food in general.

I, 108, 12. yát indrâgnî (íti) út-itâ sū́ryasya mádhye dīvá*h* svadháyâ mâdáyethe (íti).

Whether you, Indra and Agni, delight in your food at the rising of the sun or at midday.

X, 15, 12. tvám agne î*l*itá*h* *g*âta-veda*h* ávâ*t* havyā́ni surabhī́*n*i k*ri*tvī́, prá adâ*h* pit*ri*-bhya*h* svadháyâ té akshan addhí tvám deva prá-yatâ havī́*m*shi. 13. yé *k*a ihá pitára*h* yé *k*a ná ihá yā́n *k*a vidmá yā́n û*m* (íti) *k*a ná pra-vidmá, tvám vettha yáti té *g*âta-veda*h* svadhā́bhi*h* ya*gñ*ám sú-k*ri*tam *g*ushasva. 14. yé agni-dagdhā́*h* yé ánagni-dagdhâ*h* mádhye divá*h* svadháyâ mâdáyante, tébhi*h* sva-rā́*t* ásu-nîtim etā́m yathâ-vasám tanvā́m kalpayasva.

12. Thou, O Agni *G*âtavedas, hast carried, when implored, the offerings which thou hast rendered sweet: thou hast given them to the fathers, they fed on their share. Eat thou, O god, the proffered oblations. 13. Our fathers who are here, and those who are not here, our fathers whom we know and those whom we do not know, thou knowest

how many they are, O *G*âtavedas, accept the well-made sacrifice with the sacrificial portions. 14. They who, whether burnt by fire or not burnt by fire, rejoice in their offering in the midst of heaven, give to them, O king, that life, and thy (their) own body, according to thy will.

III, 4, 7. saptá p*ri*kshásа*h* svadháyâ madanti.

The seven horses delight in their food.

X, 14, 7. ubhấ rấ*g*ânâ svadháyâ mádantâ.

The two kings delighting in their food.

IX, 113, 10. yátra kấmâ*h* ni-kâmấ*h* *k*a, yátra bradhnásya vish*t*ápam, svadhấ *k*a yátra t*rí*pti*h* *k*a tátra mấm am*rí*tam k*ri*dhí.

Where wishes and desires are, where the cup of the bright Soma is (or, where the highest place of the sun is), where there is food and rejoicing, there make me immortal.

I, 154, 4. yásya trĭ́ pûr*n*ấ mádhunâ padấni ákshîyamâ*n*â svadháyâ mádanti.

He (Vish*n*u) whose three places, full of sweet, imperishable, delight or abound in food.

V, 34, 1; II, 35, 7; I, 168, 9; I, 176, 2.

In the tenth book svadhấ is used very much as it occurs in the later Sanskrit, as the name of a peculiar sacrificial rite.

X, 14, 3. yấn *k*a devấ*h* vav*ri*dhú*h* yé *k*a devấn svấhâ anyé svadháyâ anyé madanti.

Those whom the gods cherish, and those who cherish the gods, the one delight in Svâhâ, the others in Svadhâ; or, in praise and food.

Note 3. The expression garbha-tvám â-îrire is matched by that of III, 60, 3, saudhanvanấsa*h* am*ri*ta-tvám ấ îrire, the Saudhanvanas (the *Ri*bhus) obtained immortality, or became immortal. I do not think that punar erire can mean, as Ludwig supposes, they pushed away their state of garbha. The idea that the Maruts assumed the form of a garbha, lit. of an embryo or a new-born child, is only meant to express that they were born, or that the storms burst forth from the womb of the sky as soon as Indra arises to do battle against the demon of darkness. Thus we read, I, 134, 4, á*g*anaya*h* marúta*h* vakshá*n*âbhya*h*, Thou, Vâyu, hast produced the Maruts from the bowels (of the sky).

As assisting Indra in this battle, the Maruts, whose name retained for a long time its purely appellative meaning of storms, attained their rank as deities by the side of Indra, or, as the poet expresses it, they assumed their sacred name. This seems to be the whole meaning of the later legend that the Maruts, like the *Ri*bhus, were not originally gods, but became deified for their works. See also Kern, Translation of B*ri*hat-sa*m*hitâ, p. 117, note.

Other explanations are: they made that which was born within the cloud into a garbha or embryo; or, they arose with Âditya, proceeded with Savitar, and when Savitar set, they became again garbhas; see Sâma-veda II, 2, 7, 2, comm.

VÁHNI.

Verse 5.

WILSON: Associated with the conveying Maruts, the traversers of places difficult of access, thou, Indra, hast discovered the cows hidden in the cave.

BENFEY: Mit den die Festen brechenden, den Stürmenden fandst, Indra, du die Kühe in der Grotte gar.

LUDWIG: Und mit denen, die das feste sogar anbrechen, selbst im versteck, o Indra, mit den priesterlichen, fandest du die morgenstralen auf.

Note 1. Sâya*n*a explains váhnibhi*h* in the sense of Marúdbhi*h*, and he tells the oft-repeated story how the cows were carried off by the Pa*n*is from the world of the gods, and thrown into darkness, and how Indra with the Maruts conquered them and brought them back. Everybody seems to have accepted this explanation of Sâya*n*a, and I myself do not venture to depart from it. Yet it should be stated that the use of váhni as a name of the Maruts is by no means well established. Váhni is in fact a most difficult word in the Veda. In later Sanskrit it means fire, and is quoted also as a name of Agni, the god of fire, but we do not learn why a word which etymologically means carrier, from vah, to carry, should have assumed the meaning of fire. It may be that vah, which in Sanskrit, Greek, and Latin means chiefly to carry, expressed originally the idea of moving about (the German be-wegen), in which case váh-ni, fire, would have been formed with the same purpose as ag-ní, ig-nis, fire, from Sk. ag, ἀγ-ω, ag-o. In Alvis-mal, V, 94, we read, kalla Vág Vanir, the Wanes call fire Vág, i.e. wavy. But in Sanskrit Agni is so constantly represented as the carrier of the sacrificial oblation, that something may also be said in favour of the Indian scholastic interpreters who take váhni, as applied to Agni, in the sense of carrier. However that may be, it admits of no doubt that váhni, in the Veda, is distinctly applied to the bright fire or light. In some passages it looks very much like a proper name of Agni, in his various characters of terrestrial and celestial light. It is used for the sacrificial fire:

V, 50, 4. yátra váhni*h* abhí-hita*h*.

Where the sacrificial fire is placed.

It is applied to Agni:

VII, 7, 5. ásâdi *vrit*á*h* váhni*h* â-*g*aganvā̃n agní*h* brahmā̃.

The chosen light came nigh, and sat down, Agni, the priest.

Here Agni is, as usual, represented as a priest, chosen like a priest, for the performance of the sacrifice. But, for that very reason, váhni may here have the meaning of priest, which, as we shall see, it has in many places, and the translation would then be more natural: He, the chosen minister, came near and sat down, Agni, the priest.

VIII, 23, 3. váhni*h* vindate vásu.

Agni finds wealth (for those who offer sacrifices?).

More frequently váhni is applied to the celestial Agni, or other solar deities, where it is difficult to translate it in English except by an adjective:

III, 5, 1. ápa dvā̃râ támasa*h* váhni*h* âvar (íty âva*h*).

Agni opened the two doors of darkness.

I, 160, 3. sá*h* váhni*h* putrá*h* pitró*h* pavítra-vân punā̃ti dhī̃ra*h* bhúvanâni mâyáyâ.

That light, the son of the two parents, full of brightness, the wise, brightens the world by his power.

Agni is even called váhni-tama (IV, 1, 4), which hardly means more than the brightest.

II, 17, 4. ā́t ródasî (íti) *g*yótishâ váhni*h* ā́ atanot.

Then the bright (Indra) stretched out or filled heaven and earth with his light.

II, 38, 1. út û*m* (íti) syá*h* devá*h* savitā́—váhni*h* asthât.

The divine Savitar, the luminous, arose.

Besides this meaning of light or fire, however, there are clearly two other meanings of váhni which must be admitted in the Veda, first that of a carrier, vehicle, and, it may be, horse; secondly that of minister or priest.

VI, 57, 3. a*g*ā́*h* anyásya váhnaya*h* hárî (íti) anyásya sámbh*ri*tâ.

The bearers of the one (Pûshan) are goats, the bays are yoked for the other (Indra).

I, 14, 6. gh*ri*tá-p*ri*sh*th*â*h* mana*h*-yú*g*a*h* yé tvâ váhanti váhnaya*h*.

The horses with shining backs, obedient to thy will, which carry thee (Agni).

VIII, 3, 23. yásmai anyé dá*s*a práti dhúram váhanti váhnaya*h*.

A horse against whom other ten horses carry a weight; i. e. it requires ten horses to carry the weight which this one horse carries. (See X, 11, 7. váhamâna*h* á*s*vai*h*.)

II, 37, 3. médyantu te váhnaya*h* yébhi*h* ī́yase.

May thy horses be fat on which thou goest. II, 24, 13.

I, 44, 13. *s*rudhí *s*rut-kar*n*a váhni-bhi*h*.

Agni, who hast ears to hear, hear, on thy horses. Unless váhni-bhi*h* is joined with the words that follow, devai*h* sayā́va-bhi*h*.

III, 6, 2. va*k*yántâm te váhnaya*h* saptá-*g*ihvâ*h*[a].

May thy seven-tongued horses be called. Here váhnaya*h* is clearly meant for the flames of Agni, yet I doubt whether we should be justified in dropping the simile, as the plural of váhni is nowhere used in the bald sense of flames.

In one passage váhni is supposed to be used as a feminine, or at all events applied to a feminine subject:

VIII, 94, 1. yuktā́ váhni*h* ráthânâm.

---

[a] Cf. I, 58, 7. saptá *g*uhvā́*h*.

She is yoked as the drawer of the chariots. Probably, however, váhni*h* should here be changed into váhnî.

The passages in which váhni is applied to Soma in the ninth and tenth Ma*nd*alas throw little light on the subject. (IX, 9, 6; 20, 5; 6; 36, 2; 64, 19; 89, 1; X, 101, 10.)

Instead of vi*s*ấm vi*s*páti*h*, lord of men (VII, 7, 4), we find IX, 108, 10. vi*s*ấm váhni*h* ná vi*s*páti*h*. One feels inclined to translate here váhni*h* by leader, but it is more likely that váhni is here again the common name of Soma, and that it is inserted between vi*s*ấm ná vi*s*páti*h*, which is meant to form one phrase.

In IX, 97, 34, tisrá*h* vấ*k*a*h* îrayati prá váhni*h*, we may take váhni as the common appellation of Soma. But it may also mean minister or priest, as in the passages which we have now to examine. Cf. X, 11, 6.

For besides these passages in which váhni clearly means vector, carrier, drawer, horse, there is a large class of verses in which it can only be translated by minister, i. e. officiating minister, and, as it would seem, chiefly singer or reciter[a].

The verb vah was used in Sanskrit in the sense of carrying out (ud-vah, ausführen), or performing a rite, particularly as applied to the reciting of hymns. Hence such compounds as ukthá-vâhas or stóma-vâhas, offering hymns of praise, and yag*ñ*á-vâhas. Thus we read:

V, 79, 4. abhí yé tvâ vibhâ-vari stómai*h* g*rin*ánti váhnaya*h*.

The ministers who praise thee, splendid Dawn, with hymns.

I, 48, 11. yé tvâ g*rin*ánti váhnaya*h*.

The ministers who praise thee.

VII, 75, 5. ushấ*h* u*kkh*ati váhni-bhi*h* g*rin*ânấ.

The dawn lights up, praised by the ministers.

VI, 39, 1. mandrásya kavé*h* divyásya váhne*h*.

Of the sweet poet, of the heavenly priest . . . .

VII, 82, 4. yuvấm ít yut-sú p*rí*tanâsu váhnaya*h* yuvấm kshémasya pra-savé mitá-g*ñ*ava*h*, îsânấ vásva*h* ubháyasya kâráva*h* índrâvaru*n*â su-hávâ havâmahe.

[a] See Taitt. Brâhm. I, 1, 6, 10. vahnir vâ ana*d*vân, vahnir adhvaryu*h*.

We, as ministers, invoke you only in fights and battles; we, as suppliants, (invoke) you for the granting of treasure; we, as poets, (invoke) you, the lords of twofold wealth, you, Indra and Varu*n*a, who listen to our call.

VI, 32, 3. sá*h* váhni-bhi*h* *ri*kva-bhi*h* góshu *s*á*s*vat mitá-*g*ñu-bhi*h* puru-k*ri*tvâ *g*igâya.

He (Indra) was victorious often among the cows, always with celebrating and suppliant ministers.

I have placed these two passages together because they seem to me to illustrate each other, and to show that although in the second passage the celebrating and suppliant ministers may be intended for the Maruts, yet no argument could be drawn from this verse in favour of váhni by itself meaning the Maruts. See also VIII, 6, 2; 12, 15; X, 114, 2.

IV, 21, 6. hótâ yá*h* na*h* mahấn sam-vára*n*eshu váhni*h*.

The Hotar who is our great priest in the sanctuaries.

I, 128, 4. váhni*h* vedhấ*h* á*g*âyata.

Because the wise priest (Agni) was born.

The same name which in these passages is applied to Agni, is in others, and, as it will be seen, in the same sense, applied to Indra.

II, 21, 2. tuvi-gráye váhnaye.

To the strong-voiced priest or leader.

The fact that váhni is followed in several passages by ukthai*h* would seem to show that the office of the váhni was chiefly that of recitation or of addressing prayers to the gods.

III, 20, 1. agním ushásam a*s*vínâ dadhi-krấm ví-ush*t*ishu havate váhni*h* ukthai*h*.

The priest at the break of day calls with his hymns Agni, Ushas, the A*s*vins, and Dadhikrâ.

I, 184, 1. tấ vâm adyá taú aparám huvema u*kkh*ántyâm ushási váhni*h* ukthai*h*.

Let us invoke the two A*s*vins to-day and to-morrow, the priest with his hymns is there when the dawn appears.

In a similar sense, it would seem, as váhni*h* ukthai*h*, the Vedic poets frequently use the words váhni*h* âsấ. This âsấ is the instrumental singular of âs, mouth, and it is used in other phrases also of the mouth as the instrument of praise.

VI, 32, 1. vagríne sám-tamâni vákâmsi âsấ sthávirâya taksham.

I have shaped with my mouth blessed words to the wielder of the thunderbolt, the strong Indra.

X, 115, 3. âsấ váhnim ná sokíshâ vi-rapsínam.

He who sings with his flame as the poet with his mouth. See also I, 38, 14. mimîhí slókam âsyẽ, make a song in thy mouth.

Thus we find váhnih âsấ in the same place in the sixth and seventh Mandalas (VI, 16, 9; VII, 16, 9), in the phrase váhnih âsấ vidúh-tarah, applied to Agni in the sense of the priest wise with his mouth, or taking váhnih âsấ as it were one word, the wise poet.

I, 129, 5. váhnih âsấ, váhnih nah ákkha.

Indra, as a priest by his lips, as a priest coming towards us.

From the parallelism of this passage it would seem that Professor Roth concluded the meaning of âsấ[a] to be near,

[a] Âs, mouth, the Latin os, oris, has been derived from a root as, to breathe, preserved in the Sanskrit as-u, spirit, asu-ra, endowed with spirit, living, the living god. Though I agree with Curtius in admitting a primitive root as, to breathe, from which as-u, breath, must have sprung, I have always hesitated about the derivation of âs and âsya, mouth, from the same root. I do not think, however, that the lengthening of the vowel in âs is so great a difficulty as has been supposed (Kuhn, Zeitschrift, vol. xvii, p. 145). Several roots lengthen their vowel a, when used as substantives without derivative suffixes. In some cases this lengthening is restricted to the Aṅga base, as in anadvâh; in others to the Aṅga and Pada base, as in visvavât, visvavâdbhih, &c.; in others again it pervades the whole declension, as in turâshât: (see Sanskrit Grammar, §§ 210, 208, 175.) Among ordinary words vâk offers a clear instance of a lengthened vowel. In the Veda we find ritîshábham, VI, 14, 4, and ritîsháham (Samhitâ), I, 64, 15. In X, 71, 10 the Samhitâ has sabhâsâhéna, the Pada sabhâsahéna. We find vâh in apsu-vâh (Sâm. Ved.), indra-vâh, havya-vâh. Sah at the end of compounds, such as nri-sah, pritanâ-sah, bhûri-sah, satrâ-sah, vibhâ-sah, sadâ-sah, varies between a long and short â: (see Regnier, Étude sur l'idiome du

or coram. In the Nigha*n*t*u, II, 16, the right reading is evidently âsât, not âsâ; see Nirukta, ed. Satyavrata Sâma*s*rami, vol. i, p. 264. Âsã, however, is an old variant, as may be seen from Rig-veda-bhâshya I, 127, 8; X, 115, 3.

I, 76, 4. pra*g*ã-vatâ vá*k*asâ váhni*h* âsã ã *k*a huvé ní *k*a satsi ihá devaí*h*.

With words in which my people join, I, the poet, invoke, and thou (Agni) sittest down with the gods.

VI, 11, 2. pâvakáyâ *g*uhvã váhni*h* âsã.

Thou, a poet with a bright tongue, O Agni!

Grassmann thinks that vahnir âsâ can always be translated by 'vor das Angesicht bringend,' but this does not appear to be the case in his translation.

The question now arises in what sense váhni is used when applied without further definition to certain deities. Most deities in the Veda are represented as driving or driven, and many as poets or priests. When the A*s*vins are called váhnî, VIII, 8, 12; VII, 73, 4, it may mean riders. But when the Vi*s*ve Devâs are so called, I, 3, 9, or the *Ri*bhus, the exact meaning is more doubtful. The Maruts are certainly riders, and whatever other scholars may say to the contrary, it can be proved that they were supposed to sit astride on horseback, and to have the bridle through the horse's nostrils (V, 61, 2). But if in our verse I, 6, 5, we translate váhni as an epithet, rider, and not only as an epithet, but as a name of the Maruts, we cannot support our translation by independent evidence, but must rely partly on the authority of Sâya*n*a, partly on the general tenor of the text before us, where the Maruts are mentioned in the preceding verse, and, if I am right, in the verse following also. On the other hand, if váhni can thus be used as a name of

Védas, p. 111.) At all events no instance has yet been pointed out in Sanskrit, showing the same contraction which we should have to admit if, as has been proposed, we derived âs from av-as, or from an-as. From 'an' we have in the Veda âná, mouth or face, I, 52, 15. From as, to breathe, the Latin omen, originally os-men, a whisper, might likewise be derived. See Bopp, Comp. Gr. par. 909; Kuhn in Ind. Stud. I, 333.

the Maruts, there is at least one other passage which would gain in clearness by the admission of that meaning, viz.

X, 138, 1. táva tyé indra sakhyéshu váhnaya*h*—ví adardiru*h* valám.

In thy friendship, Indra, these Maruts tore asunder the cloud.

Note 2. I have translated vî*l*ú by stronghold, though it is only an adjective, meaning firm. Dr. Oscar Meyer, in his able essay Quaestiones Homericae, specimen prius, Bonnae, 1867, has tried to show that this vî*l*ú is the original form of Ἴλιος, and he has brought some further evidence to show that the siege and conquest of Troy, as I pointed out in my Lectures on the Science of Language, vol. ii, p. 470, was originally described in language borrowed from the siege and conquest of the dark night by the powers of light, or from the destruction of the cloud by the weapons of Indra. It ought to be considered, however, that vî*l*ú in the Veda has not dwindled down as yet to a mere name, and that therefore it may have originally retained its purely appellative power in Greek as well as in Sanskrit, and from meaning a stronghold in general, have come to mean the stronghold of Troy.

Note 3. The bright cows are here the cows of the morning, the dawns, or the days themselves, which are represented as rescued at the end of each night by the power of Indra, or similar solar gods. Indra's companions in that daily rescue are here the Maruts, the storms, the same companions who act even a more prominent part in the battle of Indra against the dark clouds. These two battles are often mixed up together, so that possibly usríyâ*h* may have been meant for clouds.

Verse 6.

WILSON: The reciters of praises praise the mighty (troop of Maruts), who are celebrated, and conscious of the power of bestowing wealth in like manner as they (glorify) the counsellor (Indra).

BENFEY: Nach ihrer Einsicht verherrlichend besingen Sänger den Schätzeherrn, den berühmten, gewaltigen.

LUDWIG: Als fromme heran zum liede haben die sänger ihn, der trefliches findet, berühmten gesungen.

Note 1. The reasons why I take *gírah* as a masculine in the sense of singer or praiser, may be seen in a note to I, 37, 10.

Note 2. yáthâ matím, lit. according to their mind, according to their heart's desire. Cf. II, 24, 13.

Verse 7.

WILSON: May you be seen, Maruts, accompanied by the undaunted (Indra); both rejoicing, and of equal splendour.

BENFEY: So lass mit Indra denn vereint, dem furchtlosen, erblicken dich, beide erfreu'nd und glanzesgleich.

LUDWIG: Mit Indra zusammen wirst du gesehn zusammengehend mit dem furchtlosen, mild ihr zwei, von gleichem glanze.

Note 1. The sudden transition from the plural to the singular is strange, but the host of the Maruts is frequently spoken of in the singular, and nothing else can here be intended. It may be true, as Professor Benfey suggests, that the verses here put together stood originally in a different order, or that they were taken from different sources. Yet though the Sâma veda would seem to sanction a small alteration in the order of the verses, the alteration of verses 7, 4, 5, as following each other, would not help us much. The Atharva-veda sanctions no change in the order of these verses.

The transition to the dual at the end of the verse is likewise abrupt, not more so, however, than we are prepared for in the Veda. The suggestion of the Nirukta (IV, 12) that these duals might be taken as instrumentals of the singular, is of no real value.

Note 2. D*rí*kshase, a very valuable form, well explained by d*ris*yethâ*h*, a second person singular conjunctive of the First Aorist Âtmanepada, the termination 'sase' corresponding to Greek ση, as the conjunctive takes the personal terminations of the present in both languages. Similar forms, viz. p*ri*kshase, X, 22, 7, ma*m*sase, X, 27, 10; Ath. Veda VII, 20, 2–6, and possibly vívakshase, X, 21, 1–8, 24, 1–3, 25, 1–11, will have to be considered hereafter. (Nirukta, ed. Roth, p. 30, Notes.) As Ludwig has pointed out, the Tâ*nd*ya-brâhma*n*a XII, 2, 6, 7, reads d*ri*kshuse, and explains it by ime lokâ dad*ris*ire. Sâya*n*a, however, explains d*ris*idhâto*h* karma*n*i madhyamaikava*k*ane vyatyayena se-pratyaye d*ri*kshusa iti rûpam. See Delbrück, Syntaktische Forschungen, I, p. 111. The story of Indra's being forsaken by all the gods in his battle against V*ri*tra, but being helped by the Maruts, is often mentioned; see RV. VIII, 96, 7; SV. I, 4, 1, 4, 2; Ait. Br. III, 20.

Verse 8.

WILSON: This rite is performed in adoration of the powerful Indra, along with the irreproachable, heavenward-tending, and amiable bands (of the Maruts).

BENFEY: Durch Indra's liebe Schaaren, die untadligen, himmelstürmenden, strahlet das Opfer mächtiglich.

LUDWIG: Mit den tadellosen, morgens erscheinenden singt der kämpfer sighaft, mit des Indra zu liebenden scharen.

Note 1. Ar*k*ati, which I have here translated by he cries aloud, means literally, he celebrates. I do not know of any passage where ar*k*ati, when used, as here, without an object, means to shine, as Professor Benfey translates it. The real difficulty, however, lies in makhá, which Sâya*n*a explains by sacrifice, and which I have ventured to translate by priest or sacrificer. Makhá, as an adjective, means, as far as we can judge, strong or vigorous, and is applied to various deities, such as Pûshan I, 138, 1, Savit*ri* VI, 71, 1, Soma XI, 20, 7, Indra III, 34, 2, the Maruts I, 64, 11; VI, 66, 9. By itself, makhá is never used as the name of any deity, and it cannot therefore, as Professor Roth proposes, be used in our passage as a name of Indra, or be referred to Indra as a significant adjective. In I, 119, 3, makhá is applied to men or warriors, but it does not follow that makhá by itself means warriors, though it may be connected with the Greek μαχος in σύμμαχος. See Curtius, Grundzüge, p. 293; Grassmann, in Kuhn's Zeitschrift, vol. xvi, p. 164.

There are two passages where makhá refers to an enemy of the gods, IX, 101, 13; X, 171, 2.

Among the remaining passages there is one where makhá is used in parallelism with váhni, X, 11, 6. vívakti váhni*h*, su-apasyáte makhá*h*. Here I propose to translate, The poet speaks out, the priest works well. The same meaning seems applicable likewise to the phrase makhásya dâváne, to the offering of the priest, though I should prefer to translate 'to share in the sacrifice.'

I, 134, 1. ấ yâhi dâváne, vấyo (íti), makhásya dâváne.

Come, Vâyu, to the offering, to the offering of the priest.

VIII, 7, 27. ấ na*h* makhásya dâváne—dévâsa*h* úpa gantana.

Come, gods, to the offering of our priest.

Professor Roth proposes to render makhá in these passages by 'attestation of joy, celebration, praise,' and he takes dâváne as a dative of dâván, a nomen actionis, meaning, the giving. There are some passages where one feels inclined to admit a noun dâvána, and to take dâváne as a locative sing.

VI, 71, 2. devásya vayám savitú*h* sávîmani
*s*résh*th*e syâma vásuna*h* *k*a dâváne.

May we be in the favour of the god Savitar, and in the best award of his treasure.

In II, 11, 1, and II, 11, 12, the locative would likewise be preferable; but there is a decided majority of passages in which dâváne occurs and where it is to be taken as a dative[a], nor is there any other instance in the Veda of a nomen actionis being formed by vana. It is better, therefore, in VI, 71, 2, to refer *s*résh*th*e to sávîmani, and to make allowance in the other passages for the idiomatic use of such phrases as dâváne vásûnâm or râyá*h* dâváne, whether from dâ or from do. See De Infinitivi forma et usu, by E. Wilhelm, 1873, p. 17.

[a] RV. I, 61, 10; 122, 5; 134, 2; 139, 6; II, 1, 10; IV, 29, 5; 32, 9; V, 59, 1; 4; 65, 3; VIII, 25, 20; 45, 10; (92, 26); 46, 25; 27; 63, 5; 69, 17; 70, 12; IX, 93, 4; X, 32, 5; 44, 7; 50, 7.

The termination váne explains, as has been shown by Professor Benfey, Greek infinitives such as δοῦναι, i. e. δοεναι or δοϝεναι = Sanskrit dâ-váne. The termination mane in dấ-mane, for the purpose of giving, explains, as the same scholar has proved, the ancient infinitives in Greek, such as δό-μεναι. It may be added that the regular infinitives in Greek, ending in εναι, as λελοιπ-έναι, are likewise matched by Vedic forms such as IX, 61, 30. dhűrv-ane, or VI, 61, 13. vibhv-áne, and turv-áne (Delbrück in K. Z. XVIII, p. 82; Bopp, Accent, §§ 106, 113, 117). It is hardly right to say that vibhváne in VI, 61, 13, should be taken as an instrumental, for it does not refer to the chariot, but to Sarasvatî. In the termination ειν, which stands for ενι, like εις for εσι, we have, on the contrary, not a dative, but a locative of an abstract noun in an, both cases, as we see from their juxta-position in VI, 71, 2, being equally applicable to express the relation which we are accustomed to call infinitive. See RV. I, 134, 5. ugrấ*h* isha*n*anta bhurvá*n*i, apấm ishanta bhurvá*n*i.

Note 2. Abhidyu I now translate by hastening, and derive it from div, dîvyati, in its original meaning of to throw forth, to break forth, to shine. As from this root we have didyú, weapon, what is thrown, pl. didyava*h*, and possibly didyut, the weapon, particularly Indra's weapon or thunderbolt, abhídyu might mean breaking forth, rushing forth towards us, something like prakrî*l*ína*h*, another name of the Maruts. How abhídyu could mean conquérant, maître du jour, as M. Bergaigne maintains, I do not see. Abhídyűn, I, 33, 11; 190, 4, does not differ much from ánudyűn, i.e. it is used vîpsâyâm.

Verses 9, 10.

Wilson: Therefore circumambient (troop of Maruts), come hither, whether from the region of the sky, or from the solar sphere; for, in this rite, (the priest) fully recites your praises.

Benfey: Von hier, oder vom Himmel komm ob dem Æther, Umkreisender! zu dir streben die Lieder all.

LUDWIG: Von hieher, o Pari*g*man, kom, oder von des himels glanzfirmamente her; zu disem streben unsere lieder auf.

WILSON: We invoke Indra,—whether he come from this earthly region, or from the heaven above, or from the vast firmament,—that he may give (us) wealth.

BENFEY: Von hier, oder vom Himmel ob der Erde begehren Spende wir, oder, Indra! aus weiter Luft.

LUDWIG: Von hier zu empfangen verlangen wir, oder vom himel, oder vom irdischen raume her, oder aus dem grossen luftkreis den Indra.

Note 1. Although the names for earth, sky, and heaven vary in different parts of the Veda, yet the expression divá*h* ro*k*anám occurs so frequently that we can hardly take it in this place in a sense different from its ordinary meaning. Professor Benfey thinks that ro*k*aná may here mean ether, and he translates 'come from heaven above the ether;' and in the next verse, 'come from heaven above the earth.' At first, every reader would feel inclined to take the two phrases, divá*h* vâ ro*k*anất ádhi, and divá*h* vâ pấrthivât ádhi, as parallel; yet I believe they are not quite so.

The following passages will show that the two words ro*k*anám divá*h* belong together, and that they signify the light of heaven, or the bright place of heaven.

VIII, 98, 3. ága*kkh*a*h* ro*k*anám divá*h*.

Thou (Indra) wentest to the light of heaven. I, 155, 3.

III, 6, 8. uraú vâ yé antárikshe—divá*h* vâ yé ro*k*ané.

In the wide sky, or in the light of heaven.

VIII, 82, 4. upamé ro*k*ané divá*h*.

In the highest light of heaven.

IX, 86, 27. t*ri*tī́ye p*ri*sh*th*é ádhi ro*k*ané divá*h*.

On the third ridge, in the light of heaven. See also I, 105, 5; VIII, 69, 3.

The very phrase which we find in our verse, only with *k*it instead of vâ, occurs again, I, 49, 1; VIII, 8, 7; and the same sense must probably be assigned to VIII, 1, 18, ádha *g*má*h* ádha vâ divá*h* b*r*ihatá*h* ro*k*anất ádhi.

Either from the earth, or from the light of the great heaven, increase, O Indra!

Ro*k*aná also occurs in the plural:

I, 146, 1. ví*s*vâ divá*h* ro*k*anắ.

All the bright regions of heaven.

Sâya*n*a: 'All the bright palaces of the gods.' See III, 12, 9.

The same word ro*k*aná, and in the same sense, is sometimes joined with sū́rya and nā́ka.

Thus, I, 14, 9. sū́ryasya ro*k*anā́t ví*s*vân devā́n—hótâ ihá vakshati.

May the Hotar bring the Vi*s*ve Devas hither from the light of the sun, or from the bright realm of the sun.

III, 22, 3. yā́*h* ro*k*ané parástât sū́ryasya.

The waters which are above, in the bright realm of the sun, and those which are below.

I, 19, 6. yé nā́kasya ádhi ro*k*ané, diví devā́sa*h* ā́sate.

They who in the light of the firmament, in heaven, are enthroned as gods.

Here diví, in heaven, seems to be the same as the light of the firmament, nā́kasya ro*k*ané.

Thus ro*k*aná occurs also frequently by itself, when it clearly has the meaning of heaven.

It is said of the dawn, I, 49, 4; of the sun, I, 50, 4; and of Indra, III, 44, 4.

ví*s*vam ā́ bhâti ro*k*anám, he lights up the whole sky.

We also read of three ro*k*anas, where, though it is difficult to say what is really meant, we must translate, the three skies. The cosmography of the Veda is, as I said before, somewhat vague and varying. There is, of course, the natural division of the world into heaven and earth (dyú and bhū́mi), and the threefold division into earth, sky, and heaven, where sky is meant for the region intermediate between heaven and earth (p*ri*thivī́, antáriksha, dyú). There is also a fourfold division, for instance,

VIII, 97, 5. yát vâ ási ro*k*ané divá*h*
samudrásya ádhi vish*t*ápi,
yát pā́rthive sádane v*ri*trahan-tama,
yát antárikshe ā́ gahi.

Whether thou, O greatest killer of V*ri*tra, art in the light of heaven, or in the basin of the sea, or in the place of the earth, or in the sky, come hither!

V, 52, 7. yé vav*ri*dhánta pā̆rthivâ*h* yé uraú antárikshe ā̆, v*rig*âne vâ nadī̆nâm sadhá-sthe vâ mahá*h* divá*h*.

The Maruts who grew, being on the earth, those who are in the wide sky, or in the realm of the rivers, or in the abode of the great heaven.

But very soon these three or more regions are each spoken of as threefold. Thus,

I, 102, 8. tisrá*h* bhū̆mî*h* trī̆*n*i ro*k*anā̆.

The three earths, the three skies.

II, 27, 9. trī̆ ro*k*anā̆ divyā̆ dhârayanta.

The Âdityas support the three heavenly skies.

V, 69, 1. trī̆ ro*k*anā̆ varu*n*a trī̆n utá dyū̆n trī̆*n*i mitra dhârayatha*h* rá*g*â*m*si.

Mitra and Varu*n*a, you support the three lights, and the three heavens, and the three skies.

Here there seems some confusion, which Sâya*n*a's commentary makes even worse confounded. What can ro*k*anā̆ mean as distinct from dyú and rá*g*as? The fourth verse of the same hymn throws no light on the subject, and I should feel inclined to take divyā̆-pā̆rthivasya as one word, though even then the cosmic division here adopted is by no means clear. However, there is a still more complicated division alluded to in IV, 53, 5:

trí*h* antáriksham savitā̆ mahi-tvanā̆ trī̆ rá*g*â*m*si pari-bhū̆*h* trī̆*n*i ro*k*anā̆, tisrá*h* díva*h* p*ri*thivī̆*h* tisrá*h* invati.

Here we have the sky thrice, three welkins, three lights, three heavens, three earths.

A careful consideration of all these passages will show, I think, that in our passage we must take divá*h* vâ ro*k*anā̆t ádhi in its usual sense, and that we cannot separate the two words.

In the next verse, on the contrary, it seems equally clear that divá*h* and pā̆rthivât must be separated. At all events there is no passage in the Rig-veda where pā̆rthiva is joined as an adjective with dyú. Pā̆rthiva as an adjective is frequently joined with rá*g*as, never with dyú. See I, 81,

5; 90, 7; VIII, 88, 5; IX, 72, 8: in the plural, I, 154, 1; V, 81, 3; VI, 31, 2; 49, 3.

Pā́rthivâni also occurs by itself, when it refers to the earth, as opposed to the sky and heaven.

X, 32, 2. ví indra yâsi divyā́ni rokanā́ ví pā́rthivâni rágasâ.

Indra thou goest in the sky between the heavenly lights and the earthly.

VIII, 94, 9. ā́ yé vísvâ pā́rthivâni paprâthan rokanā́ divā́h.

The Maruts who stretched out all the earthly lights, and the lights of heaven.

VI, 61, 11. â-paprúshî pā́rthivâni urú rágah antárikasham.

Sarasvatî filling the earthly places, the wide welkin, the sky. This is a doubtful passage.

Lastly, pā́rthivâni by itself seems to signify earth, sky, and heaven, if those are the three regions which Vishnu measured with his three steps; or east, the zenith, and west, if these were intended as the three steps of that deity. For we read:

I, 155, 4. yáh pā́rthivâni tri-bhíh ít vígâma-bhih urú krámishta.

He (Vishnu) who strode wide with his three strides across the regions of the earth.

These two concluding verses might also be taken as containing the actual invocation of the sacrificer, which is mentioned in verse 8. In that case the full stop at the end of verse 8 should be removed.

MANDALA I, HYMN 19.

ASHTAKA I, ADHYÂYA 1, VARGA 36-37.

TO AGNI (THE GOD OF FIRE) AND THE MARUTS (THE STORM-GODS).

1. Thou art called forth to this fair sacrifice for a draught of milk[1]; with the Maruts come hither, O Agni!

2. No god indeed, no mortal, is beyond the might[1] of thee, the mighty one; with the Maruts come hither, O Agni!

3. They who know of the great sky[1], the Visve Devas[2] without guile[3]; with those Maruts come hither, O Agni!

4. The strong ones who sing their song[1], unconquerable by force; with the Maruts come hither, O Agni!

5. They who are brilliant, of terrible designs, powerful, and devourers of foes; with the Maruts come hither, O Agni!

6. They who in heaven are enthroned as gods, in the light of the firmament[1]; with the Maruts come hither, O Agni!

7. They who toss the clouds[1] across the surging sea[2]; with the Maruts come hither, O Agni!

8. They who shoot with their darts (lightnings) across the sea with might; with the Maruts come hither, O Agni!

9. I pour out to thee for the early draught[1] the sweet (juice) of Soma; with the Maruts come hither, O Agni!

NOTES.

This hymn is ascribed to Medhâtithi, of the family of Ka*n*va. Verse I=SV I, 16.

Verse 1.

WILSON: Earnestly art thou invoked to this perfect rite, to drink the Soma juice; come, Agni, with the Maruts.

BENFEY: Zu diesem schonen Opfer wirst du gerufen, zum Trank der Milch!—Mit diesen Marut's, Agni! komm!

LUDWIG: Her zu diesem schönen opfer, gerufen wirst zum milchtrank du, mit den Marut, Agni, kom.

Note 1. Gopîthá is explained by Yâska and Sâya*n*a as drinking of Soma. I have kept to the literal signification of the word, a draught of milk. In the last verse of our hymn the libation offered to Agni and the Maruts is said to consist of Soma, but Soma was commonly mixed with milk. The other meaning assigned to gopîthá, protection, would give the sense: 'Thou art called for the sake of protection.' But pîtha has clearly the sense of drinking in soma-pîthá, RV. I, 51, 7, and may therefore be taken in the same sense in gopîthá.

Verse 2.

WILSON: No god nor man has power over a rite (dedicated) to thee, who art mighty: come, Agni, with the Maruts.

BENFEY: Denn nicht ein Gott, kein Sterblicher ragt über dein, des Grossen, Macht—Mit diesen Marut's, Agni! komm!

LUDWIG: Es überragt kein gott, kein sterblicher die einsicht dein des grossen, mit den Marut, Agni, kom.

Note 1. The Sanskrit krátu expresses power both of body and mind. Para*h* governs the accusative.

Verse 3.

WILSON: Who all are divine, and devoid of malignity,

and who know (how to cause the descent) of great waters: come, Agni, with the Maruts.

BENFEY: Die guten Götter, welche all bestehen in dem weiten Raum—Mit diesen Marut's, Agni! komm!

LUDWIG: Die wissen um den grossen raum, alle götter truges bar, mit den Marut, Agni, kom.

Note 1. The sky or welkin (rá*g*as) is the proper abode of the Maruts, and 'they who know of' means simply 'they who dwell' in the great sky. The Vedic poets distinguish commonly between the three worlds, the earth, p*ri*thivī́, f., or pā́rthiva, n.; the sky, rá*g*as; and the heaven, dyú: see I, 6, 9, note 1. The phrase mahá*h* rá*g*asa*h* occurs I, 6, 10; 168, 6, &c. Sâya*n*a takes rá*g*as for water or rain: see on this my article in Kuhn's Zeitschrift, vol. xii, p. 28. In some passages rá*g*as means 'darkness,' and might be identified with the Greek Ἔρεβος; Ath. Veda VIII, 2, 1. pâráyâmi tvâ rá*g*asa út tvâ m*ri*tyór apîparam, 'I bring thee out of darkness, out of death I brought thee.' The identification of rá*g*as with ἔρεβος (Leo Meyer, in Kuhn's Zeitschrift, vol. vi, p. 19) must however remain doubtful, until stronger evidence has been brought forward in support of a Greek β representing a Sanskrit *g*, even in the middle of a word. See my article in Kuhn's Zeitschrift, vol. xv, p. 215; Curtius. Grundzüge (fifth edition), p. 480.

Note 2. The appellation Ví*s*ve devā́*h*, all gods together, or, more properly, host-gods, is often applied to the Maruts; cf. I, 23, 8; 10. Benfey connects this line with the preceding verse, considering Ví*s*ve devā́*h*, it seems, inappropriate as an epithet of the Maruts.

Note 3. On adrúh, without guile or deceit, without hatred, see Kuhn's excellent article, Zeitschrift für die Vergleichende Sprachforschung, vol. i, pp. 179, 193. Adrúh is applied to the Maruts again in VIII, 46, 4, though in connection with other gods. It is applied to the Vi*s*ve Devas, RV. I, 3, 9; IX, 102, 5: the Âdityas, RV. VIII, 19, 34; 67, 13: the Rudras, RV. IX, 73, 7: to Heaven and Earth, RV. II, 41, 21; III, 56, 1; IV, 56, 2; VII, 66, 18: to Mitra and Varu*n*a, RV. V, 68, 4: to Agni, RV. VI, 15, 7; VIII, 44, 10. The form adhrúk occurs in the sixth Ma*nd*ala only.

Verse 4.

WILSON: Who are fierce, and send down rain, and are unsurpassed in strength: come, Ágni, with the Maruts.

BENFEY: Die schrecklich-unbesiegbaren, die mächtiglich Licht angefacht—Mit diesen Marut's, Agni, komm!

LUDWIG: Die singen, die gewaltigen, ihr lied unangegriffen durch (ihre) kraft, mit den Marut, Agni, kom.

Note 1. Sâya*n*a explains arká by water. Hence Wilson: 'Who are fierce and send down rain.' But arká has only received this meaning of water in the artificial sýstem of interpretation first started by the authors of the Brâhma*n*as, who had lost all knowledge of the natural sense of the ancient hymns. The passages in which arká is explained as water in the Brâhma*n*as are quoted by Sâya*n*a, but they require no refutation. On the singing of the Maruts, see note to I, 38, 15; also Bergaigne, Journ. As. 1884, p. 194. The perfect in the Veda, like the perfect in Homer, has frequently to be rendered in English by the present.

Verse 5.

WILSON: Who are brilliant, of terrific forms, who are possessors of great wealth, and are devourers of the malevolent: come, Agni, with the Maruts.

BENFEY: Die glänzend-grau'ngestaltigen, hochherrschend feindvernichtenden — Mit diesen Marut's, Agni! komm!

LUDWIG: Die glanzvollen, von schrecklicher gestalt, vón grosser herschaft, feindverzerer, mit den Marut, Agni, kom.

Verse 6.

WILSON: Who are divinities abiding in the radiant heaven above the sun: come, Agni, with the Maruts.

BENFEY: Die Götter die im Himmel sind ob dem Lichtkreis des Göttersitz's—Mit diesen Marut's, Agni! komm!

LUDWIG: Die ob der himmelswölbung glanz, am himel die götter sitzen, mit den Marut, Agni, kom.

Note 1. Nắka must be translated by firmament, as there

is no other word in English besides heaven, and that is wanted to render dyú. Like the Jewish firmament, the Indian nā́ka, too, is adorned with stars; cf. I, 68, 10. pipésa nā́kam str*i*bhi*h*. Dyú, heaven, is supposed to be above the rá*g*as, sky or welkin. Kuhn's Zeitschrift, vol. xii, p. 28.

Sâya*n*a: 'In the radiant heaven above the sun.' See note 1 to I, 6, 9; p. 49.

Verse 7.

WILSON: Who scatter the clouds, and agitate the sea (with waves): come, Agni, with the Maruts.

BENFEY: Welche über das wogende Meer hinjagen die Wolkenschaar—Mit diesen Marut's, Agni! komm!

LUDWIG: Die die berge wiegend hindurch durchs wogenmeer bewegen, mit den Marut, Agni, kom.

Note 1. That párvata (mountain) is used in the sense of cloud, without any further explanation, is clear from many passages:

I, 57, 6. tvám tám indra párvatam mahā́m urúm vá*g*re*n*a va*g*rin parva-*sáh k*akartitha.

Thou, Indra, hast cut this great broad cloud to pieces with thy lightning. Cf. I, 85, 10.

We actually find two similes mixed up together, such as V, 32, 2. ū́dha*h* párvatasya, the udder of the cloud. All we can do is to translate párvata by mountain, but always to remember that mountain means cloud. In the Edda, too, the rocks, said to have been fashioned out of Ymir's bones, are supposed to be intended for clouds. In Old Norse klakkr means both cloud and rock; nay, the English word cloud itself has been identified with the Anglo-Saxon clûd, rock. See Justi, Orient und Occident, vol. ii, p. 62. See Grimm, Deutsche Grammatik, I^3, 398, 424; also Kuhn, Weisse Frau, p. 12.

Note 2. Whether the surging sea is to be taken for the sea or for the air, depends on the view which we take of the earliest cosmography of the Vedic *R*ishis. Sâya*n*a explains: 'They who make the clouds to go, and stir the watery sea.' Wilson remarks that the influence of the winds upon the sea, alluded to in this and the following verse, indicates more familiarity with the ocean than we should have expected from the traditional inland position of the early Hindus, and it has therefore been supposed by others that, even in passages like our own, samudrá was meant for the sky, the waters above the firmament. But although there are passages in the Rig-veda where samudrá must be taken to mean the welkin (RV. I, 95, 3. samudrá ékam diví ékam ap-sú), this word shows in by far the larger number of passages the clear meaning of ocean. There is one famous passage, VII, 95, 2, which proves that the Vedic poets, who were supposed to have known the upper courses only of the rivers of the Penjâb, had followed the greatest and most sacred of their rivers, the Sarasvatî, as far as the Indian ocean. It is well known that, as early as the composition of the laws of the Mânavas, and possibly as early as the composition of the Sûtras on which these metrical laws are based, the river Sarasvatî had changed its course, and that the place where that river disappeared under ground was called Vina*s*ana[a], the loss. This Vina*s*ana forms, according to the laws of the Mânavas, the western frontier of Madhyade*s*a, the eastern frontier being formed by the confluence of the Gangâ and Yamunâ. Madhyade*s*a is a section of Âryâvarta, the abode of the Âryas in the widest sense. Âryâvarta shares with Madhyade*s*a the same frontiers in the north and the south, viz. the Himâlaya and Vindhya mountains, but it extends beyond Madhyade*s*a to the west and east as far as the western and eastern seas. A section of Madhyade*s*a, again, is the country described as that of the Brahmarshis, which comprises only Kurukshetra, the countries of the Matsyas, Pa*ñk*âlas (Kânyakub*g*a, according to Kullûka), and *S*ûrasenas (Mathurâ, according to Kullûka). The most sacred spot of all, however, is that section of the Brahmarshi country which lies between the rivers D*ri*shadvatî and Sarasvatî, and which in the laws of

[a] Mentioned in Lâ*t*y. *S*rauta Sûtras, X, 15, 1; Pa*ñk*avi*ms*a Brâhm. XXV, 10, 1; see Hist. A. S. L., p. 12.

the Mânavas is called Brahmâvarta. In the Sûtras which supplied the material to the authors of the metrical law-books, the Vina*s*ana is mentioned for the first time in the Baudhâyana Sûtras, I, 2, 9, 'Âryâvarta lies to the east of the region where (the Sarasvatî) disappears, to the west of the Black-forest, to the north of the Pâripâtra (mountains), to the south of the Himâlaya.' The name of the Sarasvatî is not mentioned, but no other river can be understood. What is curious, however, is, that in the Vasish*th*a Sûtras where the same frontiers of Âryâvarta are given (I, 8), the MSS. read originally prâg âdar*s*ât, i. e. east of the Âdar*s*a mountains, which was afterwards changed into prâg adar*s*anât, and interpreted 'east of the invisibility, or of the disappearance of the Sarasvatî.' Vasish*th*a quotes another authority, a Gâthâ of the Bhâllavins, which says: 'In the west the boundary river,' i. e. sindhur vidhâra*n*î. This sindhur vidhâra*n*î is another name of the old Sarasvatî, and in Baudhâyana I, 2, 12, the same verse is quoted, though the reading of vidhâra*n*î varies with vi*k*ara*n*î and visara*n*î. See Bühler, l. c. Madhyade*s*a is mentioned in one of the Pari*s*ish*t*as (MS. 510, Wilson) as a kind of model country, but it is there described as lying east of Da*s*âr*n*a[a], west of Kâmpilya[b], north of Pâriyâtra[c], and south of the Himavat, or again, in a more general way, as the Duâb of the Gangâ and Yamunâ[d].

It is very curious that while in the later Sanskrit lite-

---

[a] See Wilson's Vish*n*u-purâ*n*a, ed. Hall, pp. 154, 155, 159, 160.

[b] See Wilson's Vish*n*u-purâ*n*a, ed. Hall, p. 161.

[c] L. c., pp. 123, 127. Instead of Pâriyâtra, other MSS. read Pâripâtra; see Bühler, Vasish*th*a I, 8.

[d] Prâg da*s*âr*n*ât pratyak kâmpilyâd udak pâriyâtrâd, dakshi*n*ena himavata*h*. Gangâyamunayor antaram eke madhyade*s*am ity â*k*akshate. Medhâtithi says that Madhyade*s*a, the middle country, was not called so because it was in the middle of the earth, but because it was neither too high nor too low. Albiruny, too, remarks that Madhyade*s*a was between the sea and the northern mountains, between the hot and the cold countries, equally distant from the eastern and western frontiers. See Reinaud, Mémoire sur l'Inde, p. 46.

rature the disappearance of the Sarasvatî in the desert is a fact familiar to every writer, no mention of it should occur during the whole of the Vedic period, and it is still more curious that in one of the hymns of the Rig-veda we should have a distinct statement that the Sarasvatî fell into the sea:

VII, 95, 1–2. prá kshódasâ dhā̂yasâ sasre eshā̂ sárasvatî dharú*n*am ā̂yasî pū̂*h*, pra-bā̂badhânâ rathyā̂-iva yâti ví*s*vâ*h* apá*h* mahinā̂ síndhu*h* anyā̂*h*. éka a*k*etat sárasvatî nadī̂nâm *s*ú*k*i*h* yatī̂ girí-bhya*h* ā̂ samudrā̂t, râyá*h* *k*étantî bhúvanasya bhū̂re*h* gh*ri*tám páya*h* duduhe nā̂hushâya.

1. 'With her fertilising stream this Sarasvatî comes forth—(she is to us) a stronghold, an iron gate. Moving along as on a chariot, this river surpasses in greatness all other waters. 2. Alone among all rivers Sarasvatî listened, she who goes pure from the mountains as far as the sea. She who knows of the manifold wealth of the world, has poured out to man her fat milk.'

Here we see samudrá used clearly in the sense of sea, the Indian sea, and we have at the same time a new indication of the distance which separates the Vedic age from that of the later Sanskrit literature. Though it may not be possible to determine by geological evidence the time of the changes which modified the southern area of the Penjâb and caused the Sarasvatî to disappear in the desert, still the fact remains that the loss of the Sarasvatî is later than the Vedic age, and that at that time the waters of the Sarasvatî reached the sea. Professor Wilson had observed long ago in reference to the rivers of that part of India, that there have been, no doubt, considerable changes here, both in the nomenclature and in the courses of the rivers, and this remark has been fully confirmed by later observations. I believe it can be proved that in the Vedic age the Sarasvatî was a river as large as the Sutlej, that it was the last of the rivers of the Penjâb, and therefore the iron gate, or the real frontier against the rest of India. At present the Sarasvatî is so small a river that the epithets applied to the Sarasvatî in the Veda have become quite inapplicable to it. The Vedic *Ri*shis, though acquainted with numerous rivers, including the Indus and Ganges, call the Sarasvatî the mother of rivers (VII, 36, 6. sárasvatî saptáthî síndhu-mâtâ), the strongest of rivers (VI, 61, 13. apásâm apá*h*-tamâ), and in our passage, VII, 95, 2, we have, as far as I can judge, conclusive evidence that the old Sarasvatî reached in its course the Indian sea, either by itself, or united with the Indus[a].

But this passage, though important as showing the application of samudrá, i. e. confluvies, to the Indian sea, and proving the acquaintance of the Vedic *R*ishis with the southern coast of India, is by no means the only one in which samudrá must be translated by sea. Thus we read, VII, 49, 2:

yấ*h* ấpa*h* divyấ*h* utá vâ srávanti khanítrimâ*h* utá vâ yấ*h* svayam-*g*ấ*h*, samudrá-arthâ*h* yấ*h* *s*ú*k*aya*h* pâvakấ*h* tấ*h* ấpa*h* devī́*h* ihá mấm avantu.

The waters which are from heaven, or those which flow after being dug, or those which spring up by themselves, the bright, pure waters that tend to the sea, may those divine waters protect me here!

I, 71, 7. agním vísvâ*h* abhí p*r*íksha*h* sa*k*ante samudrám ná sraváta*h* saptá yahvī́*h*.

All kinds of food go to Agni, as the seven rivers go to the sea.

Cf. I, 190, 7. samudrám ná sraváta*h* ródha-*k*akrâ*h*.

V, 78, 8. yáthâ vấta*h* yáthâ vánam yáthâ samudrá*h* é*g*ati.

As the wind moves, as the forest moves, as the sea moves (or the sky).

In hymn X, 58, the same expression occurs which we have in our hymn, and samudrám ar*n*avám there as here admits but of one explanation, the surging sea.

Samudrá in many passages of the Rig-veda has to be taken as an adjective, in the sense of watery or flowing:

VI, 58, 3. yấs te pûshan nấva*h* antá*h* samudré hira*n*yáyî*h* antárikshe *k*áranti.

Thy golden ships, O Pûshan, which move within the watery sky.

---

[a] See 'India, what can it teach us?' pp. 170, 171.

VII, 70, 2. yá*h* vâm samudrā̃n sarítâ*h* píparti.

He who carries you across the watery rivers.

I, 161, 14. at-bhí*h* yâti váru*n*a*h* samudraí*h*.

Varu*n*a moves in the flowing waters.

In both these passages samudrá, as an adjective, does not conform to the gender of the noun. See Bollensen, Orient und Occident, vol. ii, p. 467.

II, 16, 3. ná samudraí*h* párvataí*h* indra te rátha*h* (ná pari-bhvẽ).

Thy chariot, O Indra, is not to be overcome by the watery clouds.

Verse 8.

WILSON: Who spread (through the firmament), along with the rays (of the sun), and, with their strength, agitate the ocean: come, Agni, with the Maruts.

BENFEY: Die mit Blitzen schleuderen machtig über das Meer hinaus—Mit diesen Marut's, Agni! komm!

LUDWIG: Die mit stralen ihre richtung nemen mit gewalt durchs mer, mit den Marut, Agni, kom.

Verse 9.

WILSON: I pour out the sweet Soma juice for thy drinking, (as) of old: come, Agni, with the Maruts.

BENFEY: Ich giesse zu dem ersten Trank für dich des Soma Honig aus—Mit diesen Marut's, Agni! komm!

LUDWIG: Ich giesze dir zum ersten trunk madhu mit dem soma zu; mit den Marut, Agni, kom.

Note 1. Pûrvapîti, the early draught, implies at the same time the priority of the god to whom it is given.

MANDALA I, HYMN 37.

ASHTAKA I, ADHYÂYA 3, VARGA 12-14.

To the Maruts (the Storm-gods).

1. Sing forth, O Kanvas, to the sportive host of your Maruts, brilliant on their chariots, and unscathed[1],—

2. They who were born together, self-luminous, with the spotted deer (the clouds)[1], the spears, the daggers, the glittering ornaments[2].

3. I hear their[1] whips, almost close by, when they crack them in their hands; they gain splendour[2] on their way[3].

4. Sing forth the god-given prayer to the wild[1] host of your Maruts, endowed with terrible vigour[2] and strength.

5. Celebrate the bull among the cows (the storm among the clouds)[1], for it is the sportive host of the Maruts; he grew as he tasted the rain[2].

6. Who, O ye men, is the strongest among you here, ye shakers of heaven and earth, when you shake them like the hem of a garment[1]?

7. At your approach the son of man holds himself down; the gnarled cloud[1] fled at your fierce anger.

8. They at whose racings[1] the earth, like a hoary king, trembles for fear on their ways,

9. Their birth is strong indeed: there is strength to come forth from their mother, nay, there is vigour twice enough for it[1].

10. And these sons, the singers[1], stretched out the fences in their racings[2]; the cows had to walk knee-deep.

11. They cause this long and broad unceasing rain [1] to fall on their ways.

12. O Maruts, with such strength as yours, you have caused men to tremble [1], you have caused the mountains to tremble.

13. As the Maruts pass [1] along, they talk together on the way: does any one hear them?

14. Come fast on your quick steeds! there are worshippers [1] for you among the Ka*n*vas: may you well rejoice among them.

15. Truly there is enough for your rejoicing We always are their servants, that we may live even the whole of life.

NOTES.

This hymn is ascribed to Ka*n*va, the son of Ghora.

Verse 1=TS. IV, 3, 13, 6.

Verse 3=SV. I, 135.

Verse 10=SV. I, 221.

Verse 1.

WILSON: Celebrate, Ka*n*vas, the aggregate strength of the Maruts, sportive, without horses, but shining in their car.

BENFEY: Ka*n*viden, auf! begrüsst mit Sang, die muntre Heerschaar der Marut's, die rasch'ste, wagenglänzende.

LUDWIG: Eurer spilenden schar, der Marutschar, der unangreifbaren, die auf wagen glänzt, der singt, o Ka*n*vâs, zu.

Note 1. Wilson translates anarvấ*n*am by without horses, though the commentator distinctly explains the word by without an enemy. A Brâhma*n*a passage explains: bhrât*r*ivyo vâ arvâ, ity *s*rutyantarât. See TS. IV, 3, 13, 6. Wilson considers it doubtful whether árvan can ever mean enemy. The fact is, that in the Rig-veda an-arván never means without horses, but always without hurt or free from enemies; and the commentator is perfectly right, as far as the sense is concerned, in rendering the word by without an enemy, or unopposed (apraty-*r*ita). An-arván is not formed from árvat, horse, racer, but from árvan; and this is derived from the same root which yields árus, n. a wound, *r*iti (see I, 64, 15, note), &c. The accusative of anarvat, without a horse, would be anarvantam, not anarvâ*n*am.

The root ar, in the sense of hurting, is distantly connected with the root mar: see Lectures on the Science of Language, Second Series, p. 323. It exists in the Greek ὄλλυμι, corresponding to Sanskrit *r*i*n*omi, i. e. ar*n*omi, I hurt, likewise in οὐλή, wound, which cannot be derived from ὅλη; in οὖλος, οὔλιος, hurtful, and ὀλοός, destructive: see Curtius, Grundzüge der Griechischen Etymologie (fünfte Ausgabe), p. 372. In the Veda ar has the sense of offending or injuring, particularly if preceded by upa.

X, 164, 3. yát â-*s*ásâ ni*h*-*s*ásâ abhi-*s*ásâ upa-ârimá *g*ấgrata*h* yát svapánta*h*, agní*h* ví*s*vâni ápa du*h*-*kri*tấni á*g*ush*t*âni âré asmát dadhâtu.

If we have offended, or whatever fault we have committed, by bidding, blaming, or forbidding, while waking or while sleeping, may Agni remove all wicked misdeeds far from us.

Hence upârá, injury, VII, 86, 6. ásti *g*yấyân káníyasa*h* upa-aré, the older man is there to injure, to offend, to mislead, the young: (History of Ancient Sanskrit Literature, second edition, p. 541.) Roth translates upârá by Verfehlung, missing. Ari, enemy, too, is best derived from this root, and not from râ, to give, with the negative particle, as if meaning originally, as Sâya*n*a supposes, a man who does not give. In árarivân, gen. árarusha*h*, hostile, Rosen recognised many years ago a participle of a really reduplicated perfect of ar, and he likewise traced aráru, enemy, back to the same root: see his note to I, 18, 3.

From this root ar, to hurt, árvan, hurting, as well as árus, wound, are derived in the same manner as both dhánvan and dhánus, bow, are formed from dhan; yá*g*van and yá*g*us from ya*g*, párvan and párus from par. See Kuhn, Zeitschrift, vol. ii, p. 233.

Anarván, then, is the same as ánarus, *S*at. P. Brâhma*n*a III, 1, 3, 7; and from meaning originally without a wound or without one who can wound, it takes the more general sense of uninjured, invulnerable, perfect, strong, (cf. integer, intact, and entire.) This meaning is applicable to I, 94, 2; 136, 5; II, 6, 5; V, 49, 4; VII, 20, 3; 97, 5; X, 61, 13; 65, 3. In I, 116, 16, anarván seems to be used as an adverb; in I, 51, 12, as applied to *s*lóka, it may have the more general meaning of irresistible, powerful.

There are two passages in which the nom. sing. árvân, and one in which the acc. sing. árvâ*n*am, occur, apparently meaning horse. But in I, 163, 13, and IX, 97, 25, árvân stands in the Pada text only, the Sa*m*hitâ has árvấ á*kkh*a and árvấ iva. In X, 46, 5, the text híri-*s*ma*s*rum ná árvâ*n*am dhána-ar*k*am is too doubtful to allow of any safe induction, particularly as the Sâma-veda gives a totally different reading. I do not think, therefore, that árvat, horse, admits in the nom. and acc. sing. of any forms but árvâ and árvantam[a]. Pâ*n*ini (VI, 4, 127) allows the forms arvân and arvâ*n*am, but in anarvan only, which, as we saw, has nothing in common with árvat, horse. Benfey: 'die rascheste (keinen Renner habend, uneinholbar),' the quickest (having no racer, hence not to be reached). M. Bergaigne (Journ. As. 1884, p. 188) tries to defend anarvan in the sense of ana*s*va, without considering the grammatical objections. In VI, 66, 7 (not I, 6, 7) ana*s*vá*h* does not refer to yâma*h*.

The masculine anarvấ*n*am after the neuter *s*árdhas is curious; *s*árdhas means might, but it is here used to express a might or an aggregate of strong men or gods, and the nom. plur. yé, who, in the next verse, shows the same transition of thought, not only from the singular to the plural, but also from the neuter to the masculine, which must be admitted in anarvấ*n*am[b]. It would be possible, if necessary, to explain away the irregularity of anarvấ*n*am by admitting a rapid transition from the Maruts to Indra, the eldest among the Maruts (cf. I, 23, 8. índra-*g*yesh*th*â*h* márut-ga*n*â*h*), and it would be easier still to alter *s*árdhas into *s*árdham, as an accusative singular of the masculine noun *s*árdha, which has the same meaning as the neuter *s*árdhas. There is one passage, V, 56, 9, which would seem to give ample countenance to such a conjecture:

tám va*h* *s*árdham rathe-*s*úbham—ấ huve.

I call hither this your host, brilliant on chariots.

Again, II, 30, 11, we read:

tám va*h* *s*árdham mấrutam—girấ úpa bruve.

I call with my voice on this your host of Maruts.

---

[a] See Bugge, K. Z. XIX, p. 403.

[b] Bollensen (Z. D. M. G. XXII, 603) calls it a vulgar Donatus; see, however, Lanman, Noun-Inflection, pp. 330, 526

VIII, 93, 16. *s*rutám va*h* v*ri*trahán-tamam prá *s*árdham *k*arsha*n*înā̂m, ā́ *s*ushe.

I pant for the glorious, victorious, host of the quick Maruts.

From this *s*árdha we have also the genitive *s*árdhasya, VII, 56, 8 (4):

*s*ubhrá*h* va*h* *s*úshma*h* krúdhmî mánâ*m*si dhúni*h* múni*h*-iva *s*árdhasya dh*ri*sh*n*ó*h*.

Your prowess is brilliant, your minds furious; the shout of the daring host is like one possessed.

We have likewise the dative *s*árdhâya, the instrumental *s*árdhena, and the acc. plur. *s*árdhân; and in most cases, except in two or three where *s*árdha seems to be used as an adjective, meaning strong, these words are applied to the host of the Maruts.

But the other word *s*árdhas is equally well authenticated, and we find of it, not only the nominative, accusative, and vocative sing. *s*árdhas, but likewise the nom. plur. *s*árdhâ*m*si.

The nominative singular occurs in our very hymn:

I, 37, 5. krî*l*ám yát *s*árdha*h* mā́rutam.

Which is the sportive host of the Maruts.

I, 127, 6. sá*h* hí *s*árdha*h* ná mā́rutam tuvi-sváni*h*.

For he (Agni) is strong-voiced like the host of the Maruts.

IV, 6, 10 tuvi-svanása*h* mā́rutam ná *s*árdha*h*.

Thy flames (Agni) are strong-voiced like the host of the Maruts.

V, 46, 5. utá tyát na*h* mā́rutam *s*árdha*h* ā́ gamat.

May also that host of the Maruts come to us.

II, 1, 5. tvám narā́m *s*árdha*h* asi puru-vásu*h*.

Thou (Agni), full of riches, art the host of the men.

This host of men seems to me intended again for the Maruts, although it is true that in thus identifying Agni with different gods, the poet repeats himself in the next verse:

II, 1, 6. tvám *s*árdha*h* mā́rutam.

Thou art the host of the Maruts.

If this repetition seems offensive, the first narā́m *s*árdhas might be taken for some other company of gods. Thus we find:

VII, 44, 5. *sri*nótu na*h* daívyam *s*árdha*h* agni*h* *srin*vántu ví*s*ve mahishấ*h* ámûrâ*h*.

May the divine host, may Agni, hear us, may the Vi*s*ve hear us, the strong, the wise.

Or III, 19, 4. sá*h* ấ vaha devá-tâtim yavish*th*a *s*árdha*h* yát adyá divyám yá*g*âsi.

Bring thou hither, O Agni, the gods, that you may sacrifice to-day to the divine host.

Or I, 139, 1. ấ nú tát *s*árdha*h* divyám v*rin*îmahe.

We chose for us now that divine host.

As in these last, so in many other passages, *s*árdhas is used as a neuter in the accusative. For instance,

I, 106, 1; II, 11, 14. mấrutam *s*árdha*h*.

II, 3, 3; VI, 3, 8. *s*árdha*h* marútâm.

The vocative occurs,

V, 46, 2. ágne índra váru*n*a mítra dévâ*h* *s*árdha*h* prá yanta mấruta utá vish*n*o (íti).

Agni, Indra, Varu*n*a, Mitra, gods, host of the Maruts, come forth, and Vish*n*u!

We see how throughout all these passages those in which *s*árdha and *s*árdhas are applied to the Maruts, or to some other company of gods, preponderate most decidedly. Yet passages occur in the Rig-veda where both *s*árdha and *s*árdhas are applied to other hosts or companies. Thus V, 53, 10, *s*árdha refers to chariots, while in I, 133, 3, *s*árdhas is applied to evil spirits.

If the passages hitherto examined were all that occur in the Rig-veda, we might still feel startled at the construction of our verse, where *s*árdhas is not only followed by masculine adjectives in the singular, but, in the next verse, by a pronoun in the plural. But if we take the last irregularity first, we find the same construction, viz. *s*árdhas followed by yé, in III, 32, 4:

índrasya *s*árdha*h* marúta*h* yé ấsan.

The host of Indra, that was the Maruts.

As to the change of genders, we find adjectives in the masculine after *s*árdhas, in

V, 52, 8. *s*árdha*h* mấrutam út *sam*sa satyá-*s*avasam *ri*bhvasam.

Celebrate the host of the Maruts, the truly vigorous, the brilliant.

Here, too, the poet afterwards continues in the plural, though as he uses the demonstrative, and not, as in our passage, the relative pronoun, we cannot quote this in support of the irregularity which has here to be explained. Anyhow the construction of our verse, though bold and unusual, is not so unusual as to force us to adopt conjectural remedies. In V, 58, 2, we find yé after ga*n*á*h*. On the Umbrian Çerfo Martio, as possibly the same as *s*árdha-s mấruta-s, see Grassman, Kuhn's Zeitschrift, vol. xvi, p. 190. The Zend *s*aredha, kind, species, is the same word.

Verse 2.

WILSON: Who, borne by spotted deer, were born self-radiant, with weapons, war-cries, and decorations.

BENFEY: Die mit Hirschen und Speeren gleich mit Donnern und mit Blitzen auch—selbststrahlende—geboren sind.

LUDWIG: Die mit vilfarbigen speeren, mit der schwerter glanze, sichtbar wurden mit eignem leuchten.

Note 1. The spotted deer (p*r*ishatî) are the recognised animals of the Maruts, and were originally, as it would seem, intended for the rain-clouds. Sâya*n*a is perfectly aware of the original meaning of p*r*ishatî, as clouds. The legendary school, he says, takes them for deer with white spots, the etymological school for many-coloured lines of clouds: (RV. BH. I, 64, 8.) This passage shows that although p*r*ishatî, as Roth observes, may mean a spotted cow or a spotted horse,—the Maruts, in fact, are called sometimes p*r*ishat-a*s*vâ*h*, having piebald horses, or, having p*r*ishats for their horses, VII, 40, 3,—yet the later tradition in India had distinctly declared in favour of spotted deer. The Vedic poets, however, admitted both ideas, and they speak in the same hymn, nay, in the same verse, of the fallow deer and of the horses of the Maruts. Thus V, 58, 1, the Maruts are called ấsú-a*s*vâ*h*, possessed of quick horses; and in V, 58, 6, we read yát prá áyâsish*t*a p*r*ishatîbhi*h* á*s*vai*h*—ráthebhi*h*, where the gender of p*r*ishatîbhi*h* would hardly allow us to join it with á*s*vai*h*, but where we must translate: When you come with the deer, the horses, the chariots, or with your deer, as horses. Ludwig joins p*ri*shatîbhi*h* with *ri*sh*t*ibhi*h*, and again in I, 64, 8; see note 1 to I, 87, 4.

Note 2. The spears and daggers of the Maruts are meant for the thunderbolts, and the glittering ornaments for the lightning. Sâya*n*a takes vâ*s*î in this passage for war-cries on the authority of the Nirukta, where vâ*s*î is given among the names of the voice. From other passages, however, it becomes clear that vâ*s*î is a weapon of the Maruts; and Sâya*n*a, too, explains it sometimes in that sense: cf. V, 53, 4; 57, 2. Thus I, 88, 3, the vâ*s*îs are spoken of as being on the bodies of the Maruts. In V, 53, 4, the Maruts are said to shine in their ornaments and their vâ*s*îs. Here Sâya*n*a, too, translates vâ*s*î rightly by weapon; and in his remarks on I, 88, 3, he says that vâ*s*î was a weapon commonly called ârâ, which is a shoemaker's awl. See Dhammapada, ver. 401. This reminds one of framea, which at one time was supposed to be connected with the German pfrieme. See, however, Grimm (Deutsche Grammatik, vol. i, p. 128) and Leo Meyer (Kuhn's Zeitschrift, vol. vi, p. 424). In VIII, 29, 3, the god Tvash*t*ar is said to carry an iron vâ*s*î in his hand. Grassman (Kuhn's Zeitschrift, vol. xvi, p. 163) translates vâ*s*î by axe. That a*ñg*í is to be taken in the sense of ornament, and not in the sense of ointment, is shown by passages like VIII, 29, 1, where a golden ornament is mentioned, a*ñg*í aṅkte hira*n*yáyam. Sâkám, together, is used with reference to the birth of the Maruts; see I, 64, 4. It should not be connected with vâ*s*îbhi*h*.

Verse 3.

WILSON: I hear the cracking of the whips in their hands, wonderfully inspiring (courage) in the fight.

BENFEY: Schier hier erschallt der Peitsche Knall, wenn sie in ihrer Hand erklingt; leuchtend fahr'n sie im Sturm herab.

LUDWIG: Als wäre es hier, so hört man es, wenn die geisslen in ihren händen knallen; wunderbar strecken sie auf ihrer fart sich nieder.

Note 1. Eshâm should be pronounced as a creticus; also in verses 9, 13, 15. This is a very common vyûha. On the whips as lightning, see Grimm, Donner, p. 27.

Note 2. I should have taken *k*itrám as an adverb, like Benfey, if ni *riñg* were not usually construed with an accusative. *Riñg* in the 3rd pers. plur. pres. Âtm. is treated like a verb of the Ad-class. The SV. seems to read yâmam, and the commentator explains it by ratham.

Note 3. The locative yấman is frequently used of the path on which the gods move and approach the sacrifice; hence it sometimes means, as in our passage, in the sky. Yấmam in BR., s. v. ar*g*, is wrong.

We might also translate: 'Here, close by, I hear what the whips in their hands say; they drive forth the beautiful (chariot) on the road.' See SV. I, 2, 1, 5, 1, comm.

Verse 4.

WILSON: Address the god-given prayer to those who are your strength, the destroyers of foes, the powerful, possessed of brilliant reputation.

BENFEY: Singt eurer Schaar, der wühlenden, der strahlenreichen, kräftigen ein gotterfülletes Gebet!

LUDWIG: Eurer künen schar, von blendender herlichkeit, der kraftvollen, soll ein von den göttern eingegebenes brahma gesungen werden.

Note 1. Benfey translates gh*ri*shvi by burrowing, and refers it to the thunderbolt that uproots the earth. He points out that gh*ri*shvi means also, for the same reason, the boar, as proved by Kuhn (Die Herabkunft des Feuers, S. 202). Gh*ri*sh*t*i is evidently a common name for boar, the Norse gríss, and the god of the wind, Grimnir or Grimr, is conceived as a boar, shaking the cornfield, in such phrases as 'Der Eber geht ins Korn' (Gentha, l. c. p. 14). I prefer, however, in this place the general sense assigned to the adjective gh*ri*shu and gh*ri*shvi, exuberant, brisk, wild. See Kuhn in Kuhn's Zeitschrift, vol. xi, p. 385. Wilson, after Sâya*n*a, translates destroyers of foes. On the representation of the clouds as boars, see Nir. V, 4.

Note 2. Tveshá-dyumna is difficult to render. Both

tveshá and dyumná are derived from roots that mean to shine, to be bright, to glow. Derivatives from tvish express the idea of fieriness, fierceness, and fury. In IV, 17, 2, tvish is used correlatively, with manyú, wrath. Derivatives from dyu convey the idea of brightness and briskness. Both qualities are frequently applied to the Maruts.

Verse 5.

WILSON: Praise the sportive and resistless might of the Maruts, who were born amongst kine, and whose strength has been nourished by (the enjoyment of) the milk.

BENFEY: Preist hoch die muntre Marutschaar die unbesiegbar in den Küh'n, im Schlund des Safts wuchs sie heran.

LUDWIG: Preise wie unter kühen den stier, (so) der Marut spilende schar, beim verschlingen des saftes ist sie grosz geworden.

Note 1. This translation is merely conjectural. I suppose that the wind driving the clouds before him, is here compared to a bull among cows, cf. V, 52, 3:

té syandrấsa*h* ná ukshá*n*a*h* áti skandanti *s*árvarî́*h*.

They, the Maruts, like rushing bulls, mount on the dark cows.

The last sentence states that the wind grows even stronger after it has tasted the rain (I, 85, 2. té ukshitấsa*h* mahimấnam â*s*ata).

Note 2. I take *g*ámbhe in the sense of *g*ámbhane. (On the root *g*abh and its derivatives, see Kuhn, Zeitschrift für vergleichende Sprachwissenschaft, vol. i, p. 123 seq.) It would be better to read mukhe, instead of sukhe, in the commentary. The Maruts were not born of milk for P*ris*ni, as Wilson says in a note, but from the milk of P*ris*ni. P*ris*ni is called their mother, Rudra their father: (V, 52, 16; 60, 5.)

Benfey takes the cows for clouds in which the lightnings dwell; and the abyss of the sap is by him supposed to be again the clouds.

Verse 6.

WILSON: Which is chief leader among you, agitators of heaven and earth, who shake all around, like the top (of a tree)?

BENFEY: Wer, Helden! ist der erste euch—ihr Erd- und Himmel-schütterer!—wenn ihr sie schüttelt Wipfeln gleich?

LUDWIG: Wer ist der grösste bei euch, helden, wenn vom himel und der erde, schütteler, ihr am saume gleichsam rüttelt!

Note 1. Ántam ná, literally, like an end, is explained by Sâya*n*a as the top of a tree. Wilson, Langlois, and Benfey accept that interpretation. Roth proposes, like the hem of a garment, which I prefer; for vastrânta, the end of a garment, is a common expression in later Sanskrit, while anta is never applied to a tree in the sense of the top of a tree. Here agra would be more appropriate.

Verse 7.

WILSON: The householder, in dread of your fierce and violent approach, has planted a firm (buttress); for the many-ridged mountain is shattered (before you).

BENFEY: Vor eurem Gange beuget sich, vor eurem wilden Zorn der Mann; der Hügel weichet und der Berg.

LUDWIG: Vor eurem anzug, eurem gewaltigen eifer, niederduckte sich der mensch, wich der festgeknotete [wolken]berg.

Note 1. Sâya*n*a translates: 'Man has planted a firm buttress to give stability to his dwelling.' The reading ná for ní, which Aufrecht adopted, is untenable, as Ludwig shows. It has been altered in the second edition. See also VIII, 7, 5, ní yemiré. Nidadhré is the perfect Âtmanepada, and expresses the holding down of the head or the cowering attitude of man. I have taken ugrấya manyáve over to *g*íhîta, because these words could hardly form an apposition to yấmâya. As the Vedic poets speak of the very mountains as shaken by the storms, we might translate párvato girí*h* by the gnarled or rocky mount;

but there is no authority for translating *g*ı́hîta by it is shattered, and we should have to translate, the mountain yielded or bent before your anger. Cf. V, 57, 3:

ní va*h* vánâ *g*ihate yấmanah bhiyấ.

The forests get out of your way from fear.

V, 60, 2. vánâ *k*it ugrâ*h* *g*ihate ní va*h* bhiyấ p*ri*thivı̂́ *k*it re*g*ate párvata*h* *k*it.

Even the forests, ye fearful Maruts, yield from fear of you; even the earth trembles, even the mountain.

In I, 166, 5, yát tveshá-yâmâ*h* nadáyanta párvatân, we may translate 'when they on their fiery course made the parvatas (clouds) to sound or thunder,' but it is more likely that nâdayati here means to cause to shake or vibrate, and that parvata stands for mountain. We ought to remember such poetical expressions as 1 Kings xix. 11, 'and a great, strong wind rent the mountains, and brake in pieces the rocks before the Lord.'

Verse 8.

Wilson: At whose impetuous approach earth trembles; like an enfeebled monarch, through dread (of his enemies).

Benfey: Bei deren Lauf bei deren Sturm die Erde zittert voller Furcht, wie ein altergebeugter Mann.

Ludwig: Bei deren märschen zitterte wie ein gealtet stammeshaupt die erd vor furcht auf ihren wegen.

Note 1. Á*g*ma seems to express the act of racing or running (like â*g*i, race, battle), while yấma is the road itself where the racing takes place. A very similar passage occurs in I, 87, 3. The comparison of the earth (fem.) to a king (masc.) would be considered a grave offence in the later Sanskrit literature. In I, 87, 3, vithurấ takes the place of vi*s*páti.

Verse 9.

Wilson: Stable is their birthplace, (the sky); yet the birds (are able) to issue from (the sphere of) their parent: for your strength is everywhere (divided) between two (regions,—or, heaven and earth).

BENFEY: Kaum geboren sind sie so stark, dass ihrer Mutter sie entfliehn: ist ja doch zwiefach ihre Kraft.

LUDWIG: Denn fest ist ihr geburtsort, vögel (sind sie) von der mutter fortzugehn, nach dem, wie von altersher ihre kraft.

Oder, Denn fest ist ihre kraft geworden von der mutter sich zu trennen, da schon von alters her ihre kraft diss wollte.

Note 1. A very difficult verse. The birth of the Maruts is frequently alluded to, as well as their surpassing strength, as soon as born. Hence the first sentence admits of little doubt. But what follows is very abrupt. Váyas may be the plural of vi, bird, or it may be váyas, the neuter, meaning vital strength: see Kuhn's Zeitschrift, vol. xv, p. 217. The Maruts are frequently compared to birds (cf. I, 87, 2; 88, 1), but it is usual to indicate the comparison by ná or iva. I therefore take váyas as a nom. sing. neut., in the sense of vigour, life. They are called b*ri*hadvayasa*h* in a Nivid; see Ludwig, p. 226. Nir-i is used with particular reference to the birth of a child (cf. V, 78, 7; 9).

Verse 10.

WILSON: They are the generators of speech: they spread out the waters in their courses: they urge the lowing (cattle) to enter (the water), up to their knees, (to drink.)

BENFEY: In ihrem Lauf erheben dann diese Söhne Getös und Fluth, die bis zum Knie den Kühen geht.

LUDWIG: Und dise söne, die sänger, denten auf ihren zügen ihre banen aus, so dass brüllend sie uns ganz nahe kamen.

Note 1. If we could take sûnáva*h* gíra*h* in the sense of the sons of voice, i.e. of thunder, which would remove many difficulties, the accent of gíra*h* would have to be changed. The commentator takes sûnu in the sense of utpâdaka, producers of sound. Gíra*h*, however, occurs at least once more, in the sense of singers or poets, IX, 63, 10, where gíra*h* can only be a vocative, O ye singers! In I, 6, 6, the translation of gíra*h* by singers, i.e. the Maruts, may be contested, but if we consider that gíra*h*, in the sense of hymns, is feminine, and is followed by the very word which is here used, viz. devayántah, as a feminine, viz. devayántîh, VII, 18, 3, we can hardly doubt that in I, 6, 6, gírah is a masculine and means singers. The same applies to VI, 63, 10. In VI, 52, 9, úpa nah sûnávah gírah srinvántu amrítasya yé, the construction is, of course, quite different.

Note 2. The expression that the Maruts enlarged or extended the fences of their race-course (RV. IV, 58, 7), can only mean that they swept over the whole sky, and drove the clouds away from all the corners. Kấshthâ may mean the wooden enclosures (carceres) or the wooden poles that served as turning and winning-posts (metae). The Sâma-veda has yagñeshu instead of agmeshu. That the translation of this verse is purely tentative, and far from satisfactory, was known to all Vedic scholars, but I doubt whether they will consider the interpretation which M. Bergaigne proposes with so much assurance, as less tentative and more satisfactory. He translates (Journ. As. 1884, p. 239), 'des fils ont, dans leur marche, allongé leurs chants comme des chemins, pour y marcher à genoux (sur les genoux) en mugissant (en chantant).' I shall content myself with shortly pointing out the misgivings which every Vedic scholar would feel at once in proposing such a rendering. First as to the conception itself. Can a poet say, 'The Maruts have stretched out their songs in order to march on them on their knees?' 'The roads,' as M. Bergaigne shows himself, are only a simile, and no one walks on a simile. Secondly, the idea that these Maruts widened the roads on which they march, is common enough, but that they lengthened their songs, like paths, is never said by the Vedic Rishis, nor would they in such a case have left out the particle na or iva. Lastly, though many things are said of the Maruts, I do not remember that they ever appear on their knees. I do not think, therefore, that M. Bergaigne's infallible method helps us much beyond where we were before. Conjectures are easy, but for that very reason, one does not like to bring them forward. One might propose to read sûnávah diváh, a very common name of the Maruts. One might go a step further, identify gi*h* with bhâratî, and point out that the Maruts are called the sons of Bharata, II, 36, 2. But all this leaves us in utter uncertainty, and where a scholar feels the ground so uncertain beneath his feet, he hesitates to speak with papal authority. M. Bergaigne's strong point is that abhi*g*ñú means on their knees, not up to their knees. Here again, I ask, does abhi in prepositional compounds ever mean on? If abhi*g*ñú is used in the same sense in which we use 'on our knees,' it would in Sanskrit mean only 'bowing up to the knees.' Now in I, 72, 5, abhi*g*ñu seems to express a positive expression of reverence. With regard to the other passages where abhi*g*ñu occurs, M. Bergaigne has not shown how they ought to be translated so as to give a clear sense. I do not pretend to solve the difficulties, but I think it is better to confess our difficulties than to hide them under the veil of a so-called systematic interpretation. Abhi*g*ñu, like mita*g*ñu, may have expressed a position of the knees, expressive of strength, but on such points very little information is to be gained from Indian commentators.

The last sentence expresses the result of this race, viz. the falling of so much rain that the cows had to walk up to their knees in water. This becomes still clearer from the next verse.

SÂYA*N*A: These, the producers of speech, have spread water in their courses, they cause the cows to walk up to their knees in order to drink the water.

Verse 11.

WILSON: They drive before them, in their course, the long, vast, uninjurable, rain-retaining cloud.

BENFEY: Dann treiben sie im Sturm heran jenen langen und breiten Spross der Wolke unerschöpflichen.

LUDWIG: Sogar disen langen, breiten, das kind der wolke, den unfeindlichen, schleudern auf ihren zügen sie vorwärts.

Note 1. Rain is called the offspring of the cloud, mihó nápât, and is then treated as a masculine; cf. apâm nápât, &c.

Verse 12.

WILSON: Maruts, as you have vigour, invigorate mankind: give animation to the clouds.

BENFEY: O Marut's! mit der Kraft, die ihr besitzt, werft ihr Geschöpfe um, die Berge werft ihr um sogar.

LUDWIG: O Marut, so wie eure kraft ist, warft ihr die leute nieder, warft ihr die berge nieder.

Note 1. In VIII, 72, 8, *akukyavît* is explained by vyadârayat, he tore open. A*kuk*yavîtana is the Vedic form of the 2nd pers. plur. of the reduplicated aorist.

Verse 13.

WILSON: Wherever the Maruts pass, they fill the way with clamour: every one hears their (noise).

BENFEY: Wenn die Marut's des Weges ziehn, dann sprechen mit einander sie und mancher mag sie hören.

LUDWIG: Wenn die Marut wandern, sprechen auf dem weg sie mit einander, es höret sie ein jeder.

Note 1. Yânti has to be pronounced as an amphibrachys.

Verse 14.

WILSON: Come quickly, with your swift (vehicles). The offerings of the Ka*n*vas are prepared. Be pleased with them.

BENFEY: Auf schnellen kommet schnell herbei, bei Ka*n*va's Spross sind Feste euch: da wollt euch schön ergötzen.

LUDWIG: Brecht rasch auf mit raschen rossen, bei den Ka*n*va's ist euer dienst, dort eben erfreuet euch.

Note 1. Benfey supposes that dúva*h* stands in the singular instead of the plural. But why should the plural have been used, as the singular (asti) would have created no kind of difficulty? It is better to take dúva*h* as a nominative plural of a noun dû, worshipper, derived from the same root which yielded dúva*h*, worship. We certainly find á-duva*h*, as a nom. plur., in the sense of not-worshipping:

VII, 4, 6. mā́ tvâ vayám sahasâ-van avī́râ*h* mā́ ápsava*h* pári sadâma mā́ áduva*h*.

May we not, O hero, sit round thee like men without strength, without beauty (cf. VIII, 7, 7), without worship.

Here Sâya*n*a explains áduva*h* very well by pari*k*ara*n*a-hînâ*h*, which seems better than Roth's explanation 'zögernd, ohne Eifer.'

Verse 15.

WILSON: The offering is prepared for your gratification: we are your (worshippers), that we may live all our life.

BENFEY: Gerüstet ist für euren Rausch und wir gehören, traun! euch an für unser ganzes Lebelang.

LUDWIG: Er ist euch zur trunkesfreude, und wir gleichfalls euer hier, dass unsere ganze dauer wir erleben.

MA*ND*ALA I, HYMN 38.

ASH*T*AKA I, ADHYÂYA 3, VARGA 15–17.

To the Maruts (the Storm-gods).

1. What then now? When[1] will you take (us) as a dear father takes his son by both hands, O ye gods, for whom the sacred grass has been trimmed[2]?

2. Where now? On what errand of yours are you going, in heaven, not on earth[1]? Where are your cows sporting?

3. Where are your newest favours[1], O Maruts? Where the blessings? Where all delights?

4. If you, sons of P*ri*s*n*i, were mortals, and your praiser an immortal[1],

5. Then never[1] should your praiser be unwelcome, like a deer in pasture grass[2], nor should he go on the path of Yama[3].

6. Let not one sin[1] after another, difficult to be conquered, overcome us; may it depart[2] together with greed.

7. Truly they are terrible and powerful; even to the desert the Rudriyas bring rain that is never dried up[1].

8. The lightning lows like a cow, it follows as a mother follows after her young, when the shower (of the Maruts) has been let loose[1].

9. Even by day the Maruts create darkness with the water-bearing cloud[1], when they drench the earth.

10. Then from the shouting of the Maruts over the whole space of the earth[1], men reeled forward.

11. Maruts on your strong-hoofed never-wearying[3]

steeds[1] go after those bright ones (the clouds), which are still locked up[2].

12. May your fellies be strong, the chariots, and their horses, may your reins[1] be well-fashioned.

13. Speak forth for ever with thy voice to praise the Lord of prayer[1], Agni, who is like a friend[2], the bright one.

14. Fashion a hymn in thy mouth! Expand like the cloud[1]! Sing a song of praise.

15. Worship the host of the Maruts, the terrible, the glorious, the musical[1]. May they be magnified here among us[2].

NOTES.

This hymn is ascribed to Ka*n*va, the son of Ghora. The metre is Gâyatrî throughout. Several verses, however, end in a spondee instead of the usual iambus. No attempt should be made to improve such verses by conjecture, for they are clearly meant to end in spondees. Thus in verses 2, 7, 8, and 9, all the three pâdas alike have their final spondee. In verse 7, the ionicus a minore is with an evident intention repeated thrice. No verse of the hymn occurs in SV., VS., AV.; but verse 8 = TS. III, 1, 11, 5; verse 9 = TS. II, 4, 8, 1.

Verse 1.

Note 1. Kadha-priya*h* is taken in the Padapâ*th*a as one word, and Sâya*n*a explains it by delighted by or delighting in praise, a nominative plural. A similar compound, kadha-priya, occurs in I, 30, 20, and there too the vocative sing. fem., kadhapriye, is explained by Sâya*n*a as fond of praise. In order to obtain this meaning, kadha has to be identified with kathâ, story, which is simply impossible. There is another compound, adha-priyâ, nom. dual, which occurs VIII, 8, 4, and which Sâya*n*a explains either as delighted here below, or as a corruption of kadha-priyâ.

In Boehtlingk and Roth's Dictionary, kadha-priya and kadha-prî are both taken as compounds of kadha, an interrogative adverb, and priya or prî, to love or delight, and they are explained as meaning kind or loving to whom? In the same manner adha-priya is explained as kind then and there.

It must be confessed, however, that a compound like kadha-prî, kind to whom?, is somewhat strange, and it seems preferable to separate the words, and to write kádha priyá and ádha priyá.

It should be observed that the compounds kadha-prî and kadha-priya occur always in sentences where there is another interrogative pronoun. The two interrogatives kát—kádha, what—where, and kás—kádha, who—where, occurring in the same sentence, an idiom so common in

Greek, may have puzzled the author of the Pada text, and the compound being once sanctioned by the authority of *S*âkalya, Sâya*n*a would explain it as best he could. But if we admit the double use of the interrogative in Sanskrit, as in Greek, then, in our passage, priyá*h* would be an adjective belonging to pitấ, and we might translate: 'What then now? When will you take (us), as a dear father takes his son by both hands, O ye Maruts?' In the same manner we ought to translate I, 30, 20:

ká*h* te usha*h* kádha priye bhu*g*é márta*h* amartye.

Who and where was there a mortal to be loved by thee, O beloved, immortal Dawn?

In VIII, 7, 31, where the same words are repeated as in our passage, it is likewise better to write:

kát ha nûnám kádha priyá*h* yát índram á*g*ahâtana, ká*h* va*h* sakhi-tvé ohate.

What then now? Where is there a friend, now that you have forsaken Indra? Who watches for your friendship?

Why in VIII, 8, 4, adha priyâ should have been joined into one word is more difficult to say, yet here, too, the compound might easily be separated.

Kádha does not occur again, but would be formed in analogy with ádha. It occurs in Zend as kadha.

Kuhn, Beiträge IV, p. 186, has shown that kûsh*th*a*h* (RV. V, 74, 1) is a similar monster, and stands for ku sh*th*a*h*.

The words kát ha nûnám commonly introduce an interrogative sentence, literally, What then now? cf. X, 10, 4.

Note 2. V*ri*kta-barhis is generally a name of the priest, so called because he has to trim the sacrificial grass. 'The sacred Ku*s*a grass (Poa cynosuroides), after having had the roots cut off, is spread on the Vedi or altar, and upon it the libation of Soma-juice, or oblation of clarified butter, is poured out. In other places, a tuft of it in a similar position is supposed to form a fitting seat for the deity or deities invoked to the sacrifice. According to Mr. Stevenson, it is also strewn over the floor of the chamber in which the worship is performed.'

Cf. VI, 11, 5. *vri*ñ*g*é ha yát námasâ barh*í*h agnaú, áyâmi srúk gh*ri*tá-vatî su-v*ri*kt*í*h.

When I reverentially trim the truss for Agni, when the well-trimmed ladle, full of butter, is stretched forth.

In our passage, unless we change the accent, it must be taken as an epithet of the Maruts, they for whom the grass-altar has been prepared. They are again invoked by the same name, VIII, 7, 20:

kvã nûnám su-dânava*h* mádatha v*ri*kta-barhisha*h*.

Where do ye rejoice now, you gods for whom the altar is trimmed?

Otherwise, v*ri*kta-barhisha*h* might, with a change of accent, supply an accusative to dadhidhve: 'Will you take the worshippers in your arms?' This, though decidedly better, is not absolutely necessary, because to take by the hand may be used as a neuter verb.

WILSON: Maruts, who are fond of praise, and for whom the sacred grass is trimmed, when will you take us by both hands as a father does his son?

BENFEY: Wo weilt ihr gern? was habt ihr jetzt—gleichwie ein Vater seinen Sohn—in Händen, da das Opfer harrt?

Verse 2.

Note 1. The idea of the first verse, that the Maruts should not be detained by other pursuits, is carried on in the second. The poet asks, what they have to do in the sky, instead of coming down to the earth. The last sentence seems to mean 'where tarry your herds?' viz. the clouds. Sâya*n*a translates: 'Where do worshippers, like lowing cows, praise you?' Wilson: 'Where do they who worship you cry to you, like cattle?' Benfey: 'Wo jauchzt man euch, gleich wie Stiere? (Ihre Verehrer brüllen vor Freude über ihre Gegenwart, wie Stiere.)' The verb ra*n*yati, however, when followed by an accusative, means to love, to accept with pleasure. The gods accept the offerings and the prayers:

V, 18, 1. ví*s*vâni yá*h* ámartya*h* havyã márteshu rá*n*yati.

The immortal who deigns to accept all offerings among mortals.

V, 74, 3. kásya bráhmâ*n*i ra*n*yatha*h*.

Whose prayers do ye accept?

Followed by a locative ra*n*yati means to delight in. Both the gods are said to delight in prayers (VIII, 12, 18; 33, 16), and prayers are said to delight in the gods (VIII, 16, 2). I therefore take ra*n*yanti in the sense of tarrying, disporting, and ná, if it is to be retained, in the sense of not; where do they not sport? meaning that they are to be found everywhere, except where the poet desires them to be. We thus get rid of the simile of singing poets and lowing cows, which, though not too bold for Vedic bards, would here come in too abruptly. It would be much better, however, if the negative particle could be omitted altogether. If we retain it, we must read: kvã vá*h* | gâvá*h* | na rá*n* | yantí |. But the fact is that through the whole of the Rig-veda kvã has always to be pronounced as two syllables, kuva. There is only one passage, V, 61, 2, where, before a vowel, we have to read kva: kuva vo '*s*vâ*h*, kvâbhì*s*ava*h*. In other passages, even before vowels, we always have to read kuva, e.g. I, 161, 4. kuvet=kva it; I, 105, 4. kuvartam=kva *ri*tam. In I, 35, 7, we must read either kuvedânîm sûrya*h*, making sûrya*h* trisyllabic, or kuva idânîm, leaving a hiatus. In I, 168, 6, kvâvaram is kuvâvaram: *S*âkalya, forgetting this, and wishing to improve the metre, added na, thereby, in reality, destroying both the metre and the sense. Kva occurs as dissyllabic in the Rig-veda at least forty-one times.

Verse 3.

Note 1. The meanings of sumná in the first five Ma*nd*alas are well explained by Professor Aufrecht in Kuhn's Zeitschrift, vol. iv, p. 274. As to suvitã in the plural, see X, 86, 21, and VIII, 93, 29, where Indra is said to bring all suvitas. It frequently occurs in the singular:

X, 148, 1. ã na*h* bhara suvitám yásya *k*âkán.

Verse 4.

Note 1. One might translate: 'If you, sons of P*ris*ni, were mortals, the immortal would be your worshipper. But this seems almost too deep and elaborate a compliment for a primitive age. Langlois translates: 'Quand vous ne seriez pas immortels, (faites toutefois) que votre panégyriste jouisse d'une longue vie.' Wilson's translation is obscure: 'That you, sons of P*ri*s*n*i, may become mortals, and your panegyrist become immortal.' Sâya*n*a translates: 'Though you, sons of P*ri*s*n*i, were mortal, yet your worshipper would be immortal.' Ludwig has, 'Wenn ihr, o kinder der P*ri*s*n*i, sterbliche wäret, der unsterbliche wäre euer sänger dann. Nicht werde euch unlieb der sänger, wie ein wildes tier auf der weide, nicht des Yama Pfad betrete er.' I think it best to connect the fourth and fifth verses, and I feel justified in so doing by other passages where the same or a similar idea is expressed, viz. that if the god were the poet and the poet the god, then the poet would be more liberal to the god than the god is to him. Whether syât should have the udâtta, I cannot tell. Thus I translated a passage, VII, 32, 18, in my History of Ancient Sanskrit Literature, p. 545: 'If I were lord of as much as thou, I should support the sacred bard, thou scatterer of wealth, I should not abandon him to misery. I should award wealth day by day to him who magnifies, I should award it to whosoever it be.' Another parallel passage is pointed out by Mr. J. Muir, (On the Interpretation of the Veda, p. 79; see also Sanskrit Texts, V, 303.) VIII, 19, 25: 'If, Agni, thou wert a mortal, and I were an immortal, I should not abandon thee to malediction or to wretchedness; my worshipper should not be miserable or distressed.' Still more to the point is another passage, VIII, 44, 23: 'If I were thou, and thou wert I, then thy wishes should be fulfilled.' See also VIII, 14, 1, 2.

As to the metre it is clear that we ought to read martâsa*h* syâtana.

Verse 5.

Note 1. Mấ, though it seems to stand for ná, retains its prohibitive sense.

Note 2. Yávasa is explained by Sâya*n*a as grass, and Wilson's Dictionary, too, gives to it the meaning of meadow or pasture grass, whereas yava is barley. The Greek *ζεά* or *ζειά* is likewise explained as barley or rye, fodder for horses. See I, 91, 13. gấva*h* ná yávaseshu, like cows in meadows.

Note 3. The path of Yama can only be the path first followed by Yama, or that leads to Yama, as the ruler of the departed.

X, 14, 8. sám ga*kkh*asva pit*rí*-bhi*h* sám yaména.

Meet with the fathers, meet with Yama (X, 14, 10; 15, 8).

X, 14, 7. yamám pa*s*yâsi váru*n*am *k*a devám.

Thou wilt see (there) Yama and the divine Varu*n*a.

X, 165, 4. tásmai yamấya náma*h* astu m*ri*tyáve.

Adoration to that Yama, to Death!

WILSON: Never may your worshipper be indifferent to you, as a deer (is never indifferent) to pasture, so that he may not tread the path of Yama.

BENFEY: Wer euch besingt, der sei euch nicht gleichgültig, wie das Wild im Gras, nicht wandl' er auf des Yama Pfad.

Á*g*oshya is translated insatiable by Professor Goldstücker.

Verse 6.

Note 1. One of the meanings of nír*ri*ti is sin. It is derived from the same root which yielded *ri*tá, in the sense of right. Nír*ri*ti was conceived, it would seem, as going away from the path of right, the German Vergehen. Nír*ri*ti was personified as a power of evil and destruction.

VII, 104, 9. áhaye vâ tấn pra-dádâtu sóma*h* ấ vâ dadhâtu ní*h*-*ri*te*h* upá-sthe.

May Soma hand them over to Ahi, or place them in the lap of Nir*ri*ti.

I, 117, 5. susupvấ*m*sam ná ní*h*-*ri*te*h* upá-sthe.

Like one who sleeps in the lap of Nir*ri*ti.

Here Sâya*n*a explains Nir*ri*ti as earth, and he attaches the same meaning to the word in other places which will have to be considered hereafter. Cf. Lectures on the Science of Language, Second Series, p. 562.

Wilson treats Nir*ri*ti as a male deity, and translates the last words, 'let him perish with our evil desires.'

Note 2. Padîsh*t*á is formed as an optative of the Âtmanepada, but with the additional s before the t, which, in the ordinary Sanskrit, is restricted to the so-called benedictive (Grammar, § 385; Bopp, Kritische Grammatik, ed. 1834,

§ 329, note). Pad means originally to go. Thus RV. IX, 73, 9, átra kartám áva padâti áprabhu*h*, may the impotent go down into the pit. In certain constructions it gradually assumed the meaning of to perish, and native commentators are inclined to explain it by pat, to fall. One can watch the transition of meaning from going into perishing in such phrases as VS. XI, 46, mâ pâdy âyusha*h* purâ, literally, 'may he not go before the time,' but really intended for 'may he not die before the time.' In the Rig-veda padîsh*t*á is generally qualified by some words to show that it is to be taken in malam partem. Thus in our passage, and in III, 53, 21; VII, 104, 16; 17. In I, 79, 11, however, padîsh*t*á sá*h* is by itself used in a maledictory sense, pereat, may he perish! In another, VI, 20, 5, pa᷄di by itself conveys the idea of perishing. This may have some weight in determining the origin of the Latin pestis (Corssen, Kritische Beiträge, p. 396), for it shows that, even without prepositions, such as â or vi, pad may have an ill-omened meaning. In the Aitareya-brâhma*n*a VII, 14 (History of Ancient Sanskrit Literature, p. 471), pad, as applied to a child's teeth, means to go, to fall out. With sam, however, pad has always a good meaning, and this shows that originally its meaning was neutral. Another translation, suggested by Ludwig, might be: 'Let not one dreadful Nir*ri*ti (sin) after another strike us.'

Verse 7.

Note 1. The only difficult word is avâta᷄m. Sâya*n*a explains it, 'without wind.' But it is hardly possible to understand how the Maruts, themselves the gods of the storm, the sons of Rudra, could be said to bring clouds without wind. Langlois, it is true, translates without any misgivings: 'Ces dieux peuvent sur un sol desséché faire tomber la pluie sans l'accompagner de vent.' Wilson: 'They send down rain without wind upon the desert.' Benfey saw the incongruous character of the epithet, and explained it away by saying that the winds bring rain, and after they have brought it, they moderate their violence in order not to drive it away again; hence rain without wind. Yet even this explanation, though ingenious, and, as I am told, particularly truthful in an eastern climate, is somewhat too artificial. If we changed the accent, ávâtâm, unchecked, unconquered, would be better than avâtẩm, windless. But ávâta, unconquered, does not occur in the Rig-veda, except as applied to persons. It occurs most frequently in the phrase vanván ávâta*h*, which Sâya*n*a explains well by hi*m*san ahi*m*sita*h*, hurting, but not hurt: (VI, 16, 20; 18, 1; IX, 89, 7.) In IX, 96, 8, we read p*ri*t-sú vanván ávâta*h*, in battles attacking, but not attacked, which renders the meaning of ávâta perfectly clear. In VI, 64, 5, where it is applied to Ushas, it may be translated by unconquerable, intact.

There are several passages, however, where avâta occurs with the accent on the last syllable, and where it is accordingly explained as a Bahuvrîhi, meaning either windless or motionless, from vâta, wind, or from vâta, going (I, 62, 10). In some of these passages we can hardly doubt that the accent ought to be changed, and that we ought to read ávâta. Thus in VI, 64, 4, avâte is clearly a vocative applied to Ushas, who is called ávâtâ, unconquerable, in the verse immediately following. In I, 52, 4, the Maruts are called avâtâ*h*, which can only be ávâtâ*h*, unconquerable; nor can we hesitate in VIII, 79, 7, to change avâtá*h* into ávâta*h*, as an epithet applied to Soma, and preceded by ád*ri*ptakratu*h*, of unimpaired strength, unconquerable.

But even then we find no evidence that ávâta, unconquered, could be applied to rain or to a cloud, and I therefore propose another explanation, though equally founded on the supposition that the accent of avâtâm in our passage should be on the first syllable.

I take vâta as a Vedic form instead of the later vâna, the past participle of vai, to wither. Similarly we find in the Veda *g*îta, instead of *g*îna, the latter form being sanctioned by Pâ*n*ini. Vâ means to get dry, to flag, to get exhausted; ávâta therefore, as applied to a cloud, would mean not dry, not withered, as applied to rain, not dried up, but remaining on the ground. It is important to remark that in one passage, VI, 67, 7, Sâya*n*a, too, explains ávâta, as applied to rivers, by a*s*ushka, not dry; and the same meaning would be applicable to avâtâ*h* in I, 62, 10. In this sense of not withered, not dry, ávâtâm in our passage would form a perfectly appropriate epithet of the rain, while neither windless nor unconquered would yield an appropriate sense. In the famous passage, X, 129, 2, ấnît avâtám svadháyâ tát ékam, that only One breathed breathless by itself, avâtám might be taken, in accordance with its accent, as windless or breathless, and the poet may have wished to give this antithetical point to his verse. But ávâtam, as an adverb, would here be equally appropriate, and we should then have to translate, 'that only One breathed freely by itself.' Ludwig translates, 'Als treue die blendenden, die stürmenden Rudriya auf öder fläche sogar, als brunnen die wolke schaffen.' This presupposes the conjectural reading avatám.

Verse 8.

Note 1. The peculiar structure of the metre in the seventh and eighth verses should be noted. Though we may scan

– – – – ⏑ ⏑́ – – | – – ⏑ – – ⏑́ – – | ⏑ – – – ⏑ ⏑́ – – |
– – ⏑ – – ⏑́ – – | – – ⏑ – – ⏑́ – – | ⏑ – – – ⏑ ⏑́ – –

by throwing the accent on the short antepenultimate, yet the movement of the metre becomes far more natural by throwing the accent on the long penultimate, thus reading

– –́ – –́ ⏑ ⏑ –́ – | – –́ ⏑ –́ ⏑ ⏑ –́ – | ⏑ –́ – –́ ⏑ ⏑ –́ –
– –́ ⏑ –́ – ⏑ –́ – | – –́ ⏑ –́ – ⏑ – – | ⏑ –́ – –́ ⏑ ⏑ –́ –

SÂYA*N*A : Like a cow the lightning roars, (the lightning) attends (on the Maruts) as the mother cow on her calf, because their rain is let loose at the time of lightning and thunder.

WILSON : The lightning roars like a parent cow that bellows for its calf, and hence the rain is set free by the Maruts.

BENFEY : Es blitzt—wie eine Kuh brüllt es—die Mutter folgt dem Kalb gleichsam—wenn ihr Regen losgelassen. (Der Donner folgt dem Blitz, wie eine Kuh ihrem Kalbe.)

Vâsrá as a masculine means a bull, and it is used as a name of the Maruts in some passages, VIII, 7, 3; 7. As a feminine it means a cow, particularly a cow with a calf, a milch cow. Hence also a mother, X, 119, 4. The lowing of the lightning must be intended for the distant thunder, and the idea that the lightning goes near or looks for the rain is not foreign to the Vedic poets. See I, 39, 9: 'Come to us, Maruts, with your entire help, as lightnings (come to, i. e. seek for) the rain!'

Verse 9.

Note 1. That par*g*ánya here and in other places means cloud has been well illustrated by Dr. Bühler, Orient und Occident, vol. i, p. 221. It is interesting to watch the personifying process which is very palpable in this word, and by which Par*g*anya becomes at last a friend and companion of Indra. See now, 'India, what can it teach us?' p. 183 seq.

Verse 10.

Note 1. Sádma, as a neuter, means originally a seat, and is frequently used in the sense of altar: IV, 9, 3. sá*h* sádma pári nîyate hótâ; VII, 18, 22. hótâ-iva sádma pári emi rébhan. It soon, however, assumed the more general meaning of place, as

X, 1, 1. agní*h* bhânúnâ rú*s*atâ ví*s*vâ sádmâni aprâ*h*.

Agni with brilliant light thou filledst all places.

It is lastly used with special reference to heaven and earth, the two sádmanî, I, 185, 6; III, 55, 2. In our passage sádma pā́rthivam is the same as pā́rthive sádane in VIII, 97, 5. Here the earth is mentioned together with heaven, the sea, and the sky. Sâya*n*a takes sádma as 'dwelling,' so do Wilson and Langlois. Benfey translates 'der Erde Sitz,' and makes it the subject of the sentence, which may be right: 'From the roaring of the Maruts the seat of the earth trembles, and all men tremble.' Sadman, with the accent on the last syllable, is also used as a masculine in the Rig-veda, I, 173, 1; VI, 51, 12. sadmā́nam divyám.

Verse 11.

Note 1. I have translated vî*l*u-pâ*n*íbhi*h*, as if it were vî*l*úpâ*n*ibhi*h*, for this is the right accent of a Bahuvrîhi compound. Thus the first member retains its own accent in p*ri*thú-pâ*n*i, bhū́ri-pâ*n*i, v*rí*sha-pâ*n*i, &c. It is possible that the accent may have been changed in our passage, because the compound is used, not as an adjective, but as a kind of substantive, as the name of a horse. Pâ*n*í, hand, means, as applied to horses, hoof:

II, 31, 2. p*ri*thivyā́*h* sā́nau *g*áṅghananta pâ*n*í-bhi*h*.

When they strike with their hoofs on the summit of the earth.

This meaning appears still more clearly in such compounds as dravát-pâ*n*i:

VIII, 5, 35. hira*n*yáye*n*a ráthena dravátpâ*n*i-bhi*h* ásvai*h*.

On a golden chariot, on quick-hoofed horses.

The horses of the Maruts, which in our verse are called vî*l*u-pâ*n*í, strong-hoofed, are called VIII, 7, 27. híra*n*ya-pâ*n*i, golden-hoofed:

ásvai*h* híra*n*yapâ*n*i-bhi*h* dévâsa*h* úpa gantana.

On your golden-hoofed horses come hither, O gods.

Those who retain the accent of the MSS. ought to translate, 'Maruts, with your strong hands go after the clouds.'

Note 2. Ródhasvatî is explained by Sâya*n*a as river. It does not occur again in the Rig-veda. Ródhas is enclosure or fence, the bank of a river; but it does not follow that ródhasvat, having enclosures or banks, was applicable to rivers only. II, 15, 8, it is said that he emptied or opened the artificial enclosures of Bala, these being the clouds conquered by Indra. Hence I take ródhasvatî in the sense of a cloud yet unopened, which is followed or driven on by the Maruts.

*K*itrá, bright or many-coloured, is applied to the clouds, V, 63, 3. *k*itrébhi*h* abhrái*h*.

Note 3. Roth and Ludwig take ákhidrayâman for a name of horse, which seems right. The word does not occur again in the Rig-veda.

WILSON: Maruts, with strong hands, come along the beautifully-embanked rivers with unobstructed progress.

BENFEY: Mit euren starken Händen folgt den hehren eingeschlossnen nach in unermüd'tem Gang, Maruts.

Verse 12.

Note 1. Abhîsu, rein, does not mean finger in the Rig-veda, though Sâyana frequently explains it so, misled by Yâska, who gives abhîsu among the names of finger. Wilson: 'May your fingers be well skilled (to hold the reins).'

Verse 13.

Note 1. Agni is frequently invoked together with the Maruts, and is even called marút-sakhâ, the friend of the Maruts, VIII, 92, 14. It seems better, therefore, to refer bráhmanas pátim to Agni, than, with Sâyana, to the host of the Maruts (marúdganam). Bráhmanaspáti and Brihaspáti are both varieties of Agni, the priest and purohita of gods and men, and as such he is invoked together with the Maruts in other passages, I, 40, 1. Tánâ is an adverb, meaning constantly, always, for ever. Cf. II, 2, 1; VIII, 40, 7.

WILSON: Declare in our presence (priests), with voice attuned to praise Brahmanaspati, Agni, and the beautiful Mitra.

BENFEY: Lass schallen immerfort das Lied zu grüssen Brahmanaspati, Agni, Mitra, den herrlichen.

Note 2. Mitra is never, as far as I know, invoked together with the Maruts, and it is better to take mitrám as friend. Besides ná cannot be left here untranslated. Ludwig translates, 'beautiful like Mitra,' that is, bright like the sun.

Verse 14.

Note 1. The second sentence is obscure. Sâyana translates: 'Let the choir of priests make a hymn of praise, let them utter or expand it, like as a cloud sends forth rain.' Wilson similarly: 'Utter the verse that is in your mouth, spread it out like a cloud spreading rain.' Benfey: 'Ein Preislied schaffe in dem Mund, ertöne dem Parganya gleich.' He takes Parganya for the god of thunder, and supposes the hymn of praise to be compared to it on account of its loudness. Tatanah can only be the second person singular of the conjunctive of the reduplicated perfect, of which we have also tatánat, tatánâma, tatánan, and tatánanta. Tatana*h* can be addressed either to the host of the Maruts, or to the poet. I take it in the latter sense, for a similar verse occurs VIII, 21, 18. It is said there of a patron that he alone is a king, that all others about the river Sarasvatî are only small kings, and the poet adds: 'May he spread like a cloud with the rain,' giving hundreds and thousands (par*g*ánya*h*-iva tatánat hí v*ri*sh*t*yấ). Ludwig takes tan in the sense of thundering; thunder like Par*g*anya!

Verse 15.

Note 1. It is difficult to find an appropriate rendering for arkín. It means praising, celebrating, singing, and it is in the last sense only that it is applicable to the Maruts. Wilson translates, 'entitled to adoration;' Benfey, 'flaming.' Boehtlingk and Roth admit the sense of flaming in one passage, but give to arkín in this place the meaning of praising. If it simply meant, possessed of arká, i. e. songs of praise, it would be a very lame epithet after panasyú. But other passages, like I, 19, 4; 52, 15, show that the conception of the Maruts as singers was most familiar to the Vedic *Ri*shis (I, 64, 10; Kuhn, Zeitschrift, vol. i, p. 521, note); and arká is the very name applied to their songs (I, 19, 4). In the Edda, too, 'storm and thunder are represented as a lay, as the wondrous music of the wild hunt. The dwarfs and Elbs sing the so-called Alb-leich which carries off everything, trees and mountains.' See Justi in Orient und Occident, vol. ii, p. 62; Genthe, Windgottheiten, p. 4; 11. There is no doubt therefore that arkín here means musician, and that the arká of the Maruts is the music of the winds.

Note 2. V*ri*ddhá, literally grown, is used in the Veda as an honorific epithet, with the meaning of mighty, great, or magnified:

III, 32, 7. yá*g*âma*h* ít námasâ v*ri*ddhám índram
b*ri*hántam *ri*shvám a*g*áram yúvânam.

We worship with praise the mighty Indra, the great, the exalted, the immortal, the vigorous.

Here neither is v*ri*ddhá intended to express old age,

nor yúvan young age, but both are meant as laudatory epithets. See Darmesteter, Ormazd et Ahriman, p. 91 seq.

Asan is the so-called Le*t* of as, to be. This Le*t* is properly an imperative, which gradually sinks down to a mere subjunctive, and is generally called so. Of as, we find the following Le*t* forms: belonging to the present, we have ásasi, II, 26, 2; ásati, VI, 23, 9; ásatha*h*, VI, 63, 1; and ásatha, V, 61, 4: belonging to the imperfect, ása*h*, VIII, 100, 2; ásat, I, 9, 5; ásâma, I, 173, 9; ásan, I, 89, 1. Ásam, a form quoted by Roth from Rig-veda X, 27, 4, is really ā́sam.

We find, for instance, ása*h*, with an imperative or optative meaning, in

VIII, 100, 2. ása*h k*a tvám dakshi*n*atá*h* sákhâ me
ádha v*ri*trā́*n*i *g*aṅghanâva bhū́ri.

And be thou my friend on my right hand, and we shall kill many enemies.

Here we see the transition of meaning from an imperative to the conditional. In English, too, we may say, 'Do this and you shall live,' which means nearly the same as, 'If you do this, you will live.' Thus we may translate this passage: 'And if thou be my friend on my right side, then we shall kill many enemies.'

X, 124, 1. imám na*h* agne úpa ya*gñ*ám ā́ ihi—
ása*h* havya-vā́*t* utá na*h* pura*h*-gā́*h*.

Here we have the imperative ihi and the Le*t* ása*h* used in the same sense.

Far more frequently, however, ása*h* is used in relative sentences, such as,

VI, 36, 5. ása*h* yáthâ na*h* *s*ávasâ *k*akâná*h*.

That thou mayest be ours, delighting in strength.

VII, 24, 1. ása*h* yáthâ na*h* avitā́ v*ri*dhé *k*a.

That thou mayest be our helper and for our increase.

See also X, 44, 4; 85, 26; 36.

WILSON: May they be exalted by this our worship.

BENFEY: Mögen die Hohen hier bei uns sein.

MANDALA I, HYMN 39.

ASHTAKA I, ADHYÂYA 3, VARGA 18-19.

TO THE MARUTS (THE STORM-GODS).

1. When you thus from afar cast forwards your measure[1], like a blast of fire, through whose wisdom is it, through whose design[2]? To whom do you go, to whom, ye shakers (of the earth)?

2. May your weapons be firm to attack, strong also to withstand. May yours be the more glorious power, nor that of the deceitful mortal.

3. When you overthrow what is firm, O ye men, and whirl about what is heavy, you pass[1] through the trees of the earth, through the clefts of the rocks[2].

4. No real foe of yours is known in heaven, nor on earth, ye devourers of foes! May power be yours, together with your race[1]! O Rudras, can it be defied[2]?

5. They make the rocks tremble, they tear asunder the kings of the forest[1]. Come on, Maruts, like madmen, ye gods, with your whole tribe.

6. You have harnessed the spotted deer to your chariots, a red one draws as leader[1]; even the earth listened[2] at your approach, and men were frightened.

7. O Rudras, we quickly desire your help for our race. Come now to us with help, as of yore; thus now for the sake of the frightened Kanva[1].

8. Whatever fiend, roused by you or roused by men, attacks us, deprive him of power, of strength, and of your favours[1].

9. For you, chasing and wise Maruts, have wholly

protected[1] Ka*n*va. Come to us, Maruts, with your whole favours, as lightnings[2] (go in quest of) the rain.

10. Bounteous givers, you carry whole strength, whole power, ye shakers (of the world). Send, O Maruts, against the wrathful enemy of the poets an enemy, like an arrow[1].

NOTES.

This hymn is ascribed to Ka*n*va, the son of Ghora. The metre varies between B*ri*hatî and Satob*ri*hatî, the odd verses being composed in the former, the even verses in the latter metre. Each couple of such verses is called a Bârhata Pragâtha. The B*ri*hatî consists of 8+8+12+8, the Satob*ri*hatî of 12+8+12+8 syllables. No verse of this hymn occurs in SV., VS., AV.; verse 5=TB. II, 4, 4, 3.

Verse 1.

Note 1. Mắna, which I translate by measure, is explained by Sâya*n*a as meaning strength. Wilson: 'When you direct your awful vigour downwards from afar, as light (descends from heaven).' Benfey: 'Wenn ihr aus weiter Ferne so wie Strahlen schleudert euren Stolz (das worauf ihr stolz seid: euren Blitz).' Langlois: 'Lorsque vous lancez votre souffle puissant.' I doubt whether mắna is ever used in the Rig-veda in the sense of pride, which no doubt it has, as a masculine, in later Sanskrit: cf. Halâyudha, ed. Aufrecht, iv, 37. Mắna, as a masculine, means frequently a poet in the Rig-veda, viz. a measurer, a thinker or maker; as a neuter it means a measure, or what is measured or made. Thus V, 85, 5, we read:

mắnena-iva tasthi-vắn antárikshe ví yá*h* mamé p*ri*thivĭ́m sắrye*n*a.

He (Varu*n*a) who standing in the welkin has measured the earth with the sun, as with a measure.

In this passage, as well as in ours, we must take measure, not in the abstract sense, but as a measuring line, which is cast forward to measure the distance of an object,—a simile, perfectly applicable to the Maruts, who seem with their weapons to strike the trees and mountains when they themselves are still far off. Another explanation might be given, if mắna could be taken in the sense of measure, i. e. shape or form, but this is doubtful.

Note 2. Várpas, which has generally been translated by body or form, is here explained by praise. Benfey puts Werk (i.e. Gesang, Gebet); Langlois, maison. Várpas, which, without much reason, has been compared to Latin corpus, must here be taken in a more general sense. Thus VI, 44, 14, asyá máde purú várpâ*m*si vidvấn, is applied to Indra as knowing many schemes, many thoughts, many things, when he is inspired by the Soma-juice; see I, 19, 5.

Verse 3.

Note 1. Benfey takes ví yâthana in a causative sense, you destroy, you cause the trees to go asunder. But even without assigning to yâ a causative meaning, to go through, to pierce, would convey the idea of destruction. In some passages, however, vi-yâ is certainly used in the simple sense of passing through, without involving the idea of destruction:

VIII, 73, 13. ráthah*h* viyấti ródasî (íti).

Your chariot which passes through or between heaven and earth.

In other passages the mere passing across implies conquest and destruction:

I, 116, 20. vi-bhindúnâ.... ráthena ví párvatân....ayâtam.

On your dissevering chariot you went across, or, you rent, the mountains (the clouds).

In other passages, however, a causative meaning seems equally, and even more applicable:

VIII, 7, 23. ví v*ri*trám parva-*sáh* yayu*h* ví párvatân.

They passed through V*ri*tra piecemeal, they passed through the mountains (the clouds); or, they destroyed V*ri*tra, cutting him to pieces, they destroyed the clouds.

Likewise I, 86, 10. ví yâta ví*s*vam atrí*n*am.

Walk athwart every evil spirit, or destroy every evil spirit! See before, I, 19, 7; 37, 7.

˘ – ˘ ˘ ˘ ˘ ˘ – ˘ – ˘ –

We must scan vi yâthana vanina*h* p*ri*thivyâ*h*.

Note 2. It might seem preferable to translate ấ*s*â*h* párvatânâm by the spaces of the clouds, for párvata means clouds in many places. Yet here, and still more clearly in verse 5, where párvata occurs again, the object of the poet is to show the strength of the Maruts. In that case the mere shaking or bursting of the clouds would sound very tame by the side of the shaking and breaking of the forest trees. Vedic poets do not shrink from the conception that the Maruts shake even mountains, and Indra is even said to have cut off the mountain tops: IV, 19, 4. áva abhinat kakúbha*h* párvatânâm. In the later literature, too, the same idea occurs: Mahâbh. Vana-parva, ver. 10974, dyau*h* svit patati kim bhûmir dîryate parvato nu kim, does the sky fall? is the earth torn asunder, or the mountain?

Verse 4.

Note 1. Sâya*n*a was evidently without an authoritative explanation of tánâ yu*g*ấ. He tries to explain it by 'through the union of you may strength to resist be quickly extended.' Wilson: 'May your collective strength be quickly exerted.' Benfey takes tánâ as adverb and leaves out yu*g*ấ: 'Zu allen Zeiten, O Furchtbare!—sei im Nu zu überwält'gen euch die Macht.' Yu*g*ấ, an instrumental, if used together with another instrumental, becomes in the Veda a mere preposition: cf. VII, 43, 5; 95, 4. râyấ yu*g*ấ; X, 83, 3. tápasâ yu*g*ấ; X, 102, 12. vádhri*n*â yu*g*ấ; VII, 32, 20. púram-dhyâ yu*g*ấ; VI, 56, 2. sákhyâ yu*g*ấ; VIII, 68, 9. tvấ yu*g*ấ. As to the meaning of tán, see B. R. s. v., where tán in our passage is explained as continuation. The offspring or race of the Maruts is mentioned again in the next verse.

Note 2. I take nú *k*it â-dh*r*ishe as an abrupt interrogative sentence, viz. Can it be defied? Can it be resisted? See V, 87, 2:

tát va*h* maruta*h* ná â-dh*r*ishe *s*áva*h*.

Your strength, O Maruts, is not to be defied.

Verse 5.

Note 1. Large trees of the forest are called the kings or lords of the forest. Instead of pró ârata, the Taitt. Br. II, 4, 4, 2, reads pró varata, which Sâya*n*a explains by pro, prakarshe*n*a, avârata dhâvata.

Verse 6.

Note 1. Práshți is explained by Sâyana as a sort of yoke in the middle, when three horses or other animals are harnessed to a car; róhita as a kind of red deer. Hence Wilson remarks that the sense may be, 'The red deer yoked between them aids to drag the car.' But he adds that the construction of the original is obscure, and apparently rude and ungrammatical. Benfey translates, 'Sie führt ein flammenrothes Joch,' and remarks against Wilson that Sâyana's definition of práshti as yoke is right, but that of róhita as deer, wrong. If Sâyana's authority is to be invoked at all, one might appeal from Sâyana in this place to Sâyana VIII, 7, 28, where práshti is explained by him either by quick or by pramukhe yugyamânah, harnessed in front. The verse is

yát eshâm pr*í*shatî*h* ráthe prásh*t*i*h* váhati róhita*h*.

When the red leader draws or leads their spotted deer in the chariot.

VI, 47, 24. prásh*t*i*h* is explained as tripada âdhâra*h*; tadvad vahantîti prash*t*ayo*s*vâ*h*. In I, 100, 17, prásh*t*ibhi*h*, as applied to men, means friends or supporters, or, as Sâyana explains, pâr*s*vasthair anyair *ri*shibhi*h*.

Ludwig (IV, ad 25, 8) adds some useful information. He quotes from the comm. on Taitt. S. I, 7, 8; vâmadakshi*n*ayor a*s*vayor madhya îshâdvayam prasârya tayor madhye saptyâkhyag*â*tivi*s*eshopetam a*s*va*m* yu*ñg*yât. The right horse is said to be the arvâ, the left vâ*g*î, the middle sapti*h*. Lâ*t*yâyana II, 7, 23, calls the two side-horses prash*t*î. According to Sâyana (Taitt. S. I, 7, 8, p. 1024) prash*t*i means originally a tripod for holding a pot (see above), and afterwards a chariot with three horses. In that case we should have to translate, the red chariot moves along.

Note 2. Aufrecht derives a*s*rot from *s*ru, to shake, without necessity, however; see Muir's Sanskrit Texts, IV, p. 494.

Ludwig also remarks that a*s*rot might be translated by the earth trembled or vibrated. Similar passages occur RV. I, 127, 3. vîl*ú* *k*it yásya sám-*ri*tau *s*rúvat vánâ-iva yát sthirám, at whose approach even what is firm and strong will shake, like the forests. Roth translates, the earth yielded, got out of your way.

Verse 7.

Note 1. Ka*n*va, the author of the hymn.

Verse 8.

Note 1. The abhva, fiend, or, as Benfey translates it very happily, Ungethüm, may have been sent by the Maruts themselves, or by some mortal. With reference to yushmé-shita it is said afterwards that the Maruts are to withdraw their help from him. I have adopted Wilson's and Ludwig's interpretation of vi yuyota, with the instrumental.

Verse 9.

Note 1. The verb dadá is the second pers. plur. of the perfect of dâ, and is used here in the sense of to keep, to protect, as is well shown by B. and R. s. v. dâ 4, base dad. Sâya*n*a did not understand the word, and took it for an irregular imperative; yet he assigned to the verb the proper sense of to keep, instead of to give. Hence Wilson: 'Up-hold the sacrificer Ka*n*va.' Benfey, less correctly, 'Den Ka*n*va gabt ihr,' as if Ka*n*va had been the highest gift of the Maruts.

Note 2. The simile, as lightnings go to the rain, is not very telling. It may have been suggested by the idea that the lightnings run about to find the rain, or the tertium comparationis may simply be the quickness of lightning. Wilson: 'As the lightnings bring the rain.' Benfey: '(So schnell) gleichwie der Blitz zum Regen kömmt.' Lightning precedes the rain, and may therefore be represented as looking about for the rain. Ludwig proposes some bold conjectures. He would change ká*n*vam to ra*n*vam, and take the words from asâmibhi*h* to ganta as a parenthesis. He translates: 'For nothing imperfect, you highly to be revered Maruts, no, something delightful you gave—(with perfect aids, Maruts, come to us)—as lightnings give rain.'

Verse 10.

Note 1. Wilson: 'Let loose your anger.' Sâya*n*a: 'Let loose a murderer who hates.'

Pari-manyú, which occurs but once in the Rig-veda, corresponds as nearly as possible to the Greek περίθυμος. Manyú, like θυμός, means courage, spirit, anger; and in the compound parimanyú, as in περίθυμος, the preposition pári seems to strengthen the simple notion of the word. That pári is used in that sense in later Sanskrit is well known; for instance, in parilaghu, perlevis, parikshâma, withered away: see Pott, Etymologische Forschungen, second edition, vol. i, p. 487. How pári, originally meaning round about, came to mean excessive, is difficult to explain with certainty. It may have been, because what surrounds exceeds, but it may also have been because what is done all around a thing is done thoroughly. See Curtius, Grundzüge, fifth edition, p. 274. Thus we find in the Veda, VIII, 75, 9, pári-dveshas, lit. one who hates all around, then a great hater:

mā́ na*h* . . . pári-dveshasa*h* a*m*hatí*h*, ûrmí*h* ná nā́vam ā́ vadhît.

May the grasp of the violent hater strike us not, as the wave strikes a ship.

Again, pari-sp*ri*dh means literally one who strives round about, then an eager enemy, a rival (fem.):

IX, 53, 1. nudásva yā́*h* pari-sp*rí*dha*h*.

Drive away those who are rivals.

Pari-kro*s*á means originally one who shouts at one from every side, who abuses one roundly, then an angry reviler. This word, though not mentioned in B. R.'s Dictionary, occurs in

I, 29, 7. sárvam pari-kro*s*ám *g*ahi.

Kill every reviler!

The same idea which is here expressed by pari-kro*s*á, is in other places expressed by pari-ráp, lit. one who shouts round about, who defies on every side, a calumniator, an enemy, one who 'be-rattles.'

II, 23, 3. ā́ vi-bā́dhya pari-rápa*h*.

Having struck down the enemies.

II, 23, 14. ví pari-rápa*h* ardaya.

Destroy the enemies.

In the same way as the words meaning to hate, to

oppose, to attack, are strengthened by this preposition, which conveys the idea of round about, we also find words expressive of love strengthened by the same preposition. Thus from prîtá*h*, loved, we have pári-prîta*h*, lit. loved all round, then loved very much: I, 190, 6. pári-prîta*h* ná mitrá*h*; cf. X, 27, 12. We also find IX, 72, 1. pari-príya*h*, those who love fully or all around, which may mean great lovers, or surrounding friends.

In all these cases the intensifying power of pári arises from representing the action of the verb as taking place on every side, thoroughly, excessively; but in other cases, mentioned by Professor Pott, particularly where this preposition is joined to a noun which implies some definite limit, its magnifying power is no doubt due to the fact that what is around, is outside, and therefore beyond. Thus in Greek περίμετρος expresses the same idea as ὑπέρμετρος (loc. cit. p. 488), but I doubt whether pári ever occurs in that sense in Sanskrit compounds.

MAṆḌALA I, HYMN 64.

ASHṬAKA I, ADHYÂYA 5, VARGA 6-8.

To the Maruts (the Storm-gods).

1. For the manly host, the joyful, the wise, for the Maruts bring thou, O Nodhas[1], a pure offering[2]. I prepare songs, like as a handy priest[3], wise in his mind, prepares the water, mighty at sacrifices.

2. They are born, the tall bulls of Dyu[1] (heaven), the manly youths[2] of Rudra, the divine, the blameless, pure, and bright like suns; scattering raindrops, full of terrible designs, like giants[3].

3. The youthful Rudras, they who never grow old, the slayers of the demon[1], have grown irresistible like mountains. They throw down with their strength all beings, even the strongest, on earth and in heaven.

4. They deck themselves with glittering ornaments[1] for a marvellous show; on their chests they fastened gold (chains) for beauty[2]; the spears on their shoulders pound to pieces[3]; they were born together by themselves[4], the men of Dyu.

5. They who confer power[1], the roarers[2], the devourers of foes, they made winds and lightnings by their powers. The shakers milk the heavenly udders (clouds), they sprinkle the earth all round with milk (rain).

6. The bounteous[1] Maruts pour forth[2] water, mighty at sacrifices, the fat milk (of the clouds). They seem to lead[3] about the powerful horse, the cloud, to make it rain; they milk the thundering, unceasing spring[4]

7. Mighty they are, powerful, of beautiful splendour, strong in themselves[1] like mountains, (yet) swiftly gliding along;—you chew up forests, like wild elephants[2], when you have assumed your powers among the red flames[3].

8. Like lions they roar, the wise Maruts, they are handsome like gazelles[1], the all-knowing. By night[2] with their spotted deer (rain-clouds) and with their spears (lightnings) they rouse the companions together, they whose ire through strength is like the ire of serpents.

9. You who march in companies, the friends of man, heroes, whose ire through strength is like the ire of serpents[1], salute heaven and earth[2]! On the seats on your chariots, O Maruts, the lightning stands, visible like light[3].

10. All-knowing, surrounded with wealth, endowed with powers, singers[1], men of endless prowess armed with strong rings[2], they, the archers, have taken the arrow in their fists.

11. The Maruts who with the golden tires of their wheels increase the rain, stir up the clouds like wanderers on the road. They are brisk, indefatigable[1], they move by themselves; they throw down what is firm, the Maruts with their brilliant spears make (everything) to reel[2].

12. We invoke with prayer[1] the offspring of Rudra, the brisk, the pure, the worshipful[2], the active. Cling[3] for happiness-sake to the strong company of the Maruts, the chasers of the sky[4], the powerful, the impetuous[5].

13. The mortal whom ye, Maruts, protected, he indeed surpasses people in strength through your protection. He carries off booty with his horses,

treasures with his men; he acquires honourable[1] wisdom, and he prospers[2].

14. Give, O Maruts, to our lords strength glorious, invincible in battle, brilliant, wealth-acquiring, praiseworthy, known to all men[1]. Let us foster our kith and kin during a hundred winters.

15. Will[1] you then, O Maruts, grant unto us wealth, durable, rich in men, defying all onslaughts[2]? —wealth a hundred and a thousand-fold, always increasing?—May he who is rich in prayers[3] (the host of the Maruts) come early and soon!

NOTES.

This hymn is ascribed to Nodhas, of the family of Gotama. No verse of this hymn occurs in SV., VS., AV.; but verse 6=TS. III, 1, 11, 7.

Verse 1.

Note 1. The first line is addressed by the poet to himself.

Note 2. Suv*ri*ktí is generally explained by a hymn of praise, and it cannot be denied that in this place, as in most others, that meaning would be quite satisfactory. Etymologically, however, suv*ri*ktí means the cleaning and trimming of the grass on which, as on a small altar, the oblation is offered: cf. v*ri*ktabarhis, I, 38, 1, note 2, page 84. Hence, although the same word might be metaphorically applied to a carefully trimmed, pure, and holy hymn of praise, yet wherever in the Veda the primary meaning is applicable, it seems safer to retain it: cf. III, 61, 5; VI, 11, 5.

Prof. Roth, in the Mélanges Asiatiques, vii, p. 612, calls the derivation, which he himself discovered, a 'Columbus-Egg.' He derives suv*ri*kti from su + *ri*kti, and translates it by excellent praise. He supports the insertion of v, by the analogy of su-v-ita, for su-ita. This derivation is certainly very ingenious, but there are some difficulties which have still to be accounted for. That the substantive *ri*kti does not occur by itself would not be fatal, because other words in the Veda occur as uttarapadas only. But there is the compound námov*ri*kti in X, 131, 2, which shows that v*ri*kti existed as a substantive, though it is true that the Vâ*g*asaneyins (X, 32) read namaukti instead. Taitt. S. I, 8, 21; Taitt. Br. II, 6, 1, 3; and Ath. V. XX, 125, 2, have all namov*ri*kti. There is also the compound svâv*ri*kti in RV. X, 21, 1. Are these to be separated from su-v*ri*kti, and ought we not to take into consideration also the Zend hvarsta, as pointed out by M. Darmesteter (Ormazd,

p. 10, note), meaning well performed, perfect in a liturgical sense?

Note 3. Apás, with the accent on the last syllable, is the accusative plural of ap, water, and it is so explained by Sâya*n*a. He translates: 'I show forth these hymns of praise, like water, i. e. everywhere, as Par*g*anya sends down rain at once in every place.' Benfey explains: 'I make these hymns smooth like water, i. e. so that they run smooth like water.' He compares ῥυθμός, as derived from ῥέω. Ludwig translates: 'Als ein kunstfertiger das werk im geiste, auch geschickt mit der hand mach ich schön die in der opferversammlungen mächtig wirkenden lieder.' I thought formerly that we ought either to change the accent, and read ápa*h*, or the last vowel, and read apā́*h*. In the former case the meaning would be, 'As one wise in mind and clever performs his work, so do I compose these hymns.' In the second case we should translate: 'Like a workman, wise in mind and handy, I put together these hymns.'

Still there is one point which has hitherto been overlooked by all translators, namely, that apá*h* vidátheshu âbhúva*h*, occurring in the first and sixth verses, ought to be taken in the same sense in both passages. Now apá*h* vidátheshu âbhúva*h* seems to mean water efficacious at sacrifices. In the sixth verse I now translate: 'The bounteous Maruts pour down water, mighty or efficacious at sacrifices, the fat milk (of the clouds).' Hence in the first verse I should now like to translate: 'I prepare my songs, like as a handy priest, wise in his mind, prepares the water mighty or efficacious at sacrifices.' Roth assigns to vidátha a too exclusively political meaning. Vidátha may be an assembly, a public meeting, a witenagemot, or an ἐκκλησία, but public meetings at that time had always a religious character, so that vidátha must often be translated by sacrifice.

Verse 2.

Note 1. It is difficult to say in passages like this, whether Dyu should be taken as heaven or as a personified deity. When the Maruts are called Rudrásya máryâ*h*, the boys of

Rudra (VII, 56, 1), the personification is always preserved. Hence if the same beings are called Divá*h* máryâ*h*, this too, I think, should be translated the boys of Dyu (III, 54, 13; V, 59, 6), not the sons of heaven. The bulls of Dyu is a more primitive and more vigorous expression for what we should call the fertilising winds of heaven.

Note 2. Márya is a male, particularly a young male, a young man, a bridegroom (I, 115, 2; III, 33, 10; IV, 20, 5; V, 61, 4, with vîra).

The Maruts have grown strong like well-grown manly youths. See also V, 59, 3.

V, 59, 5. máryâ*h*-iva su-v*ri*dha*h* vav*ri*dhu*h* nára*h*.

The men have grown strong like well-grown stallions.

In some passages it has simply the meaning of man:

I, 91, 13. márya*h*-iva své okyẽ.

Like a man in his own house.

Note 3. The simile, like giants, is not quite clear. Sátvan means a strong man, but it seems intended here to convey the idea of supernatural strength. Benfey translates, 'like brave warriors;' Wilson, 'like evil spirits.' Ghorávarpas is an adjective belonging to the Maruts rather than to the giants, and may mean of awful aspect, I, 19, 5, or of cruel mind; cf. I, 39, 1, note 2.

Verse 3.

Note 1. Abhog-ghána*h*, the slayers of the demon, are the slayers of the clouds, viz. of such clouds as do not yield rain. Abho*g*, not nurturing, seems to be a name of the rainless cloud, like Námu*k*i (na-mu*k*, not delivering rain), the name of another demon, killed by Indra; see Benfey, Glossar, s. v. The cloud which sends rain is called bhu*g*mán:

VIII, 50, 2. giri*h* ná bhu*g*mấ maghávat-su pinvate.

Like a feeding cloud he showers his gifts on the worshippers.

Verse 4.

Note 1. The ornaments of the Maruts are best described V, 54, 11:

á*m*seshu va*h* *ri*sh*t*áya*h* pat-sú khâdáya*h* váksha*h*-su rukmā́*h*.

On your shoulders are the spears, on your feet rings, on your chests gold ornaments. See also I, 166, 10, &c.

Rukmá as a masc. plur. is frequently used for ornaments which are worn on the breast by the Maruts. The Maruts are actually called rukmávakshasa*h*, gold-breasted (II, 34, 2; V, 55, 1; 57, 5). In the Â*s*val. *S*rauta-sûtra IX, 4, rukma is mentioned as an ornament to be given to the Hot*ri* priest; it is said to be round.

Note 2. Vápushe and *s*ubhé, as parallel expressions, occur also VI, 63, 6. Cf. Delbrück, K. Z. xviii, 96.

Note 3. Ní mim*ri*kshur does not occur again in the Rig-veda, and Roth has suggested to read ní mimikshur instead; see ni + mar*g*. He does not, however, give our passage under mya*k*, but under mraksh, and this seems indeed preferable. No doubt, there is ample analogy for mimikshu*h*, and the meaning would be, their spears stick firm to their shoulders. But as the MSS. give mim*ri*kshu*h*, and as it is possible to find a meaning for this, I do not propose to alter the text. The question is only, what does mim*ri*kshu*h* mean? Mraksh means to grind, to rub, and Roth proposes to render our passage by 'the spears rub together on our shoulders.' The objections to this translation are the preposition ni, and the active voice of the verb. I take mraksh in the sense of grinding, pounding, destroying, which is likewise appropriate to mraksha-k*ri*tvan (VIII, 61, 10), and tuvi-mrakshá (VI, 18, 2), and I translate, 'the spears on their shoulders pound to pieces.'

Note 4. The idea that the Maruts owe everything, if not their birth, at least their strength (svá-tavasa*h*, svá-bhâna-va*h*, sva-*sr*íta*h*), to themselves is of frequent occurrence in these hymns. See verse 7, note 1.

Verse 5.

Note 1. They are themselves compared to kings (I, 85, 8), and called î*s*âná, lords (I, 87, 4).

Note 2. Dhúni is connected with root dhvan, to dun or

to din. Sâyana explains it by bending or shaking, and Benfey, too, translates it by Erschütterer. Roth gives the right meaning.

Verse 6.

Note 1. I translate sudā́navah by bounteous, or good givers, for, if we have to choose between the two meanings of bounteous or endowed with liquid drops or dew, the former is the more appropriate in most passages. We might, of course, admit two words, one meaning, possessed of good water, the other, bounteous; the former derived from dā́nu, neuter, water, or rain, the other from dânú, giving. It cannot be denied, for instance, that whenever the Maruts are called sudā́navah, the meaning, possessed of good rain, would be applicable: I, 40, 1; 44, 14; 64, 6; 85, 10; II, 34, 8; III, 26, 5; V, 52, 5; 53, 6; 57, 5; VIII, 20, 18; X, 78, 5; I, 15, 2; 23, 9; 39, 10. Yet, even in these passages, while sudā́navah in the sense of possessed of good rain is possible throughout, that of good giver would sometimes be preferable, for instance, I, 15, 2, as compared with I, 15, 3. Though sudā́nu, in the sense of possessed of good water, sounds as strange as would suvrishti in the sense of possessed of good rain, or sumegha, possessed of good clouds, yet it is difficult to separate sudā́navah and gîrádânavah, both epithets of the Maruts.

When the same word is applied to Indra, VII, 31, 2; X, 23, 6; to Vishnu, VIII, 25, 12; to the Asvins, I, 112, 11; to Mitra and Varuna, V, 62, 9; to Indra and Varuna, IV, 41, 8, the meaning of giver of good rain might still seem natural. But with Agni, VI, 2, 4; the Âdityas, V, 67, 4; VIII, 18, 12; 19, 34; 67, 16; the Vasus, I, 106, 1; X, 66, 12; the Visve, X, 65, 11, such an epithet would not be appropriate, while sudā́navah, in the sense of bounteous givers, is applicable to all. The objection that dânu, giver, does not occur in the Veda, is of no force, for many words occur at the end of compounds only, and we shall see passages where sudā́nu must be translated by good giver. Nor would the accent of dânú, giver, be an obstacle, considering that the author of the Unâdi-sûtras had no Vedic authority to guide him in the determination of the accent of dânú. Several words in nu have the accent on the first syllable. But one might go even a step further, and find a more appropriate meaning for sudā́nu by identifying it with the Zend hudânu, which means, not a good giver, but a good knower, wise. True, this root dâ, to know, does not occur in the ordinary Sanskrit; and Hübschmann (Ein Zoroastrisches Lied, 1872, p. 48) tries to prove that the root dâ, to know, does not exist in Zend either. But even thus we might have the derivation in Sanskrit and Zend, while the root was kept alive in Greek only (δάημι, δάεις). This, however, is only a conjecture; what is certain is this, that apart from the passages where sudā́nu is thus applied to various deities, in the sense of bounteous or wise, it also occurs as applied to the sacrificer, where it can only mean giver. This is clear from the following passages:

I, 47, 8. su-k*ri*te su-dā́nave.

To him who acts well and gives well.

VII, 96, 4. *g*ani-yánta*h* nú ágrava*h* putri-yánta*h* su-dā́nava*h*, sárasvantam havâmahe.

We, being unmarried, and wishing for wives and wishing for sons, offering sacrifices, call now upon Sarasvat.

VIII, 103, 7. su-dā́nava*h* deva-yáva*h*.

Offering sacrifices, and longing for the gods. Cf. X, 172, 2; 3; VI, 16, 8.

IV, 4, 7. sá*h* ít agne astu su-bhága*h* su-dā́nu*h* yá*h* tvâ nítyena havíshâ yá*h* ukthai*h* píprîshati.

O Agni, let the liberal sacrificer be happy, who wishes to please thee by perpetual offerings and hymns. See also VI, 16, 8; 68, 5; X, 172, 2, 3.

It must be confessed that even the meaning of dā́nu is by no means quite clear. It is clear enough where it means demon, II, 11, 18; 12, 11; IV, 30, 7; X, 120, 6, the seven demons. In I, 32, 9; III, 30, 8, dā́nu, demon, is applied to the mother of V*ri*tra, the dark cloud. From this dā́nu we have the derivative dânavá, meaning again demon. Why the demons, conquered by Indra, were called dā́nu, is not clear, unless they were conceived originally as dark clouds, like Dânu, the mother of Indra. Dânu might mean wise, or even powerful, for this meaning also is ascribed to dânú by the author of the U*n*âdi-sûtras. If the latter meaning is authentic, and not only deduced ex post from the name of Dânu and Dânava, it might throw light on the Celtic dána, fortis, from which Zeuss derives the name of the Danube.

Sometimes dắnu, as a neuter, is explained as Soma:

X, 43, 7. ắpa*h* ná síndhum abhí yát sam-áksharan sómâsa*h* índram kulyắ*h*-iva hradám, várdhanti víprâ*h* máha*h* asya sádane yávam ná v*ri*sh*t*í*h* divyéna dắnunâ.

When the Somas run together to Indra, like water to the river, like channels to the lake, then the priests increase his greatness in the sanctuary, as rain the corn, by the heavenly Soma-juice, or by heavenly moisture.

In the next verse *g*îrádânu is explained as the sacrificer whose Soma is always alive, always ready.

In VI, 50, 13, however, dắnu pápri*h* is doubtful. As an epithet to Apắm nápât, it may mean he who wishes for Soma, or he who grants Soma; but in neither case is there any tangible sense, unless Soma is taken as a name of the fertilising rain or dew. Again, VIII, 25, 5, Mitra and Varu*n*a are called s*ri*prá-dânû, which may mean possessed of flowing rain. And in the next verse, sám yắ dắnûni yemáthu*h* may be rendered by Mitra and Varu*n*a, who brought together rain.

The fact that Mitra-Varu*n*au and the A*s*vins are called dắnunaspátî does not throw much more light on the subject, and the one passage where dắnu occurs as a feminine, I, 54, 7, dắnu*h* asmai úparâ pinvate divá*h*, may be translated by rain pours forth for him, below the sky, but the translation is by no means certain.

Dắnu*k*itra, applied to the dawn, the water of the clouds, and the three worlds (V, 59, 8; 31, 6; I, 174, 7), means most likely bright with dew or rain; and dắnumat vásu, the treasure conquered by Indra from the clouds, can be translated by the treasure of rain. Taking all the evidence together, we can hardly doubt that dắnu existed in the sense of liquid, rain, dew, and also Soma; yet it is equally certain that dắnu existed in the sense of giver, if not of gift, and that from this, in certain passages, at all events, sudânu must be derived, as a synonym of sudâvan, sudâman, &c.

Spiegel admits two words dânu in the Veda and Avesta, the one meaning enemy, the other river. Darmesteter (Ormazd, p. 220) takes dânu as a cloud, water, or river. Ludwig translates sudânu by possessed of excellent gifts.

Note 2. I thought formerly that pinvanti was here construed with two accusatives, in the sense of 'they fill the water (with) fat milk.'

Cf. VI, 63, 8. dhenúm na*h* ísham pinvatam ásakrâm.

You filled our cow (with) constant food.

Similarly duh, to milk, to extract, is construed with two accusatives: Pâ*n*. I, 4, 51. gâm dogdhi paya*h*, he milks the cow milk.

RV. IX, 107, 5. duhâná*h* ûdha*h* divyám mádhu priyám.

Milking the heavenly udder (and extracting from it) the precious sweet, i.e. the rain.

But I now prefer to translate pínvanti apá*h* by they pour out water, and I take páya*h* gh*ri*távat as a description of the water, namely, the fat milk of the clouds. After that parenthesis, vidátheshu âbhúva*h* is again an epithet of apá*h*, as it was in the first verse.

Note 3. The leading about of the clouds is intended, like the leading about of horses, to tame them, and make them obedient to the wishes of their riders, the Maruts. Átya*h* vâ*g*î is a strong horse, possibly a stallion; but this horse is here meant to signify the clouds. Thus we read:

V, 83, 6. divá*h* na*h* v*ri*sh*t*ím maruta*h* rarîdhvam prá pinvata v*rí*shna*h* ásvasya dhârâ*h*.

Give us, O Maruts, the rain of heaven, pour forth the streams of the stallion (the cloud).

In the original the simile is quite clear, and no one required to be told that the átya*h* vâ*g*î was meant for the cloud. Vâ*g*ín by itself means a horse, as I, 66, 2; 69, 3. vâ*g*î ná prîtá*h*, like a favourite horse; I, 116, 6. paidvá*h* vâ*g*î, the horse of Pedu. But being derived from vâ*g*a, strength, vâ*g*ín retained always something of its etymological meaning, and was therefore easily and naturally transferred to the cloud, the giver of strength, the source of food. Even without the ná, i. e. as if, the simile would have been understood in Sanskrit, while in English it is hardly intelligible without a commentary. Benfey discovers some additional idea in support of the poet's comparison: 'Ich bin kein Pferdekenner,' he says, 'aber ich glaube bemerkt zu haben, dass man Pferde, welche rasch gelaufen sind, zum Uriniren zu bewegen sucht. So lassen hier die Maruts die durch ihren Sturm rasch fortgetriebenen Wolken Wasser herab strömen.'

Note 4. Útsa, well, is meant again for cloud, though we should hardly be justified in classing it as a name of cloud, because the original meaning of útsa, spring, is really retained, as much as that of avatá, well, in I, 85, 10–11. The adjectives stanáyantam and ákshitam seem more applicable to cloud, yet they may be applied also to a spring. Yâska derives utsa from ut-sar, to go forth; ut-sad, to go out; ut-syand, to well out; or from ud, to wet. In V, 32, 2, the wells shut up by the seasons are identified with the udder of the cloud.

Verse 7.

Note 1. Svátavas means really having their own independent strength, a strength not derived from the support of others. The yet which I have added in brackets seems to have been in the poet's mind, though it is not expressed. In I, 87, 4, the Maruts are called sva-s*ri*t, going by themselves, i. e. moving freely, independently, wherever they list. See I, 64, 4, note 4.

Note 2. M*ri*gâ*h* hastína*h*, wild animals with a hand or a trunk, must be meant for elephants, although it has been doubted whether the poets of the Veda were acquainted with that animal. Hastín is the received name for elephant in the later Sanskrit, and it is hardly applicable to any other animal. If they are said to eat the forests, this may be understood in the sense of crushing or chewing, as well as of eating

Note 3. The chief difficulty of the last sentence has been pointed out in B. and R.'s Dictionary, s. v. âru*n*î. Âru*n*î does not occur again in the whole of the Rig-veda. If we take it with Sâya*n*a as a various reading of aru*n*î, then the

Aru*n*îs could only be the ruddy cows of the dawn or of Indra, with whom the Maruts, in this passage, can have no concern. Nor would it be intelligible why they should be called ắru*n*î in this one place only. If, as suggested by B. and R., the original text had been yadẩ aru*n*îshu, it would be difficult to understand how so simple a reading could have been corrupted.

Another difficulty is the verb áyugdhvam, which is not found again in the Rig-veda together with távishî. Távishî, vigour, is construed with dhâ, to take strength, V, 32, 2. adhatthâ*h*; V, 55, 2. dadhidhve; X, 102, 8. adhatta; also with vas, IV, 16, 14; with pat, X, 113, 5, &c. But it is not likely that to put vigour into the cows could be expressed in Sanskrit by 'you join vigour in the cows.' If távishî must be taken in the sense which it seems always to possess, viz. vigour, it would be least objectionable to translate, 'when you joined vigour, i. e. when you assumed vigour, while being among the Âru*n*îs.' The Âru*n*îs being the cows of the dawn, ắru*n*îshu might simply mean in the morning. Considering, however, that the Maruts are said to eat up forests, ắru*n*î, in this place, is best taken in the sense of red flames, viz. of fire or forest-fire (dâvâgni), so that the sense would be, 'When you, Storms, assume vigour among the flames, you eat up forests, like elephants.' Benfey: 'Wenn mit den rothen eure Kraft ihr angeschirrt. Die rothen sind die Antilopen, das Vehikel der Maruts, wegen der Schnelligkeit derselben.'

Verse 8.

Note 1. As pi*s*á does not occur again in the Rig-veda, and as Sâya*n*a, without attempting any etymological arguments, simply gives it as a name of deer, it seems best to adopt that sense till something better can be discovered. Supi*s*, too, does not occur again. In VII, 18, 2, pi*s* is explained by gold, &c.; VII, 57, 3, the Maruts are called vi*s*vapi*s*.

Note 2. Ksháp*ah* can only be the accusative plural, used in a temporal sense. It is so used in the expression kshápa*h* usrá*h* *k*a, by night and by day, lit. nights and days (VII, 15, 8). In VI, 52, 15, we find kshápa*h* usrẩ*h* in the same sense.

IV, 53, 7. kshapā́bhi*h* áha-bhi*h*, by night and by day. I, 44, 8, the loc. plur. vyúsh*t*ishu, in the mornings, is followed by ksh*á*pa*h*, the acc. plur., by night, and here the genitive kshapá*h* would certainly be preferable, in the sense of at the brightening up of the night. The acc. plur. occurs again in I, 116, 4, where tisrá*h* is used as an accusative (II, 2, 2; VIII, 41, 3). Kshapá*h*, with the accent on the last, must be taken as a genitivus temporalis, like the German Nachts (I, 79, 6). In VIII, 19, 31. kshapá*h* vástushu means at the brightening up of the night, i. e. in the morning. Thus, in III, 50, 4, Indra is called kshapā́m vastā́ *g*anitā́ sū́ryasya, the lighter up of nights, the parent of the sun. In VIII, 26, 3, áti kshapá*h*, the genitive may be governed by áti. In IV, 16, 19, however, the accusative kshápa*h* would be more natural, nor do I see how a genitive could here be accounted for:

dyā́va*h* ná dyumnai*h* abhí sánta*h* aryá*h* kshapá*h* madema *s*arláda*h* *k*a pûrvī́*h*.

May we rejoice many years, overcoming our enemies as the days overcome the nights by splendour.

The same applies to I, 70, 4, where kshapá*h* occurs with the accent on the last syllable, whereas we expect kshápa*h* as nom. or acc. plural. Here B. and R. in the Sanskrit Dictionary, s. v. kshap, rightly, I believe, suppose it to be a nom. plur. in spite of the accent.

Verse 9.

Note 1. Áhimanyu comes very near to Angra-mainyu; cf. Darmesteter, Ormazd, p. 94.

Note 2. Ródasî, a dual, though frequently followed by ubhé (I, 10, 8; 33, 9; 54, 2), means heaven and earth, excluding the antáriksha or the air between the two. Hence, if this is to be included, it has to be added: I, 73, 8. âpapri-vā́n ródasî antáriksham. Cf. V, 85, 3. We must scan ˘rodasī̆. See Kuhn, Beiträge, vol. iv, p. 193. Should rodasî stand for rodasîm, as elsewhere? She is certainly intended by what follows in the next line.

Note 3. The comparison is not quite distinct. Amáti means originally impetus, then power, e. g. V, 69, 1:

vav*ri*dhânâu amátim kshatríyasya.

Increasing the might of the warrior.

But it is most frequently used of the effulgence of the sun, (III, 38, 8; V, 45, 2; 62, 5; VII, 38, 1; 2; 45, 3.) See also V, 56, 8, where the same companion of the Maruts is called Rodasî. The comparative particle ná is used twice.

Verse 10.

Note 1. See I, 38, 14, p. 95.

Note 2. In v*rí*sha-khâdi the meaning of khâdi is by no means clear. Sâya*n*a evidently guesses, and proposes two meanings, weapon or food. In several passages where khâdi occurs, it seems to be an ornament rather than a weapon, yet if derived from khad, to bite, it may originally have signified some kind of weapon. Roth translates it by ring, and it is certain that these khâdis were to be seen not only on the arms and shoulders, but likewise on the feet of the Maruts. There is a famous weapon in India, the *k*akra or quoit, a ring with sharp edges, which is thrown from a great distance with fatal effect. Bollensen (Orient und Occident, vol. ii, p. 46) suggests for v*rí*shan the meaning of hole in the ear, and then translates the compound as having earrings in the hole of the ear. But v*rí*shan does not mean the hole in the lap of the ear, nor has v*ri*shabhá that meaning either in the Veda or elsewhere. Wilson gives for v*ri*shabha, not for v*ri*shan, the meaning of orifice of the ear, but this is very different from the hole in the lap of the ear. Benfey suggests that the khâdis were made of the teeth of wild animals, and hence their name of biters. V*rí*-shan conveys the meaning of strong, though possibly with the implied idea of rain-producing, fertilising. See p. 138. In RV. V, 87, 1, Osthoff translates sukhâdáye by jucunde praebenti, Benfey by schönverzehrendem; Muir, Sanskrit Texts, IV, 70, has the right rendering. Cf. note to I, 166, 9.

Verse 11.

Note 1. Formerly explained as 'zum Kampfe wandelnd.' See Kuhn, Zeitschrift, vol. iv, p. 19.

Note 2. WILSON: Augmenters of rain, they drive, with golden wheels, the clouds asunder; as elephants (in a herd, break down the trees in their way). They are honoured with sacrifices, visitants of the hall of offering, spontaneous assailers (of their foes), subverters of what are stable, immovable themselves, and wearers of shining weapons.

BENFEY: Weghemmnissen gleich schleudern die Fluthmehrer mit den goldnen Felgen das Gewölk empor, die nie müden Kämpfer, frei schreitend-festesstürzenden, die schweres thu'nden, lanzenstrahlenden Maruts.

Verse 12.

Note 1. Havásâ, instead of what one should expect, hávasâ, occurs but once more in another Marut hymn, VI, 66, 11.

Note 2. Vanín does not occur again as an epithet of the Maruts. It is explained by Sâya*n*a as a possessive adjective derived from vana, water, and Benfey accordingly translates it by fluthversehn. This, however, is not confirmed by any authoritative passages. Vanín, unless it means connected with the forest, a tree, in which sense it occurs frequently, is only applied to the worshippers or priests in the sense of venerating or adoring (cf. venero, venustus, &c.):

III, 40, 7. abhí dyumnâni vanína*h* índram sa*k*ante ákshitâ.
The inexhaustible treasures of the worshipper go towards Indra.

VIII, 3, 5. índram vanína*h* havâmahe.
We, the worshippers, call Indra.

Unless it can be proved by independent evidence that vanín means possessed of water, we must restrict vanín to its two meanings, of which the only one here applicable, though weak, is adoring. The Maruts are frequently represented as singers and priests, yet the epithets here applied to them stand much in need of some definite explanation, as the poet could hardly have meant to string a number of vague and ill-connected epithets together. If one might conjecture, svânínam instead of vanínam would be an improvement. It is a scarce word, and occurs but once more in the Veda, III, 26, 5, where it is used of the Maruts, in the sense of noisy, turbulent.

Note 3. Saskata, which I have here translated literally by to cling, is often used in the sense of following or revering (colere):

II, 1, 13. tvẫm râti-sẫkah adhvaréshu saskire.

The gods who are fond of offerings cling to thee, follow thee, at the sacrifices.

The Soma libation is said to reach the god:

II, 22, 1. sáh enam saskat deváh devám. The gods too are said to cling to their worshippers, i. e. to love and protect them: III, 16, 2; VII, 18, 25. The horses are said to follow their drivers: VI, 36, 3; VII, 90, 3, &c. It is used very much like the Greek ὀπάζω.

Note 4. Ragastû́h may mean rousing the dust of the earth, a very appropriate epithet of the Maruts. Sâyana explains it thus, and most translators have adopted his explanation. But as the epithets here are not simply descriptive, but laudatory, it seems preferable, in this place, to retain the usual meaning of rágas, sky. When Soma is called ragastû́h, IX, 108, 7, Sâyana too explains it by tegasâm prerakam, and IX, 48, 4, by udakasya prerakam.

Note 5. *Rig*îshín, derived from *rig*îsha. *Rig*îsha is what remains of the Soma-plant after it has once been squeezed, and what is used again for the third libation. Now as the Maruts are invoked at the third libation, they were called *rig*îshín, as drinking at their later libation the juice made of the *rig*îsha. This, at least, is the opinion of the Indian commentators. But it is much more likely that the Maruts were invoked at the third libation, because originally they had been called *rig*îshín by the Vedic poets, this *rig*îshín being derived from *rig*îsha, and *rig*îsha from *rig*, to strive, to yearn, like purîsha from prî, manîshâ from man; (see Unâdi-sûtras, p. 273.) This *rig* is the same root which we have in ὀρέγειν, to reach, ὀργή, emotion, and ὄργια, furious transports of worshippers. Thus the Maruts from being called *rig*îshín, impetuous, came to be taken for drinkers of *rig*îsha, the fermenting and overflowing Soma, and were assigned accordingly to the third libation at sacrifices.

*Rig*îshin, as an epithet, is not confined to the Maruts; it is given to Indra, with whom it could not have had a purely ceremonial meaning (VIII, 76, 5).

Verse 13.

Note 1. Âp*rikkh*ya, literally, to be asked for, to be inquired for, to be greeted and honoured. A word of an apparently modern character, but occurring again in the Rig-veda as applied to a prince, and to the vessel containing the Soma.

Note 2. Púshyati might be joined with krátu and taken in a transitive sense, he increases his strength. But púshyati is also used as an intransitive, and means he prospers:

I, 83, 3. ása*m*-yata*h* vraté te ksheti púshyati.

Without let he dwells in thy service and prospers.

Roth reads asa*m*yatta*h*, against the authority of the MSS.

Verse 14.

Note 1. The difficulty of this verse arises from the uncertainty whether the epithets dhanasp*ri*tam, ukthyâm, and vi*s*vá*k*arsha*n*im belong to *s*úshma, strength, or to toká, kith and kin. Roth and Benfey connect them with toká. Now dhanasp*ri*t is applicable to toká, yet it never occurs joined with toká again, while it is used with *s*úshma, VI, 19, 8. Ukthyâ, literally, to be praised with hymns, is not used again as an epithet of toká, though it is quite appropriate to any gift of the gods. Lastly, vi*s*vá*k*arsha*n*i is never applied to toká, while it is an epithet used, if not exactly of the strength, *s*úshma, given by the gods, yet of the fame given by them:

X, 93, 10. dhâtam vîréshu vi*s*vá-*k*arsha*n*i *s*ráva*h*.

Give to these men world-wide glory. Cf. III, 2, 15.

The next difficulty is the exact meaning of vi*s*vá-*k*arsha*n*i, and such cognate words as vi*s*vá-k*r*ish*t*i, vi*s*vá-manusha. The only intelligible meaning I can suggest for these words is, known to all men; originally, belonging to, reaching to all men; as we say, world-wide or European fame, meaning by it fame extending over the whole of Europe, or over the whole world. If Indra, Agni, and the Maruts are called by these names, they mean, as far as I can judge, known, worshipped by all men. Benfey translates allverständig.

Verse 15.

Note 1. *Ri*ti, the first element of *ri*ti-sáham, never occurs by itself in the Rig-veda. It comes from the root ar, to hurt, which was mentioned before (p. 65) in connection with ár-van, hurting, árus, wound, and ári, enemy. Sám-*ri*ti occurs I, 32, 6. *Ri*ti therefore means hurting, and *ri*ti-sáh means one who can stand an attack. In our passage rayím vîrá-vantam *ri*ti-sáham means really wealth consisting in men who are able to withstand all onslaughts.

The word is used in a similar sense, VI, 14, 4:

agní*h* apsấm *ri*ti-sáham vîrám dadâti sát-patim, yásya trásanti *s*ávasa*h* sam-*k*ákshi *s*átrava*h* bhiyấ.

Agni gives a strong son who is able to withstand all onslaughts, from fear of whose strength the enemies tremble when they see him.

In other passages *ri*ti-sáh is applied to Indra:

VIII, 45, 35. bibháya hí tvấ-vata*h* ugrất abhi-prabhaṅgína*h* dasmất ahám *ri*ti-sáha*h*.

For I stand in fear of a powerful man like thee, of one who crushes his enemies, who is strong and withstands all onslaughts.

VIII, 68, 1. tuvi-kûrmím *ri*ti-sáham índra *s*ávish*th*a sát-pate.

Thee, O most powerful Indra, of mighty strength, able to withstand all onslaughts.

VIII, 88, 1. tám va*h* dasmám *ri*ti-sáham—índram gî*h*-bhí*h* navâmahe.

We call Indra the strong, the resisting, with our songs.

Note 2. The last sentence finishes six of the hymns ascribed to Nodhas. It is more appropriate in a hymn addressed to single deities, such as Agni or Indra, than in a hymn to the Maruts. We must supply *s*ardha, in order to get a collective word in the masculine singular.

Nú, as usual, should be scanned nū̆.

Note 3. Dhiyấ-vasu, as an epithet of the gods, means rich in prayers, i. e. invoked by many worshippers. It does not occur frequently. Besides the hymns of Nodhas, it only occurs independently in I, 3, 10 (Sarasvatî), III, 3, 2, III, 28, 1 (Agni), these hymns being all ascribed to the family of Visvâmitra. In the last verse, which forms the burden of the hymns of Nodhas, it may have been intended to mean, he who is rich through the hymn just recited, or he who rejoices in the hymn, the god to whom it is addressed.

Nodhas, the poet, belongs, according to the Anukramanî, to the family of Gotama, and in the hymns which are ascribed to him, I, 58–64, the Gotamas are mentioned several times:

I, 60, 5. tám tvâ vayám pátim agne rayînâm prá samsâmah matí-bhih gótamâsah.

We, the Gotamas, praise thee with hymns, Agni, the lord of treasures.

I, 61, 16. evá te hâri-yogana su-vriktí índra bráhmâni gótamâsah akran.

Truly the Gotamas made holy prayers for thee, O Indra with brilliant horses! See also I, 63, 9.

In one passage Nodhas himself is called Gotama:

I, 62, 13. sanâ-yaté gótamah indra návyam
átakshat bráhma hari-yóganâya,
su-nîthấya nah savasâna nodhấh—
prâtáh makshú dhiyấ-vasuh gagamyât.

Gotama made a new song for the old (god) with brilliant horses, O Indra! May Nodhas be a good leader to us, O powerful Indra! May he who is rich in prayers (Indra) come early and soon!

I feel justified therefore in following the Anukramanî and taking Nodhas as a proper name. It occurs so again in

I, 61, 14. sadyáh bhuvat vîryấya nodhấh.

May Nodhas quickly attain to power!

In I, 124, 4. nodhấh-iva may mean like Nodhas, but more likely it has the general meaning of poet.

MA*ND*ALA I, HYMN 85.

ASHT*A*KÂ I, ADHYÂYA 6, VARGA 9-10.

To the Maruts (the Storm-gods).

1. Those who glance forth like wives and yoke-fellows [1], the powerful sons of Rudra on their way, they, the Maruts, have indeed made heaven and earth to grow [2]; they, the strong and wild, delight in the sacrifices.

2. When grown up [1], they attained to greatness; the Rudras have established their seat in the sky. While singing their song and increasing their vigour, the sons of P*ri*s*n*i have clothed themselves in beauty [2].

3. When these sons of the cow (P*ri*s*n*i) [1] adorn themselves with glittering ornaments, the brilliant [2] ones put bright weapons on their bodies [3]. They drive away every adversary [4]; fatness (rain) streams along their paths;—

4. When you [1], the powerful, who shine with your spears, shaking even what is unshakable by strength,—when you, O Maruts, the manly hosts [2], had yoked the spotted deer, swift as thought, to your chariots;—

5. When you had yoked the spotted deer before your chariots, hurling [1] the stone (thunderbolt) in the fight, then the streams of the red-(horse) [2] rush forth: like a skin [3] with water they water the earth.

6. May the swiftly-gliding, swift-winged horses carry you hither! Come forth with your arms [1]! Sit down on the grass-pile; a wide seat has been made for you. Rejoice, O Maruts, in the sweet food [2].

7. Strong in themselves, they grew[1] with might; they stepped to the firmament, they made their seat wide. When Vish*n*u[2] saved the enrapturing Soma, the Maruts sat down like birds on their beloved altar.

8. Like[1] heroes indeed thirsting for fight they rush about; like combatants eager for glory they have striven in battles. All beings are afraid of the Maruts; they are men terrible to behold, like kings.

9. When the clever Tvash*t*ar[1] had turned the well-made, golden, thousand-edged thunderbolt, Indra takes it to perform his manly deeds[2]; he slew V*ri*tra, he forced out the stream of water.

10. By their power they pushed the well[1] aloft, they clove asunder the rock (cloud), however strong. Blowing forth their voice[2] the bounteous Maruts performed, while drunk of Soma, their glorious deeds.

11. They pushed the well (cloud) athwart this way, they poured out the spring to the thirsty Gotama. The Maruts with beautiful splendour approach him with help, they in their own ways satisfied the desire of the sage.

12. The shelters which you have for him who praises you, grant them threefold[1] to the man who gives! Extend the same to us, O Maruts! Give us, ye heroes[2], wealth with valiant offspring!

NOTES.

This hymn is ascribed to Gotama. No verse of this hymn occurs in SV., VS.; verse 6=AV. XX, 13, 2; verse 7=TS. IV, 1, 11, 3; verse 12=TS. I, 5, 11, 5; TB. II, 8, 5, 6.

Verse 1.

Note 1. The phrase *g*ánaya*h* ná sáptaya*h* is obscure. As *g*áni has always the meaning of wife, and sápti in the singular, dual, and plural means horse, it might be supposed that *g*ánaya*h* could be connected with sáptaya*h*, so as to signify mares. But although *g*áni is coupled with patnî, I, 62, 10, in the sense of mother-wife, and though sápti is most commonly joined with some other name for horse, yet *g*ánaya*h* sáptaya*h* never occurs, for the simple reason that it would be too elaborate and almost absurd an expression for va*d*avâ*h*. We find sápti joined with vâ*g*ín, I, 162, 1; with ráthya, II, 31, 7; átyam ná sáptim, III, 22, 1; sáptî hárî, III, 35, 2; á*s*vâ sáptî-iva, VI, 59, 3.

We might then suppose the thought of the poet to have been this: What appears before us like race-horses, viz. the storms coursing through the sky, that is really the host of the Maruts. But then *g*ánaya*h* remains unexplained, and it is impossible to take *g*ánaya*h* ná sáptaya*h* as two similes, like unto horses, like unto wives.

I believe, therefore, that we must here take sápti in its original etymological sense, which would be ju-mentum, a yoked animal, a beast of draught, or rather a follower, a horse that will follow. Sápti, therefore, could never be a wild horse, but always a tamed horse, a horse that will go in harness. Cf. IX, 21, 4. hitâ*h* ná sáptaya*h* ráthe, like horses put to the chariot; or in the singular, IX, 70, 10. hitá*h* ná sápti*h*, like a harnessed horse. The root is sap, which in the Veda means to follow, to attend on, to worship. But if sápti means originally animals that will go together, it may in our passage have retained the sense of yoke-fellow (σύζυγος), and be intended as an adjective to *g*ánaya*h*, wives. There is at least one other passage where this meaning would seem to be more appropriate, viz.

VIII, 20, 23. yûyám sakhâya*h* saptaya*h*.

You (Maruts), friends and followers! or you, friends and comrades!

Here it is hardly possible to assign to sápti the sense of horse, for the Maruts, though likened to horses, are never thus barely invoked as saptaya*h*!

If then we translate, 'Those who glance forth like wives and yoke-fellows,' i.e. like wives of the same husband, the question still recurs how the simile holds good, and how the Maruts rushing forth together in all their beauty can be compared to wives. In answer to this we have to bear in mind that the idea of many wives belonging to one husband (sapatnî) is familiar to the Vedic poet, and that their impetuously rushing into the arms of their husbands, and appearing before them in all their beauty, are frequent images in their poetry. In such phrases as pátim ná *g*ánaya*h* and *g*ánayâ*h* ná gárbham, the *g*anis, the wives or mothers, are represented as running together after their husbands or children. This impetuous approach the poet may have wished to allude to in our passage also, but though it might have been understood at once by his hearers, it is almost impossible to convey this implied idea in any other language.

Wilson translates: 'The Maruts, who are going forth, decorate themselves like females: they are gliders (through the air), the sons of Rudra, and the doers of good works, by which they promote the welfare of earth and heaven. Heroes, who grind (the solid rocks), they delight in sacrifices.'

Ludwig translates: 'Die ganz besonders sich schmücken wie frauen, die renner, zu ihrem zuge,' &c. This is possible, yet the simile sounds somewhat forced.

Note 2. The meaning of this phrase, which occurs very frequently, was originally that the storms by driving away the dark clouds, made the earth and the sky to appear larger and wider. It afterwards takes a more general sense of increasing, strengthening, blessing.

Verse 2.

Note 1. Ukshitá is here a participle of vaksh or uksh, to grow, to wax; not of uksh, to sprinkle, to anoint, to inaugurate, as explained by Sâyana. Thus it is said of the Maruts, V, 55, 3. sâkám gâtấh—sâkám ukshitấh, born together, and grown up together.

Note 2. The same expression occurs VIII, 28, 5. saptó (íti) ádhi sríyah dhire. See also I, 116, 17; IX, 68, 1.

Verse 3.

Note 1. Gó-mâtri, like gó-gâta, a name of the Maruts, who are also called prísni-mâtarah, síndhu-mâtarah.

Note 2. Subhrá is applied to the Maruts, I, 19, 5. Otherwise, no doubt, it might refer, as Ludwig remarks, to virúkmatah, always supposing that virúkmat is a feminine. Whether tanûshu subhrâh can stand for tanûshu subhrâsu is more doubtful.

Note 3. Virúkmatah must be an accusative plural. It occurs I, 127, 3, as an epithet of ógas; VI, 49, 5, as an epithet of the chariot of the Asvins. In our place, however, it must be taken as a substantive, signifying something which the Maruts wear, probably armour or weapons. This follows chiefly from X, 138, 4. sátrûn asrinât virúkmatâ, Indra tore his enemies with the bright weapon. In VIII, 20, 11, where rukmá occurs as a masculine plural, ví bhrâgante rukmấsah ádhi bâhúshu, their bright things shine on their arms, it seems likewise to be meant for weapons; according to Sâyana, for chains. In V, 55, 3; X, 78, 3, the Maruts are called vi-rokínah, bright like the rays of the sun or the tongues of fire.

Note 4. Observe the short syllable in the tenth syllable of this Pâda; Benfey, Vedica, p. 124; Lanman, Noun-Inflection, pp. 378, 543.

Verse 4.

Note 1. The sudden transition from the third to the second person is not unusual in the Vedic hymns, the fact being that where we in a relative sentence should use the same person as that of the principal verb, the Vedic poets frequently use the third.

Note 2. V*ri*sha-vrâta is untranslatable for reasons stated p. 138 seq.; it means consisting of companies of v*ri*shans, in whatever sense that word be taken. Wilson in his translation mistakes á*k*yutâ for á*k*yutâ*h*, and vrâta for vrata. He translates the former by 'incapable of being overthrown,' the latter by 'entrusted with the duty of sending rain,' both against the authority of Sâya*n*a. V*ri*sha-vrăta occurs twice in the Rig-veda as an epithet of Soma only, IX, 62, 11; 64, 1.

Verse 5.

Note 1. If we take ádri for cloud, then ra*m*h might have the meaning of stirring up.

V, 32, 2. tvám utsán *ri*tú-bhi*h* badbadhânâñ ára*m*ha*h*.

Thou madest the springs to run that had been shut up by the seasons.

VIII, 19, 6. tásya ít árvanta*h* ra*m*hayante âsáva*h*.

His horses only run quick.

But ádri often means stone, in the sense of weapon, or bolt (cf. adriva*h*, voc., wielder of the thunderbolt), and ra*m*hayati would then have the meaning of hurling. This is the meaning adopted by Benfey and Ludwig.

Note 2. The red may be the dark red cloud, but arushá has almost become a proper name, and its original meaning of redness is forgotten. Nay, it is possible that arushá, as applied to the same power of darkness which is best known by the names of Vritra, Dasyu, &c., may never have had the sense of redness, but been formed straight from ar, to hurt, from which arvan, arus, &c. (see p. 65 seq.). It would then mean simply the hurter, the enemy. It is possible also to take arushá in the sense of the red horse, the leader between the two Haris, when we ought to remember that the Maruts pour forth the streams of the stallion, RV. V, 83, 6. prá pinvata v*ri*sh*n*a*h* ásvasya dhârâ*h*, and that they lead about the horse to make it rain, RV. I, 64, 6. átyam ná mihé ví nayanti vâgínam.

Note 3. Sâya*n*a explains: 'They moisten the whole earth like a hide,' a hide representing a small surface which is watered without great effort. Wilson: 'They moisten the earth, like a hide, with water.' Langlois: 'Alors les gouttes d'eau, perçant comme la peau de ce (nuage) bienfaisant viennent inonder la terre.' Benfey: 'Dann stürzen reichlich aus der rothen (Gewitterwolke) Tropfen, mit Fluth wie eine Haut die Erde netzend. (Dass die Erde so durchnässt wird, wie durchregnetes Leder.)' If the poet had intended to compare the earth, before it is moistened by rain, to a hide, he might have had in his mind the dryness of a tanned skin, or, as Professor Benfey says, of leather. If, on the contrary, the simile refers to the streams of water, then *k*árma-iva, like a skin, might either be taken in the technical acceptation of the skin through which, at the preparation of the Soma, the streams (dhârâ*h*) of that beverage are squeezed and distilled, or we may take the word in the more general sense of water-skin. In that case the comparison, though not very pointedly expressed, as it would have been by later Sanskrit poets, would still be complete. The streams of the red-(horse), i. e. of the cloud, rush forth, and they, whether the streams liberated by the Maruts, or the Maruts themselves, moisten the earth with water, like a skin, i. e. like a skin in which water is kept and from which it is poured out. The cloud itself being called a skin by Vedic poets (I, 129, 3) makes the comparison still more natural.

One other explanation might suggest itself, if the singular of *k*árma should be considered objectionable on account of the plural of the verb. Vedic poets speak of the skin of the earth. Thus:

X, 68, 4. bhū́myâ*h* udnā́-iva ví tvá*k*am bibheda.

He (B*ri*haspati) having driven the cows from the cave, cut the skin of the earth, as it were, with water, i. e. saturated it with rain.

The construction, however, if we took *k*árma in the sense of surface, would be very irregular, and we should have to translate: They moisten the earth with water like a skin, i. e. skin-deep.

We ought to scan *k*armevodabhi*h* vi undanti bhûma for *k*armeva udabhi*h* vyundanti bhûma would give an unusual cæsura.

Verse 6.

Note 1. AV. XX, 13, 2. With your arms, i.e. according to Sâya*n*a, with armfuls of gifts. Though this expression does not occur again so baldly, we read I, 166, 10, of the Maruts, that there are many gifts in their strong arms, bhûri*n*i bhadrấ náryeshu bâhúshu; nor does bâhú, as used in the plural, as far as I am able to judge, ever convey any meaning but that of arms. The idea that the Maruts are carried along by their arms as by wings, does not rest on Vedic authority, otherwise we might join raghupátvâna*h* with bâhúbhi*h*, come forth swiftly flying on your arms! As it is, and with the accent on the antepenultimate, we must refer raghupâtvâna*h* to sáptaya*h*, horses.

Note 2. The sweet food is Soma.

Verse 7.

Note 1. The initial 'a' of avardhanta must be elided, or 'té a' be pronounced as two short syllables equal to one long.

Note 2. Taitt. S. IV, 1, 11, 3. Vish*n*u, whose character in the hymns of the Veda is very different from that assumed by him in later periods of Hindu religion, must here be taken as the friend and companion of Indra. Like the Maruts, he assisted Indra in his battle against V*ri*tra and the conquest of the clouds. When Indra was forsaken by all the gods, Vish*n*u came to his help.

IV, 18, 11. utá mâtấ mahishám ánu avenat amī́ (íti) tvâ *g*ahati putra devấ*h*,
átha abravît v*ri*trám índra*h* hanishyán sákhe vish*n*o (íti) vi-tarám ví kramasva.

The mother also called after the bull, these gods forsake thee, O son; then, when going to kill V*ri*tra, Indra said, Friend, Vish*n*u, step forward!

This stepping of Vish*n*u is emblematic of the rising, the culminating, and setting of the sun; and in VIII, 12, 27,

Vish*n*u is said to perform it through the power of Indra. In VI, 20, 2, Indra is said to have killed V*ri*tra, assisted by Vish*n*u (víshnunâ sa*k*ânâ*h*). Vish*n*u is therefore invoked together with Indra, VI, 69, 8; VII, 99; with the Maruts, V, 87; VII, 36, 9. In VII, 93, 8, Indra, Vish*n*u, and the Maruts are called upon together. Nay, mấruta, belonging to the Maruts, becomes actually an epithet of Vish*n*u, V, 46, 2. mấruta utá vish*n*o (íti); and in I, 156, 4. mấrutasya vedhásah has been pointed out by Roth as an appellation of Vish*n*u. The mention of Vish*n*u in our hymn is therefore by no means exceptional, but the whole purport of this verse is nevertheless very doubtful, chiefly owing to the fact that several of the words occurring in it lend themselves to different interpretations.

The translations of Wilson, Benfey, and others have not rendered the sense which the poet intends to describe at all clear. Wilson says: 'May they for whom Vish*n*u defends (the sacrifice), that bestows all desires and confers delight, come (quickly) like birds, and sit down upon the pleasant and sacred grass.' Benfey: 'Wenn Vish*n*u schützt den rauschtriefenden tropfenden (Soma), sitzen wie Vögel sie auf der geliebten Streu.' Langlois: 'Quand Vich*n*ou vient prendre sa part de nos enivrantes libations, eux, comme des oiseaux, arrivent aussi sur le cousa qui leur est cher.' Ludwig: 'Als Vish*n*u half dem zum rauschtrank eilenden stiere, setzten sie sich wie vögel aufs liebe barhis.'

Whence all these varieties? First, because ấvat may mean, he defended or protected, but likewise, it is supposed, he descried, became aware. Secondly, because *vri*shan is one of the most vague and hence most difficult words in the Veda, and may mean Indra, Soma, or the cloud: (see the note on V*ri*shan, p. 138.) Thirdly, because the adjective belonging to v*ri*shan, which generally helps us to determine which v*ri*shan is meant, is here itself of doubtful import, and certainly applicable to Indra as well as to Soma and the A*s*vins, possibly even to the cloud. Mada-*k*yút is readily explained by the commentators as bringing down pride, a meaning which the word might well have in modern Sanskrit, but which it clearly has not in the Veda. Even where the thunderbolt of Indra is called mada*k*yút, and where the meaning of 'bringing down pride' would seem most appropriate, we ought to translate 'wildly rushing down.'

VIII, 96, 5. ấ yát vágram bâhvó*h* indra dhátse mada-*k*yútam áhaye hántavaí û*m* (íti).

When thou tookest the wildly rushing thunderbolt in thy arms in order to slay Ahi.

When applied to the gods, the meaning of mada*k*yút is by no means certain. It might mean rushing about fiercely, reeling with delight, this delight being produced by the Soma, but it may also mean sending down delight, i. e. rain or Soma. The root *k*yu is particularly applicable to the sending down of rain; cf. Taitt. Sa*m*h. II, 4, 9, 2; 10, 3; III, 3, 4, 1; and Indra and his horses, to whom this epithet is chiefly applied, are frequently asked to send down rain. However, mada*k*yút is also applied to real horses (I, 126, 4) where givers of rain would be an inappropriate epithet. I should therefore translate mada*k*yút, when applied to Indra, to his horses, to the A*s*vins, or to horses in general by furiously or wildly moving about, as if 'made or madena *k*yavate,' he moves in a state of delight, or in a state of intoxication, such as was not incompatible with the character of the ancient gods. Here again the difficulty of rendering Vedic thought in English, or any other modern language, becomes apparent, for we have no poetical word to express a high state of mental excitement produced by drinking the intoxicating juice of the Soma or other plants, which has not something opprobrious mixed up with it, while in ancient times that state of excitement was celebrated as a blessing of the gods, as not unworthy of the gods themselves, nay, as a state in which both the warrior and the poet would perform their highest achievements. The German Rausch is the nearest approach to the Sanskrit mada.

VIII, 1, 21. ví*s*veshâm tarutấram mada-*k*yútam máde hí sma dádâti na*h*.

Indra, the conqueror of all, who rushes about in rapture, for in rapture he bestows gifts upon us. Cf. I, 51, 2.

The horses of Indra are called mada*k*yút, I, 81, 3; VIII, 33, 18; 34, 9. Ordinary horses, I, 126, 4.

It is more surprising to see this epithet applied to the A*s*vins, who are generally represented as moving about with exemplary steadiness. However we read:

VIII, 22, 16. mána*h*-*g*avasấ v*ri*sha*n*ấ mada-*k*yutấ.

Ye two A*s*vins, quick as thought, powerful, wildly moving; or, as Sâya*n*a proposes, liberal givers, humblers of your enemies. See also VIII, 35, 19.

Most frequently mada*k*yút is applied to Soma, X, 30, 9; IX, 32, 1; 53, 4; 79, 2; 108, 11; where particularly the last passage deserves attention, in which Soma is called mada-*k*yútam sahásra-dhâram v*ri*shabhám.

Lastly, even the wealth itself which the Maruts are asked to send down from heaven, most likely rain, is called, VIII, 7, 13, rayím mada-*k*yútam puru-kshúm visva-dhâyasam.

In all these passages we must translate mada-*k*yút by bringing delight, showering down delight.

We have thus arrived at the conclusion that v*rí*sha*n*am mada-*k*yútam, as used in our passage I, 85, 7, might be meant either for Indra or for Soma. If the A*s*vins can be called v*rí*sha*n*au mada-*k*yútâ, the same expression would be even more applicable to Indra. On the other hand, if Soma is called v*ri*shabhá*h* mada-*k*yút, the same Soma may legitimately be called v*rí*shâ mada-*k*yút. In deciding whether Indra or Soma be meant, we must now have recourse to other hymns, in which the relations of the Maruts with Vish*n*u, Soma, and Indra are alluded to.

If Indra were intended, and if the first words meant 'When Vish*n*u perceived the approach of Indra,' we should expect, not that the Maruts sat down on the sacrificial pile, but that they rushed to the battle. The idea that the Maruts come to the sacrifice, like birds, is common enough:

VIII, 20, 10. v*ri*sha*n*a*s*véna maruta*h* v*rí*sha-psunâ ráthena v*rí*sha-nâbhinâ, ấ *s*yenấsa*h* ná pakshí*n*a*h* v*rí*thâ nara*h* havyấ na*h* vîtáye gata.

Come ye Maruts together, to eat our offerings, on your

strong-horsed, strong-shaped, strong-naved chariot, like winged hawks!

But when the Maruts thus come to a sacrifice it is to participate in it, and particularly in the Soma that is offered by the sacrificer. This Soma, it is said in other hymns, was prepared by Vish*n*u for Indra (II, 22, 1), and Vish*n*u is said to have brought the Soma for Indra (X, 113, 2). If we keep these and similar passages in mind, and consider that in the preceding verse the Maruts have been invited to sit down on the sacrificial pile and to rejoice in the sweet food, we shall see that the same train of thought is carried on in our verse, the only new idea being that the saving or, possibly, the descrying of the Soma is ascribed to Vish*n*u. See, however, Bergaigne, Journ. Asiat. 1884, p 472.

Verse 8.

Note 1. On na and iva together, see Bollensen, Orient und Occident, II, 470.

Verse 9.

Note 1. Tvásh*t*ar, the workman of the gods, frequently also the fashioner and creator.

Note 2. Nári, the loc. sing. of n*ri*, but, if so, with a wrong accent, occurs only in this phrase as used here, and as repeated in VIII, 96, 19. nári ápâ*m*si kártâ sá*h* v*ri*trahấ. Its meaning is not clear. It can hardly mean 'on man,' without some more definite application. If n*ri* could be used as a name of V*ri*tra or any other enemy, it would mean, to do his deeds against the man, on the enemy. N*ri*, however, is ordinarily an honorific term, chiefly applied to Indra, IV, 25, 4. náre náryâya n*rí*-tamâya n*rin*ấm, and hence its application to V*ri*tra would be objectionable. Sâya*n*a explains it in the sense of battle. I believe that nári stands for náryâ, the acc. plur. neut. of nárya, manly, and the frequent epithet of ápas, and I have translated accordingly. Indra is called nárya-apas, VIII, 93, 1. See also Kuhn's Zeitschrift, vol. xxv, p. 601.

Verse 10.

Note 1. Avatá, a well, here meant for cloud, like útsa, I, 64, 6.

Note 2. Dhámanta*h* vâ*n*ám is translated by Sâya*n*a as playing on the lyre, by Benfey as blowing the flute. Such a rendering, particularly the latter, would be very appropriate, but there is no authority for vâ*n*á meaning either lyre or flute in the Veda. Vâ*n*á occurs five times only. In one passage, VIII, 20, 8. góbhi*h* vâ*n*á*h* agyate, it means arrow; the arrow is sent forth from the bow-strings. The same meaning seems applicable to IX, 50, 1. vâ*n*ásya *k*odaya pavím. In another passage, IX, 97, 8. prá vadanti vâ*n*ám, they send forth their voice, is applied to the Maruts, as in our passage; in IV, 24, 9, the sense is doubtful, but here too vâ*n*á clearly does not mean a musical instrument. See III, 30, 10. Spiegel compares the Huzvaresh and Armenian vâng (Pers. bânig), voice. M. Senart (Journal Asiatique, 1874, p. 281) is in favour of taking vâ*n*a for flute.

Verse 12.

Note 1. In the Taitt. S. I, 5, 11, we have *s*a*s*amânâya, and in the Taitt. Br. II, 8, 5, 6, *s*a*m*s*s*amânâya, but Sâya*n*a explains *s*a*s*amânâya, *s*a*ms*ana*m* kurvate. He explains tridhâtûni by a*s*anam, pânam, khâdanam.

V*ri*shan.

Note 2. In v*ri*shan we have one of those words which it is almost impossible to translate accurately. It occurs over and over again in the Vedic hymns, and if we once know the various ideas which it either expresses or implies, we have little difficulty in understanding its import in a vague and general way, though we look in vain for corresponding terms in any modern language. In the Veda, and in ancient languages generally, one and the same word is frequently made to do service for many. Words retain their general meaning, though at the same time they are evidently used with a definite purpose. This is not only a peculiar phase of language, but a peculiar phase of thought, and as to us this phase has become strange and unreal, it is very difficult to transport ourselves back into it, still more to translate the pregnant terms of the Vedic poets into the definite languages which we have to use. Let us imagine a state of thought and speech in which virtus still meant manliness, though it might also be applied to the virtue of a woman; or let us try to speak and think a language which expressed the bright and the divine, the brilliant and the beautiful, the straight and the right, the bull and the hero, the shepherd and the king by the same terms, and we shall see how difficult it would be to translate such terms without losing either the key-note that was still sounding, or the harmonics which were set vibrating by it in the minds of the poets and their listeners.

I. V*ri*shan, male.

V*ri*shan, being derived from a root v*ri*sh, spargere, meant no doubt originally the male, whether applied to animals or men. In this sense v*ri*shan occurs frequently in the Veda, either as determining the sex of the animal which is mentioned, or as standing by itself and meaning the male. In either case, however, it implies the idea of strength and eminence, which we lose whether we translate it by man or male.

Thus á*s*va is horse, but VII, 69, 1, we read:

ẫ vâm rátha*h*—v*rí*sha-bhi*h* yâtu á*s*vai*h*.

May your chariot come near with powerful horses, i. e. with stallions.

The Háris, the horses of Indra, are frequently called v*rí*sha*n*â:

I, 177, 1. yuktvẫ hárî (íti) v*rí*sha*n*â.

Having yoked the bay stallions.

V*ri*shabhá, though itself originally meaning the male animal, had become fixed as the name of the bull, and in this process it had lost so much of its etymological import that the Vedic poet did not hesitate to define v*ri*shabhá itself by the addition of v*rí*shan. Thus we find:

VIII, 93, 7. sá*h* v*rí*shâ v*ri*shabhá*h* bhuvat.

May he (Indra) be a strong bull.

I, 54, 2. v*rí*shâ v*ri*sha-tvẫ v*ri*shabhá*h*.

Indra by his strength a strong bull; but, literally, Indra by his manliness a male bull.

Even v*ri*shabhá loses again its definite meaning; and as

bull in bull-calf means simply male, or in bull-trout, large, so v*ri*shabhá is added to átya, horse, to convey the meaning of large or powerful:

I, 177, 2. yé te v*rí*sha*n*a*h* v*ri*shabhẫsa*h* indra—átyâ*h*.

Thy strong and powerful horses; literally, thy male bull-horses.

When v*rí*shan and v*ri*shabhá are used as adjectives, for instance with *s*úshma, strength, they hardly differ in meaning:

VI, 19, 8. ẫ na*h* bhara v*rí*sha*n*am *s*úshmam indra.

Bring us thy manly strength, O Indra.

And in the next verse:

VI, 19, 9. ẫ te *s*úshma*h* v*ri*shabhá*h* etu.

May thy manly strength come near.

Vá*m*saga, too, which is clearly the name for bull, is defined by v*rí*shan, I, 7, 8:

v*rí*shâ yûthẫ-iva vá*m*saga*h*.

As the strong bull scares the herds.

The same applies to varẫha, which, though by itself meaning boar, is determined again by v*rí*shan:

X, 67, 7. v*rí*sha-bhi*h* varẫhai*h*.

With strong boars.

In III, 2, 11, we read:

v*rí*shâ—nẫnadat ná si*m*há*h*.

Like a roaring lion.

If used by itself, v*rí*shan, at least in the Rig-veda, can hardly be said to be the name of any special animal, though in later Sanskrit it may mean bull or horse. Thus if we read, X, 43, 8, v*rí*shâ ná kruddhá*h*, we can only translate like an angry male, though, no doubt, like a wild bull, would seem more appropriate.

I, 186, 5. yéna nápâtam apẫm *g*unẫma mana*h*-*g*úva*h* v*rí*sha*n*a*h* yám váhanti.

That we may excite the son of the water (Agni), whom the males, quick as thought, carry along.

Here the males are no doubt the horses or stallions of Agni. But, though this follows from the context, it would be wrong to say that v*rí*shan by itself means horse.

If used by itself, v*r*íshan most frequently means man, and chiefly in his sexual character. Thus:

I, 140, 6. v*r*íshâ-iva pátnî*h* abhí eti róruvat.

Agni comes roaring like a husband to his wives.

I, 179, 1. ápi ûm (íti) nú pátnî*h* v*r*íshana*h* *g*agamyu*h*.

Will the husbands now come to their wives?

II, 16, 8. sak*r*ít sú te sumatí-bhi*h*—sám pátnîbhi*h* ná v*r*íshana*h* nasîmahi.

May we for once cling firmly to thy blessings, as husbands cling to their wives.

V, 47, 6. upa-prakshé v*r*íshana*h* módamânâ*h* divá*h* pathẫ vadhvẫ*h* yanti á*kkh*a.

The exulting men come for the embrace on the path of heaven towards their wives.

In one or two passages v*r*íshan would seem to have a still more definite meaning, particularly in the formula sû̃ra*h* d*r*̃*s*îke v*r*íshana*h* *k*a paú*m*sye, which occurs IV, 41, 6; X, 92, 7. See also I, 179, 1.

In all the passages which we have hitherto examined v*r*íshan clearly retained its etymological meaning, though even then it was not always possible to translate it by male.

The same meaning has been retained in other languages in which this word can be traced. Thus, in Zend, arshan (the later gushan) is used to express the sex of animals in such expressions as a*s*pahé arshnô, gen. a male horse; varâzahe arshnô, gen. a male boar; géus arshnô, gen. a male ox; but likewise in the sense of man or hero, as arsha hu*s*rava, the hero Hu*s*rava. In Greek we find ἄρσην and ἄῤῥην used in the same way to distinguish the sex of animals, as ἄρσενες ἵπποι, βοῦν ἄρσενα. In Latin the same word may be recognised in the proper name Varro, and in vâro and bâro.

We now come to another class of passages in which v*r*íshan is clearly intended to express more than merely the masculine gender. In some of them the etymological meaning of spargere, to pour forth, seems to come out again, and it is well known that Indian commentators are very fond of explaining v*r*íshan by giver of rain, giver of good gifts, bounteous. The first of these meanings may indeed be admitted in certain passages, but in others it is more than doubtful.

II. *Vrí*shan, fertilising.

I, 181, 8. *vrí*shâ vâm meghâ*h* may be translated, your raining cloud.

I, 129, 3. dasmá*h* hí sma *vrí*sha*n*am pinvasi tvá*k*am.

Thou art strong, thou fillest the rainy skin, i. e. the cloud.

See also IV, 22, 6; and possibly V, 83, 6.

It may be that, when applied to Soma too, *vrí*shan retained something of its etymological meaning, that it meant gushing forth, poured out, though in many places it is impossible to render *vrí*shan, as applied to Soma, by anything but strong. All we can admit is that *vrí*shan, if translated by strong, means also strengthening and invigorating, an idea not entirely absent even in our expression, a strong drink.

III. *Vrí*shan, strong.

I, 80, 2. sá*h* tvâ amadat *vrí*shâ máda*h*, sóma*h*—sutá*h*.

This strong draught inspirited thee, the poured out Soma-juice.

I, 91, 2. tvám *vrí*shâ *vri*sha-tvébhi*h*.

Thou, Soma, art strong by strength.

I, 175, 1. *vrí*shâ te *vrí*sh*n*e índu*h* vâ*g*î sahasra-sâtama*h*.

For thee, the strong one, there is strong drink, powerful, omnipotent.

In the ninth Ma*nd*ala, specially dedicated to the praises of Soma, the inspiriting beverage of gods and men, the repetition of *vrí*shan, as applied to the juice and to the god who drinks it, is constant. Indo *vrí*shâ or *vrí*shâ indo are incessant invocations, and become at last perfectly meaningless.

IV. *Vrí*shan, epitheton ornans.

There can be no doubt, in fact, that already in the hymns of the Veda, *vrí*shan had dwindled away to a mere epitheton ornans, and that in order to understand it correctly, we must, as much as possible, forget its etymological colouring, and render it by hero or strong. Indra, Agni, the A*s*vins, Vish*n*u, the *Ri*bhus (IV, 35, 6), all are v*rí*shan, which means no longer male, but manly, strong.

In the following passages v*rí*shan is thus applied to Indra:

I, 54, 2. yá*h* dh*ri*sh*n*únâ *s*ávasâ ródasî (íti) ubhé (íti) v*rí*shâ v*ri*sha-tvắ v*ri*shabhá*h* ni-*riñg*áte.

(Praise Indra) who by his daring strength conquers both heaven and earth, a bull, strong in strength.

I, 100, 1. sá*h* yá*h* v*rí*shâ v*rí*sh*n*yebhi*h* sám-okâ*h* mahá*h* divá*h* p*ri*thivyắ*h* *k*a sam-rắ*t* satînâ-satvâ hávya*h* bháreshu marútvân na*h* bhavatu índra*h* ûtî́.

He who is strong, wedded to strength, who is the king of the great sky and the earth, of mighty might, to be invoked in battles,—may Indra with the Maruts come to our help!

I, 16, 1. ắ tvâ vahantu háraya*h* v*rí*sha*n*am sóma-pîtaye, índra tvâ sû́ra-*k*akshasa*h*.

May the bays bring thee hither, the strong one, to the Soma-draught, may the sunny-eyed horses (bring) thee, O Indra!

IV, 16, 20. evá ít índrâya v*ri*shabhắya v*rí*sh*n*e bráhma akarma bh*rí*gava*h* ná rátham.

Thus we have made a hymn for Indra, the strong bull, as the Bh*ri*gus make a chariot.

X, 153, 2. tvám v*ri*shan v*rí*shâ ít asi.

Thou, O hero, art indeed a hero; and not, Thou, O male, art indeed a male; still less, Thou, O bull, art indeed a bull.

I, 101, 1. avasyáva*h* v*rí*sha*n*am vá*g*ra-dakshi*n*am marútvantam sakhyắya havâmahe.

Longing for help we call as our friend the hero who wields the thunderbolt, who is accompanied by the Maruts.

VIII, 6, 14. ní *s*úsh*n*e indra dhar*n*asím vá*g*ram *g*aghantha dásyavi, v*rí*shâ hí ugra *s*r*in*vishé.

Thou, O Indra, hast struck the strong thunderbolt against *S*ush*n*a, the fiend; for, terrible one, thou art called hero!

VIII, 6, 40. vav*ri*dhâná*h* úpa dyávi v*rí*shâ va*g*rî́ aroravît, v*ri*tra-hắ soma-pắtama*h*.

Growing up by day, the hero with the thunderbolt has roared, the V*ri*tra-killer, the great Soma-drinker.

V, 35, 4. v*rí*shâ hí ási rấdhase *g*a*gñ*ishé v*rí*sh*n*i te *s*áva*h*.

Thou (Indra) art a hero, thou wast born to be bounteous; in thee, the hero, there is might.

V. Várshish*th*a, strongest, best, oldest.

It is curious to watch the last stage of the meaning of v*rí*shan in the comparative and superlative várshîyas and várshish*th*a. In the Veda, várshish*th*a still means excellent, but in later Sanskrit it is considered as the superlative of v*ri*ddha, old, so that we see v*rí*shan, from meaning originally manly, vigorous, young, assuming in the end the meaning of old. (M. M., Sanskrit Grammar, § 252.)

Yet even thus, when v*rí*shan means simply strong or hero, its sexual sense is not always forgotten, and it breaks out, for instance, in such passages as,

I, 32, 7. v*rí*sh*n*a*h* vádhri*h* prati-mấnam búbhûshan puru-trấ v*ri*trá*h* a*s*ayat ví-asta*h*.

V*ri*tra, the eunuch, trying to be like unto a man (like unto Indra), was lying, broken to many pieces.

The next passages show v*rí*shan as applied to Agni:

III, 27, 15. v*rí*sha*n*am tvâ vayám v*ri*shan v*rí*sha*n*a*h* sám idhîmahi.

O, strong one, let us the strong ones kindle thee, the strong!

V, 1, 12. ávo*k*âma kaváye médhyâya vá*k*a*h* vandấru v*ri*-shabhấya v*rí*sh*n*e.

We have spoken an adoring speech for the worshipful poet, for the strong bull (Agni).

Vish*n*u is called v*rí*shan, I, 154, 3:

prá vísh*n*ave *s*ûshám etu mánma giri-kshíte uru-gâyấya v*rí*sh*n*e.

May this hymn go forth to Vish*n*u, he who dwells in the mountain (cloud), who strides wide, the hero!

Rudra is called v*rí*shan:

II, 34, 2. rudrá*h* yát va*h* maruta*h* rukma-vakshasa*h* v*rí*shâ *g*ani p*rí*snyâ*h* *s*ukré ū́dhani.

When Rudra, the strong man, begat you, O Maruts with

bright ornaments on your chests, in the bright lap of Prisni.

That the Maruts, the sons of Rudra, are called vríshan, we have seen before, and shall see frequently again (I, 165, 1; II, 33, 13; VII, 56, 20; 21; 58, 6). The whole company of the Maruts is called vríshâ ganáh, the strong or manly host, i. e. the host of the Maruts, without any further qualification.

VI. Vríshan, name of various deities.

Here lies, indeed, the chief difficulty which is raised by the common use of vríshan in the Veda, that when it occurs by itself, it often remains doubtful who is meant by it, Indra, or Soma, or the Maruts, or some other deity. We shall examine a few of these passages, and first some where vríshan refers to Indra:

IV, 30, 10. ápa ushấh ánasah sarat sám-pishtât áha bibhyúshî, ní yát sîm sisnáthat vríshâ.

Ushas went away from her broken chariot, fearing lest the hero should do her violence.

Here vríshan is clearly meant for Indra, who, as we learn from the preceding verse, was trying to conquer Ushas, as Apollo did Daphne; and it should be observed that the word itself, by which Indra is here designated, is particularly appropriate to the circumstanccs.

I, 103, 6. bhū́ri-karmane vríshabhấya vríshne satyá-sushmâya sunavâma sómam, yáh â-drítya paripanthî́-iva sū́rah áyagvanah vi-bhágan éti védah.

Let us pour out the Soma for the strong bull, the performer of many exploits, whose strength is true, the hero who, watching like a footpad, comes to us dividing the wealth of the infidel.

Here it is clear again from the context that Indra only can be meant.

But in other passages this is more doubtful:

III, 61, 7. ritásya budhné ushásâm ishanyán vríshâ mahî́ (íti) ródasî (íti) ấ vivesa.

The hero in the depth of the heaven, yearning for the dawns, has entered the great sky and the earth.

The hero who yearns for the dawns, is generally Indra; here, however, considering that Agni is mentioned in the preceding verse, it is more likely that this god, as the light of the morning, may have been meant by the poet. That Agni, too, may be called v*ri*shan, without any other epithet to show that he is meant rather than any other god, is clear from such passages as,

VI, 3, 7. v*rí*shâ rukshá*h* óshadhîshu nûnot.

He the wild hero shouted among the plants.

In VII, 60, 9, v*ri*sha*n*au, the dual, is meant for Mitra and Varu*n*a; in the next verse, v*ri*sha*n*a*h*, the plural, must mean the same gods and their companions.

That Soma is called simply v*ri*shan, not only in the ninth Ma*nd*ala, but elsewhere, too, we see from such passages as,

III, 43, 7. índra píba v*rí*sha-dhûtasya v*rí*sh*n*a*h* (ấ yám te *s*yená*h* u*s*até *g*abhấra), yásya máde *k*yaváyasi prá k*r*ish*tî́h* yásya máde ápa gotrấ vavártha.

Indra drink of the male (the strong Soma), bruised by the males (the heavy stones), inspirited by whom thou makest the people fall down, inspirited by whom thou hast opened the stables.

Here Sâya*n*a, too, sees rightly that 'the male bruised by the males' is the Soma-plant, which, in order to yield the intoxicating juice, has to be bruised by stones, which stones are again likened to two males. But unless the words, enclosed in brackets, had stood in the text, words which clearly point to Soma, I doubt whether Sâya*n*a would have so readily admitted the definite meaning of v*ri*shan as Soma.

I, 109, 3. mấ *kh*edma ra*s*mî́n íti nấdhamânâ*h* pit*rî*n*ấ*m *s*aktî́*h* anu-yá*kkh*amânâ*h*, indrâgní-bhyâm kám v*rí*sha*n*a*h* madanti tấ hí ádrî (íti) dhishá*n*âyâ*h* upá-sthe.

We pray, let us not break the cords (which, by means of the sacrifices offered by each generation of our forefathers, unite us with the gods); we strive after the powers of our fathers. The Somas rejoice for Indra and Agni; for the two stones are in the lap of the vessel.

First, as to the construction, the fact that participles are thus used as finite verbs, and particularly when the subject changes in the next sentence, is proved by other passages, such as II, 11, 4. The sense is that the new generation does not break the sacrificial succession, but offers Soma, like their fathers. The Soma-plants are ready, and, when pressed by two stones, their juice flows into the Soma-vessel. There may be a double entendre in dhishá*n*âyâ*h* upá-sthe, which Sanskrit scholars will easily perceive.

When v*ri*shan is thus used by itself, we must be chiefly guided by the adjectives or other indications before we determine on the most plausible translation. Thus we read:

I, 55, 4. sá*h* ít váne namasyú-bhi*h* va*k*asyate *k*ắru *g*áneshu pra-bruvâ*n*á*h* indriyám, v*ri*shâ *kh*ándu*h* bhavati haryatá*h* v*ri*shâ kshéme*n*a dhénâm maghá-vâ yát ínvati.

In the first verse the subject may be Indra or Soma: 'He alone is praised by worshippers in the forest (or in the wooden vessel), he who shows forth among men his fair power.' But who is meant to be the subject of the next verse? Even Sâya*n*a is doubtful. He translates first: 'The bounteous excites the man who wishes to sacrifice; when the sacrificer, the rich, by the protection of Indra, stirs up his voice.' But he allows an optional translation for the last sentences: 'when the powerful male, Indra, by his enduring mind reaches the praise offered by the sacrificer.'

According to these suggestions, WILSON translated: He (Indra) is the granter of their wishes (to those who solicit him); he is the encourager of those who desire to worship (him), when the wealthy offerer of oblations, enjoying his protection, recites his praise.

BENFEY: The bull becomes friendly, the bull becomes desirable, when the sacrificer kindly advances praise.

LANGLOIS: When the noble Maghavan receives the homage of our hymns, his heart is flattered, and he responds to the wishes of his servant by his gifts.

As far as I know, the adjective *kh*ándu does not occur again, and can therefore give us no hint. But haryatá, which is applied to v*ri*shan in our verse, is the standing epithet of Soma. It means delicious, and occurs very frequently in the ninth Ma*nd*ala. It is likewise applied to Agni, Pûshan, the Haris, the thunderbolt, but wherever it occurs our first thought is of Soma. Thus, without quoting from the Soma-Ma*nd*ala, we read, X, 96, 1, haryatám mádam, the delicious draught, i. e. Soma.

X, 96, 9. pîtvā́ mádasya haryatásya ándhasa*h*, means having drunk of the draught of the delicious Soma.

VIII, 72, 18. padám haryatásya ni-dhânyā̂m, means the place where the delicious Soma resides.

III, 44, 1. haryatá*h* sóma*h*.

Delicious Soma.

II, 21, 1. bhara índrâya sómam ya*g*atā́ya haryatám.

Bring delicious Soma for the holy Indra.

I, 130, 2. mádâya haryatā́ya te tuví*h*-tamâya dhā́yase.

That thou mayest drink the delicious and most powerful draught, i. e. the Soma.

If, then, we know that v*r*íshan by itself is used in the sense of Soma, haryatá v*r*íshan can hardly be anything else. Va*k*asyate also is peculiar to Soma in the sense of murmuring, or as it were talking, and never occurs as a passive. I therefore should prefer to assign the whole verse to Soma, and translate: He indeed, when in the wooden vessel, talks with his worshippers, proclaiming his fair power among men; the strong Soma is pleasing, the strong Soma is delicious, when the sacrificer safely brings the cow, i. e. the milk to be mixed with the Soma.

That Indra was thirsting for Soma had been said in the second verse, and he is again called the Soma-drinker in the seventh verse. A verse dedicated to Soma therefore seems to come in quite naturally, though the Anukrama*n*î does not sanction it.

That the Maruts are called v*r*íshan, without further explanations, will appear from the following passages:

I, 85, 12. rayím na*h* dhatta v*r*isha*n*a*h* su-vī́ram.

Give us wealth, ye heroes, consisting of good offspring.

VIII, 96, 14. íshyâmi va*h* v*r*isha*n*a*h* yúdhyata â*g*aú.

I wish for you, heroes (Maruts), fight in the race!

In all the passages which we have hitherto examined, v*r*íshan was always applied to living beings, whether animals, men, or gods. But as, in Greek, ἄρσην means at last simply strong, and is applied, for instance, to the crash of the sea, κτύπος ἄρσην πόντου, so in the Veda v*r*ishan is applied to the roaring of the storms and similar objects.

V, 87, 5. svanáh v*r*íshâ.

Your powerful sound (O Maruts).

X, 47, 1. *g*ag*r*ibhmá te dákshi*n*am indra hástam vasuyáva*h* vasu-pate vásûnâm, vidmá hí tvâ gó-patim *s*ûra gónâm asmábhyam *k*itrám v*r*ísha*n*am rayím dâ*h*.

We have taken thy right hand, O Indra, wishing for treasures, treasurer of treasures, for we know thee, O hero, to be the lord of cattle; give us bright and strong wealth.

Should *k*itrá here refer to treasures, and v*r*íshan to cattle?

X, 89, 9. ní amítreshu vadhám indra túmram v*r*íshan v*r*íshâ*n*am arushám *s*i*s*îhi.

Whet, O hero, the heavy strong red weapon against the enemies.

The long â in v*r*íshâ*n*am is certainly startling, but it occurs once more, IX, 34, 3, where there can be no doubt that it is the accusative of v*r*íshan. Professor Roth takes v*r*íshan here in the sense of bull (s. v. tumra), but he does not translate the whole passage.

III, 29, 9. k*r*i*n*óta dhûmám v*r*ísha*n*am sakhâya*h*.

Make a mighty smoke, O friends!

Strength itself is called v*r*íshan, if I am right in translating the phrase v*r*ísha*n*am *s*úshmam by manly strength. It occurs,

IV, 24, 7. tásmin dadhat v*r*ísha*n*am *s*úshmam índra*h*.

Indra may give to him manly strength.

VI, 19, 8. ấ na*h* bhara v*r*ísha*n*am *s*ushmam indra.

Bring to us, O Indra, manly strength.

VII, 24, 4. asmé (íti) dádhat v*r*ísha*n*am *s*úshmam indra.

Giving to us, O Indra, manly strength.

See also VI, 19, 9, *s*úshma*h* v*r*ishabhá*h*, used in the same sense.

VII. V*r*íshan, general and empty term of praise.

This constant play on the word v*r*íshan, which we have observed in the passages hitherto examined, and which give by no means a full idea of the real frequency of its occurrence in the Veda, has evidently had its influence on the Vedic *Ri*shis, who occasionally seem to delight in the most silly and unmeaning repetitions of this word, and its compounds and derivatives. Here no language can supply any adequate translation; for though we may translate words which express thoughts, it is useless to attempt to render mere idle play with words. I shall give a few instances:

I, 177, 3. ắ tish*th*a rátham v*rí*sha*n*am v*rí*shâ te sutá*h* sóma*h* pári-siktâ mádhûni, yuktvắ v*rí*sha-bhyâm v*ri*shabha kshitînắm hári-bhyâm yâhi pra-vátâ úpa madrík.

Mount the strong car, the strong Soma is poured out for thee, sweets are sprinkled round; come down towards us, thou bull of men, with the strong bays, having yoked them.

But this is nothing yet compared to other passages, when the poet cannot get enough of v*rí*shan and v*ri*shabhá.

II, 16, 6. v*rí*shâ te vágra*h* utá te v*rí*shâ rátha*h* v*rí*sha*n*â hárî (íti) v*ri*shabhắ*n*i ắyudhâ, v*rí*sh*n*a*h* mádasya v*ri*shabha tvám îsishe índra sómasya v*ri*shabhásya t*ri*p*n*uhi.

Thy thunderbolt is strong, and thy car is strong, strong are the bays, the weapons are powerful, thou, bull, art lord of the strong draught, Indra rejoice in the powerful Soma!

V, 36, 5. v*rí*shâ tvâ v*rí*sha*n*am vardhatu dyaú*h* v*rí*shâ v*rí*sha-bhyâm vahase hári-bhyâm, sá*h* na*h* v*rí*shâ v*rí*sha-ratha*h* su-*s*ipra v*rí*sha-krato (íti) v*rí*shâ vagrin bháre dhâ*h*.

May the strong sky increase thee, the strong; a strong one thou art, carried by two strong bays; do thou who art strong, with a strong car, O thou of strong might, strong holder of the thunderbolt, keep us in battle!

V, 40, 2–3. v*rí*shâ grắvâ v*rí*shâ máda*h* v*rí*shâ sóma*h* ayám sutá*h*, v*rí*shan indra v*rí*sha-bhi*h* v*ri*trahan-tama, v*rí*shâ tvâ v*rí*sha*n*am huve.

The stone is strong, the draught is strong, this Soma that has been poured out is strong, O thou strong Indra, who killest V*ri*tra with the strong ones (the Maruts), I, the strong, call thee, the strong.

VIII, 13, 31–33. v*rí*shâ ayám indra te rátha*h* utó (íti) te v*r*isha*n*â hárî (íti), v*r*íshâ tvám *s*ata-krato (íti) v*r*íshâ hávа*h*. v*r*íshâ grā́vâ v*r*íshâ máda*h* v*r*íshâ sóma*h* ayám sutá*h*, v*r*íshâ yag*ñ*á*h* yám ínvasi v*r*íshâ háva*h*. v*r*íshâ tvâ v*r*ísha*n*am huve vágrin *k*itrā́bhi*h* ûtí-bhi*h*, vavántha hí práti-stutim v*r*íshâ háva*h*.

This thy car is strong, O Indra, and thy bays are strong; thou art strong, O omnipotent, our call is strong. The stone is strong, the draught is strong, the Soma is strong, which is here poured out; the sacrifice which thou orderest is strong, our call is strong. I, the strong, call thee, the strong, thou holder of the thunderbolt, with manifold blessings; for thou hast desired our praise; our call is strong.

There are other passages of the same kind, but they are too tedious to be here repeated. The commentator, throughout, gives to each v*r*íshan its full meaning either of showering down or bounteous, or male or bull; but a word which can thus be used at random has clearly lost its definite power, and cannot call forth any definite ideas in the mind of the listener. It cannot be denied that here and there the original meaning of v*r*íshan would be appropriate even where the poet is only pouring out a stream of majestic sound, but we are not called upon to impart sense to what are verba et praeterquam nihil. When we read, I, 122, 3, vā́ta*h* apā́m v*r*isha*n*-vân, we are justified, no doubt, in translating, 'the wind who pours forth water;' and X, 93, 5, apā́m v*r*isha*n*-vasû (íti) sū́ryâmā́sâ, means 'Sun and Moon, givers of water.' But even in some passages where v*r*íshan is followed by the word v*r*ish, it is curious to observe that v*r*ish is not necessarily used in the sense of raining or pouring forth, but rather in the sense of drinking.

VI, 68, 11. índrâvaru*n*â mádhumat-tamasya v*r*íshn*a*h sómasya v*r*isha*n*â[a] ā́ v*r*ishethâm.

[a] The dual v*r*isha*n*au occurs only when the next word begins with a vowel. Before an initial a, â, i, the au is always changed into âv in the Sa*m*hitâ (I, 108, 7–12; 116, 21; 117, 19; 153, 2; 157, 5; 158, 1; 180, 7; VII, 61, 5). Before u the preceding au becomes â in the Sa*m*hitâ, but the Pada gives au, in order to show that no Sandhi can take place between the two vowels (VII, 60, 9;

Indra and Varu*n*a, you strong ones, may you drink of the sweetest strong Soma.

That â-v*ri*sh means to drink or to eat, was known to Sâya*n*a and to the author of the *S*atapatha-brâhma*n*a, who paraphrases â v*ri*shâyadhvam by a*s*nîta, eat.

The same phrase occurs I, 108, 3.

I, 104, 9. uru-vyá*k*â*h* *g*a*th*áre ấ v*ri*shasva.

Thou of vast extent, drink (the Soma) in thy stomach.

The same phrase occurs X, 96, 13.

VIII, 61, 3. ấ v*ri*shasva—sutásya indra ándhasa*h*.

Drink, Indra, of the Soma that is poured out.

In conclusion, a few passages may be pointed out in which v*rí*shan seems to be the proper name of a pious worshipper:

I, 36, 10. yám tvâ devấsa*h* mánave dadhú*h* ihá yá*g*ish*th*am havya-vâhana, yám ká*n*va*h* médhya-atithi*h* dhanaspr*í*tam yám v*rí*shâ yám upa-stutá*h*.

Thee, O Agni, whom the gods placed here for man, the most worthy of worship, O carrier of oblations, thee whom Ka*n*va, thee whom Medhyâtithi placed, as the giver of wealth, thee whom V*ri*shan placed and Upastuta.

Here the commentator takes V*ri*shan as Indra, but this would break the symmetry of the sentence. That Upastutá*h* is here to be taken as a proper name, as Upastuta, the son of V*ri*sh*t*ihavya, is clear from verse 17:

agní*h* pra âvat mitrấ utá médhya-atithim agní*h* sâtấ upastutám.

Agni protected also the two friends, Medhyâtithi and Upastuta, in battle.

The fact is that whenever upastutá has the accent on the last syllable, it is intended as a proper name, while, if used as a participle, in the sense of praised, it has the accent on the first.

X, 66, 7). Before consonants the dual always ends in â, both in the Sa*m*hitâ and Pada. But there are a few passages where the final â occurs before initial vowels, and where the two vowels are allowed to form one syllable. In four passages this happens before an initial â (I, 108, 3; VI, 68, 11; I, 177, 1; II, 16, 5). Once, and once only, it happens before u, in VIII, 22, 12.

VIII, 5, 25. yáthâ *k*it ká*n*vam ấvatam priyá-medham upa-stutám.

As you have protected Ka*n*va, Priyamedha, Upastutá. Cf. I, 112, 15.

VIII, 103, 8. prá má*m*hish*th*âya gâyata—úpa-stutâsa*h* agnáye (accent of the vocative).

Sing, O Upastutás, to the worthiest, to Agni!

X, 115, 9. íti tvâ agne v*ri*sh*t*i-hávyasya putrấ*h* upa-stutấsa*h* *rí*shaya*h* avo*k*an.

By these names, O Agni, did the sons of V*ri*sh*t*ihavya, the Upastutás, the *Ri*shis, speak to you.

V*ri*shan occurs once more as a proper name in VI, 16, 14 and 15:

tám û*m* (íti) tvâ dadhyáṅ *rí*shi*h* putrá*h* îdhe átharva*n*a*h*, v*ri*tra-hánam puram-darám.

tám û*m* (íti) tvâ pâthyá*h* v*rí*shâ sám îdhe dasyuhán-tamam, dhanam-*g*ayám rá*n*e-ra*n*e.

Thee, O Agni, did Dadhya*k* kindle, the *Ri*shi, the son of Atharvan, thee the killer of V*ri*tra, the destroyer of towns;

Thee, O Agni, did V*ri*shan Pâthya kindle, thee the best killer of enemies, the conqueror of wealth in every battle.

Here the context can leave no doubt that Dadhya*k* and V*ri*shan were both intended as proper names. Yet as early as the composition of the *S*atapatha-brâhma*n*a, this was entirely misunderstood. Dadhya*k*, the son of Atharvan, is explained as speech, V*ri*shan Pâthya as mind (*S*at. Br. VI, 3, 3, 4). On this Mahîdhara, in his remarks on Vâ*g*. Sa*m*h. XI, 34, improves still further. For though he allows his personality to Dadhya*k*, the son of Atharvan, he says that Pâthya comes from pathin, path, and means he who moves on the right path; or it comes from pâthas, which means sky, and is here used in the sense of the sky of the heart. He then takes v*ri*shan as mind, and translates the mind of the heart. Such is a small chapter in the history of the rise and fall of the Indian mind!

MANDALA I, HYMN 86.

ASHTAKA I, ADHYÂYA 6, VARGA 11-12.

To the Maruts (the Storm-gods).

1. O Maruts, that man in whose dwelling you drink (the Soma), ye mighty (sons) of heaven, he indeed has the best guardians [1].

2. You who are propitiated [1] either by sacrifices or from the prayers of the sage, hear the call, O Maruts!

3. Aye, the powerful man to whom you have granted a sage, he will live in a stable rich in cattle [1].

4. On the altar of this strong man (here) [1] Soma is poured out in daily sacrifices; praise and joy are sung.

5. To him let the mighty [1] Maruts listen, to him who surpasses all men, as the flowing rain-clouds [2] pass over the sun.

6. For we, O Maruts, have sacrificed at many harvests, through the mercies [1] of the swift gods (the storm-gods).

7. May that mortal be blessed, O chasing Maruts, whose offerings you carry off [1].

8. You take notice either of the sweat of him who praises you, ye men of true strength, or of the desire of the suppliant [1].

9. O ye of true strength, make this manifest with might! strike the fiend [1] with your lightning!

10. Hide the hideous darkness, destroy [1] every tusky [2] fiend. Make the light which we long for!

NOTES.

This hymn is ascribed to Gotama.

Verse 1=VS. VIII, 31; AV. XX, 1, 2; TS. IV, 2, 11, 1.
Verse 2=TS. IV, 2, 11, 2.
Verse 6=TS. IV, 3, 13, 5.
Verse 8=SV. II, 944.

Verse 1.

Note 1. Vímahas occurs only once more as an epithet of the Maruts, V, 87, 4. Being an adjective derived from máhas, strength, it means very strong. The strong ones of heaven is an expression analogous to I, 64, 2. divá*h* *ri*sh-vâsa*h* ukshá*n*a*h*; I, 64, 4. divá*h* nára*h*. The Ait. Brâhma*n*a VI, 10, takes gopâ, guardian, as Indra.

Verse 2.

Note 1. The construction of this verse is not clear. Yag*ñ*á-vâhas has two meanings in the Veda. It is applied to the priest who carries or performs the sacrifice:

III, 8, 3, and 24, 1. vár*k*a*h* dhâ*h* yag*ñ*á-vâhase.
Grant splendour to the sacrificer!

But it is also used of the gods who carry off the sacrifice, and in that case it means hardly more than worshipped or propitiated; I, 15, 11 (A*s*vinau); IV, 47, 4 (Indra and Vâyu); VIII, 12, 20 (Indra). In our verse it is used in the latter sense, and it is properly construed with the instrumental yag*ñ*ai*h*. The difficulty is the gen. plur. matî-nẫm, instead of matíbhi*h*. The sense, however, seems to allow of but one construction, and we may suppose that the genitive depends on the yag*ñ*a in yag*ñ*ávâhas, 'accepting the worship of the prayers of the priest.' Benfey refers yag*ñ*ai*h* to the preceding verse, and joins hávam to víprasya matînẫm: 'Durch Opfer—Opferfördrer ihr!—oder ihr hört —Maruts—den Ruf der Lieder, die der Priester schuf.'

The Sa*m*hitâ text lengthens the last syllable of *s*ri*n*utá, as suggested by the metre.

If the accent allowed yag*ñ*avâhasa*h* to be taken as a genitive, the translation, as suggested by Ludwig, might be, 'Either for the sake of the sacrifices of the sacrificer, or because of the prayers of the sage, O Maruts, hear the call.'

Verse 3.

Note 1. The genitive yásya vâgína*h* depends on vípra. Anu-taksh, like anu-grah, anu-g*ñ*â, seems to convey the meaning of doing in behalf or for the benefit of a person. Gántâ might also be translated in a hostile sense, he will go into, he will conquer many a stable full of cows.

Verse 4.

Note 1. Ludwig has pointed out that asyá may refer to the present sacrificer.

Verse 5.

Note 1. I have altered ấ bhúva*h* into âbhúva*h*, for I do not think that bhuva*h*, the second pers. sing., even if it were bhúvat, the third pers., could be joined with the relative pronoun yá*h* in the second pada. The phrase vísvâ*h* yá*h* *k*arsha*n*ī́*h* abhí occurs more than once, and is never preceded by the verb bhuva*h* or bhuvat. Âbhúva*h*, on the contrary, is applied to the Maruts, I, 64, 6, vidátheshu âbhúva*h*; and as there can be no doubt who are the deities invoked, âbhúva*h*, the strong ones, is as appropriate an epithet as vímahas in the first verse.

Note 2. Sasrúshî*h* ísha*h*, as connected with sū́ra, the sun, can only be meant for the flowing waters, the rain-clouds, the givers of ish or vigour. They are called divyā́*h* ísha*h*: VIII, 5, 21. utá na*h* divyā́*h* ísha*h* utá síndhûn varshatha*h*. You rain down on us the heavenly waters and the rivers.

WILSON translates: May the Maruts, victorious over all men, hear (the praises) of this (their worshipper); and may (abundant) food be obtained by him who praises them.

BENFEY: Ihn, der ob allen Menschen ragt, sollen hören die Labungen, und nahn, die irgend Weisen nahn.

LUDWIG: Hören sollen von ihm, der über allen menschen ist, die erden, seine bis zur sonne gelangten kräfte. In his notes he would prefer: Von ihm sollen sie gegenwartig hören, von ihm der alle menschen übertrift (und die in die sonne wegegangenen), die darbringungen.

*S*roshantu does not occur again; but we find *s*róshan, I, 68, 5; *s*róshamâ*n*a, III, 8, 10; VII, 51, 1; VII, 7, 6.

Verse 6.

Note 1. The expression ávobhi*h*, with the help, the blessings, the mercies, is generally used with reference to divine assistance; (I, 117, 19; 167, 2; 185, 10; 11; IV, 22, 7; 41, 6; V, 74, 6; VI, 47, 12; VII, 20, 1; 35, 1, &c.) It seems best therefore to take *k*arsha*n*i as a name or epithet of the Maruts, although, after the invocation of the Maruts by name, this repetition is somewhat unusual. I should have preferred, 'with the help of our men, of our active and busy companions,' for *k*arsha*n*i is used in that sense also. Only ávobhi*h* would not be in its right place then. The same applies to the various reading in TS. IV, 3, 13, 5, where instead of ávobhi*h* we find máhobhi*h*. This too is used with reference to gods, and particularly to the Maruts; see I, 165, 5, note.

Verse 7.

Note 1. Par, with ati, means to carry over (I, 97, 8; 99, 1; 174, 9; III, 15, 3; 20, 4; IV, 39, 1; V, 25, 9; 73, 8; VII, 40, 4; 97, 4; VIII, 26, 5; 67, 2, &c.); with apa, to remove (I, 129, 5); with ni*h*, to throw down. Hence, if used by itself, unless it means to overrun, as frequently, it can only have the general sense of carrying, taking, accepting, or accomplishing.

Verse 8.

Note 1. Vidá as second pers. plur. perf. is frequent, generally with the final 'a' long in the Sa*m*hitâ, I, 156, 3; V, 41, 13; 55, 2.

Verse 9.

Note 1. Observe the long penultimate in rákshah*,* instead of the usual short syllable. Cf. I, 12, 5, and see Kuhn, Beiträge, vol. iii, p. 456.

Verse 10.

Note 1. See note 1 to I, 39, 3.

Note 2. Atrín, which stands for attrín, is one of the many names assigned to the powers of darkness and mischief. It is derived from atrá, which means tooth or jaw, and therefore meant originally an ogre with large teeth or jaws, a devourer. Besides atrá, we also find in the Veda átra, with the accent on the first syllable, and meaning what serves for eating, or food :

X, 79, 2. átrâ*n*i asmai pa*t*-bhí*k* sám bhâranti.

They bring together food for him (Agni) with their feet.

With the accent on the last syllable, atrá in one passage means an eater or an ogre, like atrín :

V, 32, 8. apā̆dam atrám—m*ri*dhrá-vâ*k*am.

Indra killed the footless ogre, the babbler.

It means tooth or jaw :

I, 129, 8. svayám sā̆ rishayádhyai yā̆ na*h* upa-îshé atraí*h*.

May she herself go to destruction who attacks us with her teeth.

It is probably from atrá in the sense of tooth (cf. ὀδόντες = ἐδόντες) that atrín is derived, meaning ogre or a devouring devil. In the later Sanskrit, too, the Asuras are represented as having large tusks, Mahâbh. V, 3572, da*m*sh*t*ri*n*o bhîmavegâ*s k*a.

Thus we read I, 21, 5, that Indra and Agni destroy the Rakshas, and the poet continues :

ápra*g*â*h* santu atrí*n*a*h*.

May the ogres be without offspring!

IX, 86, 48. *g*ahí vís*v*ân rakshása*h* indo (íti) atrí*n*a*h*.

Kill, O Soma, all the tusky Rakshas. Cf. IX, 104, 6; 105, 6.

VI, 51, 14. *g*ahí ní atrí*n*am pa*n*ím.

Kill, O Soma, the tusky Pa*n*i.

I, 94, 9. vadhaí*h* du*h*-sá*m*sân ápa du*h*-dhyā̆*h g*ahi
dûré vâ yé ánti vâ ké *k*it atrí*n*a*h*.

Strike with thy blows, O Agni, the evil-spoken, evil-minded (spirits), the ogres, those who are far or who are near.

See also I, 36, 14; 20; VI, 16, 28; VII, 104, 1; 5; VIII, 12, 1; 19, 15; X, 36, 4; 118, 1.

MANDALA I, HYMN 87.

ASHTAKA I, ADHYÂYA 6, VARGA 13.

TO THE MARUTS (THE STORM-GODS).

1. Endowed with exceeding vigour and power, the singers, the never flinching, the immovable, the impetuous, the most beloved and most manly, have decked themselves with their glittering ornaments, a few only [1], like the heavens with the stars.

2. When you have seen your way through the clefts, like birds, O Maruts, on whatever road it be [1], then the casks (clouds) on your chariots trickle everywhere, and you pour out the honey-like fatness (the rain) for him who praises you.

3. At their racings the earth shakes, as if broken [1], when on the (heavenly) paths they harness (their deer) for victory [2]. They the sportive, the roaring, with bright spears, the shakers (of the clouds) have themselves glorified their greatness.

4. That youthful company (of the Maruts), with their spotted horses [1], moves by itself; hence [2] it exercises lordship, invested with powers. Thou indeed art true, thou searchest out sin [3], thou art without blemish. Therefore the manly host will help this prayer.

5. We speak after the kind of our old father, our tongue goes forth at the sight [1] of the Soma: when the singers (the Maruts) had joined Indra in deed [2], then only they took their holy names;—

6. These Maruts, armed with beautiful rings, obtained splendours for their glory [1], they obtained [2] rays, and men to celebrate them; nay, armed with daggers, speeding along, and fearless, they found the beloved domain of the Maruts [3].

NOTES.

This hymn is ascribed to Gotama. No verse in SV., VS., AV.

Verse 2=TS. IV, 3, 13, 7.
Verse 3=TS. IV, 3, 13, 7.
Verse 6=TS. II, 1, 11, 2; IV, 2, 11, 2.

Verse 1.

Note 1. Ké *k*it refers to the Maruts, who are represented as gradually rising, or just showing themselves, as yet only few in number, like the first stars in the sky. Ké *k*it, some, is opposed to sarve, all. The same expression occurs again, V, 52, 12, where the Maruts are compared to a few thieves. B. and R., and those who follow them, translate usrắ*h* iva st*rí*-bhi*h* by 'like cows marked with stars on their foreheads.' Such cows no doubt exist, but they can hardly be said to become visible by these frontal stars, as the Maruts by their ornaments. We must take usrắ*h* here in the same sense as dyắva*h*; II, 34, 2, it is said that the Maruts were perceived dyắva*h* ná st*rí*-bhi*h*, like the heavens with the stars.

I, 166, 11. dûre-d*rí*sa*h* yé divyắ*h*-iva st*rí*-bhi*h*.

Who are visible far away, like the heavens (or heavenly beings) by the stars.

And the same is said of Agni, II, 2, 5. dyaú*h* ná st*rí*-bhi*h* *k*itayat ródasî (íti) ánu. Ṣt*rí*bhi*h* occurs I, 68, 5; IV, 7, 3; VI, 49, 3; 12. It always means stars, and the meaning of rays (strahl) rests, as yet, on etymological authority only. The evening sky would, no doubt, be more appropriate than usrắ*h*, which applies chiefly to the dawn. But in the Indian mind, the two dawns, i. e. the dawn and the gloaming, are so closely united and identified, that their names, too, are frequently interchangeable.

Verse 2.

Note 1. I translate yayí not by a goer, a traveller, i. e. the cloud (this is the explanation proposed by Sâya*n*a, and adopted by Professor Benfey), but by path. Sâya*n*a (TS. IV, 3, 13, 7) renders yayim by gatim. Etymologically yayí may mean either, and in some passages I feel doubtful as to which is the more appropriate meaning. But in parallel passages yayí is clearly replaced by yā̆ma. Thus:

VIII, 7, 2. yát—yā̆mam *s*ubhrâ*h* á*k*idhvam.

When you, bright Maruts, have seen your way.

See also VIII, 7, 4. yát yā̆mam yā̆nti vâyú-bhi*h*.

When they (the Maruts) go on their path with the winds.

VIII, 7, 14. ádhi-iva yát girî*n*ā̆m yā̆mam *s*ubhrâ*h* á*k*idhvam.

When you, bright Maruts, had seen your way, as it were, from above the mountains.

The same phrase occurs, even without yā̆ma or yayí, in

V, 55, 7. ná párvatâ*h* ná nadyā̆*h* varanta va*h* yátra á*k*idhvam maruta*h* gá*kkh*ata ít u tát.

Not mountains, not rivers, keep you back; where you have seen (your way), there you go.

Though yayí does not occur frequently in the Rig-veda, the meaning of path seems throughout more applicable than that of traveller.

V, 87, 5. tvesha*h* yayí*h*.

Your path, O Maruts, is blazing.

V, 73, 7. ugrá*h* vâm kakuhá*h* yayí*h*.

Fearful is your pass on high.

I, 51, 11. ugrá*h* yayím ní*h* apá*h* srótasâ as*r*i*g*at.

The fearful Indra sent the waters forth on their way streaming.

X, 92, 5. prá—yayínâ yanti síndhava*h*.

The waters go forth on their path.

Ludwig takes *k*ó*s*a as buckets on the chariots of the Maruts, which seems right.

Verse 3.

Note 1. Cf. I, 37, 8, page 75. There is no authority for Sâya*n*a's explanation of vithurā̆-iva, the earth trembles like a widow. Vithurā̆ occurs several times in the Rig-veda, but never in the sense of widow. Thus:

I, 168, 6. yát *k*yaváyatha vithurā́-iva sám-hitam.

When you, Maruts, throw down what is compact, like brittle things.

I, 186, 2; VI, 25, 3; 46, 6; VIII, 96, 2; X, 77, 4 (vithuryáti). The Maruts themselves are called ávithura in verse 1. Spiegel compares the Zend aiwithura. As to á*g*ma and yā́ma, see I, 37, 8, page 75.

Note 2. *S*úbh is one of those words to which it is very difficult always to assign a definite special meaning. Being derived from *s*ubh, to shine, the commentator has no difficulty in explaining it by splendour, beauty; sometimes by water. But although *s*úbh means originally splendour, and is used in that sense in many passages, yet there are others where so vague a meaning seems very inappropriate. In our verse Sâya*n*a proposes two translations, either, 'When the Maruts harness the clouds,' or, 'When the Maruts harness their chariots, for the bright rain-water.' Now the idea that the Maruts harness their chariots in order to make the clouds yield their rain, can hardly be expressed by the simple word *s*ubhé, i. e. for brightness' sake. As the Maruts are frequently praised for their glittering ornaments, their splendour might be intended in this passage, as it certainly is in others. Thus:

I, 85, 3. yát *s*ubháyante a*ñg*í-bhi*h* tanū́shu *s*ubhrā́*h* dadhire virúkmata*h*.

When the Maruts adorn themselves with glittering ornaments, the brilliant ones put bright weapons on their bodies.

VII, 56, 6. *s*ubhā́ *s*óbhish*th*â*h*, *s*riyā́ sám-mi*s*lâ*h*, ó*g*a*h*-bhi*h* ugrā́*h*.

The most brilliant by their brilliancy, united with beauty, terrible by terrors.

In I, 64, 4, I have translated váksha*h*-su rukmā́n ádhi yetire *s*ubhé by 'they fix gold (chains) on their chests for beauty.' And the same meaning is applicable to I, 117, 5, *s*ubhé rukmám ná dar*s*atám ní-khâtam, and other passages: IV, 51, 6; VI, 63, 6.

But in our verse and others which we shall examine, beauty and brilliancy would be very weak renderings for *s*ubhé. 'When they harnessed their chariots or their deer for the sake of beauty,' means nothing, or, at least, very little. I take, therefore, *s*ubhé in this and similar phrases in the sense of triumph or glory or victory. 'When they harness their chariots for to conquer,' implies brilliancy, glory, victory, but it conveys at the same time a tangible meaning. Let us now see whether the same meaning is appropriate in other passages:

I, 23, 11. *g*áyatâm-iva tanyatu*h* marútâm eti dh*ri*sh*n*u-yā́ yát *s*úbham yâthána nara*h*.

The thundering voice of the Maruts comes fiercely, like that of conquerors, when you go to conquer, O men!

Sâya*n*a: 'When you go to the brilliant place of sacrifice.' Wilson: 'When you accept the auspicious (offering).' Benfey: 'Wenn ihr euren Schmuck nehmt.'

V, 57, 2. yâthana *s*úbham, you go to conquer. Cf. V, 55, 1.

Sâya*n*a: 'For the sake of water, or, in a chariot.'

V, 52, 8. *s*árdha*h* mā́rutam út *sam*sa—utá sma té *s*ubhe nára*h* prá syandrā́*h* yu*g*ata tmánâ.

Praise the host of the Maruts, whether they, the men, the quickly moving, have by themselves harnessed (the chariots) for conquest.

Sâya*n*a: 'For the sake of water.' Cf. X, 105, 3.

V, 57, 3. *s*ubhé yát ugrâ*h* p*rí*shatî*h* áyugdhvam.

When you have harnessed the deer for conquest.

Sâya*n*a: 'For the sake of water.'

III, 26, 4. *s*ubhé—p*rí*shatî*h* ayukshata.

They had harnessed the deer for victory.

Sâya*n*a: 'They had harnessed in the water the deer together (with the fires).'

V, 63, 5. rátham yuñ*g*ate marúta*h* *s*ubhé su-khám *s*ū́ra*h* ná—gó-ish*t*ishu.

The Maruts harness the chariot meet for conquest, like a hero in battles.

Sâya*n*a: 'For the sake of water.'

I, 88, 2. *s*ubhé kám yânti—á*s*vai*h*.

The Maruts go on their horses towards conquest.

Sâya*n*a: 'In order to brighten the worshipper, or, for the sake of water.'

I, 119, 3. sám yát mitháh paspridhânấsah ágmata subhé makhấh ámitâh gâyávah ráne.

When striving with each other they came together, for the sake of glory, the brisk (Maruts), immeasurable (in strength), panting for victory in the fight.

Sâyana : 'For the sake of brilliant wealth.'

VII, 82, 5. marút-bhih ugráh súbham anyáh îyate.

The other, the fearful (Indra), goes with the Maruts to glory.

Sâyana : 'He takes brilliant decoration.'

I, 167, 6. ấ asthâpayanta yuvatím yúvânah subhé nímislâm.

The Maruts, the youths, placed the maid (lightning on their chariot), their companion for victory (subhé nímislâm).

Sâyana: 'For the sake of water, or, on the brilliant chariot.' Cf. I, 127, 6; 165, 1.

VI, 62, 4. súbham príksham ísham ū́rgam váhantâ.

The Asvins bringing glory, wealth, drink, and food.

VIII, 26, 13. subhé kakrâte, you bring him to glory.

Subham-yấvan is an epithet of the Maruts, I, 89, 7; V, 61, 13. Cf. subhra-yâvânâ, VIII, 26, 19 (Asvinau).

Subham-yấ, of the wind, IV, 3, 6.

Subham-yú, of the rays of the dawn, X, 78, 7.

Verse 4.

Note 1. Sâyana : 'With spotted deer for their horses.' See I, 37, 2, note 1, page 70 ; as Pûshan is called agâsva, having goats for his horses, RV. V, 58, 2.

That the Maruts have not only prishatîs, but horses for their chariots, we have seen before. In I, 88, 1, we have ásvaparnaih ráthebhih.

Note 2. Ayấ is a word of very rare occurrence in the Rig-veda. It is the instrum. sing. of the feminine pronominal base a or î, and as a pronoun followed by a noun it is frequently to be met with ; V, 45, 11. ayấ dhiyấ, &c. But in our verse it is irregular in form as not entering into Sandhi with îsânáh. This irregularity, however, which might have led us to suppose an original ayấh, indefatigable, corresponding with the following ási, is vouched for by the Pada text, in such matters a better authority than the Sa*m*hitâ text, and certainly in this case fully borne out by the Prâti*s*âkhya, I, 163, 10. Unless we read ayắ*h*, we must take ayắ as an adverb, in the sense of thus or hence; cf. VI, 66, 4. In some passages where ayắ seems thus to be used as an adverb, it would be better to supply a noun from the preceding verse. Thus in II, 6, 2, ayắ refers to samídham in II, 6, 1. In VI, 17, 15, a similar noun, samídhâ or girắ, should be supplied. But there are other passages where, unless we suppose that the verse was meant to illustrate a ceremonial act, such as the placing of a samídh, and that ayắ pointed to it, we must take it as a simple adverb, like the Greek τῷ: RV. III, 12, 2; IX, 53, 2; 106, 14. In X, 116, 9, the Pada reads áyâ*h*-iva, not áyâ, as given by Roth; in VI, 66, 4, áyâ nú, the accent is likewise on the first.

Note 3. *Rin*a-yắvan is well explained by B. and R. as going after debt, searching out sin. Sâya*n*a, though he explains *rin*a-yắvan by removing sin, derives it nevertheless correctly from *rin*a and yâ, and not from yu. The same formation is found in *s*ubham-yắvan, &c.; and as there is *rin*a-yắ besides *rin*a-yắvan, so we find *s*ubham-yắ besides *s*ubham-yắvan. Ludwig prefers the derivation from yu.

Verse 5.

Note 1. The Soma-juice inspires the poet with eloquence.

Note 2. *S*ámi occurs again in II, 31, 6; III, 55, 3; VIII, 45, 27; X, 40, 1. Grassmann has shown that it may be taken as an instrum. of *s*ámî, meaning work, but with special reference to the toil of the battle-field or the sacrifice. It is used in the former sense in

VIII, 45, 27. ví âna*t* turvá*n*e *s*ámi.

He (Indra) was able to overcome, lit. he reached to, or he arrived at the overcoming or at victory by toil.

But, like other words which have the general meaning of working or toiling, *s*ámî is used both in a general sense, and in the more special sense of sacrifice.

X, 40, 1. vásto*h*-vasto*h* váhamânam dhiyắ *s*ámi.

Your chariot, O A*s*vins, driven along every morning by thought and deed.

II, 31, 6. apā̂m nápât â*s*u-hémâ dhiyā̂ *s*ámi.

Apâm napât (Agni) moving quickly by thought and deed.

In these two passages it might be possible, with a slight alteration of the accent, to read dhiyâ-*s*ámi as one word. Dhiyâ-*s*ám would mean the sacrificer who is engaged in prayer; cf. dhiyâ-*g*úr, V, 43, 15. Thus we read:

VI, 2, 4. yá*h* te su-dā̂nave dhiyā̂ márta*h* *s*a*s*ámate.

The mortal who toils for thee, the liberal god, with prayer.

There is no necessity, however, for such a change, and the authority of the MSS. is against it. See also IX, 74, 7.

In III, 55, 3, *s*ámi á*kkh*a dîdye pûrvyā̂*n*i, Roth takes *s*ámi as an acc. plur. neut., Lanman as an instrum., Grassmann as a locative.

I glance back at the former sacrifices. See B. R. s.v. dî and *s*ámi.

In other passages the feminine *s*ámî seems to mean work, sacrificial work, but, as far as we can see, not simply sacrifice. Thus the *Ri*bhus and others are said to have acquired immortality by their work or works, *s*ámî or *s*ámîbhi*h*, I, 20, 2; 110, 4; III, 60, 3; IV, 33, 4. Cf. IV, 22, 8; 17, 18; V, 42, 10; 77, 4; VI, 52, 1; VIII, 75, 14; IX, 74, 7; X, 28, 12. In VI, 3, 2, we read:

îgé yag*ñ*ébhi*h* *s*a*s*amé *s*ámîbhi*h*.

I have sacrificed with sacrifices, I have worked with pious works.

Here the verb *s*am must be taken in the sense of working, or performing ceremonial worship, while in other places (III, 29, 16; V, 2, 7) it may be perhaps taken in the more special sense of singing songs of praise. The Greek κάμ-νω, to work, to labour, to tire (Sanskrit *s*âmyati), the Greek κομιδή and κομίζω, to labour for or take care of a person, and possibly even the Greek κῶμος, a song or a festival (not a village song), may all find their explanation in the Sanskrit root *s*am.

The idea that the Maruts did not originally enjoy divine

honours will occur again and again: cf. I, 6, 4; 72, 3. A similar expression is used of the *Ri*bhus, I, 20, 8, &c. But while originally the expression of obtaining sacred names meant no more than obtaining a sacred or divine character, it was soon taken literally, and a number of names were invented for the Maruts which even in the Vâ*g*asan. Sa*m*hitâ XVII, 80–85 amount to 49, i.e. 7 × 7. Ya*gñ*íya, properly 'worthy of sacrifice,' has the meaning of divine or sacred. The Greek ἅγιος has been compared with yâ*g*ya, sacrificio colendus, which is not a Vedic word.

Verse 6.

Note 1. *S*riyáse kám seems to be the same as the more frequent *s*riyé kám. *S*riyáse only occurs twice more, V, 59, 3. The chief irregularity consists in the absence of Gu*n*a, which is provided for by Pâ*n*ini's kasen (III, 4, 9). Similar infinitives, if they may so be called, are bhiyáse, V, 29, 4; v*ri*dháse, V, 64, 5; dhruváse, VII, 70, 1; tu*g*áse, IV, 23, 7; *riñg*áse, VIII, 4, 17; v*riñg*áse, VIII, 76, 1; *rik*áse, VII, 61, 6. In VI, 39, 5, *rik*áse may be a dat. sing. of the masculine, to the praiser.

Note 2. Mimikshire from myaksh, to be united with. Ra*s*mí, rays, after bhânú, splendour, may seem weak. It might be possible to assign to ra*s*mí the meaning of reins, and take *ri*kvabhir in the sense of sounding or tinkling. In V, 79, 8, ar*k*í is used in juxtaposition with ra*s*mí.

Note 3. The bearing of this concluding verse is not quite clear, unless we take it as a continuation of the preceding verse. It was there said that the Maruts (the *rí*kvâ*n*a*h*) obtained their holy names after having joined Indra in his work, which means that they then and there became what they are. Having thus obtained their true character and a place among the gods, they may be said to have won at the same time splendour, and worshippers to sing their praises, and to have established themselves in what became afterwards known as their own domain, their own place among the gods who are invoked at the sacrifice. See VII, 58, 1.

The metre requires that we should read dhâmana*h*.

BENFEY translates: Gedeih'n zu spenden woll'n die schöngeschmücketen mit Lichtern, Strahlen mit Lobsängern regenen; die brüllenden, furchtlosen, stürmischen, sie sind bekannt als Glieder des geliebten Marutstamms.

WILSON: Combining with the solar rays, they have willingly poured down (rain) for the welfare (of mankind), and, hymned by the priests, have been pleased partakers of the (sacrificial food). Addressed with praises, moving swiftly, and exempt from fear, they have become possessed of a station agreeable and suitable to the Maruts.

LUDWIG: Zu herlichkeit haben dise sich mit liechtglanz versehen, mit sausenden zügeln die schönberingten, schwertbewaffnet die kraftvollen, ohne furcht besitzen sie die freundliche Marutmacht.

MANDALA I, HYMN 88.

ASHTAKA I, ADHYÂYA 6, VARGA 14.

To the Maruts (the Storm-gods).

1. Come hither, Maruts, on your chariots charged with lightning, resounding with beautiful songs[1], stored with spears, and winged with horses! Fly[3] to us like birds, with your best food[2], you mighty ones!

2. They come gloriously on their red, or, it may be, on their tawny horses which hasten their chariots. He who holds the axe[1] is brilliant like gold;—with the tire[2] of the chariot they have struck the earth.

3. On your bodies there are daggers for beauty; may they stir up our minds[1] as they stir up the forests. For yourselves, O well-born Maruts, the vigorous (among you) shake[2] the stone (for distilling Soma).

4. Days went round you and came back[1], O hawks, back to this prayer, and to this sacred rite; the Gotamas making prayer with songs, pushed up the lid of the well (the cloud) for to drink.

5. No such hymn[1] was ever known as this which Gotama sounded for you, O Maruts, when he saw you on golden wheels, wild boars[2] rushing about with iron tusks.

6. This comforting speech rushes sounding towards you, like the speech of a suppliant: it rushed freely from our hands as our speeches are wont to do.

NOTES.

This hymn is ascribed to Gotama, the son of Rahûga*n*a. The metre varies. Verses 1 and 6 are put down as Prastâra-paṅkti, i.e. as 12 + 12 + 8 + 8. By merely counting the syllables, and dissolving semivowels, it is just possible to get twenty-four syllables in the first line of verses 1 and 6. The old metricians must have scanned verse 1:

â vidyunmat-bhi*h* mârutâ*h* sû-arkai*h*
rathebhi*h* yâta⁀*ri*sh*t*imat-bhi*h* a*s*va-par*n*ai*h*.

Again verse 6: eshâ syâ va*h* mârutâ*h* anu-bhartrî
prati stobhati vâghata*h* na vâ*n*î.

But the general character of these lines shows that they were intended for hendecasyllabics, each ending in a bacchius, though even then they are not free from irregularities. The first verse would scan:

â vidyunmat-bhi*h* mârutâ*h* sû-arkai*h*
rathebhi*h* yâta⁀*ri*sh*t*imat-(bhi*h*) a*s*va-par*n*ai*h*.

And verse 6: eshâ syâ va*h* mâruta*h*⁀anu-bhartrî
prati stobhati vâghata*h* na vâ*n*î.

Our only difficulty would be the termination bhi*h* of *ri*sh*t*i-mat-bhi*h*. I cannot adopt Professor Kuhn's suggestion to drop the Visarga of bhi*h* and change i into y (Beiträge, vol. iv, p. 198), for this would be a license without any parallel. It is different with sa*h*, originally sa, or with feminines in i*h*, where parallel forms in î are intelligible. The simplest correction would be to read rathebhi*h* yâta⁀*ri*sh*t*i-mânta*h*⁀a*s*va-par*n*ai*h*. One might urge in support of this reading that in all other passages where *ri*sh*t*imat occurs, it refers to the Maruts themselves, and never to their chariots. Yet the difficulty remains, how could so simple a reading have been replaced by a more difficult one?

In the two Gâyatrî pâdas which follow I feel equally reluctant to alter. I therefore scan

â varshishthayâ nah ishâ vayah na paptata su-mâyâh,

taking the dactyl of paptata as representing a spondee, and admitting the exceptional bacchius instead of the amphimacer at the end of the line.

The last line of verse 6 should be scanned:

astobhayat vrithâ âsâm anu svadhâm gabhastyoh.

There are two other verses in this hymn where the metre is difficult. In the last pâda of verse 5 we have seven syllables instead of eleven. Again, I say, it would be most easy to insert one of the many tetrasyllabic epithets of the Maruts. But this would have been equally easy for the collectors of the Veda. Now the authors of the Anukramanîs distinctly state that this fifth verse is virâdrûpâ, i. e. that one of its pâdas consists of eight syllables. How they would have made eight syllables out of vi-dhâvatah varâhûn does not appear, but at all events they knew that last pâda to be imperfect. The rhythm does not suffer by this omission, as long as we scan vi-dhâvatah varâhûn.

Lastly, there is the third pâda of the second verse, rukmah na kitrah svadhiti-vân. It would not be possible to get eleven syllables out of this, unless we admitted vyûha not only in svadhitivân or svadhitî-vân, but also in kitrah. Kuhn (Beiträge, vol. iv, p. 192) proposes to scan rukmaü na kitarah svadhitivân. Nothing would be easier than to insert eshâm after kitrah, but the question occurs again, how could eshâm be lost, or why, if by some accident it had been lost, was not so obvious a correction made by Saunaka and Kâtyâyana?

No verse of this hymn occurs in SV., VS., AV., TS., TB.

Verse 1.

Note 1. Alluding to the music of the Maruts, and not to the splendour of the lightning which is mentioned before. See Wolf, Beiträge zur Deutschen Mythologie, vol. ii, p. 137. 'Das Ross und den Wagen des Gottes begleitet munterer Hörnerschall, entweder stösst er selbst ins Horn, oder sein Gefolge. Oft vernimmt man auch eine liebliche Musik, der keine auf Erden gleich kommt (Müllenhof, 582). Das wird das Pfeifen und Heulen des Sturmes sein, nur in idealisirter Art.' Ibid. p. 158.

Note 2. Várshish*th*a, which is generally explained as the superlative of v*ri*ddha, old (Pâ*n*. VI, 4, 157), has in most passages of the Rig-veda the more general meaning of strong or excellent: VI, 47, 9. ísham ấ vakshi ishấm várshish*th*âm; III, 13, 7 (vásu); III, 26, 8 (rátná); III, 16, 3 (raí); IV, 31, 15; VIII, 46, 24 (*s*rávā*h*); IV, 22, 9 (n*ri*m*n*á); V, 67, 1 (kshatrá); VI, 45, 31 (mûrdhán). In some passages, however, it may be taken in the sense of oldest (I, 37, 6; V, 7, 1), though by no means necessarily. Várshish*th*a is derived in reality from v*ri*shan, in the sense of strong, excellent See note to I, 85, 12, page 144.

Note 3. Paptata, the second person plural of the imperative of what is commonly, though without much reason, called the aorist of the causative of pat. It is curiously like the Greek πίπτετε, but it has the meaning of flying rather than falling; see Curtius, Grundzüge, p. 190. Two other forms formed on the same principle occur in the Rig-veda, papta*h* and paptan:

II, 31, 1. prá yát váya*h* ná páptan.

That they may fly to us like birds.

VI, 63, 6. prá vâm váya*h*—ánu paptan.

May your birds fly after you.

X, 95, 15. púrûrava*h* mấ m*ri*thâ*h* mấ prá papta*h*.

Purûravas, do not die, do not go away!

Verse 2.

Note 1. Though svadhiti-vân does not occur again, it can only mean he who holds the axe, or, it may be, the sword or the thunderbolt, the latter particularly, if Indra is here intended. Svadhiti signifies axe:

III, 2, 10. svá-dhitim ná té*g*ase.

They adorned Agni like an axe to shine or to cut.

The svádhiti is used by the butcher, I, 162, 9; 18; 20; and by the wood-cutter or carpenter, III, 8, 6; 11; X, 89, 7, &c. Roth (s. v.) takes svadhiti as meaning also a tree, possibly the oak, and he translates svadhitivân in our passage by a chariot made of the wood of the Svadhiti tree. In RV. IX, 96, 6, svádhitir vánânâm may well mean 'the strong axe among woods,' the axe being naturally made of the strongest wood. In V, 32, 10, a devī́ svádhiti*h* is mentioned, possibly the lightning, the companion of Indra and the Maruts.

Note 2. The tire of the chariot of the Maruts is frequently mentioned. It was considered not only as an essential part of their chariot, but likewise as useful for crushing the enemy:

V, 52, 9. utá pavyā́ ráthânâm ádrim bhindanti ó*g*asâ.

They cut the mountain (cloud) with the tire of their chariots.

I, 166, 10. pavíshu kshurā́*h* ádhi.

On their tires are sharp edges.

In V, 31, 5, tires are mentioned without horses and chariot, which were turned by Indra against the Dasyus (I, 64, 11). I doubt, however, whether in India or elsewhere the tires or the wheels of chariots were ever used as weapons of attack, as detached from the chariot; (see M. M., On Pavîrava, in Beiträge zur Vergleichenden Sprachforschung, vol. iii, p. 447.) If we translate the figurative language of the Vedic poets into matter-of-fact terms, the tires of the chariots of the Maruts may be renderėd by thunderbolts; yet by the poets of the Veda, as by the ancient people of Germany, thunder was really supposed to be the noise of the chariot of a god, and it was but a continuation of the same belief that the sharp wheels of that chariot were supposed to cut and crush the clouds; (see M. M., loc. cit., p. 444.)

Verse 3.

Note 1. That the vā́*s*is are small weapons, knives or daggers, we saw before, p. 71. Sâya*n*a here explains vā́*s*î by a weapon commonly called âra, or an awl. In X, 101, 10, vā́*s*îs are mentioned, made of stone, a*s*man-máyî.

The difficulty begins with the second half. Medhā́, as here written in the Pada text, could only be a plural of a neuter medhá, but such a neuter does nowhere exist in the Veda. We only find the masculine médha, sacrifice, which is out of the question here, on account of its accent. Hence the passage III, 58, 2, ûrdhvā́*h* bhavanti pitárâ-iva médhâ*h*, is of no assistance, unless we alter the accent. The feminine medhā́ means will, thought, prayer: I, 18, 6; II, 34, 7; IV, 33, 10; V, 27, 4; 42, 13; VII, 104, 6; VIII, 6, 10; 52, 9; IX, 9, 9; 26, 3; 32, 6; 65, 16; 107, 25; X, 91, 8. The construction does not allow us to take medhā́ as a Vedic instrumental instead of medháyâ, nor does such a form occur anywhere else in the Rig-veda. Nothing remains, I believe, but to have recourse to conjecture, and the addition of a single Visarga in the Pada would remove all difficulty. In the next line, if tuvi-dyumnā́sa*h* be the subject, it would signify the priests. This, however, is again without any warrant from the Rig-veda, where tuvi-dyumná is always used as an epithet of gods. I therefore take it as referring to the Maruts, as an adjective in the nominative, following the vocatives maruta*h* su-*g*âtâ*h*. The conception that the Maruts stir up the forests is not of unfrequent occurrence in the Rig-veda: cf. I, 171, 3. That ûrdhvá is used of the mind, in the sense of roused, may be seen in I, 119, 2; 134, 1; 144, 1; VII, 64, 4. The idea in the poet's mind seems to have been that the thunderbolts of the Maruts rouse up men to prayer as they stir the tops of the forest trees. Ludwig takes medha, masc., in the sense of lance, comparing it with Icelandic meidhr, but the two words cannot well be the same. Possibly vana may be meant for lances: 'May they raise our minds, like lances;' see note to I, 171, 3.

Note 2. On dhan in the sense of to agitate, see B. and R. s. v. The shaking of the stone may be the shaking of the stone for distilling the heavenly Soma or the rain; but adri may also be meant for the thunderbolt. I now take tuvidyumna for an adjective referring to the Maruts, because it is a divine rather than a human epithet. Still, the passage is doubtful.

Verse 4.

Note 1. The first question is, which is the subject, áhâni or g*ri*dh̆râ*h*? If g*ri*dhrâ*h* were the subject, then we should have to translate it by the eager poets, and take áhâni in the sense of vi*s*vâ ahâni. The sense then might be: 'Day by day did the eager poets sing around you this prayer.' There would be several objections, however, to this rendering. First, g*ri*dhrâ*h*, though metaphorically applicable to poets, never occurs again as signifying poets or priests. One passage only could be quoted in support, IX, 97, 57, kaváyah ná g*ri*dhrâ*h* (not g*ri*dhrā́*h*), like greedy poets. But even here, if indeed the translation is right, the adjective is explained by kaví, and does not stand by itself. Secondly, áhâni by itself is never used adverbially in the sense of day after day. The only similar passage that might be quoted is III, 34, 10, and that is very doubtful. To take áhâni as a totally different word, viz. as á+h̆âni, without ceasing, without wearying, would be too bold in the present state of Vedic interpretation. If then we take áhâni as the subject, g*ri*dhrâ*h* would have to be taken as a vocative, and intended for the Maruts. Now, it is perfectly true, that by itself g*ri*dhra, hawk, does not occur again as a name of the Maruts, but *s*yená, hawk, and particularly a strong hawk (IX, 96, 6), is not only a common simile applied to the Maruts, but is actually used as one of their names:

VII, 56, 3. abhí sva-pū́bhi*h* mithá*h* vapanta vā́ta-svanasa*h* *s*yenā́*h* asp*ri*dhran.

They plucked each other with their beaks (?), the hawks, rushing like the wind, strove together.

Agu*h* might be the aorist of gai, to sing, or of gâ, to go:

I, 174, 8. sánâ tā́ te indra návyâ*h* ā́ agu*h*.

New poets, O Indra, sang these thy old deeds.

III, 56, 2. gā́va*h* ā́ agu*h*.

The cows approached.

If then the sense of the first line is, 'Days went and came back to you,' the next question is whether we are to extend the construction to the next words, imā́m dhíyam vârkâryā́m *k*a devī́m, or whether these words are to be joined to k*ri*nvánta*h*, like bráhma. The meaning of vârkâryā́ is, of course, unknown. Sâyaṇa's interpretation as 'what is to be made by means of water' is merely etymological, and does not help us much. It is true that the object of the hymn, which is addressed to the Maruts, is rain, and that literally vârkâryā́ might be explained as 'that the effect of which is rain.' But this is far too artificial a word for Vedic poets. Possibly there was some other word that had become unintelligible and which, by a slight change, was turned into vârkâryā́, in order to give the meaning of rain-producing. It might have been *k*arkârya, glorious, or the song of a poet called Vârkara, or, as Ludwig suggests, V*ri*kâri. The most likely supposition is that vârkâryā́ was the name given to some famous hymn, some pæan or song of triumph belonging to the Gotamas, possibly to some verses of the very hymn before us. In this case the epithet devī́ would be quite appropriate, for it is frequently used for a sacred or sacrificial song: IV, 43, 1. devī́m su-stutím; III, 18, 3. imā́m dhíyam *s*ata-séyâya devī́m. See, however, the note to verse 6.

The purport of the whole line would then be that many days have gone for the Maruts as well as for the famous hymn once addressed to them by Gotama, or, in other words, that the Gotamas have long been devoted to the Maruts, an idea frequently recurring in the hymns of the Veda, and, in our case, carried on in the next verse, where it is said that the present hymn is like one that Gotama composed when he saw the Maruts or spoke of them as wild boars with iron tusks. The pushing up the lid of the well for to drink, means that they obtained rain from the cloud, which is here, as before, represented as a covered well.

See another explanation in Haug, Über die ursprüngliche Bedeutung des Wortes Brahma, 1868, p. 5.

Verse 5.

Note 1. Yó*g*ana commonly means a chariot:

VI, 62, 6. are*n*ú-bhi*h* yó*g*anebhi*h* bhu*g*ántâ.

You who possess dustless chariots.

VIII, 72, 6. á*s*va-vat yó*g*anam b*ri*hát.

The great chariot with horses.

It then became the name for a distance to be accomplished without unharnessing the horses, just as the Latin jugum, a yoke, then a juger of land, 'quod uno jugo boum uno die exarari posset,' Pliny XVIII, 3, 3, 9.

In our passage, however, yó*g*ana means a hymn, lit. a composition, which is clearly its meaning in

VIII, 90, 3. bráhma te indra girva*nah* kriyánte ánatidbhutâ, imấ *g*ushasva hari-a*s*va yó*g*anâ índra yấ te ámanmahi.

Unequalled prayers are made for thee, praiseworthy Indra; accept these hymns which we have devised for thee, O Indra with bright horses!

Note 2. Varấhu has here the same meaning as varâhá, wild boar (VIII, 77, 10; X, 28, 4). It occurs once more, I, 121, 11, as applied to V*ri*tra, who is also called varâhá, I, 61, 7; X, 99, 6. In X, 67, 7, v*rí*sha-bhi*h* varấhai*h* (with the accent on the penultimate) is intended for the Maruts[a]. Except in this passage, varâha has the accent on the last syllable. In IX, 97, 7, varâhá is applied to Soma.

Verse 6.

This last verse is almost unintelligible to me. I give, however, the various attempts that have been made to explain it.

WILSON: This is that praise, Maruts, which, suited (to your merits), glorifies every one of you. The speech of the priest has now glorified you, without difficulty, with sacred verses, since (you have placed) food in our hands.

BENFEY: Dies Lied—Maruts!—das hinter euch emporstrebt, es klingt zurück gleich eines Beters Stimme. Mühlos schuf solche Lieder er, entsprechend eurer Arme Kraft. (Note: Der zum Himmel schallende Lobgesang findet seinen Widerhall (wirklich, 'bebt zurück') in dem Sturm-

[a] See Genthe, Die Windgottheiten, 1861, p. 14; Grimm, Deutsche Mythologie, p. 689. Grimm mentions eburðrung (boar-throng) as a name of Orion, the star that betokens storm.

geheul der Maruts, welches mit dem Geheul des Betenden verglichen wird.)

LUDWIG: Dises lied, o Marut, euch unterstützend (aufnemend) als eines priesters braust euch entgegen, nachbrausen hat es gemacht ohne mühe in (die) der nähe die göttliche weise (ihrer) arme.

My own translation is to a great extent conjectural. It seems to me from verse 3, that the poet offers both a hymn of praise and a libation of Soma. Possibly vârkâryâ in verse 4 might be taken in the sense of Soma-juice, and be derived from valkala, which in later Sanskrit means the bark of trees. In that case verse 5 would again refer to the hymn of Gotama, and verse 6 to the libation which is to accompany it. Anu-bhartrî̆ does not occur again, but it can only mean what supports or refreshes, and therefore would be applicable to a libation of Soma which supports the gods. The verb stobhati would well express the rushing sound of the Soma, as in I, 168, 8, it expresses the rushing noise of the waters against the fellies of the chariots. The next line adds little beyond stating that this libation of Soma rushes forth freely from the hands, the gabhastis being specially mentioned in other passages where the crushing of the Soma-plant is described:

IX, 71, 3. ádri-bhi*h* sutá*h* pavate gábhastyo*h*.

The Soma squeezed by the stones runs from the hands.

The translation would then be: O Maruts, this comforting draught (of Sŏma) rushes towards you, like the speech of a suppliant; it rushed freely from our hands, as our draughts (of Soma) are wont to do.

On svadhâ̆, see p. 32.

MANDALA I, HYMN 165.

ASHTAKA II, ADHYÂYA 3, VARGA 24–26.

TO THE MARUTS AND INDRA.

The Prologue.

The sacrificer speaks:

1. To what splendour do the Maruts all equally[1] cling[2], they who are of the same age, and dwell in the same nest? With what thoughts?—from whence are they come[3]? Do these heroes sing forth their (own) strength[4], wishing for wealth?

2. Whose prayers have the youths accepted? Who has turned the Maruts to his own sacrifice? By what strong desire[1] may we arrest them, they who float through the air like hawks?

The Dialogue.

The Maruts speak:

3. From whence[1], O Indra, dost thou come alone, thou who art mighty? O lord of men[2], what has thus happened to thee? Thou greetest (us)[3] when thou comest together with (us), the bright (Maruts)[4]. Tell us then, thou with thy bay horses, what thou hast against us!

Indra speaks:

4. The sacred songs are mine, (mine are) the prayers[1]; sweet[2] are the libations! My strength rises[3], my thunderbolt is hurled forth. They call for me, the hymns yearn for me. Here are my horses, they carry me hither.

The Maruts speak:

5. From thence, in company with our strong

friends[1], having adorned our bodies, we now harness our fallow deer[2] with all our might[3];—for, Indra, according to custom, thou hast come to be with us.

Indra speaks:

6. Where, O Maruts, was that custom with you, when you left me alone in the killing of Ahi? I indeed am terrible, powerful, strong,—I escaped from the blows of every enemy[1].

The Maruts speak:

7. Thou hast achieved much with us as companions[1]. With equal valour, O hero! let us achieve then many things, O thou most powerful, O Indra! whatever we, O Maruts, wish with our mind[2].

Indra speaks:

8. I slew V*ri*tra, O Maruts, with (Indra's) might, having grown powerful through my own vigour; I, who hold the thunderbolt in my arms, have made these all-brilliant waters to flow freely for man[1].

The Maruts speak:

9. Nothing, O mighty lord, is strong[1] before thee: no one is known among the gods[2] like unto thee. No one who is now born[3] comes near, no one who has been born. Do what thou wilt do[4], thou who art grown so strong.

Indra speaks:

10. Almighty strength be mine alone, whatever I may do, daring in my heart[1]; for I indeed, O Maruts, am known as terrible: of all that I threw down, I, Indra, am the lord.

Indra speaks:

11. O Maruts, now your praise has pleased me, the glorious hymn which you have made for me, ye

men!—for me, for Indra, for the joyful hero, as friends for a friend, for your own sake, and by your own efforts[1].

Indra speaks:

12. Truly, there they are, shining towards me, bringing blameless glory, bringing food. O Maruts, wherever I have looked for you, you have appeared to me in bright splendour: appear to me also now!

The Epilogue.

The sacrificer speaks:

13. Who has magnified you here, O Maruts? Come hither, O friends, towards your friends. Ye brilliant Maruts, welcoming[1] these prayers, be mindful[2] of these my rites.

14. The wisdom of Mânya has brought us hither, that he should help as the poet helps the performer of a sacrifice[1]: turn hither quickly[2]! Maruts, on to the sage! the singer has recited these prayers for you.

15. May this your praise, O Maruts, this song of Mândârya, the son of Mâna[1], the poet, bring offspring[2] for ourselves with food. May we have an invigorating autumn, with quickening rain[3].

NOTES.

A critical examination of Professor von Roth's remarks on this hymn, together with some supplementary notes of my own, will be found in the Preface to this volume.

According to the Anukrama*n*ikâ this hymn is a dialogue between Agastya, the Maruts, and Indra. A careful consideration of the hymn would probably have led us to a similar conclusion, but I doubt whether it would have led us to adopt the same distribution of the verses among the poet, the Maruts, and Indra, as that adopted by the author of the Anukrama*n*ikâ. He assigns the first two verses to Indra, the third, fifth, seventh, and ninth to the Maruts, the fourth, sixth, eighth, tenth, eleventh, and twelfth to Indra, and the three concluding verses to Agastya. I think that the two verses in the beginning, as well as the three concluding verses, belong certainly to Agastya or to whoever else the real performer of the sacrifice may have been. The two verses in the beginning cannot be ascribed to Indra, who, to judge from his language, would never say: 'By what strong desire may we arrest the Maruts?' It might seem, in fact, as if the three following verses too should be ascribed to the sacrificer, so that the dialogue between Indra and the Maruts would begin only with the sixth verse. The third verse might well be addressed to Indra by the sacrificer, and in the fourth verse we might see a description of all that he had done for Indra. What is against this view, however, is the phrase prábh*ri*ta*h* me ádri*h*. If used by the sacrificer, it might seem to mean, 'my stone, i.e. the stone used for squeezing the Soma, has been brought forth.' But though Professor Roth assigns this meaning to prábh*ri*ta in our passage, I doubt whether, in connection with ádri, or with vá*g*ra, prábh*ri*ta can mean anything but hurled. Thus we read:

I, 61, 12. asmaí ít ûm (íti) prá bhara—v*ri*trấya vá*g*ram.

Hurl thou, Indra, the thunderbolt against this V*ri*tra.

V, 32, 7. yát îm vá*g*rasya prá-bh*ri*tau dadấbha.

When Indra conquered him in the hurling of the thunderbolt.

I therefore suppose the dialogue to begin with verse 3, and I find that Langlois, though it may be from different reasons, arrived at the same conclusion.

There can be little doubt that the other verses, to verse 12, are rightly apportioned between Indra and the Maruts. Verse 12 might perhaps be attributed again to the worshipper of the Maruts, but as there is no absolute necessity for assigning it to him, it is better to follow the tradition and to take it as the last verse of Indra's speech. It would seem, in fact, as if these ten verses, from 3 to 12, formed an independent poem, which was intended to show the divine power of the Maruts. That their divine power was sometimes denied, and that Indra's occasional contempt of them was well known to the Vedic poets, will become evident from other hymns. This dialogue seems therefore to have been distinctly intended to show that, in spite of occasional misunderstandings between the Maruts and the all-powerful Indra, Indra himself had fully recognised their power and accepted their friendship. If we suppose that this dialogue was repeated at sacrifices in honour of the Maruts, or that possibly it was acted by two parties, one representing Indra, the other the Maruts and their followers, then the two verses in the beginning and the three at the end ought to be placed in the mouth of the actual sacrificer, whoever he was. He begins by asking, Who has attracted the Maruts to his sacrifice, and by what act of praise and worship can they be delighted? Then follows the dialogue in honour of the Maruts, and after it the sacrificer asks again, 'Who has magnified the Maruts, i. e. have not we magnified them?' and he implores them to grant him their friendship in recognition of his acts of worship. If then we suppose that the dialogue was the work of Mândârya Mânya, the fourteenth verse, too, would lose something of its obscurity. Coming from the mouth of the actual sacrificer, it would mean, 'the wisdom, or the poetical power, of Mânya has brought us to this, has induced us to do this, i. e. to perform this dialogue of Mânya, so that he, Mânya, should assist, as a poet assists the priest at a sacrifice.' Of course all this is and can only be guess-work.

We do not know the age of Mânya nor that of Agastya. We do not know whether they were contemporaries or not. But supposing that Mânya was present at the sacrifice, vípra might be meant for Mânya; and in the last words, too, 'the singer has recited these prayers for you,' the singer (*g*aritấ) might again be Mânya, the powerful poet whose services the sacrificer had engaged, and whose famous dialogue between Indra and the Maruts was considered a safe means of winning their favour. It would be in keeping with all this, if in the last verse the sacrificer once more informed the Maruts that this hymn of praise was the work of the famous poet Mândârya, the son of Mâna, and if he then concluded with the usual prayer for safety, food, and progeny.

No verse of this hymn occurs in the Sâma-veda; verse 3 = VS. XXXIII, 27; verse 4 = VS. XXXIII, 78; verse 6 = TB. II, 8, 3, 5; verse 8 = TB. II, 8, 3, 6; verse 9 = VS. XXXIII, 79.

Verse 1.

Note 1. As samânī́ occurs in the Veda as the feminine of samâna (cf. IV, 51, 9; X, 191, 3; 4), samânyấ might, no doubt, be taken as an instrumental, belonging to *s*ubhấ. We should then have to translate: 'With what equal splendour are the Maruts endowed?' Sâya*n*a adopts the same explanation, while Wilson, who seems to have read samânyâ*h*, translates 'of one dignity.' Professor Roth, s. v. myaksh, would seem to take samânyấ as some kind of substantive, and he refers to another passage, I, 167, 4, sâdhâra*n*yấ-iva marúta*h* mimikshu*h*, without, however, detailing his interpretation of these passages.

It cannot be said that Sâya*n*a's explanation is objectionable, yet there is something awkward in qualifying by an adjective, however indefinite, what forms the subject of an interrogative sentence, and it would be possible to avoid this, by taking samânyấ as an adverb. It is clearly used as an adverb in III, 54, 7; VIII, 83, 8.

Note 2. Mimikshu*h* is the perfect of myaksh, in the sense of to be firmly joined with something. It has therefore a more definite meaning than the Latin miscere and the Greek μίσγειν, which come from the same source, i. e.

from a root mik or mig, in Sanskrit also mis in mis-ra; (see Curtius, Grundzüge, p. 300.) There may be indeed one or two passages in the Veda where myaksh seems to have the simple meaning of mixing, but it will be seen that they constitute a small minority compared with those where myaksh has the meaning of holding to, sticking to; I mean

X, 104, 2. mimikshú*h* yám ádraya*h* indra túbhyam.

The Soma which the stones have mixed for thee.

This form cannot be derived from mimiksh, but is the 3rd pers. plur. perf. Parasm. of myaksh. It may, however, be translated, 'This Soma which the stones have grasped or squeezed for thee,' as may be seen from passages quoted hereafter, in which myaksh is construed with an accusative.

II, 3, 11. gh*ri*tám mimikshe.

The butter has been mixed.

This form cannot be derived from mimiksh, but is the 3rd pers. sing. perf. Âtm. of myaksh. If the meaning of mixing should be considered inadmissible, we might in this verse also translate, 'The butter has become fixed, solid, or coagulated.'

Leaving out of consideration for the present the forms which are derived from mimiksh, we find the following passages in which myaksh occurs. Its original meaning must have been to be mixed with, to be joined to, and in many passages that original sense is still to be recognised, only with the additional idea of being firmly joined, of sticking to, or, in an active sense, laying hold of, grasping firmly.

1. Without any case:

I, 169, 3. ámyak sấ te indra *ri*sh*t*í*h* asmé (íti).

This thy spear, O Indra, sat firm for us.

This would mean that Indra held his weapon well, as a soldier ought to hold his spear. Ámyak is the 3rd pers. sing. of a second aor. Parasm., ámyaksham, ámyak(sh + t); (Sây. prâpnoti.) Cf. VIII, 61, 18.

2. With locative:

X, 44, 2. mimyáksha vágra*h* n*ri*-pate gabhástau.

In thy fist, O king, the thunderbolt rests firmly.

I, 167, 3. mimyáksha yéshu sú-dhitâ—*ri*sh*tí*h.

To whom clings the well-grasped spear.

VI, 50, 5. mimyáksha yéshu rodasî́ nú devî́.

To whom the goddess Rodasî clings. (Sây. sa*m*ga*kkh*ate.)

VI, 11, 5. ámyakshi sádma sádane p*ri*thivyấ*h*.

The seat was firmly set on the seat of the earth. (Sây. gamyate, parig*ri*hyate.) It is the 3rd pers. sing. aor. pass.

VI, 29, 2. ấ yásmin háste náryâ*h* mimikshú*h* ấ ráthe hira*n*yáye rathe-sthấ*h*, ấ ra*s*máya*h* gábhastyo*h* sthûráyo*h* ấ ádhvan á*s*vâsa*h* v*rí*sha*n*a*h* yu*g*ânấ*h*.

To whose hand men cling, in whose golden chariot the drivers stand firm, in whose strong fists the reins are well held, on whose path the harnessed stallions hold together. (Sây. âsi*k*yante, âpûryante; or âsi*ñk*anti, pûrayanti.)

X, 96, 3. índre ní rûpấ háritâ mimikshire.

Bright colours stuck or clung or settled on Indra. (Sây. nishiktâni babhûvu*h*; mihe*h* sanantât karma*n*i rûpam.)

3. With instrumental:

I, 165, 1. káyâ *s*ubhấ marúta*h* sám mimikshu*h*.

To what splendour do the Maruts cling; or, what splendour clings to them?

V, 58, 5. sváyâ matyấ marúta*h* sám mimikshu*h*. (See also I, 165, 1.)

The Maruts cling to their own thought or will. (Sây. v*ri*sh*t*yâ samyak si*ñk*anti.)

I, 167, 4. yavyấ sâdhâra*n*yấ-iva marúta*h* mimikshu*h*.

The Maruts cling to the young maid, as if she belonged to all. See I, 173, 12; VIII, 98, 8; or VI, 27, 6.

I, 87, 6. bhânú-bhi*h* sám mimikshire.

The Maruts were joined with splendour. (Sây. me*dh*um i*kkh*anti.)

4. With accusative:

VIII, 61, 18. ní yấ vá*g*ram mimikshátu*h*.

Thy two arms which have firmly grasped the thunderbolt. (Say. parig*ri*h*n*îta*h*.)

Here I should also prefer to place VII, 20, 4, if we might read mimikshe or mimyáksha, for it is impossible to take mímikshan for anything but a participle of the desiderative of mih, which does not yield an appropriate meaning.

ní vá*g*ram índra*h* mímikshan.

Grasping firmly the thunderbolt. (Sây. *s*atrushu prâpayan.)

VI, 29, 3. *s*riyé te pádâ dúva*h* â mimikshu*h*.

Thy servants embrace thy feet for their happiness. (Sây. âsi*ñk*anti, samarpayanti.)

Like other verbs which mean to join, myaksh, if accompanied by prepositions expressive of separation, means to separate. (Cf. vi-yukta, se-junctus.)

II, 28, 6. ápo (íti) sú myaksha varu*n*a bhiyásam mát.

Remove well from me, O Varu*n*a, terror. (Sây. apagamaya.)

Quite distinct from this is the desiderative or inchoative verb mimiksh, from mih, in the sense of to sprinkle, or to shower, chiefly used with reference to the gods who are asked to sprinkle the sacrifice with rain. Thus we read:

I, 142, 3. mádhvâ ya*gñ*ám mimikshati.

(Narâ*s*a*m*sa) sprinkles the sacrifice with rain.

IX, 107, 6. mádhvâ ya*gñ*ám mimiksha na*h*.

Sprinkle (O Soma) our sacrifice with rain.

I, 34, 3. trí*h* adyá ya*gñ*ám mádhunâ mimikshatam.

O A*s*vins, sprinkle the sacrifice with rain thrice to-day!

I, 47, 4. mádhvâ ya*gñ*ám mimikshatam.

O A*s*vins, sprinkle the sacrifice with rain!

5. Without mádhu:

I, 22, 13. mahí dyaú*h* p*ri*thiví *k*a na*h* imám ya*gñ*ám mimikshatâm.

May the great heaven and earth sprinkle this our sacrifice.

6. With mádhu in the accusative:

VI, 70, 5. mádhu na*h* dyávâp*ri*thiví (íti) mimikshatâm.

May heaven and earth shower down rain for us.

Very frequently the A*s*vins are asked to sprinkle the sacrifice with their whip. This whip seems originally, like the whip of the Maruts, to have been intended for the cracking noise of the storm, preceding the rain. Then as whips had possibly some similarity to the instruments used for sprinkling butter on the sacrificial viands, the A*s*vins are asked to sprinkle the sacrifice with their whip, i. e. to give rain:

I, 157, 4. mádhu-matyâ na*h* ká*s*ayâ mimikshatam.

O A*s*vins, sprinkle us with your rain-giving whip.

I, 22, 3. táyâ ya*gñ*ám mimikshatam.

O A*s*vins, sprinkle the sacrifice with it (your whip).

7. Lastly, we find such phrases as,

I, 48, 16. sám na*h* râyấ—mimikshvá.

Sprinkle us with wealth, i. e. shower wealth down upon us. Here mih is really treated as a Hu-verb in the Âtmanepada, though others take it for mimikshasva.

As an adjective, mimikshú is applied to Indra (III, 50, 3), and mimikshá to Soma (VI, 34, 4).

Note 3. I do not see how étâsa*h* can here be taken in any sense but that suggested by the Pada, ấ-itâsa*h*, come near. Professor Roth thinks it not impossible that it may be meant for étâ*h*, the fallow deer, the usual team of the Maruts. These Etas are mentioned in verse 5, but there the Pada gives quite correctly étân, not ấ-itân, and Sâya*n*a explains it accordingly by gantûn.

Note 4. The idea that the Maruts proclaim their own strength occurred before, I, 87, 3. It is a perfectly natural conception, for the louder the voice of the wind, the greater its strength, and vice versa.

Verse 2.

Note 1. Mánas here, as elsewhere, is used in the sense of thought preceding speech, desire, or devotion not yet expressed in prayer. See Taitt. Sa*m*h. V, 1, 3, 3. yat purusho manasâbhiga*kkh*ati tad vâ*k*â vadati, what a man grasps in his mind, that he expresses by speech. Professor Roth suggests an emendation which is ingenious, but not necessary, viz. mahấ námasâ, with great adoration, an expression which occurs, if not in VI, 52, 17, at least in VII, 12, 1. We find, however, the phrase mahấ mánasâ in

VI, 40, 4. ấ yâhi *s*á*s*vat u*s*atấ yayâtha índra mahấ mánasâ soma-péyam,

úpa bráhmâ*n*i *s*ri*n*ava*h* imấ na*h* átha te ya*gñ*á*h* tanvẽ váya*h* dhât.

Come hither, thou hast always come, Indra, to our libation through our yearning great desire. Mayest thou hear these our prayers, and may then the sacrifice put vigour in thy body.

It is curious to observe that throughout the Rig-veda the instrumental singular mahā́ is always used as an adjective belonging to some term or other for praise and prayer. Besides the passages mentioned, we find:

II, 24, 1. ayā́ vidhema návayâ mahā́ girā́.

Let us sacrifice with this new great song.

VI, 52, 17. su-ukténa mahā́ námasâ ā́ vivâse.

I worship with a hymn with great adoration, or I worship with a great hymn in adoration. VIII, 46, 14. gâya girā́ mahā́ ví-*k*etasam. Celebrate the wise Indra with a great song. Otherwise we might translate, Thou hast always come with a great yearning desire.

Verse 3.

Note 1. We ought to scan kŭtā*h* t̆văm īnd̆rā̆ mâhĭnā*h* san, because yâsi, being anudâtta, could not begin a new pâda. It would be more natural to translate kúta*h* by why? for the Maruts evidently wish to express their surprise at Indra's going to do battle alone and without their assistance. I do not think, however, that in the Rig-veda, even in the latest hymns, kúta*h* has as yet a causal meaning, and I have therefore translated it in the same sense in which it occurs before in the poet's address to the Maruts.

Note 2. Sat-pati, lord of men, means lord of real men, of heroes, and should not be translated by good lord. Sat by itself is frequently used in the sense of heroes, of men physically rather than morally good:

II, 1, 3. tvám agne índra*h* v*ri*shabhá*h* satā́m asi.

Thou, Agni, art Indra, the hero among heroes.

I, 173, 7. samát-su tvâ *s*ûra satā́m urâ*n*ám.

Thee, O hero, in battles the protector of (good and true) men.

Note 3. The meaning of sám p*rikkh*ase is very much the same as that of sám vadasva in I, 170, 5.

Note 4. *S*ubhâná is evidently meant as a name for the

Maruts, who thus speak of themselves in the third person, which is by no means unusual in the Rig-veda.

Mahîdhara explains *s*ubhânai*h* by *s*obhanair va*k*anai*h*.

Verse 4.

Indra certainly addresses his old friends, the Maruts, very unceremoniously, but this, though at first startling, was evidently the intention of the poet. He wished to represent a squabble between Indra and the Maruts, such as they were familiar with in their own village life, and this was to be followed by a reconciliation. The boorish rudeness, selfishness, and boastfulness here ascribed to Indra may seem offensive to those who cannot divest themselves of the modern meaning of deities, but looked upon from the right point of view, it is really full of interest.

Note 1. Bráhmâ*n*i and matáya*h* are here mentioned separately in the same way as a distinction is made between bráhman, stóma, and ukthá, IV, 22, 1; VI, 23, 1; between bráhmâ*n*i and gíra*h*, III, 51, 6; between bráhma, gíra*h*, and stóma*h*, VI, 38, 3; between bráhma, gíra*h*, ukthấ, and mánma, VI, 38, 4, &c.

Note 2. *S*ám, which I have here translated by sweet, is a difficult word to render. It is used as a substantive, as an adjective, and as an adverb; and in several instances it must remain doubtful whether it was meant for one or the other. The adverbial character is almost always, if not always, applicable, though in English there is no adverb of such general import as *s*ám, and we must therefore render it differently, although we are able to perceive that in the mind of the poet it might still have been conceived as an adverb, in the sense of 'well.' I shall arrange the principal passages in which *s*ám occurs according to the verbs with which it is construed.

1. With bhû:

VIII, 79, 7. bháva na*h* soma *s*ám h*ri*dé.

Be thou, Soma, well (pleasant) to our heart. Cf. VIII, 82, 3.

VIII, 48, 4. *s*ám na*h* bhava h*ri*dé ấ pîtá*h* indo (íti).

Be thou well (sweet) to our heart, when drunk, O Soma! Cf. X, 9, 4.

I, 90, 9. *s*ám na*h* bhavatu aryamā́.

May Aryaman be well (kind) to us!

VI, 74, 1. *s*ám na*h* bhûtam dvi-páde *s*ám *k*átu*h*-pade.

May Soma and Rudra be well (kind) to our men and cattle. Here *s*ám might be rendered as an adverb, or as an adjective, or even as a substantive, in the sense of health or blessing.

Cf. VII, 54, 1; IX, 69, 7. The expression dvipád and *k*átu*h*-pad is curiously like what occurs in the prayers of the Eugubian tables, Fisovie San*s*ie, ditu ocre Fisi, tote Jovine, ocrer Fisie, totar Jovinar dupursus, peturpursus fato fito (Umbrische Sprachdenkmäler, ed. Aufrecht, p. 198); and also in the edicts of Piyadasi, dupada-*k*atupadesu pakhivâlí*k*alesu, 'aux bipèdes, aux quadrupèdes, aux volatiles, aux animaux qui se meuvent dans les eaux.' See Burnouf, Lotus, p. 667.

II, 38, 11. *s*ám yát stot*ri*-bhya*h* âpáye bhávâti.

What may be well (a pleasure) for the praisers, for the friend.

X, 37, 10. *s*ám na*h* bhava *k*ákshasâ.

Be kind to us with thy light!

2. With as:

VIII, 17, 6. sóma*h* *s*ám astu te h*ri*dé.

May the Soma be well (agreeable) to thy heart!

I, 5, 7. *s*ám te santu prá-*k*etase.

May the Somas be well (pleasing) to thee, the wise!

V, 11, 5. túbhyam manîshā́ iyám astu *s*ám h*ri*dé.

May this prayer be well (acceptable) to thy heart!

I, 114, 1. yáthâ *s*ám ásat dvi-páde *k*átu*h*-pade.

That it may be well for our men and cattle. Cf. X, 165, 1; 3.

VII, 86, 8. *s*ám na*h* kshéme *s*ám û*m* (íti) yóge na*h* astu.

May it be well with us in keeping and acquiring!

V, 7, 9. ā́ yá*h* te—agne *s*ám ásti dhā́yase.

He who is lief to thee to support, i.e. he whom thou likest to support.

V, 74, 9. *s*ám û*m* (íti) sú vâm—asmā́kam astu *k*ark*ri*tí*h*.

Let there be happiness to you—glory to us!

3. With as or bhû understood:

VI, 45, 22. *s*ám yát gáve ná *s*âkíne.

A song which is pleasant to the mighty Indra, as food to an ox.

VIII, 13, 11. *s*ám ít hí te.

For it is well for thee.

X, 86, 15. mantthá*h* te indra *s*ám h*ri*dé.

The mixture is pleasant to thy heart, O Indra!

X, 97, 18. áram kấmâya, *s*ám h*ri*dé.

Enough for love, pleasant to the heart.

VI, 34, 3. *s*ám tát asmai.

That is pleasant to him.

VI, 21, 4. ká*h* te ya*g*ñá*h* mánase *s*ám várâya.

What sacrifice seems to thy mind pleasant to select?

4. With kar:

I, 43, 6. *s*ám na*h* karati árvate.

May he do well to our horse, i.e. may he benefit our horses.

IV, 1, 3. tokấya tu*g*é—*s*ám k*ri*dhi.

Do good to our children and progeny, or bless us for the procreation of children.

VIII, 18, 8. *s*ám na*h* karata*h* a*s*vínâ.

May the two A*s*vins do us good!

5. With vah:

I, 157, 3. *s*ám na*h* ấ vakshat dvi-páde *k*átu*h*-pade.

May he bring blessing to us for man and cattle.

VIII, 5, 20. téna na*h*—pá*s*ve tokấya *s*ám gáve, váhatam pî́varî*h* ísha*h*.

Bring to us rich food, a blessing to cattle, to children, and to the ox.

6. With verbs, such as pû, vâ, and others, where it is clearly used as an adverb:

IX, 11, 3. sá*h* na*h* pavasva *s*ám gáve *s*ám *g*ánâya *s*ám árvate, *s*ám râ*g*an óshadhîbhya*h*.

Do thou, king Soma, stream upon us, a blessing for the ox, a blessing for man, a blessing for the horse, a blessing for the plants. Cf. IX, 11, 7; 60, 4; 61, 15; 109, 5.

VII, 35, 4. *s*ám na*h* ishirá*h* abhí vâtu vấta*h*.

May the brisk wind blow kindly upon us, or blow a blessing upon us!

VII, 35, 6. *s*ám na*h* tvásh*t*â gnấbhi*h* ihá *sr*i*n*otu.

May Tvash*t*ar with the goddesses hear us here well, i. e. auspiciously!

VII, 35, 8. *s*ám na*h* sũrya*h*—út etu.

May the sun rise auspiciously for us!

VIII, 18, 9. *s*ám na*h* tapatu sũrya*h*.

May the sun warm us well!

III, 13, 6. *s*ám na*h* *s*o*k*a—ágne.

Shine well for us, O Agni!

*S*ám Yó*h*.

*S*ám also occurs in a phrase that has puzzled the interpreters of the Veda very much, viz. *s*ám yó*h*. These are two words, and must both be taken as substantives, though originally they may have been adverbs. Their meaning seems to have been much the same, and in English they may safely be rendered by health and wealth, in the old acceptation of these words:

I, 93, 7. dhattam yá*g*amânâya *s*ám yó*h*.

Give, Agni and Soma, to the sacrificer health and wealth.

I, 106, 5. *s*ám yó*h* yát te mánu*h*-hitam tát îmahe.

B*ri*haspati, we ask for health and wealth which thou gavest to Manu.

I, 114, 2. yát *s*ám *k*a yó*h* *k*a mánu*h* â-yegé pitấ tát a*s*yâma táva rudra prá-nîtishu.

Rudra, the health and wealth which Manu, the father, obtained, may we reach it under thy guidance.

II, 33, 13. yấni mánu*h* ávri*n*îta pitấ na*h* tấ *s*ám *k*a yó*h* *k*a rudrásya va*s*mi.

The medicines which our father Manu chose, those I desire, the health and wealth of Rudra.

I, 189, 2. bháva tokấya tánayâya *s*ám yó*h*.

Be to our offspring health and wealth!

IV, 12, 5. yá*kkh*a tokấya tánayâya *s*ám yó*h*.

Give to our offspring health and wealth!

V, 69, 3. î*l*e tokâya tánayâya *s*ám yó*h*.

I ask for our offspring health and wealth.

VI, 50, 7. dhâ̆ta tokâ̆ya tánayâya *s*ám yó*h*.

Give to our offspring health and wealth!

X, 182, 1. átha karat yá*g*amânâya *s*ám yó*h*.

May he then produce for the sacrificer health and wealth.

VII, 69, 5. téna na*h* *s*ám yó*h*—ní a*s*vinâ vahatam.

On that chariot bring to us, A*s*vins, health and wealth.

III, 17, 3. átha bhava yá*g*amânâya *s*ám yó*h*.

Then, Agni, be health and wealth to the sacrificer.

III, 18, 4. b*ri*hát váya*h* sa*s*amânéshu dhehi, revát agne vi*s*vâ̆mitreshu *s*ám yó*h*.

Give, Agni, much food to those who praise thee, give to the Vi*s*vâmitras richly health and wealth.

X, 15, 4. átha na*h* *s*ám yó*h* arapá*h* dadhâta.

And give us health and wealth without a flaw! Cf. X, 59, 8.

X, 37, 11. tát asmé *s*ám yó*h* arapá*h* dadhâtana.

And give to us health and wealth without a flaw!

V, 47, 7. tát astu mitra-varu*n*â tát agne *s*ám yó*h* asmábhyam idám astu *s*astám.

Let this, O Mitra-Varu*n*a, let this, O Agni, be health and wealth to us; may this be auspicious!

V, 53, 14. v*r*ish*t*vî̆ *s*ám yó*h* â̆pa*h* usrí bhesha*g*ám syâ̆ma maruta*h* sahá.

Let us be together with you, O Maruts, after health, wealth, water, and medicine have been showered down in the morning.

VIII, 39, 4. *s*ám *k*a yó*h* *k*a máya*h* dadhe.

He gave health, wealth, and happiness.

VIII, 71, 15. agním *s*ám yó*h* *k*a dâ̆tave.

We ask Agni to give us health and wealth.

X, 9, 4. *s*ám yó*h* abhí sravantu na*h*.

May the waters come to us, as health and wealth, or may they run towards us auspiciously.

Note 3. If we retain the reading of the MSS. *s*úshma*h* iyarti, we must take it as an independent phrase, and translate it by 'my strength rises.' For *s*úshma, though in this and other places it is frequently explained as an adjective, meaning powerful, is, as far as I can see, always a substantive, and means breath, strength. There may be a few passages in which, as there occur several words for strength, it might be possible to translate *s*úshma by strong. But even there it is better to keep to the general meaning of *s*úshma, and translate it as a substantive.

Iyarti means to rise and to raise. It is particularly applied to prayers raised by the poet in honour of the gods, and the similes used in connection with this, show clearly what the action implied by iyarti really is. For instance,

I, 116, 1. stómâ*n* iyarmi abhríyâ-iva vấta*h*.

I stir up hymns as the wind stirs the clouds.

X, 116, 9. su-va*k*asyấm iyarmi síndhau-iva prá îrayam nấvam arkai*h*.

I stir up sweet praise, as if I rowed a ship on the river with hymns.

In the sense of rising it occurs,

X, 140, 2. pâvaká-var*k*â*h* *s*ukrá-var*k*â*h* ánûna-var*k*â*h* út iyarshi bhânúnâ.

Thou risest up with splendour, Agni, thou of bright, resplendent, undiminished majesty.

We might therefore safely translate in our verse 'my strength rises,' although it is true that such a phrase does not occur again, and that in other passages where iyarti and *s*úshma occur together, the former governs the latter in the accusative. Cf. IV, 17, 12; X, 75, 3.

Mahîdhara translates, 'my held-up thunderbolt moves on destroying everything,' but he admits another rendering in which adri would mean the stone used for pressing the Soma.

Verse 5.

Note 1. If, as we can hardly avoid, we ascribe this verse to the Maruts, we must recognise in it the usual offer of help to Indra on the part of the Maruts. The question then only is, who are the strong friends in whose company they appear? It would be well if one could render antamébhi*h* by horses, as Sâya*n*a does, but there is no authority for it. Svá-kshatra is an adjective, meaning endowed with independent strength, synonymous with svá-tavas, I, 166, 2. It is applied to the mind of Indra, I, 54, 3; V, 35, 4; to the Maruts, V, 48, 1, but never to horses. As it stands, we can only suppose that a distinction is made between the Maruts and their followers, and that after calling together their followers, and adorning themselves for battle, they proceed to harness their chariots. Cf. I, 107, 2.

Note 2. Etân, in all MSS. which I consulted, has here the accent on the first syllable, and Professor Aufrecht ought not to have altered the word into etấn. If the accent had not been preserved by the tradition of the schools, the later interpreters would certainly have taken etân for the demonstrative pronoun. As it is, in spite of accent and termination, Sâya*n*a in I, 166, 10, seems to take étâ*h* for eté. In other passages, however, Sâya*n*a, too, has perceived the difference, and in I, 169, 6, he explains the word very fully as p*ri*shadvar*n*â gantâro vâ a*s*vâ vâ. In this passage the Etas are clearly the deer of the Maruts, the P*ri*shatîs:

I, 169, 6. ádha yát eshâm p*ri*thu-budhnấsa*h* étâ*h*.

In the next verse, however, éta seems applied to the Maruts themselves:

I, 169, 7. práti ghorấ*n*âm étânâm ayấsâm marútâm *srin*ve â-yatấm upabdí*h*.

The sound of the terrible, speckled, indefatigable Maruts is heard, as they approach; unless we translate:

The noise of the terrible deer of the indefatigable Maruts is heard, as they approach.

In I, 166, 10, á*m*seshu étâ*h*, I adopt Professor Roth's conjecture, that étâ*h* means the skins of the fallow deer, so that we should have to translate: On their shoulders are the deer-skins.

In the other passages where éta occurs it is used as a simile only, and therefore throws no light on the relation of the Etas to the Maruts. In both passages, however (V, 54, 5; X, 77, 2), the simile refers to the Maruts, though to their speed only, and not to their colour.

Note 3. Máha*h*-bhi*h*, which I have translated 'with all our might,' seems to be used almost as an adverb, mightily or quickly (makshu), although the original meaning, with our powers, through our might, is likewise applicable. The original meaning is quite perceptible in passages like

V, 62, 3. ádhârayatam p*ri*thivî́m utá dyấm mítra-râ*g*ânâ varu*n*â máha*h*-bhi*h*.

Kings Mitra and Varu*n*a, you have supported heaven and earth by your powers.

VII, 3, 7. tébhi*h* na*h* agne ámitai*h* máha*h*-bhi*h* *s*atám pûrbhí*h* ẫyasîbhi*h* ní pâhi.

With those immeasurable powers, O Agni, protect us, with a hundred iron strongholds.

I, 90, 2. té—máha*h*-bhi*h*, vratẫ rakshante vi*s*vẫhâ.

They always protect the laws by their powers.

VII, 71, 1. tvám na*h* agne máha*h*-bhi*h* pâhí.

Protect us, Agni, with thy power.

In other passages, however, we see máha*h*-bhi*h* used of the light or of the flames of Agni and of the dawn:

IV, 14, 1. devá*h* ró*k*amâna*h* máha*h*-bhi*h*.

Agni, the god, brilliant with his powers.

VI, 64, 2. devi ró*k*amânâ máha*h*-bhi*h*.

O goddess, brilliant with thy powers.

The powers of the Maruts are referred to by the same name in the following passages:

V, 58, 5. prá-pra *g*âyante—máha*h*-bhi*h*.

The Maruts are born with their powers.

VII, 58, 2. prá yé máha*h*-bhi*h* ó*g*asâ utá sánti.

The Maruts who excel in power and strength. Cf. III, 4, 6.

Verse 6.

Note 1. Indra in this dialogue is evidently represented as claiming everything for himself alone. He affects contempt for the help proffered by the Maruts, and seems to deny that he was at any time beholden to their assistance. By asking, Where was that custom that I should be with you and you with me in battle? he implies that it was not always their custom, and that he can dispense with their succour now. He wants to be alone, as in his former battle with Ahi, and does not wish that they should join him (cf. I, 33, 4). Professor Roth takes sam-ádhatta in the sense of implicating, but it can hardly be said that the Maruts ever implicated Indra in his fight against Ahi. Certainly this is not in keeping with the general tenor of this dialogue where, on the contrary, Indra shuns the company of the Maruts. But while on this point I differ from Professor Roth, I think he has rightly interpreted the meaning of ánamam. Out of the four passages in which badhasnai*h* occurs, it is three times joined with nam, and every time has the sense of to bend away from, to escape from. See also Sonne, in Kuhn's Zeitschrift, vol. xii, p. 348.

Verse 7.

Note 1. See VII, 39, 6. sakshîmáhi yú*g*yebhi*h* nú devai*h*.

Note 2. The last words leave no doubt as to their meaning, for the phrase is one of frequent occurrence. The only difficulty is the vocative maruta*h*, where we should expect the nominative. It is quite possible, however, that the Maruts should here address themselves, though, no doubt, it would be easy to alter the accent. As to the phrase itself, see

VIII, 61, 4. táthâ ít asat índra krátvâ yáthâ vá*s*a*h*.

May it be so, O Indra, as thou mayest desire by thy mind.

VIII, 66, 4. va*gr*ī́—ít karat índra*h* krátvâ yáthâ vá*s*at.

May Indra with the thunderbolt act as he may desire in his mind. Cf. VIII, 20, 17; 28, 4, &c.

Verse 8.

Note 1. Here again Indra claims everything for himself, denying that the Maruts in any way assisted him while performing his great deeds. These deeds are the killing of V*ri*tra, who withholds the waters, i. e. the rain from the earth, and the consequent liberation of the waters, so that they flow down freely for the benefit of Manu, that is, of man.

When Indra says that he slew V*ri*tra indriyé*n*a, he evidently chooses that word with a purpose, and we must therefore translate it here, not only by might, but by Indra's peculiar might. Indriyá, as derived from índra, means originally Indra-hood, then power in general, just as verethraghna in Zend means victory in general, though originally it meant the slaying of V*ri*tra.

On bádhîm, see Bollensen, Z. D. M. G. XXII, p. 594.

He takes bádhîm for a contraction of badhisham, in analogy with badhîs and badhît. He refers to akramîm, X, 166, 5, and badhîm, X, 28, 7.

Verse 9.

Note 1. Ánutta, in the sense of 'not shaken,' not shakeable, inébranlable, is strange; likewise the genitive, where we expect the instrumental. Still, nud, by itself, occurs in similar phrases, e. g. VI, 17, 5, nutthấ*h* á*k*yutam, thou shookest what is unshakeable, which might have been expressed by á*k*u*k*yava*h* ánuttam, and I cannot bring myself to believe that in our passage Aufrecht's conjectural emendation is called for. He (K. Z. XXVI, 611) takes ánutta for ánudatta, like pratta for pradatta, &c., and proposes to omit the negative particle, translating the verse: 'Certainly it is conceded to thee, there is none among the gods like unto thee.'

But though I cannot adopt this emendation here, I think that in other passages Aufrecht's rendering of ánutta is far more appropriate than to take it for a-nutta; for instance, I, 80, 7; III, 31, 13; VII, 34, 11.

There remains one verse in which anutta seems to mean not shaken, not overcome, namely, VIII, 90, 5, tvám v*ri*trấ*n*i ha*m*si apratî́ni éka*h* ít ánuttâ *k*arsha*n*i-dh*rí*tâ, thou, being alone, killest the irresistible enemies with the thunderbolt (?). However, anudâ, in the sense of conceding, yielding, nachgeben, is certainly a very familiar idea in Vedic poetry.

II, 12, 10. yá*h* *s*árdhate ná anu-dádâti *sri*dhyấm, who does not forgive the hurter his hurt.

I, 53, 8; II, 21, 4; 23, 11; X, 38, 5, Indra is called ananudá*h*, not yielding, not surrendering.

We must therefore admit two anuttas, one á-nutta, the other ánu(da)tta. In ánutta-manyu I prefer the former, 'of irresistible fury,' while Aufrecht prefers the latter, 'of recognised, or universally-admitted fury.'

Note 2. Devátâ in the ordinary sense of a deity never occurs in the Rig-veda. The word, in fact, as a feminine substantive occurs but twice, and in the tenth Ma*nd*ala only. But even there it does not mean deity. In X, 24, 6, devâ*h* devátayâ means, O gods, by your godhead, i. e. by your divine power. In X, 98, 1, b*ri*haspate práti me devátâm ihi, I take devátâ in the same sense as devátâti, and translate, O B*ri*haspati, come to my sacrifice.

In all other places where devátâ occurs in the Rig-veda it is a local adverb, and means among the gods. I shall only quote those passages in which Professor Roth assigns to devátâ a different meaning :

I, 55, 3. prá vîryḗ*n*a devátâ áti *k*ekite.

He is pre-eminent among the gods by his strength.

I, 22, 5. sá*h* *k*éttâ devátâ padám.

He knows the place among the gods.

I, 100, 15. ná yásya devā́*h* devátâ ná mártâ*h* ā́pa*h* *k*aná *s*ávasa*h* ántam âpú*h*.

He, the end of whose power neither the gods among the gods, nor mortals, nor even the waters have reached.

Here the translation of devátâ in the sense of 'by their godhead,' would be equally applicable, yet nothing would be gained as, in either case, devátâ is a weak repetition.

VI, 4, 7. índram ná tvâ *s*ávasâ devátâ vâyúm p*rin*anti rā́dhasâ n*ri*-tamâ*h*.

The best among men celebrate thee, O Agni, as like unto Indra in strength among the gods, as like unto Vâyu in liberality. See also devatâti, VIII, 74, 3; X, 8, 2.

Note 3. The juxta-position of *g*ā́yamâna*h* and *g*âtá*h* would seem to show that, if the latter had a past, the former had a future meaning. To us, 'No one who will be born and no one who has been born,' would certainly sound more natural. The Hindu, however, is familiar with the idea as here expressed, and in order to comprehend all beings, he speaks of those who are born and those who are being born. Thus in a Pada*s*ish*t*a of the Pâvamânîs (IX, 67) we read :

yan me garbhe vasata*h* pâpam ugram,
ya*g* *g*âyamânasya *k*a ki*mk*id anyat,
*g*âtasya *k*a ya*k* *k*âpi vardhato me,
tat pâvamânîbhir aham punâmi.

Note 4. Karishyā́ is written in all the MSS. without a

Visarga, and unless we add the Visarga on our own authority, we should have to take it as an entirely anomalous acc. plur. neut. of a passive participle of the future, karishyám standing for kâryãm, facie ndum. It is much easier, however, to explain this form if we add the Visarga, and read karishyã*h*, which would then be a second person singular of a Vedic conjunctive of the future. This form occurs at least once more in the Veda:

IV, 30, 23. utá nûnám yát indriyám karishyã*h* indra paú*m*syam, adyá náki*h* tát ã minat.

O Indra, let no man destroy to-day whatever manly feat thou art now going to achieve.

Verse 10.

Note 1. As I have translated these words, they sound rather abrupt. The meaning, however, would be clear enough, viz. almighty power belongs to me, therefore I can dare and do. If this abrupt expression should offend, it may be avoided, by taking the participle dadh*ri*shvãn as a finite verb, and translating, Whatever I have been daring, I shall do according to my will.

Verse 11.

Note 1. In this verse Indra, after having declined with no uncertain sound the friendship of the Maruts, seems to repent himself of his unkindness towards his old friends. The words of praise which they addressed to him in verse 9, in spite of the rebuff they had received from Indra, have touched his heart, and we may suppose that, after this, their reconciliation was complete. The words of Indra are clear enough, the only difficulty occurs in the last words, which are so idiomatic that it is impossible to render them in English. In tanvẽ tanûbhi*h*, literally for the body by the bodies, tanû is used like the pronoun self. Both must therefore refer to the same subject. We cannot translate 'for myself made by yourselves,' but must take the two words together, so that they should mean, 'the hymn which you have made for your own benefit and by your own exertions.'

Verse 13.

Note 1. Spiegel, in his review, called my attention to the Zend api-vat, which Burnouf discussed in his 'Études,' p. 328. Burnouf tries to show that vat in Zend has the meaning of knowing, and that it occurs with the preposition api, in apivatahê and apivatâiti. If this is the same word as in Sanskrit, then apivâtayati would be a causative, meaning to make known. The meaning of vat, however, is doubtful in Zend, and hardly appropriate in the few passages where it occurs in the Veda. Roth, in the Dictionary, explains vat by verstehn, begreifen, the causative by begreiflich machen; but in our passage he translates it by belebend, Ludwig by aufspürend. Till we get more light, I shall feel content to translate apivat by to approach, to obtain, and the causative by to make approach, to invite, to welcome.

The following are the passages in which api-vat occurs:

VII, 3, 10. ápi krátum su-*k*étasam vatema.

May we obtain an excellent understanding; not, Awaken in us a good sense.

VII, 60, 6. ápi krátum su-*k*étasam vátanta*h*.

They (Mitra and Varu*n*a) obtaining an excellent understanding.

I, 128, 2. tám ya*gñ*a-sâdham ápi vâtayâmasi.

Him, Agni, the performer of the sacrifice, we make approach, we invite.

X, 20, 1; 25, 1. bhádram na*h* ápi vâtaya mána*h*, dáksham utá krátum.

Bring to us, i. e. give us, a good mind, and a strong understanding.

X, 13, 5. pitré putrâsa*h* ápi avîvatan *ri*tam.

The sons obtained the right for the father (an obscure verse).

As to svapivâta, VII, 46, 3, I should derive it from van, in the sense of implored, desired; see, however, Muir, Sanskrit Texts, IV, p. 314, note; Nirukta, ed. Roth, p. 135.

Note 2. On návedâ*h*, see IV, 23, 4.

Verse 14.

Note 1. This is a verse which, without some conjectural

alterations, it seems impossible to translate. Sâya*n*a, of course, has a translation ready for it, so has M. Langlois, but both of them offend against the simplest rules of grammar and logic. The first question is, who is meant by asmā́n (which is here used as an amphimacer), the sacrificers or the Maruts? The verb ā́ *k*akré would well apply to the medhā́ mânyásya, the hymn of Mânya, which is intended to bring the Maruts to the sacrifice, this bringing to the sacrifice being the very meaning of â kar. But then we have the vocative maruta*h* in the next line, and even if we changed the vocative into the accusative, we should not gain much, as the Maruts could hardly call upon anybody to turn them towards the sage.

If, on the contrary, we admit that asmā́n refers to those who offer the sacrifice, then we must make a distinction, which, it is true, is not an unusual one, between those who here speak of themselves in the first person, and who provide the sacrifice, and the poet Mâ*n*dârya Mânya, who was employed by them to compose or to recite this hymn.

But even if we adopt this alternative, many difficulties still remain. First of all, we have to change the accent of *k*akré into *k*akre, which may seem a slight change, but is not the less objectionable when we consider that in our emendations of the Vedic hymns we must think rather of accidents that might happen in oral traditions than of the lapsus calami of later scribes. Secondly, we must suppose that the hymn of Mândârya Mânya ends with verse 13, and that the last verses were supplied by the sacrificers themselves. Possibly the dialogue only, from verse 3 to verse 12, was the work of Mânya, and the rest added at some solemn occasion.

Other difficulties, however, remain. Duvasyā́t is taken by Sâya*n*a as an ablative of duvasyá, worthy of dúvas, i. e. of worship, of sacrifice. Unfortunately this duvasyá does not occur again, though it would be formed quite regularly, like namasyā̃, worthy of worship, from námas, worship.

If we take duvasyā́t as the 3rd pers. sing. of the present in the Vedic conjunctive, we must also confess that this conjunctive does not occur again. But the verb duvasyati occurs frequently. It seems to have two meanings. It is derived from dúvas, which in the Vedic language means worship or sacrifice, just as karma, work, has assumed the special sense of sacrifice. Derived from dúvas in this sense, duvasyati means to worship. But dúvas meant originally any opus operatum. The root from which dúvas is derived, is lost in Sanskrit, but it exists in other languages. It must have been du or dû in the sense of acting, or sedulously working. It exists in Zend as du, to do, in Gothic as táujan, gataujan, Old High-German zawjan, Modern German zauen (Grimm, Gram. i^2. p. 1041). The Gothic tavi, opus, Old High-German zouwi, Middle High-German gezöuwe (Grimm, Gram. iii. p. 499), come from the same source; and it is possible, too, that the Old Norse taufr, modern töfrar, incantamenta, the Old High-German zoupar, Middle High-German zouber, both neuter, and the modern Zauber, may find their explanation in the Sanskrit dúvas. Derived from dúvas, in the sense of work, we have duvasyati in the sense of helping, providing, the German schaffen and verschaffen.

In the sense of worshipping, duvasyati occurs,

III, 2, 8. duvasyáta—*g*âtá-vedasam.

Worship *G*âtavedas.

V, 28, 6. ā́ *g*uhota duvasyáta agním.

Invoke, worship Agni. Cf. III, 13, 3; 1, 13.

III, 3, 1. agní*h* hí devā́n—duvasyáti.

Agni performs the worship of the gods. Cf. VII, 82, 5.

I, 167, 6. sutá-soma*h* duvasyán.

He who has poured out Soma and worships.

In many passages duvasyati is joined with an instrumental:

V, 42, 11. náma*h*-bhi*h* devám—duvasya.

Worship the god with praises.

I, 78, 2. tám u tvâ gótama*h* girā́—duvasyati.

Gotama worships thee with a song.

V, 49, 2. su-uktai*h* devám—duvasya.

Worship the god with hymns.

VI, 16, 46. vîtī́ yá*h* devám—duvasyét.

He who worships the god with a feast.

X, 14, 1. yamám—havíshâ duvasya.

Worship Yama with an oblation.

VI, 15, 6. agním-agnim va*h* samídhâ duvasyata.

Worship Agni with your log of wood. Cf. VIII, 44, 1.

III, 1, 2. samít-bhi*h* agním námasâ duvasyan.

They worshipped Agni with logs of wood, with praise.

In the more general and, I suppose, more original sense of caring for, attending, we find duvasyati:

III, 51, 3. anehása*h* stúbha*h* índra*h* duvasyati.

Indra provides for the matchless worshippers.

I, 112, 15. kalím yā̆bhi*h*—duvasyátha*h*.

By the succours with which you help Kali. Cf. I, 112, 21.

I, 62, 10. duvasyánti svásâra*h* áhrayâ*n*am.

The sisters attend the proud (Agni).

I, 119, 10. yuvám pedáve—*s*vetám—duvasyatha*h*.

You provide for Pedu the white horse.

If, then, we take duvasyati in the sense of working for, assisting, it may be with the special sense of assisting at a sacred act, like διακονεῖν; and if we take duvás, as it has the accent on the last syllable, as the performer of a sacrifice, we may venture to translate, 'that he should help, as the singer helps the performer of the sacrifice[a].' The singer or the poet may be called the assistant at a sacrifice, for his presence was not necessary at all sacrifices, the songs constituting an ornament rather than an essential part in most sacred acts. But though I think it right to offer this conjectural interpretation, I am far from supposing that it gives us the real sense of this difficult verse. Duvasyā́t may be, as Sâya*n*a suggests, an ablative of duvasyá; and duvasyá, like namasyā́, if we change the accent, may mean he who is to be worshipped, or worshipping. In this way a different interpretation might suggest itself, though I confess I do not see that any other interpretation as yet suggested is satisfactory. Some happy thought may some day or other clear up this difficulty, when those who have

---

[a] Kar in the sense of officiating at a sacrifice is equally construed with a dative, X, 97, 22. yásmai k*ri*n*ó*ti brâhma*n*á*h*, he for whom a Brâhma*n*a performs a sacrifice.

toiled, but toiled in a wrong direction, will receive scant thanks for the trouble they have taken. See Bollensen, Z. D. M. G. XVIII, p. 606.

Note 2. In the second line, the words ó sú varta remind us of similar phrases in the Veda, but we want an accusative, governed by varta; whereas maruta*h*, to judge from its accent, can only be a vocative. Thus we read:

I, 138, 4. ó (íti) sú tvâ vav*ri*tîmahi stómebhi*h*.

May we turn thee quickly hither by our praises!

VIII, 7, 33. ó (íti) sú vr*í*sh*n*a*h*--vav*ri*tyấm.

May I turn the heroes quickly hither!

Compare also passages like III, 33, 8:

ó (íti) sú svasâra*h* kâráve *srin*ota.

Listen quickly, O sisters, to the poet.

I, 139, 7. ó (íti) sú na*h* agne *srin*uhi.

Hear us quickly, O Agni.

Cf. I, 182, 1; II, 34, 15; VII, 59, 5; VIII, 2, 19; X, 179, 2.

Unless we change the accent, we must translate, 'Bring hither quickly!' and we must take these words as addressed to the kârú, the poet, whose hymn is supposed to attract the gods to the sacrifice. By a quick transition, the next words, maruta*h* vípram á*kkh*a, would then have to be taken as addressed to the gods, 'Maruts, on to the sage!' and the last words would become intelligible by laying stress on the va*h*, 'for you, and not for Indra or any other god, has the singer recited these hymns.' See, however, Preface, p. xxi.

Verse 15.

Note 1. I translate Mânya, the son of Mâna, because the poet, so called in I, 189, 8, is in all probability the same as our Mândârya Mânya. But it may also be Mânya, the descendant of Mandâri. The Mânas are mentioned I, 172, 5; 182, 8.

Note 2. Vâ*g*. S. XXXIV, 48. The second line is difficult, owing to the uncertain meaning of vayấm.

Ấ ishấ[a] yâsîsh*t*a has been rendered, 'Come hither with

[a] There was a misprint in the Sa*m*hitâ text, eshấ instead of éshấ, which was afterwards repeated whenever the same verse occurred again.

water or drink or rain,' yâsîsh*t*a being the aorist without the augment and with the intermediate vowel lengthened. The indicative occurs in

V, 58, 6. yát prá áyâsish*t*a p*ri*shatîbhi*h* ásvai*h*.

When you Maruts came forth with your fallow deer and your horses.

But what is the meaning of vayã́m? Vayā́ means a germ, a sprout, an offshoot, a branch, as may be seen from the following passages:

II, 5, 4. vidvā́n asya vratā́ dhruvā́ vayā́*h*-iva ánu rohate.

He who knows his eternal laws, springs up like young sprouts. (Better vayā́-iva.)

VI, 7, 6. tásya ít û*m* (íti) vísvâ bhúvanâ ádhi mûrdháni vayā́*h*-iva ruruhu*h*.

From above the head of Vaisvanara all worlds have grown, like young sprouts.

VIII, 13, 6. stotā́—vayā́*h*-iva ánu rohate. (Better vayā́-iva.)

The worshipper grows up like young sprouts.

VIII, 13, 17. índram ksho*n*ī́*h* avardhayan vayā́*h*-iva.

The people made Indra to grow like young sprouts.

VIII, 19, 33. yásya te agne anyé agnáya*h* upa-kshíta*h* vayā́*h*-iva.

Agni, of whom the other fires are like parasitical shoots.

I, 59, 1. vayā́*h* ít agne agnáya*h* te anyé.

O Agni, the other fires are indeed offshoots of thee.

II, 35, 8. vayā́*h* ít anyā́ bhúvanâni asya.

The other worlds are indeed his (the rising sun's) offshoots.

VI, 13, 1. tvát vísvâ—saúbhagâni ágne ví yanti vanína*h* ná vayā́*h*.

From thee O Agni, spring all happinesses, as the sprouts of a tree.

VI, 24, 3. v*ri*kshásya nú (ná?) te—vayā́*h* ví ûtáya*h* ruruhu*h*.

Succours sprang from thee, like the branches of a tree.

V, 1, 1. yahvā́*h*-iva prá vayā́m ut-*g*íhânâ*h* prá bhânáva*h* sisrate nā́kam á*kkh*a.

Like birds (?) flying up to a branch, the flames of Agni went up to heaven; (or like strong men reaching up to.)

VI, 57, 5. tā́m pû́sh*n*á*h* su-matím vayám v*ri*kshásya prá vayā́m-iva índrasya *k*a ā́ rabhâmahe.

Let us reach this favour of Pûshan and of Indra, as one reaches forth to the branch of a tree.

There remain some doubtful passages in which vayā́ occurs, VII, 40, 5, and X, 92, 3; 134, 6. In the first passage, as in our own, vayā́*h* is trisyllabic.

If vayā́ can be used in the sense of offshoot or sprout, we may conclude that the same word, used in the singular, might mean offspring, particularly when joined with tanvè̄. 'Give a branch to our body,' would be understood even in languages less metaphorical than that of the Vedas; and as the prayer for 'olive branches' is a constant theme of the Vedic poets, the very absence of that prayer here, might justify us in assigning this sense to vayā́m. In VI, 2, 5, the expression vayā́vantam ksháyam, a house with branches, means the same as n*ri*vántam, a house with children and men. See M. M., On Βίος and váyas, in Kuhn's Zeitschrift, vol. xv, p. 215. Benfey (Endungen in îans, p. 37) takes vayâm as a genitive plural, referring it to the Maruts, as closely connected with each other, like branches of a tree. This is much the same interpretation as that of Mahîdhara (VS. XXXIV, 48), who translates 'come near for the body, i. e. for the bodily strength of the fellows, the Maruts.' Ludwig takes it as a possible instrumental of vayam.

It is preferable, however, to take yâsîsh*t*a as a precative Âtm., in order to account for the long î, and to accept it as a third person singular, referring to stóma*h*.

Note 3. V*rig*ána means an enclosure, a νομός, whether it be derived from v*rig*, to ward off, like arx from arcere, or from v*rig*, in the sense of clearing, as in v*ri*kta-barhis, barhí*h* prá v*riñg*e, I, 116, 1. In either case the meaning remains much the same, viz. a field, cleared for pasture or agriculture,—a clearing, as it is called in America, or a camp,—enclosed with hurdles or walls, so as to be capable of defence against wild animals or against enemies. In this sense, however, v*rig*ana is a neuter, while as a masculine it means powerful, invigorating. See Preface, p. xx.

MAN*D*ALA I, HYMN 166.

ASH*T*AKA II, ADHYÂYA 4, VARGA 1–3.

TO THE MARUTS (THE STORM-GODS).

1. Let us now proclaim for the robust[1] host, for the herald[2] of the powerful (Indra), their ancient greatness! O ye strong-voiced Maruts, you heroes, prove your powers on your march, as with a torch, as with a sword[3]!

2. Like parents bringing a dainty to[1] their own[2] son, the wild (Maruts) play playfully at the sacrifices. The Rudras reach the worshipper with their protection, strong in themselves, they do not fail the sacrificer.

3. For him to whom the immortal guardians have given fulness of wealth, and who is himself a giver of oblations, the Maruts, who gladden men with the milk (of rain), pour out, like friends, many clouds.

4. You who have stirred[1] up the clouds with might, your horses rushed[2] forth, self-guided. All beings who dwell in houses[3] are afraid of you, your march is brilliant with your spears thrust forth.

5. When they whose march is terrible have caused the rocks to tremble[1], or when the manly Maruts have shaken the back of heaven, then every lord of the forest fears at your racing, each shrub flies out of your way[2], whirling like chariot-wheels[3].

6. You, O terrible Maruts, whose ranks are never broken, favourably[1] fulfil our prayer[2]! Wherever your gory-toothed[3] lightning bites[4], it crunches[5] cattle, like a well-aimed bolt[6].

7. The Maruts whose gifts are firm, whose bounties are never ceasing, who do not revile[1], and who are highly praised at the sacrifices, they sing their song[2] for to drink the sweet juice: they know the first manly deeds of the hero (Indra).

8. The man whom you have guarded, O Maruts, shield him with hundredfold strongholds from injury[1] and mischief,—the man whom you, O fearful, powerful singers, protect from reproach in the prosperity of his children.

9. On your chariots, O Maruts, there are all good things, strong weapons[1] are piled up clashing against each other. When you are on your journeys, you carry the rings[2] on your shoulders, and your axle turns the two wheels at once[3].

10. In their manly arms there are many good things, on their chests golden chains[1], flaring[2] ornaments, on their shoulders speckled deer-skins[3], on their fellies sharp edges[4]; as birds spread their wings, they spread out splendours behind.

11. They, mighty by might, all-powerful powers[1], visible from afar like the heavens[2] with the stars, sweet-toned, soft-tongued singers with their mouths[3], the Maruts, united with Indra, shout all around.

12. This is your greatness[1], O well-born Maruts!—your bounty[3] extends far, as the sway[2] of Aditi[4]. Not even[5] Indra in his scorn[6] can injure that bounty, on whatever man you have bestowed it for his good deeds.

13. This is your kinship (with us), O Maruts, that you, immortals, in former years have often protected the singer[1]. Having through this prayer granted a hearing to man, all these heroes together have become well-known by their valiant deeds.

14. That we may long flourish, O Maruts, with your wealth, O ye racers, that our men may spread in the camp, therefore let me achieve the rite with these offerings.

15. May this praise, O Maruts, this song of Mândârya, the son of Mâna, the poet, ask you with food for offspring for ourselves! May we have an invigorating autumn, with quickening rain!

NOTES.

This hymn is ascribed to Agastya, the reputed son of Mitrâvaru*n*au, and brother of Vasish*th*a. The metre in verses 1–13 is *G*agatî, in 14, 15 Trish*t*ubh. No verse of this hymn occurs in SV., VS., AV., TS., TB.

Verse 1.

Note 1. Rabhasá, an adjective of rábhas, and this again from the root rabh, to rush upon a thing, â-rabh, to begin a thing. From this root rabh we have the Latin robur, in the general sense of strength, while in rabies the original meaning of impetuous motion has been more clearly preserved. The Greek λάβρος, too, as pointed out by Cowell, comes from this root. In the Vedic Sanskrit, derivatives from the root rabh convey the meaning both of quickness and of strength. Quickness in ancient languages frequently implies strength, and strength implies quickness, as we see, for instance, from the German snël, which, from meaning originally strong, comes to mean in modern German quick, and quick only. The German bald again, meaning soon, comes from the Gothic balths, the English bold. Thus we read:

I, 145, 3. *s*í*s*u*h* ấ adatta sám rábha*h*.

The child (Agni) acquired vigour.

Indra is called rabha*h*-dấ*h*, giver of strength; and rabhasá, vigorous, is applied not only to the Maruts, who in V, 58, 5, are called rábhish*th*â*h*, the most vigorous, but also to Agni, II, 10, 4, and to Indra, III, 31, 12.

In the sense of rabid, furious, it occurs in

X, 95, 14. ádha enam v*r*í*k*â*h* rabhasấsa*h* adyú*h*.

May rabid wolves eat him!

In the next verse rabhasá, the epithet of the wolves, is replaced by á*s*iva, which means unlucky, uncanny.

In our hymn rabhasá occurs once more, and is applied there, in verse 10, to the a*ñg*í or glittering ornaments of the Maruts. Here Sâya*n*a translates it by lovely, and it was most likely intended to convey the idea of lively or brilliant splendour, though it may mean also strong. See also IX, 96, 1.

Note 2. Ketú, derived from an old root ki, in Sanskrit *k*i, to perceive, from which also *k*itra, conspicuous, kenspeckled, beautiful, means originally that by which a thing is perceived or known, whether a sign, or a flag, or a herald. It is the Gothic haidu, species. It then takes the more general sense of light and splendour. In our passage, herald seems to me the most appropriate rendering, though B. and R. prefer the sense of banner. The Maruts come before Indra, they announce the arrival of Indra, they are the first of his army.

Note 3. The real difficulty of our verse lies in the two comparisons aidhấ-iva and yudhấ-iva. Neither of them occurs again in the Rig-veda. B. and R. explain aidhấ as an instrumental of aídh, flaming, or flame, and derive it from the root idh, to kindle, with the preposition â. Professor Bollensen in his excellent article Zur Herstellung des Veda (Orient und Occident, vol. iii, p. 473) says: 'The analysis of the text given in the Pada, viz. aidhấ-iva and yudhấ-iva, is contrary to all sense. The common predicate is tavishấ*n*i kartana, exercise your power, you roarers. i. e. blow as if you meant to kindle the fire on the altar, show your power as if you went to battle. We ought therefore to read aidhé va and yudhé | va. Both are infinitives, aidh is nothing but the root idh + â, to kindle, to light.' Now this is certainly a very ingenious explanation, but it rests on a supposition which I cannot consider as proved, viz. that in the Veda, as in Pâli, the comparative particle iva may be changed, as shown in the preface to the first edition, to va. It must be admitted that the two short syllables of iva are occasionally counted in the Veda as one, but yudhé-iva, though it might become yudhá iva, would never in the Veda become yudhéva.

As yudhấ occurs frequently in the Veda, we may begin by admitting that the parallel form aidhấ must be explained in analogy to yudhấ. Now yúdh is a verbal noun and means fighting. We have the accusative yúdham, I, 53, 7; the genitive yudhá*h*, VIII, 27, 17; the dative yudhé, I, 61, 13; the locative yudhí, I, 8, 3; the instrumental yudhấ, I, 53, 7, &c.; loc. plur. yut-sú, I, 91, 21. As long as yúdh retains the general predicative meaning of fighting, some of these cases may be called infinitives. But yúdh soon assumes not only the meaning of battle, battle-ground, but also of instrument of fighting, weapon. In another passage, X, 103, 2, yúdha*h* may be taken as a vocative plural, meaning fighters. Passages in which yúdh means clearly weapon, are, for instance,

V, 52, 6. ấ rukmai*h* ấ yudhấ nára*h* *ri*shvấ*h* *ri*sh*t*ī́*h* as*ri*kshata.

With their bright chains, with their weapon, the tall men have stretched forth the spears.

X, 55, 8. pîtvī́ sómasya divá*h* ấ v*ri*dhânấ*h* *s*ū́ra*h* ní*h* yudhấ adhamat dásyûn.

The hero, growing, after drinking the Soma, blew away from the sky the enemies with his weapon. See also X, 103, 4.

I therefore take yúdh in our passage also in the sense of weapon or sword, and, in accordance with this, I assign to aídh the meaning of torch. Whether aídh comes from idh with the preposition â, which, after all, would only give edh, or whether we have in the Sanskrit aídh the same peculiar strengthening which this very root shows in Greek and Latin[a], would be difficult to decide. The torch of the Maruts is the lightning, the weapon the thunderbolt, and by both they manifest their strength; ferro et igne, as Ludwig remarks.

WILSON: We proclaim eagerly, Maruts, your ancient greatness, for (the sake of inducing) your prompt appearance, as the indication of (the approach of) the showerer (of benefits). Loud-roaring and mighty Maruts, you exert your vigorous energies for the advance (to the sacrifice), as if it was to battle.

Verse 2.

Note 1. That úpa can be construed with the accusative is clear from many passages:

III, 35, 2. úpa imám ya*g*ñám ấ vahâta*h* índram.

Bring Indra to this sacrifice!

I, 25, 4. váya*h* ná vasatī́*h* úpa.

As birds (fly) to their nests.

[a] Schleicher, Compendium, § 36, αἴθω, αἰθήρ, αἴθουσα; and § 49. aides, aidilis aestas.

Note 2. Nítya, from ni + tya[a], means originally what is inside, internus, then what is one's own; and is opposed to níshtya, from nis + tya, what is outside, strange, or hostile. Nítya has been well compared with nigá, literally eingeboren, then, like nítya, one's own. What is inside, or in a thing or place, is its own, is peculiar to it, does not move or change, and hence the secondary meanings of nítya, one's own, unchanging, eternal. Thus we find nítya used in the sense of internal or domestic:

I, 73, 4. tám tvâ nára*h* dáme ấ nítyam iddhám ágne sá*k*anta kshitíshu dhruvấsu.

Our men worshipped thee, O Agni, lighted within the house in safe places.

This I believe to be a more appropriate rendering than if we take nítya in the sense of always, continuously lighted, or, as some propose, in the sense of eternal, everlasting.

VII, 1, 2. dakshấyya*h* yá*h* dáme ấsa nítya*h*.

Agni who is to be pleased within the house, i. e. as belonging to the house, and, in that sense, who is to be pleased always. Cf. I, 140, 7; 141, 2; X, 12, 2, and III, 25, 5, where nítya*h*, however, may have been intended as an adjective belonging to the vocative sûno.

Most frequently nítya occurs with sûnú, I, 66, 1; 185, 2; tánaya, III, 15, 2; X, 39, 14; toká, II, 2, 11; âpí, VII, 88, 6; páti, I, 71, 1, and has always the meaning of one's own, very much like the later Sanskrit niga, which never occurs in the Rig-veda, though it makes its appearance in the Âtharva*n*a.

Nísh*t*ya, extraneus, occurs three times in the Rig-veda:

VI, 75, 19. yá*h* na*h* svá*h* ára*n*a*h* yá*h* *k*a nísh*t*ya*h* gíghâ*m*sati.

Whoever wishes to hurt us, our own friend or a stranger from without.

X, 133, 5. yá*h* na*h* indra abhi-dấsati sá-nâbhi*h* yá*h* *k*a nísh*t*ya*h*.

He who infests us, O Indra, whether a relative or a stranger.

VIII, 1, 13. mấ bhûma nísh*t*yâ*h*-iva índra tvád ára*n*â*h*-iva.

---

[a] Ápa-tya; cf. Bopp, Accentuationssystem, § 138, ἔπι-σσαι, Nachkommen.

Let us not be like outsiders, O Indra, not like strangers to thee.

Wilson: Ever accepting the sweet (libation), as (they would) a son, they sport playfully at sacrifices, demolishing (all intruders).

Ludwig: Wie einen nicht absterbenden Sohn das Madhu bringend.

Verse 4.

Note 1. Ávyata, a Vedic second aorist of vî (a*g*), to stir up, to excite. From it pravaya*n*a, a goad, pra-vetar, a driver. The Greek οἶ-σ-τρος, gad-fly, has been referred to the same root. See Fick, Wörterbuch, p. 170.

Roth (Wenzel, Instrumental, p. 54) translates: 'While you quickly throw yourselves into the mists;' from a verb vyâ.

Note 2. Adhra*g*an, from dhra*g*, a root which, by metathesis of aspiration, would assume the form of dra*gh* or dragh. In Greek, the final medial aspirate being hardened, reacts on the initial media, and changes it to t, as bâhu becomes πῆχυς, budh πυθ, bandh πευθ. This would give us τρεχ, the Greek root for running, Goth. thrag-jan.

Note 3. Harmyá is used here as an adjective of bhúvana, and can only mean living in houses. It does not, however, occur again in the same sense, though it occurs several times as a substantive, meaning house. Its original meaning is fire-pit, then hearth, then house, a transition of meaning analogous to that of aedes. Most of the ancient nations begin their kitchen with a fire-pit. 'They dig a hole in the ground, take a piece of the animal's raw hide, and press it down with their hands close to the sides of the hole, which thus becomes a sort of pot or basin. This they fill with water, and they make a number of stones red-hot in a fire close by. The meat is put into the water, and the stones dropped in till the meat is boiled. Catlin describes the process as awkward and tedious, and says that since the Assinaboins had learnt from the Mandans to make pottery, and had been supplied with vessels by the traders, they had entirely done away the custom, "excepting at public festivals; where they seem, like all others of the human family, to take pleasure in cherishing and perpetuating their ancient customs[a].''' This pit was called harmyá[b] or gharmá, which is the Latin formus. Thus we read:

VII, 56, 16. té harmye-sthấ*h* sís*avah* ná *s*ubhrấ*h*.

The Maruts bright like boys standing by the hearth.

From meaning fire-pit, or hearth, harmyá afterwards takes the more general sense of house:

VII, 55, 6. téshâm sám hanma*h* akshấ*n*i yáthâ idám harmyám táthâ.

We shut their eyes as we shut this house (possibly, this oven).

VII, 76, 2. pratî*k*ī́ ấ agât ádhi harmyébhya*h*.

The dawn comes near, over the house-tops.

X, 46, 3. *g*âtá*h* ấ harmyéshu.

Agni, born in the houses.

X, 73, 10. manyó*h* iyâya harmyéshu tasthau.

He came from Manyu, he remained in the houses.

In some of these passages harmyá might be taken in the sense of householder; but as harmyá in VII, 55, 6, has clearly the meaning of a building, it seems better not to assign to it unnecessarily any new significations.

If harmya or *harma meant originally a fire-pit, then a hearth, a house, we see the close connection between harma and gharma, harmya and gharmya. Thus by the side of harmyesh*th*a we find gharmyesh*th*a (RV. X, 106, 5). We find gharma meaning, not only heat in general, but fire-pit, hearth; and we find the same word used for what we should call the pit, a place of torture and punishment from which the gods save their worshippers, or into which they throw the evil-doers.

V, 32, 5. yúyutsantam támasi harmyé dhấ*h*.

---

[a] Tylor, Early History of Mankind, p. 262.

[b] Spiegel, who had formerly identified harmyá with the Zend zairimya in zairimya*n*ura, has afterwards recalled this identification; see Spiegel, Av. Übers. I, p. 190; Commentar über den Avesta, I, p. 297: Justi, Handbuch, p. 119; Haug, Pahlavi Glossary, p. 22. According to the Parsis, the Hairimya*n*ura, a daêva animal which appears at the rising of the sun, is the turtle, and Darmesteter (Ormazd et Ahriman, p. 283) identifies zair in zair-imya with the Greek χελ-ύς, Sanskrit har-mu*t*a.

When thou, Indra, hadst placed *S*ush*n*a, who was anxious to fight, in the darkness of the pit.

In the next verse we find

asûryé támasi, in the ghastly darkness.

VIII, 5, 23. yuvám ká*n*vâya nâsatyâ ápi-riptâya harmyé *s*á*s*vat ûtî*h* da*s*asyatha*h*.

You, Nâsatyas, always grant your aid to Ka*n*va when thrown into the pit.

This fiery pit into which Atri is thrown, and whence he, too, was saved by the A*s*vins, is likewise called gharmá, I, 112, 7; 119, 6; VIII, 73, 3; X, 80, 3.

Lastly we find:

X, 114, 10. yadấ yamá*h* bhávati harmyé hitá*h*.

When Yama is seated in the house, or in the nether world.

When the Pitars, too, the spirits of the departed, the Manes, are called gharma-sád, this is probably intended to mean, dwelling on the hearth (X, 15, 9 and 10), and not dwelling in the abode of Yama.

Kuhn, Zeitschrift, vol. ii, p. 234: 'Die ihr die Luft erfüllt mit eurer Kraft, hervorstürmt ihr selbst-gelenkten Laufes.'

Verse 5.

Note 1. Nad certainly means to sound, and the causative might be translated by 'to make cry or shriek.' If we took párvata in the sense of cloud, we might translate, 'When you make the clouds roar;' if we took párvata for mountain, we might, with Professor Wilson, render the passage by 'When your brilliant coursers make the mountains echo.' But nad, like other roots which afterwards take the meaning of sounding, means originally to vibrate, to shake; and if we compare analogous passages where nad occurs, we shall see that in our verse, too, the Vedic poet undoubtedly meant n̤ad to be taken in that sense:

VIII, 20, 5. á*k*yutâ *k*it va*h* ágman ấ nấnadati párvatâsa*h* vánaspáti*h*, bhû́mi*h* yấmeshu regate.

At your racing even things that are immovable vibrate, the rocks, the lord of the forest; the earth quivers on your ways. (See I, 37, 7, note 1.) Grassmann here translates nadáyanta by e r s c h ü t t e r n, but in VIII, 20, 5 by e r d r ö h n t.

Note 2. See I, 37, 7, note 1.

Note 3. Rathiyántî-iva does not occur again. Sâya*n*a explains it, like a woman who wishes for a chariot, or who rides in a chariot. I join it with óshadhi, and take it in the sense of upamânâd â*k*âre (Pâ*n*. III, 1, 10), i.e. to behave like or to be like a chariot, whether the comparison is meant to express simply the quickness of chariots or the whirling of their wheels. The Pada has rathiyántî, whereas the more regular form is that of the Sa*m*hitâ, rathîyántî. Cf. Prâti*s*âkhya, 587.

Verse 6.

Note 1. Su-*k*etúnâ, the instrumental of su-*k*etú, kindness, good-mindedness, favour. This word occurs in the instrumental only, and always refers to the kindness of the gods; not, like sumatí, to the kindness of the worshipper also:

I, 79, 9. ấ na*h* agne su-*k*etúnâ rayím vi*s*vấyu-poshasam, mâr*d*îkám dhehi *g*îváse.

Give us, O Agni, through thy favour wealth which supports our whole life, give us grace to live.

I, 127, 11. sá*h* na*h* nédish*th*am dád*risa*na*h* ấ bhara ágne devébhi*h* sá-*k*anâ*h* su-*k*etúnâ mahá*h* râyá*h* su-*k*etúnâ.

Thou, O Agni, seen close to us, bring to us, in union with the gods, by thy favour, great riches, by thy favour!

I, 159, 5. asmábhyam dyâvâp*ri*thivî (íti) su-*k*etúnâ rayím dhattam vásu-mantam *s*ata-gvínam.

Give to us, O Dyâvâp*ri*thivî, by your favour, wealth, consisting of treasures and many flocks.

V, 51, 11. svastí dyâvâp*ri*thivî (íti) su-*k*etúnâ.

Give us, O Dyâvâp*ri*thivî, happiness through your favour!

V, 64, 2. tấ bâhávâ su-*k*etúnâ prá yantam asmai ár*k*ate.

Stretch out your arms with kindness to this worshipper!

In one passage of the ninth Ma*nd*ala (IX, 65, 30) we meet with su-*k*etúnam, as an accusative, referring to Soma, the gracious, and this would pre-suppose a substantive *k*etúna, which, however, does not exist.

Note 2. Sumatí has, no doubt, in most passages in the Rig-veda, the meaning of favour, the favour of the gods. 'Let us obtain your favour, let us be in your favour,' are familiar expressions of the Vedic poets. But there are also numerous passages where that meaning is inapplicable, and where, as in our passage, we must translate sumatí by prayer or desire.

In the following passages sumatí is clearly used in its original sense of favour, blessing, or even gift:

I, 73, 6 (7). su-matím bhíkshamâ*n*â*h*.

Begging for thy favour.

I, 171, 1. su-ukténa bhikshe su-matím turấ*n*âm.

With a hymn I beg for the favour of the quick Maruts.

I, 114, 3. a*s*yấma te su-matím.

May we obtain thy favour! Cf. I, 114, 9.

I, 114, 4. su-matím ít vayám asya ấ v*ri**n*îmahe.

We choose his favour. Cf. III, 33, 11.

I, 117, 23. sádâ kavî (íti) su-matím ấ *k*ake vâm.

I always desire your favour, O ye wise A*s*vins.

I, 156, 3. mahá*h* te vish*n*o (íti) su-matím bha*g*âmahe.

May we, O Vish*n*u, enjoy the favour of thee, the mighty!

Bhiksh, to beg, used above, is an old desiderative form of bha*g*, and means to wish to enjoy.

III, 4, 1. su-matím râsi vásva*h*.

Thou grantest the favour of wealth.

VII, 39, 1. ûrdhvá*h* agní*h* su-matím vásva*h* a*s*ret.

The lighted fire went up for the favour of wealth. Cf. VII, 60, 11; IX, 97, 26.

III, 57, 6. váso (íti) rấsva su-matím vi*s*vá-*g*anyâm.

Grant us, O Vasu, thy favour, which is glorious among men!

VII, 100, 2. tvám vish*n*o (íti) su-matím vi*s*vá-*g*anyâm—dâ*h*.

Mayest thou, Vish*n*u, give thy favour, which is glorious among men!

X, 11, 7. yá*h* te agne su-matím márta*h* ákshat.

The mortal who obtained thy favour, O Agni.

II, 34, 15. arvấ*k*î sấ maruta*h* yấ va*h* ûtí*h* ó (íti) sú vâ*s*rấ-iva su-matí*h* *g*igâtu.

Your help, O Maruts, which is to usward, your favour may it come near, like a cow!

VIII, 22, 4. asmấn á*kkh*a su-matí*h* vâm *s*ubha*h* patî (íti) â dhenú*h*-iva dhâvatu.

May your favour, O A*s*vins, hasten towards us, like a cow!

But this meaning is by no means the invariable meaning of sumatí, and it will easily be seen that, in the following passages, the word must be translated by prayer. Thus when Sarasvatî is called (I, 3, 11) *k*étantî su-matînắm, this can only mean she who knows of the prayers, as before she is called *k*odayitrî sûn*rí*tânâm, she who excites songs of praise:

I, 151, 7. á*kkh*a gíra*h* su-matím gantam asma-yű (íti).

Come towards the songs, towards the prayer, you who are longing for us. Cf. X, 20, 10.

II, 43, 3. tûsh*n*ī́m ā́sîna*h* su-matím *k*ikiddhi na*h*.

Sitting quiet, listen, O *S*akuni (bird), to our prayer!

V, 1, 10. ā́ bhándish*th*asya su-matím *k*ikiddhi.

Take notice of the prayer of thy best praiser! Cf. V, 33, 1.

VII, 18, 4. ā́ na*h* índra*h* su-matím gantu á*kkh*a.

May Indra come to our prayer!

VII, 31, 10. prá-*k*etase prá su-matím kri*n*udhvam.

Make a prayer for the wise god!

IX, 96, 2. su-matím yâti á*kkh*a.

He (Soma) goes near to the prayer.

X, 148, 3. *rí*shî*n*âm vípra*h* su-matím *k*akâná*h*.

Thou, the wise, desiring the prayer of the *Ri*shis.

VIII, 22, 6. tā́ vâm adyá sumatí-bhi*h* *s*ubha*h* patî (íti) á*s*vinâ prá stuvîmahi.

Let us praise to-day the glorious A*s*vins with our prayers.

IX, 74, 1. tám îmahe su-matī́.

We implore him with prayer.

In our passage the verb pipartana, fill or fulfil, indicates in what sense sumatí ought to be taken. Su-matím pipartana is no more than kā́mam pipartana, fulfil our desire! See VII, 62, 3. ā́ na*h* kā́mam pûpurantu; I, 158, 2. kâmapré*n*a-iva mánasâ. On sumná, see Burnouf, Études, p. 91, and Aufrecht, in Kuhn's Zeitschrift, vol. iv, p. 274.

Note 3. Krívi*h*-datî has been a crux to ancient and modern interpreters. It is mentioned as a difficult word in the Nigha*n*t*u, and all that Yâska has to say is that it means possessed of cutting teeth (Nir. VI, 30. krivirdatî vikartanadantî). Professor Roth, in his note to this passage, says that krivi can never have the meaning of well, which is ascribed to it in the Nigha*n*t*u III, 23, but seems rather to mean an animal, perhaps the wild boar, κάπρος, with metathesis of v and r. He translates our passage: 'Where your lightning with boar-teeth tears.' In his Dictionary, however, he only says, 'krivis, perhaps the name of an animal, and dant, tooth.' Sâya*n*a contents himself with explaining krívirdatî by vikshepa*n*a*s*îladantî, having teeth that scatter about.

My own translation is founded on the supposition that krívis, the first portion of krívirdatî, has nothing to do with krivi, but is a dialectic variety of kravís, raw flesh, the Greek *κρέας*, Latin caro, cruor. It means what is raw, bloody, or gory. From it the adjective krûra, horrible, cruentus (Curtius, Grundzüge, p. 142; Kuhn, Zeitschrift, vol. ii, p. 235). A name of the goddess Durgâ in later Sanskrit is krûradantî, and with a similar conception the lightning, I believe, is here called krívirdatî, with gory teeth.

Note 4. It should be observed that in rádati the simile of the teeth of the lightning is carried on. For rádati may be supposed to have had in the Veda, too, the original meaning of râdere and rôdere, to scratch, to gnaw. Rada and radana in the later Sanskrit mean tooth. It is curious, however, that there is no other passage in the Rig-veda where rad clearly means to bite. It means to cut, in

I, 61, 12. gó*h* ná párva ví rada tira*sk*ấ.

Cut his joint through, as the joint of an ox.

But in most passages where rad occurs in the Veda, it has the meaning of giving. It is not the same which we have in the Zend râd, to give, and which Justi rightly identifies with the root râdh. But rad, to divide, may, like the German theilen in zutheilen, have taken the meaning of giving. Greek *δαίω* means to divide, but yields *δαίς*, portion, meal, just as Sanskrit day, to divide, yields dâyas, share, i. e. inheritance.

This meaning is evident in the following passages:

VII, 79, 4. tấvat usha*h* rấdha*h* asmábhyam râsva yấvat stot*rí*-bhya*h* árada*h* g*rin*ânấ.

Grant us, Ushas, so much wealth as thou hast given to the singers, when praised.

I, 116, 7. kakshívate aradatam púram-dhim.

You gave wisdom to Kakshîvat.

I, 169, 8. ráda marút-bhi*h* *s*urúdha*h* gó-agrâ*h*.

Give to the Maruts gifts, rich in cattle.

VII, 62, 3. ví na*h* sahásram *s*urúdha*h* radantu.

May they (the gods) give to us a thousand gifts!

I, 117, 11. vā́*g*am víprâya—rádantâ.

Giving spoil to the sage!

VI, 61, 6. ráda pûshā́-iva na*h* saním.

Give us, Sarasvatî, wealth, like Pûshan!

IX, 93, 4. rada índo (íti) rayím.

Give us, O Indra, wealth!

VII, 32, 18. rada-vaso (íti).

Indra, thou who givest wealth!

In many passages, however, this verb rad is connected with words meaning way or path, and it then becomes a question whether it simply means to grant a way, or to cut a way open for some one. In Zend, too, the same idiom occurs, and Professor Justi explains it by 'prepare a way.' I subjoin the principal passages:

VI, 30, 3. yát ấbhya*h* árada*h* gâtúm indra.

That thou hast cut a way for them (the rivers). Cf. VII, 74, 4.

IV, 19, 2. prá vartanī́*h* arada*h* vi*s*vá-dhenâ*h*.

Thou (Indra) hast cut open the paths for all the cows.

X, 75, 2. prá te aradat váru*n*a*h* yā́tave pathá*h*.

Varu*n*a cut the paths for thee to go.

VII, 87, 1. rádat pathá*h* váru*n*a*h* sū́ryâya.

Varu*n*a cut paths for Sûrya.

V, 80, 3. pathá*h* rádantî suvitā́ya devī́.

She, the dawn, cutting open the paths for welfare.

VII, 60, 4. yásmai âdityā́*h* ádhvana*h* rádanti.

For whom the Âdityas cut roads.

II, 30, 2. pathá*h* rádantî*h*—dhúnaya*h* yanti ártham.

Cutting their paths, the rivers go to their goal.

This last verse seems to show that the cutting open of a road is really the idea expressed by rad in all these passages. And thus we find the rivers themselves saying that Indra cut them out or delivered them:

III, 33, 6. índra*h* asmā́n aradat vá*g*ra-bâhu*h*. Cf. X, 89, 7.

Note 5. Ri*n*ā́ti, like the preceding expressions krívirdatî and rádati, is not chosen at random, for though it has the general meaning of crushing or destroying, it is used by the Vedic poets with special reference to the chewing or crunching by means of the teeth. For instance,

I, 148, 4. purū́*n*i dasmá*h* ní ri*n*âti *g*ámbhai*h*.

Agni crunches many things with his jaws.

I, 127, 4. sthirấ *k*it ánnâ ní ri*n*âti ó*g*asâ.

Even tough morsels he (Agni) crunches fiercely.

In a more general sense we find it used,

V, 41, 10. *s*o*k*í*h*-ke*s*a*h* ní ri*n*âti vánâ.

Agni with flaming hair swallows or destroys the forests.

IV, 19, 3. áhim vá*g*re*n*a ví ri*n*â*h*.

Thou destroyedst Ahi with the thunderbolt.

X, 120, 1. sadyá*h* *g*a*g*ñâná*h* ní ri*n*âti *s*átrûn.

As soon as born he destroys his enemies.

Note 6. Súdhitâ-iva barhá*n*â. I think the explanation of this phrase given by Sâya*n*a may be retained. He explains súdhitâ by suhitâ, i. e. sush*th*u preritâ, well thrown, well levelled, and barhá*n*â by hatis, tatsâdhanâ hetir vâ, a blow or its instrument, a weapon. Professor Roth takes barhá*n*â as an instrumental, used adverbially, in the sense of powerfully, but he does not explain in what sense súdhitâ-iva ought then to be taken. We cannot well refer it to didyút, lightning, on account of the iva, which requires something that can form a simile of the lightning. Nor is su-dhitâ ever used as a substantive so as to take the place of svádhitîva. Sú-dhita has apparently many meanings, but they all centre in one common conception. Sú-dhita means well placed, of a thing which is at rest, well arranged, well ordered, secure; or it means well sent, well thrown, of a thing which has been in motion. Applied to human beings, it means well disposed or kind.

III, 23, 1. ní*h*-mathita*h* sú-dhita*h* ấ sadhá-sthe.

Agni produced by rubbing, and well placed in his abode.

VII, 42, 4. sú-prîta*h* agní*h* sú-dhita*h* dáme ấ.

Agni, who is cherished and well placed in the house.

III, 29, 2. ará*n*yo*h* ní-hita*h* *g*âtá-vedâ*h* gárbha*h*-iva *s*u-dhita*h* garbhí*n*îshu.

Agni placed in the two fire-sticks, well placed like an embryo in the mothers. Cf. X, 27, 16.

VIII, 60, 4. abhí práyâ*m*si sú-dhitâ ấ vaso (íti) gahi.

Come, O Vasu, to these well-placed offerings. Cf. I, 135, 4; VI, 15, 15; X, 53, 2.

X, 70, 8. sú-dhitâ havī́*m*shi.

The well-placed offerings.

IV, 2, 10 (adhvarám). VII, 7, 3 (barhí*h*).

As applied to ấyus, life, súdhita may be translated by well established, safe:

II, 27, 10. a*s*yấma ấyû*m*shi sú-dhitâni pū́rvâ.

May we obtain the happy long lives of our forefathers.

IV, 50, 8. sá*h* ít ksheti sú-dhita*h* ókasi své.

That man dwells secure in his own house.

Applied to a missile weapon, súdhita may mean well placed, as it were, well shouldered, well held, before it is thrown; or well levelled, well aimed, when it is thrown:

I, 167, 3. mimyáksha yéshu sú-dhitâ—*r*ish*t*í*h*.

To whom the well held spear sticks fast.

VI, 33, 3. tvám tấn indra ubháyân amítrân dấsâ v*r*itrấ*n*i ấryâ *k*a *s*ûra, vádhî*h* vánâ-iva sú-dhitebhi*h* átkai*h*.

Thou, Indra, O hero, struckest both enemies, the barbarous and the Aryan fiends, like forests with well-aimed weapons.

Applied to a poem, súdhita means well arranged or perfect:

I, 140, 11. idám agne sú-dhitam dú*h*-dhitât ádhi priyất û*m* (íti) *k*it mánmana*h* préya*h* astu te.

May this perfect prayer be more agreeable to thee than an imperfect one, though thou likest it.

VII, 32, 13. mántram ákharvam sú-dhitam.

A poem, not mean, well contrived.

As applied to men, súdhita means very much the same as hitá, well disposed, kind:

IV, 6, 7. ádha mitrá*h* ná sú-dhita*h* pâvaká*h* agní*h* dîdâya mấnushîshu vikshú.

Then, like a kind friend, Agni shone among the children of man.

V, 3, 2. mitrám sú-dhitam.

VI, 15, 2. mitrám ná yám sú-dhitam.

VIII, 23, 8. mitrám ná *g*áne sú-dhitam *r*itá-vani.

X, 115, 7. mitrấsa*h* ná yé sú-dhitâ*h*.

At last sú-dhita, without reference to human beings, takes the general sense of kind, good:

III, 11, 8. pári vísvâni sú-dhitâ agné*h* a*s*yâma mánmabhi*h*.

May we obtain through our prayers all the goods of Agni.

Here, however, práyâ*m*si may have to be supplied, and in that case this passage, too, should be classed with those mentioned above, VIII, 60, 4, &c.

If then we consider that súdhita, as applied to weapons, means well held or well aimed, we can hardly doubt that barhá*n*â is here, as Sâya*n*a says, some kind of weapon. I should derive it from barhayati, to crush, which we have, for instance,

I, 133, 5. pi*s*áṅga-bh*r*ish*t*im ambhri*n*ám pi*s*ấ*k*im indra sám m*ri*n*a, sárvam ráksha*h* ní barhaya.

Pound together the fearful Pi*s*â*k*i with his fiery weapons, strike down every Rakshas.

II, 23, 8. b*rí*haspate deva-nída*h* ní barhaya.

B*ri*haspati strike down the scoffers of the gods. Cf. VI, 61, 3.

Barhá*n*â would therefore mean a weapon intended to crush an enemy, a block of stone, it may be, or a heavy club, and in that sense barhá*n*â occurs at least once more:

VIII, 63, 7. yát pấñ*k*a-*g*anyayâ vi*s*ấ índre ghóshâ*h* ás*ri*kshata, ást*ri*n*ât barhá*n*â vipá*h*.

When shouts have been sent up to Indra by the people of the five clans, then the club scattered the spears; or, then he scattered the spears with his club.

In other passages Professor Roth is no doubt right when he assigns to barhá*n*â an adverbial meaning, but I do not think that this meaning would be appropriate in our verse. Grassmann also translates, 'ein wohlgezielter Pfeil.'

Verse 7.

Note 1. Alât*ri*n*ấsa*h*, a word which occurs but once more, and which had evidently become unintelligible even at the time of Yâska. He (Nir. VI, 2) explains it by alamâtardano megha*h*, the cloud which opens easily. This, at least, is the translation given by Professor Roth, though not without hesitation. Alamâtardana*h*, as a compound, is explained by the commentator as âtardanaparyâpta*h*, alam âtardayitum udakam, i. e. capable of letting off the water. But Devarâ*g*ayaya*g*van explains it differently. He says: alam paryâptam âtardanam hi*m*sâ yasya, bahûdakatvâ*kkh*abalo megho vi*s*eshyate, i. e. whose injuring is great; the dark cloud is so called because it contains much water. Sâya*n*a, too, attempts several explanations. In III, 30, 10, he seems to derive it from t*r*i*h*, to kill, not, like Yâska, from t*r*id, and he explains its meaning as the cloud which is exceedingly hurt by reason of its holding so much water. In our passage he explains it either as anât*r*i*n*a, free from injury, or good hurters of enemies, or good givers of rewards.

From all this I am afraid we gain nothing. Let us now see what modern commentators have proposed in order to discover an appropriate meaning in this word. Professor Roth suggests that the word may be derived from râ, to give, and the suffix t*r*i*n*a, and the negative particle, thus meaning, one who does not give or yield anything. But, if so, how is this adjective applicable to the Maruts, who in this very verse are praised for their generosity? Langlois in our passage translates, 'heureux de nos louanges;' in III, 30, 10, 'qui laissait flétrir les plantes.' Wilson in our passage translates, 'devoid of malevolence;' but in III, 30, 10, 'heavy.'

I do not pretend to solve all these difficulties, but I may say this in defence of my own explanation that it fulfils the condition of being applicable both to the Maruts and to the demon Bala. The suffix t*r*i*n*a is certainly irregular, and I should much prefer to write alât*r*i*n*a, for in that case we might derive lâtrin from lâtra, and to this lâtra, i. e. râtra, I should ascribe the sense of barking. The root rai or râ means to bark, and has been connected by Professor Aufrecht with Latin rire, inrire, and possibly inritare[a],

[a] Kuhn, Zeitschrift, vol. ix, p. 233.

thus showing a transition of meaning from barking, to provoking or attacking. The same root râ explains also the Latin lâtrare, to bark, allatrare, to assail; and, whatever ancient etymologists may say to the contrary, the Latin latro, an assailer. The old derivation 'latrones eos antiqui dicebant, qui conducti militabant, ἀπὸ τῆς λατρείας,' seems to me one of those etymologies in which the scholars of Rome, who had learnt a little Greek, delighted as much as scholars who know a little Sanskrit delight in finding some plausible derivation for any Greek or Latin word in Sanskrit. I know that Curtius (Grundzüge, p. 326) and Corssen (Kritische Nachträge, p. 239) take a different view; but a foreign word, derived from λάτρον, pay, hire, would never have proved so fertile as latro has been in Latin.

If then we could write alâtri*n*ã́sa*h*, we should have an appropriate epithet of the Maruts, in the sense of not assailing or not reviling, in fact, free from malevolence, as Wilson translated the word, or rather Sâya*n*a's explanation of it, âtardanarahita. What gives me some confidence in this explanation is this, that it is equally applicable to the other passage where alât*rin*a occurs, III, 30, 10:

alât*rináh* valá*h* indra vra*gáh* gó*h* purã́ hánto*h* bháyamâna*h* ví âra.

Without barking did Vala, the keeper of the cow, full of fear, open, before thou struckest him.

If it should be objected that vra*gá* means always stable, and is not used again in the sense of keeper, one might reply that vra*gáh*, in the nom. sing., occurs in this one single passage only, and that bháyamâna*h*, fearing, clearly implies a personification. Otherwise, one might translate: 'Vala was quiet, O Indra, and the stable of the cow came open, full of fear, before thou struckest.' The meaning of alât*riná* would remain the same, the not-barking being here used as a sign that Indra's enemy was cowed, and no longer inclined to revile or defy the power of Indra. Hom. hymn. in Merc. 145, οὐδὲ κύνες λελάκοντο.

Note 2. See I, 38, 15, note 1, page 95.

Verse 8.

Note 1. Abhí-hruti seems to have the meaning of assault, injury, insult. It occurs but once, but abhí-hrut, a feminine substantive with the same meaning, occurs several times. The verb hru, which is not mentioned in the Dhâtupâ*th*a, but has been identified with hvar, occurs in our hymn, verse 12:

I, 128, 5. sá*h* na*h* trâsate du*h*-itā́t abhi-hrúta*h* sá*m*sât aghā́t abhi-hrúta*h*.

He protects us from evil, from assault, from evil speaking, from assault.

X, 63, 11. trā́yadhvam na*h* du*h*-évâyâ*h* abhi-hrúta*h*.

Protect us from mischievous injury!

I, 189, 6. abhi-hrútâm ási hí deva vishpá*t*.

For thou, god, art the deliverer from all assaults. Vishpá*t*, deliverer, from vi and spa*s*, to bind.

Ví-hruta, which occurs twice, means evidently what has been injured or spoiled:

VIII, 1, 12. íshkartâ ví-hrutam púnar (íti).

He who sets right what has been injured. Cf. VIII, 20, 26.

Ávi-hruta again clearly means uninjured, intact, entire:

V, 66, 2. tā́ hí kshatrám ávi-hrutam—ā́sâte.

For they both have obtained uninjured power.

X, 170, 1. ā́yu*h* dádhat ya*gñ*á-patau ávi-hrutam.

Giving uninjured life to the lord of the sacrifice.

Verse 9.

Note 1. Tavishá certainly means strength, and that it is used in the plural in the sense of acts of strength, we can see from the first verse of our hymn and other passages. But when we read that tavishā́*n*i are placed on the chariots of the Maruts, just as before bhadrā́, good things, food, &c., are mentioned, it is clear that so abstract a meaning as strength or powers would not be applicable here. We might take it in the modern sense of forces, i. e. your armies, your companions are on your chariots, striving with each other; but as the word is a neuter, weapons, as the means of strength, seemed a preferable rendering. As to mithaspr*i*dhya, see I, 119, 3, p. 164.

Note 2. The rendering of this passage must depend on the question whether the khâdís, whatever they are, can be carried on the shoulders or not. We saw before (p. 120) that khâdís were used both as ornaments and as weapons, and that, when used as weapons, they were most likely rings or quoits with sharp edges. There is at least one other passage where these khâdís are said to be worn on the shoulders:

VII, 56, 13. á*m*seshu ấ maruta*h* khâdáya*h* va*h* váksha*h*-su rukmấ*h* upa-*s*i*s*riyâ*n*ấ*h*.

On your shoulders are the quoits, on your chests the golden chains are fastened.

In other places the khâdís are said to be in the hands, hásteshu, but this would only show that they are there when actually used for fighting. Thus we read:

I, 168, 3. ấ eshâm á*m*seshu rambhínî-iva rarabhe, hásteshu khâdí*h* *k*a kr*i*tí*h* *k*a sám dadhe.

To their shoulders there clings as if a clinging wife, in their hands the quoit is held and the dagger.

In V, 58, 2, the Maruts are called khấdi-hasta, holding the quoits in their hands. There is one passage which was mentioned before (p. 112), where the khâdís are said to be on the feet of the Maruts, and on the strength of this passage Professor Roth proposes to alter prá-patheshu to prá-padeshu, and to translate, 'The khâdís are on your forefeet.' I do not think this emendation necessary. Though we do not know the exact shape and character of the khâdí, we know that it was a weapon, most likely a ring, occasionally used for ornament, and carried along either on the feet or on the shoulders, but in actual battle held in the hand. The weapon which Vish*n*u holds in one of his right hands, the so-called *k*akra, may be the modern representation of the ancient khâdí. What, however, is quite certain is this, that khâdí in the Veda never means food, as Sâya*n*a optionally interprets it. This interpretation is accepted by Wilson, who translates, 'At your resting-places on the road refreshments (are ready).' Nay, he goes on in a note to use this passage as a proof of the advanced civilisation of India at the time of the Vedic *Ri*shis. 'The expression,' he says, 'is worthy of note, as indicating the existence of accommodations for the use of travellers: the prapatha is the choltri of the south of India, the sarái of the Mohammedans, a place by the road-side where the travellers may find shelter and provisions.'

Note 3. This last passage shows that the poet is really representing to himself the Maruts as on their journey, and he therefore adds, 'your axle turns the two (IV, 30, 2) wheels together,' which probably means no more than, 'your chariot is going smoothly or quickly.' Though the expression seems to us hardly correct, yet one can well imagine how the axle was supposed to turn the wheels as the horses were drawing the axle, and the axle acted on the wheels. Anyhow, no other translation seems possible. Samáyâ in the Veda means together, at once, and is the Greek ὁμῇ, generally ὁμοῦ or ὁμῶς, the Latin simul. Cf. I, 56, 6; 73, 6; 113, 10; 163, 3; VII, 66, 15; IX, 75, 4; 85, 5; 97, 56.

V*ri*t means to turn, and is frequently used with reference to the wheels:

VIII, 46, 23. dá*s*a syâvā́*h*—nemím ní vav*ri*tu*h*.

The ten black horses turn down the felly or the wheel.

IV, 30, 2. satrā́ te ánu k*r*ish*t*áya*h* ví*s*vâ*h* *k*akrā́-iva vav*ri*tu*h*.

All men turn always round thee, like wheels.

That the Âtmanepada of v*ri*t may be used in an active sense we see from

I, 191, 15. táta*h* vishám prá vav*ri*te.

I turn the poison out from here.

All the words used in this sentence are very old words, and we can with few exceptions turn them into Greek or Latin. In Latin we should have axis vos(ter) circos simul divertit. In Greek ἄξων ὑ(μῶν) κύκλω ὁμῇ . . . .

Verse 10.

Note 1. See I, 64, 4, note 1, page 111.

Note 2. See I, 166, 1, note 1, page 212.

Note 3. On éta in the sense of fallow deer, or, it may be, antelope, see I, 165, 5, note 2, page 196.

Éta originally means variegated, and thus becomes a name of any speckled deer, it being difficult to say what exact species is meant. Sâya*n*a in our passage explains étâ*h* by *s*uklavar*n*â mâlâ*h*, many-coloured wreaths or chains, which may be right. Yet the suggestion of Professor Roth that étâ*h*, deer, stands here for the skins of fallow deer, is certainly more poetical, and quite in accordance with the Vedic idiom, which uses, for instance, go, cow, not only in the sense of milk,—that is done even in more homely English,—but also for leather, and thong. It is likewise in accordance with what we know of the earliest dress of the Vedic Indians, that deer-skins should here be mentioned. We learn from Â*s*valâyana's G*ri*hya-sûtras, of which we now possess an excellent edition by Professor Stenzler, and a reprint of the text and commentary by Râma Nârâya*n*a Vidyâratna, in the Bibliotheca Indica, that a boy when he was brought to his tutor, i. e. from the eighth to possibly the twenty-fourth year, had to be well combed, and attired in a new dress. A Brâhma*n*a should wear the skin of an antelope (ai*n*eya), the Kshatriya the skin of a deer (raurava), the Vai*s*ya the skin of a goat (â*g*a). If they wore dresses, that of the Brâhma*n*a should be dark red (kâshâya), that of the Kshatriya bright red (mâ*ñ*gish*th*a), that of the Vai*s*ya yellow (hâridra). The girdle of the Brâhma*n*a should be of Mu*ñg*a grass, that of the Kshatriya a bow-string, that of the Vai*s*ya made of sheep's wool. The same regulations occur in other Sûtras, as, for instance, the Dharma-sûtras of the Âpastambîyas and Gautamas, though there are certain characteristic differences in each, which may be due either to local or to chronological causes. Thus according to the Âpastambîya-sûtras, which have been published by Professor Bühler, the Brâhma*n*a may wear the skin of the hari*n*a deer, or that of the antelope (ai*n*eyam), but the latter must be from the black antelope (k*ri*sh*n*am), and, a proviso is added, that if a man wears the black antelope skin, he must never spread it out to sit or sleep on it. As materials for the dress, Âpastamba allows *sana*, hemp[a], or kshumâ, flax, and he adds that woollen dresses are allowed to all castes, as well as the kambala (masc.), which seems to be any cloth made of vegetable substances (darbhâdinirmitam *k*îram kambalam). He then adds a curious remark, which would seem to show

[a] *Sana* is an old Aryan word, though its meanings differ. Hesychius and Eustathius mention *κάννα* as being synonymous with *ψίαθος*, reed. Pollux gives two forms, *κάννα* and *κάνα*, (Pollux X. 166, *πτανάκα δέ ἐστι ψίαθος ἡ ἐν τοῖς ἀκατίοις ἣν καὶ κάναν καλοῦσιν.* VII, 176, *κάνναι δὲ τὸ ἐκ καναβῶν πλέγμα.*) This is important, because the same difference of spelling occurs also in *κάνναβις* and *κάναβος* or *κάνναβος*, a model, a lay figure, which Lobeck derives from *κάνναι*. In Old Norse we have hanp-r, in A. S. hænep, hemp, Old High-Germ. hanaf.

The occurrence of the word *sana* is of importance as showing at how early a time the Aryans of India were acquainted with the uses and the name of hemp. Our word hemp, the A. S. hænep, the Old Norse hanp-r, are all borrowed from Latin cannabis, which, like other borrowed words, has undergone the regular changes required by Grimm's law in Low-German, and also in High-German, hanaf. The Slavonic nations seem to have borrowed their word for hemp (Lith. kanapẽ) from the Goths, the Celtic nations (Ir. canaib) from the Romans (cf. Kuhn, Beiträge, vol. ii, p. 382). The Latin cannabis is borrowed from Greek, and the Greeks, to judge from the account of Herodotus, most likely adopted the word from the Aryan Thracians and Scythians (Her. IV, 74; Pictet, Les Aryens, vol. i, p. 314). *Κάνναβις* being a foreign word, it would be useless to attempt an explanation of the final element bis, which is added to *sana*, the Sanskrit word for hemp. It may be visa, fibre, or it may be anything else. Certain it is that the main element in the name of hemp was the same among the settlers in Northern India, and among the Thracians and Scythians through whom the Greeks first became acquainted with hemp.

The history of the word *κάνναβις* must be kept distinct from that of the Greek *κάννα* or *κάνα*, reed. Both spellings occur, for Pollux, X, 166, writes *πτανάκα δέ ἐστι ψίαθος ἡ ἐν τοῖς ἀκατίοις ἣν καὶ κάναν καλοῦσιν*, but VII, 176, *κάνναι δὲ τὸ ἐκ καναβῶν πλέγμα*. This word *κάννα* may be the same as the Sanskrit *sana*, only with this difference, that it was retained as common property by Greeks and Indians before they separated, and was applied differently in later times by the one and the other.

that the Brâhma*n*as preferred skins, and the Kshatriyas clothes, for he says that those who wish well to the Brâhma*n*as should wear a*g*ina, skins, and those who wish well to the Kshatriyas should wear vastra, clothes, and those who wish well to both should wear both, but, in that case, the skin should always form the outer garment. The Dharma-sûtras of the Gautamas, which were published in India, prescribe likewise for the Brâhma*n*a the black antelope skin, and allow clothes of hemp or linen (*sâ*n*a*kshauma*k*îra) as well as kutapas (woollen cloth) for all. What is new among the Gautamas is, that they add the kârpâsa, the cotton dress, which is important as showing an early knowledge of this manufacture. The kârpâsa dress occurs once more as a present to be given to the Potar priest (Â*s*v. *S*rauta-sûtras IX, 4), and was evidently considered as a valuable present, taking precedence of the kshaumî or linen dress. It is provided that the cotton dress should not be dyed, for this, I suppose, is the meaning of avik*ri*ta. Immediately after, however, it is said, that some authorities say the dress should be dyed red (kâshâyam apy eke), the very expression which occurred in Âpastamba, and that, in that case, the red for the Brâhma*n*a's dress should be taken from the bark of trees (vârksha). Manu, who here, as elsewhere, simply paraphrases the ancient Sûtras, says, II, 41:

kârsh*n*arauravabâstâni *k*armâ*n*i brahma*k*âri*n*a*h*
vasîrann ânupûrvye*n*a *sâ*n*a*kshaumâvikâni *k*a.

'Let Brahma*k*ârins wear (as outer garments) the skins of the black antelope, the deer, the goat, (as under garments) dresses of hemp, flax, and sheep's wool, in the order of the three castes.'

The Sanskrit name for a dressed skin is a*g*ina, a word which does not occur in the Rig-veda, but which, if Bopp is right in deriving it from a*g*á, goat, as *αἰγίς* from *αἴξ*, would have meant originally, not skin in general, but a goat-skin. The skins of the éta, here ascribed to the Maruts, would be identical with the ai*n*eya, which Â*s*valâyana ascribes to the Brâhma*n*a, not, as we should expect, to the Kshatriya, if, as has been supposed, ai*n*eya is derived from ena, which is a secondary form, particularly in the feminine enî, of eta. There is, however, another word, e*d*a, a kind of sheep, which, but for Festus, might be haedus, and by its side e*n*a, a kind of antelope. These two forms pre-suppose an earlier er*n*a or ar*n*a, and point therefore in a different direction, though hardly to ἄρνες.

Note 4. I translate kshurá by sharp edges, but it might have been translated literally by razors, for, strange as it may sound, razors were known, not only during the Vedic period, but even previous to the Aryan separation. The Sanskrit kshurá is the Greek ξυρός or ξυρόν. In the Veda we have clear allusions to shaving:

X, 142, 4. yadā́ te vā́ta*h* anu-vā́ti *s*o*k*í*h*, váptâ-iva *s*má*s*ru vapasi prá bhū́ma.

When the wind blows after thy blast, then thou shavest the earth as a barber shaves the beard. Cf. I, 65, 4.

If, as B. and R. suggest, vaptar, barber, is connected with the more modern name for barber in Sanskrit, viz. nâpita, we should have to admit a root svap, in the sense of tearing or pulling, vellere, from which we might derive the Vedic svapū́ (VII, 56, 3), beak. Corresponding to this we find in Old High-German snabul, beak, (schnepfe, snipe,) and in Old Norse nef. The Anglo-Saxon neb means mouth and nose, while in modern English neb or nib is used for the bill or beak of a bird[a]. Another derivation of nâpita, proposed by Professor Weber (Kuhn's Beiträge, vol. i, p. 505), who takes nâpita as a dialectic form of snâpitar, balneator, or lavator, might be admitted if it could be proved that in India also the barber was at the same time a balneator. Burnouf, Lotus, p. 452, translating from the Sâma*ññ*a-phala Sutta, mentions among the different professions of the people those of 'portier,' 'barbier,' and 'baigneur.'

Verse 11.

Note 1. Ví-bhûtaya*h* is properly a substantive, meaning

---

[a] Grimm, Deutsche Grammatik, vol. iii, pp. 400, 409. There is not yet sufficient evidence to show that Sanskrit sv, German sn, and Sanskrit n are interchangeable, but there is at least one case that may be analogous. Sanskrit sva*ñ*g, to embrace, to twist round a person, German slango, Schlange, snake, and Sanskrit nâga, snake. Grimm, Deutsche Grammatik, vol. iii, p. 364.

power, but, like other substantives[a], and particularly substantives with prepositions, it can be used as an adjective, and is, in fact, more frequently used as an adjective than as a substantive. In English we may translate it by power. It is a substantive,

I, 8, 9. evá hí te ví-bhûtaya*h* ûtáya*h* indra mấ-vate sadyá*h* *k*it sánti dâ*s*úshe.

For indeed thy powers, O Indra, are at once shelters for a sacrificer, like me.

But it is an adjective,

I, 30, 5. ví-bhûti*h* astu sûn*ri*tâ.

May the prayer be powerful.

VI, 17, 4. mahẫm ánûnam tavásam ví-bhûtim matsarẫsa*h* *g*arh*ri*shanta pra-sáham.

The sweet draughts of Soma delighted the great, the perfect, the strong, the powerful, the unyielding Indra. Cf. VIII, 49, 6; 50, 6.

Vibhvẫ*h*, with the Svarita on the last syllable, has to be pronounced vibhúà*h*. In III, 6, 9, we find vi-bháva*h*.

Note 2. See I, 87, 1, note 1, page 160.

Note 3. See I, 6, 5, note 1, page 41.

Verse 12.

Note 1. Mahi-tvanám, greatness, is formed by the suffix tvaná, which Professor Aufrecht has identified with the Greek σύνη (συνον); see Kuhn's Zeitschrift, vol. i, p. 482. The origin of this suffix has been explained by Professor Benfey, ibid. vol. vii, p. 120, who traces it back to the suffix tvan, for instance, i-tvan, goer, in prâta*h*-ítvâ = prâta*h*-yẫvâ.

Note 2. Vratá is one of the many words which, though we may perceive their one central idea, and their original purport, we have to translate by various terms in order to make them intelligible in every passage where they occur. Vratá (from v*ri*, v*rin*oti), I believe, meant originally what is enclosed, protected, set apart, the Greek νομός:

1. V, 46, 7. yẫ*h* pẫrthivâsa*h* yẫ*h* apẫm ápi vraté tẫ*h* na*h* devî*h* su-havâ*h* *s*árma ya*kkh*ata.

---

[a] See Benfey, Kuhn's Zeitschrift, vol. ii, p. 216.

O ye gracious goddesses, who are on the earth or in the realm of the waters, grant us your protection!

Here vratá is used like v*ri*gána, see I, 165, 15, note 3, page 208.

X, 114, 2. tấsâm ní *k*ikyu*h* kaváya*h* ni-dấnam páreshu yấ*h* gúhyeshu vratéshu.

The poets discovered their (the Nir*ri*tis') origin, who are in the far hidden chambers.

I, 163, 3. ási tritá*h* gúhyena vraténa.

Thou art Trita within the hidden place, or with the secret work.

Dr. Muir sent me another passage:

III, 54, 5. dád*ri*s*re eshâm avamấ sádâ*m*si páreshu yấ gúhyeshu vratéshu.

2. Vratá means what is fenced off or forbidden, what is determined, what is settled, and hence, like dhárman, law, ordinance. Vârayati means to prohibit. In this sense vratá occurs very frequently:

I, 25, 1. yát *k*it hí te vís*a*h* yathâ prá deva varu*n*a vratám, minîmási dyávi-dyavi.

Whatever law of thine we break, O Varu*n*a, day by day, men as we are.

II, 8, 3. yásya vratám ná mîyate.

Whose law is not broken.

III, 32, 8. índrasya kárma sú-k*ri*tâ purû*n*i vratấni devấ*h* ná minanti vísve.

The deeds of Indra are well done and many, all the gods do not break his laws, or do not injure his ordinances.

II, 24, 12. vísvam satyám maghavânâ yuvó*h* ít ấpa*h* *k*aná prá minanti vratám vâm.

All that is yours, O powerful gods, is true; even the waters do not break your law.

II, 38, 7. náki*h*-asya tấni vratấ devásya savitú*h* minanti.

No one breaks these laws of this god Savitar. Cf. II, 38, 9.

I, 92, 12. áminatî daívyâni vratấni.

Not injuring the divine ordinances. Cf. I, 124, 2.

X, 12, 5. kát asya áti vratám *k*akrima.

Which of his laws have we overstepped?

VIII, 25, 16. tásya vratấni ánu vaḥ *k*arâmasi.

His ordinances we follow.

X, 33, 9. ná devấnâm áti vratám *s*atá-âtmâ *k*aná *g*îvati.

No one lives beyond the statute of the gods, even if he had a hundred lives.

VII, 5, 4. táva tri-dhấtu p*ri*thivī́ utá dyaú*h* vaí*s*vânara vratám agne sa*k*anta.

The earth and the sky followed thy threefold law, O Agni Vai*s*vânara.

VII, 87, 7. yá*h* m*rí*láyâti *k*akrúshe *k*it ấga*h* vayám syâma váru*n*e ánâgâ*h*, ánu vratấni ádite*h* *ri*dhánta*h*.

Let us be sinless before Varu*n*a, who is gracious even to him who has committed sin, performing the laws of Aditi!

II, 28, 8. náma*h* purấ te varu*n*a utá nûnám utá aparám tuvi-*g*âta bravâma, tvé hí kam párvate ná *s*ritấni ápra-*k*yutâni du*h*-dabha vratấni.

Formerly, and now, and also in future let us give praise to thee, O Varu*n*a; for in thee, O unconquerable, all laws are grounded, immovable as on a rock.

A very frequent expression is ánu vratám, according to the command of a god, II, 38, 3; 6; VIII, 40, 8; or simply ánu vratám, according to law and order:

I, 136, 5. tám aryamấ abhí rakshati *ri*gu-yántam ánu vratám.

Aryaman protects him who acts uprightly according to law.

Cf. III, 61, 1; IV, 13, 2; V, 69, 1.

3. The laws or ordinances or institutions of the gods are sometimes taken for the sacrifices which are supposed to be enjoined by the gods, and the performance of which is, in a certain sense, the performance of the divine will.

I, 93, 8. yá*h* agnī́shómâ havíshâ saparyất devadrī́*k*â mánasâ yá*h* gh*ri*téna, tásya vratám rakshatam pâtám á*m*-hasa*h*.

He who worships Agni and Soma with oblations, with a godly mind, or with an offering, protect his sacrifice, shield him from evil!

I, 31, 2. tvám agne prathamá*h* áṅgira*h*-tama*h* kaví*h* devấnâm pári bhûshasi vratám.

Agni, the first and wisest of poets, thou performest the sacrifice of the gods.

III, 3, 9. tásya vratấni bhûri-poshí*n*a*h* vayám úpa bhûshema dáme ấ suvr*i*ktí-bhi*h*.

Let us, who possess much wealth, perform with prayers the sacrifices of Agni within our house.

In another acceptation the vratas of the gods are what they perform and establish themselves, their own deeds:

III, 6, 5. vratấ te agne mahatá*h* mahấni táva krátvâ ródasî (íti) ấ tatantha.

The deeds of thee, the great Agni, are great, by thy power thou hast stretched out heaven and earth.

VIII, 42, 1. ástabhnât dyấm ásura*h* vi*s*vá-vedâ*h* ámimîta varimấ*n*am p*r*ithivyấ*h*, ấ asîdat ví*s*vâ bhúvanâni sam-rấ*t* ví*s*vâ ít tấni váru*n*asya vratấni.

The wise spirit established the sky, and made the width of the earth, as king he approached all beings,—all these are the works of Varu*n*a.

VI, 14, 3. tû́rvanta*h* dásyum âyáva*h* vratai*h* sî́kshanta*h* avratám.

Men fight the fiend, trying to overcome by their deeds him who performs no sacrifices; or, the lawless enemy.

Lastly, vratá comes to mean sway, power, or work, and the expression vraté táva signifies, at thy command, under thy auspices:

I, 24, 15. átha vayám âditya vraté táva ánâgasa*h* áditaye syâma.

Then, O Âditya, under thy auspices may we be guiltless before Aditi.

VI, 54, 9. pû́shan táva vraté vayám ná rishyema kádâ *k*aná.

O Pûshan, may we never fail under thy protection.

X, 36, 13. yé savitú*h* satyá-savasya ví*s*ve mitrásya vraté váru*n*asya devấ*h*.

All the gods who are in the power of Savitar, Mitra, and Varu*n*a.

V, 83, 5. yásya vraté p*r*ithivî́ námnamîti yásya vraté *s*aphá-vat *g*árbhurîti, yásya vraté óshadhî*h* vi*s*vá-rûpâ*h* sá*h* na*h* par*g*anya máhi *s*árma ya*kkh*a.

At whose bidding the earth bows down, at whose bidding hoofed animals run about, at whose bidding the plants assume all shapes, mayest thou, O Par*g*anya, yield us great protection!

Note 3. Dâtrá, if derived from dâ, would mean gift, and that meaning is certainly the most applicable in some passages where it occurs:

IX, 97, 55. ási bhága*h* ási dâtrásya dâtấ.

Thou art Bhaga, thou art the giver of the gift.

In other passages, too, particularly in those where the verb dâ or some similar verb occurs in the same verse, it can hardly be doubted that the poet took dâtrá, like dátra or dáttra, in the sense of gift, bounty, largess:

I, 116, 6. yám a*s*vinâ dadáthu*h* *s*vetám á*s*vam—tát vâm dâtrám máhi kîrtényam bhût.

The white horse, O A*s*vins, which you gave, that your gift was great and to be praised.

I, 185, 3. anehá*h* dâtrám ádite*h* anarvám huvé.

I call for the unrivalled, the uninjured bounty of Aditi.

VII, 56, 21. mấ va*h* dâtrất maruta*h* ní*h* arâma.

May we not fall away from your bounty, O Maruts!

III, 54, 16. yuvám hí sthá*h* rayi-daú na*h* rayî*n*ấm dâtrám rakshethe.

For you, Nâsatyas, are our givers of riches, you protect the gift.

VI, 20, 7. *rigís*vane dâtrám dâ*s*úshe dâ*h*.

To *Rigis*van, the giver, thou givest the gift.

VIII, 43, 33. tát te sahasva îmahe dâtrám yát ná upadásyati, tvát agne vấryam vásu.

We ask thee, strong hero, for the gift which does not perish; we ask from thee the precious wealth.

X, 69, 4. dâtrám rakshasva yát idám te asmé (íti).

Protect this gift of thine which thou hast given to us.

VIII, 44, 18. ī́*s*ishe vấryasya hí dâtrásya agne svã*h*-pati*h*.

For thou, O Agni, lord of heaven, art the master of the precious gift. Cf. IV, 38, 1.

Professor Roth considers that dâtrá is derived rather from dâ, to divide, and that it means share, lot, possession. But there is not a single passage where the meaning of gift or bounty does not answer all purposes. In VII, 56, 21, mấ va*h* dâtrất maruta*h* ní*h* arâma, is surely best translated by, 'let us not fall away from your bounty,' and in our own passage the same meaning should be assigned to dâtrá. The idea of dâtrá, bounty, is by no means incompatible with vratá, realm, dominion, sway, if we consider that the sphere within which the bounty of a king or a god is exercised and accepted, is in one sense his realm. What the poet therefore says in our passage is simply this, that the bounty of the Maruts extends as far as the realm of Aditi, i. e. is endless, or extends everywhere, Aditi being in its original conception the deity of the unbounded world beyond, the earliest attempt at expressing the Infinite.

As to dấtra occurring once with the accent on the first syllable in the sense of sickle, see M. M., 'Über eine Stelle in Yâska's Commentar zum Naigha*nt*uka,' Zeitschrift der Deutschen Morgenländischen Gesellschaft, 1853, vol. vii, p. 375.

VIII, 78, 10. táva ít indra ahám â-sásâ háste dấtram *k*aná ấ dade.

Trusting in thee alone, O Indra, I take the sickle in my hand.

This dấtra, sickle, is derived from do, to cut.

Aditi, the Infinite.

Note 4. Aditi, an ancient god or goddess, is in reality the earliest name invented to express the Infinite; not the Infinite as the result of a long process of abstract reasoning, but the visible Infinite, visible, as it were, to the naked eye, the endless expanse beyond the earth, beyond the clouds, beyond the sky. That was called A-diti, the un-bound, the un-bounded; one might almost say, but for fear of misunderstandings, the Absolute, for it is derived from diti, bond, and the negative particle, and meant therefore originally what is free from bonds of any kind, whether of space or time, free from physical weakness, free from moral guilt. Such a conception became of necessity a being, a person, a god. To us such a name and such a conception seem decidedly modern, and to find in the Veda Aditi, the

Infinite, as the mother of the principal gods, is certainly, at first sight, startling. But the fact is that the thoughts of primitive humanity were not only different from our thoughts, but different also from what we think their thoughts ought to have been. The poets of the Veda indulged freely in theogonic speculations, without being frightened by any contradictions. They knew of Indra as the greatest of gods, they knew of Agni as the god of gods, they knew of Varu*n*a as the ruler of all, but they were by no means startled at the idea that their Indra had a mother, or that their Agni was born like a babe from the friction of two fire-sticks, or that Varu*n*a and his brother Mitra were nursed in the lap of Aditi. Some poet would take hold of the idea of an unbounded power, of Aditi, originally without any reference to other gods. Very soon these ideas met, and, without any misgivings, either the gods were made subordinate to, and represented as the sons of Aditi, or where Indra was to be praised as supreme, Aditi was represented as doing him homage.

VIII, 12, 14. utá sva-râ*g*e áditi*h* stómam índrâya *g*î*g*anat.
And Aditi produced a hymn for Indra, the king.

Here Professor Roth takes Aditi as an epithet of Agni, not as the name of the goddess Aditi, while Dr. Muir rightly takes it in the latter sense, and likewise retains stómam instead of sómam, as printed by Professor Aufrecht. Cf. VII, 38, 4.

The idea of the Infinite, as I have tried to show elsewhere, was most powerfully impressed on the awakening mind, or, as we now say, was revealed, by the East[a]. 'It is impossible to enter fully into all the thoughts and feelings that passed through the minds of the early poets when they formed names for that far, far East from whence even the early dawn, the sun, the day, their own life, seemed to spring. A new life flashed up every morning before their eyes, and the fresh breezes of the dawn reached them like greetings from the distant lands beyond the mountains, beyond the clouds, beyond the dawn, beyond "the immortal

[a] Lectures on the Science of Language, Second Series, p. 499.

sea which brought us hither." The dawn seemed to them to open golden gates for the sun to pass in triumph, and while those gates were open, their eyes and their mind strove in their childish way to pierce beyond the limits of this finite world. That silent aspect awakened in the human mind the conception of the Infinite, the Immortal, the Divine.' Aditi is a name for that distant East, but Aditi is more than the dawn. Aditi is beyond the dawn, and in one place (I, 113, 19) the dawn is called 'the face of Aditi,' áditer ánîkam. Thus we read:

V, 62, 8. híra*n*ya-rûpam ushása*h* ví-ush*t*au áya*h*-sthû*n*am út-itâ sû́ryasya, ấ rohatha*h* varu*n*a mitra gártam áta*h* *k*akshâthe (íti) áditim dítim *k*a.

Mitra and Varu*n*a, you mount your chariot, which is golden, when the dawn bursts forth, and has iron poles at the setting of the sun: from thence you see Aditi and Diti, i. e. what is yonder and what is here.

If we keep this original conception of Aditi clearly before our mind, the various forms which Aditi assumes, even in the hymns of the Veda, will not seem incoherent. Aditi is not a prominent deity in the Veda, she is celebrated rather in her sons, the Âdityas, than in her own person. While there are so many hymns addressed to Ushas, the dawn, or Indra, or Agni, or Savitar, there is but one hymn, X, 72, which from our point of view, though not from that of Indian theologians, might be called a hymn to Aditi. Nevertheless Aditi is a familiar name; a name of the past, whether in time or in thought only, and a name that lives on in the name of the Âdityas, the sons of Aditi, including the principal deities of the Veda.

Aditi and the Âdityas.

Thus we read:

I, 107, 2. úpa na*h* devấ*h* ávasâ ấ gamantu áṅgirasâm sấma-bhi*h* stûyámânâ*h*, índra*h* indriyaí*h* marúta*h* marútbhi*h* âdityaí*h* na*h* áditi*h* *s*árma ya*m*sat.

May the gods come to us with their help, praised by the songs of the Aṅgiras,—Indra with his powers, the Maruts with the storms, may Aditi with the Âdityas give us protection!

X, 66, 3. índra*h* vásu-bhi*h* pári pâtu na*h* gáyam âdityaí*h* na*h* áditi*h* *s*árma ya*kkh*atu, rudrá*h* rudrébhi*h* devá*h* m*ril*a-yâti na*h* tvásh*t*â na*h* gnấbhi*h* suvitấya *g*invatu.

May Indra with the Vasus watch our house, may Aditi with the Âdityas give us protection, may the divine Rudra with the Rudras have mercy upon us, may Tvash*t*ar with the mothers bring us to happiness!

III, 54, 20. âdityaí*h* na*h* áditi*h* *sri*n*o*tu yá*kkh*antu na*h* marúta*h* *s*árma bhadrám.

May Aditi with the Âdityas hear us, may the Maruts give us good protection!

In another passage Varu*n*a takes the place of Aditi as the leader of the Âdityas:

VII, 35, 6. *s*ám na*h* índra*h* vásu-bhi*h* devá*h* astu *s*ám âdityébhi*h* váru*n*a*h* su-*s*á*m*sa*h*, *s*ám na*h* rudrá*h* rudrébhi*h* *g*álâsha*h* *s*ám na*h* tvásh*t*â gnấbhi*h* ihá *sri*n*o*tu.

May Indra bless us, the god with the Vasus! May Varu*n*a, the glorious, bless us with the Âdityas! May the relieving Rudra with the Rudras bless us! May Tvash*t*ar with the mothers kindly hear us here!

Even in passages where the poet seems to profess an exclusive worship of Aditi, as in

V, 69, 3. prâtá*h* devī́m áditim *g*ohavîmi madhyándine út-itâ sū́ryasya,

I invoke the divine Aditi early in the morning, at noon, and at the setting of the sun,

Mitra and Varu*n*a, her principal sons, are mentioned immediately after, and implored, like her, to bestow blessings on their worshipper.

Her exclusive worship appears once, in VIII, 19, 14.

A very frequent expression is that of âdityấ*h* áditi*h* without any copula, to signify the Âdityas and Aditi:

IV, 25, 3. ká*h* devấnâm áva*h* adyá v*ri*n*î*te ká*h* âdityấn áditim *g*yóti*h* î*tt*e.

Who does choose now the protection of the gods? Who asks the Âdityas, Aditi, for their light?

VI, 51, 5. vísve âdityâ*h* adite sa-*g*óshâ*h* asmábhyam *s*árma bahulám ví yanta.

All ye Âdityas, Aditi together, grant to us your manifold protection!

X, 39, 11. ná tám râ*g*ânau adite kúta*h* *k*aná ná á*m*ha*h* a*s*noti du*h*-itám náki*h* bhayám.

O ye two kings (the A*s*vins), Aditi, no evil reaches him from anywhere, no misfortune, no fear (whom you protect). Cf. VII, 66, 6.

X, 63, 5. tấn ấ vivâsa námasâ suv*ri*ktí-bhi*h* mahá*h* âdityấn áditim svastáye.

I cherish them with worship and with hymns, the great Âdityas, Aditi, for happiness' sake.

X, 63, 17. evá platé*h* sûnú*h* avîv*ri*dhat va*h* ví*s*ve âdityâ*h* adite manîshî́.

The wise son of Plati magnified you, all ye Âdityas, Aditi!

X, 65, 9. par*g*ányâvấtâ v*ri*shabhấ purîshí*n*â indravâyū́ (íti) váru*n*a*h* mitrá*h* aryamấ, devấn âdityấn áditim havâmahe yé pấrthivâsa*h* divyấsa*h* ap-sú yé.

There are Par*g*anya and Vâta, the powerful, the givers of rain, Indra and Vâyu, Varu*n*a, Mitra, Aryaman, we call the divine Âdityas, Aditi, those who dwell on the earth, in heaven, in the waters.

We may not be justified in saying that there ever was a period in the history of the religious thought of India, a period preceding the worship of the Âdityas, when Aditi, the Infinite, was worshipped, though to the sage who first coined this name, it expressed, no doubt, for a time the principal, if not the only object of his faith and worship.

Aditi and Daksha.

Soon, however, the same mental process which led on later speculators from the earth to the elephant, and from the elephant to the tortoise, led the Vedic poets beyond Aditi, the Infinite. There was something beyond that Infinite which for a time they had grasped by the name of Aditi, and this, whether intentionally or by a mere accident of language, they called dáksha, literally power or the powerful. All this, no doubt, sounds strikingly modern, yet, though the passages in which this dáksha is mentioned are few in number, I should not venture to say that they are necessarily modern, even if by modern we mean only later than 1000 B.C. Nothing can bring the perplexity of the ancient mind, if once drawn into this vortex of speculation, more clearly before us than if we read:

X, 72, 4–5. ádite*h* dáksha*h* a*g*âyata dákshât û*m* (íti) áditi*h* pári,—áditi*h* hí á*g*anish*t*a dáksha yā́ duhitā́ táva, tā́m devā́*h* ánu a*g*âyanta bhadrā́*h* am*rí*ta-bandhava*h*.

Daksha was born of Aditi, and Aditi from Daksha. For Aditi was born, O Daksha, she who is thy daughter; after her the gods were born, the blessed, who share in immortality.

Or, in more mythological language:

X, 64, 5. dákshasya vâ adite *g*ánmani vraté rā́*g*ânâ mitrā́-váru*n*â ā́ vivâsasi.

Or thou, O Aditi, nursest in the birthplace of Daksha the two kings, Mitra and Varu*n*a.

Nay, even this does not suffice. There is something again beyond Aditi and Daksha, and one poet says:

X, 5, 7. ásat *k*a sát *k*a paramé ví-oman dákshasya *g*ánman ádite*h* upá-sthe.

Not-being and Being are in the highest heaven, in the birthplace of Daksha, in the lap of Aditi.

At last something like a theogony, though full of contradictions, was imagined, and in the same hymn from which we have already quoted, the poet says:

X, 72, 1–4. devā́nâm nú vayám *g*ā́nâ prá vo*k*âma vipanyáyâ, ukthéshu *s*asyámâneshu yá*h* (yát?) pá*s*yât ut-tare yugé. 1.

bráhma*n*a*h* páti*h* etā́ sám karmā́ra*h*-iva adhamat, devā́nâm pûrvyé yugé ásata*h* sát a*g*âyata. 2.

devā́nâm yugé prathamé ásata*h* sát a*g*âyata, tát ā́*s*â*h* ánu a*g*âyanta tát uttâná-pada*h* pári. 3.

bhū́*h* *g*a*g*ñe uttâná-pada*h*, bhuvá*h* ā́*s*â*h* a*g*âyanta, ádite*h* dáksha*h* a*g*âyata, dákshât û*m* (íti) áditi*h* pári. 4.

1. Let us now with praise proclaim the births of the gods, that a man may see them in a future age, whenever these hymns are sung.

2. Brahma*n*aspati[a] blew them together like a smith (with

[a] Bráhma*n*aspáti, literally the lord of prayer, or the lord of the sacrifice, sometimes a representative of Agni (I, 38, 13, note), but

his bellows); in a former age of the gods, Being was born from Not-being.

3. In the first age of the gods, Being was born from Not-being, after it were born the Regions (space), from them Uttânapada;

4. From Uttânapad the Earth was born, the Regions were born from the Earth. Daksha was born of Aditi, and Aditi from Daksha.

The ideas of Being and Not-being (τὸ ὄν and τὸ μὴ ὄν) are familiar to the Hindus from a very early time in their intellectual growth, and they can only have been the result of abstract speculation. Therefore dáksha, too, in the sense of power or potentia, may have been a metaphysical conception. But it may also have been suggested by a mere accident of language, a never-failing source of ancient thoughts. The name dáksha-pitara*h*, an epithet of the gods, has generally been translated by 'those who have Daksha for their father.' But it may have been used originally in a very different sense. Professor Roth has, I think, convincingly proved that this epithet dáksha-pitar, as given to certain gods, does not mean, the gods who have Daksha for their father, but that it had originally the simpler meaning of fathers of strength, or, as he translates it, 'preserving, possessing, granting faculties[a].' This is particularly clear in one passage:

III, 27, 9. bhûtắnâm gárbham ấ dadhe, dákshasya pitáram.

I place Agni, the source of all beings, the father of strength . . . . .

---

by no means identical with him (see VII, 41, 1); sometimes performing the deeds of Indra, but again by no means identical with him (see II, 23, 18. índre*n*a yugắ—ní*h* apấm aubga*h* ar*n*avám; cf. VIII, 96, 15). In II, 26, 3, he is called father of the gods (devắnâm pitáram); in II, 23, 2, the creator of all beings (vís*v*eshâm *g*anitắ).

[a] The accent in this case cannot help us in determining whether dáksha-pitar means having Daksha for their father (Λοκροπάτωρ), or father of strength. In the first case dáksha would rightly retain its accent (dáksha-pitar) as a Bahuvrîhi; in the second, the analogy of such Tatpurusha compounds as g*ri*há-pati (Pâ*n*. VI, 2, 18) would be sufficient to justify the pûrvapadaprak*ri*tisvaratvam.

After this we can hardly hesitate how to translate the next verse:

VI, 50, 2. su-*g*yótisha*h*—dáksha-pit*r*ín—devấn.

The resplendent gods, the fathers of strength.

It may seem more doubtful, when we come to gods like Mitra and Varu*n*a, whom we are so much accustomed to regard as Âdityas, or sons of Aditi, and who therefore, according to the theogony mentioned before, would have the best claim to the name of sons of Daksha; yet here, too, the original and simple meaning is preferable; nay, it is most likely that from passages like this, the later explanation, which makes Mitra and Varu*n*a the sons of Daksha, may have sprung.

VII, 66, 2. yấ—su-dákshâ dáksha-pitarâ.

Mitra and Varu*n*a, who are of good strength, the fathers of strength.

Lastly, even men may claim this name; for, unless we change the accent, we must translate:

VIII, 63, 10. avasyáva*h* yushmấbhi*h* dáksha-pitara*h*.

We suppliants, being, through your aid, fathers of strength.

But whatever view we take, whether we take dáksha in the sense of power, as a personification of a philosophical conception, or as the result of a mythological misunderstanding occasioned by the name of dáksha-pitar, the fact remains that in certain hymns of the Rig-veda (VIII, 25, 5) Dáksha, like Áditi, has become a divine person, and has retained his place as one of the Âdityas to the very latest time of Purâ*n*ic tradition.

Aditi in her Cosmic Character.

But to return to Aditi. Let us look upon her as the Infinite personified, and most passages, even those where she is presented as a subordinate deity, will become intelligible.

Aditi, in her cosmic character, is the Beyond, the unbounded realm beyond earth, sky, and heaven, and originally she was distinct from the sky, the earth, and the ocean. Aditi is mentioned by the side of heaven and earth, which shows that, though in more general language she may be identified with heaven and earth in their unlimited character, her original conception was different. This we see in passages where different deities or powers are invoked together, particularly if they are invoked together in the same verse, and where Aditi holds a separate place by the side of heaven and earth:

I, 94, 16 (final). tát na*h* mitrá*h* váru*n*a*h* mamahantâm áditi*h* síndhu*h* p*ri*thivī́ utá dyaú*h*.

May Mitra and Varu*n*a grant us this, may Aditi, Sindhu (sea), the Earth, and the Sky!

In other passages, too, where Aditi has assumed a more personal character, she still holds her own by the side of heaven and earth; cf. IX, 97, 58 (final):

I, 191, 6. dyaú*h* va*h* pitā́ p*ri*thivī́ mâtā́ sóma*h* bhrā́tâ áditi*h* svásâ.

The Sky is your father, the Earth your mother, Soma your brother, Aditi your sister.

VIII, 101, 15. mâtā́ rudrā́*n*âm duhitā́ vásûnâm svásâ âdityā́nâm am*ri*tasya nā́bhi*h*, prá nú vo*k*am *k*ikitúshe *g*ánâya mā́ gā́m ánâgâm áditim vadhish*t*a.

The mother of the Rudras, the daughter of the Vasus, the sister of the Âdityas, the source of immortality, I tell it forth to the man of understanding, may he not offend the cow, the guiltless Aditi! Cf. I, 153, 3; IX, 96, 15; Vâ*g*asan. Sa*m*hitâ XIII, 49.

VI, 51, 5. dyaû*h* pítar (íti) p*ri*thivi mā́ta*h* ádhruk ágne bhrâta*h* vasava*h* m*ril*áta na*h*, víśve âdityâ*h* adite sa-*g*óshâ*h* asmábhyam *s*árma bahulám vi yanta.

Sky, father, Earth, kind mother, Fire, brother, bright gods, have mercy upon us! All Âdityas (and) Aditi together, grant us your manifold protection!

X, 63, 10. su-trā́mâ*n*am p*ri*thivī́m dyā́m anehásam su-*s*árma*n*am áditim su-pránîtim, daívîm nā́vam su-aritrā́m ánâgasam ásravantîm ā́ruhema svastáye.

Let us for welfare step into the divine boat, with good oars, faultless and leakless—the well-protecting Earth, the peerless Sky, the sheltering, well-guiding Aditi!

X, 66, 4. áditi*h* dyā́vâp*ri*thivī́ (íti).

Aditi, and Heaven and Earth.

Where two or more verses come together, the fact that Aditi is mentioned by the side of Heaven and Earth may seem less convincing, because in these Nivids or long strings of invocations different names or representatives of one and the same power are not unfrequently put together. For instance,

X, 36, 1–3. ushásânáktâ b*ri*hatī́ (íti) su-pé*s*asâ dyā́vâ-kshā́mâ váru*n*a*h* mitrá*h* aryamā́, índram huve marúta*h* párvatân apá*h* âdityā́n dyā́vâp*ri*thivī́ (íti) apá*h* svā̃r (íti svā̃*h*). 1.

dyaú*h* *k*a na*h* p*ri*thivī́ *k*a prá-*k*etasâ *ri*távarî (íty ritá-varî) rakshatâm á*m*hasa*h* rishá*h*, mā́ du*h*-vidátrâ ní*h*-*ri*ti*h* na*h* î*s*ata tát devā́nâm áva*h* adyá v*rin*îmahe. 2.

ví*s*vasmât na*h* áditi*h* pâtu á*m*hasa*h* mâtā́ mitrásya váru-*n*asya revúta*h* svā̃*h*-vat *g*yóti*h* av*ri*kám na*s*îmahi. 3.

1. There are the grand and beautiful Morning and Night, Heaven and Earth, Varu*n*a, Mitra, Aryaman; I call Indra, the Maruts, the Waters, the Âdityas, Heaven and Earth, the Waters, the Heaven.

2. May Heaven and Earth, the provident, the righteous, preserve us from sin and mischief! May the malevolent Nir*ri*ti not rule over us! This blessing of the gods we ask for to-day.

3. May Aditi protect us from all sin, the mother of Mitra and of the rich Varu*n*a! May we obtain heavenly light without enemies! This blessing of the gods we ask for to-day.

Here we cannot but admit that Dyā́vâkshā́mâ, heaven and earth, is meant for the same divine couple as Dyā́vâp*ri*thivī́, heaven and earth, although under slightly differing names they are invoked separately. The waters are invoked twice in the same verse and under the same name; nor is there any indication that, as in other passages, the waters of the sky are meant as distinct from the waters of the sea. Nevertheless even here, Aditi, who in the third verse is called distinctly the mother of Mitra and Varu*n*a, cannot well have been meant for the same deity as Heaven and Earth, mentioned in the second verse; and the author of these two verses, while asking the same blessing from both, must have been aware of the original independent character of Aditi.

Aditi as Mother.

In this character of a deity of the far East, of an Orient in the true sense of the word, Aditi was naturally thought of as the mother of certain gods, particularly of those that were connected with the daily rising and setting of the sun. If it was asked whence comes the dawn, or the sun, or whence come day and night, or Mitra and Varu*n*a, or any of the bright, solar, eastern deities, the natural answer was that they come from the Orient, that they are the sons of Aditi. Thus we read in

IX, 74, 3. urvī́ gávyûti*h* ádite*h* *ri*tám yaté.

Wide is the space for him who goes on the right path of Aditi.

In VIII, 25, 3, we are told that Aditi bore Mitra and Varu*n*a, and these in verse 5 are called the sons of Daksha (power), and the grandsons of *S*avas, which again means might: nápâtâ *s*ávasa*h* mahá*h* sûnū́ (íti) dákshasya su-krátû (íti). In X, 36, 3, Aditi is called the mother of Mitra and Varu*n*a; likewise in X, 132, 6; see also VI, 67, 4. In VIII, 47, 9, Aditi is called the mother of Mitra, Aryaman, Varu*n*a, who in VII, 60, 5 are called her sons. In X, 11, 1, Varu*n*a is called yahvá*h* ádite*h*, the son of Aditi (cf. VIII, 19, 12); in VII, 41, 2, Bhaga is mentioned as her son. In X, 72, 8, we hear of eight sons of Aditi, but it is added that she approached the gods with seven sons only, and that the eighth (mârtâ*nd*á, addled egg) was thrown away: ash*t*aú putrā́sa*h* ádite*h* yé *g*âtā́*h* tanvā̀*h* pári, devā́n úpa prá ait saptá-bhi*h* párâ mârtâ*nd*ám âsyat.

In X, 63, 2, the gods in general are represented as born from Aditi, the waters, and the earth: yé sthá *g*âtā́*h* ádite*h* at-bhyá*h* pári yé p*ri*thivyā́*h* té me ihá *s*ruta hávam.

You who are born of Aditi, from the water, you who are born of the earth, hear ye all my call!

The number seven, with regard to the Âdityas, occurs also in

IX, 114, 3. saptá dísa*h* nắnâ-sûryâ*h* saptá hótâra*h* *ri*tvíga*h*, devắ*h* âdityắ*h* yé saptá tébhi*h* soma abhí raksha na*h*.

There are seven regions with their different suns, there are seven Hotars as priests, those who are the seven gods, the Âdityas, with them, O Soma, protect us!

The Seven Âdityas.

This number of seven Âdityas requires an explanation. To say that seven is a solemn or sacred number is to say very little, for however solemn or sacred that number may be elsewhere, it is not more sacred than any other number in the Veda. The often-mentioned seven rivers have a real geographical foundation, like the seven hills of Rome. The seven flames or treasures of Agni (V, 1, 5) and of Soma and Rudra (VI, 74, 1), the seven paridhis or logs at certain sacrifices (X, 90, 15), the seven Harits or horses of the sun, the seven Hotar priests (III, 7, 7; 10, 4), the seven cities of the enemy destroyed by Indra (I, 63, 7), and even the seven *Ri*shis (X, 82, 2; 109, 4), all these do not prove that the number of seven was more sacred than the number of one or three or five or ten used in the Veda in a very similar way. With regard to the seven Âdityas, however, we are still able to see that their number of seven or eight had something to do with solar movements. If their number had always been eight, we should feel inclined to trace the number of the Âdityas back to the eight regions, or the eight cardinal points of the heaven. Thus we read:

I, 35, 8. ash*t*aú ví akhyat kakúbha*h* p*ri*thivyắ*h*.

The god Savitar lighted up the eight points of the earth (not the eight hills).

But we have seen already that though the number of Âdityas was originally supposed to have been eight, it was reduced to seven, and this could hardly be said in any sense of the eight points of the compass. Cf. Taitt. Âr. I, 7, 6.

As we cannot think in ancient India of the seven planets, I can only suggest the seven days or tithis of the four parvans of the lunar month as a possible prototype of the

Âdityas. This might even explain the destruction of the eighth Âditya, considering that the eighth day of each parvan, owing to its uncertainty, might be represented as exposed to decay and destruction. This would explain such passages as,

IV, 7, 5. yá*g*ish*th*am saptá dhã́ma-bhi*h*.

Agni, most worthy of sacrifice in the seven stations.

IX, 102, 2. ya*gñ*ásya saptá dhã́ma-bhi*h*.

In the seven stations of the sacrifice.

The seven threads of the sacrifice may have the same origin:

II, 5, 2. ã́ yásmin saptá ra*s*máya*h* tatã́*h* ya*gñ*ásya netári, manushvát daívyam ash*t*amám.

In whom, as the leader of the sacrifice, the seven threads are stretched out,—the eighth divine being is manlike (?).

The sacrifice itself is called, X, 124, 1, saptá-tantu, having seven threads.

X, 122, 3. saptá dhã́mâni pari-yán ámartya*h*.

Agni, the immortal, who goes round the seven stations.

X, 8, 4. ushá*h*-usha*h* hí vaso (íti) ágram éshi tvám yamáyo*h* abhava*h* vi-bhã́vâ, *ri*tã́ya saptá dadhishe padã́ni *g*anáyan mitrám tanvẽ́ svã́yai.

For thou, Vasu (Agni), comest first every morning, thou art the illuminator of the twins (day and night). Thou holdest the seven places for the sacrifice, creating Mitra (the sun) for thy own body.

X, 5, 6. saptá maryã́dâ*h* kaváya*h* tatakshu*h* tã́sâm ékâm ít abhí a*m*hurá*h* gât.

The sages established the seven divisions, but mischief befell one of them.

I, 22, 16. áta*h* devã́*h* avantu na*h* yáta*h* víshnu*h* vi-*k*akramé p*ri*thivyã́*h* saptá dhã́ma-bhi*h*.

May the gods protect us from whence Vish*n*u strode forth, by the seven stations of the earth!

Even the names of the seven or eight Âdityas are not definitely known, at least not from the hymns of the Rigveda. In II, 27, 1, we have a list of six names: Mitrá, Aryamán, Bhága, Váru*n*a, Dáksha, Á*m*sa*h*. These with Áditi would give us seven. In VI, 50, 1, we have Áditi,

Váru*n*a, Mitrá, Agní, Aryamán, Savitár, and Bhága. In I, 89, 3, Bhága, Mitrá, Áditi, Dáksha, Aryamán, Váru*n*a, Sóma, A*s*vínâ, and Sárasvatî are invoked together with an old invocation, pū́rvayâ ni-vídâ. In the Taittirîya-âra*n*yaka, I, 13, 3, we find the following list: 1. Mitra, 2. Varu*n*a, 3. Dhâtar, 4. Aryaman, 5. A*ms*a, 6. Bhaga, 7. Indra, 8. Vivasvat, but there, too, the eighth son is said to be Mârtâ*n*da, or, according to the commentator, Âditya.

The character of Aditi as the mother of certain gods is also indicated by some of her epithets, such as rā́*g*a-putrâ, having kings for her sons; su-putrā́, having good sons; ugrá-putrâ, having terrible sons:

II, 27, 7. pípartu na*h* áditi*h* rā́*g*a-putrâ áti dvéshâ*m*si aryamā́ su-gébhi*h*, b*ri*hát mitrásya váru*n*asya *s*árma úpa syâma puru-vī́râ*h* árish*t*â*h*.

May Aditi with her royal sons, may Aryaman carry us on easy roads across the hatreds; may we with many sons and without hurt obtain the great protection of Mitra and Varu*n*a!

III, 4, 11. barhí*h* na*h* âstâm áditi*h* su-putrā́.

May Aditi with her excellent sons sit on our sacred pile!

VIII, 67, 11. párshi dîné gabhîré ā́ úgra-putre *g*ighâ*m*sata*h*, mā́ki*h* tokásya na*h* rishat.

Protect us, O goddess with terrible sons, from the enemy in shallow or deep water, and no one will hurt our offspring!

Aditi identified with other Deities.

Aditi, however, for the very reason that she was originally intended for the Infinite, for something beyond the visible world, was liable to be identified with a number of finite deities which might all be represented as resting on Aditi, as participating in Aditi, as being Aditi. Thus we read:

I, 89, 10 (final). áditi*h* dyaú*h* áditi*h* antáriksham áditi*h* mâtā́ sá*h* pitā́ sá*h* putrá*h*, ví*s*ve devā́*h* áditi*h* páñ*k*a *g*ánâ*h* áditi*h* *g*âtám áditi*h* *g*áni-tvam.

Aditi is the heaven, Aditi the sky, Aditi the mother, the

father, the son. All the gods are Aditi, the five clans, the past is Aditi, Aditi is the future.

But although Aditi may thus be said to be everything, heaven, sky, and all the gods, no passage occurs, in the Rig-veda at least, where the special meaning of heaven or earth is expressed by Aditi. In X, 63, 3, where Aditi seems to mean sky, we shall see that it ought to be taken as a masculine, either in the sense of Âditya, or as an epithet, unbounded, immortal. In I, 72, 9, we ought probably to read p*ri*thvī́ and pronounce p*ri*thuvī́, and translate 'the wide Aditi, the mother with her sons;' and not, as Benfey does, 'the Earth, the eternal mother.'

It is more difficult to determine whether in one passage Aditi has not been used in the sense of life after life, or as the name of the place whither people went after death, or of the deity presiding over that place. In a well-known hymn, supposed to have been uttered by *S*una*hs*epa when on the point of being sacrificed by his own father, the following verse occurs:

I, 24, 1. ká*h* na*h* mahyaí áditaye púna*h* dât, pitáram *k*a d*ri*séyam mâtáram *k*a.

Who will give us back to the great Aditi, that I may see father and mother?

As the supposed utterer of this hymn is still among the living, Aditi can hardly be taken in the sense of earth, nor would the wish to see father and mother be intelligible in the mouth of one who is going to be sacrificed by his own father. If we discard the story of *S*una*hs*epa, and take the hymn as uttered by any poet who craves for the protection of the gods in the presence of danger and death, then we may choose between the two meanings of earth or liberty, and translate, either, Who will give us back to the great earth? or, Who will restore us to the great Aditi, the goddess of freedom?

Aditi and Diti.

There is one other passage which might receive light if we could take Aditi in the sense of Hades, but I give this translation as a mere guess:

IV, 2, 11. râyé *k*a na*h* su-apatyấya deva dítim *k*a rấsva áditim urushya.

That we may enjoy our wealth and healthy offspring, give us this life on earth, keep off the life to come! Cf. I, 152, 6.

It should be borne in mind that Diti occurs in the Rig-veda thrice only, and in one passage it should, I believe, be changed into Aditi. This passage occurs in VII, 15, 12. tvám agne vîrá-vat yá*s*a*h* devá*h* *k*a savitấ bhága*h*, díti*h* *k*a dâti vấryam. Here the name of Diti is so unusual, and that of Aditi, on the contrary, so natural, that I have little doubt that the poet had put the name of Aditi; and that later reciters, not aware of the occasional license of putting two short syllables instead of one, changed it into Aditi. If we remove this passage, then Diti, in the Rig-veda at least, occurs twice only, and each time together or in contrast with Aditi; cf. V, 62, 8, page 243. I have no doubt, therefore, that Professor Roth is right when he says that Diti is a being without any definite conception, a mere reflex of Aditi. We can clearly watch her first emergence into existence through what is hardly more than a play of words, whereas in the epic and Purâ*n*ic literature this Diti (like the Suras) has grown into a definite person, one of the daughters of Daksha, the wife of Ka*s*yapa, the mother of the enemies of the gods, the Daityas. Such is the growth of legend, mythology and religion!

Aditi in her Moral Character.

Besides the cosmical character of Aditi, which we have hitherto examined, this goddess has also assumed a very prominent moral character. Aditi, like Varu*n*a, delivers from sin. Why this should be so, we can still understand if we watch the transition which led from a purely cosmical to a moral conception of Aditi. Sin in the Veda is frequently conceived as a bond or a chain from which the repentant sinner wishes to be freed:

VII, 86, 5. áva drugdhấni pítryâ *s*r*i*g*a na*h* áva yấ vayám *k*ak*ri*má tanû́bhi*h*, áva râ*g*an pa*s*u-t*ri*pam ná tâyúm *s*r*i*gá vatsám ná dấmna*h* vásish*th*am.

Absolve us from the sins of our fathers, and from those

which we have committed with our own bodies. Release Vasish*th*a, O king, like a thief who has feasted on stolen cattle; release him like a calf from the rope[a].

VIII, 67, 14. té na*h* âsná*h* v*rí*kâ*n*âm ā̃dityâsa*h* mumó*k*ata stenám baddhám-iva adite.

O Âdityas, deliver us from the mouth of the wolves, like a bound thief, O Aditi! Cf. VIII, 67, 18.

*S*una*hs*epa, who, as we saw before, wishes to be restored to the great Aditi, is represented as bound (dita) by ropes, and in V, 2, 7, we read:

*s*úna*h*-*s*épam *k*it ní-ditam sahásrât yū̃pât amu*ñk*a*h* á*s*amish*t*a hí sá*h*, evá asmát agne ví mumugdhi pā̃*s*ân hótar (íti) *k*ikitva*h* ihá tú ni-sádya.

O Agni, thou hast released the bound *S*una*hs*epa from the stake, for he had prayed; thus take from us, too, these ropes, O sagacious Hotar, after thou hast settled here.

Expressions like these, words like dā̃man, bond, ní-dita, bound, naturally suggested á-diti, the un-bound or unbounded, as one of those deities who could best remove the bonds of sin or misery. If we once realise this concatenation of thought and language, many passages of the Veda that seemed obscure, will become intelligible.

VII, 51, 1. âdityā̃nâm ávasâ nū̃tanena sakshîmáhi *s*árma*n*â *s*ám-tamena, anâgâ*h*-tvé aditi-tvé turā̃sa*h* imám yag*ñ*ám dadhatu *s*róshamâ*n*â*h*.

May we obtain the new favour of the Âdityas, their best protection; may the quick Maruts listen and place this sacrifice in guiltlessness and Aditi-hood.

I have translated the last words literally, in order to make their meaning quite clear. Ā̃gas has the same meaning as the Greek ἄγος, guilt, abomination; an-âgâs-tvá, therefore, as applied to a sacrifice or to the man who makes it, means guiltlessness, purity. Aditi-tvá, Aditi-hood, has a similar meaning, it means freedom from bonds, from anything that hinders the proper performance of a religious act; it may come to mean perfection or holiness.

---

[a] See M. M., History of Ancient Sanskrit Literature, 2nd ed., p. 541.

Aditi having once been conceived as granting this adititvá, soon assumed a very definite moral character, and hence the following invocations:

I, 24, 15. út ut-tamám varu*n*a pấ*s*am asmát áva adhamám ví madhyamám *s*rathaya, átha vayám âditya vraté táva ánâgasa*h* áditaye syâma.

O Varu*n*a, lift the highest rope, draw off the lowest, remove the middle; then, O Âditya, let us be in thy service free of guilt before Aditi.

V, 82, 6. ánâgasa*h* áditaye devásya savitú*h* savé, ví*s*vâ vâmấni dhîmahi.

May we, guiltless before Aditi, and in the keeping of the god Savitar, obtain all goods! Professor Roth here translates Aditi by freedom or security.

I, 162, 22. anâgâ*h*-tvám na*h* áditi*h* k*rin*otu.

May Aditi give us sinlessness! Cf. VII, 51, 1.

IV, 12, 4. yát *k*it hí te purusha-trấ yavish*th*a á*k*itti-bhi*h* *k*ak*ri*má kát *k*it âgâ*h*, k*ri*dhí sú asmấn ádite*h* ánâgân ví énâ*m*si si*s*ratha*h* víshvak agne.

Whatever, O youthful god, we have committed against thee, men as we are, whatever sin through thoughtlessness, make us guiltless of Aditi, loosen the sins on all sides, O Agni!

VII, 93, 7. sá*h* agne enấ námasâ sám-iddha*h* á*kkh*a mitrám váru*n*am índram vo*k*e*h*, yát sîm âgâ*h* *k*ak*ri*má tát sú m*ril*a tát aryamấ áditi*h* si*s*rathantu.

O Agni, thou who hast been kindled with this adoration, greet Mitra, Varu*n*a, and Indra. Whatever sin we have committed, do thou pardon it! May Aryaman, Aditi loose it!

Here the plural si*s*rathantu should be observed, instead of the dual.

VIII, 18, 6–7. áditi*h* na*h* dívâ pa*s*úm áditi*h* náktam ádvayâ*h*, áditi*h* pâtu á*m*hasa*h* sadấ-v*ri*dhâ.

utá syấ na*h* dívâ matí*h* áditi*h* ûtyấ ấ gamat, sâ *s*ám-tâti máya*h* karat ápa srídha*h*.

May Aditi by day protect our cattle, may she, who never deceives, protect by night; may she, with steady increase, protect us from evil!

And may she, the thoughtful Aditi, come with help to

us by day; may she kindly bring happiness to us, and carry away all enemies! Cf. X, 36, 3, page 251.

X, 87, 18. ấ vri*sk*yantâm áditaye du*h*-évâ*h*.

May the evil-doers be cut off from Aditi! or literally, may they be rooted out before Aditi!

II, 27, 14. ádite mítra váru*n*a utá m*ri*l*a* yát va*h* vayám *k*ak*ri*má kát *k*it ấga*h*, urú a*s*yâm ábhayam *g*yóti*h* indra mấ na*h* dîrghấ*h* abhí na*s*an támisrâ*h*.

Aditi, Mitra, and also Varu*n*a forgive, if we have committed any sin against you. May I obtain the wide and fearless light, O Indra! May not the long darkness reach us!

VII, 87, 7. yá*h* m*ril*áyâti *k*akrúshe *k*it ấga*h* vayám syâma váru*n*e ánâgâ*h*, ánu vratấni ádite*h* *ri*dhánta*h* yuyám pâta svastí-bhi*h* sádâ na*h*.

May we be sinless before Varu*n*a, who is gracious even to him who has committed sin, and may we follow the laws of Aditi! Protect us always with your blessings!

Lastly, Aditi, like all other gods, is represented as a giver of worldly goods, and implored to bestow them on her worshippers, or to protect them by her power:

I, 43, 2. yáthâ na*h* áditi*h* kárat pá*s*ve n*rí*-bhya*h* yáthâ gáve, yáthâ tokấya rudríyam.

That Aditi may bring Rudra's favour to our cattle, our men, our cow, our offspring.

I, 153, 3. pîpấya dhenú*h* áditi*h* *ri*tấya *g*ánâya mitrâvaru*n*â havi*h*-dé.

Aditi, the cow, gives food to the righteous man, O Mitra and Varu*n*a, who makes offerings to the gods. Cf. VIII, 101, 15.

I, 185, 3. anehá*h* dâtrám ádite*h* anarvám huvé.

I call for the unrivalled, uninjured gift of Aditi. Here Professor Roth again assigns to Aditi the meaning of freedom or security.

VII, 40, 2. dídesh*t*u devī́ áditi*h* rékna*h*.

May the divine Aditi assign wealth!

X, 100, 1. ấ sarvá-tâtim áditim v*rin*îmahe.

We implore Aditi for health and wealth.

I, 94, 15. yásmai tvám su-dravi*n*a*h* dádâ*s*a*h* anâgâ*h*-tvám aditc sarvá-tâtâ, yám bhadré*n*a sávasâ *k*odáyâsi pra*g*ấ-vatâ rấdhasâ té syâma.

To whom thou, possessor of good treasures, grantest guiltlessness, O Aditi, in health and wealth[a], whom thou quickenest with precious strength and with riches in progeny, may we be they! Cf. II, 40, 6; IV, 25, 5; X, 11, 2.

The principal epithets of Aditi have been mentioned in the passages quoted above, and they throw no further light on the nature of the goddess. She was called devî́, goddess, again and again; another frequent epithet is anarván, uninjured, unscathed. Being invoked to grant light (VII, 82, 10), she is herself called luminous, *g*yótishmatî, I, 136, 3; and svấrvatî, heavenly. Being the goddess of the infinite expanse, she, even with greater right than the dawn, is called úrû*k*î, VIII, 67, 12; uruvyá*k*as, V, 46, 6; uruvra*g*â, VIII, 67, 12; and possibly p*ri*thvî́ in I, 72, 9. As supporting everything, she is called dhârayátkshiti, supporting the earth, I, 136, 3; and vi*s*vá*g*anyâ, VII, 10, 4. To her sons she owes the names of rấ*g*aputrâ, II, 27, 7; suputrấ, III, 4, 11; and ugráputrâ, VIII, 67, 11: to her wealth that of sudravi*n*as, I, 94, 15, though others refer this epithet to Agni. There remains one name pastyấ, IV, 55, 3; VIII, 27, 5, meaning housewife, which again indicates her character as mother of the gods.

I have thus given all the evidence that can be collected from the Rig-veda as throwing light on the character of the goddess Aditi, and I have carefully excluded everything that rests only on the authority of the Ya*g*ur- or Atharva-vedas, or of the Brâhma*n*as and Âra*n*yakas, because in all they give beyond the repetitions from the Rig-veda, they seem to me to represent a later phase of thought that ought not to be mixed up with the more primitive conceptions of the Rig-veda. Not that the Rig-veda is free from what seems decidedly modern, or at all events secondary and late. But it is well to keep the great collections, as such,

[a] On sarvátâti, salus, see Benfey's excellent remarks in Orient und Occident, vol. ii, p. 519. Professor Roth takes aditi here as an epithet of Agni.

separate, whatever our opinions may be as to the age of their component parts.

In the Atharva-veda Aditi appears more unintelligible, more completely mythological, than in the Rig-veda. We read, for instance, Atharva-veda VII, 6, 1:

'Aditi is the sky, Aditi is the welkin, Aditi is mother, is father, is son; all the gods are Aditi, and the five clans of men; Aditi is what was, Aditi is what will be.

'We invoke for our protection the great mother of the well-ruling gods, the wife of *Ri*ta, the powerful, never-aging, far-spreading, the sheltering, well-guiding Aditi.'

In the Taittirîya-âra*n*yaka and similar works the mythological confusion becomes greater still. Much valuable material for an analytical study of Aditi may be found in B. and R.'s Dictionary, and in several of Dr. Muir's excellent contributions to a knowledge of Vedic theogony and mythology.

Aditi as an Adjective.

But although the foregoing remarks give as complete a description of Aditi as can be gathered from the hymns of the Rig-veda, a few words have to be added on certain passages where the word áditi occurs, and where it clearly cannot mean the goddess Aditi, as a feminine, but must be taken either as the name of a corresponding masculine deity, or as an adjective in the sense of unrestrained, independent, free.

V, 59, 8. mímâtu dyaú*h* áditi*h* vîtáye na*h*.

May the boundless Dyú (sky) help us to our repast!

Here áditi must either be taken in the sense of Âditya, or better in its original sense of unbounded, as an adjective belonging to Dyú, the masculine deity of the sky.

Dyú or the sky is called áditi or unbounded in another passage, X, 63, 3:

yébhya*h* mâtā́ mádhu-mat pínvate páya*h* pîyū́sham dyaú*h* áditi*h* ádri-barhâ*h*.

The gods to whom their mother yields the sweet milk, and the unbounded sky, as firm as a rock, their food.

IV, 3, 8. kathā́ *s*árdhâya marútâm *ri*tā́ya kathā́ sûré b*ri*haté p*rikkh*yámâna*h*, práti brava*h* áditaye turā́ya.

How wilt thou tell it to the host of the Maruts, how to the bright heaven, when thou art asked? How to the quick Aditi?

Here Aditi cannot be the goddess, partly on account of the masculine gender of turấya, partly because she is never called quick. Aditi must here be the name of one of the Âdityas, or it may refer back to sûré b*ri*haté. It can hardly be joined, as Professor Roth proposes, with *s*árdhâya marútâm, owing to the intervening sûré b*ri*haté.

In several passages áditi, as an epithet, refers to Agni:

IV, 1, 20 (final). ví*s*veshâm áditi*h* yag*ñ*íyânâm ví*s*veshâm átithi*h* mấnushâ*n*âm.

He, Agni, the Aditi, or the freest, among all the gods; he the guest among all men.

The same play on the words áditi and átithi occurs again:

VII, 9, 3. ámûra*h* kaví*h* áditi*h* vivásvân su-sa*m*sát mitrá*h* átithi*h* *s*ivá*h* na*h*, *k*itrá-bhânu*h* ushásâm bhâti ágre.

The wise poet, Aditi, Vivasvat, Mitra with his good company, our welcome guest, he (Agni) with brilliant light came at the head of the dawns.

Here, though I admit that several renderings are possible, Aditi is meant as a name of Agni, to whom the whole hymn is addressed, and who, as usual, is identified with other gods, or, at all events, invoked by their names. We may translate áditi*h* vivásvân by 'the brilliant Aditi,' or 'the unchecked, the brilliant,' or by 'the boundless Vivasvat,' but on no account can we take áditi here as the female goddess. The same applies to VIII, 19, 14, where Aditi, unless we suppose the goddess brought in in the most abrupt way, must be taken as a name of Agni; while in X, 92, 14, áditim anarvá*n*am, to judge from other epithets given in the same verse, has most likely to be taken again as an appellative of Agni. In some passages it would, no doubt, be possible to take Aditi as the name of a female deity, if it were certain that no other meaning could be assigned to this word. But if we once know that Aditi was the name of a male deity also, the structure of these passages becomes far more perfect, if we take Aditi in that sense:

IV, 39, 3. ánâgasam tám áditi*h* kri*n*otu sá*h* mitré*n*a váru*n*ena sa-*g*óshâ*h*.

May Aditi make him free from sin, he who is allied with Mitra and Varu*n*a.

We have had several passages in which Aditi, the female deity, is represented as sa*g*óshâ*h* or allied with other Âdityas, but if sá*h* is the right reading here, Aditi in this verse can only be the male deity. The pronoun sá cannot refer to tám.

With regard to other passages, such as IX, 81, 5; VI, 51, 3, and even some of those translated above in which Aditi has been taken as a female goddess, the question must be left open till further evidence can be obtained. There is only one more passage which has been often discussed, and where áditi was supposed to have the meaning of earth:

VII, 18, 8. du*h*-âdhyâ*h* áditim srevâyanta*h* a*k*etása*h* ví *g*ag*ri*bhre párush*n*îm.

Professor Roth in one of his earliest essays translated this line, 'The evil-disposed wished to dry the earth, the fools split the Parush*n*î,' and he supposed its meaning to have been that the enemies of Sudâs swam across the Parush*n*î in order to attack Sudâs. We might accept this translation, if it could be explained how by throwing themselves into the river, the enemies made the earth dry, though even then there would remain this difficulty that, with the exception of one other doubtful passage, discussed before, áditi never means earth. We might possibly translate: 'The evil-disposed, the fools, laid dry and divided the boundless river Parush*n*î.' This would be a description of a stratagem very common in ancient warfare, viz. diverting the course of a river and laying its original bed dry by digging a new channel, and thus dividing the old river. This is also the sense accepted by Sâya*n*a, who does not say that vigraha means dividing the waves of a river, as Professor Roth renders kûlabheda, but that it means dividing or cutting through its banks. In the Dictionary Professor Roth assigns to áditi in this passage the meaning of endless, inexhaustible.

*K*aná.

Note 5. Nothing is more difficult in the interpretation of the Veda than to gain an accurate knowledge of the power of particles and conjunctions. The particle *k*aná, we are told, is used both affirmatively and negatively, a statement which shows better than anything else the uncertainty to which every translation of Vedic hymns is as yet exposed. It is perfectly true that in the text of the Rig-veda, as we now read it, *k*aná means both indeed and no. But this very fact shows that we ought to distinguish where the first collectors of the Vedic hymns have not distinguished, and that while in the former case we read *k*aná, we ought in the latter to read *k*a ná.

I begin with those passages in which *k*aná is used emphatically, though originally it may have been a double negation.

I a. In negative sentences:

I, 18, 7. yásmât *ri*té ná sídhyati ya*gñáh* vipa*h*-*k*íta*h* *k*aná.

Without whom the sacrifice does not succeed, not even that of the sage.

V, 34, 5. ná ásunvatâ sa*k*ate púshyatâ *k*aná.

He does not cling to a man who offers no libations, even though he be thriving.

I, 24, 6. nahí te kshatrám ná sáha*h* ná manyúm váya*h* *k*aná amî́ (íti) patáyanta*h* âpú*h*.

For thy power, thy strength, thy anger even these birds which fly up, do not reach. Cf. I, 100, 15.

I, 155, 5. t*ri*tî́yam asya náki*h* ấ dadharshati váya*h* *k*aná patáyanta*h* patatrí*n*a*h*.

This third step no one approaches, not even the winged birds which fly up.

I, 55, 1. divá*h* *k*it asya varimấ ví papratha, índram ná mahnấ p*ri*thivî́ *k*aná práti.

The width of the heavens is stretched out, even the earth in her greatness is no match for Indra.

I b. In positive sentences:

VII, 32, 13. pûrvî́*h* *k*aná prá-sitaya*h* taranti tám yá*h* índre kárma*n*â bhúvat.

Even many snares pass him who is with Indra in his work.

VIII, 2, 14. ukthám *k*aná *s*asyámânam ágo*h* arí*h* ấ *k*iketa, ná gâyatrám gîyámânam.

He (Indra) marks indeed a poor man's prayer that is recited, but not a hymn that is sung. (Doubtful.)

VIII, 78, 10. táva ít indra ahám â-*s*ásâ háste dấtram *k*aná ấ dade.

Hoping in thee alone, O Indra, I take even this sickle in my hand.

I, 55, 5. ádha *k*aná *s*rát dadhati tvíshi-mate índrâya vá*g*ram ni-ghánighnate vadhám.

Then indeed they believe in Indra, the majestic, when he hurls the bolt to strike.

I, 152, 2. etát *k*aná tva*h* ví *k*iketat eshâm.

Does one of them understand even this?

IV, 18, 9. mámat *k*aná used in the same sense as mámat *k*it.

I, 139, 2. dhíbhi*h* *k*aná mánasâ svébhi*h* akshá-bhi*h*.

V, 41, 13. váya*h* *k*aná su-bhvấ*h* ấ áva yanti.

VII, 18, 9. â*s*ú*h* *k*aná ít abhi-pitvám *g*agâma.

VIII, 91, 3. ấ *k*aná tvâ *k*ikitsâma*h* ádhi *k*aná tvâ ná imasi.

We wish to know thee, indeed, but we cannot understand thee.

X, 49, 5. ahám randhayam m*ri*gayam *s*rutárva*n*e yát mâ á*g*ihita vayúnâ *k*aná ânu-shák.

VI, 26, 7. ahám *k*aná tát sûrí-bhi*h* âna*s*yâm.

May I also obtain this with the lords.

I c. Frequently *k*aná occurs after interrogative pronouns, to which it imparts an indefinite meaning, and principally in negative sentences:

I, 74, 7. ná yó*h* upabdí*h* ásvya*h* *s*ri*n*vé ráthasya kát *k*aná, yát agne yấsi dûtyấm.

No sound of horses is heard, and no sound of the chariot, when thou, O Agni, goest on thy message.

I, 81, 5. ná tvấ-vân indra ká*h* *k*aná ná *g*âtá*h* ná *g*anishyaté.

No one is like thee, O Indra, no one has been born, no one will be!

I, 84, 20. mā́ te rā́dhâ*m*si mā́ te ûtáya*h* vaso (íti) asmā́n kádâ *k*aná dabhan.

May thy gifts, may thy help, O Vasu, never fail us!

Many more passages might be given to illustrate the use of *k*aná or ká*s* *k*aná and its derivatives in negative sentences.

Cf. I, 105, 3; 136, 1; 139, 5; II, 16, 3; 23, 5; 28, 6; III, 36, 4; IV, 31, 9; V, 42, 6; 82, 2; VI, 3, 2; 20, 4; 47, 1; 3; 48, 17; 54, 9; 59, 4; 69, 8; 75, 16; VII, 32, 1; 19; 59, 3; 82, 7; 104, 3; VIII, 19, 6; 23, 15; 24, 15; 28, 4; 47, 7; 64, 2; 66, 13; 68, 19; IX, 61, 27; 69, 6; 114, 4; X, 33, 9; 39, 11; 48, 5; 49, 10; 59, 8; 62, 9; 85, 3; 86, 11; 95, 1; 112, 9; 119, 6; 7; 128, 4; 129, 2; 152, 1; 168, 3; 185, 2.

I d. In a few passages, however, we find the indefinite pronoun ká*s* *k*aná used in sentences which are not negative:

III, 30, 1. títikshante abhí-*s*astim *g*ánânâm índra tvát ā́ ká*h* *k*aná hí pra-ketá*h*.

They bear the scoffing of men; for, Indra, from thee comes every wisdom.

I, 113, 8. ushā́*h* m*ri*tám kám *k*aná bodháyantî.

Ushas, who wakes every dead (or one who is as if dead).

I, 191, 7. ád*ri*sh*t*â*h* kím *k*aná ihá va*h* sárve sâkám ní *g*asyata.

Invisible ones, whatever you are, vanish all together!

II. We now come to passages in which *k*aná stands for *k*a ná, and therefore renders the sentence negative without any further negative particle. It might seem possible to escape from this admission, by taking certain sentences in an interrogative sense. But this would apply to certain sentences only, and would seem forced even there:

II, 16, 2. yásmât índrât b*ri*hatá*h* kím *k*aná îm *ri*té.

Beside whom, (beside) the great Indra, there is not anything.

II, 24, 12. ví*s*vam satyám magha-vânâ yuvó*h* ít ā́pa*h* *k*aná prá minanti vratám vâm.

Everything, you mighty ones, belongs indeed to you; even the waters do not transgress your law.

IV, 30, 3. víśve *k*aná ít anấ tvâ devấsa*h* indra yuyudhu*h*.

Even all the gods do not ever fight thee, O Indra.

V, 34, 7. du*h*-gé *k*aná dhriyate víśva*h* ấ purú *g*ána*h* yá*h* asya távishîm á*k*ukrudhat.

Even in a stronghold many a man is not often preserved who has excited his anger.

VII, 83, 2. yásmin â*g*ấ bhávati kím *k*aná priyám.

In which struggle there is nothing good whatsoever.

VII, 86, 6. svápna*h* *k*aná ít án*ri*tasya pra-yotấ.

Even sleep does not remove all evil.

In this passage I formerly took *k*aná as affirmative, not as negative, and therefore assigned to prayotấ the same meaning which Sâya*n*a assigns to it, one who brings or mixes, whereas it ought to be, as rightly seen by Roth, one who removes.

VIII, 1, 5. mahé *k*aná tvấm adri-va*h* párâ *s*ulkấya deyâm, ná sahásrâya ná ayútâya va*g*ri-va*h* ná *s*atấya *s*ata-magha.

I should not give thee up, wielder of the thunderbolt, even for a great price, not for a thousand, not for ten thousand (?), not for a hundred, O Indra, thou who art possessed of a hundred powers!

VIII, 51, 7. kadấ *k*aná starî*h* asi.

Thou art never sterile.

VIII, 52, 7. kadấ *k*aná prá yu*kkh*asi.

Thou art never weary.

VIII, 55, 5. *k*ákshushâ *k*aná sam-náśe.

Not to be reached even with eye.

X, 56, 4. mahimná*h* eshâm pitára*h* *k*aná îśire.

Note 6. Considering the particular circumstances mentioned in this and the preceding hymn, of Indra's forsaking his companions, the Maruts, or even scorning their help, one feels strongly tempted to take tyá*g*as in its etymological sense of leaving or forsaking, and to translate, by his forsaking you, or, if he should forsake you. The poet may have meant the word to convey that idea, which no doubt would be most appropriate here; but it must be confessed, at the same time, that in other passages where tyá*g*as occurs, that meaning could hardly be ascribed to it. Strange as it may seem, no one who is acquainted with the general train of thought in the Vedic hymns can fail to see that tyá*g*as in most passages means attack, onslaught; it may be even the instrument of an attack, a weapon. How it should come to take this meaning is indeed difficult to explain, and I do not wonder that Professor Roth in his Dictionary simply renders the word by forlornness, need, danger, or by estrangement, unkindness, malignity. But let us look at the passages, and we shall see that these abstract conceptions are quite out of place:

VIII, 47, 7. ná tám tigmám *k*aná tyá*g*a*h* ná drâsad abhí tám gurú.

No sharp blow, no heavy one, shall come near him whom you protect.

Here the two adjectives tigmá, sharp, and gurú, heavy, point to something tangible, and I feel much inclined to take tyá*g*as in this passage as a weapon, as something that is let off with violence, rather than in the more abstract sense of onslaught.

I, 169, 1. mahá*h* *k*it asi tyá*g*asa*h* varûtấ.

Thou art the shielder from a great attack.

IV, 43, 4. ká*h* vâm mahá*h* *k*it tyá*g*asa*h* abhī́ke urushyátam mâdhvî dasrâ na*h* ûtī́.

Who is against your great attack? Protect us with your help, O A*s*vins, ye strong ones.

Here Professor Roth seems to join mahá*h* *k*it tyá*g*asa*h* abhī́ke urushyátam, but in that case it would be impossible to construe the first words, ká*h* vâm.

I, 119, 8. ága*kkh*atam k*r*í pamâ*n*am parâ-váti pitú*h* svásya tyá*g*asâ ní-bâdhitam.

You went from afar to the suppliant, who had been struck down by the violence of his own father.

According to Professor Roth tyá*g*as would here mean forlornness, need, or danger. But níbâdhita is a strong verb, as we may see in

VIII, 64, 2. padấ pa*n*ī́n arâdhása*h* ní bâdhasva mahā́n asi.

Strike the useless Pa*n*is down with thy foot, for thou art great.

X, 18, 11. út sva*ñ**k*asva p*r*ithivi mấ ní bâdhathâ*h*.

Open, O earth, do not press on him (i.e. the dead, who is

to be buried; cf. M. M., Über Todtenbestattung, Zeitschrift der D. M. G., vol. ix, p. xv).

VII, 83, 6. yátra rā́ga-bhi*h* da*s*á-bhi*h* ní-bâdhitam prá su-dā́sam ā́vatam t*r*í tsu-bhi*h* sahá.

Where you protected Sudâs with the T*r*itsus, when he was pressed or set upon by the ten kings.

Another passage in which tyá*g*as occurs is,

VI, 62, 10. sánutyena tyá*g*asâ mártyasya vanushyatā́m ápi *s*îrshā́ vav*r*iktam.

By your covert attack turn back the heads of those even who harass the mortal.

Though this passage may seem less decisive, yet it is difficult to see how tyá*g*asâ could here, according to Professor Roth, be rendered by forlornness or danger. Something is required by which enemies can be turned back. Nor can it be doubtful that *s*îrshā́ is governed by vav*r*iktam, meaning turn back their heads, for the same expression occurs again in I, 33, 5. párâ *k*it *s*îrshā́ vav*r*i*g*u*h* té indra áya*g*vâna*h* yá*g*va-bhi*h* spárdhamânâ*h*.

Professor Benfey translates this verse by, 'Kopfüber flohn sie alle vor dir;' but it may be rendered more literally, 'These lawless people fighting with the pious turned away their heads.'

X, 144, 6. evá tát índra*h* índunâ devéshu *k*it dhârayâte máhi tyá*g*a*h*.

Indeed through this draught Indra can hold out against that great attack even among the gods.

X, 79, 6. kím devéshu tyá*g*a*h* éna*h* *k*akartha.

What insult, what sin hast thou committed among the gods?

In these two passages the meaning of tyá*g*as as attack or assault is at least as appropriate as that proposed by Professor Roth, estrangement, malignity.

There remains one passage, VI, 3, 1. yám tvám mitré*n*a váru*n*a*h* sa-*g*ósha*h* déva pā́si tyá*g*asâ mártam á*m*ha*h*.

I confess that the construction of this verse is not clear to me, and I doubt whether it is possible to use tyá*g*asâ as a verbal noun governing an accusative. If this were possible, one might translate, 'The mortal whom thou, O God (Agni),

Varu*n*a, together with Mitra, protectest by pushing back evil.' More probably we should translate, 'Whom thou protectest from evil by thy might.'

If it be asked how tyá*g*as can possibly have the meaning which has been assigned to it in all the passages in which it occurs, viz. that of forcibly attacking or pushing away, we can only account for it by supposing that tya*g*, before it came to mean to leave, meant to push off, to drive away with violence (verstossen instead of verlassen). This meaning may still be perceived occasionally in the use of tya*g*; e.g. devâs tya*g*antu mâm, may the gods forsake me! i.e. may the gods drive me away! Even in the latest Sanskrit tya*g* is used with regard to an arrow that is let off. 'To expel' is expressed by nis-tya*g*. Those who believe in the production of new roots by the addition of prepositional prefixes might possibly see in tya*g* an original ati-a*g*, to drive off; but, however that may be, there is evidence enough to show that tya*g* expressed originally a more violent act of separation than it does in ordinary Sanskrit, though here, too, passages occur in which tya*g* may be translated by to throw, to fling; for instance, khe dhûli*m* yas tya*g*ed u*kk*air mûrdhni tasyaiva sâ patet, he who throws up dust in the air, it will fall on his head. Ind. Spr. 1582.

Mu*k*, too, is used in a similar manner; for instance, va*g*ram mokshyate te' mahendra*h*, Mahâbh. XIV, 263. Cf. Dhammapada, ver. 389.

Verse 13.

Note 1. *Sám*sa, masc., means a spell, whether for good or for evil, a blessing as well as a curse. It means a curse, or, at all events, a calumny:

I, 18, 3. mấ na*h* *sámsah* árarusha*h* dhûrtí*h* prá*n*ak mártyasya.

Let not the curse of the enemy, the onslaught of a mortal hurt us.

I, 94, 8. asmấkam *sámsah* abhí astu du*h*-dhyã*h*.

May our curse overcome the wicked!

III, 18, 2. tápa *sám*sam ára rusha*h*.

Burn the curse of the enemy!

VII, 25, 2. âré tám *sám*sam k*ri*nuhi ninitsó*h*.

Take far away the curse of the reviler! Cf. VII, 34, 12.

It means blessing:

II, 31, 6. utá va*h* *sám*sam u*s*í*g*âm-iva *s*masi.

We desire your blessing as a blessing for suppliants.

X, 31, 1. ấ na*h* devắnâm úpa vetu *sám*sa*h*.

May the blessing of the gods come to us!

X, 7, 1. urushyá na*h* urú-bhi*h* deva *sám*sai*h*.

Protect us, god, with thy wide blessings!

II, 23, 10. mấ na*h* du*h*-*sám*sa*h* abhi-dipsú*h* î*s*ata prá su-*sám*sâ*h* matí-bhi*h* târishîmahi.

Let not an evil-speaking enemy conquer us; may we, enjoying good report, increase by our prayers!

In some passages, however, as pointed out by Grassmann, *sám*sa may best be rendered by singer, praiser. Grassmann marks one passage only,

II, 26, 1. *rigúh* ít *sám*sa*h* vanavat vanushyatá*h*.

May the righteous singer conquer his enemies.

He admits, however, doubtfully, the explanation of B. R., that *rigúh sám*sa*h* may be taken as one word, meaning, 'requiring the right.' This explanation seems surrendered by B. R. in the second edition of their Dictionary, and I doubt whether *sám*sa*h* can mean here anything but singer. That being so, the same meaning seems more appropriate in other verses also, which I formerly translated differently, e. g.

VII, 56, 19. imé *sám*sam vanushyatá*h* ní pânti.

They, the Maruts, protect the singer from his enemy.

Lastly, *sám*sa means praise, the spell addressed by men to the gods, or prayer:

I, 33, 7. prá sunvatá*h* stuvatá*h* *sám*sam âva*h*.

Thou hast regarded the prayer of him who offers libation and praise.

X, 42, 6. yásmin vayám dadhimá *sám*sam índre.

Indra in whom we place our hope. Cf. â*sam*s, Westergaard, Radices Linguae Sanscritae, s. v. *sam*s.

MAN*D*ALA I, HYMN 167.

ASH*T*AKA II, ADHYÂYA 4, VARGA 4-5.

TO THE MARUTS (THE STORM-GODS).

1. O Indra, a thousand have been thy helps accorded to us, a thousand, O driver of the bays, have been thy most delightful viands. May thousands of treasures richly to enjoy, may goods [1] come to us a thousandfold.

2. May the Maruts come towards us with their aids, the mighty ones, or with their best aids from the great heaven, now that their furthest steeds have rushed forth on the distant shore of the sea;

3. There clings [1] to the Maruts one who moves in secret, like a man's wife (the lightning [2]), and who is like a spear carried behind [3], well grasped, resplendent, gold-adorned; there is also with them Vâ*k* (the voice of thunder), like unto a courtly, eloquent woman.

4. Far away the brilliant, untiring Maruts cling to their young maid, as if she belonged to them all [1]; but the terrible ones did not drive away Rodasî (the lightning), for they wished her to grow [2] their friend.

5. When the divine Rodasî with dishevelled locks, the manly-minded, wished to follow them, she went, like Sûryâ (the Dawn), to the chariot of her servant, with terrible look, as with the pace of a cloud.

6. As soon as the poet with the libations, O Maruts, had sung his song at the sacrifice, pouring out Soma, the youthful men (the Maruts) placed the young maid (in their chariot) as their companion for victory, mighty in assemblies.

7. I praise what is the praiseworthy true greatness of those Maruts, that the manly-minded, proud, and strong one (Rodasî) drives with them towards the blessed mothers.

8. They protect[1] Mitra and Varuna from the unspeakable, and Aryaman also finds out the infamous. Even what is firm and unshakable is being shaken[2]; but he who dispenses treasures[3], O Maruts, has grown (in strength).

9. No people indeed, whether near to us, or from afar, have ever found the end of your strength, O Maruts! The Maruts, strong in daring strength, have, like the sea, boldly[1] surrounded their haters.

10. May we to-day, may we to-morrow in battle be called the most beloved of Indra. We were so formerly, may we truly be so day by day, and may the lord of the Maruts be with us.

11. May this praise, O Maruts, this song of Mândârya, the son of Mâna, the poet, ask you with food for offspring for ourselves! May we have an invigorating autumn, with quickening rain!

NOTES.

Ascribed to Agastya, addressed to the Maruts, but the first verse to Indra. Metre Trish*t*ubh throughout.

No verse of this hymn occurs in the Sâma-veda, nor in the other Sa*m*hitâs.

Verse 1.

Note 1. We must keep vâ*g*a, as a general term, distinct from a*s*va, horses, and go, cows, for the poets themselves distinguish between gavyánta*h*, a*s*vayánta*h*, and vâ*g*ayánta*h*; see IV, 17, 16; VI, 8, 6.

Verse 3.

Note 1. On mimyaksha, see before, I, 165, 1, note 2.

Note 2. The spear of the Maruts is meant for the lightning, and we actually find *r*ish*t*í-vidyuta*h*, having the lightning for their spear, as an epithet of the Maruts, I, 168, 5; V, 52, 13.

The rest of this verse is difficult, and has been variously rendered by different scholars. We must remember that the lightning is represented as the wife or the beloved of the Maruts. In that character she is called Rodasî́, with the accent on the last syllable, and kept distinct from ródasî, the dual, with the accent on the antepenultimate, which means heaven and earth.

This Rodasî́ occurs:

V, 56, 8. ấ yásmin tastháu su-rá*n*âni bíbhratî sá*k*â marútsu rodasî́.

The chariot on which, carrying pleasant gifts, stands Rodasî among the Maruts.

VI, 50, 5. mimyáksha yéshu rodasî́ nú devî́.

To whom clings the divine Rodasî.

VI, 66, 6. ádha sma eshu rodasî́ svá-*s*o*k*i*h* ấ ámavatsu tasthau ná róka*h*.

When they (the Maruts) had joined the two Rodas, i.e. heaven and earth, then the self-brilliant Rodasî came among the strong ones.

The name of Ródasî, heaven and earth, is so much more frequent in the Rig-veda than that of Rodasî́, that in several passages the iti which stands after duals, has been wrongly inserted after Rodasî in the singular. It is so in our hymn, verse 4, where we must read rodasîm instead of rodasî íti, and again in X, 92, 11.

Besides the lightning, however, the thunder also may be said to be in the company of the Maruts, to be their friend or their wife, and it is this double relationship which seems to be hinted at in our hymn.

The thunder is called Vâ*k*, voice, the voice of heaven, also called by the author of the Anukrama*n*î, Âmbh*rin*î. It was natural to identify this ambh*rin*a with Greek ὄβριμος, terrible, particularly as it is used of the thunder, ὄβριμον ἐβρόντησε, Hes. Th. 839, and is applied to Athene as ὀβριμοπάτρη. But there are difficulties pointed out by Curtius, Grundzüge, p. 532, which have not yet been removed. This Vâ*k* says of herself (X, 125, 12) that she stretched the bow for Rudra, the father of the Maruts, that her birth-place is in the waters (clouds), and that she fills heaven and earth. See also X, 114, 8.

In I, 173, 3. antá*h* dûtá*h* ná ródasî *k*arat vấk.

The voice (thunder) moved between heaven and earth, like a messenger.

In VIII, 100, 10 and 11, after it has been said that the thunderbolt lies hidden in the water, the poet says: yát vấk vádantî avi-*k*etanấni rấsh*t*rî devấnâm ni-sasấda mandrâ, when the voice, the queen of the gods, the delightful, uttering incomprehensible sounds, sat down. If, in our verse, we take Vâ*k* in the sense of thunder, but as a feminine, it seems to me that the poet, speaking of the lightning and thunder as the two companions of the Maruts, represents the first, Rodasî, or the lightning, as the recognised wife, hiding herself in the house, while the other, the loud thunder, is represented as a more public companion of the Maruts, distinctly called vidatheshu pa*g*râ (verse 6), a good speaker at assemblies. This contrast, if it is really what the poet intended, throws a curious light on the social character of the Vedic times, as it presupposes two classes of wives, not necessarily simultaneous, however,—a house-wife, who stays at home and is not much seen, and a wife who appears in public and takes part in the society and conversation of the sabhâ, the assembly-room, and the vidathas, the meetings. The loud voice of the thunder as well as the usual hiding of the lightning might well suggest this comparison. That good manners, such as are required in public, and ready speech, were highly esteemed in Vedic times, we learn from such words as sabhéya and vidathyã. Sabhéya, from sabhâ, assembly, court, comes to mean courtly, polite: vidathyã, from vidatha, assembly, experienced, learned.

VIII, 4, 9. *k*andrá*h* yâti sabhấm úpa.

Thy friend, Indra, goes brilliant towards the assembly.

X, 34, 6. sabhấm eti kitavá*h*.

The gambler goes to the assembly.

VI, 28, 6. b*ri*hát va*h* váya*h* u*ky*ate sabhấsu.

Your great strength is spoken of in the assemblies.

Wealth is described as consisting in sabhâs, houses, IV, 2, 5; and a friend is described as sabhâsaha, strong in the assembly, X, 71, 10.

Sabhéya is used as an epithet of vipra (II, 24, 13), and a son is praised as sabheya, vidathya, and sadanya, i.e. as distinguished in the assemblies.

Vidathyã, in fact, means much the same as sabheya, namely, good for, distinguished at vidathas, meetings for social, political, or religious purposes, IV, 21, 2; VII, 36, 8, &c.

Note 3. Úparâ ná *rishtih*. I do not see how uparâ can here mean the cloud, if it ever has that meaning. I take úpara as opposed to pûrva, i. e. behind, as opposed to before. In that sense úpara is used, X, 77, 3; X, 15, 2; 44, 7, &c. It would therefore mean the spear on the back, or the spear drawn back before it is hurled forward.

B. R. propose to read sa*m*-vâk, colloquium, but they give no explanation. The reference to VS. IX, 2, is wrong.

Verse 4.

Note 1. The fourth verse carries on the same ideas which were hinted at in the third. We must again change rodasî, the dual, into rodasîm, which is sufficiently indicated by the accent. Yavyâ I take as an instrumental of yavî, or of yavyâ. It means the youthful maid, and corresponds to yuvati in verse 6. Yavyâ would be the exact form which Curtius (Grundzüge, p. 589) postulated as the Sanskrit prototype of Hebe[a]. Now, if the Maruts correspond to Mars in Latin, and to Ares in Greek, the fact that in the Iliad Hebe bathes and clothes Ares[b], may be of some significance. Sâdhâra*n*î is used in the sense of uxor communis, and would show a familiarity with the idea of polyandry recognised in the epic poetry of the Mahâbhârata.

But although the Maruts cling to this maid (the Vâ*k*, or thunder), they do not cast off Rodasî, their lawful wife, the lightning, but wish her to grow for their friendship, i. e. as their friend.

Ayấsa*h* yavyấ must be scanned ⏑ ⏓ ⏑ – ⏑ – –. In VI 66, 5, ayấsa*h* mahnấ must be scanned as ⏑ ⏓ ⏑ – ⏑ – – (mahimnâ ?).

Note 2. V*ri*dham, as the accent shows, is here an infinitive governed by *g*ushanta.

Verse 5.

See von Bradke, Dyaus Asura, p. 76.

Verse 6.

I translate arká by poet. The construction would become too cumbersome if we translated, 'as soon as the hymn with the libations was there for you, as soon as the sacrificer sang his song.'

Verse 7.

The meaning of the second line is obscure, unless we adopt Ludwig's ingenious view that Rodasî is here conceived as Eileithyia, the goddess who helps mothers in childbirth. I confess that it is a bold conjecture, and there is nothing in Vedic literature to support it. All I can say is that Eileithyia is in Greek, like Hebe (Yavyâ) and Ares (Marut), a child of Hera, and that lightning as well as dawn might become a symbol of birth. The etymology and the

[a] Wir müssen ein vorgriechisches yâvâ oder möglicherweise yâvyâ annehmen.

[b] Il. V, 905.

very form of Εἰλείθυια is doubtful, and so is that of Rodasî. It is tempting to connect rodasî, in the sense of heaven and earth, with O. S. radur, A. S. rôdor (Grimm, Myth. p. 662), but that is impossible. Cf. I, 101, 7.

Verse 8.

Note 1. I do not see how pânti, the plural, can refer to Mitra and Varu*n*a, nor how these gods could here be introduced as acting the part of the Maruts. I therefore refer pânti to the Maruts, who may be said to protect Mitra and Varu*n*a, day and night, and all that belongs to them, from evil and disgrace. Aryaman is then brought in, as being constantly connected with Mitrâ-varu*n*au, and the finding out, the perceiving from a distance, of the infamous enemies, who might injure Mitrâ-varu*n*au, is parenthetically ascribed to him. See Ludwig, Anmerkungen, p. 239.

Note 2. *K*yavante cannot and need not be taken for *k*yâvayanti, though a*k*yuta*k*ut is a common epithet of the Maruts. It is quite true that the shaking of the unshakable mountains is the work of the Maruts, but that is understood, even though it is not expressed. In V, 60, 3, we read, párvata*h* *k*it máhi v*ri*ddhá*h* bibhâya, even the very great mountain feared, i. e. the Maruts.

Note 3. Dâti in dấtivâra has been derived by certain Sanskrit scholars from dâ, to give. It means, no doubt, gift, but it is derived from dâ (do, dyati), to share, and means first, a share, and then a gift. Dấtivâra is applied to the Maruts, V, 58, 2; III, 51, 9, and must therefore be applied to them in our passage also, though the construction becomes thereby extremely difficult. It means possessed of a treasure of goods which they distribute. The growing, too, which is here predicated by vav*ri*dhe, leads us to think of the Maruts, as in I, 37, 5, or of their friend Indra, I, 52, 2; 81, 1; VI, 30, 1. It is never, so far as I know, applied to the sacrificer.

Verse 9.

Note 1. Dh*ri*shatấ is used as an adverb; see I, 71, 5; 174, 4; II, 30, 4, &c. Perhaps tmanấ may be supplied as in I, 54, 4.

MANDALA I, HYMN 168.

ASHTAKA I, ADHYÂYA 4, VARGA 6-7.

To the Maruts (the Storm-gods).

1. To every sacrifice[1] you hasten together[2], you accept prayer after prayer, O quick Maruts! Let me therefore bring you hither by my prayers from heaven and earth, for our welfare, and for our great protection;

2. The shakers who were born to bring food and light[1], self-born and self-supported, like springs[2], like thousandfold waves of water, aye, visibly like unto excellent bulls[3],

3. Those Maruts, like Soma-drops[1], which squeezed from ripe stems dwell, when drunk, in the hearts of the worshipper—see how on their shoulders there clings as if a clinging wife; in their hands the quoit is held and the sword.

4. Lightly they have come down from heaven of their own accord: Immortals, stir yourselves with the whip! The mighty Maruts on dustless paths, armed with brilliant spears, have shaken down even the strong places.

5. O ye Maruts, who are armed with lightning-spears, who stirs you from within by himself, as the jaws are stirred by the tongue[1]? You shake the sky[2], as if on the search for food; you are invoked by many[3], like the (solar) horse of the day[4].

6. Where, O Maruts, is the top, where the bottom of the mighty sky where you came? When you throw down with the thunderbolt what is strong, like brittle things, you fly across the terrible sea!

7. As your conquest is violent, splendid, terrible, full and crushing, so, O Maruts, is your gift delightful, like the largess of a liberal worshipper, wide-spreading, laughing like heavenly lightning.

8. From the tires of their chariot-wheels streams gush forth, when they send out the voice of the clouds; the lightnings smiled upon the earth, when the Maruts shower down fatness (fertile rain).

9. P*ri*s*ni[1] brought forth for the great fight the terrible train of the untiring Maruts: when fed they produced the dark cloud[3], and then looked about for invigorating food[2].

10. May this praise, O Maruts, this song of Mândârya, the son of Mâna, the poet, ask you with food for offspring for ourselves! May we have an invigorating autumn, with quickening rain!

NOTES.

This hymn is ascribed to Agastya. Verses 1-7, *G*agatî; 8-10, Trish*t*ubh. No verse of this hymn occurs in the SV., VS., TS., AS.

Verse 1.

There can be little doubt that the text of the first line is corrupt. Ludwig admits this, but both he and Grassmann translate the verse.

GRASSMANN: Durch stetes Opfer möcht ich euch gewinnen recht, Gebet, das zu euch Göttern drengt, empfangt ihr gern.

LUDWIG: Bei jedem opfer ist zusammen mit euch der siegreich thätige, in jedem lied hat der fromme an euch gedacht.

Ludwig proposes to read âdîdhiye or devayâ*d* â dîdhiye, but even then the construction remains difficult.

Note 1. Ya*gñ*ấ-ya*gñ*ấ, an adverbial expression, much the same as ya*gñ*e ya*gñ*e (I, 136, 1); it occurs once more in VI, 48, 1.

Note 2. Tuturvá*n*i*h* does occur here only, but is formed like *g*ugurvá*n*i, I, 142, 8, and su*s*ukváni, VIII, 23, 5. Possibly tuturva*n*i*h* might stand for the host of the Maruts in the singular, 'you hasten together to every sacrifice.' As to dadhidhve, used in a similar sense, see IV, 34, 3; 37, 1.

As a conjecture, though no more, I propose to read evayâ*h* u.

Éva, in the sense of going, quick, is used of the horses of the Maruts, I, 166, 4. More frequently it has the sense of going, moving, than of manner (mos), and as an adverb eva and evam mean in this way (K. Z. II, 235). From this is derived evayâ*h*, in the sense of quickly moving, an epithet applied to Vish*n*u, I, 156, 1, and to the Maruts, V, 41, 16: kathấ dâ*s*ema námasâ su-dấnûn eva-yấ marúta*h* a*kkh*a-ukthai*h*, How shall we worship with praise and invocations the liberal quick-moving Maruts? I read, with Roth, eva-yấ*h*; otherwise we should have to take evayâ as an adverbial instrumental, like âsayấ from âsâ; see Grassmann, s. v. âsayâ.

In one hymn (V, 87) Evayâ-marut, as one word, has become an invocation, reminding us of ἤιε Φοῖβε, or Evoe Bacche, and similar forms. Possibly ἤια may be viatica, though the vowels do not correspond regularly (see yayi, I, 87, 2, note 1).

From eva we have also eva-yâvan (fem. evayấvari, VI, 48, 12), which Benfey proposed to divide into evayâ-van, quick, again an epithet of Vishnu and the Maruts. If then we read evayâ*h* u, without the accent on the last syllable, we should have a proper invocation of the Maruts, 'You, quick Maruts, accept prayer after prayer.'

Verse 2.

Note 1. Ísham svãr are joined again in VII, 66, 9. sahá ísham svã*h* *k*a dhîmahi. It seems to mean food and light, or water and light, water being considered as invigorating and supporting. Abhigâyanta governs the accusative.

Note 2. The meaning of spring was first assigned to vavra by Grassmann.

Note 3. Though I cannot find gấva*h* and ukshá*n*a*h* again, used in apposition to each other, I have little doubt that Grassmann is right in taking both as one word, like ταῦρος βοῦς in Greek.

Verse 3.

Note 1. The first line of this verse is extremely difficult. GRASSMANN translates:

Den Somasäften gleichen sie, den kräftigen,
Die eingeschlürft sich regen, nimmer wirkungslos.

LUDWIG: Die wie Soma, das gepresst aus saftvollen stengel, aufgenommen ins innere freundlich weilen.

It may be that the Maruts are likened to Somas, because they refresh and strengthen. So we read VIII, 48, 9:

tvám hí na*h* tanvã*h* Soma gopấ*h* gấtre-gâtre ni-sasáttha.

For thou, O Soma, has sat down as a guardian in every member of our body.

It is possible, therefore, though I shall say no more, that the poet wished to say that the Maruts, bringing rain and cooling the air, are like Somas in their refreshing and invigorating power, when stirring the hearts of men. In X, 78, 2, the Maruts are once more compared with Somas, su-*s*ármâ*n*a*h* ná sómâ*h* *ri*tám yaté. Should there be a dative hidden in ấsate?

Rambhi*n*î I now take with Sâya*n*a in the sense of a wife clinging to the shoulders of her husband, though what is meant is the spear, or some other weapon, slung over the shoulders; see I, 167, 3.

Verse 5.

Note 1. Hánvâ-iva *g*ihváyâ gives no sense, if we take hanvâ as an instrum. sing. Hanu is generally used in the dual, in the Rig-veda always, meaning the two jaws or the two lips. Thus Ait. Br. VII, 11. hanû sa*g*ihve; AV. X, 2, 7. hanvor hi *g*ihvâm adadhâ*h*, he placed the tongue in the jaws. I should therefore prefer to read hanû iva, which would improve the metre also, or take hanvâ for a dual, as Sâya*n*a does.

One might also translate, 'Who amongst you, O Maruts, moves by himself, as the jaws by the tongue,' but the simile would not be so perfect. The meaning is the same as in the preceding verse, viz. that the Maruts are self-born, self-determined, and that they move along without horses and chariots. In X, 78, 2, the Maruts are called svayu*g*, like the winds.

Note 2. I feel doubtful about dhanva*k*yút, and feel inclined towards Sâya*n*a's explanation, who takes dhanvan for antariksha. It would then correspond to parvata-*k*yút, dhruva-*k*yút, &c.

Note 3. Purupraisha may also be, You who have the command of many.

Note 4. As to ahanyấ*h* ná éta*s*a*h*, see V, 1, 4. *s*vetá*h* vâ*g*ī́ *g*âyate ágre áhnâm.

Verse 6.

Vithura translated before, I, 87, 3, by broken, means also breakable or brittle. Sâya*n*a explains it by grass, which may be true, though I see no authority for it. Grassmann translates it by leaves. It is derived from vyath.

Verse 7.

Sâtí and râtí are used on purpose, the former meaning the acquisition or conquest of good things, the latter the giving away of them. The onslaught of the Maruts is first described as violent and crushing; their liberality in giving away what they have conquered, chiefly rain, is represented as delightful, like the gifts of a liberal worshipper. Then follows p*ri*thu*g*ráyî asuryẽva *g*áñ*g*atî. Here asuryâ reminds us of the asuryâ in the preceding hymn, where it occurred as an epithet of Rodasî, the lightning. P*ri*thu*g*ráyî, wide-spreading, seems to apply best to the rain, that is, the râti, though it might also apply to the lightning. However, the râti is the storm with rain and lightning, and I therefore propose to read *g*á*ggh*atî for *g*áñ*g*atî. *Gañg* is a root which occurs here only, and *gaggh* too is a root which is unknown to most students of Sanskrit. Benfey[a], to whom we owe so much, was the first to point out that *g*a*ggh*, which Yâska explains by to make a noise and applies to murmuring waters, is a popular form of *g*aksh, to laugh, a reduplicated form of has. He shows that ksh is changed into *kkh* in a*kkh*â for akshâ, and into *gh* and *ggh*, in Pâli and Prakrit, e.g. *gh*â for kshâ. The original form *g*aksh, to laugh, occurs I, 33, 7. tvám etấn rudatá*h* *g*ákshata*h* *k*a áyodhaya*h*, thou foughtest them, the crying and the laughing.

That the lightning is often represented as laughing we see from the very next verse, áva smayanta vidyúta*h*, the lightnings laughed down; and the very fact that this idea occurs in the next verse confirms me in the view that it was in the poet's mind in the preceding one. See also I, 23, 12. haskârất vidyúta*h* pári áta*h* *g*âtấ*h* avantu na*h* marúta*h* m*ri*-*l*ayantu na*h*.

In the only other passage where *gañg* occurs, VIII, 43, 8, ar*k*íshâ *g*añ*g*anâbhávan, applied to Agni, admits of the same correction, *g*a*ggh*anâbhávan, and of the same translation, 'laughing with splendour.'

Benfey' objection to the spelling of *gaghgh* with two

[a] Gött. Nachr., 1876, No. 13, s. 324.

aspirates is just with regard to pronunciation, but this would hardly justify our changing the style of our MSS., which, in this and in other cases, write the two aspirates, though intending them for non-aspirate and aspirate.

Verse 9.

Note 1. P*ris*ni, the mother of the Maruts, who are often called P*rí*s*ni-mâtara*h*, gó-mâtara*h*, and síndhu-mâtara*h*.

Note 2. As to svadhâ in the sense of food, see before, I, 6, 4, note 2, and X, 157, 5.

Note 3. Abhva is more than dark clouds, it is the dark gathering of clouds before a storm, ein Unwetter, or, if conceived as a masculine, as in I, 39, 8, ein Ungethüm. Such words are simply untranslatable.

MAN*D*ALA I, HYMN 170.

ASHT*A*KA I, ADHYÂYA 4, VARGA 8–9.

DIALOGUE BETWEEN INDRA AND HIS WORSHIPPER, AGASTYA.

1. Indra: There is no such thing to-day, nor will it be so to-morrow. Who knows what strange thing [1] this is? We must consult the thought of another, for even what we once knew seems to vanish.

2. Agastya: Why dost thou wish to kill us, O Indra? the Maruts are thy brothers; fare kindly with them, and do not strike [1] us in battle.

3. The Maruts: O brother Agastya, why, being a friend, dost thou despise us? We know quite well what thy mind was. Dost thou not wish to give to us?

4. Agastya: Let them prepare the altar, let them light the fire in front! Here we two will spread [2] for thee the sacrifice, to be seen [1] by the immortal.

5. Agastya: Thou rulest, O lord of treasures; thou, lord of friends, art the most generous. Indra, speak again with the Maruts, and then consume our offerings at the right season

NOTES.

Although this hymn is not directly addressed to the Maruts, yet as it refers to the before-mentioned rivalry between the Maruts and Indra, and as the author is supposed to be the same, namely Agastya, I give its translation here.

None of its verses occurs in SV., VS., TS., AV.

The Anukrama*n*ikâ ascribes verses 1, 3, 4 to Indra, 2 and 5 to Agastya; Ludwig assigns verses 1 and 3 to the Maruts, 2, 4, and 5 to Agastya; Grassmann gives verse 1 to Indra, 2 and 3 to the Maruts, and 4 and 5 to Agastya.

The hymn admits of several explanations. There was a sacrifice in which Indra and the Maruts were invoked together, and it is quite possible that our hymn may owe its origin to this. But it is possible also that the sacrifice may be the embodiment of the same ideas which were originally expressed in this and similar hymns, namely, that Indra, however powerful by himself, could not dispense with the assistance of the storm-gods. I prefer to take the latter view, but I do not consider the former so untenable as I did formerly. The idea that a great god like Indra did not like to be praised together with others is an old idea, and we find traces of it in the hymns themselves, e. g. II, 33, 4. mấ dú*h*stutî, mấ sáhûtî.

It is quite possible, therefore, that our hymn contains the libretto of a little ceremonial drama in which different choruses of priests are introduced as preparing a sacrifice for the Maruts and for Indra, and as trying to appease the great Indra, who is supposed to feel slighted. Possibly Indra and the Maruts too may have been actually represented by some actors, so that here, as elsewhere, the first seeds of the drama would be found in sacrificial performances.

I propose, though this can only be hypothetical, to take the first verse as a vehement complaint of Indra, when asked to share the sacrifice with the Maruts. In the second verse Agastya is introduced as trying to pacify Indra. The third verse is most likely an appeal of the Maruts to remind Indra that the sacrifice was originally intended for them. Verses 4 and 5 belong to Agastya, who, though frightened into obedience to Indra, still implores him to make his peace with the Maruts.

Verse 1.

Note 1. In the first verse Indra expresses his surprise in disconnected sentences, saying that such a thing has never happened before. I do not take ádbhuta (nie da gewesen) in the sense of future, because that is already contained in *s*vas. The second line expresses that Indra does not remember such a thing, and must ask some one else, whether he remembers anything like it. We ought to take abhisa*m*kāré*n*ya as one word, and probably in the sense of to be approached or to be accepted. Abhisa*mk*ârin, however, means also changeable.

Verse 2.

Note 1. Vadhî*h* is the augmentless indicative, not subjunctive; see, however, Delbrück, Synt. Forsch. I, pp. 21, 115.

Verse 4.

Note 1. *K*etana refers to ya*gñ*a as in VIII, 13, 8. It means that which attracts the attention of the gods (IV, 7, 2), and might be translated by beacon.

Note 2. The dual tanavâvahai is strange. It may refer, as Grassmann supposes, to Agastya and his wife, Lopamudrâ, but even that is very unusual. See Oldenberg, K. Z. XXXIX, 62. Professor Oldenberg (K. Z. XXXIX, 60 seq.) takes this and the next hymn as parts of the same Âkhyâna hymn, and as intimately connected with the Marutvatîya *S*âstra of the midday Savana, in the Soma sacrifice.

MAN*D*ALA I, HYMN 171.

ASH*T*AKA II, ADHYÂYA 4, VARGA 11.

TO THE MARUTS (THE STORM-GODS).

1. I come to you with this adoration, with a hymn I implore the favour[1] of the quick (Maruts). O Maruts, you have rejoiced[2] in it clearly[3], put down then all anger and unharness your horses!

2. This reverent praise of yours, O Maruts, fashioned in the heart, has been offered by the mind[1], O gods! Come to it, pleased in your mind, for you give increase to (our) worship[2].

3. May the Maruts when they have been praised be gracious to us, and likewise Maghavat (Indra), the best giver of happiness, when he has been praised. May our trees (our lances)[1] through our valour stand always erect, O Maruts!

4. I am afraid of this powerful one, and trembling in fear of Indra. For you the offerings were prepared,—we have now put them away, forgive us!

5. Thou through whom the Mânas[1] see the mornings, whenever the eternal dawns flash forth with power[2], O Indra, O strong hero, grant thou glory to us with the Maruts, terrible with the terrible ones, strong and a giver of victory.

6. O Indra, protect thou these bravest of men[1] (the Maruts), let thy anger be turned away[2] from the Maruts, for thou hast become[3] victorious together with those brilliant heroes. May we have an invigorating autumn, with quickening rain!

NOTES.

The Anukrama*n*î assigns verses 1 and 2 to the Maruts, the rest to Indra Marutvat. The poet is again Agastya. The whole hymn corresponds to the situation as described in the preceding hymns, and leads on to a kind of compromise between the Maruts, who seem really the favourite gods of the poet, and Indra, an irresistible and supreme deity whose claims cannot be disregarded.

None of the verses of this hymn occurs in SV., VS., TS., AV.

Verse 1.

Note 1. Sumati here means clearly favour, as in I, 73, 6, 7; while in I, 166, 6 it means equally clearly prayer.

Note 2. Ludwig takes rarâ*n*átâ as referring to sûkténa and námasâ. The accent of rarâ*n*átâ is irregular, and likewise the retaining of the final long â in the Pada text. Otherwise the form is perfectly regular, namely the 2 p. plural of the reduplicated aorist, or the so-called aorist of the causative[a]. Pâ*n*ini (VII, 4, 2, 3) gives a number of verbs which form that aorist as ∪ ∪ –, and not as ∪ – ∪, e. g. a*s*a*s*âsat, not a*s*î*s*asat; ababâdhat, ayayâ*k*at, &c. Some verbs may take both forms, e. g. abibhra*g*at and ababhrâ*g*at. This option applies to all Kâ*n*yâdi verbs, and one of these is ra*n*, which therefore at the time of Kâtyâyana was supposed to have formed its reduplicated aorist both as árarâ*n*at and as árîra*n*at. Without the augment we expect rîra*n*ata or rárâ*n*ata. The question is why the final a should have been lengthened not only in the Sa*m*hitâ, that would be explicable, but in the Pada text also. The conjunctive of the perfect would be rârá*n*ata. See also Delbrück, Verbum, p. 111.

Note 3. Vedyâbhis, which Ludwig translates here by um dessentwillen, was ihr erfaren sollt, I have translated by clearly, though tentatively only.

---

[a] See Sanskrit Grammar, § 372, note.

Verse 2.

Note 1. The same idea is expressed in X, 47, 7. h*ri*di-sp*r*í*s*a*h* mánasâ va*k*yámânâ*h*.

Note 2. Námasa*h* v*r*idhásá*h* is intended to convey the idea that the Maruts increase or bless those who worship them.

Verse 3.

Note 1. The second line has given rise to various interpretations.

GRASSMANN:

Uns mögen aufrecht stehn wie schöne Bäume
Nach unsrem Wunsch, O Maruts, alle Tage.

LUDWIG: Hoch mögen sein unsere kämpfenden lanzen, alle tage, O Marut, sigesstreben.

As komyâ never occurs again, it must for the present be left unexplained.

There was another difficult passage, I, 88, 3. medhá váná ná k*r*i*n*avante ûrdhvâ, which I translated, 'May the Maruts stir up our minds as they stir up the forests.' I pointed out there that ûrdhva means not only upright, but straight and strong (I, 172, 3; II, 30, 3), and I conjectured that the erect trees might have been used as a symbol of strength and triumph. Vana, however, may have been used poetically for anything made of wood, just as cow is used for leather or anything made of leather. In that case vana might be meant for the wooden walls of houses, or even for lances (like δούρατα from δόρυ = Sk. dâru), and the adjective would probably have to determine the true meaning. If connected with komala it might have the same meaning as εὔξεστος.

Prof. Oldenberg suggests that vanâni may be meant for the wooden vessels containing the Soma.

Verse 5.

Note 1. The Mânas are the people of Mânya, see I, 165, 15, note 1, and there is no necessity for taking mâna, with Grassmann, as a general name for poet (Kuhn's Zeitschrift, vol. xvi, p. 174).

Note 2. It is doubtful to which word *s*avasâ belongs. I take it to be used adverbially with vyush*t*ishu.

Verse 6.

Note 1. We might also translate, 'protect men from the stronger one,' as we read I, 120, 4. pâtám *k*a sáhyasa*h* yuvám *k*a rábhyasa*h* na*h*; and still more clearly in IV, 55, 1. sáhîyasa*h* varu*n*a mitra mártât. But I doubt whether n*r*în by itself would be used in the sense of our men, while nara*h* is a common name of the Maruts, whether as divá*h* nára*h*, I, 64, 4, or as nára*h* by themselves, I, 64, 10; 166, 13, &c.

Note 2. On the meaning of avayâ in ávayâtahe*l*â*h*, see Introduction, p. xx.

Note 3. On dadhána*h*, see VIII, 97, 13, &c.

MA*ND*ALA I, HYMN 172.

ASH*T*AKA II, ADHYÂYA 4, VARGA 12.

To the Maruts (the Storm-gods).

1. May your march be brilliant, brilliant through your protection, O Maruts, you bounteous givers, shining like snakes!

2. May that straightforward shaft of yours, O Maruts, bounteous givers, be far from us, and far the stone which you hurl!

3. Spare, O bounteous givers, the people of T*rin*askanda, lift us up that we may live!

NOTES.

The hymn is ascribed to Agastya, the metre is Gâyatrî. None of its verses occurs in SV., VS., TS., AV.

Verse 1.

Prof. Oldenberg conjectures *k*itrā́ ûtí*h*, and possibly mahibhânava*h* for ahibhânava*h*. See for yā́ma*h* *k*itrá*h* ûtī́ V, 52, 2. té yā́man pânti; also VI, 48, 9.

MANDALA II, HYMN 34.

ASHTAKA II, ADHYÂYA 7, VARGA 19-21.

TO THE MARUTS (THE STORM-GODS).

1. The Maruts charged with rain[1], endowed with fierce force, terrible like wild beasts[2], blazing[3] in their strength[4], brilliant like fires, and impetuous[5], have uncovered the (rain-giving) cows by blowing away the cloud[6].

2. The (Maruts) with their rings[1] appeared like the heavens with their stars[2], they shone wide like streams from clouds as soon as Rudra, the strong man, was born for you, O golden-breasted Maruts, in the bright lap of *Pris*ni[3].

3. They wash[1] their horses like racers in the courses, they hasten with the points of the reed[2] on their quick steeds. O golden-jawed[3] Maruts, violently shaking (your jaws), you go quick[4] with your spotted deer[5], being friends of one mind.

4. Those Maruts have grown to feed[1] all these beings, or, it may be, (they have come) hither for the sake of a friend, they who always bring quickening rain. They have spotted horses, their bounties cannot be taken away, they are like headlong charioteers on their ways[2].

5. O Maruts, wielding your brilliant spears, come hither on smooth[1] roads with your fiery[2] cows (clouds) whose udders are swelling; (come hither), being of one mind, like swans toward their nests, to enjoy the sweet offering.

6. O one-minded Maruts, come to our prayers, come to our libations like (Indra) praised by men[1]!

Fulfil (our prayer) like the udder of a barren cow[2], and make the prayer glorious by booty to the singer.

7. Grant us this strong horse for our chariot, a draught[1] that rouses our prayers, from day to day, food to the singers, and to the poet in our homesteads[2] luck[3], wisdom, inviolable and invincible strength.

8. When the gold-breasted Maruts harness the horses to their chariots, bounteous[1] in wealth, then it is as if a cow in the folds poured out[2] to her calf copious food, to every man who has offered libations.

9. Whatever mortal enemy may have placed us among wolves[1], shield us from hurt, ye Vasus! Turn the wheels with burning heat[2] against him, and strike down the weapon of the impious fiend, O Rudras!

10. Your march, O Maruts, appears brilliant, whether even friends have milked the udder of P*ris*ni, or whether, O sons of Rudra, you mean to blame him who praises you, and to weaken those who are weakening Trita, O unbeguiled heroes[1].

11. We invoke you, the great Maruts, the constant wanderers, at the offering of the rapid Vish*n*u[1]; holding ladles (full of libations) and prayerful we ask the golden-coloured and exalted Maruts for glorious wealth.

12. The Da*s*agvas (Maruts?)[1] carried on[2] the sacrifice first; may they rouse us at the break of dawn. Like the dawn, they uncover the dark nights with the red (rays), the strong ones, with their brilliant light, as with a sea of milk.

13. With the (morning) clouds, as if with glittering red ornaments[1], these Maruts have grown great in the sacred places[2]. Streaming down with rush-

ing splendour[3], they have assumed their bright and brilliant colour.

14. Approaching[1] them for their great protection to help us, we invoke them with this worship, they whom Trita may bring near, like the five Hot*ri* priests for victory[2], descending on their chariot to help.

15. May that grace of yours by which you help the wretched[1] across all anguish, and by which you deliver the worshipper from the reviler, come hither, O Maruts; may your favour approach us like a cow (going to her calf)!

NOTES.

Hymn ascribed to *Gri*tsamada. Metre, 1–14 *G*agatî, 15 Trish*t*ubh, according to the paribhâshâ in the Sarvânukrama*n*î 12, 13. See also Ludwig, III, p. 59; Bergaigne, Recherches sur l'histoire de la liturgie védique, 1889, pp. 66 seq.; Oldenberg, Prolegomena, p. 144. None of its verses occurs in SV., VS., AV. The first verse is found in TB. II, 5, 5, 4, with three various readings, viz. tavishébhir ûrmíbhi*h* instead of távishîbhir ar*k*ína*h*, bhrúmim instead of bh*rí*mim, and rípa instead of ápa.

Verse 1.

Note 1. Dhârâvarấ*h*, a word of doubtful import, possibly meaning wishing for rain, or the suitors of the streams of rain. The Maruts are sometimes represented as varas or suitors; cf. V, 60, 4.

Note 2. Cf. II, 33, 11.

Note 3. Bergaigne, II, 381, translates ar*k*ína*h* by chantres, singers, deriving it, as it would seem, from arka which, as he maintains (Journ. Asiat. 1884, IV, pp. 194 seq.), means always song in the RV. (Rel. Véd. I, 279). This, however, is not the case, as has been well shown by Pischel, Ved. Stud. I, pp. 23 seq. Besides, unless we change ar*k*ina*h* into arki*n*a*h*, we must connect it with ar*k*i, light. Thus we read VIII, 41, 8, ar*k*ínâ padấ.

Note 4. Tavishébhir ûrmíbhi*h*, the reading of the Taittirîyas, is explained by Sâya*n*a by balavadbhir gamanai*h*. It may have been taken from RV. VI, 61, 2.

Note 5. On *rig*îshín, see I, 64, 12[5]; I, 87, 1.

Note 6. Bh*rí*mi seems to me a name of the cloud, driven about by the wind. The Taittirîyas read bhrúmim, and Sâya*n*a explains it by megha*m* dhamanta*s* *k*âlayanta*h*. In most passages, no doubt, bh*ri*mi means quick, fresh, and is opposed to radhra, IV, 32, 2; VII, 56, 20. In I, 31, 16, as applied to Agni, it may mean quick. But in our passage that meaning is impossible, and I prefer the traditional meaning of cloud to that of storm-wind, adopted by Benfey and Roth. The expression 'to blow a storm-wind' is not usual, while dham is used in the sense of blowing away clouds and darkness. The cows would then be the waters in the clouds. It is possible, however, that Sâya*n*a's explanation, according to which bh*ri*mi is a musical instrument, may rest on some traditional authority. In this case it would correspond to dhámanta*h* vâ*n*ám; in I, 85, 10[2].

Verse 2.

Note 1. On khâdin, see I, 166, 9, note 2. On rukmavakshas, I, 64, 4, note 1. Golden-breasted is meant for armed with golden chest-plates. The meaning seems to be that the Maruts with their brilliant khâdis appear like the heavens with their brilliant stars. The Maruts are not themselves lightning and rain, but they are seen in them, as Agni is not the fire, but present in the fire, or the god of fire. Thus we read, RV. III, 26, 6. agné*h* bhấmam marútâm óga*h*, 'The splendour of Agni, the strength of the Maruts,' i. e. the lightning. It must be admitted, however, that a conjecture, proposed by Bollensen (Z.D.M.G. XLI, p. 501), would improve the verse. He proposes to read *ri*sh*t*aya*h* instead of v*ri*sh*t*aya*h*. We should then have to translate, 'Their spears shone like lightnings from the clouds.' These *ri*sh*t*is or spears are mentioned by the side of khâdi and rukma in RV. V, 54, 11, and the compound *ri*sh*t*ívidyuta*h* is applied to the Maruts in I, 168, 5 and V, 52, 13. The difficulty which remains is abhriyâ*h*.

Note 2. On dyấvo ná st*ri*bhi*h*, see note to I, 87, 1.

Note 3. The second line is full of difficulties. No doubt the Maruts are represented as the sons of Rudra (V, 60, 5; VI, 66, 3), and as the sons of P*ris*ni, fem., being called P*rí*sni-mâtara*h*. Their birth is sometimes spoken of as unknown (VII, 56, 2), but hardly as mysterious. Who knows their birth, hardly means more than 'the wind bloweth where it listeth, and thou hearest the sound thereof, but canst not tell whence it cometh.' P*ris*ni as a feminine is the speckled sky, and the cloud may have been conceived as the udder at the same time that P*ris*ni was conceived as a cow (I, 160, 3). Nothing seems therefore more natural than that we should translate, 'When Rudra had begotten you in the bright lap of P*ris*ni.' The bright lap, *s*ukrám ū́dha*h*, is an idiomatic expression (VI, 66, 1; IV, 3, 10), and I see no reason why we should with Roth, K.Z. XXVI, 49, change the *s*ukré of the padapâ*th*a into *s*ukrá*h* and refer it to v*ŕ*ishâ.

The real difficulty lies in á*g*ani. Can it mean he begot, as Bergaigne (Religion Védique, III, 35) interprets it? Wherever á*g*ani occurs it means he was born, and I doubt whether it can mean anything else. It is easy to suggest a*g*anît, for though the third person of the aorist never occurs in the RV., the other persons, such as a*g*anish*t*a, *g*anish*th*â*h*, are there. But, as the verse now stands, we must translate, 'When Rudra was born for you, he the strong one in the bright udder of P*ris*ni.' Could Rudra be here conceived as the son, he who in other passages is represented as the husband of P*ris*ni? There is another passage which may yield the same sense, VI, 66, 3. vidé hí mâtā́ mahá*h* mahī́ sā́, sā́ ít p*ŕ*sni*h* subhvẽ́ gárbham ā́ adhât, 'for she, the great, is known as the mother of the great, that very P*ris*ni conceived the germ (the Maruts) for the strong one.'

Verse 3.

Note 1. Ukshánte is explained by washing, cleaning the horses, before they start for a new race. See V, 59, 1. ukshánte á*s*vân, followed by tárushante ā́ rá*g*a*h*; IX, 109, 10. á*s*va*h* ná niktá*h* vâ*g*ī́ dhánâya; *S*atap. Br. XI, 5, 5, 13. Pischel (Ved. Stud. I, 189) supposes that it always refers to the washing after a race.

Note 2. Nadásya kár*n*ai*h* is very difficult. Sâya*n*a's explanation, meghasya madhyaprade*s*ai*h*, 'through the hollows of the cloud,' presupposes that nada by itself can in the RV. be used in the sense of cloud, and that kar*n*a, ear, may have the meaning of a hole or a passage. To take, as BR. propose, kár*n*a in the sense of kar*n*á, eared, with long ears, would not help us much. Grassmann's translation, 'mit der Wolke schnellen Fittigen,' is based on a conjectural reading, nadasya par*n*ai*h*. Ludwig's translation, 'mit des fluszes wellen den raschen eilen sie,' is ingenious, but too bold, for kar*n*a never means waves, nor nada river in the Rig-veda. The Vedârthayatna gives: 'they rush with steeds that make the roar,' taking kar*n*ai*h* for kart*ri*bhi*h*, which again is simply impossible. The best explanation is that suggested by Pischel, Ved. Stud., p. 189. He takes nada for reed, and points out that whips were made of reeds. The kar*n*a would be the sharp point of the reed, most useful for a whip. I cannot, however, follow him in taking â*s*úbhi*h* in the sense of accelerating. I think it refers to a*s*va in the preceding pâda.

Note 3. Híra*n*ya*s*iprâ*h*. *S*iprâ, in the dual *s*ipre, is intended for the jaws, the upper and lower jaws, as in RV. I, 101, 10. ví syasva *s*ípre, open the jaws. See Zimmer, Altindisches Leben, p. 249, note. RV. III, 32, 1; V, 36, 2, *s*ípre and hánû; VIII, 76, 10; X, 96, 9. *s*ípre hári*n*î dávidhvata*h*; X, 105, 5. *s*íprâbhyâm *s*iprí*n*îvân. In the plural, however, *s*iprâ*h*, V, 54, 11 (*s*íprâ*h* *s*îrshásu vítatâ*h* hira*n*yáyî*h*), VIII, 7, 25, is intended for something worn on the head, made of gold or gold threads. As we speak of the ears of a cap, that is, lappets which protect the ears, or of the cheeks of a machine, so in this case the jaws seem to have been intended for what protects the jaws, and not necessarily for the real jaw-bones of an animal, used as an helmet, and afterwards imitated in any kind of metal. As to *s*iprin it may mean helmeted or possessed of jaws. To be possessed of jaws is no peculiar distinction, yet in several of the passages where *s*iprin occurs, there is a clear reference to eating and drinking; see VI, 44, 14; VIII, 2, 28; 17, 4; 32, 24; 33, 7; 92, 4; see also *s*ípravân in VI, 17, 2. It is possible therefore that like su*s*ipra, *s*iprin also was used in the sense of possessed of jaw-bones, i.e. of strong jaw-bones. Even such epithets as híra*n*ya-*s*ipra, hári-*s*ipra, híri-*s*ipra may mean possessed of golden, possibly of strong jaws. (M. M., Biographies of Words, p. 263, note.) Roth takes hári*s*ipra as yellow-jawed, híri*s*ipra as golden-cheeked, or with golden helmet, hira*n*ya*s*ipra, with golden helmet. A decision between golden-jawed or golden-helmeted is difficult, yet golden-jawed is applicable in all cases.

In our passage we must be guided by dávidhvata*h*, which together with *s*ípra occurs again X, 96, 9. *s*ípre vá*g*âya hári*n*î dávidhvata*h*, shaking the golden jaws, and it seems best to translate: O ye golden-jawed Maruts, shaking (your jaws), you go to feed.

Note 4. If we retain the accent in p*ri*kshám, we shall have to take it as an adverb, from p*ri*kshá, quick, vigorous, like the German snël. This view is supported by Pischel, Ved. Stud. I, 96. If, however, we could change the accent into p*rí*ksham, we might defend Sâya*n*a's interpretation. We should have to take p*rí*ksham as the accusative of p*ri*ksh, corresponding to the dative p*ri*kshé in the next verse. P*ri*ksh is used together with *s*ubh, ish, ûr*g* (VI, 62, 4), and as we have *s*ubham yâ, we might take p*rí*ksham yâ in the sense of going for food, in search of food. But it is better to take p*ri*kshám as an adverb. In the next verse p*ri*kshé is really a kind of infinitive, governing bhúvanâ.

Note 5. Tradition explains the P*ri*shatîs as spotted deer, but p*ri*shada*s*va, as an epithet of the Maruts, need not mean having P*ri*shatîs for their horses, but having spotted horses. See Bergaigne, Rel. Véd. II, p. 378, note.

Verse 4.

Note 1. Ludwig translates: Zu narung haben sie alle dise wesen gebracht; Grassmann: Zur Labung netzten alle diese Wesen sie. Ludwig suggests *k*itrâya for mitrâya; Oldenberg, far better, mitrâyáva*h*, looking for friends, like mitrâyúva*h*, in I, 173, 10.

Note 2. On vayúna, see Pischel in Vedische Studien, p. 301. But why does Pischel translate *ri*gipyá by bulls, referring to VI, 67, 11?

Verse 5.

Note 1. Adhvasmábhi*h* seems to mean unimpeded or smooth. Cf. IX, 91, 3.

Note 2. The meaning of índhanvabhi*h* is very doubtful.

Verse 6.

Note 1. Narấ*m* ná sá*m*sa*h*, the original form of Narâ-sa*m*sa*h*, I take here as a proper name, Männerlob (like Frauenlob, the poet) referring to Indra. Bergaigne, I, p. 305, doubts whether Narâ*s*a*m*sa can be a proper name in our passage, but on p. 308 he calls it an appellation of Indra.

Note 2. Á*s*vâm iva, gives a sense, but one quite inappropriate to the Veda. It would mean, 'fill the cow in her udder like a mare.' I therefore propose to read asvā̃m iva (asuam iva), from asû, a cow that is barren, or a cow that has not yet calved. Thus we read, I, 112, 3. yā̃bhi*h* dhenúm asvā̃m pínvatha*h*, 'with the same help with which you nourish a barren cow.' Cf. I, 116, 22. staryā̃m pipyathu*h* gā̃m, 'you have filled the barren cow.' If asvā̃m iva dhenúm is a simile, we want an object to which it refers, and this we find in dhíyam. Thus we read, V, 71, 2; VII, 94, 2; IX, 19, 2, pipyatam dhíya*h*, to fulfil prayers. I know, of course, that such changes in the sacred text will for the present seem most objectionable to my friends in India, but I doubt not that the time will come when they will see that such emendations are inevitable. I see that in the appendix to the Petersburg Dictionary, s.v. asû, the same conjecture has been suggested.

Verse 7.

Note 1. Here again I have taken great liberties. Âpânám is explained by Sâya*n*a as a participle for âpnuvantam. This participle, though quite correct (see Lindner, Altindische Nominalbildung, p. 54), does not occur again in the RV., nor does it yield a proper meaning. It could only mean, 'give us a horse to the chariot, an obtaining prayer, rousing the attention (of the gods) day by day.' Âpâna may mean a drinking or carousing, and I do not see why we should not take it in that sense. Sacrifices in ancient times were often festivals; VII, 22, 3. imā̃ bráhma sadhamā̃de *g*ushasva, 'accept these prayers at our feast.' If we suppose that âpâna refers to the drinking of Soma, then nothing is more appropriate than to call the drinking *k*itáyat, exciting, bráhma, a hymn. Anyhow I can discover no better meaning in this line. Grassmann, who knows that *k*itayati means to excite, yet translates: 'Gebt Gebet, das durchdringt, euch erinnernd Tag für Tag.' Ludwig: 'Das erfolgreiche brahma, das erinnernde tag für tag.' Possibly we should have to change the accent from âpâná to âpắna. Âpâná in IX, 10, 5 is equally obscure.

Note 2. On v*ri*gana, see I, 165, 15[3]. For fuller discussions of the various meanings of v*ri*gana, see Geldner, Ved. Stud. I, 139; Oldenberg, Göttinger gel. Anzeigen, 1890, pp. 410 seq.; Ph. Colinet, Les principes de l'exégèse védique d'après MM. Pischel et Geldner, p. 28; Ludwig, Über Methode bei Interpretation des Rigveda, 1890, pp. 27 seq.

Note 3. Saní means acquiring, success, luck, gain, and is often placed in juxtaposition with medhắ, wisdom. If they are thus placed side by side, saní looks almost like an adjective, meaning efficient. RV. I, 18, 6. saním medhắm ayâsisham, 'I had asked for efficient, true, real wisdom,' or, 'I had asked for success and wisdom.' In such passages, however, as V, 27, 4. dádat *rik*ắ saním yaté dádat medhắm *ri*tâyaté, it is clear that saní was considered as independent and different from medhắ (*rik*âyaté = *ri*tâyaté).

Verse 8.

Note 1. On sudắnava*h*, see note to I, 64, 6. It must often be left open whether sudắnu was understood as bounteous, or as having good rain or good Soma.

Note 2. Pinvate, lit. to make swell or abound.

Verse 9.

Note 1. V*ri*katắti is an old locative of v*ri*katât, wolfhood. To place us in wolfhood means to treat us as wolves, or as vogelfrei. Others take it to mean treating us as a wolf would treat us.

Note 2. Tápushâ *k*akríyâ. According to Lanman (p. 571) tápushâ might be taken as an acc. dual fem. I know, however, of no strictly analogous cases, and prefer to take tápushâ as an instrumental, this being its usual employment.

Verse 10.

Note 1. The second line is obscure. Neither Grassmann nor Ludwig nor Sâya*n*a can extract any intelligible meaning from it. I have translated it, but I am far from satisfied. There may be an antithesis between the friends (the Maruts themselves, see V, 53, 2), milking the udder of P*r*i*s*ni, and the Maruts coming to blame their friends for not offering them sacrifices, or for offering them sacrifices in common with Indra. In the first case when they, as friends, milk the cloud, their approach is brilliant and auspicious. In the second case, when they come to blame those who ought to celebrate them, or those who are actually hostile to them by causing the ruin or decay of a friend of the Maruts, such as Trita, their approach is likewise brilliant, but not auspicious. Trita is a friend of the Maruts whom they assist in battle, and it is possible that this legend may be alluded to here. Sometimes Trita seems also connected with the third libation which was offered at sunset, just as Vish*n*u represented the second libation which was offered at noon[a]. Thus we read, VIII, 12, 16. yát sómam indra vísh*n*avi yát vâ gha trité âptyé yát vâ marútsu mándase, 'whether you, Indra, enjoy the Soma near Vish*n*u, or near Trita Âptya, or among the Maruts.' *S*âkapû*n*i, as quoted by Yâska (Nir. XII, 19), explains the three steps of Vish*n*u as earth, sky, and heaven; Aur*n*avâbha distinguishes Samâroha*n*a, Vish*n*upada, and Gaya*s*iras. But all this does not help us to disentangle our verse. It should be added that Bergaigne makes Tritám to be governed by duhú*h* (Rel. Véd. II, 327). We should then have to translate, 'or whether they milk Trita in order to blame the singer, to make them old who make

[a] Oðinn is styled Thridi, by the side of Hâr and Tafnhâr (the high and the even high) as the Third High. At other times he is Tveggi (secundus). Grimm's Teutonic Mythology, vol. i, p. 162.

others old, or who themselves become old.' This, however, does not help us much. Professor Oldenberg conjectures that possibly *g*uratā́m might be changed to *g*urátâm, and that the dual of the verb might refer to Rudra and P*ri*s*n*i; or we might read *g*urátâ for *g*uráta, if it refers to Rudriyas. Návamânasya might also be used in the sense of making a noise (see I, 29, 5), and possibly návamânasya nidé might have been intended for shouting and laughing to scorn. But all this leaves the true meaning of the verse as unfathomable as ever.

Verse 11.

Note 1. Vísh*n*or eshásya prabh*ri*thé is obscure. At the offering of the rapid Vish*n*u is supposed to mean, when the rapid Vish*n*u offers Soma. The same phrase occurs again, VII, 40, 5. In VIII, 20, 3, we can translate, 'we know the strength of the Maruts, and of the hasting Vish*n*u, the bounteous gods.' In VII, 39, 5, the reading is vísh*n*um eshâm. Bergaigne (II, 419) is inclined to take vish*n*u esha as Soma. We should then translate, 'at the offering of Soma.'

Verse 12.

Note 1. The Da*s*agvas are mentioned as an old priestly family, like the Aṅgiras, and they seem also, like the Aṅgiras, to have their prototypes or their ancestors among the divine hosts. Could they here be identified with the Maruts? They are said to have been the first to carry on the sacrifice, and they are asked to rouse men at the break of the day. Now the same may be said of the Maruts. They are often connected with the dawn, probably because the storms break forth with greater vigour in the morning, or, it may be, because the chasing away of the darkness of the night recalls the struggle between the darkness of the thunderstorm and the brightness of the sun. The matutinal character of the Maruts appears, for instance, in V, 53, 14 (usrí bhesha*g*ám), and their father Dyaus is likewise called v*ri*shabhá*h* usríya*h*, V, 58, 6. In the second line ûr*n*ute, though in the singular, refers also to the Maruts in the plural; see Bergaigne, Mélanges Renier,

Paris, 1886, p. 80. There still remain two difficult words, mahá*h* and gó-ar*n*asâ. The former (see Lanman, p. 501) may be taken as an adjective referring to the Da*s*agvas or Maruts, unless we take it as an adverb, quickly, like makshu. If we could change it into mahấ, it would form an appropriate adjective to *g*yotishâ, as in IV, 50, 4. On gó-ar*n*asâ all that can be said is that it mostly occurs where something is uncovered or revealed, so I, 112, 18; X, 38, 2.

Note 2. On ya*gñ*am vah, to carry on the sacrifice like a wagon, see Bergaigne, Rel. Véd. II, 259–260. See also RV. VIII, 26, 15; 58, 1, and ya*gñ*a-vâhas.

Verse 13.

Note 1. In interpreting this obscure verse we must begin with what is clear. The aru*n*ấ*h* a*ñg*áya*h* are the well-known ornaments of the Maruts, mentioned I, 37, 2, note; I, 64, 4, note, &c. The Maruts shine in these ornaments or paints, I, 85, 3; 87, 1; V, 56, 1; X, 78, 7. Though we do not know their special character, we know that, like the daggers, spears, and bracelets of the Maruts, they were supposed to contribute to their beautiful appearance. Again, we know that when the Maruts are said to grow (vav*ri*dhu*h*), that means that they grow in strength, in spirits, and in splendour, or, in a physical sense, that the storms increase, that the thunder roars, and the lightnings flash, see V, 55, 3; 59, 5. Now if it is said that the Rudras grew with ksho*n*îs, as if with bright red ornaments, we must have in these ksho*n*îs the physical prototype of what are metaphorically called their glittering ornaments. And here we can only think either of the bright morning clouds (referring to ushấ*h* ná râmî́*h* aru*n*ai*h* ápa ûr*n*ute in the preceding verse), or lightnings. These bright clouds of heaven are sometimes conceived as the mothers (III, 9, 2. apá*h* mât*rî́h*), and more especially the mothers of the Maruts, who are in consequence called Síndhu-mâtara*h*, X, 78, 6, a name elsewhere given to Soma, IX, 61, 7, and to the A*s*vins, I, 46, 2. It is said of a well-known hero, Purûravas (originally a solar hero), that as soon as he was born the women (gnâ*h*) were there, and immediately afterwards that the rivers increased or cherished him, X, 95, 7. In other passages too these celestial rivers or waters or clouds are represented as women, whether mothers or wives (X, 124, 7). A number of names are given to these beings, when introduced as the companions of the Apsaras Urva*s*î, and it is said of them that they came along like a*ñg*áya*h* aru*n*áya*h*, like bright red ornaments, X, 95, 6. It seems clear therefore that the aru*n*â*h* a*ñg*áya*h* of the Maruts have to be explained by the bright red clouds of the morning, or in more mythological language, by the Apsaras, who are said to be like aru*n*áya*h* a*ñg*áya*h*. Hence, whatever its etymology may have been, ksho*n*îbhi*h* in our passage must refer to the clouds of heaven, and the verse can only be translated, 'the Rudras grew with the clouds as with their red ornaments,' that is, the clouds were their red ornaments, and as the clouds grew in splendour, the Maruts grew with their splendid ornaments.

Professor Geldner arrived at a similar conclusion. In Bezzenberger's Beiträge, XI, p. 327, and more recently in Ved. Stud., p. 277, he assigned to ksho*n*î the meaning of woman, which is quite possible, and would make it a synonym of the celestial gnâs. But he translates, 'the Maruts excite themselves with red colours as with women.' These are hardly Vedic thoughts, and the position of ná would remain anomalous. Nor should we gain much if we read te ksho*n*aya*h* aru*n*ebhi*h* na a*ñg*ibhi*h*, 'these Rudras were delighted like wives by bright ornaments.' The bright ornaments have once for all a settled meaning, they are peculiar to the Maruts, and cannot in a Marut hymn be taken in any other sense.

Then comes the question, how is the meaning assigned to ksho*n*î, namely cloud, or, as personified, Apsaras, applicable to other passages? In X, 95, 9, it seems most appropriate: 'So long as the mortal (Purûravas), longing for the immortal (Apsaras), does not come near with strength to those ksho*n*îs, i. e. those Apsaras, or morning clouds, they beautified their bodies like ducks' (an excellent image, if one watches ducks cleaning themselves in the water), 'like sporting horses biting each other.' Geldner translates this verse somewhat differently, Ved. Stud. I, p. 276.

Having disposed of these two passages where kshonî occurs in the plural, we have next to consider those where it stands in the dual. Here kshonî always means heaven and earth, like rodasî, dyâvâprithivî, &c.

VIII, 7, 22. sám u tyé mahatī̀h apáh sám kshonī̀ sám u sū̀ryam . . . parvasáh dadhuh. They, the Maruts, set the great waters (the sky), heaven and earth and the sun piecemeal (or, they put them together piece by piece).

VIII, 52, 10. sám índrah rā̀yah brihatī̀h adhûnuta sám kshonī̀ sám u sū̀ryam. Indra shook the great treasures, heaven and earth, and the sun.

VIII, 99, 6. ánu te súshmam turáyantam îyatuh kshonī̀ sísum ná mâtárâ. Heaven and earth followed thy rapid strength, like mother-cows their calf.

II, 16, 3. ná kshonī̀bhyâm paribhvḕ te indriyám. Thy strength is not to be compassed by heaven and earth.

If after this we look at the passage translated by Professor Geldner, I, 180, 5. apáh kshonī̀ sakate mā̀hinâ vâm, we see at once that apáh and kshonī̀ cannot be separated, and that we must translate, your Mâhinâ reaches heaven and earth and the sky. Mâhinâ, according to Professor Geldner, means the magnificent woman, namely Sûryâ, but it is possible that it may have been meant for 'mahimâ, your greatness reaches heaven and earth and the sky.' Apáh, which Professor Geldner translates 'from the water,' is the acc. plural, meaning the waters between heaven and earth, or the sky. It occurs again in connection with heaven and earth, the sun, heaven, and generally without any copula. Thus, VIII, 7, 22. apáh, kshonī̀, sū̀ryam, i.e. the waters (the sky), heaven and earth, the sun. I, 36, 8. ródasî apáh, heaven and earth and the waters; cf. V, 31, 6. Likewise I, 52, 12. apáh svā̀h paribhū̀h eshi ā̀ dívam; V, 14, 4. ávindat gā̀h apáh svā̀h; VI, 47, 14. apáh gā̀h; cf. VI, 60, 2. VII, 44, 1. dyā̀vâprithivī̀ apáh svā̀h, cf. X, 36, 1; IX, 90, 4; 91, 6.

There remain five passages where kshonîh occurs, and where Professor Geldner's conjecture that it means women holds good. In I, 54, 1, it may mean real women, or the women of the clouds. In I, 57, 4; 173, 7; VIII, 3, 10; 13, 17; also in X, 22, 9, women seems the most plausible translation.

Note 2. *Ri*tasya sádanâni is almost impossible to translate. It may be the places in heaven where the Maruts are supposed to be, or the places where sacrifices are offered to them.

Note 3. Átyena pấgasâ has been explained in different ways. Sâya*n*a renders it by always moving power; Grassmann by 'mit schnell erregtem Schimmer;' Ludwig, 'mit eilender kraft,' though he is no longer satisfied with this meaning, and suggests 'net for catching.' Roth has touched several times on this word. In the Allgemeine Monatsschrift of 1851, p. 87, he suggested for pấgas the meaning of 'impression of a foot or of a carriage, perhaps also reflection.' In his Notes on the Nirukta, p. 78 seq., he is very hard on the Indian commentators who explain the word by strength, but who never go conscientiously through all the passages in which a word occurs. He then still maintained that the word ought to be translated by track.

It seems, however, that the most appropriate meaning in the passages in which pấgas occurs is splendour, though of course a stream of light may be conceived as a bright train or path. In some the meaning of light seems quite inevitable, for instance, III, 15, 1. ví pấgasâ p*ri*thúnâ sósu*k*âna*h*. Agni, shining with broad light.

VIII, 46, 25. ấ . . . yâhí makhấya pấgase. Come hither, Vâyu, for strong light.

III, 14, 1. (agní*h*) p*ri*thivyấm pấga*h* as*r*et. Agni assumed (or spread) splendour on earth.

VII, 10, 1. ushá*h* ná *g*ârá*h* p*ri*thú pấga*h* as*r*et. (Agni,) like the lover of the dawn, assumed (or spread) wide splendour.

III, 61, 5. ûrdhvám madhudhấ diví pấga*h* as*r*et. The dawn assumed rising splendour in the sky.

VII, 3, 4. ví yásya te p*ri*thivyấm pấga*h* ás*r*et. Thou (Agni) whose splendour spread on earth.

IX, 68, 3. abhivrá*g*an ákshitam pá̂*g*a*h* á̂ dade. (Soma) approaching assumed imperishable splendour. This splendour of Soma is also mentioned in IX, 109, 21, and the expression that he shakes his splendour (v*ri*thâ kar) occurs IX, 76, 1; 88, 5. (Cf. Geldner, Ved. Stud. I, p. 117.)

In VI, 21, 7. abhí tvâ pá̂*g*a*h* rakshása*h* ví tasthe, it would, no doubt, seem preferable to translate, 'the power of the Rakshas came upon thee,' but the ugrám pá̂*g*a*h*, the fierce light, is not out of place either, while in most of the passages which we have examined, the meaning of power would be entirely out of place.

In I, 121, 11, heaven and earth seem to be called pá̂*g*asî, the two splendours. Pischel, Ved. Stud. p. 87, translates átyena pá̂*g*asâ by 'durch das stattliche Ross,' namely the Soma, but pá̂*g*as seems to be something that belongs to Soma, not Soma himself.

Verse 14.

Note 1. Grassmann suggests iyânấ*h* instead of iyânấ*h*.

Note 2. Abhísh*t*aye, for superiority or victory, rather than for assistance. Abhish*t*í, with accent on the last syllable, means conqueror or victorious; see RV. I, 9, 1; III, 34, 4; X, 100, 12; 104, 10.

Verse 15.

Note 1. On radhra and its various applications, see Pischel, Ved. Stud. I, p. 124.

MA*ND*ALA V, HYMN 52.

ASH*T*AKA IV, ADHYÂYA 3, VARGA 8–10.

TO THE MARUTS (THE STORM-GODS).

1. O *S*yâvâ*s*va, sing boldly with[1] the Maruts, the singers who, worthy themselves of sacrifice, rejoice in their guileless glory[2] according to their nature.

2. They are indeed boldly the friends of strong power; they on their march protect all who by themselves are full of daring[1].

3. Like rushing bulls, these Maruts spring over[1] the dark cows (the clouds)[2], and then we perceive the might of the Maruts in heaven and on earth.

4. Let us boldly offer praise and sacrifice to your Maruts, to all them who protect the generation of men, who protect the mortal from injury.

5. They who are worthy, bounteous, men of perfect strength, to those heavenly Maruts who are worthy of sacrifice, praise the sacrifice!

6. The tall men[1], coming near with their bright chains, and their weapon, have hurled forth their spears. Behind these Maruts there came by itself the splendour of heaven, like laughing lightnings[2].

7. Those who have grown up on earth, or in the wide sky, or in the realm of the rivers, or in the abode of the great heaven,

8. Praise that host of the Maruts, endowed with true strength and boldness[1], whether those rushing heroes have by themselves harnessed (their horses) for triumph,

9. Or whether these brilliant Maruts have in the (speckled) cloud clothed themselves in wool[1], or

whether by their strength they cut the mountain asunder with the tire of their chariot;

10. Call them comers, or goers, or enterers, or followers, under all these names, they watch on the straw[1] for my sacrifice.

11. The men (the Maruts) watch, and their steeds watch. Then, so brilliant are their forms to be seen, that people say, Look at the strangers[1]!

12. In measured steps[1] and wildly shouting[2] the gleemen[3] have danced toward the well (the cloud). They who appeared one by one like thieves, were helpers to me to see the light[4].

13. Worship, therefore, O seer, that host of Maruts, and keep and delight them with your voice, they who are themselves wise[1] poets, tall heroes armed with lightning-spears.

14. Approach, O seer, the host of Maruts, as a woman approaches a friend, for a gift[1]; and you, Maruts, bold in your strength[2], hasten hither, even from heaven, when you have been praised by our hymns.

15. If he, after perceiving them, has approached them as gods with an offering, then may he for a gift remain united with the brilliant (Maruts), who by their ornaments are glorious on their march.

16. They, the wise[1] Maruts, the lords, who, when there was inquiry for their kindred, told me of the cow, they told me of P*ri*sni as their mother, and of the strong Rudra as their father.

17. The seven and seven heroes[1] gave me each a hundred. On the Yamunâ I clear off glorious wealth in cows, I clear wealth in horses.

NOTES.

This hymn is ascribed to *S*yâvâ*s*va Âtreya. Metre, Anush*t*ubh, 1–5, 7–15; Paṅkti, 6, 16, and 17. Sâya*n*a seems to take verse 16 as an Anush*t*ubh, which of course is a mistake. No verse of this hymn occurs in SV., VS., TS., TB., MS., AV.

Verse 1.

Note 1. One expects the dative or accusative after ar*k*a. The instrumental leaves us no choice but to translate, 'Sing with the Maruts, who are themselves famous as singers.' Cf. I, 6, 8; V, 60, 8.

Note 2. On *s*ráva*h* mádanti, see Gaedicke, Accusativ, p. 75.

Verse 2.

Note 1. Dh*ri*shadvínas may also refer to the Maruts.

Verse 3.

Note 1. One expects ádhi instead of áti, see Gaedicke, Accusativ, p. 95 seq.

Note 2. See note to I, 37, 5; also, Bartholomae in Bezzenberger's Beiträge, XV, 211. The whole verse has been discussed by Benfey, Vedica und Verwandtes, p. 152 seq.

Verse 6.

Note 1. This verse has been discussed before, I, 168, 7, note. Benfey (Nachrichten der K. Ges. der Wiss. zu Göttingen, 1876, 28 Juni; comp. Vedica und Verwandtes, p. 141) translated it: 'Heran . . . haben die Helden, die hehren, ihre Speere geschleudert; ihnen, den Maruts, nach (erheben sich) traun gleichsam lachende Blitze, erhebt sich selbst des Himmels Glanz.' *Ri*shvấ*h* seems here, as in verse 13, to refer to the Maruts, as in IV, 19, 1, *ri*shvám refers to Indra, though it can be used of weapons also, see VI, 18, 10. As to the instrumentalis comitativus in rukmaí*h* and yudhấ, see Lanman, p. 335.

Note 2. Benfey's explanation of *gághghatîh* is ingenious, though it leaves some difficulties. The writing of *ghgh* in Devanâgarî may have been meant for *ggh*, as in akhkhalîkrítya, VII, 103, 3. But there remains the fact that *g*aksh occurs in the sense of laughing, I, 33, 7, and one does not see why it should have undergone a Prakritic change in our passage, and not there. It might be a mimetic word, to express the sound of rattling and clattering ; cf. *gañg*anâbhávan, VIII, 43, 8.

Verse 8.

Note 1. As to the adjective in the masculine gender after *s*árdhas, see I, 37, 1, note. The meaning of *ri*bhvas, bold, rabid, is doubtful; see Bergaigne, Rel. Véd. II, 408.

Verse 9.

Note 1. Sâya*n*a takes Parush*n*î as the name of one of the rivers of the Punjâb, called the Irâvatî, and at present the Ravi. Parush*n*î might mean speckled, muddy, as a synonym of p*risn*i. Roth has suggested that parush*n*î might here mean cloud. But what is the meaning of parush*n*î in a similar passage, IV, 22, 2. (Índra*h*) *s*riyé párush*n*îm ushámâ*n*a*h* ũr*n*âm yásyâ*h* párvâ*n*i sakhyâya vivyé? If it means that Indra clothed himself in speckled wool, that wool might be intended for what we call woolly or fleecy clouds. As the Maruts often perform the same acts as Indra, we might read in our verse utá sma té párush*n*îs ũr*n*â*h*, and pronounce utá sma té párush*n*ia ũr*n*â*h*, though Lanman, p. 395, objects to ias for îs in the acc. plur. See, however, hetĩ*h* ádevî*h* in VIII, 61, 16. The instrumental singular is possible, but again unusual with vas, párush*n*yâ ũr*n*â. Possibly the original meaning of parush*n*î may have been forgotten, and if the name of the river Parush*n*î was generally known, it might easily have taken the place of parush*n*î, the cloud. For other explanations see Roth, Über gewisse Kürzungen, Wien, 1887; Bartholomae, in Kuhn's Zeitschrift, XXIX, 583; Schmidt, Die Pluralbildungen der indogermanischen Neutra, 1889, p. 307.

Verse 10.

Note 1. Vish*t*ârá*h* does not occur again, and Lanman is therefore quite justified in assigning to it the meaning of straw (p. 339). He paraphrases: 'Let their customs carry them where they may, yet when I sacrifice, they wait quietly on the straw, i.e. the altar, for it.' He reads in the Pada text vi-stâré for vi-stârá*h*. Vish*t*árín, which occurs AV. IV, 34, 1, does not throw much light on the exact meaning of vish*t*âra in this place. If we retain vish*t*ârá*h*, the nominative, we must assign to it the meaning of crowd, and refer it to the Maruts.

Verse 11.

Note 1. Pârâvata is a turtle-dove (VS. XXIV, 25), and it is just possible that the Maruts might have been compared to them. But pârâvata is used in VIII, 100, 6, as an epithet of vasu, wealth, and in VIII, 34, 18, we read of râtis (not râtris), i.e. gifts of Pârâvata. The river Sarasvatî is called pârâvataghnî, killing Pârâvata, VI, 61, 2, and in the Pa*ñk*av. Br. IX, 4, 11, we hear that Tura*s*ravas and the Pârâvatas offered their Somas together. I am therefore inclined to take Pârâvata, lit. distant people, extranei, strangers, as a name of an Aryan border clan with whom the Vedic Âryas were sometimes at war, sometimes at peace. In that case the frontier-river, the Sarasvatî, might be called the destroyer or enemy of the Pârâvatas. As their wealth and gifts have been mentioned, to compare the Maruts with the Pârâvatas may mean no more than that the Maruts also are rich and generous. Ludwig thinks of the Παρυῆται, which seems more doubtful. For a different interpretation see Delbrück, Syntax, p. 531.

Verse 12.

Note 1. I take *kh*anda*h*stúbh in the sense of stepping (according to) a measure, as explained in my Preface (1st ed.), p. cii, though I do not doubt that that meaning was afterwards forgotten, and replaced by the technical meaning of stubh, to shout. See Böhtlingk-Roth, s.v. stubh, and stobhagrantha, Sâma-veda, Bibl. Ind., II, p. 519. It can hardly be supposed that such artificial performances of Vedic hymns, as are preserved in the Sâma-veda, could have suggested the first names of the ancient metres.

Note 2. Kubhanyú can only be derived from bhan, to shout.

Note 3. The kîrí*n*a*h* are probably intended here for strolling minstrels who, when they approached the well of a village (here the cloud), might be taken either for friends or foes.

Note 4. D*r*isí tvishé. Grassmann translates: 'Wie Räuberbanden schienen sie geschart zum Andrang meinem Blick.' Ludwig better: 'Helfer waren sie, glanz zu sehn.' We must either read d*r*isé tvishé, to see the light, or d*r*isé tvishí, to be seen by light. See, however, P. G., Ved. Stud. p. 225.

Verse 13.

Note 1. Vedhas, wise. The different possible meanings of this word have been discussed by Ludwig, Z. D. M. G. XL, p. 716; and by Bartholomae, in Kuhn's Zeitschrift, XXVII, p. 361.

Verse 14.

Note 1. On dânắ, see Lanman, pp. 533, 335; P. G., Ved. Stud. p. 101.

Note 2. Dh*r*ish*n*ava*h* ó*g*asâ to be read – ◡ – ◡ –.

Verse 15.

This verse, as Roth says, is very obscure, and the translation is purely tentative. Grassmann derives vakshá*n*â from vah in the sense of an offering. It may more easily be derived from vaksh, i. e. what gives increase, and be taken as an instrumental. Pischel shows that in many passages vaksha*n*â in the plural has the meaning of yoni, also of the yoni on the altar. But even this meaning does not throw much light on our passage. The first pâda may possibly be taken in an interrogative and conditional sense, or we may translate: 'Now, having perceived them, may he, as a refreshing draught goes to the gods, come together with the Maruts for his reward.' Whatever the verse may mean, eshâm devấn cannot mean the gods of the Maruts, or prove the existence of idols, as Bollensen (Z. D. M. G. XXII, 587) and even Muir (S. T. V, 454) imagined. The translation of Pischel, Ved. Stud. p. 101, sûríbhi*h* a*ñg*íbhi*h* mit 'Herren, die schmieren, d. h. ordentlich bezahlen,' seems too exclusively German. Could a*ñg*in be an adjective, in the sense of possessed of a*ñg*is?

Verse 16.

Note 1. If *s*íkvas is not to be derived from *s*ak (see Hübschmann, Vocalsystem, pp. 64, 186), we should have to derive ni*s*, night, from a root altogether different from that which yields nakt, nákta, &c. But how does *s*íkvas come to mean, according to Ludwig, both bunch of flowers, and flaming? Does he connect it with *s*ikhấ? Surely, if *s*iksh may stand for *s*i*s*ak-s, why not *s*ik-vas for **s*i*s*ak-vas? 'Bright' leaves it doubtful whether it means clever or flaming.

Verse 17.

Note 1. The seven, seven heroes need not be the Maruts, but some liberal patrons who rewarded *S*yâvâ*s*va. See Bergaigne, Rel. Véd. II, 371.

MANDALA V, HYMN 53.

ASHTAKA IV, ADHYÂYA 3, VARGA 11-13.

To the Maruts (the Storm-gods).

1. Who knows their birth? or who was of yore in the favour of the Maruts, when they harnessed the spotted deer[1]?

2. Who has heard them when they had mounted their chariots, how they went forth? For the sake of what liberal giver (Sudâs) did they run, and their comrades followed[1], (as) streams of rain (filled) with food?

3. They themselves said to me when day by day[1] they came to the feast with their birds[2]: they (the Maruts) are manly youths and blameless; seeing them, praise them thus;

4. They who shine by themselves in their ornaments[1], their daggers, their garlands, their golden chains, their rings, going[2] on their chariots and on dry land.

5. O Maruts, givers of quickening rain, I am made to rejoice, following after your chariots, as after days[1] going with rain.

6. The bucket which the bounteous heroes shook down from heaven for their worshipper, that cloud they send[1] along heaven and earth, and showers follow on the dry land.

7. The rivers having pierced[1] the air with a rush of water, went forth like milk-cows; when your spotted deer roll about[2] like horses that have hasted to the resting-place on their road.

8. Come hither, O Maruts, from heaven, from the sky, even from near[1]; do not go far away!

9. Let not the Rasâ, the Anitabhâ, the Kubhâ, the Krumu, let not the Sindhu delay you! Let not the marshy Sarayu prevent you! May your favour be with us alone!

10. The showers come forth after the host of your chariots, after the terrible Marut-host of the ever-youthful heroes [1].

11. Let us then follow with our praises and our prayers each host of yours, each troop, each company [1].

12. To what well-born generous worshipper have the Maruts gone to-day on that march,

13. On which you bring to kith and kin the never-failing seed of corn? Give us that for which we ask you, wealth and everlasting happiness!

14. Let us safely pass through our revilers, leaving behind the unspeakable and the enemies. Let us be with you when in the morning [1] you shower down health, wealth [2], water, and medicine, O Maruts!

15. That mortal, O men, O Maruts, whom you protect, may well be always beloved by the gods, and rich in valiant offspring. May we be such!

16. Praise the liberal Maruts, and may they delight on the path of this man here who praises them, like cows in fodder. When they go, call after them as for old friends, praise them who love you, with your song!

NOTES.

Ascribed to *S*yâvâ*s*va Âtreya. Metre, 1, 5, 10, 11, 15 Kakubh; 2 Br*i*hatî; 3 Anush*t*ubh; 4 Pura-ush*n*ih; 6, 7, 9, 13, 14, 16 Satobr*i*hatî; 8, 12 Gâyatrî. No verse of this hymn occurs in SV., VS., AV.; the sixth verse is found in TS. II, 4, 8, 1; MS. II, 4, 7; Kâ*th*aka XI, 9.

Verse 1.

Note 1. Kilâsî, as fem. of kilâsa, does not occur again. It seems to have meant spotted or marked with pocks, and would be intended for the pr*i*shatîs. Does Kailâsa come from the same source?

Verse 2.

Note 1. Kásmai sasru*h* is much the same as kásmai adyá sú*g*âtâya ... prá yayu*h*, in verse 12. We must then begin a new sentence, ánu âpáya*h*, their comrades after, namely sasru*h*. Thus we read in verse 10 tám va*h* *s*árdham ... ánu prá yanti vr*i*sh*t*áya*h*, where the streams of rain are represented as the followers of the Maruts. We might also translate in our sentence: For what liberal giver did their comrades, the streams of rain with food follow after (the Maruts).

Verse 3.

Note 1. Úpa dyúbhi*h* occurs again VIII, 40, 8, and seems to mean from day to day.

Note 2. The birds of the Maruts, probably of the same character as the birds of the A*s*vins.

Verse 4.

Note 1. I translate a*ñg*i by ornament in general, not by paint or ointment, though that may have been its original meaning.

Note 2. On *s*râya, see Pâ*n*. III, 3, 24. Dhánvasu may possibly have been intended as governed by svábhânava*h*, and not by *s*râyấ*h*; see, however, VIII, 33, 6. *s*má*s*rushu *s*ritá*h*.

Verse 5.

Note 1. On dyấvah, nom. plur., and ráthân, acc. plur., compare Bergaigne, Mélanges Renier, p. 88. The text is doubtful, and may be a corruption of vrishtî́h dyấvah yatî́h iva.

Verse 6.

Note 1. The Taittirîyas, TS. II, 4, 8, 1, read pargányâh; the Maitreyas, prá pargányah srigatâm and yantu.

Verse 7.

Note 1. Tatridâná, as trid occurs in the Veda in the Parasmaipada only, may be intended for a passive, bored, dug out, tapped. One would, however, expect in that case an instrumental, marudbhih, by whom they were brought forth.

Note 2. The words ví yád vártanta enyấh have received various explanations. Wilson translates: 'When the rivers rush in various directions.' Sâyana admits also another meaning: 'When the rivers grow.' Ludwig translates: 'Sich verteilend gehn die schimmernden auszeinander.' Grassmann, very boldly: 'Wie Hengste träufelnd, wenn vom Wege heimgekehrt, sie zu den bunten Stuten gehn.' Vi-vrit seems, however, to have a very special meaning, namely, rolling on the ground, and this the spotted deer are here said to have done, like horses at the end of their journey. We read of the sacrificial horse, Sat. Br. XIII, 5, 1, 16. sa yady ava vâ gighred vi vâ varteta, samriddho me yagña iti ha vidyât; cf. XI, 2, 5, 3. In the TS. VII, 1, 19, 3, the commentator explains vivartanam by nirgatya bhûmau vilunthanam, the rolling on the ground. The same meaning is applicable to Mahâparinibbâna Sutta, p. 66 (Childers), where the Bhikkhus are said to roll on the ground when they hear of Buddha's death; also to Mahâbh. III, 11953 (of a wild boar). The meaning therefore in our passage seems to be, when the deer roll on the ground, as horses are wont to do at the end of a journey.

Verse 8.

Note 1. Amất corresponds here to prithivî in other places. Originally it may have meant from the home.

Verse 9.

This verse has often been discussed on account of the names of the rivers which it contains. *S*yâvâ*s*va had mentioned the Yamunâ in 52, 17, and some interpreters have been inclined to give to parush*n*î in 52, 9 a geographical meaning, taking it for the river Ravi, instead of translating it by cloud. The geographical names are certainly interesting, but they have been discussed so often that I need not dwell on them here. (See M. M., India. p. 163.)

The Rasâ, known to the Zoroastrians as the Ra*n*hâ, was originally the name of a real river, but when the Âryas moved away from it into the Punjâb, it assumed a mythical character, and became a kind of Okeanos, surrounding the extreme limits of the world.

Anitabhâ seems to be the name of a new river or part of a river. It can hardly be taken as an epithet of Rasâ, as Ludwig suggests. Anitabhâ, whose splendour has not departed (Ludwig), or, amitabhâ, of endless splendour, would hardly be Vedic formations. (Chips, I, p. 157; Hibbert Lect., p. 207; India, pp. 166, 173, notes.)

Kubhâ is the Κωφήν or Κωφής of the Greeks, the Kabul river. The Krumu I take to be the Kurrum. (India. p. 177, note.)

The Sindhu is the Indus, though it is difficult to say which part of it, while the Sarayu has been supposed to be the Sarayû, the affluent of the Gaṅgâ, but may also be a more general name for some more northern river in the Punjâb. (See Zimmer, Altindisches Leben, pp. 17 f., 45; Muir, S. T. II, p. xxv, note.)

Verse 10.

Note 1. Návyasînâm has been a puzzle to all interpreters. Sâya*n*a seems to me to give the right interpretation, namely, nûtanânâm. As from a*ñ*gasâ, instr. sing., straightway, a*ñ*gasîna was formed, straightforward; from návyasâ, instr. sing., anew, návyasîna seems to have been formed in the sense of new. Návyasînâm might then be a somewhat irregular gen. plur., referring to ga*n*ám mā́rutam, the Marut-host of the young men; see V, 58, 1. Lanman (p. 515) takes it for a gen. plur. fem., but in that case it could not refer to ráthânâm. Zimmer translates endlos, Bergaigne (II, 400) thinks of new or rejuvenescent mothers.

Verse 11.

Note 1. See III, 26, 6.

Verse 14.

Note 1. Usrí, in the morning. Lanman (p. 427) proposes to read ushári, but the metre would be better preserved by reading v*r*ish*t*vī́ as trisyllabic. The difficulty is the construction of the gerund v*r*ish*t*vī́, which refers to the Maruts, and syā́ma sahá, which refers to the sacrificers.

Note 2. On *s*ám yó*h*, see I, 165, 4, note 2.

The metrical structure of this hymn is interesting. If we represent the foot of eight syllables by a, that of twelve by b, we find the following succession:

I	1	a b a
	2	a a b a
II	3	a a a a
	4	b a a
III	5	a a a
	6	b a b a
	7	b a b a
IV	8	a a a
	9	b a b a
V	10	a b a
	11	a b a
VI	12	a a a
	13	b a b a
	14	b a b a
VII	15	a b a
	16	b a b a

We find that I contains the question, II the answer, III description of rain, IV prayer and invitation, V praise of the companions, VI prayer, VII conclusion. Comp. Oldenberg's Prolegomena, p. 106 seq.

MANDALA V, HYMN 54.

ASHTAKA IV, ADHYÂYA 3, VARGA 14–16.

TO THE MARUTS (THE STORM-GODS).

1. You have fashioned[1] this speech for the brilliant Marut-host which shakes the mountains: celebrate then the great manhood in honour of that host who praises the warm milk (of the sacrifice), and sacrifices on the height of heaven[2], whose glory is brilliant.

2. O Maruts, your powerful men (came) forth searching for water, invigorating, harnessing their horses, swarming around. When they aim with the lightning, Trita shouts, and the waters murmur, running around on their course.

3. These Maruts are men brilliant with lightning, they shoot with thunderbolts, they blaze with the wind, they shake the mountains, and suddenly, when wishing to give water[1], they whirl the hail; they have thundering strength, they are robust, they are ever-powerful.

4. When you drive forth[1] the nights, O Rudras, the days, O powerful men, the sky, the mists, ye shakers, the plains, like ships, and the strongholds, O Maruts, you suffer nowhere.

5. That strength of yours, O Maruts, that greatness extended far as the sun extends its daily course, when you, like your deer on their march, went down to the (western) mountain with untouched splendour[1]

6. Your host, O Maruts, shone forth when, O sages, you strip, like a caterpillar, the waving tree[1]

Conduct then, O friends, our service [2] to a good end, as the eye conducts the man in walking.

7. That man, O Maruts, is not overpowered, he is not killed, he does not fail, he does not shake, he does not drop, his goods do not perish, nor his protections, if you lead him rightly, whether he be a seer or a king.

8. The men with their steeds, like conquerors of clans, like Aryaman (Mitra and Varu*n*a) [1], the Maruts, carrying waterskins [2], fill the well; when the strong ones roar, they moisten the earth with the juice of sweetness [3].

9. When the Maruts come forth this earth bows, the heaven bows, the paths in the sky bow, and the cloud-mountains with their quickening rain.

10. When you rejoice at sunrise, O Maruts, toiling together [1], men of Svar (sun-light), men of Dyu (heaven), your horses never tire in running, and you quickly reach the end of your journey.

11. On your shoulders are the spears, on your feet rings, on your chests golden chains, O Maruts, on your chariot gems; fiery lightnings in your fists, and golden headbands tied round your heads [1].

12. O Maruts, you shake the red apple [1] from the firmament, whose splendour no enemy [2] can touch; the hamlets bowed when the Maruts blazed, and the pious people (the Maruts) intoned their far-reaching shout.

13. O wise Maruts, let us carry off [1] the wealth of food which you have bestowed on us; give us [2], O Maruts, such thousandfold wealth as never fails [3], like the star Tishya [4] from heaven!

14. O Maruts, you protect our wealth of excellent men, and the seer, clever in song; you give to

Bharata (the warrior)[1] a strong horse[2], you make the king to be obeyed[3].

15. O you who are quickly ready to help, I implore you for wealth whereby we may overshadow all men, like the sky. O Maruts, be pleased with this word of mine, and let us speed by its speed over a hundred winters!

NOTES.

The same poet, *S*yâvâ*s*va Âtreya. Metre, 1–13, 15 *G*agatî; 14 Trish*t*ubh. None of the verses of this hymn occurs in SV., VS., AV., TS., TB., MS.

Verse 1.

Note 1. Ana*g*a, explained as a 2nd pers. plur. perf., referring to the same people who are addressed by ar*k*ata. It may be also the first person of the imperative; see Benfey, Über die Entstehung der mit r anlautenden Personalendungen, p. 5, note.

Note 2. Possibly the second line of this verse may refer to ceremonial technicalities. Gharma means heat and summer, but also the sacrificial vessel (formus) in which the milk is heated, and the warm milk itself. Ya*g*van can only mean sacrificing, and diva*h* p*r*ish*th*a is the back of heaven, the highest roof of heaven; see trip*r*ish*th*a. Thus we read, I, 115, 3. harîta*h* . . . divá*h* ấ p*r*ish*th*ám asthu*h*. See also I, 164, 10; 166, 5; III, 2, 12; IX, 36, 6; 66, 5; 69, 5; 83, 2; 86, 27. It would seem therefore as if the Maruts themselves were here represented as performing sacrificial acts in the highest heaven, praising the milk, that is, the rain, which they pour down from heaven to earth. Possibly the text is corrupt. If ya*g*yu could have the same meaning as praya*g*yu, I should like to conjecture, divá*h* ấ p*r*ish*th*ám yá*g*yave. In IX, 61, 12. índrâya yá*g*yave seems to mean 'to the chasing Indra.' See also âya*g*i (erjagend), obtaining. Might we conjecture divá ấ p*r*ikshayấvane? P*r*ikshayâma occurs as a name; see also II, 34, 3.

Verse 3.

Note 1. Abdâ, wish to give water, is very doubtful. Both abda and abdi, in abdimat, mean cloud. The text seems corrupt.

Verse 4.

Note 1. The meaning of vyag is doubtful. It may simply mean to make visible.

Verse 5.

Note 1. The last words ána*s*vadâm yát ní áyâtana girím are difficult. Sâya*n*a has an explanation ready, viz. when you throw down the cloud or the mountain which gives no water or which does not give up the horses carried off by the Pa*n*is. Grassmann too is ready with an explanation: 'Als ihr unnahbar glänzend, Hirschen gleich, den Berg auf eurer Fahrt durchranntet, den kein Ross erreicht.' Ludwig: 'Als ihr nider gehn machtet den nicht vergängliches gebenden (d. i. die waszer; oder: die rosse verweigernden?) berg.'

Giri may be the cloud, and nothing could be more appropriate than that the Maruts should come down upon the cloud or go over it, in order to make it give up the rain. But a*s*vadâ means 'giving horses,' and though rain-clouds may be compared to horses, it does not follow that a*s*va by itself could mean rain. A*s*vadâ is used of the dawn, I, 113, 18, possibly as giving horses, that is, wealth, but possibly also, as bringing the horses to the morning sun. These horses start with the dawn or the sun in the morning, and they rest in the evening. The legend that Agni hid himself in an A*s*vattha tree (Sâya*n*a, RV. I, 65, 1) may owe its origin to a*s*vattha, i.e. horse-stable, having been a name of the West (K. Z. I, 467); cf. tish*th*adgu, at sunset. In X, 8, 3, the Dawns are called á*s*vabudhnâ*h*, which may mean that they had their resting-place among the horses. The Maruts, more particularly, are said to dwell in the A*s*vattha tree, when Indra called them to his help against V*ri*tra; cf. *S*at. Brâhm. IV, 3, 3, 6; Pâr. G*ri*hy. II, 15, 4. Possibly therefore, though I say no more, possibly the Dawn or the East might have been called a*s*vadâ, the West ana*s*vadâ, and in that case it might be said that the Maruts are of unsullied splendour, when they go down to the western mountain. M. Bergaigne explains, 'La montagne qui ne donne pas, qui retient le cheval, le cheval mythique, soleil ou éclair.' My own impression, however, is that ana*s*vadâm is an old mistake, though I cannot accept Ludwig's conjecture a-na*s*va-dâm. Why not ánu svadhâm, or ana*s*va-yâ*h*, moving without horses? cf. V, 42, 10.

Verse 6.

Note 1. This is, no doubt, a bold simile, but a very true one. In one night caterpillars will eat off the whole foliage of a tree, and in the same way a violent storm in the autumn will strip every leaf. Ar*n*asám as an adjective, with the accent on the last syllable, does not occur again, but it can hardly mean anything but waving. If it will stand for the sea, we might translate, 'When you clear the waving sea (or air), as the caterpillar a tree.'

Note 2. Arámati seems here to mean service or obedience, not a person who is willing to serve.

Verse 8.

Note 1. To translate aryamá*n*a*h* by friends is unsatisfactory. Bergaigne takes it for Aryaman, Mitra, and Varu*n*a, the three Aryamans, as we say the two Mitras, and points out that these three gods do send rain, in I, 79, 3; VII, 40, 4.

Note 2. It ought to be kavandhína*h* as much as kávandha, V, 85, 3.

Note 3. Mádhva*h* ándhasâ; Grassmann, 'mit des Honigs Seim.'

Verse 10.

Note 1. Sabharas is evidently a recognised epithet of the Maruts, see VS. XVII, 81 and 84, but its meaning is doubtful. We have vi*s*vábharasam, IV, 1, 19, as an epithet of Agni, which does not help us much. If bharas means burden, sabharas may mean those who work together, companions, friends.

Verse 11.

Note 1. See Muir, S. T. V, p. 149. On *s*ipr*â*h &c., see II, 34, 3, note.

Verse 12.

Note 1. The red apple to be shaken from the firmament can only be the lightning. Vi-dhû is construed with two accusatives, as in III, 45, 4; V, 57, 3. Gaedicke, Accusativ, p. 266.

Note 2. Aryá*h* cannot be a vocative, on account of the accent, nor a nominative on account of the context. There remains nothing but to take it as a genitive, and connect it with ag*ri*bhîta, though such a construction has few parallels, except perhaps in such sentences as hávya*h* *k*arsha*n*înâm, VI, 22, 1, &c. Possibly it may be intended as an epithet of the Maruts. Bergaigne (Journ. As. 1884, p. 190), 'au profit du pauvre.' Geldner (Ved. Stud. I, p. 148) proposes a very bold translation: 'The sacrificial nets are being contracted, when the Maruts rush on. The priests (*ri*tâyu) roar their (as catching-net) extended shouting.' The sense is said to be that when the Maruts appear, all priests try to catch them by shouting. See, however, Oldenberg in Gött. Gel. Anzeigen, 1890, p. 414.

Verse 13.

Note 1. For rathyã*h*, see II, 24, 15. râyá*h* syâma rathyã*h* vayasvata*h*; VI, 48, 9.

Note 2. Râranta, 2nd pers. plur. imp. intens., but Pada has raranta. Why not rarâta?

Note 3. Yu*kkh*ati has been compared by Kuhn (K. Z. III, 328) with δύσκει; but see Brugmann, Grundriss, I, pp. 110, 118.

Note 4. Tishya must be the name of a star, hardly, as Sâya*n*a suggests, of the sun. It ought to be a star which does not set. See Weber, Über alte iranische Sternnamen, p. 14. Ludwig quotes from TS. II, 2, 10, 1 seq., an identification of Tishya with Rudra.

Verse 14.

Note 1. Grassmann marks this verse as late, Ludwig defends it. We must know what is meant by late before we decide. Bharata may mean simply a warrior, or a Bharata; see Ludwig, III, 175–176; Oldenberg, Buddha (1st edition), p. 413.

Note 2. Árvantam vấ*g*am, a horse, his strength. See Bergaigne, Rel. Véd. II, 405; Pischel, Ved. Stud. p. 46.

Note 3. Could *s*rush*t*imat here mean obedient?

MAN*D*ALA V, HYMN 55.

ASH*T*AKA IV, ADHYÂYA 3, VARGA 17–18.

To the Maruts (the Storm-gods).

1. The chasing[1] Maruts with gleaming spears, the golden-breasted, have gained great strength, they move along on quick well-broken horses;—when they went in triumph, the chariots followed.

2. You have yourselves, you know, acquired power; you shine bright and wide, you great ones. They have even measured the sky with their strength;—when they went in triumph, the chariots followed.

3. The strong heroes, born together, and nourished together, have further grown to real beauty. They shine brilliantly like the rays of the sun;—when they went in triumph, the chariots followed.

4. Your greatness, O Maruts, is to be honoured, it is to be yearned for like the sight of the sun. Place us also in immortality;—when they went in triumph, the chariots followed.

5. O Maruts you raise[1] the rain from the sea, and rain it down, O yeomen[2]! Your milch-cows, O destroyers[3], are never destroyed;—when they went in triumph, the chariots followed.

6. When you have joined the deer as horses[1] to the shafts, and have clothed yourselves in golden garments, then, O Maruts, you scatter all enemies;—when they went in triumph, the chariots followed.

7. Not mountains, not rivers have kept you back, wherever you see, O Maruts, there you go. You

go even round heaven and earth;—when they went in triumph, the chariots followed.

8. Be it old, O Maruts, or be it new, be it spoken, O Vasus, or be it recited, you take cognisance of it all;—when they went in triumph, the chariots followed.

9. Have mercy on us, O Maruts, do not strike us, extend to us your manifold protection. Do remember the praise, the friendship;—when they went in triumph, the chariots followed.

10. Lead us, O Maruts, towards greater wealth, and out of tribulations, when you have been praised. O worshipful Maruts, accept our offering, and let us be lords of treasures!

NOTES.

The same poet, *S*yâvâ*s*va Âtreya. Metre, 1–9 *G*agatî; 10 Trish*t*ubh. None of the verses occurs in SV., VS., AV. Verse 5 is found in TS. II, 4, 8, 2; MS. II, 4, 7. The refrain probably means that when the Maruts march in triumph, the chariots of their army, or the chariots of other gods, follow. The latter view is taken by Sâya*n*a, TS. II, 4, 8, 2.

Verse 1.

Note 1. Práya*g*yu, generally explained by rushing forward, but in that sense hardly to be derived from ya*g*, to sacrifice, may stand for an old Vedic form prayakshyu, changed into praya*g*yu by priests who had forgotten the root yaksh, and thought of nothing but sacrifices. This root yaksh has been identified by Grassmann with OHG. jagôn (venari, persequi), originally to rush after, to hunt, to try to injure or kill (cf. m*ri*ga*n*yáva*h*, X, 40, 4). This would explain most derivations from yaksh, not excepting the later Yakshas, and would yield an excellent sense for prayakshyu, as an epithet of the Maruts. See note to VII, 56, 16. Pischel, Ved. Stud. I, p. 98, is satisfied with deriving praya*g*yu and p*ri*sh*th*apraya*g* from the root ya*g*, to sacrifice, and translates it by sacrificing, but in the sense of causing sacrifices to be offered.

Verse 5.

Note 1. The verb îrayatha is transitive; see Gaedicke, Accusativ, p. 54, and compare AV. IV, 27, 4. apá*h* samudrā́d dívam úd vahanti.

Note 2. I have translated purîshi*n*a*h* by yeomen, in the sense of cultivators of the land. I have followed Roth, who shows that purîsha means soil, and that purîshin is used for an occupier of the soil, a landlord. See K. Z. XXVI, p. 65.

Note 3. Dasra, powerful, a common epithet of the A*s*vins, seems here, when joined with dasyanti, to retain something of its etymological meaning, which comes out clearly in dâs, to attack, unless it is derived from da*m*s.

Verse 6.

Note 1. I prefer to translate here 'the deer as horses,' not 'the speckled horses.' See, however, II, 34, 4, and Pischel, Ved. Stud. p. 226.

MANDALA V, HYMN 56.

ASHTAKA IV, ADHYÂYA 3, VARGA 19–20.

TO THE MARUTS (THE STORM-GODS).

1. O Agni, on to the strong host (of the Maruts), bedecked with golden chains and ornaments[1]. To-day I call the folk of the Maruts down from the light of heaven.

2. As thou (Agni) thinkest in thine heart, to the same object my wishes have gone. Strengthen thou these Maruts, terrible to behold, who have come nearest to thy invocations.

3. Like a bountiful lady[1], the earth comes towards us, staggering, yet rejoicing; for your onslaught, O Maruts, is vigorous, like a bear, and fearful, like a wild bull.

4. They who by their strength disperse wildly[1] like bulls, impatient of the yoke, they by their marches make the heavenly stone, the rocky mountain (cloud)[2] to shake.

5. Arise, for now I call with my hymns[1] the troop of these Maruts, grown strong together, the manifold, the incomparable, as if calling a drove of bulls.

6. Harness the red mares to the chariot, harness the ruddy horses to the chariots, harness the two bays, ready to drive in the yoke, most vehement to drive in the yoke.

7. And this red stallion too, loudly neighing, has been placed here, beautiful to behold; may it not cause you delay on your marches, O Maruts; spur him forth on your chariots.

8. We call towards us the glorious chariot of the Maruts, whereon there stands also Rodasî[1], carrying delightful gifts, among the Maruts.

9. I call hither this your host, brilliant on chariots, terrible and glorious, among which she, the well-born and fortunate, the bounteous lady, is also magnified among the Maruts.

NOTES.

The same poet and deity, though Agni is invoked in the first, possibly in the second verse also. Metre, 1, 2, 4-6, 8, 9 B*ri*hatî; 3, 7 Satob*ri*hatî. None of the verses occurs in SV., VS., AV., TS., MS.

Verse 1.

Note 1. Here again some interpreters of the Veda take a*ñ*gi in the sense of paint, war-paint. It may be so, but the more general meaning of colours or ornament seems, as yet, safer.

Verse 3.

Note 1. The earth is frequently represented as trembling under the fury of the Maruts. Here she is first called mî*lh*úshmatî, a curious compound which, in our verse, may possibly have a more special meaning. As the earth is not only struck down by the storm, but at the same time covered with water and fertilised, she is represented as struck down and staggering, but likewise as rejoicing, possibly, as drunk.

Verse 4.

Note 1. V*ri*thâ means pell-mell, confusedly, wildly; see also Geldner, Ved. Ṣtud. p. 115.

Note 2. Á*s*mâ svaryã*h* seems to mean the thunderbolt like vágra*h* svaryã*h* in I, 32, 2; 61, 6. See also V, 30, 8. In that case we should have to translate, 'they let the heavenly bolt fall down on the rocky mountain.' But *k*yâvayati is never used for the hurling of the thunderbolt, nor is it construed with two accusatives. It always means to shake what is firm, and we have therefore to translate, 'they shake the heavenly stone (the sky), the rocky mountain (the cloud).' Parvata and giri often occur together, as in I, 37, 7; VIII, 64, 5.

Verse 5.

Note 1. Stómai*h* may possibly refer to sámukshitânâm.

Verse 8.

Note 1. On Rodasî, see before, I, 167, 3.

MAN*D*ALA V, HYMN 57.

ASHT*A*KA IV, ADHYÂYA 3, VARGA 21-22.

To the Maruts (the Storm-gods).

1. O Rudras, joined by Indra, friends on golden chariots, come hither for our welfare! This prayer from us is acceptable to you like the springs of heaven to a thirsty soul longing for water.

2. O you sons of P*ris*ni, you are armed with daggers and spears, you are wise, carrying good bows and arrows and quivers, possessed of good horses and chariots. With your good weapons, O Maruts, you go to triumph!

3. You shake[1] the sky and the mountains (clouds) for wealth to the liberal giver; the forests bend down out of your way from fear[2], O sons of P*ris*ni, you rouse the earth when you, O terrible ones, have harnessed the spotted deer for triumph!

4. The Maruts, blazing with the wind, clothed in rain, are as like one another as twins, and well adorned. They have tawny horses, and red horses, they are faultless, endowed with exceeding vigour; they are in greatness wide as the heaven.

5. Rich in rain-drops, well adorned, bounteous, terrible to behold, of inexhaustible wealth, noble by birth, golden-breasted, these singers of the sky[1] have obtained their immortal name[2].

6. Spears are on your two shoulders, in your arms are placed strength, power, and might. Manly thoughts dwell in your heads, on your chariots are weapons, and every beauty has been laid on your bodies.

7. O Maruts, you have given us wealth of cows, horses, chariots, and heroes, golden wealth! O men of Rudra, bestow on us great praise, and may I enjoy your divine protection!

8. Hark, O heroes, O Maruts! Be gracious to us! You who are of great bounty, immortal, righteous, truly listening to us, poets, young, dwelling on mighty mountains[1], and grown mighty.

NOTES.

The same poet and deity. Metre, 1-6 *G*agatî; 7, 8 Trish*t*ubh. None of its verses occurs in SV., VS., AV., TS.; verse 6 in MS. IV, 11, 4.

Verse 3.

Note 1. Dhû is construed with two accusatives, see RV. III, 45, 4; otherwise vásu might be connected with dâ*s*úshe. The third pâda is almost literally repeated soon after, V, 60, 2; see note 1 to I, 37, 7.

Note 2. Yắmana*h* bhiyắ may be from fear of your approach.

Verse 5.

Note 1. In divá*h* arkắ*h* even Bergaigne allows that arká may mean singer, not song.

Note 2. Nắma, name, is here as elsewhere what is meant by the name, therefore immortal being or immortality.

Verse 8.

Note 1. B*ri*hadgiraya*h* cannot well mean with a powerful voice. The Maruts are called girish*th*a, VIII, 94, 12, dwelling on mountains, and like b*ri*haddiva, b*ri*hadgiri seems to have been intended for dwelling on high mountains.

MANDALA V, HYMN 58.

ASHTAKA IV, ADHYÂYA 3, VARGA 23.

To the Maruts (the Storm-gods).

1. I praise[1] now the powerful company of these ever-young Maruts, who drive violently along with quick horses; aye, the sovereigns are lords of Amrita (the immortal).

2. The terrible company, the powerful, adorned with quoits on their hands, given to roaring, potent, dispensing treasures, they who are beneficent, infinite in greatness, praise, O poet, these men of great wealth!

3. May your water-carriers come here to-day, all the Maruts who stir up the rain. That fire which has been lighted for you, O Maruts, accept it, O young singers!

4. O worshipful Maruts, you create for man an active king, fashioned by Vibhvan[1]; from you comes the man who can fight with his fist, and is quick with his arm, from you the man with good horses and valiant heroes.

5. Like the spokes of a wheel, no one is last, like the days they are born on and on, not deficient in might. The very high sons of Prisni are full of fury, the Maruts cling firmly to their own will[1].

6. When you have come forth with your speckled deer as horses[1] on strong-fellied chariots, O Maruts, the waters gush, the forests go asunder[2];—let Dyu[3] (Sky) roar down, the bull of the Dawn.

7. At their approach, even the earth opened wide,

and they placed (sowed) their own[1] strength (the rain), as a husband the germ. Indeed they have harnessed the winds as horses to the yoke, and the men of Rudra have changed their sweat into rain.

8. Hark, O heroes, O Maruts! Be gracious to us! You who are of great bounty, immortal, righteous, truly listening to us, poets, young, dwelling on mighty mountains, and grown mighty.

NOTES.

The same poet and deity. Metre, Trish*t*ubh. None of the verses occurs in SV., VS., AV., TS. Verses 3 and 5 are found in TB. II, 5, 5, 3; II, 8, 5, 7; MS. IV, 11, 2; IV, 4, 18.

Verse 1.

Note 1. On stushé, see M. M., Selected Essays, I, p. 162; Wilhelm, De infinitivi forma et usu, p. 10; Bartholomae. in Bezzenberger's Beiträge, XV, p. 219. I take stushé as 1 pers. sing. Aor. Âtm. (not, as Avery, of the Present) in many places where it has been taken as an infinitive. For instance, II, 31, 5; VI, 49, 1; 51, 3 (with vo*k*e); 62, 1 (with huve); VIII, 5, 4; 7, 32; 74, 1; 84, 1 (here the second pâda must begin with stushé). It may be an indicative or a subjunctive. As to stushe, without an accent, its character cannot be doubtful; see I, 122, 8; 159, 1; V, 33, 6; VI, 21, 2; 48, 14; VIII, 21, 9; 23, 2; 23, 7 (g*ri*n*e*). In II, 20, 4, tám u stushe índram tám g*ri*n*î*she, g*ri*n*î*she is an aorist with vikara*n*a, like punîshé, I praise that Indra, I laud him. In I, 46, 1, stushé may be the infinitive, but not necessarily. It is an infinitive in I, 122, 7. stushé sâ vâm varu*n*a mitra râtí*h*, your gift, Varu*n*a and Mitra, is to be praised. Likewise in VIII, 4, 17 (see BR. s. v. sâman); 24, 1; 63, 3, though in several of these passages it must remain doubtful whether stushé should be taken as an absolute infinitive, or as a finite verb. In VIII, 65, 5, índra g*ri*n*î*shé u stushé, means, 'Indra, I laud and praise,' as in II, 20, 4.

Verse 4.

Note 1. Vibhva-tash*t*á is generally explained as made by a master, or by Vibhvan, one of the *Ri*bhus. This may be so, though it seems a bold expression (see Bergaigne, II, 410–411). But may it not be a mere synonym of sutash*t*a, and intended for vibhvane tash*t*a? see Selected Essays, I, p. 143.

Verse 5.

Note 1. See Taitt. Br. II, 8, 5, 7. As to mimikshu*h*, see note to I, 165, 1.

Verse 6.

Note 1. On p*r*ishatîbhi*h* á*s*vai*h*, see II, 34, 4; V, 55, 6. Bergaigne's note (II, p. 378) does not settle the question whether the horses of the Maruts were speckled, or whether they had speckled deer for their horses.

Note 2. On ri*n*até vánâni, see V, 57, 3.

Note 3. Dyaus, the father of the Maruts, the oldest and highest god of heaven, the strong bull, or, it may be, the man of the dawn. See v. Bradke, Dyaus Asura, p. 63; Bergaigne, I, p. 316.

Verse 7.

Note 1. Roth conjectures svâm for svám, taking it as a locative of sû, genetrix. This is not without difficulties, nor is it necessary. That we find in the Rig-veda no other locative in âm after monosyllabic stems in û is perhaps no serious objection. But the text as it stands can be translated, 'as a husband the germ, they have placed (sown) their own strength.' *S*ávas is the same as v*r*ísh*n*yam and v*r*ísh*n*i *s*áva*h* in VIII, 3, 8; 10. Dhu*h* is used like dhâ in retodhâ.

MANDALA V, HYMN 59.

ASHTAKA IV, ADHYÂYA 3, VARGA 24.

To the Maruts (the Storm-gods).

1. They truly[1] tried to make you grant them welfare. Do thou sing[2] praises to Heaven (Dyu), I offer sacrifice (*ri*ta) to the Earth. The Maruts wash their horses and race to the air, they soften their splendour by waving mists.

2. The earth trembles with fear from their onset. She sways like a full ship, that goes rolling[1]. The heroes who appear on their marches, visible from afar, strive together within the great (sacrificial) assembly[2].

3. Your horn is exalted for glory[1], as the horns of cows; your eye is like the sun[2], when the mist is scattered. Like strong racers, you are beautiful, O heroes, you think of glory, like manly youths[3].

4. Who could reach, O Maruts, the great wise thoughts, who the great manly deeds of you, great ones? You shake the earth like a speck of dust, when you are carried forth for granting welfare.

5. These kinsmen[1] (the Maruts) are like red horses, like heroes eager for battle, and they have rushed forward to fight. They are like well-grown manly youths, and the men have grown strong, with streams of rain they dim the eye of the sun.

6. At their outbreak there is none among them who is the eldest, or the youngest, or the middle: they have grown by their own might, these sons of P*ris*ṇi, noble by birth, the boys of Dyaus; come hither to us!

7. Those who like birds flew with strength in rows [1] from the ridge of the mighty heaven to its ends, their horses shook the springs [2] of the mountain (cloud) so that people on both sides [3] knew it.

8. May [1] Dyaus Aditi (the unbounded) [2] roar for our feast, may the dew-lighted Dawns come striving together; these, the Maruts, O poet, (the sons) of Rudra, have shaken the heavenly bucket (cloud), when they had been praised.

NOTES.

The same poet and deity. Metre, 1–7 *G*agatî; 8 Trish*t*ubh. None of the verses occurs in SV., VS., AV., TB., TS., MS.

Verse 1.

Note 1. If we accept the text as it stands, we have to translate, 'The spy called out to you to grant welfare.' The spy is then either Agni (Bergaigne, II, p. 378) or the priest. See also VIII, 61, 15; X, 35, 8. But there are many objections to this. Pra-krand is not used in that sense, and we should expect pra krânt suvitâya. Pra-kar, when it is construed with a dative, means generally to prepare some one for something, to cause some one to do a thing. Thus, I, 186, 10. pró a*s*vínau ávase k*rin*udhvam, get the A*s*vins to protect. VI, 21, 9. prá ûtáye váru*n*am mitrám índram marúta*h* k*ri*shva ávase na*h* adyá, make Varu*n*a, Mitra, and Indra to protect, make the Maruts to protect us to-day. X, 64, 7. prá va*h* vâyúm—stómai*h* k*rin*udhvam sakhyấya pûshá*n*am, make Vâyu by your praises to be your friend. I, 112, 8. prá andhám *s*ro*n*ám *k*ákshase étave k*ri*thá*h*, whereby you make the blind and lame to see and to walk. The poet therefore seems to have said in our verse also, 'They (my men or priests) made you or wished you to give them welfare.' What spa*t* can mean in such a sentence, is difficult to say. Till we know better, we must simply accept it as a particle of asseveration, like ba*t*.

Note 2. Ár*k*â may also be the first person.

Verse 2.

Note 1. With regard to vyáthir yatî́, cf. I, 117, 15. samudrám avyathír *g*aganvấn, and VIII, 45, 19. vyáthir *g*aganvấ*m*sa*h*: Bergaigne, Journ. As. 1884, p. 490.

Note 2. Mahé vidáthe must be taken as a locative sing. It occurs again X, 96, 1. We have similar forms in mahé rá*n*e, IX, 66, 13. &c. The locative is governed by antá*h*.

as in II, 27, 8. vidáthe antá*h* eshâm. The etymology and the meaning of vidatha have been often discussed, for the last time by M. Regnaud, Revue de l'histoire des religions, 1890. Prof. Roth. as M. Regnaud states, explains it by conseil, avis, réunion où l'on délibère, assemblée, troupe, armée. Grassmann takes it generally for réunion, rencontre, combat. Geldner derives it from vid, in the sense of art, science. Ludwig derives it likewise from vid, but in the sense of Bekanntschaft, then Gesellschaft, and lastly as synonymous with yag*ñ*a, sacrifice, assemblage. M. Regnaud differs from all his predecessors, and derives vidatha from vidh, to sacrifice. He maintains that *vidhatha would become vidatha, like adhak from dah or dhagh, and phaliga for parigha. I know nothing about the etymology of phaliga, but if it stands for parigha, the second aspirate has lost its aspiration and thrown it on the initial. In adhak, the final has lost its aspiration, and thus allowed its appearance in the initial. But in vidatha, if it stood for vidhatha, there would be no phonetic excuse whatever for changing dh into d, at least in Sanskrit. It is possible that in Sanskrit such a form as vidhatha might have been avoided, but there is no phonetic law to prevent the formation of such a word as vidhatha, like u*k*atha, yagatha, &c. We say vidhatha in the 2 pers. plur., as we say bodhatha. No Sanskrit grammarian could derive vidatha from vidh. If therefore vidatha signifies sacrifice, this is not because it is derived from vidh, to sacrifice. Vidatha may have been the name of a sacred act, as veda is of sacred knowledge. But the fact remains that it is best translated by assembly, particularly an assembly for sacrificial purposes.

Verse 3.

Note 1. On *s*riyáse, see I, 87, 6.

Note 2. I see no necessity for changing sûrya*h* into sûra*h*, see Bergaigne, Mélanges Renier, p. 94. He would translate, 'they are like the eye of the sun.'

Note 3. Máryâ*h* may be bridegrooms, as in V, 60, 4

(varā́*h* iva), but there is nothing to indicate that meaning here. The difficulty is to find a word to express *s*riyáse. It means to shine, but at the same time to excel. Possibly it may have even a more definite meaning, such as to shine in battle, or to triumph.

Verse 5.

Note 1. As to sabandhu, see VIII, 20, 21.

Verse 7.

Note 1. On *srénîh*, see Gaedicke, p. 164; Bergaigne, Mél. Renier, p. 94.

Note 2. The meaning of nabhanú, spring, is doubtful.

Note 3. Ubháye refers to many on both sides, and cannot be taken for ubhe, heaven and earth. It may mean all, particularly when there are two sides only, as in a battle.

Verse 8.

Note 1. Ludwig seems to have seen the true meaning of this verse, namely that, though Dyaus may roar for the feast, and though the Dawns may strive to come near. the Maruts alone deserve the sacrifice, because they opened the chest of rain.

Note 2. On Dyaus Aditi, see note to I, 166, 12, p. 261, where the translation has to be corrected.

MA*ND*ALA V, HYMN 60.

ASH*T*AKA IV, ADHYÂYA 3, VARGA 25.

To Agni and the Maruts.

1. I implore[1] Agni, the gracious, with salutations, may he sit down here, and gather what we have made[2]. I offer[3] (him sacrifice) as with racing chariots; may I, turning to the right, accomplish this hymn to the Maruts.

2. Those who approached on their glorious deer, on their easy chariots, the Rudras, the Maruts,—through fear of you, ye terrible ones, the forests even bend down, the earth shakes, and also the mountain (cloud).

3. At your shouting, even the mountain (cloud), grown large, fears, and the ridge of heaven trembles. When you play together, O Maruts, armed with spears, you run together like waters.

4. Like rich suitors the Maruts have themselves[1] adorned their bodies with golden ornaments; more glorious for glory[2], and powerful on their chariots, they have brought together splendours on their bodies.

5. As brothers, no one being the eldest or the youngest, they have grown up together to happiness. Young is their clever father Rudra, flowing with plenty is P*ri*sni (their mother), always kind to the Maruts.

6. O happy Maruts, whether you are in the highest, or in the middle, or in the lowest heaven, from thence, O Rudras, or thou also, O Agni, take notice of this libation which we offer.

7. When Agni, and you, wealthy Maruts, drive down from the higher heaven over the ridges, give then, if pleased, you roarers, O destroyers of enemies[1], wealth to the sacrificer who prepares (Soma-juice).

8. Agni, be pleased to drink Soma with the brilliant Maruts, the singers, approaching in companies[1], with the men (Âyus[2]), who brighten and enliven everything; do this, O Vaisvânara (Agni), thou who art always endowed with splendour.

NOTES.

This hymn, by the same poet, is supposed to be addressed either to the Maruts alone, or to the Maruts and Agni. The same might have been said of hymn 56 and others which are used for the Âgnimâruta *S*astra. See Bergaigne, Recherches sur l'histoire de la liturgie védique, p. 38. Metre, 1-6 Trish*t*ubh ; 7, 8 *G*agatî. No verse of this hymn occurs in SV., VS., AV., TS., TB., except verse 1 in AV. VII, 50, 3; TB. II, 7, 12, 4; MS. IV, 14, 11; verse 3 in TS. III, 1, 11, 5; MS. IV, 12, 5; verse 6 in TB. II, 7, 12, 4.

Verse 1.

The AV. reads svấvasum, prasaktó, pradakshi*n*ám, all of them inferior readings. The TB. agrees with RV., except that it seems to read prasaptá*h* (prakarshe*n*a samâgata*h*).

Note 1. That î*l* or î*d* has originally the meaning of imploring, asking, begging, we see from such passages as RV. III, 48, 3. upasthâya mâtáram ánnam ai*tt*a, 'he, having approached his mother, asked for food,' unless we prefer to construe î*d* with two accusatives, 'he, having approached, asked his mother for food.' The same verb is also construed with the accusative of the god implored, the dative of the object, and the instrumental of the means by which he is implored. See RV. VIII, 71, 14. agním î*l*ishva ávase gấthâbhi*h*, implore Agni with songs for his protection. Whether the root î*d* is distantly connected with either ish, to desire (Brugmann, I, 591), or with ard, to stir, or with ar, to go, is a question which admits of many, or of no answer.

Note 2. Vi*k*i k*ri*tam seems to have the settled meaning of gathering in what one has made at play, or in battle; see X, 42, 9; 43, 5; IX, 97, 58; X, 102, 2. The same meaning is applicable here, though we may also translate, 'Take notice of our k*ri*ta or our karma, i. e. the sacrifice.' A similar thought is expressed in verse 6. Sâya*n*a explains vi*g*ânâtu and vi*k*inuyât.

Note 3. Perhaps prá bhare means, 'I am carried forth,' as in V, 59, 4, where it is applied to the Maruts.

Verse 4.

Note 1. See note 2 to I, 6, 4. Instead of svadhā́bhi*h* we have svayám in VII, 56, 11.

Note 2. *S*riyé *s*réyâ*ms*a*h* is difficult to translate ; cf. II, 33, 3. *s*résh*th*a*h* *s*riyā́ asi. Ludwig translates, zu herlichkeit die herlichen.

Verse 7.

Note 1. On ri*s*âdas, see Aufrecht, Bezzenb. Beitr. XIV, p. 32.

Verse 8.

Note 1. On ga*n*a*s*rī́, see BR. s. v.; Lanman, 372; Benfey Vedica und Verwandtes, p. 108; Pischel, Ved. Stud. I, 53 seq. Ludwig translates scharenherlich, but what does that mean? Shining in their companies' is a possible meaning, but the analogy of abhi*s*rī́ and adhvara*s*rī́ points in another direction.

Note 2. On the Âyus as a proper name, see Bergaigne, Rel. Véd. I, 62; II, 323.

MA*ND*ALA V, HYMN 61.

ASH*T*AKA IV, ADHYÂYA 3, VARGA 26–29.

TO THE MARUTS (THE STORM-GODS).

1. Who are you, O men, the very best, who have approached one by one, from the furthest distance [1]?

2. Where are your horses, where the bridles? How could you, how did you come?—the seat on the back, the rein in the nostrils?

3. Their goad is on the croup [1], the heroes stretched their legs apart [2]. . .

4. Move along, heroes, young men, the sons of an excellent mother [1], so that you may warm yourselves at our fire [2].

5. (1.) May the woman, if she stretched out her arm [1] as a rest for the hero, praised by *S*yâvâ*s*va [2], gain cattle consisting of horses, cows, and a hundred sheep.

6. (2.) Many a woman is even more often kindlier than a godless and miserly man,

7. (3.) A woman who finds out the weak, the thirsty, the needy, and is mindful of the gods.

8. (4.) Even though many an unpraiseworthy miser (Pa*n*i) is called a man, she is worth as much in weregild.

9. (5.) Also the young woman joyfully whispered to me, to *S*yâva, the road,—and the two bays went straight to Purumî*lh*a [1], the wise, the far-famed,

10. (6.) Who gave me a hundred cows, like Vaidada*s*vi, like Taranta, in magnificence.

11. (1.) The Maruts, who drive on their quick horses, drinking the delightful mead, have gained glory here;

12. (2.) They on whose chariots Rodasî[1] glitters in glory[2], like the golden disk above in heaven;

13. (3.) That youthful company of the Maruts, with blazing chariots, blameless, triumphant, irresistible.

14. (4.) Who now knows of them where the strikers rejoice, the well-born, the faultless?

15. (5.) You who are fond of praise, become the leaders of the mortal, listening to his imploring invocations, thus is my thought[1].

16. (6.) Bring then to us delightful and resplendent[1] treasures, ye worshipful Maruts, destroyers of enemies.

17. (1.) O night, like a charioteer, carry away this hymn to Dârbhya, and these songs, O goddess.

18. (2.) And then tell him thus from me, 'When Rathavîti offers Soma, my desire never goes away from me.'

19. (3.) That mighty Rathavîti dwells among people rich in cattle[1], retired among the mountains.

NOTES.

This hymn is of a very composite nature. It is addressed to the Maruts by *S*yâvâ*s*va. According to the Anukrama*n*î, however, the Maruts are addressed in vv. 1–4, 11–16 only; vv. 5–8 are addressed to *S*a*s*îyasî Tarantamahishî, 9 to Purumî*l*h*a Vaidada*s*vi, 10 to Taranta Vaidada*s*vi, 17–19 to Rathavîti Dârbhya. None of the verses occurs in SV., VS., AV., TS., TB., MS. Metre, 1–4, 6–8, 10–19 Gâyatrî; 5 Anush*t*ubh; 9 Satob*ri*hatî.

It has been pointed out that in the hymns addressed to the Maruts beginning with V, 52, and ending with V, 60, there is the usual decrease in the number of verses of each successive hymn, viz. 17, 16, 15, 10, 9, 8, 8, 8, 8. Our hymn, however, which is the last in the collection of hymns addressed by *S*yâvâ*s*va to the Maruts, breaks the rule, and it has been suggested with great plausibility that it contains a number of verses thrown together at random. Possibly the four verses in the beginning formed an independent hymn, addressed to the Maruts, and again 5–10, and 11–16, followed by an appendix, 17–19. These verses refer to a legend which will have to be discussed at verse 5.

Verse 1.

Note 1. As to paramásyâ*h* parâváta*h*, see TS. IV, 1, 9, 3, where we also find (IV, 1, 9, 2) párasyâ ádhi sa*m*váta*h*.

Verse 3.

Note 1. *G*aghâne, like *g*aghanata*h*, may mean simply behind, as agre and agrata*h* mean before.

Note 2. It is clear that the Maruts are here supposed to sit astride on their horses. This is also shown by p*ri*sh*th*é sádas (v. 2), and by putrak*ri*thé ná *g*ánaya*h*, they stretched out their legs, ὡς γυναῖκες ἐν τεκνοποιίᾳ. Zimmer (p. 230) says, 'Zum Reiten wurde das Ross nicht benutzt.' On p. 295 he modifies this by saying, 'Keine einzige klare Stelle des Rigveda ist mir bekannt, wo das Reiten beim Kampfe erwähnt würde; man fährt immer zu Wagen, wie die Griechen in homerischen Zeiten.'

Verse 4.

Note 1. Bhádraǵânayaḥ, generally rendered by 'possessed of beautiful wives,' seems really to mean 'possessed of an excellent mother.' *G*âni clearly means mother, when Agni dvimâtâ, having two mothers, is called dviǵâni*h*; for it is never said that he has two wives. Besides, the Maruts are constantly addressed as the sons of their mother, P*ris*ni, while their wives are mentioned but rarely. However, the other meaning is not impossible. See also Bergaigne, II, 387 seq.

Note 2. The fire here intended is, I suppose, the sacrificial fire, to which the Maruts are here invited as they had been in former hymns.

Verse 5.

Note 1. Ludwig compares the A. S. expression healsgebedde; see also RV. X, 10, 10.

Note 2. I have very little belief in the legends which are told in the Brâhma*n*as and in the Anukrama*n*î in illustration of certain apparently personal and historical allusions in the hymns of the Veda. It is clear in many cases that they are made up from indications contained in the hymns, as in IX, 58, 3, and it seems best therefore to forget them altogether in interpreting the words of the Vedic hymns.

The story told in the introductory verses, quoted by Sâya*n*a, is this:—'Ar*k*anânas Âtreya was chosen by Rathavîti Dârbhya to be his *R*itvig priest. At the sacrifice Ar*k*anânas saw the daughter of Rathavîti and asked her in marriage for his son *S*yâvâ*s*va. Rathavîti consulted his wife, but she declined on the ground that no daughter of theirs had ever been given to a man who was not a poet (*R*ishi). Thereupon *S*yâvâ*s*va performed penance, and travelled about collecting alms. He thus came to *S*a*s*îyasî, who recommended him, as a *R*ishi, to her husband, king Taranta. King Taranta was very generous to him, and sent him on to his younger brother, Purumî*lh*a. On his way to Purumî*lh*a, *S*yâvâ*s*va saw the Maruts, and composed a hymn in their praise (vv. 11–16). He had thus become a real poet or *R*ishi, and on returning home, he received from Rathavîti his daughter in marriage.'

*S*aunaka confirms the same story, see Sâya*n*a's commentary to V, 61, 17. Here therefore we have to deal with two princely brothers, both Vaidada*s*vis, namely Taranta and Purumî*l*h*a. They both give presents to *S*yâvâ*s*va, who is a Brâhma*n*a, and he marries the daughter of another prince, Rathavîti Dârbhya.

In the Tâ*nd*ya-Brâhma*n*a, however, XIII, 7, 12, another story is told, which I quoted in my edition of the Rig-veda at IX, 58, 3 (vol. v, p. xxxiii). Here Dhvasra and Purushanti are introduced as wishing to give presents to the two Vaidada*s*vis, Taranta and Purumî*l*h*a. These hesitate for a while, because they have no right to accept a present without deserving it or having done something for it. They then compose a hymn in praise of Dhvasra and Purushanti, and after that feel justified in accepting their present.

Here therefore the Vaidada*s*vis are receivers, not givers of presents, therefore of princely, not, as has been supposed, of priestly rank, and this would agree better with the words of verse 9, purumî*l*h*ấya víprâya. See on all this Oldenberg in Z. D. M. G. XLII, p. 232.

If we accept this story, we have to take *sás*îyasî in verse 6 as a proper name.

But *sás*îyasî may be a comparative of *sas*-vat (see B.-R. s.v.), and would then mean, more frequent. We expect, no doubt, an adverb rather like *sas*vat, but a feminine corresponding to vásyasî is perhaps admissible. In that case we should have simply to deal with some woman, tvâ strî̋, who, as the poet says, is as good as, if not better than, many a man.

Verse 8.

This verse is very obscure. Sâya*n*a translates: 'And the other half (the husband of *S*a*s*îyasî, viz. Taranta) is a man not praised (enough), thus I, the poet, say: and that Taranta is equal or just in the giving of wealth.' Grassmann translates: 'Und dagegen ist mancher nicht lobenswerth geizig, der ein Mann sich nennt, ein solcher ist der Strafe verfallen.' Ludwig: 'Auch mancher halbmensch, ungepriesen, der "mensch" zwar heiszt, doch ein Pa*n*i ist, der ist auf böse gabe nur bedacht.'

The first light that was thrown on this verse came from Prof. Roth. He showed (Z. D. M. G. XLI, p. 673) that vairadeya means weregild, the German wergelt, the price to be given for a man killed. Vaira would here be derived from vîra, man, the Goth. waír, the Latin vir, and vairadeya would mean what is to be given as the value of a man. Still I doubt whether Prof. Roth has discovered the true meaning of the verse. He translates: 'So ist auch mancher Mann nicht zu loben, mehr ein Pa*n*i (unfromm, gegen die Götter karg, zugleich Bezeichnung habsüchtiger Dämonen), obschon man ihn einen Menschen nennt—nur am Wergeld steht er den andern gleich.' I confess I do not see much point in this. It is quite clear that the poet praises a charitable woman, and wishes to say that she is sometimes better than a man, if he gives nothing. Now the weregild, if we may say so, for women was generally, though not always, less than that for men, and I therefore propose to read sấ vaíradeye ít samấ, and translate: 'Even though many an unpraiseworthy miser (Pa*n*i) is called man, she is like him in weregild, i.e. she is worth as much, even though she is a woman.' On uta, see Delbrück, Syntaktische Forschungen, V, p. 528.

Verse 9.

Note 1. Purumî*lh*a is here clearly the man from whom benefits are expected, and therefore could not be the same as Purumî*lh*a Vaidada*s*vi, mentioned by the commentator, who accepted gifts from Dhvasra and Purushanti. Nor can Taranta Vaidada*s*vi in the next verse be taken for a recipient, but only for a giver, and therefore, most likely, a prince. The whole story, however, is by no means clear, and I doubt whether the commentator drew his information from any source except his own brain.

Verse 11.

I agree with Ludwig that a new hymn begins with verse 11.

Verse 12.

Note 1. I have adopted the reading Rodasî vibhrấgate in my translation; cf. VI, 66, 6, where Rodasî is compared with a rókaḥ.

Note 2. Roth (K.Z. XXVI, 51) takes *s*riyấdhi as *s*riyás ádhi, but such a sandhi has not yet been established in the hymns of the Rig-veda, see Oldenberg, Proleg. p. 459, Anm. 1. Oldenberg himself suggests *s*ríyo-dhi, and would translate, 'They whose charms shine over the two worlds on their chariots.' Pischel (Ved. Stud. p. 54) translates yéshâm *s*riyấ by 'for whose sake.'

Verse 15.

Note 1. On itthấ dhiyấ, see Pischel, Ved. Stud. p. 184.

Verse 16.

Note 1. The Pada ought to have puru-*k*andrấ, as suggested by Grassmann and Ludwig.

Verses 17–19.

These verses are very peculiar, and may refer to historical events, for Dâlbhya or Dârbhya and Rathavîti sound like real names. Of course the Indian commentators are never at a loss to tell us what it all refers to, but we can never say how little they knew, and how much they invented. The invocation of Ûrmyâ, if it is meant for the Night, and the request that she may convey the hymn to Dârbhya, is different from the usual style of the hymns. See, however, VIII, 24, 28, and Oldenberg, Z.D.M.G. XXXIX, 89.

The following names, occurring in our hymn, have the sanction of the Anukrama*n*î: *S*a*s*îyasî Tarantamahishî (V, 61, 5; 8), Purumî*ll*ha Vaidada*s*vi (V, 61, 9), Taranta Vaidada*s*vi (V, 61, 10), Rathavîti Dâlbhya (V, 61, 17–19). There is another Purumî*ll*ha, a Sauhotra, in IV, 43, and a Purumî*ll*ha Âṅgirasa in VIII, 71.

Verse 19.

Note 1. See Oldenberg, Z.D.M.G. XXXIX, 89. He corrects gómatî*h* to gómatîm, the name of a river, mentioned in a very similar way in VIII, 24, 30.

MANDALA V, HYMN 87.

ASHTAKA IV, ADHYÂYA 4, VARGA 33–34.

TO THE MARUTS (THE STORM-GODS).

1. Let your voice-born[1] prayers go forth to the great Vishnu, accompanied by the Maruts, Evayâmarut, and to the chasing host, adorned with good rings, the strong, in their jubilant throng, to the shouting power (of the Maruts).

2. O Maruts, you who are born great, and proclaim it yourselves by knowledge, Evayâmarut, that power of yours cannot be approached by wisdom, that (power) of theirs (cannot be approached) by gift or might[1]; they are like unapproachable mountains.

3. They who are heard with their voice from the high heaven, the brilliant and strong, Evayâmarut, in whose council no tyrant[1] reigns, the rushing chariots[2] of these roaring Maruts come forth[3], like fires with their own lightning.

4. The wide-striding (Vishnu)[1] strode forth from the great common seat, Evayâmarut. When he has started by himself from his own place along the ridges, O ye striving, mighty[2] Maruts, he goes together with the heroes (the Maruts), conferring blessings.

5. Impetuous, like your own shout, the strong one (Vishnu) made everything tremble, the terrible, the wanderer[1], the mighty, Evayâmarut; strong with him you advanced self-luminous, with firm reins, golden coloured, well-armed[2], speeding along.

6. Your greatness is infinite, ye Maruts, endowed

with full power, may that terrible power help, Evayâmarut. In your raid[1] you are indeed to be seen as charioteers; deliver us therefore from the enemy, like shining fires.

7. May then these Rudras, lively like fires and with vigorous shine, help, Evayâmarut. The seat of the earth is stretched out far and wide[1], when the hosts of these faultless Maruts come quickly to the races.

8. Come kindly on your path, O Maruts, listen to the call of him who praises you, Evayâmarut. Confidants of the great Vishnu, may you together, like charioteers, keep all hateful things far[1], by your wonderful skill.

9. Come zealously[1] to our sacrifice, ye worshipful, hear our guileless call, Evayâmarut. Like the oldest mountains in the sky, O wise guardians, prove yourselves for him irresistible to the enemy.

NOTES.

This hymn is evidently a later addition at the end of the fifth Ma*nd*ala. It is addressed to the Maruts, and is ascribed to Evayâmarut Âtreya. None of its verses occurs in SV., VS., AV., TS., TB., MS., except the first, which is found in SV. I, 462. Metre, Ati*g*agatî.

The name of the poet is due to the refrain Evayắmarut which occurs in every verse, and sometimes as an integral portion of the verse. Evayắmarut is a sacrificial shout, much like Εὐοῖ in Greek, Evoe in Latin, though I do not mean to say that the two are identical. Evayâ*h*, as I explained in note to I, 168, 1, is an epithet of Vish*n*u, as well as of the Maruts, meaning quickly moving. Evayâmarut, therefore, may mean the 'quick Marut.' This is strange, no doubt, because in the Rig-veda the Maruts always occur in the plural, except in some doubtful passages. Still Evayâmarut, the quick Marut, might be a name of Vish*n*u. It cannot be taken as a Dvandva, Vish*n*u and the Maruts.

This hymn was translated by Benfey in his glossary to the Sâma-veda, p. 39. Benfey takes evayâ as identical with εὐοῖ, and explains it as an adverbial instrumental, like â*s*uyâ, in the sense of stürmisch. But this would leave evayâvan unexplained.

Verse 1.

Note 1. Giri-*g*ắ*h* may mean 'produced on the mountains,' but it may also mean 'produced in the throat or voice,' and it is so explained elsewhere, for instance in SV. I, 462 (Bibl. Ind., vol. i, p. 922). girau vâ*k*i nishpannâ*h*; [also by another commentator, h*ri*daye *g*âtâ, ya*gñag*âtâ vâ ity uktam]. Oldenberg suggests giri*g*e, which would be much better, considering how Vish*n*u is called girikshit, girish*th*â, &c.; see Bergaigne, II, 47. Most of the epithets have occurred before. I take *s*ávase as a substantive, like *s*ardhas, not as an adjective. As to dhúnivrata, see V, 58, 2; as to práya*g*yu, V, 55, 1.

Verse 2.

Note 1. Krátvâ, dânắ, and mahnắ seem to me in this place to belong together. The difficulty lies in the transition from va*h* to eshâm, but this is not uncommon. On mahinắ = mahimnâ, dânắ, and mahnắ, see Wenzel, Instrumentalis, p. 17; Lanman, p. 533. Pischel, Ved. Stud. p. 101, translates, 'Ihre Macht gereicht ihnen zu grosser Gabe.' See also VIII, 20, 14. *G*âtắ*h* mahinắ, born by greatness, seems to mean born in greatness, or born great. It would be easy to write mahínâ*h*.

Verse 3.

Note 1. The translation of írî is purely conjectural.

Note 2. Syandrắsa*h*, as suggested by Oldenberg, are probably meant for rathâ*h*. Syandana is a carriage in later Sanskrit. In VIII, 20, 2, we have to supply rathai*h*; in VI, 66, 2, rathâ*h*.

Note 3. Prá, with the verb understood, they come forth; cf. VII, 87, 1. prá ár*n*â*m*si samudríyâ nadī́nâm; X, 75, 1. Dhuni, like dhûti, has become almost a name of the Maruts, see I, 64, 5.

Verse 4.

Note 1. The god here meant seems to be Vish*n*u, mentioned already in verse 1, and probably recalled by the Evayâ in Evayâmarut.

Note 2. We must either take víspardhasa*h* and vímahasa*h* with Benfey as names of the horses, or accept them as vocatives, addressed to the Maruts. Vimahas is used as an epithet of the Maruts, see I, 86, 1.

Verse 5.

Note 1. On yayí*h*, see note to I, 87, 2; but it seems better to take it here as an adjective.

Note 2. On svâyudha, see Geldner, Ved. Stud. I, p. 143; Oldenberg, Gött. Gel. Anzeigen, 1890, p. 424.

Verse 6.

Note 1. Prásiti may be, as Ludwig translates it, fangschnur, a noose, but it can hardly mean Noth, as Grassmann suggests. I take it here in the sense of shooting forth, onslaught, raid; cf. VII, 46, 4. Geldner, Ved. Stud. I, p. 139, takes it for a trap. Lanman, p. 386, is right in considering the locative in au before consonants a sure sign of the modern origin of this hymn.

Verse 7.

Note 1. The idea that the earth is stretched out or becomes large during a thunderstorm has been met with before, V, 58, 7. We read I, 37, 8; 87, 3, that at the racings of the Maruts the earth trembled, and that the Maruts enlarged the fences in their races. I therefore translate, though tentatively only, that the earth is opened far and wide, as a race-course for the faultless Maruts, whose hosts ấ, appear, á*g*meshu, on the courses, mahá*h*, quickly. If the accent of paprathe could be changed, we might translate, 'at whose coursings (á*g*meshu ấ) the seat of the earth is quickly stretched out far and wide,' and then take *s*árdhâ*m*si ádbhutainasâm in apposition to rudrấsa*h*. Adbhutainas, in whom no fault is seen.

Bergaigne translates, 'faisant du mal mystérieusement.' See Geldner, in K. Z. XXVIII, 199, Anm. 2; Bezzenberger's Beiträge, III, 169.

Verse 8.

Note 1. Cf. VI, 48, 10.

Verse 9.

Note 1. Su*s*ámi, generally explained as a shortened instrumental, for su*s*amî = su*s*amyâ, used in an adverbial sense. Su*s*ámi has a short i here, because it stands at the end of a pâda, otherwise the i is long, see VII, 16, 2; X, 28, 12, even before a vowel. The same applies in the Rig-veda to *s*ami; it has short i at the end of a pâda, see II, 31, 6; VIII, 45, 27; X, 40, 1. The phrase dhiyấ *s*ấmi, which has short i in II, 31, 6; X, 40, 1, has long i in IX, 74, 7. dhiyấ *s*ámî. It is shortened, however, before vowels in the middle of a pâda, and written *s*amy; see I, 87, 5; III, 55, 3.

MAN*D*ALA VI, HYMN 66.

ASHT*A*KA V, ADHYÂYA 1, VARGA 7–8.

To the Maruts (the Storm-gods).

1. This may well be a marvel, even to an intelligent man, that anything should have taken the same name dhenu, cow:—the one is always brimming to give milk among men, but P*ris*ni (the cloud, the mother of the Maruts) poured out her bright udder once (only).

2. The Maruts who shone like kindled fires, as they grew stronger twice and thrice,—their golden, dustless (chariots [1]) became full of manly courage and strength.

3. They who [1] are the sons of the bounteous Rudra, and whom she indeed was strong enough to bear; for she, the great, is known as the mother of the great, that very P*ris*ni conceived the germ for the strong one (Rudra).

4. They who do not shrink from being born in this way [1], and who within (the womb) clean themselves from all impurity [2], when they have been brought forth brilliant, according to their pleasure, they sprinkle their bodies with splendour.

5. Among them there is no one who does not strive to be brought forth quickly; and they assume the defiant name of Maruts. They who are not (unkind [1]), never tiring in strength [2], will the generous sacrificer be able to bring down these fierce ones?

6. Fierce in strength, followed by daring armies, these Maruts have brought together heaven and earth [1], both firmly established [2]; then the self-

shining Rodasî stood among the impetuous Maruts, like [3] a light.

7. Even though your carriage, O Maruts, be without your deer [1], without horses, and not driven by any charioteer, without drag [2], and without reins, yet, crossing the air [3], it passes between heaven and earth, finishing its courses.

8. No one can stop, no one can overcome him whom you, O Maruts, protect in battle. He whom you protect in his kith, his cattle, his kin, and his waters, he breaks the stronghold at the close of the day [1].

9. Offer a beautiful song to the host of the Maruts, the singers, the quick, the strong, who resist violence with violence; O Agni, the earth trembles before the champions.

10. Blazing like the flame of the sacrifices, flickering like the tongues of the fire, shouters, like roaring fighters, the flame-born Maruts are unassailable.

11. I invite with my call this strong and Marut-like son of Rudra [1], armed with flaming spears. Bright thoughts, like wild waters from the mountain [2], strove to reach the host of heaven.

NOTES.

Hymn ascribed to Bharadvâga Bârhaspatya. None of its verses occurs in SV., VS., AV. Verse 2 in MS. IV, 14, 11. Verse 9 in TS. IV, 1, 11, 3; TB. II, 8, 5, 5; MS. IV, 10, 3. Verse 10 in MS. IV, 14, 11. Metre, Trish*t*ubh.

Verse 1.

The meaning seems to be that it is strange that two things, namely, a real cow and the cloud, i.e. P*ris*ni, the mother of the Maruts, should both be called dhenu, cow; that the one should always yield milk to men, while the other has her bright udder milked but once. This may mean that dhenu, a cow, yields her milk always, that dhenu, a cloud, yields rain but once, or, that P*ris*ni gave birth but once to the Maruts. See also VI, 48, 22; Gaedicke, Accusativ, p. 19; Delbrück, Tempuslehre, p. 102. Dhenu must be taken as the neuter form, and as a nominative, as is shown by II, 37, 2. dadí*h* yá*h* nấma pátyate.

Verse 2.

Note 1. It seems necessary to take are*n*áva*h* hira*n*yáyâsa*h* for rathấ*h*, chariots, as in V, 87, 3. Sâya*n*a takes the same view, and I do not see how the verse gives sense in any other way. The first pâda might be referred to the Maruts, or to the chariots.

Verse 3.

Note 1. The relative pronouns may be supposed to carry on the subject, viz. Marúta*h*, from the preceding verse, unless we supply eshâm mâtấ. I am doubtful about mahó mahī́; cf. I, 102, 1; II, 33, 8. Grassmann proposes to read mahâm, gen. plur.; Ludwig thinks of garbha. It may also be a compound, as in mahâmaha, mahâmahivrata, or an adverb, but the construction remains difficult throughout. Oldenberg suggests that the second pâda may have been yân *k*o nú p*rís*ni*h* dấdh*r*ivi*h* bháradhyai.

Verse 4.

Note 1. A tentative rendering and no more. I take áyâ for ayā́ as an adverb in the sense of thus, in this way, see I, 87, 4, note 2. Grassmann seems to take it as an instr. fem., dependent on *g*anúsha*h*, which is possible, but without analogy. Lanman, p. 358, takes it for áyâ*h*, nom. plur. of aya, wanderer, and translates, 'as long as the ones now wanderers quit not their birth.' Grassmann: 'Die nicht verleugnen die Geburt aus jener.' But is *g*an with instrumental ever used of a woman giving birth to a child? Ludwig: 'Die sich nicht weigern der geburt.'

Note 2. Pû with accusative occurs AV. XIX, 33, 3.

Verse 5.

This verse is again very obscure. It would be more honest to say that it is untranslatable. Possibly the poet may have taken doháse in the same sense as duhré in verse 4. The Maruts are born as by being milked from the udder of P*ris*ni. It would then mean, 'Among whom there is no one not striving to be born quickly.'

Note 1. Stauna is an unknown word. Sâya*n*a explains it as stena, thieves. It probably meant something not favourable, something that must be denied of the Maruts. This is all we can say. It cannot be a corruption of stavânâ*h*, praised.

Note 2. Ayā́s can hardly refer to P*ris*ni, never tiring to suckle the Maruts. In B.-R. ayâs is explained as sich nicht anstrengend, behende, leicht, unermüdlich. See also Windisch, K. Z. XXVII, 170; also Johansson, Bezzenb. Beitr. XV, p. 180.

Verse 6.

Note 1. To join together heaven and earth is, as Bergaigne remarks (II, p. 374, n. 1), the apparent effect of a thunderstorm, when the clouds cover both in impenetrable darkness. We have the same expression in VIII, 20, 4.

Note 2. On suméke, see Geldner, K. Z. XXIV, 145; and Windisch, Festgruss an Böhtlingk, p. 114.

Note 3. The ná, placed before róka*h*, is irregular, see Bergaigne, Mélanges Renier, p. 79. Oldenberg suggests narokâ*h* = n*ri*-okâ*h*, 'she who is fond of the men,' namely, of the Maruts. The corruption may be due to the writers of our text.

Verse 7.

Note 1. Anená*h* is strange, and might be changed into anetá*h*; it cannot be anenấ*h*, without guilt.

Note 2. If avasa in an-avasa comes from ava-so, it may mean the step for descending or ascending, or possibly a drag. Bergaigne explains it by sine viatico.

Note 3. Ra*g*a*h*-tû̃*h*, according to Ludwig, den Staub aufwirbelnd, which seems too much opposed to are*n*u, dustless. Ra*g*as + tar means to pass through the air, and in that sense only conquering the air. Geldner, Ved. Stud. p. 123, ignores the various shades of meaning in tur at the end of compounds.

Verse 8.

Note 1. Pấrye dyó*h*, according to Grassmann, 'on the decisive day,' like pấrye diví.

Verse 11.

Note 1. I have translated Rudrásya sûnúm by the son of Rudra. It is true that a single Marut, as the son of Rudra, is not mentioned; but on the other hand, one could hardly call the whole company of the Maruts, the mâruta scil. ga*n*a, the son of Rudra. In I, 64, 12, we have Rudrasya sûnu in one pâda, and mâruta ga*n*a in the next. The *Ri*bhus also are called in the same line *s*avasa*h* napâta*h*, and indrasya sûno, IV, 37, 4. Here sûnu corresponds almost to the English offspring, only it is masculine.

Note 2. Giráya*h* may have been meant for girya*h*, a possible ablative of giri; see Lanman, p. 383. Ugrấ*h* would then refer to ấpa*h*, unless we break the sentence into two, viz. 'my bright thoughts tend to the host of heaven,' and 'the fierce Maruts strive like waters from the mountain.' If we compare, however, IX, 95, 3. apấm iva íd ûrmáya*h* tárturâ*n*â*h* prá manîshấ*h* îrate sómam á*kkh*a, we see that the whole verse forms one sentence. All would be right if we could change giraya*h* into giribhya*h*, but is not this a conjecture nimis facilis?

MAN*D*ALA VII, HYMN 56.

ASHT*A*KA V, ADHYÂYA 4, VARGA 23–26.

To the Maruts (the Storm-gods).

1. Who are these resplendent men, dwelling together, the boys of Rudra, also [1] with good horses?

2. No one indeed knows their births, they alone know each other's birthplace.

3. They plucked each other with their beaks [1]; the hawks, rushing like the wind, strove together.

4. A wise man understands these secrets [1], that P*ris*ni, the great, bore an udder.

5. May that clan be rich in heroes by the Maruts, always victorious, rich in manhood!

6. They are quickest to go, most splendid with splendour, endowed with beauty, strong with strength.

7. Strong is your strength, steadfast your powers, and thus by the Maruts is this clan mighty.

8. Resplendent is your breath, furious are the minds of the wild host, like a shouting maniac [1].

9. Keep from us entirely your flame, let not your hatred reach us here.

10. I call on the dear names of your swift ones, so that the greedy should be satisfied [1], O Maruts,

11. The well-armed, the swift, decked with beautiful chains, who themselves adorn their bodies.

12. Bright are the libations for you, the bright ones, O Maruts, a bright sacrifice I prepare for the bright. In proper order came those who truly follow the order, the bright born, the bright, the pure.

13. On your shoulders, O Maruts, are the rings,

on your chests the golden chains are fastened; far-shining like lightnings with showers[1], you wield your weapons, according to your wont.

14. Your hidden[1] splendours come forth; spread out your powers (names), O racers! Accept, O Maruts, this thousandfold, domestic share, as an offering for the house-gods[2].

15. If you thus listen, O Maruts, to this praise, at the invocation of the powerful sage, give him quickly a share of wealth in plentiful offspring, which no selfish enemy shall be able to hurt.

16. The Maruts, who are fleet like racers, the manly youths, shone like Yakshas[1]; they are beautiful like boys standing round the hearth, they play about like calves who are still sucking.

17. May the bounteous Maruts be gracious to us, opening up to us the firm heaven and earth. May that bolt of yours which kills cattle and men, be far from us! Incline to us, O Vasus, with your favours.

18. The Hot*ri* priest calls on you again and again, sitting down and praising your common gift, O Maruts. O strong ones, he who is the guardian of so much wealth, he calls on you with praises, free from guile.

19. These Maruts stop the swift, they bend strength by strength[1], they ward off the curse of the plotter, and turn[2] their heavy hatred on the enemy.

20. These Maruts stir up even the sluggard[1], even the vagrant[2], as the gods[3] pleased. O strong ones, drive away the darkness, and grant us all our kith and kin.

21. May we not fall away from your bounty, O

Maruts, may we not stay behind, O charioteers, in the distribution of your gifts. Let us share in the brilliant wealth, the well-acquired, that belongs to you, O strong ones.

22. When valiant men fiercely fight together, for rivers, plants, and houses[1], then, O Maruts, sons of Rudra, be in battles our protectors from the enemy.

23. O Maruts, you have valued[1] the praises which our fathers have formerly recited to you; with the Maruts the victor is terrible in battle, with the Maruts alone the racer wins the prize.

24. O Maruts, may we have a strong son, who is lord among men, a ruler, through whom we may cross the waters to dwell in safety, and then obtain our own home for you[1].

25. May Indra then, Varu*n*a, Mitra, Agni, the waters, the plants, the trees of the forest be pleased with us. Let us be in the keeping, in the lap of the Maruts; protect us always with your favours.

NOTES.

Ascribed to Vasish*th*a. Verse 1 occurs in SV. I, 433; verse 10 in TS. II, 1, 11, 1; MS. IV, 11, 2; verse 12 in TB. II, 8, 5, 5; MS. IV, 14, 18; verse 13 in TB. II, 8, 5, 5; MS. IV, 14, 18; verse 14 in TS. IV, 3, 13, 6; MS. IV, 10, 5; verse 16 in TS. IV, 3, 13, 7; MS. IV, 10, 5; verse 19 in TB. II, 8, 5, 6; MS. IV, 14, 18. Metre, 1–11 Dvipadâ Virâ*g*; 12–25 Trish*t*ubh.

Verse 1.

Note 1. The SV. reads athâ for the older adhâ. Sanîkâ in the edition of the Bibl. Ind. is a misprint for sanî*l*â.

Verse 3.

Note 1. Sva-pû is explained by Roth as possibly a broom, raising the dust. Grassmann translates it by light, Ludwig by blowing. I suggest to take it for *vapû, in the sense of beak or claw, from vap, which follows immediately. See note to I, 88, 4. I do not see how the other meanings assigned to svapû give any sense. Oldenberg therefore suggests pavanta, 'Sie strömten hell auf einander zu mit ihren svapûs.'

Verse 4.

Note 1. Sâya*n*a explains etấni ni*n*yấ by *s*vetavar*n*âni marudâtmakâni bhûtâni. He takes ûdhas as a locative.

Verse 8.

Note 1. Geldner translates: 'Der Spielmann des wilden Heeres ist wie ein Muni,' and adds, 'Aber was ist ein Muni im Veda?'

Verse 10.

Note 1. I read t*r*ipán for t*r*ipát of the Pada text, and refer vâva*s*ânấ*h* to the Maruts. The TS. has t*r*ipát, and the commentary explains it by t*r*iptim. The first line is Virâ*g*, the second Trish*t*ubh, and the Trish*t*ubh metre is afterwards carried on.

Verse 11.

This verse refers to the Maruts, not, as Ludwig thinks, to the priests. Dr. v. Bradke (Dyaus Asura, p. 65) proposes to join verses 10 and 11 into one Trish*t*ubh, and possibly to insert ấ before huve. I doubt whether for the present such changes are justified. On the structure of this hymn, see Oldenberg, Prol. 96, Anm. 3; 200, Anm. 5.

Verse 13.

Note 1. TB. II, 8, 5, 6, reads vy*ri*sh*t*ibhi*h* (not v*ri*sh*t*ibhi*h*), and the commentator explains, vy*ri*sh*t*ibhir âyudhavi*s*eshair vy*ri*sh*t*yâkhyair, vi*s*eshe*n*a ro*k*amânâ*h* sthitâ*h*. And again, *ri*sh*t*aya eva vi*s*ish*t*atvâd vy*ri*sh*t*aya ity u*k*yante. Bollensen, Z. D. M. G. XLI, 501, conjectures *ri*sh*t*ibhi*h* for v*ri*sh*t*ibhi*h*, which is very ingenious. See also note 1 to II, 34, 2.

Verse 14.

Note 1. Budhnyã, explained by budhne bhavâni, and also by kâlaprav*ri*ttâni.

Note 2. G*ri*hamedhîya may refer to the Maruts as g*ri*hamedhâs or g*ri*hamedhinas; see RV. VII, 59, 10; VS. XXIV, 16. The g*ri*hamedhîyâ ish*t*i in *S*at. Br. XI, 5, 2, 4, is meant for the Maruts.

Verse 16.

Note 1. Yakshad*rís*a*h* is explained as wishing to see a sacrifice or feast. Ludwig retains this meaning. Grassmann translates, 'wie feurige Blitze funkeln.' Yaksha may mean a shooting star or any meteor, literally what shoots or hastens along; see VII, 61, 5. ná yấsu *k*itrám dád*ri*s*e ná yakshám; also note to V, 55, 1. But d*ris* is not sad*ris*. If we follow the later Sanskrit, yaksha would mean a class of spirits, followers of Kuvera, also ghosts in general. If this is not too modern a conception for the Rig-veda, we might translate yakshad*ris*, 'appearing as ghosts' (see Kau*s*. Sûtra 95 in BR.), or, considering the expression átya*h* ná ya*m*sat yakshabh*rí*t ví*k*etâ*h*, I, 190, 4, take it for a name of horses.

Verse 19.

Note 1. Does not sáhasa ấ stand for sáhasâ ấ, and not for sáhasa*h* ấ? Comp. Oldenberg, Prolegomena, 465 seq.

Note 2. On dadhanti, see Hübschmann, Indogerm. Vocalsystem, p. 12.

Verse 20.

Note 1. On radhra, see Pischel, Ved. Stud. pp. 124 seq.

Note 2. Bh*ri*mi is doubtful, but as it stands by the side of radhra, it seems to have a bad meaning, such as a vagrant, unsteady.

Note 3. The Vasus are often mentioned with the Âdityas and Rudras, see III, 8, 8; X, 66, 12; 128, 9. By themselves they became almost synonymous with the Devas. Thus in VII, 11, 4, we read that Agni became the master of all sacrifices, krátum hí asya Vásava*h* *g*ushánta átha devấ*h* dadhire havyavấham, 'for the Vasus liked his wisdom, therefore the Devas made him the carrier of offerings.' See also V, 3, 10. pitấ Vaso yádi tát *g*osháyâse. In one passage, VI, 50, 4, Vasava*h* means the Maruts. In our passage it seems better to take it in the sense of gods, but we might also refer it to the Maruts.

Verse 22.

Note 1. With pâda b, compare VII, 70, 3 b.

Verse 23.

Note 1. I have taken bhû́ri *k*akra in the sense of magni facere, though I can find no analogous passages.

Verse 24.

Note 1. This verse has been well explained by Dr. v. Bradke, Dyaus Asura, p. 66. Svám óka*h*, our own home, occurs IV, 50, 8; V, 33, 4; VI, 41, 1; VIII, 72, 14. Abhyas means generally to obtain what is not our own. See also VII, 48, 2. Va*h*, which I have translated 'for you,' may also mean 'from you.'

Verse 25.

This verse is marked as a galita taken from VII, 34, 25, while the last pâda is a galita taken from VII, 1, 25.

MANDALA VII, HYMN 57.

ASHTAKA V, ADHYÂYA 4, VARGA 27.

TO THE MARUTS (THE STORM-GODS).

1. O ye worshipful, your company of Maruts is fond of honey, they who delight in their strength at the sacrifices, the Maruts, who shake even the wide heaven and earth, and fill the well, when they move about, the terrible ones.

2. Truly the Maruts find out the man who praises them, and guide the thoughts of the sacrificer. Sit down then to rejoice to-day, on the altar[1] in our assemblies[2] well pleased.

3. Others do not shine so much as these Maruts with their golden chains, their weapons, and their own bodies; the all-adorned, adorning heaven and earth, brighten themselves with the same brightness, when starting for triumph.

4. May your shining thunderbolt be far from us, O Maruts, whatever sin we may commit against you, men as we are: O worshipful, let us not fall under[1] its power, let your best favour rest on us.

5. May the Maruts be pleased with whatever little we have done here, they the faultless, the bright, the pure. Protect us, ye worshipful, with your favours, lead us to prosperity through booty.

6. And let the manly Maruts, when they have been praised, under whatever names, enjoy these offerings! Grant that our offspring may not die[1], raise up for us riches[2], glory, and wealth.

7. O Maruts, when you have thus been praised, come all together with help towards our lords who with their hundredfold wealth freely prosper us;—protect us always with your favours!

NOTES.

Ascribed to Vasish*th*a. None of its verses occurs in SV., VS., AV., TS., TB., MS. Metre, Trish*t*ubh.

Verse 1.

This hymn has been translated by Geldner and Kaegi. The first verse is most difficult. G.-K. avoid all difficulties by translating, 'Beim Fest des süssen Trankes weiss man tüchtig euch zu begeistern, hehre Schaar der Marut.' Ludwig grapples with them by translating: 'An eures madhu kraft, o zu vererende, freut bei den opfern sich der Marut geschlecht.' I doubt, however, whether *s*avas is ever ascribed to madhu, though it is ascribed to Soma. Oldenberg suggests, 'The sweet ones' is your Marut-name, O worshipful, they who rejoice in their strength at the sacrifices.' Here the difficulty would be that Mârutam nâma is the recognised term for the name, i.e. the kin of the Maruts. Still, unless we venture on a conjecture, this would seem to be the best rendering. Could we change mádhva*h* va*h* nấma mấrutam into madhvád va*h* nấma mấrutam? Madhvád is a Vedic word, though it occurs once only, in I, 164, 22, and as trisyllabic. Its very rarity would help to account for the change. The meaning would then be, 'your Marut kin eats honey, is fond of honey.'

It has been proved that the present mádati is always neutral, meaning to rejoice, while mand (Par.) is transitive, to make rejoice. Otherwise madhva*h* might possibly have been taken in the sense of sweet things, as in I, 180, 4; IX, 89, 3, and construed with madanti.

Verse 2.

Note 1. Barhis, which I translate by altar, is the simplest form of an altar, mere turf or ku*s*a-grass, on which the offerings are placed. See note to VII, 46, 4.

Note 2. On vidatha, see my note, V, 59, 2.

Verse 3.

See Gaedicke, Accusativ, p. 241; his rendering would be acceptable but for the â. Without any verb of motion â ragas can hardly mean 'through the air,' nor ấ ródasî 'through the worlds.'

Verse 4.

Note 1. On api bhû and api as, see B.-R. s. v.

Verse 6.

Note 1. Am*ri*ta cannot be rendered by immortality in our sense, it simply means not dying.

Note 2. *G*ig*ri*tá, imp. aor. caus. of gar. Râyá*h*, acc. plur.

MANDALA VII, HYMN 58.

ASHTAKA V, ADHYÂYA 4, VARGA 28.

To the Maruts (the Storm-gods).

1. Sing to the company (of the Maruts), growing up together, the strong among the divine host[1]: they stir heaven and earth by their might, they mount up to the firmament from the abyss of Nirriti[2].

2. Even your birth[1] was with fire and fury, O Maruts! You, terrible, wrathful, never tiring! You who stand forth with might and strength; every one who sees the sun[2], fears at your coming.

3. Grant mighty strength to our lords, if the Maruts are pleased with our praise. As a trodden path furthers a man, may they further us; help us with your brilliant favours.

4. Favoured by you, O Maruts, a wise man wins a hundred, favoured by you a strong racer wins a thousand, favoured by you a king also kills his enemy: may that gift of yours prevail, O ye shakers.

5. I invite these bounteous sons of Rudra[1], will these Maruts turn again to us? Whatever they hated secretly or openly, that sin we pray the swift ones to forgive.

6. This praise of our lords has been spoken: may the Maruts be pleased with this hymn. Keep far from us, O strong ones, all hatred, protect us always with your favours!

NOTES.

Ascribed to Vasish*th*a. None of its verses occurs in SV., VS., AV., TS., TB., MS. Metre, Trish*t*ubh.

Verse 1.

Note 1. Dhâman is one of the cruces of translators, and it remains so after all that has been written on the subject by Bergaigne, III, 210 seq. There are many words in the Veda which it is simply impossible to translate, because their meaning has not yet been differentiated, and they convey such general or rather vague concepts that it is utterly impossible to match them in our modern languages. Translators are often blamed that they do not always render the same Vedic by the same English word. It would be simply impossible to do so, because, according to the different surroundings in which it occurs, the same word receives different shades of meaning which in English can only be approximately expressed by different words. Bergaigne is, no doubt, right when he says that dhâ-man is derived from dhâ, to set or settle, and that it therefore meant at first what is settled. From this he proceeds to argue that the original meaning of dhâman, from which all others are derived, is law. But law is a very late and very abstract word, and we must never forget that words always progress from the concrete to the abstract, from the material to the spiritual, and but seldom, and at a much later time, in an opposite direction. Now even if we were to admit that dhâman does not occur in the Veda in the sense of settlement, i.e. abode, this is certainly its most general meaning afterwards, and no one would maintain that a settlement, i.e. a household, was called dhâman, because it involved a settlement, i.e. laws. The same applies to vratá. Bergaigne (III, 213) agrees with me that vrata should be derived from var, to surround, to guard, and not from var, to choose, but he thinks that it meant at once 'garde, protection,' and not 'lieu clos.' I still hold that like νομός, vrata must have meant first a real hedge, or ἕρκος, and then only an abstract enclosure, i.e. a law, νόμος. In this case we can see the actual transition of thought. People would begin by saying, 'there is a fence here against your cattle,' and this would in time assume the meaning 'there is a defence against your cattle straying on my meadow.' But it would be impossible to begin, as Bergaigne (p. 216) does, with the abstract meaning of protection, law, and then return and use the word in such phrases as V, 46, 7. apā́m vraté, 'within the pale of the waters.'

Dhâman, therefore, meant originally, I still believe, what was actually laid down or settled, hence an abode. When, as in the Veda, it means law, I do not say that this was necessarily derived from the meaning of abode. I only maintain that it was a second, if not a secondary, meaning, and that, at all events, the meaning of abode cannot be derived from that of law.

After dhâman meant what is settled, it has sometimes to be translated by law, by nature, sometimes by class, or clan, where it comes very near to nâman, name, while sometimes it may best be rendered by a general and abstract suffix, or even by a plural. Thus in our passage, daívyasya dhā́mna*h* is not very different from devânâm.

What is peculiar to our passage is the genitive governed by tuvishmân. After all the learning which Bergaigne has expended on the analysis of dhâman, he does not help us to a translation of our sentence. If we translate 'of the divine law, powerful,' we have words, but no sense. I take daívyasya dhā́mna*h* as a genitivus partitivus, such as AV. IV, 37, 5. óshadhînâm vîrúdhâm vîryā̂vatî. See Kuhn, Zeitschrift XIII, 120; Siecke, Genitivus, p. 14. Grassmann: 'Die mächtig walten in der Götter Wohnsitz.' Ludwig: 'Die von göttlicher natur, die starke.' He denies that tuvishmân could be followed by the genitive. I do not maintain that I am satisfied on that point. All I say in this as in many other cases is that my translation gives something which we can understand. Let others give us something better.

Note 2. On Nir*ri*ti, see Hibbert Lectures, p. 245; Lect. Science of Lang., vol. ii, p. 562. Ava*m*sá, literally without beams of support, or bottomless.

Verse 2.

Note 1. On *g*anûs, see Lanman, p. 571.

Note 2. Svard*ri*k, according to Grassmann, der lichte Himmel; according to Ludwig, jeder der das licht schaut. Sâya*n*a, among other meanings, gives that of tree. See VII, 83, 2.

Verse 3.

On the construction of this verse, see Delbrück, Syntax p. 384, and Bergaigne, Mélanges Renier, p. 82.

Verse 5.

Note 1. With regard to tấn mî*lh*úsha*h* rudrásya, 'these bounteous (sons) of Rudra,' see VIII, 20, 3.

MAN*D*ALA VII, HYMN 59.

ASH*T*AKA V, ADHYÂYA 4, VARGA 29-30.

TO THE MARUTS AND RUDRA.

1. Whom you protect again and again, O gods, and whom you lead, to him, O Agni, Varu*n*a, Mitra, Aryaman, and Maruts, yield your protection.

2. He who sacrifices, O gods, overcomes his enemies by your protection on a happy day. He who gives to your delight, spreads forth his dwelling, spreads out much food.

3. This Vasish*th*a will not despise even the last among you, O Maruts; drink[1] all of you, to-day, at my libation here, full of desire.

4. Your help does not indeed fail that man in battle to whom you granted it, O men! Your newest favour has turned hither, come quick then, ye who wish to drink.

5. O ye whose gifts are cheering, come to drink the (juice of the Soma) flowers: these are your libations, O Maruts, for I gave them to you, do not go elsewhere!

6. Sit down on our altar and protect[1] us, to give us brilliant riches. O Maruts, who never miss the Soma mead, hail to you here to enjoy yourselves.

7. Having adorned their bodies, the swans with dark blue backs came flying in secret[1]—the whole flock sat down all around me, like gay men, delighting in the Soma offering.

8. O Maruts, that hateful man who beyond our thoughts tries to hurt us, O Vasus, may he catch the snares of Druh, kill him with your hottest bolt!

9. O you Maruts, full of heat, here is the libation; be pleased to accept it, O you who destroy the enemies by your help[1].

10. O you who accept the domestic sacrifices[1], come hither, O Maruts, do not keep away, you who are bounteous by your help[2].

11. O Maruts, strong and wise, with sun-bright skins, I choose the sacrifice for you here and there[1]

12. We sacrifice to Tryambaka[1], the sweet-scented, wealth-increasing (Rudra). May I be detached from death, like a gourd from its stem, but not[2] from the immortal[3].

NOTES.

Ascribed to Vasish*th*a. Verse 12 addressed to Rudra. Verse 3 occurs SV. I, 241; verse 8, AV. VII, 77, 2; TS. IV, 3, 13, 3; MS. IV, 10, 5; verse 9, AV. VII, 77, 1; TS. IV, 3, 13, 3; MS. IV, 10, 5; verse 10, TS. IV, 3, 13, 5; MS. IV, 10, 5; verse 11, TÂ. I, 4, 3; MS. IV, 10, 3; verse 12, VS. III, 60; AV. XIV, 1, 17; TS. I, 8, 6, 2; MS. I, 10, 4; TÂ. X, 56; *S*at. Br. II, 6, 2, 12.

Metre, 1, 3, 5 B*ri*hatî; 2, 4, 6 Satob*ri*hatî; 7, 8 Trish*t*ubh; 9, 10, 11 Gâyatrî; 12 Anush*t*ubh.

Verse 2.

With pâda a compare I, 110, 7; with c and d, VIII, 27, 16.

Verse 3.

Note 1. SV. has pibantu, and as a various reading the comment. gives pivanta. Suté sá*k*â is a standing phrase.

Verse 6.

Note 1. I cannot see how avitá can stand for avish*t*a (Delbrück, Verb, 186; Whitney, Gram. § 908). I translate as if the text gave ávatâ.

Verse 7.

Note 1. On the secret approach of the Maruts, see I, 88, 5.

Verse 8.

The text in the AV. VII, 77, 2, is bad, yó no márto maruto durh*rin*âyús, práti mu*ñk*atâm sá*h*, and tápasâ for hánmanâ. The TS. IV, 3, 13, 3, has tirá*h* satyấni. It reads besides, yó no márto vasavo durh*rin*âyús tirá*h* satyấni maruta*h* *g*ígha*m̐*sât druhá*h* pấ*s*am, and tápasâ. Tirá*h* *k*ittấni may mean 'beyond all conception,' as Grassmann takes it, or 'unobserved,' as B.-R. suggest. Tirá*h* satyấni might mean 'in spite of all pledges,' but that is probably an emendation. All this shows the unsettled state of Vedic tradition, outside that of the Rig-veda; see Oldenberg, Prolegomena, p. 328.

Verse 9.

Note 1. Ûtî́, taken here as a dative, by Lanman, p. 382.

Verse 10.

Note 1. On the Maruts g*ri*hamedhina*h*, see *S*at. Br. II, 5, 3, 4. Possibly the Maruts may be called g*ri*hamedhas, i.e. g*ri*hasthas, performing the G*ri*hya sacrifices. See on these names TS. I, 8, 4, 1; 2.

Note 2. The last pâda in the TS. is pramu*ñk*ánto no á*m*hasa*h*.

Verse 11.

Note 1. On ihéha, see Delbrück, Syntax, p. 51. It means 'here and there,' that is, 'again and again.'

Verse 12.

Note 1. Tryambaka is a name of Rudra, but its original meaning is doubtful. Some commentators explain it by 'three-eyed,' but its natural meaning would be 'having three mothers.' The *S*at. Br. II, 6, 2, 9, derives it from Stry-ambikâ, because Ambikâ, Rudra's sister, shares the sacrifice with him.

Note 2. On mâ with optative, see Delbrück, Synt. Forsch. I, 194; Syntax, 338, 361, Anm. 1.

Note 3. That am*ri*tât is right, not, as Grassmann suggests, am*ri*ta, is clear from the parallel forms, prétó mu*ñk*âmi nấmúta*h*, or itó mukshîya mấmúta*h*. Pischel in Z.D.M.G. XL, 121, demands too much logical accuracy from a poet; see AV. XIV, 1, 17; VS. III, 60.

All scholars seem to agree that this hymn is a composite hymn, and that it breaks the law of decrease in the number of verses. It begins with three Pragâthas, verses 1 and 2, 3 and 4, 5 and 6, which may be in their right place. Then follow two Trish*t*ubhs, 7 and 8, which may form a hymn by themselves. The next three Gâyatrîs, which clearly belong together, are a later addition; so is the last verse, which ought to stand in the Atharva rather than in the Rig-veda. The Pada text does not divide this last verse. See on this subject, Oldenberg, Z.D.M.G. XXXVIII, 449 seq., Proleg. 200; 511; Bergaigne, Recherches sur l'histoire de la Samhitâ, II, 10.

MAN*D*ALA VIII, HYMN 7.

ASH*T*AKA V, ADHYÂYA 8, VARGA 18–24.

To the Maruts (the Storm-gods).

1. When the sage has poured out the threefold [1] draught to you, O Maruts, then you shine forth in the mountains (clouds).

2. Aye, when, O bright Maruts, growing in strength, you have seen your way, then the mountains (clouds) have gone down [1].

3. The sons of P*ri*s*n*i, the bulls, have risen together with the winds, they have drawn forth the swelling draught.

4. The Maruts sow the mist, they shake the mountains (clouds), when they go their way with the winds,

5. When the mountain bent down before your march, the rivers before your rule, before your great power (blast).

6. We invoke you by night for our protection, you by day, you while the sacrifice proceeds.

7. And they rise up on their courses, the beautiful, of reddish hue [1], the bulls, above the ridge of the sky.

8. With might they send forth a ray of light, that the sun may have a path to walk [1]: they have spread far and wide with their lights.

9. Accept, O Maruts, this my speech, this hymn of praise, O *Ri*bhukshans [1], this my call.

10. The P*ri*s*n*is [1] (the clouds) yielded three lakes (from their udders) as mead for the wielder of the thunderbolt (Indra), the well, the water-skin, the watering-pot [2].

11. O Maruts, whenever we call you from heaven, wishing for your favour, come hither towards us.

12. For you are bounteous[1], in our house, O Rudras, *Ri*bhukshans: you are attentive, when you enjoy (the libations).

13. O Maruts, bring to us from heaven enrapturing wealth, which nourishes many, which satisfies all.

14. When you have seen your way, brilliant Maruts, as it were from above[1] the mountains, you rejoice in the (Soma) drops which have been pressed out.

15. Let the mortal with his prayers ask the favour of that immense, unconquerable (host)[1] of them,

16. Who like torrents[1] foam along heaven and earth with their streams of rain, drawing the inexhaustible well.

17. These sons of P*ris*ni rise up together with rattlings, with chariots, with the winds, and with songs of praise.

18. That (help) with which you helped Turva*s*a, Yadu, and Ka*n*va when he carried off riches, that we pray for, greatly for our wealth.

19. O bounteous Maruts, may these draughts, swelling like butter, strengthen you, together with the prayers of Kâ*n*va.

20. Where do you rejoice now, O bounteous Maruts, when an altar has been prepared for you? What priest serves you?

21. For you for whom we have prepared an altar, do not, as it was with you formerly, in return for these praises, gladden the companies of our sacrifice.

22. These Maruts have brought together piece

by piece[1] the great waters, heaven and earth, the sun, and the thunderbolt;

23. And, while performing their manly work, they have trodden V*ri*tra to pieces, and the dark mountains (clouds).

24. They protected the strength and intelligence of the fighting Trita, they protected Indra in his struggle with V*ri*tra.

25. Holding lightnings in their hands, they hasten heavenward, golden helmets[1] are on their head; the brilliant Maruts have adorned themselves for beauty.

26. When with U*s*anâ[2] you have come from afar to Uksh*n*orandhra (ox-hollow)[1], he roared from fear, like Dyu (the sky).

27. O gods, come to us with your golden-hoofed horses, for the offering of the sacrifice[1].

28. When the red leader leads their spotted deer in their chariot, the brilliant Maruts approach and let the waters run.

29. The heroes went downwards to *S*arya*n*âvat, to Sushoma, to Âr*g*îka, to Pastyâvat.

30. When will you come hither, O Maruts, to the sage who calls you so, with your consolations to the suppliant?

31. What then now? Where are your friends, now that you have forsaken Indra? Who is counted in your friendship?

32. O Kâ*n*vas, I praise Agni, together with our Maruts, who carry the thunderbolt in their hands, and are armed with golden daggers.

33. Might I succeed in bringing hither the strong hunters, hither with their splendid booty for the newest blessings.

34. The hills even sink low, as if they thought themselves valleys, the mountains even bow themselves down.

35. The crossing (horses) bring them hither, flying through the air; they bestow strength on the man who praises them.

36. The old fire[1] has been born, like the shine[2] by the splendour of the sun, and the Maruts have spread far and wide with their lights.

NOTES.

Ascribed to Punarvatsa Kâ*n*va. Verse 8 occurs MS. IV, 12, 5; verse 11 in TS. I, 5, 11, 4; MS. IV, 10, 4; verse 28 in AV. XIII, 1, 21. Metre, Gâyatrî.

Verse 1.

Note 1. Trish*t*úbham is an adjective belonging to ísham. The same expression occurs again, VIII, 69, 1, as a galita, and is therefore of little help. In IX, 62, 24, the ísha*h* are called parish*t*úbha*h*, which seems to mean something like parisrut, i. e. standing round about. I therefore take trish*t*ubh in our passage simply as threefold, referring probably to the morning, noon, and evening sacrifice. The sacrifice is often called triv*ri*t, X, 52, 4; 124, 1. Some scholars ascribe to stubh in trish*t*ubh the meaning of liturgical shouting.

Verse 2.

Note 1. Besides ní ahâsata, we find úd ahâsata, I, 9, 4, and ápa ahâsata, IX, 73, 6. On *k*i, see verse 14, and V, 55, 7. It is often impossible to say whether the Vedic Aorist should be translated in English by the perfect or the imperfect. If we take the verse as describing an historical fact, it would be, 'When you saw your way, or, as soon as you had seen your way, the clouds fell.' If it is meant as a repeated event, it would be, 'when, i. e. whenever you have seen your way, the clouds have fallen.' The difficulty lies in English, and though the grammars lay down rules, usage does not conform to them. The difference in the use of tenses in English is so great that in the revised version of the Bible, a number of passages had to be translated differently for the English and for the American public. Thus in Rom. ii. 12, the English edition gives, 'For as many as have sinned without law, shall perish without law.' The American edition changes this into 'As many as sinned without the law.' Gal. iii. 22, English: 'The scripture hath shut up;' American: 'The scripture shut up.' It was on account of this and other changes of idiom which have sprung up between English and American, that different editions of the revised version had actually to be printed for England and America. No wonder, therefore, that an American critic should in his innocence have charged me with not knowing the difference between the aorist, the imperfect, and the perfect in Vedic Sanskrit!

Verse 7.

Note 1. Aru*n*apsu, perhaps reddish-coloured, an epithet of the dawn, here applied to the Maruts. The Maruts are sometimes called v*ri*shapsu, ahrutapsu, I, 52, 4; VIII, 20, 7.

Verse 8.

Note 1. The relation between the light cast forth by the Maruts and the path of the sun is not quite clear, except that in other places also the Maruts are connected with the morning. The darkness preceding a thunderstorm may be identified with the darkness of the night, preceding the sunrise. See Bergaigne, II, 379 seq.

Verse 9.

Note 1. The meaning of *ri*bhukshan is doubtful. It is applied to Indra and the Maruts. See Bergaigne, II, 403; 404 note; 412.

Verse 10.

Note 1. The P*ris*nis in the plural fem. are the clouds, see VIII, 6, 19. Mythologically there is but one P*ris*ni, the mother of the Maruts. See also Bergaigne, II, 397.

Note 2. I am doubtful about the three lakes of Madhu, here of rain, poured from their udders by the clouds. The number three is common enough, and Ludwig has pointed out a parallel passage from the AV. X, 10, 10–12, where we read of three pâtras, filled with milk and Soma. Many similar passages have been collected by Bergaigne, I, 177, but again without a definite result. The question is whether the three words utsa, kavandha, and udrin are meant as names of the three pâtras, in our passage, of the three lakes, or whether they should be taken as an apposition, the three lakes, namely, the well (of the sky), the skin full of water, and udrin, the watering-pot. Udrin is elsewhere an adjective only, but I think we must here translate, 'the well, the water-skin, the watering-pot.'

Verse 12.

Note 1. On sudânava*h* as vocative, see Delbrück, Syntax, p. 106.

Verse 14.

Note 1. For adhi with genitive, one expects ati. But Delbrück doubts whether ati can govern the genitive. See Altind. Syntax, p. 440.

Verse 15.

Note 1. As ádâbhyasya can only refer to etấvata*h*, I have taken etâvat in the sense of ga*n*a, followed by eshâm. But I am not certain that the rendering is right.

Verse 16.

Note 1. I have ventured to translate drapsâ*h* by torrents. Neither drops nor sparks nor banners seem to yield an appropriate simile, but I feel very doubtful. See VIII, 96, 13; IX, 73, 1.

Verse 22.

Note 1. I thought at first that by sám parva*s*á*h* dadhu*h* was meant the mixing or confounding together of heaven and earth; it being impossible, during a storm, to distinguish the two. But there is clearly, as Ludwig points out, an opposition between sám dadhu*h* and ví yayu*h*. I therefore take parva*s*á*h* in verse 22 in the sense of piece by piece, as in AV. IV, 12, 7. sám dadhat párushâ páru*h*, while in verse 23 it means in pieces.

Verse 25.

Note 1. On *s*iprâ*h*, see note to II, 34, 3.

Verse 26.

Note 1. Uksh*n*á*h* rándhram, 'the hollow of the bull,' whatever that may be, is not mentioned again. If it is meant for the dark cloud which hides the rain, then the roar of the bull would be the thunder of the cloud, stirred by the Maruts. Aukshnorandhra, however, is the technical name of certain Sâmans, so that Ukshnorandhra may have been, like Usanâ (later Usanas), a proper name. See Tândya Br. XIII, 9, 18; 19.

Note 2. If usánâ stands for usanayâ it might mean, 'with desire,' but it seems more likely that it refers to the *Ri*shi, who is called Usanâ in the Rig-veda, and Usanas in later writings. See Lanman, p. 562, l. 21; Bergaigne, II, 338, n. 3; Schmidt, K. Z. XXVI, 402, n. 1.

Verse 27.

Note 1. On makhásya dâváne, see note to I, 6, 8, where I accepted the old explanation, 'Come to the offering of the priest.' But does makha mean priest? In later Sanskrit it means sacrifice, so that makhásya dâváne has been translated, 'for the offering of the sacrifice,' that is, 'that we may be able to offer you sacrifice.' If makha means glad and refers to Soma, which is doubtful, the sense would be the same. Possibly dâváne may here be derived from do, to divide, but this would not help us much.

Verse 28.

The AV. reads yám tvâ p*ri*shatî ráthe prásh*t*ir váhati rohita, subhấ yâsi ri*n*ánn apá*h*, which yields no help.

Verse 29.

This verse is very difficult. First of all, ní*k*akrayâ can hardly mean 'without a chariot' (B.-R.), but seems an adverb, meaning downwards. But the chief difficulty lies in this, that we must decide, once for all, whether words, such as sushoma, sarya*n*âvat, âr*g*îka, pastyâvat, &c., are to be interpreted in their natural sense, as expressing localities, well known to the poet, or in their technical sense, as names of sacrificial vessels. That this decision is by no means easy, may be inferred from the fact that two scholars, Roth and Ludwig, differ completely, the former preferring the technical, the latter the geographical meaning. We must remember that in the hymns to the Maruts the poets speak occasionally of the countries, far and near, visited by the storm-winds. We must also bear in mind that in our very passage the poet asks the Maruts to come to him, and not to tarry with other people. When, therefore, he says, that they went to *S*arya*n*âvat, &c., is that likely to be meant for a tank of Soma at his own or any other sacrifice?

*S*arya*n*âvat is derived from *s*arya, this from *s*ara. *S*ara means reed, arrow; *s*arya, made of reeds, *s*aryâ, an arrow, but also reeds tied together and used at the sacrifice for carrying Soma-oblations. From it, *s*arya*n*a, which, according to Sâya*n*a, means lands in Kurukshetra (RV. VIII, 6, 39), and from which *S*arya*n*âvat is derived, as the name of a lake in that neighbourhood (not a Landstrich, B.-R.). When this *s*arya*n*âvat occurs in the Rig-veda, the question is, does it mean that lake, evidently a famous lake and a holy place in the early settlements of the Vedic Âryas, or does it mean, as others suppose, a sacrificial vessel made of reeds? It occurs in the Rig-veda seven times.

In I, 84, 14, Indra is said to have found the head of the horse, which had been removed among the mountains (clouds) at *S*arya*n*âvat. This seems to me the lake in which the sun sets. In the 8th Ma*nd*ala *s*arya*n*âvat occurs three times. In VIII, 6, 39, Indra is invoked to rejoice at *S*arya*n*âvat, or, according to others, in a vessel full of Soma. In our passage the Maruts went to *S*arya*n*âvat, to Sushoma, Âr*g*îka, and Pastyâvat, countries, it would seem, not vessels. In VIII, 64, 11, after saying that the Soma had been prepared among the Pûrus, it is added that the Soma is sweetest in *S*arya*n*âvat, on the Sushomâ, and in Âr*g*îkîya. In IX, 65, 22, we read of Somas prepared far and near, and at *S*arya*n*âvat, and in the next verse we read of Somas to be found either among the Âr*g*îkas, among the Pastyâs, or among the Five Tribes. In IX, 113, 1; 2, Indra is asked to drink Soma at *S*arya*n*âvat, and the Soma is asked to come from Âr*g*îka. In X, 35, 2, the aid is implored of heaven and earth, of the rivers and the mountains, and these mountains are called *s*arya*n*âvata*h*.

Ârgîkîyâ, besides the three passages mentioned already, occurs X, 75, 5, where it is clearly a river as well as Sushomâ, while in IX, 65, 23, the Ârgikas, in the plural, could only be the name of a people.

Taking all this into account, it seems to me that we ought to accept the tradition that *S*arya*n*âvat was a lake and the adjoining district in Kurukshetra, that Ârgîkâ was the name of a river, Ârgîka the name of the adjoining country, Ârgîkâ*h*, of the inhabitants, Ârgîkîyâ another name of Ârgîkâ, the river, and Ârgîkîyam another name of the country Ârgîka. Sushoma in our passage is probably the name of the country near the Sushomâ, and Pastyâvat, though it might be an adjective meaning filled with hamlets, is probably another geographical name; see, however, IX, 65, 23. Ludwig takes *S*arya*n*âvat as a name of the Eastern Sarasvatî; see Zimmer, Altindisches Leben, p. 19; but we should expect *S*arya*n*âvatî as the name of a river. See also Bergaigne, I, 206, who, according to his system, takes all these names as 'préparateurs célestes du Soma.'

Verse 31.

See I, 38, 1, note 1.

Verse 36.

Note 1. Sâya*n*a may be right in stating that this verse was intended for an Âgnimâruta sacrifice, and that therefore Agni was praised first, and afterwards the Maruts. In that case pûrvya might mean first.

Note 2. *Kh*andas is doubtful; see, however, I, 92, 6.

MAN*D*ALA VIII, HYMN 20.

ASH*T*AKA VI, ADHYÂYA 1, VARGA 36-40.

To the Maruts (the Storm-gods).

1. Come hither, do not fail, when you march forward! Do not stay away, O united friends, you who can bend even what is firm.

2. O Maruts, *Ri*bhukshans, come hither on your flaming strong fellies [1], O Rudras, come to us to-day with food, you much-desired ones, come to the sacrifice, you friends of the Sobharis [2].

3. For we know indeed the terrible strength of the sons of Rudra, of the vigorous Maruts, the liberal givers [1] of Soma [2] (rain).

4. The islands (clouds) were scattered, but the monster remained [1], heaven and earth were joined together. O you who are armed with bright rings, the tracts (of the sky) [2] expanded, whenever you stir, radiant with your own splendour.

5. Even things that cannot be thrown down resound at your race, the mountains, the lord of the forest,—the earth quivers on your marches.

6. The upper sky makes wide room, to let your violence pass, O Maruts, when these strong-armed heroes display their energies in their own bodies.

7. According to their wont these men, exceeding terrible, impetuous, with strong and unbending forms [1], bring with them beautiful light [2].

8. The arrow of the Sobharis is shot from the bowstrings at the golden chest on the chariot of the Maruts [1]. They, the kindred of the cow (P*ri*sni),

the well-born, should enjoy their food, the great ones should help us.

9. Bring forward, O strongly-anointed[1] (priests), your libations to the strong host of the Maruts, the strongly advancing.

10. O Maruts, O heroes, come quickly hither, like winged hawks, on your chariot with strong horses, of strong shape, with strong naves, to enjoy our libations.

11. Their anointing is the same, the golden chains shine on their arms, their spears sparkle.

12. These strong, manly, strong-armed Maruts, do not strive among themselves; firm are the bows, the weapons on your chariot, and on your faces are splendours.

13. They whose terrible name[1], wide-spreading like the ocean, is the one of all that is of use, whose strength is like the vigour of their father,

14. Worship these Maruts, and praise them! Of these shouters, as of moving spokes[1], no one is the last; this is theirs by gift, by greatness[2] is it theirs.

15. Happy is he who was under your protection, O Maruts, in former mornings, or who may be so even now.

16. Or he, O men, whose libations you went to enjoy; that mighty one, O shakers, will obtain your favours with brilliant riches and booty.

17. As the sons of Rudra, the servants of the divine Dyu[1], will it, O youths, so shall it be.

18. Whatever liberal givers may worship[1] the Maruts, and move about together as generous[2] benefactors, even from them turn[3] towards us with a kinder heart, you youths!

19. O Sobhari, call loud with your newest song

the young, strong, and pure Maruts, as the plougher calls the cows.

20. Worship the Maruts with a song, they who are strong like a boxer, called in to assist those who call[1] for him in all fights; (worship them) the most glorious, like bright-shining bulls.

21. Yes, O united friends, kindred, O Maruts, by a common birth, the oxen lick one another's humps[1].

22. O ye dancers, with golden ornaments on your chests, even a mortal comes (to ask) for your brotherhood[1]; take care of us, ye Maruts, for your friendship lasts for ever.

23. O bounteous Maruts, bring us some of your Marut-medicine, you friends, and (quick, like) steeds.

24. With the favours whereby you favour the Sindhu, whereby you save, whereby you help Krivi[1], with those propitious favours be our delight, O delightful ones, ye who never hate your followers[2].

25. O Maruts, for whom we have prepared good altars, whatever medicine[1] there is on the Sindhu, on the Asiknî, in the seas, on the mountains,

26. Seeing it, you carry it all on your bodies. Bless us with it! Down to the earth, O Maruts[1], with what hurts our sick one,—straighten what is crooked!

NOTES.

Ascribed to Sobhari Kâ*n*va ; metre, Kâkubha pragâtha. Verse 1 = SV. I, 401 ; verse 21 = SV. I, 404.

Verse 1.

SV. reads sthâta, and d*ridh*â *k*id yamayish*n*ava*h*.

Verse 2.

Note 1. It might be better to supply rathai*h*, but the poet may have used pars pro toto.

Note 2. The Sobharis, who are mentioned in the 8th Ma*nd*ala only, are clearly a clan of that name, and their hymns form a small collection by itself. See Oldenberg, Prolegomena, p. 209 seq.

Verse 3.

Note 1. Mi*l*hvas is sometimes used by itself in the sense of patron or benefactor, VII, 86, 7 ; 97, 2. Whether it can govern a genitive is doubtful, but see VII, 58, 5, note.

Note 2. Here again, as in II, 34, 11, Vish*n*u esha seems to mean Soma, possibly the food, or even the seed (retas) of Vish*n*u. Sâya*n*a too takes Vish*n*u as a name of rain. In I, 154, 5, we read that the spring of madhu is in the highest place of Vish*n*u. Could it mean the generous sons of Vish*n*u?

Verse 4.

Note 1. My translation is purely conjectural. I take dvîpa for isolated or scattered clouds, different from the du*kkh*unâ, which I take for the black mass of storm-clouds, threatening destruction. Grassmann: 'Die Wolkeninseln stoben und das Unheil floh.' Ludwig: 'Empor stigen gewaltig die waszerinseln, still stand das unglück.'

Note 2. The coming together of heaven and earth and their apparent widening have been ascribed to the Maruts before. It seems hardly possible to translate dhanvâni here by bows. I take it for the wide expanse, as if the desert, of the sky.

Verse 7.

Note 1. On psu in v*ri*shapsu, see note to VIII, 7, 7.

Note 2. Possibly *s*ríyam váhante has to be taken like *s*ubham yâ, see Gaedicke, Accusativ, p. 163.

Verse 8.

Note 1. In support of the translation which I proposed in I, 85, 10, note 2, all I can say is that a*g* is a verb used for shooting forth an arrow, see I, 112, 16, and that vâ*n*a may be used in the sense of bâ*n*a, reed and arrow, and that go is used for bowstring, see B.-R. s. v. The question, however, arises, how does this verse come in here? How does the fact that the Sobharis, who are praising the storm-gods, shoot their arrow at the golden chest on their chariot, agree with what precedes and follows?

Let us look first whether a more natural translation can be found. B.-R. translate: 'The sacrificial music of the Sobharis is furnished and therefore made more attractive by draughts of milk (or animal food).' In order to support such a translation, it should be proved, first, that vâ*n*a ever means sacrificial music, and that such sacrificial music can be spoken of as a*g*yate (it is furnished), gobhi*h* (by milk-draughts). Grassmann translates: 'Durch Milchtrank wird der Sobharis Musik belohnt.' Here again it must be proved that vâ*n*a can mean sacrificial music, and a*g*yate, it is rewarded. Ludwig translates: 'Mit der milch wird gesalbt den Sobhari der zapfen am wagen am goldnen korbe.' This is explained to mean that 'the bolt on the chariot of the Maruts is to be greased with milk, so that the milk may stream down on the Sobharis.' I doubt whether vâ*n*a can mean bolt, and I do not see that the intention of the poet, namely to ask for rain, would be conveyed by such words.

Sâya*n*a interprets: 'Through the cows, i. e. the hymns, of the Sobharis the lyre of the Maruts is made evident;' or, 'by the cows, i. e. the Maruts, the lyre is manifested for the sake of the Sobharis.'

In support of my own translation I can only appeal to a

custom ascribed by Herodotus (IV, 94) to another ancient Aryan tribe, namely the Thracians, who, when there is thunder and lightning, shoot arrows against the sky. Herodotus in trying to find a motive for this says they do it to threaten the god. because they believe in no other god but their own. This may be so; the only question is whether in shooting their arrows against the sky, they hoped to drive the clouds away, or wished them to give up their treasure, namely the rain. I should feel inclined to take the latter view, but in either case we see that what the Thracians did, was exactly what the Sobharis are said to do here, namely to shoot an arrow at the golden chest or treasure on the chariot of the Maruts. This is, of course. no more than a conjecture, and I shall gladly give it up, if a more appropriate meaning can be elicited from this line. What is against it is the frequent occurrence of a*ñg* with gobhi*h* in the sense of covering with milk, see IX, 45, 3; V, 3, 2, &c. As to ráthe kó*s*e hira*n*yáye, see VIII, 22, 9.

Verse 9.

Note 1. V*ri*shad-a*ñg*aya*h* for v*ri*sha*n*-a*ñg*aya*h*, see J Schmidt, K. Z. XXVI, 358. It cannot mean 'raining down ointments,' as Grassmann supposes, because that would be varshad-a*ñg*aya*h*, if it existed at all. Besides. the a*ñg*is are never poured down, nor are they sacrificial viands. The repetition of the word v*ri*shan is intentional. and has been discussed before.

Verse 13.

Note 1. Nâman is, of course, more than the mere name; but name can be used in much the same sense.

Verse 14.

Note 1. The simile of the aras, as in V, 58, 5, seems to require another negative.

Note 2. See V, 87, 2, on dânấ and mahnấ.

Verse 17.

Note 1. On divá*h* ásurasya vedhása*h*, see von Bradke. Dyaus Asura, pp. 44 and 46. It should be remembered.

however, that vedhas and medhas interchange. Thus in RV. IX, 102, 4, we have vedhā́m, in SV. I, 101, medhā́m. On medhâs, the Zend mazdâ, see Darmesteter, Ormazd, p. 29. I take servant in the sense of worshipper, from vidh.

Verse 18.

Note 1. Arhanti, in the sense of arhayanti, to worship, seems better than to be worthy of, or to have a right to.

Note 2. Mî*lh*úsha*h* can be nominative, see Lanman, p. 511; but it may also refer to the Maruts, and then be accusative.

Note 3. Instead of ā́ vav*ri*dhvam, which Ludwig translates, Nemt uns für euch in besitz, Grassmann translates, Wendet euch zu uns her. He read therefore ā́ vav*ri*ddhvam, and this, the plural corresponding to ā́ vav*ri*tsva, seems to be the right reading.

Verse 20.

Note 1. Grassmann proposes to change p*ri*tsú hót*ri*shu into yutsú p*ri*tsúshu. But may not hót*ri*shu be used here in a sense corresponding to that of hávya? Hávya has almost the technical meaning of an ally who is to be called for assistance. Thus IV, 24, 2. sá*h* v*ri*trahátye hávya*h*; VII, 32, 24. bháre-bhare *k*a hávya*h*, &c. Now a hávya*h*, one who is called, presupposes a hót*ri*, one who calls for assistance. It is true that hot*ri*, from hu, to pour out, has so completely become a technical name that it seems strange to see it used here, in a new etymological sense, as caller. But the connection with havya may justify what may have been meant as a play on the words. Wilson seems to have taken the verse in a similar sense, when he translates: 'and like a boxer who has been challenged over his challengers.' He, like Ludwig, takes hot*ri* as a challenger. I prefer to take it as calling for aid. I am not satisfied, however, with either translation, nor does Grassmann or Ludwig offer anything useful.

Verse 21.

Note 1. In the SV. marúta*h* and riháte have the accent

on the second syllable. Sábandhava*h* was used before of the Maruts, V, 59, 5; according to its accent it would here refer to gấva*h*. I can see no meaning in this verse except a very naturalistic one, namely that the Maruts, who are described as friends and brothers, as never quarrelling and always of one mind, are here compared to oxen, grazing in the same field, and so far from fighting, actually licking the humps on each other's backs.

Verse 22.

Note 1. Grassmann, 'geht euch an um eure Brüderschaft;' possibly, 'becomes your brother.'

Verse 24.

Note 1. It is, no doubt, very tempting to change tűrvatha into turvá*s*am, as Ludwig proposes. The difficulty is to understand how such a change should have come about. Sindhu may mean here, not so much the river, as the people living on its shores. Krivi is said to be an old name of the Pa*ñk*âlas (*S*at. Br. XIII, 5, 4, 7). But, because the Pa*ñk*âlas were called Krivis, and because in later times we often hear of Kuru-Pa*ñk*âlas, it does in no way follow that the Krivis were identical with the Kurus. It proves rather the contrary. Kuru may be derived from kar, and may have meant active, but it may also have had a very different original meaning. A derivation of krivi from kar is still more objectionable.

Note 2. Asa*k*advisha*h*, which I translate by not hating your followers, is translated by Ludwig: 'ihr, denen kein haszer folgt.' It may also be rendered by 'hating those who do not follow you.'

Verse 25.

Note 1. The medicines are generally brought by Rudra, and by his sons, the Maruts.

Verse 26.

Note 1. As to kshamấ rápa*h*, see X, 59, 8–10; AV VI, 57, 3; as to íshkarta, VIII, 1, 12.

MANDALA VIII, HYMN 94.

ASHTAKA VI, ADHYÂYA 6, VARGA 28-29.

To the Maruts (the Storm-gods).

1. The cow, wishing for glory, the mother of the bounteous Maruts, sends forth her milk; the two horses [1] have been harnessed to the chariots,—

2. She in whose lap [1] all gods observe their duties, sun and moon (also), that they may be seen;

3. Therefore all our friends [1], the singers, invite the Maruts always, to drink (our) Soma.

4. This Soma here has been prepared, the Maruts drink of it, the Asvins also drink of the lord (Soma) [1].

5. Mitra, Aryaman, Varuna drink of the Soma which is continually [1] clarified, dwelling in three abodes [2], procuring offspring.

6. May Indra also rejoice to his satisfaction in this pressed juice, mixed with milk, like a Hotri [1] at the morning-sacrifice.

7. Did the brilliant lords flare up? Endowed with pure strength they rush, like water, through their enemies.

8. Shall I now choose the favour of you, the great gods, who by yourselves shine forth marvellously,

9. The Maruts, who, when going to drink Soma, spread out the whole earth and the lights of heaven.

10. I call now them who are endowed with pure strength, you, O Maruts, from heaven, that you may drink the Soma here;

11. I call now those Maruts who hold heaven and earth asunder, that they may drink the Soma here;

12. I call now that manly company of the Maruts, dwelling in the mountains, that they may drink the Soma here.

NOTES.

Ascribed to Bindu or Pûtadaksha. Metre, Gâyatrî. Verse 1=SV. I, 149; verse 4=SV. I, 174; II, 1135; verse 5=SV. II, 1136; verse 6=SV. II, 1137. The whole hymn can easily be divided into t*rik*as.

Verse 1.

Note 1. I adopt Ludwig's correction of the Pada, changing váhni*h* to váhnî iti, though it interrupts somewhat the connection between the first and second verses. Still it seems as impossible to change P*ris*ni, the mother of the Maruts, into a cart-horse as into a sucking-calf. This we should have to do, if we took dhayati in its usual sense of sucking. Still dhayati means to suck, not to suckle. The commentary to the SV. explains vahni*h* as vo*dh*ri, the driver.

Verse 2.

Note 1. I should prefer to take upásthe in the sense of proximity, which, as in the case of v*ri*kshopasthe, may be translated by shadow, or protection.

Verse 3.

Note 1. I cannot believe that we can take aryá ấ in our passage as aryé ấ, and translate it with Pischel (Z.D.M.G. XL, p. 125) by 'our singers among the Aryas.' With the plural kâráva*h* we should expect aryéshu ấ, not aryé ấ: see also Bergaigne, III, 287; II, 218. Pâda a and b are galita, see VI, 45, 33.

Verse 4.

Note 1. Svarâ*g* seems to be meant for Soma as lord, not as brilliant.

Verse 5.

Note 1. Tánâ is generally explained by ûr*n*âstukanirmita da*s*âpavitra; see also Bergaigne, I, 179.

Note 2. The three abodes are either the morning, noon,

and evening sacrifices, or the three Soma-vessels, the D*ro*n*akalas*a, Âdhavanîya, and Pûtabh*ri*t.

Verse 6.

Note 1. I do not see why hótâ-iva should not mean 'like the priest,' for the priest also rejoices in the libation; see Arthasa*m*graha, ed. Thibaut, pp. 10 and 20. Ludwig prefers to take hótâ for Agni, fire.

Verse 9.

Note 1. See note to I, 6, 9, and 10, note 1.

MAṆḌALA X, HYMN 77.

ASHṬAKA VIII, ADHYÂYA 3, VARGA 10-11.

To the Maruts (the Storm-gods).

1. Let me with my voice shower[1] wealth like cloud-showers[2], like sacrifices of a sage, rich in oblations. I have praised the goodly host of the Maruts[3], so that they may be worthy of a Brahman[4] so that they may be glorious.

2. These boys have prepared their ornaments for beauty, the goodly host of the Maruts, through many nights; the sons of Dyu struggled, like harts, they, the Âdityas, grew high, like banners[1].

3. They who by their own might seem to have risen above heaven and earth, like the sun above the cloud, they are glorious, like brilliant heroes, they shine forth like foe-destroying youths.

4. When you move along on the bottom of the waters, the earth seems to break and to melt[1]. This perfect sacrifice is meet for you, come hither together, as if enjoying our offerings.

5. You are as drivers[1] on the poles with their reins, and as brilliant with light at daybreak; like hawks, you are famous destroyers of foes; like wells[2] springing forth, you scatter moisture.

6. When you, O Maruts, come from afar, knowing the great treasure of the hidden place, O Vasus, the treasure which has to be gained, then keep away also from afar all who hate us.

7. The man who, firm in his sacrifice, offers gifts to the Maruts to the end of the ceremony[1], he

gains health and wealth, blessed with offspring; he shall also be in the keeping of the gods.

8. They are indeed our guardians, to be worshipped at all sacrifices, most blissful by their name of Âdityas; may they, swiftly driving on their chariots, protect our prayer, quick even on their march, delighting in our sacrifice.

NOTES.

Ascribed to Syûmarasmi Bhârgava. On the metre, see Rig-veda, translation, Introd. p. civ; Benfey, Quantitätsversch. IV, 2; 38–39; Oldenberg, Prolegomena, 92. This hymn and the next belong closely together. They are both so artificial and obscure that a translation of them can only be tentative. None of its verses occurs in SV., VS., AV., TS., TB., MS.

Verse 1.

Note 1. I take prushâ for prushâ*n*i.

Note 2. I do not think that abhraprúsha*h* can be meant for the Maruts.

Note 3. The ná in many of the verses seems to be due to a mere trick, and untranslatable.

Note 4. Or, 'I have praised the priestly host, so that they may be worthy of good Marut-hood.'

Verse 2.

Note 1. Akrấ*h*, banners, Grassmann; columns, Ludwig. The meaning is utterly unknown.

Verse 4.

Note 1. See Aurel Mayr, Beiträge aus dem Rig-Veda p. 12. 'The earth melted,' see Ps. xlvi. 6.

Verse 5.

Note 1. Prayu*g* seems to mean here a driver; pra-yu*g* is often used of the Maruts as harnessing or driving their horses; see I, 85, 5; V, 52, 8.

Note 2. Prava has been derived from pru, to float. I should prefer to derive it from pra-van, from which we have pra-va*n*a, precipice, possibly the Latin adjective pronus, and, very irregularly, Greek πρηνής. Stems in radical n frequently enter the class of stems in â and a, and pravan would become pravâ*h* or prava*h*, as -*g*an becomes -*g*â*h* and -*g*a*h*; cf. Lanman,

p. 478. Others take vana for a mere suffix like vat. Prava, rushing forward, would have been a good name for a spring. This, of course, is a mere conjecture. Others derive pravâ-s from vâ, to blow. As a substantive pravâ as well as upavâ occurs AV. XII, 1, 51. vấtasya pravấm upavấm ánu vâty ar*k*i*h*. But these words mean the blowing before and the blowing after, and not blowers. There are the verbs pravâ and anuvâ in Tâ*nd*ya Br. I, 9, 7; TS. III, 5, 2, 3; IV, 4, 1, 1. They are there referred to dawn and night. These passages, however, seem too technical to allow us to fix the original meaning of prava-*h*. Pravâ in RV. I, 34, 8, remains unexplained.

Verse 7.

Note 1. On ud*r*i*h*i, see Ludwig's note.

MA*ND*ALA X, HYMN 78.

ASH*T*AKA VIII, ADHYÂYA 3, VARGA 12-13.

TO THE MARUTS (THE STORM-GODS).

1. Full of devotion like priests with their prayers, wealthy like pious men, who please the gods with their offerings, beautiful to behold like brilliant kings, without a blemish like the youths of our hamlets—

2. They who are gold-breasted like Agni with his splendour, quick to help like self-harnessed winds, good leaders like the oldest experts, they are to the righteous man like Somas, that yield the best protection.

3. They who are roaring and hasting like winds, brilliant like the tongues of fires, powerful like mailed soldiers, full of blessings like the prayers of our fathers,

4. Who hold together like the spokes of chariot-wheels, who glance forward like victorious heroes, who scatter gh*ri*ta[1] like wooing youths, who chant beautifully like singers, intoning a hymn of praise,

5. Who are swift like the best of horses, who are bounteous like lords of chariots on a suit, who are hastening on like water with downward floods, who are like the manifold[1] Aṅgiras with their (numerous) songs.

6. These noble sons of Sindhu[1] are like grinding-stones, they are always like Soma-stones[2], tearing everything to pieces; these sons of a good mother are like playful children, they are by their glare like a great troop on its march.

7. Illumining the sacrifice[1] like the rays of the dawn, they shone forth in their ornaments like triumphant warriors; the Maruts with bright spears seem like running rivers, from afar they measure many miles.

8. O gods, make us happy and rich, prospering us, your praisers, O Maruts! Remember our praise and our friendship, for from of old there are always with you gifts of treasures.

NOTES.

Ascribed to Syûmara*s*mi Bhârgava. None of its verses occurs elsewhere. Metre, 1, 3, 4, 8 Trish*t*ubh; 2, 5–7 *G*agatî.

Verse 4.

Note 1. Gh*ri*taprush, Fett sprühend, Gluth austheilend, according to Grassmann; gh*ri*ta-sprühend, according to Ludwig. Sâya*n*a takes vareyáva*h* as wishing to give presents, and explains that such gifts were preceded by a gift of water, so that gh*ri*taprúsha*h* would mean, giving water or rain. The real meaning is difficult.

Verse 5.

Note 1. Vi*s*varûpa may have been meant in a more special and mythological sense.

Verse 6.

Note 1. Síndhu-mâtara*h* may be a synonym of P*ris*ni-mâtara*h*, sindhu being used as a name of the water in the sky. It may also mean, having the river Sindhu for their mother, i. e. coming from the region of the river. Bergaigne translates (II, 397), 'qui ont pour mère la rivière céleste. Cette rivière peut être une des formes de la vache qui passe aussi pour leur mère.'

Note 2. The grâvâ*n*a*h* and ádraya*h* are probably meant for stones used for pounding corn and squeezing Soma.

Verse 7.

Note 1. On adhvara*s*rî, see Pischel, Ved. Stud. p. 53.

MAN*D*ALA I, HYMN 43.

ASHT*A*KA I, ADHYÂYA 3, VARGA 26–27.

To Rudra.

1. What could we say to Rudra, the wise, the most liberal, the most powerful, that is most welcome to his heart,—

2. So that Aditi[1] may bring Rudra's healing to the cattle, to men, to cow, and kith,

3. So that Mitra, that Varu*n*a, that Rudra hear us, and all the united Maruts[1].

4. We implore Rudra, the lord of songs, the lord of animal sacrifices[1], the possessor of healing medicines[2], for health, wealth[3], and his favour.

5. He who shines like the bright sun, and like gold, who is the best Vasu among the gods,

6. May he bring health to our horse, welfare to ram and ewe, to men, to women, and to the cow!

7. Bestow on us, O Soma, the happiness of a hundred men, great glory of strong manhood[1];

8. O Soma[1], let not those who harass and injure overthrow us; O Indu, help us to booty!

9. Whatever beings are thine, the immortal, in the highest place of the law, on its summit[1], in its centre, O Soma, cherish them, remember them who honour thee.

NOTES.

Ascribed to Ka*n*va Ghaura, and addressed to Rudra (1, 2, 4–6), to Rudra and Mitrâ-Varu*n*au (3), and to Soma (7–9). Metre, Gâyatrî (1–8); Anush*t*ubh (9). Verse 2 in TS. III, 4, 11, 2; MS. IV, 12, 6.

The hymn may be divided into two, the first from 1–6, the second from 7–9. See, however, Bergaigne, III, 32, n. 1; and Recherches sur l'hist. de la Sa*m*hitâ, I, 65. He would prefer to divide the whole into three hymns.

Verse 1.

See TÂ. X, 17, 1; Delbrück, Synt. Forsch. I, 246.

Verse 2.

Note 1. Ludwig takes Aditi here as a name of Rudra; also Hillebrandt, Über die Göttin Aditi, p. 6.

Verse 3.

Note 1. The vísve sa*g*óshasa*h*, following on Rudra, can hardly be meant for any but the Maruts, who are often called sa*g*óshasa*h*. But it may also have been intended for all the gods together.

Verse 4.

Note 1. Gâthápatim and medhápatim are both difficult. We expect gâthắpatim and medhắpatim. If, as Ludwig maintains, gâtha in Zend is equivalent to *ri*tu, season, then gâthapati might be *ri*tupati, a name of Agni, X, 2, 1. But this is extremely doubtful. We must derive gâthápati from gâthă, I, 167, 6, and medhápati from medhă, animal sacrifice, till we know more on the subject.

Note 2. *G*álâsha-bheshagam, an epithet of Rudra; see VIII, 29, 5, where Rudra is intended. In II, 33, 7, the arm of Rudra is called bhesha*g*á*h* *g*álâsha*h*; in VII, 35, 6, Rudra himself is called *g*álâsha*h*. *G*álâsha seems connected with *g*ala, water. Bergaigne, III, 32, translates it by adoucissant.

Note 3. On sa*m*yó*h*, see note 2 to I, 165, 4.

Verse 7.

Note 1. Tuvi-n*ri*m*n*a would seem more appropriate as a vocative. In verse 8, too, I should prefer to take Soma as a vocative, like Benfey and Grassmann.

Verse 8.

Note 1. I read Soma, paribấdha*h*. See Delbrück, Synt. Forsch. p. 116.

Verse 9.

Note 1. Unless we can take mûrdhấ for a locative, attracted by nấbhâ, I should propose to read mûrdhán nấbhâ. It can hardly be an adverbial Dvandva, mûrdhâ-nâbhâ, nor do I see how it can be applied as a nominative to Rudra. The whole verse is difficult, possibly a later addition. On *ri*tásya am*ri*tasya dhấman, see IX, 97, 32; 110, 4 (dhárman).

MANDALA I, HYMN 114.

ASHTAKA I, ADHYÂYA 8, VARGA 5-6.

To Rudra.

1. We offer these prayers[1] to Rudra, the strong, whose hair is braided[2], who rules over heroes[3], that he may be a blessing to man and beast, that everything in this our village may be prosperous and free from disease.

2. Be gracious to us, O Rudra, and give us joy, and we shall honour thee, the ruler of heroes, with worship. What health and wealth father Manu acquired by his sacrifices, may we obtain the same, O Rudra, under thy guidance.

3. O bounteous Rudra, may we by sacrifice obtain the goodwill of thee, the ruler of heroes; come to our clans, well-disposed, and, with unharmed men, we shall offer our libation to thee.

4. We call down for our help the fierce Rudra, who fulfils our sacrifice, the swift, the wise; may he drive far away from us the anger of the gods; we desire his goodwill only.

5. We call down with worship the red boar of the sky, the god with braided hair, the blazing form; may he who carries in his hand the best medicines grant us protection, shield, and shelter!

6. This speech is spoken for the father of the Maruts, sweeter than sweet, a joy[1] to Rudra; grant to us also, O immortal, the food of mortals, be gracious to us and to our kith and kin!

7. Do not slay our great or our small ones, our

growing or our grown ones, our father or our mother and do not hurt our own[1] bodies, O Rudra!

8. O Rudra, hurt us not in our kith and kin, nor in our own life, not in our cows, nor in our horses! Do not slay our men in thy wrath: carrying libations, we call on thee always.

9. Like a shepherd[1], I have driven these praises near to thee; O father of the Maruts, grant us thy favour! For thy goodwill is auspicious, and most gracious, hence we desire thy protection alone.

10. Let thy cow-slaying and thy man-slaying be far away[1], and let thy favour be with us, O ruler of heroes! Be gracious to us, and bless us, O god, and then give us twofold protection[2].

11. We have uttered our supplication to him, desiring his help; may Rudra with the Maruts hear our call. May Mitra, Varu*n*a, Aditi, the River, Earth, and the Sky grant us this!

NOTES.

Ascribed to Kutsa Âṅgirasa. Metre, 1–9 *G*agatî; 10, 11 Trish*t*ubh. Verse 1 = VS. XVI, 48; TS. IV, 5, 10, 1; MS. II, 9, 9 (yáthâ na*h* *s*ám); verse 2 = TS. IV, 5, 10, 2; verse 7 = VS. XVI, 15; TS. IV, 5, 10, 2; verse 8 = VS. XVI, 16; TS. III, 4, 11, 2; IV, 5, 10, 3; MS. IV, 12, 6 (ấyushi; havíshmanto námasâ vidhema te); verse 10 = TS. IV, 5, 10, 3.

Verse 1.

Note 1. TS. reads imấm matím, and yáthâ na*h* *s*ám.

Note 2. Kapardin is an epithet not only of Rudra, but also of Pûshan (VI, 55, 2; IX, 67, 11), and of a Vedic clan, the T*ri*tsus (VII, 83, 8) or Vasish*th*as; see Roth, Zur Literatur und Geschichte des Weda, pp. 94 seq.; Oldenberg, Z.D.M.G. XLII, p. 207. Kaparda is the name of a shell, and the hair twisted together in the form of a shell seems to have suggested the name of kapardin.

Note 3. Kshayád-vîra means 'ruling over heroes,' just as mandád-vîra (VIII, 69, 1) means 'delighting heroes.' This meaning is applicable to all passages where kshayád-vîra occurs, and there is no reason why we should translate it by 'destroyer of heroes,' which can hardly be considered as an epitheton ornans. No doubt, a god who rules and protects can also be conceived as punishing and destroying, and this is particularly the case with Rudra. Hence in certain passages Rudra may well be invoked as n*ri*hán (IV 3, 6), just as we read of the Maruts (VII, 56, 17): 'May that bolt of yours which kills cattle and men be far from us! Incline to us, O Vasu, with your favours!' See Muir, S.T. IV, p. 301, note.

Verse 2.

TS. reads âyag*é* and prá*n*îtau. See Ludwig, Notes, p. 265.

Verse 6.

Note 1. On the meaning of vardhana and v*ri*dh in Zend, see Darmesteter, Ormazd, pp. 41, 6; 92, 1.

Verse 7.

Note 1. TS. reads priyấ mấ nas tanúva*h* rudra rîrisha*h*. Priya, dear, used like *φίλος*, in the sense of our own. See Bergaigne, III, 152.

Verse 8.

See Colebrooke, Misc. Ess. I, p. 141 (ed. 1837); and *S*vetâ*s*vat. Up. in S. B. E. XV, p. 254, note. Ấyushi for âyaú is supported by VS. and TS. I propose to read ấyau for âyaú. Bhâmitá*h* is supported by TS. and *S*vet. Up., while VS. reads bhâmína*h*, which Mahîdhara refers to vîrấn. The last line is the same in RV. and VS., but the TS. reads havíshmanto námasâ vidhema te, while the *S*vet. Up. reads havishmanta*h* sadasi tvâ havâmahe.

Verse 9.

Note 1. As to the simile, see RV. X, 127, 8, and Muir S.T. IV, p. 304, note.

Verse 10.

Note 1. TS. reads ârất te, goghná (°é), purushaghné, kshayádvîrâya, rákshâ for m*r*i*l*ấ, deva brûhi.

Note 2. I take dvibárhâ*h*, which stands for dvibárha*h*, as an adjective to *s*árma, or possibly as an adverb, see Lanman, p. 560. It can hardly refer to Rudra, as Grassmann supposes. See J. Schmidt, Pluralbildungen der Neutra, pp. 132 seq.

MAN*D*ALA II, HYMN 33.

ASH*T*AKA II, ADHYÂYA 7, VARGA 16–18.

To Rudra, the Father of the Maruts (the Storm-gods).

1. O father of the Maruts, let thy favour come near, and do not deprive us of the sight of the sun; may the hero (Rudra) be gracious to our horse [1], and may we increase in offspring, O Rudra!

2. May I attain to a hundred winters through the most blissful medicines which thou hast given! Put away far [1] from us all hatred, put away anguish, put away sicknesses in all directions!

3. In beauty thou art the most beautiful of all that exists, O Rudra, the strongest of the strong, thou wielder of the thunderbolt! Carry us happily to the other shore of our anguish, and ward off all assaults of mischief [1].

4. Let us not incense thee, O Rudra, by our worship, not by bad praise, O hero, and not by divided praise! Raise up our men by thy medicines, for I hear thou art the best of all physicians.

5. He who is invoked [1] by invocations and libations, may I pay off [2] that Rudra with my hymns of praise. Let not him who is kind-hearted [3], who readily hears our call, the tawny, with beautiful cheeks, deliver us to this wrath!

6. The manly hero with the Maruts has gladdened me, the suppliant, with more vigorous health. May I without mischief find shade, as if from sunshine [1], may I gain the favour of Rudra!

7. O Rudra, where is thy softly stroking hand which cures and relieves[1]? Thou, the remover of all heaven-sent mischief, wilt thou, O strong hero, bear with me?

8. I send forth a great, great hymn of praise to the bright tawny bull. Let me reverence[1] the fiery god[2] with prostrations; we celebrate the flaring name[3] of Rudra.

9. He, the fierce god, with strong limbs, assuming many forms, the tawny Rudra, decked himself with brilliant golden ornaments. From Rudra, who is lord of this wide world, divine power[1] will never depart.

10. Worthily thou bearest arrows and bow, worthily, O worshipful[1], the golden, variegated chain; worthily thou cuttest every fiend[2] here to pieces, for there is nothing indeed stronger than thou, O Rudra.

11. Praise him, the famous, sitting in his chariot[1], the youthful, who is fierce and attacks like a terrible wild beast[2] (the lion). And when thou hast been praised, O Rudra, be gracious to him who magnifies thee, and let thy armies[3] mow down others than us!

12. O Rudra, a boy indeed makes obeisance to his father who comes to greet him[1]: I praise the lord of brave men, the giver of many gifts, and thou, when thou hast been praised, wilt give us thy medicines.

13. O Maruts, those pure medicines of yours, the most beneficent and delightful, O heroes, those which Manu[1], our father, chose, those I crave from Rudra, as health and wealth.

14. May the weapon of Rudra avoid us[1], may the great anger of the flaring one pass us by.

Unstring thy strong bows[2] for the sake of our liberal lords, O bounteous Rudra, be gracious to our kith and kin.

15. Thus, O tawny and manly god, showing thyself[1], so as neither to be angry nor to kill, be mindful of our invocations[2], and, rich in brave sons, we shall magnify thee in the congregation.

NOTES.

Ascribed to G*ri*tsamada. Metre, Trish*t*ubh. See Muir, S. T. IV, 309; Geldner and Kaegi, p. 90. Bergaigne, III, 153; Leop. v. Schroeder, Indiens Literatur und Cultur, 343. Verse 1=TB. II, 8, 6, 9; verse 2=TB. II, 8, 6, 8; verse 10=TÂ. IV, 5, 7; verse 11=TS. IV, 5, 10, 3; AV. XVIII, 1, 40; verse 14=VS. XVI, 50; TS. IV, 5, 10. 4; verse 15=TB. II, 8, 6, 9.

Verse 1.

Note 1. The words abhí na*h* vîrá*h* árvati kshameta admit of different interpretation. Grassmann has: 'Der Held sei huldreich unsren schnellen Rossen;' Muir: 'May the hero spare our horses;' Ludwig: 'Unser held möge tüchtig zu Rosse sein.' The passages quoted by Ludwig from the *S*at. Br. III, 7, 3, 1, and IV, 3, 4, 14, do not bear out the meaning of tüchtig sein, to be strong, they rather mean, to suffer, to submit to, with a dative. Yet vîrá*h* by itself may mean son or offspring (III, 4, 9; VII, 1, 21; 56, 24), and if abhi-ksham in our passage could mean to be capable and strong, Ludwig's translation would be justified. But if we take vîrá, hero, as intended for Rudra, as Indra also is often called simply vîra, abhi kshameta would lend itself to the translation of 'to be gracious,' or 'to spare,' and I therefore translate: 'May the hero (Rudra) be gracious to our horse.' It should be understood in the same sense in verse 7, at least I see no reason to vary the translation as Geldner does, and also Ludwig, while Muir is right and consistent. Our poet uses the verb abhiksham frequently, II, 28, 3; 29, 2 (abhikshantâra*h*?). It seems confined to the second Ma*nd*ala.

Verse 2.

Note 1. Vitarám, wherever it occurs, is always joined with ví in the Rig-veda.

Verse 3.

Note 1. If rápas is derived from rap, to whisper, it would have meant originally what is whispered, that is, slander, accusation, and then only crime. Latin crîmen also meant originally what is heard, Leumund. Crîmen is not connected with the Greek *κρίνω*. The î in crîmen has to be accounted for like the î in lîber, from lubh (libh). The r is irregular, unless we find an analogy in increpare.

Verse 5.

Note 1. Hávate, we expect hûyáte. Ludwig's explanation has not solved the difficulty, and suháva*h* points back to yo havate. Oldenberg suggests an anacoluthon, He who invokes—may I.

Note 2. I formerly took áva dishîya in the sense of 'to unloose,' used originally with reference to tethered horses. As horses are unloosed before they can do their work, so the gods are, as it were, unloosed by prayer, or set off, so that they may fulfil what they are asked to do; see RV. I, 25, 3. In the passage quoted by Ludwig from the TS. I, 8, 6, 2, the same meaning seemed quite appropriate: áva Rudrám adimahi—yáthâ na*h* *s*réyasa*h* kárat, 'We unloosed Rudra, that he might make us happier.' Ludwig takes it to mean, 'We have bound, tied, or obliged Rudra, so that he make us happy,' but the preposition ava is against this interpretation. Muir proposes 'to avert' or 'to propitiate,' the latter being adopted by Geldner.

However, in an article lately published by Roth on Wergeld in the Veda (Z.D.M.G. XLI, 672), ava-day has been recognised as an almost technical legal term, meaning 'to pay off, to compound.' Thus, Tâ*nd*ya Br. XVI, 1, 12, we read yâ*h* *s*ata*m* vaira*m* tad devân avadayate, 'He portions off, i.e. he satisfies, or pacifies, the gods who were offended, by giving a hundred cows.' With ni*h*, we find TB. I, 6, 10, 1. pra*g*ấ rudrấn nír áva dayate; the same occurs in Maitr. S. I, 10, 20, where we also read, *gri*heshv eva Rudram nir ava dayata esha te Rudra bhâgas. See also Ait. Br. II, 7, 1. There is a verse quoted, ávâmba Rudrám adimahi, in TS. I, 8, 6, 2;

and again in MS. I, 10, 4; Kâ*th*. IX, 7; Kap. S. VIII, 10; VS. III, 58, and this gives us the right key to our verse, namely, 'May I pay off, may I pacify, Rudra with my songs of praise,' dishîya being the optat. of the aorist, adimahi the aor. ind.

Note 3. On *ri*dûdára*h*, see Benfey, Quantitätsversch. V, 1; p. 25; Geldner, K.Z. XXVIII, 201; Ludwig, Süsses in seinem bauche habend; Bergaigne, miséricordieux. The meaning is doubtful.

Verse 6.

Note 1. Gh*rín*îva, divided into gh*rín*i-iva, is a difficult form. Various attempts have been made to explain it. Grassmann translates: 'Wie Schatten von der Gluth mög unversehrt ich des Rudra Huld erreichen,' preferring to write gh*rin*er va. Ludwig, in his notes: 'Bei hitze,' taking gh*rin*i as a locative. Muir: 'Shade in the heat.' Geldner: 'Vor Sonnengluth den Schatten,' taking gh*rin*i as an instrumental. Lanman (p. 379) takes the same view, though he admits that this would be the only example of an instrumental in the masculine, contracted to î. He translates: 'As by the heat unharmed, to shelter bring me.' He adds: 'It may be ablative with elision and crasis,' and this is likewise Roth's view. Weber thinks that we may retain gh*rin*îva in the Sa*m*hitâ text, but should divide it into gh*rin*î-iva, 'like a man suffering from heat' (Ind. Stud. XIII, p. 58). I think we must take into account a parallel passage, VI, 16, 38. úpa *kh*âyấm iva gh*ríneh* áganma *s*árma te vayám, see M.M., Preface to translation of Rig-veda, p. cxliii. Probably the apparent irregularity of the metre led to the change of gh*rín*er iva to gh*rín*îva, but gh*rín*er iva can be scanned ◡ – ◡; see M.M., l.c., p. cxlviii.

Verse 7.

Note 1. *G*álâsha by itself occurs but once more as an epithet of Rudra, VII, 35, 6, and twice in composition, *g*álâshabhesha*g*a; see I, 43, 4. The second pâda begins with hásta*h*.

Verse 8.

Note 1. Namasyá is difficult, but we can hardly take it for namasyâmasi, masi being supplied from g*rin*îmasi. Nor do we gain by taking namasyấ for an instrumental. Perhaps it is best to take it as a 1st pers. of the imperative.

Note 2. The meaning of kalmalîkin is unknown.

Note 3. I think it is best to translate nấma by name, though, no doubt, it implies more than the mere name. Geldner's 'majestätisch Wesen' is right, but it is only one side of nâma. See VIII, 20, 13, note 1.

Verse 9.

Note 1. On vai, see Delbrück, Syntax, p. 483. On asurya, see von Bradke, Dyaus Asura, pp. 29, 34.

Verse 10.

Note 1. I have changed ya*g*atám into ya*g*ata.

Note 2. Árhan idám dayase ví*s*vam ábhvam has been rendered in different ways. Grassmann: 'Du theilst alle diese Macht aus.' Ludwig: 'Du besitzest all dise gewalt.' Geldner: 'Du besitzest höchste Macht.' Muir: 'Thou possessest all this vast world.' Dayase is used, no doubt, in the sense of cutting and distributing, but never in the sense of possessing. In several places, however, it has been translated by to cut and to destroy, e.g. X, 80, 2. agní*h* v*ri*trấ*n*i dayate purû*n*i, 'Agni cuts up many enemies.' VI, 22, 9. ví*s*vâ*h* a*g*urya dayase ví mâyấ*h*, 'thou destroyest all deceits.' See also IV, 7, 10; VI, 6, 5. As to ábhva in the sense of fiend, we had it before in I, 39, 8. ấ yá*h* na*h* ábhva*h* ī́shate, ví tám yuyota. In other places it assumes a more neutral character, meaning monster, or monstrous power; see B.-R. s.v. 'To distribute power' is not a Vedic conception, nor does ábhva ever mean power in the sense of 'ungeheure Macht, or Urkraft' (Delbrück, Chrest. p. 49).

Verse 11.

Note 1. AV. XVIII, 1, 40, has gartasádam *g*ánânâm rấ*g*ânam, and anyám asmát te. Garta-sad, literally, sitting in the hole, probably the place of the chariot where the king sat, separated from the driver. These divided chariots can be seen in the ancient monuments of Assyria and Babylon. The king seems to stand in a box of his own, fighting, while the charioteer holds the reins, so as not to interfere with the king. See, however, Bergaigne, III, 122 seq.; Z. D. M. G. XL, 681.

Note 2. The m*ri*gá bhîmá is probably meant for the lion, cf. I, 154, 2, and Zimmer, Altindisches Leben, p. 78.

Note 3. As to the senâs of Rudra, see TS. IV, 5, 2, 1, senânî; AV. XI, 2, 31; Pâr. G*ri*hy. III, 8, 11.

Verse 12.

Note 1. The sense would be better if vándamânam could be changed to vándamâna*h*.

Verse 13.

Note 1. That father Manu obtained health and wealth from Rudra was mentioned before, I, 114, 2, and it is curious that the Vedic authority of Manu's Sm*ri*ti should be based on the well-known sentence, yat ki*m*k*a Manur abravît tad bheshagam, Taitt. Sa*m*h. II, 2, 10, 2; cf. M. M., Hist. of Anc. Sansk. Lit. p. 89.

Verse 14.

Note 1. The VS. reads pári no rudrásya hetír v*rin*aktu, pári tveshásya durmatír aghâyó*h*. V*rig*yâ*h* is the 3rd pers. sing. in s of the aor. opt.

Note 2. Rudra is called sthiradhanvan; see also IV, 4, 5; VIII, 19, 20; X, 116, 5; 6; 120, 4; 134, 2; Maitr. S. II, 9, 9.

Verse 15.

Note 1. *K*ekitâna, the vocative of the participle.

Note 2. Muir seems to translate bodhi, which Sâya*n*a explains by budhyasva, by 'think of us now.' The TB. reads havana*s*rû*h*.

MAN*D*ALA VI, HYMN 74.

ASH*T*AKA V, ADHYÂYA 1, VARGA 18.

TO SOMA AND RUDRA.

1. Soma and Rudra, may you maintain your divine dominion, and may the oblations reach you properly. Bringing the seven treasures to every house, be kind to our children and our cattle.

2. Soma and Rudra, draw far away in every direction [1] the disease [2] which has entered our house. Drive far away Nir*ri*ti [3], and may auspicious glories belong to us!

3. Soma and Rudra, bestow all these remedies on our bodies. Tear away and remove from us [1] whatever evil we have committed, which clings to our bodies.

4. Soma and Rudra, wielding sharp weapons and sharp bolts, kind friends, be gracious unto us here! Deliver us from the snare of Varu*n*a, and guard us, as kind-hearted gods!

NOTES.

Ascribed to Bhâradvâga Bârhaspatya. Verse 2 occurs TS. I, 8, 22, 5; AV. VII, 42, 1; verse 3, TS. I, 8, 22, 5; AV. VII, 42, 2. All the four verses, but in a different order (3, 1, 2, 4), in MS. IV, 11, 2; see also Kâth. XI, 12. Metre, Trishtubh.

This is the only hymn addressed to Soma and Rudra. In the Khândogya Up. III, 7 and 9, the Rudras are said to have Indra, while the Maruts have Soma at their head.

It is translated by Geldner and Kaegi.

The whole hymn betrays its secondary character; first by violating the law of decrease, secondly by duals in au before consonants, and thirdly by using a very large number of passages from other hymns. Compare verse 1, pâda c, with V, 1, 5, c; verse 2, pâda c, with I, 24, 9, c; verse 2, pâda d, with VI, 1, 12, d. Phrases like verse 1, pâda d, sám nah bhûtam dvipáde sám kátuhpade, occur again and again, with slight modifications; see I, 114, 1; 157, 3; VII, 54, 1; X, 165, 1. Sumanasyámânâ also is suspicious. It occurs again in the next hymn, the last of the Mandala, in VII, 33, 14, likewise a suspected hymn, and in the tenth Mandala, X, 51, 5; 7.

Verse 2.

Note 1. On víshûkîm, see II, 33, 2.

Note 2. Ámîvâ has been identified with ἀνία by Fick, Orient und Occident, III, p. 121. The difficulty is m=n.

Note 3. The AV. reads bấdhethâm dûrám nírritim, the AV. and TS. read parâkaih kritám kid énah prá mumuktam asmát.

Verse 3.

Note 1. AV. reads asmát for asmé, and ásat for ásti.

Verse 4.

In the Maitr. S. the second half of this verse is, mumuktám asmā́n grasitā́n abhī́ke prá yakkhatam vrishanâ sántamâni.

MAṆḌALA VII, HYMN 46.

ASHṬAKA V, ADHYÂYA 4, VARGA 13.

To Rudra.

1. Offer ye these songs to Rudra whose bow is strong, whose arrows are swift, the self-dependent[1] god, the unconquered conqueror, the intelligent, whose weapons are sharp—may he hear us!

2. For, being the lord[1], he looks after what is born on earth; being the universal ruler, he looks after what is born in heaven. Protecting us, come to our protecting doors, be without illness among our people, O Rudra!

3. May that thunderbolt of thine, which, sent from heaven, traverses the earth, pass us by! A thousand medicines are thine, O thou who art freely accessible[1]; do not hurt us in our kith and kin!

4. Do not strike us, O Rudra, do not forsake us! May we not be in thy way when thou rushest forth furiously. Let us have our altar and a good report among men[1]—protect us always with your favours!

NOTES.

Ascribed to Vasish*th*a. Verse 1 occurs TB. II, 8, 6, 8. Metre, 1–3 *G*agati; 4 Trish*t*ubh.

Verse 1.

Note 1. The TB. has svadhā́mne for svadhā́vne, mî*dh*úshe for vedháse, and *srin*otana for *srin*otu na*h*. The commentator explains both svadhâmne = svakîyasthânayuktâya and svadhâvne = svadhâ*s*abdavâ*k*yenânnena yuktâya vâ. On vedhas, see Bartholomae, K. Z. XXVII, 361; Ludwig, Z. D. M. G. XL, 716.

Verse 2.

Note 1. Geldner translates kshaye*n*a by 'from his high seat.' The meaning of kshaya in this place seems defined by the parallel expression *s*ā́mrâ*g*yena.

Verse 3.

Note 1. Svapivâta has been variously translated. Grassmann gives Vielbegehrter; Ludwig, des windhauch in schlaf versenkt; Roth, wohl verstehend, denkend; Geldner, freundlicher; Muir, thou who art easy of access, which seems to me the right rendering; cf. sûpâyana. It is derived from api + vat, which occurs six times in the Rig-veda. As a simple verb it means 'to go near, to attend,' as a causative, the same, or 'to bring near.' Thus, VII, 3, 10. ápi krátum su-*k*étasam vatema, may we obtain wisdom, full of good thoughts. VII, 60, 6. ápi krátum su-*k*étasam vátanta*h*, (the gods) obtaining wisdom, full of good thoughts (for their worshippers). X, 20, 1 (X, 25, 1). bhadrám na*h* ápi vâtaya mána*h*, let us obtain a good mind. I, 128, 2. tám ya*gñ*a-sā́dham ápi vâtayâmasi, we go near to, or we bring near Agni, the performer of the sacrifice. I, 165, 13. mánmâni—api-vâtáyanta*h*, bringing the prayers near, or attending to the prayers. X, 13, 5. pitré putrā́sa*h* ápi avîvatan *ri*tám, the sons brought the sacrifice to the father.

Api-vâta would then mean approach, or in a more

spiritual sense, attention, regard, and su-apivâta would mean either of easy approach, opposed to durdharsha, or full of kind attention and regard. See Muir, S.T. IV, p. 314, note. Bergaigne, III, 306, does not help us much, though he points out where the difficulty lies.

The following are the Zend passages in which api-vat occurs, with some notes sent me by Dr. Stein: Apivatahê, Y. 9, 25, 2. p. sg. med. c. Gen. 'Hom, du verstehst dich auf rechte Preissprüche' d.h. 'kannst sie würdigen;' apivatâitê daênayâo mâzdayaçnôis, V. 9, 2, 47, 'vertraut mit dem Gesetz;' daênãm zarazca dâṭ apaéca aotât, yt. 9, 26: 'wer das Gesetz lernt und in dasselbe eindringt;' verezyôtûca frâcâ vatôyôtû, Y. 35, 6, 'das richtig erkannte führe er aus und theile es mit;' Y. 44, 18 scheint apivaiti 1. p. sg. med. in der Bedeutung: 'in Erfahrung gebracht haben;' die Stelle ist indess sehr dunkel.

Verse 4.

Note 1. Ã na*h* bhaga barhíshi *g*îva*s*a*m*sé seems a very simple sentence. It has been translated without any misgivings by Grassmann, Ludwig, Geldner and Kaegi and others.

Grassmann translates: 'Lass lange lebend uns die Streu noch schmücken.'

Ludwig: 'Gib uns anteil an dem barhis als verheiszung des lebens.'

Kaegi and Geldner (or Roth): 'Verstatt uns Theil an Opfer und an Herrschaft.'

Bergaigne often points to such translations with scorn, but after he has written several pages on the words in question, here on *g*îva*s*a*m*sa, he is indeed very positive that it means 'formule qui donne la vie' (I, p. 306), but what such a 'formule' is, and how this meaning fits the whole sentence, he does not tell us.

Let us begin with what is clear. Ã bha*g*a na*h* with locative, means 'appoint us to something,' i.e. 'give us something.' Thus I, 121, 15. á na*h* bha*g*a góshu, means 'divide us, distribute us, appoint us to cows,' i.e. 'give us cows as our share.' The same expression is used when instead of cows or riches, the gods are asked to give long life, glory, or sinlessness. Thus we read, I, 104, 6. sá*h* tvám na*h* indra sū́rye sá*h* apsú anâgâstvé ā́ bhaga *g*îva*s*a*m*sé, that is, 'Indra, allow us to share and rejoice in the sun, in water, in sinlessness and praise of men.' X, 45, 10. ā́ tám bha*g*a sau*s*ravaséshu, 'give him, let him share in, good renown.'

When we are once familiar with this phraseology, we cannot doubt that in our passage also we have to translate, 'let us have our barhis, our homely altar, and good report among men.'

Another word narâ*s*a*m*sa had originally the same meaning as *g*îva*s*a*m*sa, but it was chiefly used as a name of Agni. He was called Narâ*s*a*m*sa, i. e. Männerlob, or dyó*h* *s*á*m*sa, Himmelslob, as a German poet was once called Frauenlob, not only because he praised women, but because he was praised by women. As we can say, God is my song, the Vedic Rishis might call any god the *s*a*m*sa, i. e. the praise or song of men, of the fathers, or of the gods. So far from agreeing with Bergaigne, 'on comprendrait moins bien qu'une locution dont le sens propre aurait été "éloge mortel" eût désigné celui qui est loué par le mortel,' nothing is easier and better confirmed by other languages, while the invocation of 'une formule sacrée' is almost unintelligible. If in a later hymn Indra is called *g*yésh*th*a*h* mántra*h*, in X, 50, 4, I should translate, 'thou art the oldest or the best song,' that is, 'the theme of the oldest song,' but not thou art a magic formula. There is no necessity therefore for taking narâ*s*a*m*sa as a possessive compound, possessed of the praise of men, nor must we forget that in words which become almost proper names the accent is by no means always a safe guide.

MAN*D*ALA I, HYMN 2.

ASH*T*AKA I, ADHYÂYA 1, VARGA 3-4.

To Vâyu.

1. Come hither, O Vâyu, thou beautiful one[1]! These Somas are ready, drink of them, hear our call!

2. O Vâyu, the praisers celebrate thee with hymns, they who know the feast-days[1], and have prepared the Soma.

3. O Vâyu, thy satisfying stream[1] goes to the worshipper, wide-reaching, to the Soma-draught.

4. O Indra and Vâyu, these (libations of Soma) are poured out; come hither for the sake of[1] our offerings, for the drops (of Soma) long for you.

5. O Indra and Vâyu, you perceive the libations, you who are rich in booty[1]; come then quickly hither!

6. O Vâyu and Indra, come near to the work[1] of the sacrificer, quick, thus is my prayer[2], O ye men!

7. I call Mitra, endowed with holy strength[1], and Varu*n*a, who destroys all enemies; who both fulfil a prayer accompanied by fat offerings[2].

8. On the right way, O Mitra and Varu*n*a, you have obtained great wisdom, you who increase the right and adhere to the right[1];

9. These two sages, Mitra and Varu*n*a, the mighty, wide-ruling, give us efficient strength.

NOTES.

Ascribed to Madhu*kkh*andas Vai*s*vâmitra, and addressed to Vâyu (1–3), Indra and Vâyu (4–6), and to Mitra and Varu*n*a (7–9). Metre, Gâyatrî. Verse 4=VS. VII, 8; XXXIII, 56; TS. I, 4, 4, 1; MS. I. 3, 6. Verse 7=SV. II, 197; VS. XXXIII, 57. Verse 8=SV. II, 198. Verse 9=SV. II, 199.

This hymn, with the hymn I, 3, belongs to the Pra-uga ceremony. It consists of three t*rik*as.

Verse 1.

Note 1. Dar*s*ata, as applied to the wind, may be intended for visible, but its more general meaning is conspicuous, clarus, insignis.

Verse 2.

Note 1. Aharvid, which Benfey translates by tagekundig, Grassmann, die des Tages (Anbruch) kundig, seems to have two meanings. When applied to men, poets or priests, it means those who know (vid) the right days or seasons for every sacrifice, but when it is applied to certain deities, particularly those of the morning, it means finding (vind), bringing back the day, like lucifer. Thus the A*s*vins are called aharvidâ (VIII, 5, 9; 21). The power (daksha) of Vish*n*u is called aharvid, conquering, or bringing, the light of the day (I, 156, 4). The priests, as inviting these gods, might possibly themselves be called aharvid, bringing back the light of day, but this seems doubtful.

Verse 3.

Note 1. This verse, though it seems easy, is really full of difficulties. The meaning of dhenâ is very doubtful. It is explained as lips by native authorities, and would in that case be derived from dhe, to suck. But though this meaning is possible in some passages, particularly where dhene occurs in the dual, in other passages dhenâ seems clearly to mean a stream of milk, or of some other liquid, poured out (vis*ri*sh*t*a) from the clouds or at a sacrifice. It often occurs in the dual dhene, and has then been taken as the upper and lower lips (not the nares, as Roth suggests), distinguished from *s*ipre, the upper and lower jaws. See note on II, 34, 3. Sâya*n*a (Rv. Bh. I, 101, 10) explains it by *g*ihvopa*g*ihvike. Durga adds (Nirukta Bhâshya, VI, 17) âdhastye da*m*sh*t*re vâ *g*ihvopa*g*ihvike vâ, ity eke, tayor hy anna*m* dhîyate.

Benfey translates: 'Vâyu, deine vorkostende Lippe schreitet zum Opferer, weit hingestreckt zum Somatrank.' Prap*riñk*atî can hardly mean vorkostend.

Verse 4.

Note 1. The instrumental práyobhi*h* is best translated here by 'for the sake of;' see Wenzel, Instrumental, p. 104.

Verse 5.

Note 1. On vâ*g*inî and vâ*g*a, see 'India, what can it teach us?' pp. 164, 166. The transition of meaning from vâ*g*a, booty, to vâ*g*a, wealth in general, finds an analogy in the German kriegen, to obtain, also in Gewinn, and A.S. winnan, to strive, to fight, to obtain. Vâ*g*inîvasû, in the dual, is a frequent epithet of the A*s*vins, II, 37, 5; V, 74, 6; 7; 75, 3; 78, 3; VIII, 5, 3; 12; 20; 8, 10; 9, 4; 10, 5; 22, 7; 14; 18; 26, 3; 85, 3; 101, 8; of Indra, III, 42, 5; X, 96, 8.

It differs little from vâ*g*inîvat, which is likewise applied to the A*s*vins, I, 120, 10, and comes to mean simply wealthy, liberal; cf. I, 122, 8; VII, 69, 1. Vâ*g*inîvatî is an epithet of Ushas, Sarasvatî, and Sindhu. A common phrase is vấ*g*ebhi*h* vâ*g*ínîvatî, lit. wealthy in wealth, cf. I, 3, 10. Vâ*g*inî occurs as the feminine of vâ*g*in, wealthy, or strong, but never in the sense of mare; cf. III, 61, 1, úsha*h* vấ*g*ena vâ*g*ini, Ushas wealthy by wealth or booty; VI, 61, 6. Sarasvati vấgeshu vâ*g*ini, Sarasvati, strong in battles; cf. I, 4, 8; 9. Native commentators generally explain vâ*g*inî by sacrifice, vâ*g*inîvasu, by dwelling in the sacrifice. I take vâ*g*inî in compounds like vâ*g*inîvasu as a collective substantive, like padminî, ûhinî, vâhinî, tretinî, anîkinî, &c., and in the sense of wealth; unless we may look upon vâ*g*inîvat as formed in analogy to such words as tavishî-mat, only that in this case tavishî exists in the sense of strength. Pischel's explanation, Ved. Stud. p. 9, rich in mares, takes for granted the existence of vâ*g*inî in the sense of mare. I have not found any passage where vâ*g*inî has necessarily that sense.

Verse 6.

Note 1. Nishk*ri*ta can hardly mean here what it means in later Sanskrit, a rendezvous.

Note 2. On ítthā́ dhiyā́, see Pischel, Ved. Stud. p. 184.

Verse 7.

Note 1. Pûtádaksha, cf. pûtákratu, VIII, 68, 17.

Note 2. Gh*ri*tâ*k*î seems to be taken here in a technical sense, like gh*ri*tavat, i.e. with oblations of butter thrown into the fire. In I, 167, 3, I took gh*ri*tâ*k*î in the more general sense of bright, resplendent, while others ascribed to it the meaning of bringing fatness, i.e. rain. It may also mean accompanied by ghee. See B.-R. s. v.

Verse 8.

Note 1. *Ri*tasp*ri*s, probably not very different from *ri*tasā́p.

MA*ND*ALA I, HYMN 134.

ASH*T*AKA II, ADHYÂYA 1, VARGA 23.

To Vâyu.

1. O Vâyu, may the quick racers bring thee towards the offerings, to the early drink[1] here, to the early drink of Soma! May Sûn*ri*tâ[2] (the Dawn) stand erect, approving thy mind! Come near on thy harnessed chariot to share, O Vâyu, to share in the sacrifice[3]!

2. May the delightful drops of Soma delight thee, the drops made by us, well-made, and heaven-directed, yes, made with milk, and heaven-directed. When his performed aids assume strength for achievement, our prayers implore the assembled steeds for gifts, yes, the prayers implore them.

3. Vâyu yokes the two ruddy, Vâyu yokes the two red horses, Vâyu yokes to the chariot the two swift horses to draw in the yoke, the strongest to draw in the yoke. Awake Purandhi (the Morning)[1] as a lover wakes a sleeping maid, reveal heaven and earth, brighten the dawn, yes, for glory brighten the dawn.

4. For thee the bright dawns spread out in the distance beautiful garments, in their houses[1], in their rays, beautiful in their new rays. To thee the juice-yielding[2] cow pours out all treasures. Thou hast brought forth the Maruts from the flanks[3], yes, from the flanks of heaven.

5. For thee the white, bright, rushing Somas, strong in raptures, have rushed to the whirl, they

have rushed to the whirl of the waters. The tired hunter asks luck of thee in the chase[1]; thou shieldest[2] by thy power from every being, yes, thou shieldest by thy power from powerful spirits[3].

6. Thou, O Vâyu, art worthy as the first before all others to drink these our Somas, thou art worthy to drink these poured-out Somas. Among the people also who invoke thee and have turned to thee[1], all the cows pour out the milk, they pour out butter and milk (for the Soma).

NOTES.

Ascribed to Paru*kkh*epa Daivodâsi, and addressed to Vâyu. Metre, 1–5 Atyash*t*i; 6 Ash*t*i. No verse occurs in the other Vedas.

Verse 1.

Note 1. Pûrvapîti may here imply that Vâyu receives his libation first, before the other gods, see verse 6.

Note 2. Whatever the etymology of sûn*ri*tâ may be, in our passage, which describes the morning sacrifice and the arrival of Vâyu as the first of the gods, it can hardly mean anything but dawn. Ûrdhvâ sthâ is an expression applied frequently to the rise of the dawn or the morning, see III, 55, 14; 61, 3; VIII, 45, 12. In the last passage sûn*ri*tâ is simply the dawn. Ludwig translates, 'deine treflichkeit erhebe sich, günstig aufnemend die absicht.' He, like Bergaigne, III, 295, takes sûn*ri*tâ as su-n*ri*-tâ, virtue. It seems to me that sûn*ri*ta may be formed irregularly in analogy to an-*ri*ta, and then mean true, good. In other places sûn*ri*tam seems to mean hymn, like *ri*tavâka, IX, 113, 2. In places where it occurs as a name of Ushas, one feels tempted to conjecture su-n*ri*tûs. See also Bartholomae, in Bezzenb. Beitr. XV, 24.

Note 3. On makhásya dâváne, see note to I, 6, 8; but also note to VIII, 7, 27.

Verse 2.

My translation is purely tentative, and I doubt whether the text can be correct. I have taken krâ*n*a here in the sense of made, but I am quite aware that this meaning becomes incongruous in our very verse, when repeated for the third time. On its other meanings, see Pischel, Ved. Stud. p. 67. For the whole verse, compare VI, 36, 3. Grassmann translates:

Die lust'gen Indu's mögen, Vâyu, dich erfreuen,
Die starken, die wir schön gebraut, die himmlischen,
Die milchgemischten, himmlischen;
Wenn Tränke tüchtig deinen Sinn

Uns zu gewinnen, bei dir sind,
Dann fordere Lieder die vereinte Rosseschar,
Die Speisen zu empfangen auf.

Ludwig: Erfreuen sollen dich die frohen tropfen, Vâyu, von uns bereitet, die morgendlichen, mit milch bereitet, die morgendlichen, dasz der (opfer) tüchtigkeit zukomen hilfleistungen zum gelingen, gewärt, die insgesammt herwärts gerichteten gespanne (antworten) zur (mit) beschenkung den liedern, ihn sprechen an die lieder.

These translations may serve to show that certain verses in the Veda are simply hopeless, and that the translators must not be held responsible if they cannot achieve the impossible.

Verse 3.

Note 1. Purandhi may have meant originally doorkeeper or bar-holder (cardo), from pû*h* and dhi, being formed like ishudhí, v*rí*shandhi, *s*evadhí, &c. Purandhrî also may have been *πυλωρός*, janitor, or rather janitrix, then housewife. Grassmann translates it by Segensfülle, Ludwig by Fülle; Bergaigne, III, 476, has a long note on purandhi, as one of the many names of 'la femelle.' Whatever it meant etymologically, in our passage, where she is to be woke by the wind in the morning (cf. ushása*h* budhí, I, 137, 2), it is again a characteristic epithet of the dawn, *πολιοῦχος*, *πολιάς*, *πολαῖτις*. See also Pischel, Vedica, p. 202; Hillebrandt, Wiener Zeitschrift, III, 188; 259.

Verse 4.

Note 1. I have translated da*m*su as a locative; could it be a nom. plur. of da*m*su, *δασυ*, referring to vastrâ, the terminations being left out? see Lanman, p. 415.

Note 2. Sabardúghâ, juice-yielding. Roth explains it as quickly yielding, identifying sabar with Greek *ἄφαρ*. But Greek *φ* never represents Sanskrit b. Sabar, juice, milk, water, would really seem to yield the true source of A. S. sæp, O. H. G. saf, sap, for it is clear that neither *ὀπός*, nor Lat. sucus, would correspond with A. S. sæp; see Brugmann, Grundriss, vol. i, § 328; also Bartholomae, in Bezzenb. Beitr. XV, 17.

Note 3. Vakshá*n*âbhya*h*, from the flanks. It would be better if we could refer váksha*n*âbhya*h* to Dhenu, the cow, the mother of the Maruts, while Dyaus is their father, see V, 52, 16. Here, however, Vâyu is conceived as their father, and dyaus (fem.) as their mother.

Verse 5.

Note 1. I have followed Ludwig in his explanation of tsârî, hunter, watcher, and takvavîya, chase of the takva, whatever animal it may be.

Note 2. Oldenberg suggests prâsi for pâsi, which on many accounts would be excellent.

Note 3. On asuryă, see von Bradke, Dyaus Asura, p. 39, and Bergaigne, Journal Asiatique, 1884, p. 510.

Verse 6.

Note 1. Vihutmat is translated by Roth as not sacrificing. But vihutmat can hardly be separated from vihava and vihavya, and seems to mean therefore invoking, possibly, invoking towards different sides. Hu, to sacrifice, does not take the preposition vi. Vavar*g*ushî is doubtful. Without some other words, it can hardly mean 'those who have turned towards the gods,' as we read in X, 120, 3 (tvé krátum ápi v*riñg*anti ví*s*ve); nor is it likely to be the same as v*ri*kta-barhis, 'those who have prepared the barhis.' I have translated it in the former sense. See Geldner, Ved. Stud. p. 144, and Oldenberg, Gött. Gel. Anz. 1890, p. 414.

MANDALA X, HYMN 168.

ASHTAKA VIII, ADHYÂYA 8, VARGA 26.

To Vâta.

1. Now for the greatness of the chariot of Vâta [1]! Its roar goes crashing and thundering. It moves touching the sky, and creating red sheens [2], or it goes scattering the dust of the earth.

2. Afterwards there rise the gusts of Vâta [1], they go towards him, like women to a feast [2]. The god goes with them on the same chariot, he, the king of the whole of this world.

3. When he moves on his paths along the sky, he rests not even a single day [1]; the friend of the waters, the first-born, the holy, where was he born, whence did he spring?

4. The breath of the gods, the germ [1] of the world, that god moves wherever he listeth; his roars indeed are heard, not his form—let us offer sacrifice to that Vâta!

NOTES.

Ascribed to Anila Vâtâyana, and addressed to Vâyu, here called Vâta. The metre is Trish*t*ubh. This hymn does not occur in the other Vedas. See Muir, Sanskrit Texts, V, p. 145; Geldner and Kaegi, p. 95.

Verse 1.

Note 1. For this use of the accusative, see Pischel, Ved. Stud. p. 13.

Note 2. Aru*n*âni is explained by Geldner, Ved. Stud. p. 274, as the reddish colours of the lightning.

Verse 2.

Note 1. Vish*th*â means kind or variety. Anu seems to refer to ratha, which I take as the subject of the whole of the first verse.

Note 2. 'Sie gehn mit einander zum Tanz,' Geldner and Kaegi.

Verse 3.

Note 1. Geldner and Kaegi propose aha for aha*h*.

Verse 4.

Note 1. Vâta seems to be called the garbha of the world, in the sense of being its source or life.

MAN*D*ALA X, HYMN 186.

ASH*T*AKA VIII, ADHYÂYA 8, VARGA 44.

TO VÂTA.

1. May Vâta waft medicine, healthful, delightful to our heart; may he prolong our lives!

2. Thou, O Vâta, art our father, and our brother, and our friend; do thou grant us to live!

3. O Vâta, from that treasure of the immortal which is placed in thy house yonder, give us to live!

NOTES.

Ascribed to Ula Vâtâyana, and addressed to Vâyu, under the name of Vâta. The metre is Gâyatrî. Verse 1 occurs in SV. I, 184; II, 1190; Taitt. Br. II, 4, 1, 8; Taitt. Âr. IV, 42, 8. Verse 3 in SV. II, 1192; Taitt. Br. II, 4, 1, 8; Taitt. Âr. IV, 42, 7.

APPENDICES.

I. INDEX OF WORDS.

II. LIST OF THE MORE IMPORTANT PASSAGES QUOTED IN THE PREFACE AND IN THE NOTES.

III. A BIBLIOGRAPHICAL LIST OF THE MORE IMPORTANT PUBLICATIONS ON THE RIG-VEDA.

THE following Index of Words was commenced by Professor Thibaut, and continued and finished by Dr. Winternitz. I beg to express my gratitude to both of them, more particularly to Dr. Winternitz, who has spared no pains in order to make the Index as complete and as accurate as possible.—F. M. M.

The Index contains all the words of the hymns translated in this volume, and besides, all the words about which something is said in the Notes.

The lists of passages are complete, except when three dots (. . .) are put after the word (e. g. á*kkh*a . . .).

Three figures refer to Ma*nd*ala, hymn, and verse, a small figure to a note, e. g. X, 77, 2[1], stands for Ma*nd*ala X, hymn 77, verse 2, note 1 (the word occurs in X, 77, 2, and also in note 1).

If a word occurs in a note only, the passage is put in parentheses, e. g. (V, 61, 4[1]) means that the word occurs in note 1 on V, 61, 4, but *not* in V, 61, 4.

In the case of longer notes, it seemed advisable to refer to the page. *One* number refers to the page, e. g. (287) means that the word occurs in a note on page 287.

I. INDEX OF WORDS.

a*k*yuta-*k*yút, shaking the unshakable: epithet of Indra [not of the Maruts, correct on p. 278], (I, 167, 8[2].)

ag:
ágati, he drives, VI, 66, 7.—vâ*n*á*h* agyate, the arrow is shot, VIII, 20, 8[1]; (I, 85, 10[2].)—ví ágatha, you drive forth, V, 54, 4[1].

agá, goat:
(234.)

agá-a*s*va, having goats for his horses: ep. of Pûshan, (I, 87, 4[1].)

agára, never growing old:
agárâ*h*, I, 64, 3.

agina, skin:
(234.)

agirá, ready, swift (horses):
agirā́, I, 134, 3; V, 56, 6.

ágoshya, unwelcome:
ágoshya*h*, I, 38, 5[3].

ágma, racing:
ágmeshu, I, 37, 8[1]; 10[2]; 87, 3; V, 87, 7[1].

ágman, racing:
ágman (Loc.), I, 166, 5; VIII, 20, 5.

agyesh*th*á:
agyesh*th*ā́*h*, among whom none is the eldest, V, 59, 6; agyesh*th*ā́sa*h*, V, 60, 5.

ágra, a plain:
ágrân, V, 54, 4.

a*ñk*, to bow:
sám a*k*yanta, V, 54, 12.

a*ñg*:
a*ñg*ate (a*ñg*í), they brighten themselves, VII, 57, 3.—a*ñg*, with góbhi*h*, to cover with milk, (VIII, 20, 8[1]; 405.)—prá anaga, you have fashioned, V, 54, 1.—with ví, to deck, adorn oneself; ví a*ñg*ate, I, 64, 4; ví ânagre, I, 87, 1; ví a*ñg*ata, VIII, 7, 25.—sám a*ñg*e, I prepare, I, 64, 1.

á*ñg*asâ, straightway, and a*ñg*asína, straightforward:
(V, 53, 10[1].)

a*ñg*í:
a*ñg*í a*ñg*ate, they brighten themselves with brightness, VII, 57, 3; samânám a*ñg*í, their anointing is the same, VIII, 20, 11.—pl. the glittering ornaments of the Maruts, a*ñg*áya*h*, I, 166, 10; a*ñg*ín, X, 77, 2; a*ñg*í-bhi*h*, I, 37, 2[2]; 64, 4[1]; 85, 3; 87, 1; V, 52, 15[1]; 56, 1[1]; X, 78, 7; (aru*n*ébhi*h*) II, 34, 13[1]; (307; 308); a*ñg*íshu, V, 53, 4[1].—(VIII, 20, 9[1].)

a*ñg*in, possessed of a*ñg*is?
(V, 52, 15[1].)

a*ñg*i-mát, well-adorned:
a*ñg*i-mánta*h*, V, 57, 5.

átas:
áta*h*, from yonder, I, 6, 9; from thence, I, 165, 5; V, 60, 6; áta*h* *k*it, even from them, VIII, 20, 18.

áti:
gánân áti tasthau, I, 64, 13; across, II, 34, 15.—áti = ádhi? V, 52, 3[1]; (VIII, 7, 14[1].)—pûrví*h* áti kshápa*h*, through many nights, X, 77, 2; áti kshapá*h*, Gen., (I, 64, 8[2].)

átithi, guest:
play on the words átithi and áditi, (262.)

átka, garment:
átkân, V, 55, 6.

átya, rushing, horse, racer:
átyam, I, 64, 6[3]; atyám ná sáptim, (I, 85, 1[1]); v*r*isha*n*a*h* v*r*ishabhā́sa*h* átyâ*h*, strong and powerful horses (140); átyâ*h*-iva, V, 59, 3; átyâsa*h* ná, VII, 56, 16; átyân iva âgíshu, II, 34, 3.—átyena pā́gasâ, with rushing splendour, II, 34, 13[3].

átra:
now, I, 165, 11; here, I, 165, 13; V, 61, 11; VII, 57, 5.

átra, food:
(I, 86, 10[2].)

atrá, tooth, jaw, eater, ogre:
(I, 86, 10[2].)

atrín, tusky fiend:
atrí*n*am, I, 86, 10[2].

átha, therefore:
I, 87, 4; 114, 9; (VII, 56, 1[1].)

adás, yonder:
X, 186, 3.

ádâbhya, unbeguiled, unconquerable:
adâbhyâ*h*, II, 34, 10; ádâbhyasya, VIII, 7, 15[1].

Aditi:
Aditi, (241 seqq.); âdityā́*h* áditi*h*, (244); earth, (255; 263); as adj. unbound, unbounded, (257); unrestrained, independent, free,

Ánitabhâ, N. of a river:
V, 53, 9[1].
ánîka:
áditer ánîkam, the face of Aditi (the dawn), (243.)—marútâm ánîkam, the train of the Maruts, I, 168, 9.—ánîkeshu ádhi, on the faces, VIII, 20, 12.
ánu, prep. . . . :
according to, svadhắm ánu, see svadhắ; ánu *g*ósham, according to pleasure, VI, 66, 4.—ánu dyűn, day by day, I, 167, 10; (I, 6, 8[2].)—ánu átakshata, I, 86, 3[1]; ánu scil. sasru*h*, V, 53, 2[1].—after, X, 168, 2[1].—synizesis, p. cxxii
ánutta, not shaken, strong:
ánuttam, I, 165, 9[1].
ánutta-manyu, of irresistible fury:
(I, 165, 9[1].)
ánu-patha, follower:
ánu-pathâ*h*, V, 52, 10.
anu-bhartrí, comforting:
anu-bhartrî, I, 88, 6[1]; (178.)
anu-stubh:
Anush*t*ubh = 'After-step,' p. xcvi.
anu-svadhám, according to their nature:
V, 52, 1.
anetá:
anená*h* for anetá*h*? (VI, 66, 7[1].)
ánedya, blameless:
ánedya*h*, I, 87, 4; 165, 12; V, 61, 13; p. xviii seq.
anená, without deer:
anená*h*, VI, 66, 7[1].
anenás, without guilt:
anená*h*, (VI, 66, 7[1].)
ánta, end:
ántam, the hem of a garment, I, 37, 6[1].—*s*ávasa*h* ántam, I, 167, 9.—ántân divá*h*, V, 59, 7.
ánta*h*-patha, enterer:
ánta*h*-pathâ*h*, V, 52, 10.
antamá, friend:
antamébhi*h*, I, 165, 5[1].
antár:
antá*h*, from within, I, 168, 5.—c. Loc. within, V, 59, 2[2].—antá*h* sánta*h*, within (the womb), VI, 66, 4.
antáriksha, sky, air:
antáriksham, V, 54, 4; 55, 2; divá*h* ấ antárikshât, V, 53, 8; uraú antárikshe, V, 52, 7; antárikshe rágasa*h*, the air in the sky, X, 121, 5[2]; antárikshe, through the air, I, 165, 2; X, 168, 3; antáriksheṇa, VIII, 7, 35.—antáriksha, p*ri*thivî, and dyú, (50); ródasî antáriksham, (I, 64, 9[2].)
antárikshya:
antárikshyâ*h* pathyẫ*h*, the paths in the sky, V, 54, 9.
ánti, near:
I, 167, 9.
ándhas, (Soma) juice:
ándhasa*h* (mádhva*h*), I, 85, 6[2]; ándhasâ (mádhva*h*), V, 54, 8[3]; ándhâ*m*si pîtáye, to drink the (juice of the Soma) flowers, VII, 59, 5.
anyá, other . . . :
ná tvád anyá*h*, no other than thou, X, 121, 10.—anyá*h*, enemy, VII, 56, 15.
anyátas, to a different place:
anyáta*h*, p. xl.
anyátra, elsewhere:
VII, 59, 5.
áp, water:
ấpa*h*, V, 54, 2; 58, 6; VII, 56, 25; ấpa*h*-iva, V, 60, 3; VIII, 94, 7; giráya*h* ná ấpa*h* ugrấ*h*, VI, 66, 11[2]; ấpa*h* ná, X, 78, 5; ấpa*h* b*ri*hatî*h*, the great waters, X, 121, 7[1]; 8; 9; mahatî*h* apá*h*, VIII, 7, 22; apá*h* mât*ri*̂*h*, (307); apá*h*, I, 165, 8; VIII, 7, 28.—apá*h* tárema, cross the waters, VII, 56, 24.—apá*h*, the waters (at sacrifices), I, 64, 1[3]; 6[2].—apẫm ar*n*avám, I, 85, 9; apẫm ná ûrmáya*h*, I, 168, 2; apẫm budhné, X, 77, 4; bhurvá*n*i apẫm, I, 134, 5; apẫm sákhâ, the friend of the waters (Vâta), X, 168, 3.—ap-sú, VI, 66, 8.—apá*h*, the waters between heaven and earth, the sky, (309.)—ấpa*h*, Acc. (cf. Lanman, 483), V, 53, 14.
ápatya, 'Nachkommen':
(215, note [a].)
apa-bhart*ri*, the remover:
apa-bhartấ (rápasa*h*), II, 33, 7.
ápas, n., work, deed:
ápa*h*, (I, 64, 1[3]); ápâ*m*si (nári), I, 85, 9.
apás, m., workman:
apấ*h*, (I, 64, 1[3]); apásam (dáksham), efficient, I, 2, 9.

amr*í*ta, immortal, pl. the immortals:
amr*í*ta*h*, I, 38, 4; amr*i*ta (Rudra), I, 114, 6; amr*í*tasya (Indra), I, 170, 4; (Rudra), I, 43, 9[1].—amr*í*tam nãma, V, 57, 5.—amr*í*tâ*h* (Maruts), I, 166, 3; amr*i*tâsa*h*, I, 166, 13; ámr*i*tâ*h*, V, 57, 8; 58, 8.

amr*í*ta, n., the immortal, immortality, not dying:
amr*í*tam, X, 121, 2; amr*í*tasya, V, 58, 1; VII, 57, 6[1]; X, 186, 3; amr*í*tât, VII, 59, 12[3].

amr*i*ta-tvá, immortality:
amr*i*ta-tvám ã́ îrire, they became immortal (I, 6, 4[3]); amr*i*ta-tvé dadhâtana, V, 55, 4.

ámr*i*dhra, unceasing:
ámr*i*dhram (rain), I, 37, 11.

ambhr*i*n*á*, ὄβριμος? (275.)

áya, wanderer:
áyâ*h*, (VI, 66, 4[1].)

ayá, going:
ayãsa*h*, (I, 64, 11[1].)

áya*h*-da*m*sh*t*ra, with iron tusks:
áya*h*-da*m*sh*t*rân, I, 88, 5.

ayã́, adv., hence:
I, 87, 4[2].—Instrum., ayã́ dhiyã́, through this prayer, I, 166, 13. áyâ for ayã́, VI, 66, 4[1].

ayã́s, untiring:
ayã́*h*, (I, 87, 4[2]); ayã́sa*h*, I, 64, 11[1]; 167, 4[1]; VI, 66, 5[2]; áyâsa*h*, VII, 58, 2; ayã́sâm, I, 168, 9.—ayã́*h*, not striving (?), VI, 66, 5[2].

ar, to hurt:
(65 seq.; I, 64, 15[1]; 85, 5[2]); upa-ârimá, we have offended, (66.)

ará, spoke:
arã́*h*-iva, like the spokes of a wheel, V, 58, 5; ráthânâm ná arã́*h*, X, 78, 4; arã́*n*âm ná *k*aramá*h*, as of moving spokes no one is the last, VIII, 20, 14[1].

arakshás, guileless:
araksha*h*, V, 87, 9.

árathî, not a charioteer:
árathî*h*, VI, 66, 7.

arapás, without mischief:
arapã́*h*, II, 33, 6.

áram, properly:
VI, 74, 1; áram kr*i*n*vantu, let them prepare, I, 170, 4; áram-kr*i*tâ*h*, ready, I, 2, 1.

arámati, service:
arámatim, V, 54, 6[2].

ákrarivas, hostile:
ákrarushe, on the enemy, VII, 56, 19; (66.)

aráru, enemy:
(66.)

arâ*g*ín, dark:
arâ*g*ína*h* (párvatân), VIII, 7, 23.

árâti, enemy:
árâtî*h*, V, 53, 14; árâtaya*h*, I, 43, 8.

arâdhás, miserly:
arâdhása*h*, V, 61, 6.

árâvan, selfish:
árâvâ, VII, 56, 15.

ári, friend:
ví*s*ve aryá*h*, VIII, 94, 3[1].

ári, enemy:
aryá*h*, Gen., V, 54, 12[2]; Abl., VII, 56, 22.—(66); (I, 64, 15.[1])—arí*h* = arî*h* = araya*h*, pp. xxxix; xli.

árish*t*a, inviolable:
árish*t*am (sáha*h*), II, 34, 7.

árish*t*a-grâma, whose ranks are never broken:
árish*t*a-grâmâ*h*, I, 166, 6.

árish*t*a-vîra, with unharmed men:
árish*t*a-vîrâ*h*, I, 114, 3.

aru*n*á, red:
aru*n*ébhi*h* a*ñg*í-bhi*h*, II, 34, 13[1]: aru*n*aí*h*, with the red (rays), II, 34, 12.—Red (horses), aru*n*ébhi*h*, I, 88, 2; aru*n*â, I, 134, 3. —aru*n*ãni, red sheens, X, 168, 1[2].

aru*n*á-a*s*va, having red horses:
aru*n*á-a*s*vâ*h*, V, 57, 4.

aru*n*á-psu, reddish-coloured:
aru*n*á-psava*h* (Maruts), VIII, 7, 7[1].

aru*n*í, red:
aru*n*ĩ́, the ruddy cows, (I, 64, 7[3].) —a*ñg*áya*h* aru*n*áya*h*, bright red ornaments, (308.)

arushá, red; m. f., red horse:
arushám (horse), I, 6, 1[1]; arushásya, I, 85, 5[2]; árushî*h*, red mares, V, 56, 6; arushá*h* vâ*g*ĩ́, V, 56, 7; arushã́sa*h* á*s*vâ*h*, V, 59, 5; arushám varâhám, I, 114, 5.—(See 17 seqq.) Adj. red, (17–19): white, bright, (19, 24); vr*í*shan arushá, fire in the shape of lightning, (18); the red hero, (18, 25): the red horses of the Sun and of Agni, (19 seq.); the cloud as one of the horses of the Maruts, (20.)

ávayâta-he*l*as:
  ávayâta-he*l*â*h* bháva, let thy anger be turned away from (Instr.), I, 171, 6[2].
ávara:
  ávaram, the bottom, I, 168, 6; ávarân, descending, II, 34, 14.
ávas, help, protection:
  áva*h*, I, 39, 7; VIII, 94, 8; I, 114, 9; ávasâ, I, 39, 7; 85, 11; 166, 2; VII, 59, 2; ávase, I, 168, 1; II, 34, 14; I, 114, 4; ávasa*h*, V, 57, 7; áva*h*-bhi*h*, I, 86, 6[1]; 167, 2.—ávasâ, by (his) will, X, 121, 6.
avasá, drag (?):
  (VI, 66, 7[2].)
avasyú, desiring help:
  avasyáva*h*, I, 114, 11.
ávâta, unconquered, (90.)
avâtá (or ávâta), never dried up:
  avâtã́m, I, 38, 7[1].
avik*ri*ta, not dyed:
  (234.)
ávithura, immovable:
  ávithurâ*h*, I, 87, 1; (I, 87, 3[1].)
ávi-hruta, uninjured, intact:
  (I, 166, 8[1].)
a*s*, to eat:
  prá a*s*âna, I, 170, 5.
a*s*, to reach, to attain to:
  â*s*ata, I, 85, 2; 87, 5; â*s*âthe, I, 2, 8; a*s*nutha, V, 54, 10; a*s*yâma, I, 114, 2; 3; a*s*iya, II, 33, 2; 6.—abhí a*s*yâm, I, 166, 14.—út a*s*navat, V, 59, 4.—prá a*s*nuvantu, VI, 74, 1.
a*s*ás, impious fiend:
  a*s*ása*h*, II, 34, 9.
á*s*iva, unlucky, uncanny:
  (I, 166, 1[1].)
á*s*ma-didyu, shooting with thunderbolts:
  á*s*ma-didyava*h*, V, 54, 3.
á*s*man, stone:
  á*s*mâ, I, 172, 2.—á*s*mânam svaryàm, the heavenly stone (the sky), V, 56, 4[2].
a*s*man-máya, made of stone:
  a*s*man-máyî (vã́*s*î), (I, 88, 3[1].)
á*s*va, horse:
  á*s*vâ*h*-iva, V, 53, 7; 59, 5; á*s*vâsa*h* ná *g*yésh*th*âsa*h*, X, 78, 5; á*s*vâ sápti-iva, (I, 85, 1[1]); góshu, á*s*veshu, I, 114, 8; v*ri*shabhi*h* á*s*vai*h*, stallions, (139); a*s*va and vâ*g*a, (I, 167, 1[1].)—For á*s*vâm-iva, read asvãm-iva, II, 34, 6[2].—The horses of the Maruts, á*s*vâsa*h*, I, 38, 12; V, 59, 7; á*s*vâ*h*, V, 54, 10; 61, 2; á*s*vân, I, 171, 1; II, 34, 3; 8; V, 55, 6[1]; 58, 7; 59, 1; á*s*vai*h*, I, 88, 2; V, 55, 1; VIII, 7, 27; p*ri*shatîbhi*h* á*s*vai*h*, V, 58, 6[1]; (I, 37, 2[1].)
a*s*vatthá, horse-stable, i.e. West:
  (V, 54, 5[1].)
a*s*va-dã́, giving horses, the dawn, the East (?):
  (V, 54, 5[1].)
á*s*va-par*n*a, winged with horses:
  á*s*va-par*n*ai*h*, (I, 87, 4[1]); I, 88, 1.
á*s*va-budhna, having their resting-place among the horses:
  á*s*va-budhnâ*h*, the Dawns (V, 54, 5[1].)
a*s*va-yát, wishing horses:
  a*s*vayánta*h*, (I, 167, 1[1].)
a*s*va-yú*g*, harnessing horses:
  a*s*va-yú*g*a*h*, V, 54, 2.
á*s*va-vat:
  á*s*va-vat rã́dha*h*, wealth of horses, V, 57, 7.
A*s*vín:
  a*s*vínâ, the A*s*vins, VIII, 94, 4.
á*s*vya, consisting of horses:
  á*s*vyam (rã́dha*h*), V, 52, 17; á*s*vyam pa*s*úm, V, 61, 5.
áshâ*lh*a, unconquered:
  áshâ*lh*âya, VII, 46, 1.
as, to throw:
  ásyatha, you hurl, I, 172, 2; asyatu âré asmát, may he drive far away from us, I, 114, 4; ásyan, scattering, X, 168, 1.—prá ásyatha, you cast forwards, I, 39, 1.—ví asyatha, you scatter, V, 55, 6.
as, to be . . .:
  na*h* astu, may it be ours, X, 121, 10; yushmã́kam astu, may yours be, I, 39, 2; 4.—va*h* santu, I, 38, 12; 39, 2; smási eshâm, we are their servants, I, 37, 15; me astu, I, 165, 10; va*h* sánti, you have for (dat.), I, 85, 12.—sánti, there are, I, 37, 14; ásti (with dat.), there is enough for, I, 37, 15; ná ásti, there is no such thing, I, 170, 1.—yát syã́tana, syât, I, 38, 4[1]; syã́ma té, may we be such, V, 53, 15.—asan, may they be, I, 38, 15[2];

gárbha, germ :
gárbham, X, 121, 7 ; V, 58, 7 ; VI, 66, 3[1] ; bhúvanasya gárbha*h*, the germ of the world, X, 168, 4[1].

garbha-tvá, the form of new-born babes :
garbha-tvám, I, 6, 4[3].

gávya, consisting of cows :
(rã́dha*h*) gávyam, V, 52, 17 ; pa*s*úm gávyam, V, 61, 5.

gavyát, desirous of cows :
gavyánta*h*, (I, 167, 1[1].)

gâ, to go :
*g*ígâti, V, 87, 4 ; I, 2, 3.—ádhi gâtana, do remember (c. Gen.), V, 55, 9 ; ádhi gâta, VIII, 20, 22 ; X, 78, 8.—ã́ gât, she went to, I, 167, 5 ; ó *g*igâtu, II, 34, 15 ; ã́ *g*igâtana, V, 59, 6; ã́ *g*igâta, VII, 57, 7.—úpa gât, I, 38, 5.—pári ã́ va*h* ã́ agu*h*, they went round you and came back to, I, 88, 4[1] ; pári gât, may it pass by, II, 33, 14.—prá *g*igâta, come forth, I, 85, 6 ; prá *g*igâti, I, 87, 5.

gâtú, path :
gâtúm, V, 87, 8.

gâthá, song :
gâthám, I, 167, 6 ; (I, 43, 4[1].)

gâthá-pati, lord of songs :
gâthá-patim (rudrám), I, 43, 4[1].

gâyatrá, song :
gâyatrám (ukthyã́m), I, 38, 14.

gír, speech, song :
iyám gî́*h*, I, 165, 15 ; 166, 15 ; 167, 11 ; 168, 10 ; imã́m me gíram, VIII, 7, 9 ; girã́, I, 38, 13 ; V, 52, 13 ; 53, 16 ; 87, 3 ; VIII, 20, 19 ; 20 ; gíra*h*, I, 64, 1 ; V, 61, 17 ; VII, 46, 1 ; (I, 37, 10[1]; 165, 4[1].)

gír, singer :
gíra*h* (the Maruts), I, 6, 6[1] ; 9 ; 37, 10[1].

girí, mountain, cloud :
girí*h*, VIII, 7, 5 ; girî́n, I, 37, 12 ; giráya*h*, I, 64, 7; VIII, 7, 34 ; girím ána*s*va-dâm, western mountain, V, 54, 5[1] ; giráya*h* for girya*h* (?), VI, 66, 11[2] ; ádhi-iva girî*n*ã́m, VIII, 7, 14.—girí*h* (párvata*h*), gnarled (cloud), I, 37, 7[1] ; párvatam girím, V, 56, 4[2].

giri-kshít, ep. of Vish*n*u :
(V, 87, 1[1].)

giri-*g*ã́, voice-born :
giri-*g*ã́*h*, V, 87, 1[1].

giri-sthã́, dwelling on mountains :
giri-sthã́m (mã́rutam ga*n*ám), VIII, 94, 12 ; (V, 57, 8[1]; 87, 1[1].)

gurú, heavy :
gurú, I, 39, 3 ; VII, 56, 19 ; laghu and guru, light and heavy syllables, p. xcvii.

guh, to hide :
gṹhata, I, 86, 10.

gúha, hiding-place :
gúhã́, I, 6, 5 ; gúhâ (*k*árantî), in secret, I, 167, 3.

gúhya, hideous :
gúhyam, I, 86, 10.

gûrtá-tama, most delightful :
gûrtá-tamâ*h*, I, 167, 1.

g*ri* (gar), caus., to raise up :
*g*ig*ri*tá, VII, 57, 6[2].

g*rí*dhra, hawk :
g*rí*dhrâ*h*, I, 88, 4[1].

g*ri*há, house :
g*ri*hé, X, 186, 3.

g*rí*ha-medha, accepting the domestic sacrifices :
g*rí*ha-medhâsa*h*, VII, 59, 10[1] ; (VII, 56, 14[2].)

g*ri*hamedhin :
maruta*h* g*ri*hamedhina*h*, (VII, 56, 14[2]; 59, 10[1].)

g*ri*ha-medhîya, offering for the house-gods :
g*ri*ha-medhî́yam, VII, 56, 14[2].

g*rî*, to praise :
g*ri*nî́masi, I, 64, 12 ; II, 33, 8 ; g*ri*nántam, VII, 57, 2 ; g*ri*naté, VI, 66, 9 ; g*ri*nî́hi, V, 53, 16 ; g*ri*nî́she, (V, 58, 1[1]) ; II, 33, 12 ; g*ri*nânã́*h*, V, 55, 10 ; 59, 8 ; g*ri*nâná*h*, VII, 56, 18.—ã́ g*ri*nanti, they invite, VIII, 94, 3.—úpa g*ri*nî́masi, II, 34, 14.

gai, to sing :
gã́ya, I, 38, 14 ; gã́yat, I, 167, 6 ; agu*h*, (175.)—abhí gã́ya, VIII, 20, 19.—prá gâyata, I, 37, 1 ; 4.

gó, cow, bull :
gaú*h*-iva, V, 56, 3 ; gã́va*h* ná, I, 38, 2 ; V, 53, 16 ; 56, 4 ; gã́va*h* ná ukshá*n*a*h*, I, 168, 2[3] ; gã́va*h*, VIII, 20, 21[1] ; gã́*h*-iva, VIII, 20, 19 ; gávâm sárgam-iva, V, 56, 5 ; gávâm-iva, V, 59, 3.—gáve, I, 43, 2 ; 6 ; góshu, VI, 66, 8 ; I, 114, 8.—góshu, among the cows

dadhé (vrikâ-tâti), II, 34, 9[1]; dhuh, V, 58, 7[1]; dadhanti, VII, 56, 19[2].—dadhidhvé, will you take, I, 38, 1; dadhidhve, you accept, I, 168, 1[2]; dádhânâh, X, 121, 7; 8; I, 6, 4; távishîh dhâ, to take strength, (I, 64, 7[3]); dadhire (várnam), they have assumed, II, 34, 13; dádhânah, having become, I, 171, 6[3]; dadhe mudé, I am made to rejoice, V, 53, 5.—ấ dádhânâh, bringing, I, 165, 12; p. xviii; ấ dádhânâh nấma, assuming a name, VI, 66, 5; gárbham ấ adhât, she conceived the germ, VI, 66, 3; ấ-hitâ, piled up, I, 166, 9.—ní dhattá, put down, I, 171, 1; ádhi ní dhehi asmé, bestow on us, I, 43, 7.—samádhatta mấm ékam, you left me alone, I, 165, 6[1]; p. xvi; sám dadhe, it is held, I, 168, 3; sám vi-dyútâ dádhati, they aim with the lightning, V, 54, 2; sám dadhuh parva-sáh, they have brought together piece by piece, VIII, 7, 22[1].—See dhấtri, and dhyâ for dhîmahi.

dhấtri, bestowing:
dhấtârah, VIII, 7, 35.

dhânyấ:
dhânyấm bîgam, the seed of corn, V, 53, 13.

dhấman, abode, law, company:
dhấma-bhih, in their own ways, I, 85, 11.—dhấmnah (mấrutasya), domain, I, 87, 6[3]; (daívyasya), host, VII, 58, 1[1].—párasmin dhấman ritásya, in the highest place of the law, I, 43, 9[1].—(27; 383 seq.)

dhârayát-kshiti, supporting the earth: ep. of Aditi, (260.)

dhấrâ, stream:
dhấrâh, I, 85, 5[2,3].

dhârâvará, charged with rain:
dhârâvarấh, II, 34, 1[1].

dhâv, to run:
vi-dhấvatah, rushing about, I, 88, 5.

dhiyấ-vasu, rich in prayers:
dhiyấ-vasuh, I, 64, 15[3].

dhiyâ-sám, engaged in prayer:
(166.)

dhî, prayer:
dhíyam, I, 88, 4; II, 34, 6[2]; I, 2, 7; dhíyam-dhiyam, prayer after prayer, I, 168, 1; dhiyấ, I, 166, 13; dhiyấ-sámî, (V, 87, 9[1]); (166); dhíyah, I, 134, 2 (bis); dhiyáh, I, 87, 4; dhîbhíh, V, 52, 14.—itthấ dhiyấ, thus is my thought, V, 61, 15[1]; I, 2, 6[2].

dhîtí, prayer:
dhîtí-bhih, V, 53, 11.

dhîra, wise:
dhîrah, I, 64, 1; VII, 56, 4.

dhúni, roaring:
dhúnayah, the roarers (Maruts), I, 64, 5[2]; 87, 3; V, 60, 7; VI, 66, 10; X, 78, 3; dhúnînâm, V, 87, 3[3]; VIII, 20, 14.—dhúnih, shouting, VII, 56, 8[1].

dhúni-vrata, given to roaring:
dhúni-vratam, V, 58, 2; dhúni-vratâya, V, 87, 1.

dhúr, shaft, yoke:
dhûh-sú, V, 55, 6; X, 77, 5; dhurí, V, 56, 6 (bis); 58, 7; I, 134, 3 (bis).

dhû, to shake (with two Acc.):
dhûnuthá, I, 37, 6; V, 57, 3[1].—ví dhûnutha, V, 54, 12[1].

dhûh-sád, charioteer:
dhûh-sádah, II, 34, 4.

dhûti, shaker:
dhûtayah (Maruts), I, 37, 6; 39, 1; 10; V, 54, 4; VII, 58, 4; VIII, 20, 16; (V, 87, 3[3]); dhûtayah, I, 64, 5; 87, 3; 168, 2; V, 61, 14.

dhûrv:
dhûrvane, (48.)

dhri, to hold:
dadhire, I, 64, 10; 85, 3; (nấmâni), I, 87, 5; dâdhâra, he established, X, 121, 1; dhârá-yante vratấ, they observe their duties, VIII, 94, 2; dhâráye-thâm, may you maintain, VI, 74, 1.—ádhi sríyah dadhire, they clothed themselves in beauty, I, 85, 2[2].—ví ánu dhire, they spread out behind, I, 166, 10.—ní dadhré, he holds himself down (Dat.), I, 37, 7[1].

dhrish, to defy:
â-dhríshe, I, 39, 4[2]; V, 87, 2.—da-dhrishvấn, daring, I, 165, 10[1].

dhrishatấ, adv., boldly:
I, 167, 9[1].

dhrishat-vín, full of daring:
dhrishat-vínah, V, 52, 2[1].

pat, to fly:
paptú*h*, V, 59, 7; pátata*h*, VIII, 7, 35.—ā́ paptata, fly to, I, 88, 1[3]; ā́ apaptan, VII, 59, 7.—ví patatha, you fly across, I, 168, 6; ví pā́patan, they were scattered, VIII, 20, 4.

pat (patyate):
pátyamânam, having taken (a name), VI, 66, 1; távishî*h* pat, (I, 64, 7[3].)

páti, lord:
bhûtásya páti*h*, X, 121, 1; bráhma*n*a*h* pátim, I, 38, 13[1]; pátaya*h* rayî*n*ā́m, X, 121, 10; V, 55, 10.

pátnî, wife:
gáni with pátnî, (I, 85, 1[1].)

pathín, path:
patha (yamásya), on the path, I, 38, 5[3]; kéna *k*it pathā́, I, 87, 2; pathí-bhi*h*, II, 34, 5; X, 168, 3; pánthâm sū́ryâya yā́tave, a path for the sun to walk, VIII, 7, 8[1].

pathyā́, path, course:
pathyā̀*h*, V, 54, 9; VI, 66, 7.

pad, to go, depart:
padish*t*á, I, 38, 6[2].

pad, foot:
pat-sú, V, 54, 11.

pan, to glorify:
panayanta, I, 87, 3.

panasyú, praiseworthy, glorious.
panasyúm, I, 38, 15; V, 56, 9; panasyáva*h*, X, 77, 3.

pánîyas, more glorious:
pánîyasî (távishî), I, 39, 2.

paya*h*-dhā́, sucking:
paya*h*-dhā́*h*, VII, 56, 16.

paya*h*-v*r*ídh, increasing the rain:
paya*h*-v*r*ídha*h*, I, 64, 11.

páyas, milk (rain):
páyasâ, I, 64, 5; 166, 3; páya*h* gh*r*itá-vat, I, 64, 6[2].

par, see p*r*î.

pára, highest:
párasmin dhā́man, I, 43, 9; páram, top, I, 168, 6.—páre yugé, in former years, I, 166, 13.

pára-para, one after another:
párâ-parâ, I, 38, 6.

paramá, further:
paramā́*h*, I, 167, 2; paramásyâ*h*, V, 61, 1[1].

parás, beyond (c. Acc.):
pará*h*, I, 19, 2.

párâ, prep. . . . :
adv., far away, I, 167, 4.

parâkā́t, from afar:
X, 77, 6.

parâ*k*aís, far away:
âré parâ*k*aí*h*, VI, 74, 2.

parâ-vát, far:
parâ-váta*h*, from afar, I, 39, 1; VIII, 7, 26; X, 78, 7; far, V, 53, 8; paramásyâ*h* parâ-váta*h*, from the furthest distance, V, 61, 1[1]; parâ-váti, in the distance, I, 134, 4.

pári, prep. . . . :
pári (tasthúsha*h*), round, I, 6, 1[2]; (agu*h*), I, 88, 4.—With Abl., from, V, 59, 7; VII, 46, 3.—pari-, excessive, (104 seq.)—Synizesis of pári, p. cxxiii.

pari-krosá, reviler:
pari-krosám, (104.)

parikshâma, withered away:
(104.)

pári-gman, traveller:
pari-gman (Indra), I, 6, 9.

pári-gri, running, swarming around:
pári-graya*h*, I, 64, 5; V, 54, 2 (bis).

pári-dveshas, a great hater:
pári-dveshasa*h*, (104.)

pari-prī́:
pari-príya*h*, great lovers or surrounding friends, (105.)

pári-prîta, loved very much:
pári-prîta*h*, (105.)

pari-prúsh, scattering moisture:
pari-prúsha*h*, X, 77, 5.

pari-bā́dh, harasser:
pari-bā́dha*h*, I, 43, 8[1].

pari-manyú, wrathful:
pari-manyáve, I, 39, 10[1].

pari-ráp, enemy:
pari-rápa*h*, (104.)

parilaghu, perlevis:
(104.)

parish*th*âna, abode:
(I, 6, 1[2]); (29.)

pari-stúbh:
pari-stúbha*h*, shouting all around, I, 166, 11.—pari-stúbha*h* (ísha*h*), standing round about, (VIII, 7, 1[1].)

pari-sp*r*ídh, rival:
pari-sp*r*ídha*h*, (104.)

pari-srut:
pari-stubh = pari-srut, (VIII, 7, 1[1].)

bâhú-ogas, strong-armed:
bâhú-ogasa*h*, VIII, 20, 6.
bâhú-gûta, quick with his arm:
bâhú-gûta*h*, V, 58, 4.
bī́ga, seed:
bī́gam, V, 53, 13.
budh, to awake:
Sâya*n*a, bodhi = budhyasva, (II, 33, 15[2].)—prá bodhaya, awake, I, 134, 3.
budhná, bottom:
budhné apā́m, X, 77, 4.
budhnyā̀, hidden:
budhnyā̀, VII, 56, 14[1]
b*r*ih:
barhayati, to crush, (226.)—upa-bárb*r*ihat, she stretched out (dó*h*, her arm), V, 61, 5[1].—Cf. v*r*ih.
b*r*ihát, great, mighty:
b*r*ihát, V, 55, 1; 2; 57, 8; 58, 8; b*r*ihát váya*h*, VII, 58, 3; b*r*ihát gíhite, VIII, 20, 6; b*r*ihát vadema, we shall magnify, II, 33, 15; b*r*ihántam krátum, I, 2, 8; ā́pa*h* b*r*ihatī́*h*, X, 121, 7[1]; 9; b*r*ihatá*h* divá*h*, V, 59, 7; 87, 3.
b*r*íhat-giri, dwelling on mighty mountains:
b*r*íhat-giraya*h*, V, 57, 8[1]; 58, 8.
b*r*ihát-diva, coming from the great heaven:
b*r*ihát-divai*h*, I, 167, 2; (V, 57, 8[1].)
b*r*ihat-vayas, of great strength:
b*r*ihat-vayasa*h* (the Maruts), (I, 37, 9[1].)
B*r*íhaspáti, a variety of Agni:
(I, 38, 13[1].)
bradhná, bright:
bradhnám, I, 6, 1[1].
Bráhma*n*aspáti, lord of prayer: N. of Agni, (I, 38, 13[1]); (246, note[a].)
brahma*n*yát, prayerful:
brahma*n*yánta*h*, II, 34, 11.
brahmán, m. priest:
brahmā́ ká*h*, VIII, 7, 20; brahmā́*n*am, X, 77, 1[4].
bráhman, n., prayer, hymn:
bráhma, I, 37, 4; 88, 4; 165, 11; II, 34, 7[1]; bráhmâ*n*i, I, 165, 2; 4[1]; 14; II, 34, 6; brā́hmana*h* pátim, lord of prayer, I, 38, 13[1].
brû, to speak:
bruve (púmân íti), he is called, V, 61, 8.—ádhi brûhi na*h*, bless us, I, 114, 10.—úpa bruvate, they implore, I, 134, 2.—prá bruváte, they proclaim, V, 87, 2.—sám bruvate, they talk together, I, 37, 13.

bhaksh, to enjoy:
bhakshîyá (c. Gen.), V, 57, 7.
bhága, luck:
bhágam, luck, I, 134, 5; bháge ā́, in wealth, II, 34, 8.
bhag, to obtain:
bhegire, V, 57, 5.—ā́ bhaga na*h*, appoint us to, give us, help us to (Loc.), I, 43, 8; VII, 46, 4[1]; ā́ bhagatana, VII, 56, 21.—Desider., bhiksh, (220.)
bhadrá, good, auspicious:
bhadrā́, good things, I, 166, 9[1]; 10; (sau*s*ravasâni), VI, 74, 2; (vástrâ), beautiful, I, 134, 4; bhadrā́ (râtí*h*), I, 168, 7[1]; (sumatí*h*), I, 114, 9.
bhádra-gâni, having an excellent mother:
bhádra-gânaya*h*, V, 61, 4[1].
bhan, to shout:
(V, 52, 12[2].)
bhandát-ish*t*i, in jubilant throng:
bhandát-ish*t*aye, V, 87, 1.
bharatá, Bharata (the warrior):
bharatā́ya, V, 54, 14[1].
bharas, burden (?):
(V, 54, 10[1].)
bhártri, husband:
bhártâ-iva, V, 58, 7.
bhâ, to shine:
vi-bhā́ti, he shines forth, X, 121, 6.
bhâgá, share:
bhâgám, VII, 56, 14.
bhânú, splendour:
bhânú*h* divá*h*, V, 52, 6; bhânúm, V, 59, 1; bhânú-bhi*h*, I, 87, 6; VIII, 7, 8; 36.
bhâm, to be in wrath:
bhâmitá*h*, I, 114, 8[1].
bhā́ma, vigour:
bhā́mena, I, 165, 8.
bhâmín:
bhâmína*h*, VS. for bhâmitá*h*, (I, 114, 8[1].)
bhā́s, light:
bhâsā́, X, 77, 5.
bhiksh, to beg, to implore:
(220); bhikshe, I, 171, 1; bhiksheta, VIII, 7, 15.

súshma, breath, strength:
súshmah, I, 165, 4^{3}; p. xv; breath, VII, 56, 8; súshmam, I, 64, 14; 165, 1^{4}; pp. xiii seq.; xxi; VIII, 7, 24; 20, 3; súshmâya, power (blast), VIII, 7, 5; súshma with vríshan and vrishabhá, (140; 149.)

sushmín, strong:
sushmî́, VII, 56, 24; sushmíne, I, 37, 4.

sû́ra, hero:
sûrâh, I, 64, 9; sû́râh-iva, I, 85, 8; V, 59, 5; gánâsah sû́râh, VII, 56, 22; gigîvấmsah ná sû́râh, X, 78, 4.

sûsu-vás, always increasing:
sûsu-vấmsam, I, 64, 15; sûsu-vấmsah, strong, I, 167, 9.

srínga, horn:
sríngam, V, 59, 3.

sridh, strong:
sárdhantam, V, 56, 1.

sé-vridh, conferring blessings:
sé-vridhah, V, 87, 4.

so:
ní-sitâni, prepared, I, 171, 4.

sokís, blast of fire:
sokíh, I, 39, 1.

sóna, brown:
sónâ, I, 6, 2.

sobhás, see sumbh.

sóbhishtha, most splendid:
sóbhishthâh, VII, 56, 6.

skut, to trickle:
skótanti, I, 87, 2.

Syâvá:
syâvấya, V, 61, 9.

Syâvá-asva:
syâva-asva, V, 52, 1; (V, 61, 5^{2}); (359 seq.)

Syâvấsva-stuta, praised by Syâvâsva:
syâvấsva-stutâya, V, 61, 5^{2}.

syená, hawk:
syenấh, VII, 56, 3; syenấsah ná pakshínah, like winged hawks, VIII, 20, 10; syenấsah, X, 77, 5; syenấn-iva, I, 165, 2; (175.)

srath:
srathayanta, they tire, V, 54, 10.—srathayante, they soften, V, 59, 1.—sisrathantu, may they loose it (plural instead of dual), (258.)

srathary, to melt:
sratharyáti, X, 77, 4^{1}.

srávas, glory:
srávah, I, 165, 12; 171, 5; V, 52, 1^{2}; I, 43, 7; srávâmsi, V, 61, 11; srávase, I, 134, 3.

sravasyú, eager for glory:
sravasyúh, VIII, 94, 1; sravasyávah, I, 85, 8.—sravasyúm, glorious, V, 56, 8.

srâyá, going:
srâyấh, V, 53, 4^{2}.

sri:
ápa-sritah, retired, V, 61, 19.—upa-sisriyâṅấh, fastened, VII, 56, 13.

sriyáse, see srî́.

srî́, splendour, beauty, glory:
srî́h, V, 57, 6; sriyấ, V, 61, 12^{2}; VI, 66, 4; VII, 56, 6; sriyấ sréshthah, II, 33, 3; sriyé, I, 88, 3; V, 55, 3; VIII, 7, 25; X, 77, 2; sriyé sréyâmsah, V, 60, 4^{2}; sriyáse, I, 87, 6^{1}; V, 59, 3^{3} (bis); srîyah, I, 85, 2^{2}; 166, 10; VIII, 20, 12; srîyam váhante, they bring with them beautiful light, VIII, 20, 7^{2}.—srîyam, happiness, I, 43, 7; sriyé, for happiness sake, I, 64, 12.

sru, to hear:
srinve, I, 37, 3; srinóti, I, 37, 13; srinutá, I, 86, 2^{1}; sróta, V, 87, 8; 9; srudhí, I, 2, 1; srinótu, I, 114, 11; VII, 46, 1^{1}; susrâva, V, 53, 2; srinvire, V, 87, 3; X, 168, 4; srinomi (with two Acc.), I hear thou art —, II, 33, 4.—ấ asrot, listened, I, 39, 6^{1}; sroshantu ấ, I, 86, 5^{2}.—See srótri.

srutá, glorious:
srutám, I, 6, 6; V, 52, 17; II, 33, 11; srutấsu, V, 60, 2.

srútya, glorious:
srútyam, I, 165, 11.

srushtí, a hearing:
srushtím, I, 166, 13.

srushti-mát, to be obeyed:
srushti-mántam, V, 54, 14^{3}.

sréni, row:
srénîh, V, 59, 7^{1}.

sréyas:
sriyé sréyâmsah, glorious for glory, V, 60, 4^{2}.

sréshtha, best:
sréshthah, I, 43, 5.—sréshthah sriyấ, the most beautiful in beauty, II, 33, 3.

sấm-râ*g*ya, the being the universal ruler:
sấm-râ*g*yena, VII, 46, 2[1].
sấyaka, arrow:
sấyakâni, II, 33, 10.
sâsahí, see sasahí.
si*m*há, lion:
si*m*hấ*h*-iva, I, 64, 8; v*ŕi*shâ si*m*há*h*, (140.)
si*ñk*, to pour out:
ási*ñk*an, I, 85, 11.
síndhu, stream, river:
síndhava*h*, I, 168, 8; V, 53, 7; VIII, 7, 5; X, 78, 7; (X, 78, 6[1].)—síndhu*h*, the Indus, V, 53, 9[1]; the river, I, 114, 11; síndhum, VIII, 20, 24[1]; síndhau, VIII, 20, 25
síndhu-mât*ri*, pl., the sons of Sindhu, N. of the Maruts:
síndhu-mâtara*h*, X, 78, 6[1]; (I, 85, 3[1]; 168, 9[1]); (307.)
sîm, particle:
I, 37, 6; 9.
su, to press out, to pour out (Soma):
suvâna, dissyllabic, p. cxxi; suvânaí*h* (índu-bhi*h*), VIII, 7, 14; sunvaté, V, 60, 7; sunvatá*h*, I, 2, 6; sutá*h*, I, 86, 4; VIII, 94, 4; sutấ*h*, I, 2, 4; 168, 3; sutấnâm sómânâm, I, 134, 6.—See also sutá.
sú, well:
I, 37, 14; 38, 6; V, 54, 15; VIII, 94, 3; X, 77, 4; VI, 74, 4; quickly, I, 165, 14; loud, VIII, 20, 19; greatly, VIII, 7, 18; ó sú, II, 34, 15; VII, 59, 5; VIII, 7, 33; mó sú, VII, 59, 5; sahó sú, VIII, 7, 32.
su-á*k*, fleet:
su-á*ñk*a*h*, VII, 56, 16.
su-ápas, clever:
su-ápâ*h*, I, 85, 9; V, 60, 5.
su-apivâta, implored, desired:
su-apivâta (Rudra), freely accessible, VII, 46, 3[1]; (I, 165, 13[1]); see vat.
su-ápnas, wealthy:
su-ápnasa*h*, X, 78, 1.
su-arká, resounding with beautiful songs:
su-arkaí*h*, I, 88, 1[1].
su-ávas, gracious:
su-ávasam, V, 60, 1; su-ávân, svavadbhi*h*, (I, 6, 3[2].)
su-á*s*va, possessed of good horses:
su-á*s*vâ*h*, V, 57, 2; VII, 56, 1.
su-âdhí, full of devotion:
su-âdhyấ*h*, X, 78, 1.
su-âyudhá, with good weapons:
su-âyudhấ*h*, V, 57, 2; su-âyudhấsa*h*, V, 87, 5[2]; VII, 56, 11.
su-uktá, hymn:
su-ukténa, I, 171, 1; su-uktám, VII, 58, 6.
su-upâyana:
(VII, 46, 3[1].)
su-k*ŕi*t, good deeds:
su-k*ŕi*te, I, 166, 12.
sú-k*ri*ta, well-made:
sú-k*ri*tam, I, 85, 9; sú-k*ri*tâ*h*, I, 134, 2.
su-kshatrá, powerful:
su-kshatrấsa*h*, I, 19, 5.
su-kshití, dwelling in safety:
su-kshitáye, VII, 56, 24.
su-khá, easy:
su-khéshu (rátheshu), V, 60, 2.
su-khâdí, armed with beautiful rings:
su-khâdáye, (I, 64, 10[2]); V, 87, 1; su-khâdáya*h*, I, 87, 6.
su-gá, flowing freely:
su-gấ*h*, I, 165, 8.—su-gám, to a good end, V, 54, 6; su-gám, welfare, I, 43, 6.
su-gándhi, sweet-scented:
sugándhim, VII, 59, 12.
su-gopấtama, having the best guardians:
su-gopấtama*h*, I, 86, 1[1].
su-*k*andrá, bright:
su-*k*andrám, II, 34, 13.
su-*k*etú, kindness:
su-*k*etúnâ, I, 166, 6[1].
su-*k*etúna, gracious:
su-*k*etúnam (Soma), (I, 166, 6[1].)
sú-*g*âta, well-born:
sú-*g*âtâya, V, 53, 12; sú-*g*âtâ, V, 56, 9; su-*g*âtấsa*h* *g*anúshâ, V, 57, 5; 59, 6; VIII, 20, 8; su-*g*âtâ*h*, I, 88, 3; 166, 12; su-*g*âtám, well-acquired, VII, 56, 21.
su-*g*ihvá, soft-tongued:
su-*g*ihvấ*h*, I, 166, 11.
sutá, the pressed juice (of Soma), libation:
asya sutásya, VIII, 94, 6; suté sá*k*â, VII, 59, 3[1]; sutấsa*h*, I, 165, 4; sutấnâm, I, 2, 5.

II. LIST OF THE MORE IMPORTANT PASSAGES QUOTED IN THE PREFACE AND IN THE NOTES.

RIG-VEDA.

ATHARVA-VEDA.

VÂ*G*ASANEYI-SA*M*HITÂ.

TAITTIRÎYA-SA*M*HITÂ.

AITAREYA-BRÂHMA*N*A.

*S*ATAPATHA-BRÂHMA*N*A.

TÂ*ND*YA-BRÂHMA*N*A.

TAITTIRÎYA-ÂRA*N*YAKA.

Â*S*VALÂYANA *S*RAUTA-SÛTRA.

III.

A BIBLIOGRAPHICAL LIST OF THE MORE IMPORTANT PUBLICATIONS ON THE RIG-VEDA.

I have often stated how much I was indebted to the labours of others in all I have endeavoured to do for the Veda. I have to make the same acknowledgment once more. Many indeed of those with whom I once worked side by side have ceased from their labours, but the gaps which death has caused have been filled by many young and equally valiant soldiers. I am almost afraid to mention names, lest I should seem forgetful of some by whose labours I have benefitted. The elaborate publications of M. Bergaigne occupy a prominent place, and seem to me to have hardly received the credit which they deserve. Scholars are too apt to forget that we may differ from the results arrived at by our colleagues, and yet admire their industry, their acumen, their genius. Professor Ludwig has continued his work, undismayed by the unjust and unseemly attacks of his rivals. Professor Oldenberg's contributions, Das altindische Âkhyâna, 1883; Ṛigveda-Saṃhitâ und Sâmavedârcika, 1884; Die Adhyâyatheilung des Ṛigveda, 1887, and lastly, the Prolegomena to his Hymnen des Ṛigveda, 1888, have opened new and important fields of critical investigation. Different views have been ably represented by Pischel and Geldner in their Vedische Studien.

Professor Avery's Contributions to the History of Verb-Inflection in Sanskrit (1875), Professor Lanman's Statistical Account of Noun-inflection in the Veda (1877), are indispensable helps to every student of the Veda. Professor Delbrück's Syntaktische Forschungen (1871–1879) und Das Altindische Verbum (1874) marked a decided advance in critical scholarship. Almost every case of the noun in the Veda has found its special investigator, the Dative in Delbrück (1867), the Genitive in Siecke (1869), the Vocative in Benfey (1872), the Instrumental in Wenzel (1879), the Accusative in Gaedicke (1880). The nominal suffixes have been treated by Bruno Lindner in his Altindische Nominalbildung (1878); the suffixes of the Infinitive by Professor Ludwig (1871) and Professor Wilhelm (1870 and 1873). Geldner and Professor Kaegi have given a popular and useful account of the results of Vedic studies in Siebenzig Lieder des Rigveda (1875), and Der Rigveda (1881).

The following is a list of the more important publications on the Rig-veda which have proved useful to myself and will prove useful to others. This list does not pretend to be complete, but even in its incomplete form, I hope that it may be serviceable to students of the Rig-veda.

The following abbreviations have been used :—

Bezz. Beitr. = Beiträge zur Kunde der indogermanischen Sprachen, herausgegeben von A. Bezzenberger.

Festgruss an Böhtlingk = Festgruss an Otto von Böhtlingk zum Doctor-Jubiläum von seinen Freunden. Stuttgart, 1888.

Journ. Amer. Or. Soc. = Journal of the American Oriental Society.

KZ. = Kuhn's Zeitschrift für vergleichende Sprachforschung.

Rev. hist. rel. = Revue de l'histoire des religions, publiée by M. Jean Reville. Paris.

ZDMG. = Zeitschrift der deutschen morgenländischen Gesellschaft.

ARROWSMITH, R. The Rigveda. By Adolf Kaegi. Translation. Boston, 1886.

AUFRECHT, TH. KZ. XXV, 435, 601; XXVI, 610; XXVII, 609.—Zur Kenntniss des Ṛgveda: Festgruss an Böhtlingk, 1–3.—Erklärung vedischer Stellen: Bezz. Beitr. XIV, 29–33.—ZDMG. XLV, 305.

AVERY, JOHN. Contributions to the History of Verb-Inflection in Sanskrit, 1875. (Journ. Amer. Or. Soc., Vol. X, No. 10.)

—— The Unaugmented Verb-Forms of the Rig- and Atharva-Vedas (Journ. Amer. Or. Soc., Vol. XI, No. 2, 1885.)

BARTHOLOMAE, CHR. Rv. I, 171, 1: KZ. XXIX, 279.—Arisches: Bezz. Beitr. XV, 1–43, 185–247.—ZDMG. XLIII, 664–668.

—— Studien zur indogermanischen Sprachgeschichte. Halle, 1890. See Pischel in Götting. Gel. Anz., No. 13, 20 Juni 1890, pp. 529 ff.

Benfey, Theodor. Die Quantitätsverschiedenheiten in den Samhitâ- und Pada-Texten der Veden. 6 Theile. Göttingen, 1874–81.

—— Ueber die Entstehung des indogermanischen Vokativs. Göttingen, 1872.

—— Vedica und Verwandtes. Strassburg, 1879

—— Ueber einige Wörter mit dem Bindevocal î im Rigveda. Göttingen, 1879.

—— Vedica und Linguistica. Strassburg, 1880.

—— Behandlung des auslautenden a in na 'wie' und na 'nicht' im Rigveda, mit Bemerkungen über die Aussprache der Wörter im Veda. Göttingen, 1881.

—— Uebersetzung des Rigveda (I, 1–118): Orient und Occident, 1862–64.

—— Rigveda, X, 10, 7: Bezz. Beitr. I, 47–51.—Uebersetzung des Rigveda (I, 119–130): Bezz. Beitr. VII, 286–309.

—— Kleinere Schriften, herausgegeben von A. Bezzenberger, I, 109, 120, 265, 278, 295, 305, 314, 316; II, 172, 177. Berlin, 1890.

Bergaigne, A. La religion védique d'après les hymnes du Rig-Veda. Vols. I–III. Paris, 1878–83.

—— Quelques Observations sur les figures de rhétorique dans le Rig-Veda. (Mémoires de la Société de linguistique, tome IV, 2e fascicule.) Paris, 1880.

—— Recherches sur l'histoire de la Samhitâ du Rig-Veda I. La Samhitâ primitive. Paris, 1887. (Journal Asiatique, 1886. Extrait.)

—— Nouvelles recherches sur l'histoire de la Samhitâ du Rig-Veda II–IV. Supplément au Mémoire sur la Samhitâ primitive; les différents couches d'interprétations; le classement du Mandala VIII. Paris, 1887. (Journal Asiatique, IX, 191–287. Extrait.)

—— Deuxième note additionnelle à l'article Recherches sur l'histoire de la Samhitâ du Rig-Veda. (Journal Asiatique, IX, 518 f.)

—— La syntaxe des comparisons védiques: Bibliothèque de l'école des hautes études, LXXII, pp. 75–101. (Mél. Renier, Paris, 1887.)

—— Recherches sur l'histoire de la liturgie védique. La forme métrique des hymns du Rig-Veda. (Ac. des Inscr., C—R, XVI, 1888, Mai-Juin, pp. 232–238.)

—— Recherches sur l'histoire de la liturgie védique. (Journal Asiatique, XIII, 2, 121–197. 1889.)

—— La division en Adhyâyas du Rig-Veda: Journal Asiatique, X, 3, 488–495. (Extrait. Paris, 1888.)

—— et V. Henry. Manuel pour le Sanscrit Védique. Paris, 1890.

BLOOMFIELD, M. Final *as* before Sonants in Sanskrit. Baltimore, 1882. (Amer. Journal of Philology, Vol. III, No. 1.)

—— On certain Irregular Vedic Subjunctives or Imperatives. Baltimore, 1884. (Amer. Journal of Philology, Vol. V, No. 1.)

—— On the Vedic Instrumental pa*d*bhís. (Proc. Amer. Or. Soc. Oct. 1889, pp. clii–clvi.)

—— Contributions to the Interpretation of the Veda. Second Series. Baltimore, 1890.

BOLLENSEN, F. Zur Vedametrik: ZDMG. XXXV, 448–445.—Die Betonungssysteme des Rig- und Sâmaveda: ZDMG. XXXV, 456–72.—Beiträge zur Kritik des Veda: ZDMG. XLI, 494–507; XLV, 204.

P. VON BRADKE. Beiträge zur altindischen Religions- und Sprachgeschichte: ZDMG. XL, 347 ff., 655 ff.

—— Dyâus Asura, Ahura Mazdâ und die Asuras. Halle, 1885.

BRUNNHOFER, H. Erwähnung der Pfahlbauten im Rigveda: Fernschau, Jahrb. der Mittelschweiz, Geogr.-Commerz. Ges. in Aarau, II (1888).

—— Dialektspuren (Infinitiv): KZ. XXV, 329.—Ueber Infinitive des Veda und Avesta: Bezz. Beitr. XV, 262–270.

COLINET, PH. Les principes de l'exégèse védique d'après MM. Pischel et K. Geldner (Muséon, IX, 1890, pp. 250–267 and 372–388).

—— Purandhi, the goddess of abundance, in the Rigveda. (Babyl. and Oriental Record, II, 11 (1888), pp. 245–254.)

—— Purandhi *is* the goddess of abundance in the Rigveda. (Babyl. and Oriental Record, 1890, IV, 6, pp. 121–130.)

COLLITZ, H. Ueber eine besondere Art vedischer Composita, Verhandlungen des Vten intern. Or. Congr. zu Berlin, 1881. II, 287–298.

DELBRÜCK, B. De usu dativi in carminibus Rigvedae. Halle, 1867.

—— Syntaktische Forschungen. Halle, 1871–79.—Bd. V, Altindische Syntax. Halle, 1888.

—— Das Altindische Verbum. Halle, 1874.

—— Vedische Chrestomathie. Halle, 1874.

EATON, A. J. The Âtmanepada in the Rigveda. Leipzig, 1884.

D'ECKSTEIN, BARON. Études sur la Grammaire Védique. (Revue Archéologique.) Paris, 1859.

EDGREN, A. H. On the Relation in the Rig-Veda between the Palatal and Labial Vowels and their Corresponding Semivowels, 1878. (Journ. Amer. Or. Soc., Vol. XI, 1880.)

EHNI, J. Der Vedische Mythus des Yama. Strassburg, 1890.

—— Rv. X, 85, die Vermählung des Soma und der Sûryâ: ZDMG. XXXIII, 166–176.

GAEDICKE, CARL. Der Accusativ im Veda. Breslau, 1880.

GARBE, R. Accentuationssystem der altindischen Nominalcomposita: KZ. XXIII, 470.

GELDNER, K. Conjectanea Vedica (kshonî): Bezz. Beitr. XI, 327–331.—Ueber das vedische Wort meni: Festgruss an Böhtlingk, 31–33.—Conjectanea Vedica: KZ. XXVII, 215 ff.

GELDNER, K., u. A. KAEGI. Siebenzig Lieder des Rigveda. Tübingen, 1875.

GRASSMANN, H. Wörterbuch zum Rig-Veda. Leipzig, 1873.

—— Rigveda, übersetzt. 2 Vols. Leipzig, 1876–77.

GRIFFITH, R. T. H. The Hymns of the Rigveda, translated with a Popular Commentary. Vols. I, II. Benares, 1889–90.

GURU DATTA, Vidyârthî. The Terminology of the Vedas, Part I. Lahore, New Indian Press, 1888.

HAPPEL, JULIUS. An Varuna, Rigveda I, 25, übersetzt: Zeitschr. f. Missionskunde u. Religionswissenschaft, V, 1, p. 28 f.

HAUG, M. The Origin of Brahmanism. Poona, 1863.

—— A Contribution towards a Right Understanding of the Rigveda. Bombay, 1863.

—— Brahma und die Brahmanen. München, 1871.

—— On the Interpretation of the Veda: Report of the Proc. of the 2nd intern. Çongr. of Or. in London, 1874, pp. 24–27. Cf. Delbrück in Jenaer Literaturzeitung, Jahrgang 1874, Art. 785, and 1875, Art. 137.

—— Ueber das Wesen und den Werth des wedischen Accents. München, 1874.

—— Vedische Räthselfragen und Räthselsprüche. Uebersetzung und Erklärung des Dîrghatamas-Liedes Rigv. I, 164. München, 1876.

HILLEBRANDT, A. Ueber die Göttin Aditi. Breslau, 1876.

—— Varuṇa und Mitra. Breslau, 1877.

—— Das altindische Neu- u. Vollmondsopfer. Jena, 1880.

—— Die beiden arischen Accentsysteme. 1882–85.

—— Veda-Chrestomathie mit Glossar. Berlin, 1885.

—— Zu Rv. V, 2, 1–6: ZDMG. XXXIII, 248–251.—Zu Rv. I, 162: ZDMG. XXXVII, 521–524.—Miscelle aus dem Vedaritual: ZDMG. XL, 708–712.

HILLEBRANDT, A. Spuren einer älteren Ṛigvedarecension: Bezz. Beitr. VIII, 195–203.—Uktham madas ka sasyate: Bezz. Beitr. IX, 192.

—— Vedica. Vienna Oriental Journal, III, 188–194, 259–273.

—— Nationale Opfer in Altindien: Festgruss an Böhtlingk, 40–43.

—— Die Sonnwendfeste in Altindien: Romanische Forschungen, V. 1889, 299 seqq.

—— Vedische Mythologie I. Soma und verwandte Götter. Breslau, 1891.

HIRZEL, A. Gleichnisse und Metaphern im Ṛgveda. Leipzig, 1890.

KAEGI, A. Der Rigveda, die aelteste Literatur der Inder. 2te Aufl. Leipzig, 1881. See Arrowsmith.

—— Vasta usrâḥ: Festgruss an Böhtlingk, 48 seq.

KERBAKER, M. Varuna e gli Aditya, saggio di esegesi vedica, memoria (Atti della R. Acad. di archeol. lettere e belle arti, 1884–86). Napoli, 1887, pp. 105–144.—App. II al Vol. XIII, degli Atti &c. Napoli, 1889.

KIRSTE, J. Études sur les Prâtiśâkhyas. Paris, 1883.

KOULIKOWSKI, D. Les trois feux sacrés du Rig-Véda: Rev. hist. rel XX, 2, pp. 151–179.

KÜHNAU, R. Die Trishṭubh-Jagatî-Familie. Göttingen, 1886.

—— Rhythmus und indische Metrik. Göttingen, 1887.

LANGLOIS, M. Rig-Véda, ou Livre des Hymnes, traduit du Sanscrit, 4 tom. Paris, 1848–51.

LANMAN, CHARLES R. A Statistical Account of Noun-Inflection in the Veda. (Journ. Amer. Or. Soc., Vol. X, No. 11.) New Haven, 1880. Cf. Collitz in Bezz. Beitr. VII, 176–184.

LIGNANA, GIACOMO. I Navagvâḥ e i Dáṣagvâḥ del Ṛigveda: Verhandlungen des VIIten internat. Or. Congr. in Wien, 1886. Arische Section, pp. 59–68.

LINDNER, BRUNO. Altindische Nominalbildung. Jena, 1878.

LUDWIG, A. Der Infinitiv im Veda. Prag, 1871.

—— Ueber die unflectierten Formen auf â des verbum finitum im Rigveda. Prag, 1874. (Sitzungsber. d. Kgl. böhm. Ges. d. Wiss.)

—— Die philosophischen und religiösen Anschauungen des Veda. Prag, 1875.

—— Der Rigveda, Deutsch mit Commentar und Einleitung, Vols. 1–6. Prag, 1876–88.

—— Über die Erwähnung von Sonnenfinsternissen im Rigveda. Sitzungsber. der Kgl. böhm. Ges. der Wiss. Prag, 1885.

Ludwig, A. Die Ironie im Mahâbhârata und im Ṛgveda: Festgruss an Böhtlingk, 82–87.

—— Ueber die Kritik des Rgveda Textes. Prag, 1889.

—— Ueber Methode bei Interpretationen des Rgveda. Prag, 1890.

—— dhâman und svadhâ: KZ. XXVIII, 240.

—— Bedeutungen vedischer Wörter: ZDMG. XL, 715–717.—Drei Ṛgvedastellen: ZDMG. XL, 713.

Macdonell, A. A. Kâtyâyana's Sarvânukrama*n*î of the *Ri*gveda. Oxford, 1886.

Max Müller, F. Rig-Veda oder die heiligen Lieder der Brahmanen. I: Text und Uebersetzung des Prâtisâkhya oder der ältesten Phonetik und Grammatik. Leipzig, 1856.

—— Rig-Veda-Sa*m*hitâ. The Sacred Hymns of the Brahmans. Translated and explained. Vol. I. London, 1869.

Mayr, Aurel. Beiträge aus dem Rg-Veda zur Accentuirung des Verbum finitum. Wien, 1871.

Meyer, Rudolf. Ṛgvidhâna. Berlin, 1878.

Muir, John. Original Sanskrit Texts, Vols. I–V, London, 1868–1871 (2nd ed.).

Myriantheus, L. Die Aśvins oder Arischen Dioskuren. München, 1876.

Neisser, W. Zur vedischen Verballehre I: Bezz. Beitr. VII, 211–241. —Vorvedisches im Veda: Bezz. Beitr. XVII, 244–256.

Nève, M. F. Études sur les hymnes du Rig-Vêda. Paris, 1842.

—— Essai sur le Mythe des Ṛibhavas. Paris, 1847.

Oldenberg, H. Das altindische Âkhyâna: ZDMG. XXXVII, 54–86.

—— Ṛigveda-Saṃhitâ und Sâmavedârcika: ZDMG. XXXVIII, 439–480.

—— Âkhyâna-Hymnen im Ṛigveda: ZDMG. XXXIX, 52–90.

—— Die Adhyâyatheilung des Ṛigveda: ZDMG. XLI, 508–515; XLII, 362–365.

—— Ueber die Liedverfasser des Ṛigveda. ZDMG. XLII, 199–247.

—— Der Abhinihita Sandhi im Ṛigveda, ZDMG. XLIV, 321–338.

—— Der Ṛigveda. Band I: Metrische und textgeschichtliche Prolegomena. Berlin, 1888. [Cf. Review by A. Hillebrandt, in Goetting. Gel. Anz., Mai 1889, pp. 387–424.—See Sabbathier.]

—— The Interpretation of the Veda, and the Hindu Epic: Open Court (Chicago), 1889, April 11 (Translated from the Deutsche Rundschau).

PERRY, E. D. Indra in the Rigveda: Journ. Amer. Or. Soc., Vol. XI, pp. 117–208. New Haven, 1882. (See Hillebrandt in E. Kuhns Literatur-Blatt für Orientalische Philologie, II, 1.)

PERTSCH, W. Upalekha, de Kramapâṭha libellus. Berol. 1854.

PETERSON, P. Hymns from the Rigveda, edited with Sâyaṇa's Commentary, notes and a translation. Bombay, 1888 (B. S. S.).

—— Handbook to the Study of the Rigveda. Part I. Bombay, 1890 (B. S. S.).

PISCHEL, R. Miscellanea: ZDMG. XXXV, 711–724.—Vedica: ZDMG. XL, 111–126.

—— Zur Lehre vom Dativ: Bezz. Beitr. I, 111–120.

PISCHEL, R., u. K. F. GELDNER. Vedische Studien I. Stuttgart, 1888. [Cf. Reviews by: V. HENRY: Revue critique (1890), 5, pp. 81–85.—H. OLDENBERG: Götting. Gel. Anz. 1890. 10.—BARTHOLOMAE: Deutsche Litztg. 23 (1890).—VECKENSTEDT: Zeitschr. f. Volkskunde II, 6, pp. 244–248.—See Colinet.]

REGNAUD, PAUL. Le mot védique ṛta: Rev. hist. rel. XVI, 1887, pp. 26–27.

—— Le caractère et l'origine des jeux des mots védiques: Rev. hist. rel. XVI, 2, pp. 166–169.

—— Un épithète des dieux dans le Rig-Veda (amûra): Rev. hist. rel. XV, 1887, pp. 46–51.

—— Etymologies védiques: Rev. hist. rel. XIX, 1, pp. 79–84.

—— Le Rig Veda et les origines de la mythologie indo-européenne: Rev. hist. rel. XIX, 3, pp. 333–352.

—— Études védiques. Traduction d'un hymn à l'Aurore (I, 123 du Rig-Véda): Rev. hist. rel. XXI, 1, pp. 63–96.

—— Études védiques. Deux appréciations récentes du Rig-Veda: Rev. hist. rel. XXI, 3, pp. 301–311.

—— Études védiques. L'hymne III, 1 du Rig-Véda; Rev. hist. rel. XXII, 302.

REGNIER, A. Étude sur l'idiome des Védas et les origines de la langue Sanscrite. Paris, 1855.

—— Études sur la grammaire védique. Prâtiśâkhya du Rig-Véda. Paris, 1857.

RIG-VEDA. Rigveda Sanhita, liber primus, ed. F. Rosen. London, 1838.

—— Rig-Veda-Sanhita, the Sacred Hymns of the Brahmans, together with the Commentary of Sayanacharya. Edited by F. Max Müller. 6 vols. London, 1849–1874. Second Edition, Vols. I, II. London, 1890.

RIG-VEDA. The Hymns of the Rig-Veda in the Sa*m*hitâ Text. Reprinted from the editio princeps, by F. Max Müller. London, 1873.

—— The Hymns of the Rig-Veda in the Pada Text. Reprinted from the editio princeps, by F. Max Müller. London, 1873.

—— Die Hymnen des Ṛigveda. Herausgegeben von Th. Aufrecht. 2 Theile. 2te Auflage. Bonn, 1877.

—— *Ri*ksa*m*hitâ Sâya*n*â*k*ârya-vira*k*ita-Bhâshya-sahitâ, Padapâ*th*ayuktâ *k*a, edited by Râ*g*ârâma *S*âstri Bodas and *S*ivarâma *S*âstri Gore. 8 vols. Bombay, 1889.

—— Rigveda Samhitâ, ed. by Prasanna Kumâra Vidyâratna. Vol. I. Calcutta, 1888–9.

—— Rigvedasya Sâya*n*â*k*ârya-vira*k*itam Mâdhavîya-Vedârtha-Prakâ*s*âkhyam Bhâshyam. Edited by Prasanna Kumâra Vidyâratna. Calcutta, 1889.

—— Rig-Veda Sanhita, the first and second Adhyâyas of the first Ashtaka, with notes and explanations, and an introductory essay on the study of the Vedas. By K. M. Banerjea. Calcutta, 1875.

—— Rig Veda Samhitâ, Vols. I–VII. Bengali Translation, with notes, by R. C. Datta. Calcutta, 1887.

—— The Vedârthayatna, Marâthi and English Translation of the Vedas. Parts 1–22. Bombay, 1876–80.

ROTH, R. Zur Litteratur und Geschichte des Weda. Stuttgart, 1846.

—— Ueber gewisse Kürzungen des Wortendes im Veda: Verhandlungen des VIIten intern. Or. Congr. in Wien, 1886. Arische Section, pp. 1–10.

—— Ueber den Soma: ZDMG. XXXV, 680–692.—Wo wächst der Soma? ZDMG. XXXVIII, 134–139.—Der Adler mit dem Soma: ZDMG. XXXVI, 353–360.—Lösung eines Räthsels im Veda: ZDMG. XXXVII, 109–112.—Wergeld im Veda: ZDMG. XLI, 672–676.

—— Vedische Studien: KZ. XXVI, 45.

SABBATHIER, R. Une édition critique du Ṛig-Veda par M. Oldenberg: Rev. hist. rel. XX, 3, pp. 297–331.—Rev. de ling. XXIII, 1, 93–97.

SCHERMAN, LUCIAN. Philosophische Hymnen aus der Ṛig- und Atharva-Veda-Sanhitâ. Strassburg, 1887.

SCHMIDT, J. Pluralbildungen der indog. Neutra (Weimar, 1889), p. 127 to Rv. I, 171, 1.—p. 128 seq. on krâ*n*â.—p. 307 seq. to Rv. V, 52, 9.—p. 314 to Rv. X, 77, 8.

L. VON SCHRÖDER. Nominalcomposita: KZ. XXIV, 101.

SCHWAB, JULIUS. Das altindische Thieropfer. Erlangen, 1886.

SIECKE, E. De genitivi in lingua Sanscrita imprimis Vedica usu. Berol. 1869.

SIMON, RICHARD. Beiträge zur Kenntniss der vedischen Schulen. Kiel, 1889.

THIBAUT, G. Das Jaṭâpaṭala. Lpzg. 1870.

TURRINI, GIUSÈPPE. All' Auròra ínno dí Práskaṇva Kâṇva recáto di Sáṁskṛito in volgáre. Bologna, 1889.

WALLIS, H. W. The Cosmology of the Ṛigveda. London, 1887.

WEBER, A. Vedische Hochzeitsprüche: Indische Studien, V, 177–226.

—— Ueber die Metrik der Inder. Berlin, 1863 (Indische Studien, VIII).

WENZEL, H. Ueber den Instrumentalis im Rigveda. Tübingen, 1879.

WHITNEY, W. D. On the History of the Vedic Texts: Journ. Amer. Or. Soc. 1853.

WILHELM, EUGEN. De infinitivi linguarum Sanscritae, Bactriae, etc. forma et usu. Isenaci, 1873.

WILSON, H. H. Rig-Veda-Sanhitá. Translated, completed by E. B. Cowell. London, 1850–66.

WINDISCH, E. Zwölf Hymnen des Rigveda mit Sâyaṇa's Commentar. Leipzig, 1883.

—— Vedisches: Festgruss an Böhtlingk, 114–118.

WINDISCHMANN, FR. Ueber den Somacultus der Arier: Abhandlungen der Münchener Ak. der Wiss. IV. B. Abh. 2.

ZIMMER, HEINRICH. Altindisches Leben. Berlin, 1879.

ZUBATÝ, JOSEF. Der Quantitätswechsel im Auslaute vedischer Wörter: Vienna Oriental Journal, II, 53–62, 309–318; III, 86–92, 151–162, 281–312; IV, 1–16, 89–112.

CORRIGENDA.

Page 123, line 6 from below, *read* visvá-mânusha *for* visvá-manusha
„ 138, „ 19, *read* samsamânâya *for* samsa°
„ 138, „ 20, *read* samsanam *for* samsanam
„ 173, „ 4 from below, *read* ârâ *for* âra
„ 278, „ 17 seq., *read* of Indra *for* of the Maruts
„ 315, „ 8, *read* gañgana- *for* gañganâ-

TRANSLITERATION OF ORIENTAL ALPHABETS ADOPTED FOR THE TRANSLATIONS OF THE SACRED BOOKS OF THE EAST.

CONSONANTS.	MISSIONARY ALPHABET. I Class.	II Class.	III Class.	Sanskrit.	Zend.	Pehlevi.	Persian.	Arabic.	Hebrew.	Chinese.
Gutturales.										
1 Tenuis	k	...	...	क	𐬐	[illegible]	ک	ك	כּ	k
2 „ aspirata	kh	...	...	ख	𐬑	[illegible]	...	...	כ	kh
3 Media	g	...	...	ग	𐬔	[illegible]	گ	...	גּ	...
4 „ aspirata	gh	...	...	घ	𐬖	[illegible]	...	...	ג	...
5 Gutturo-labialis	q	...	...	...	...	...	ق	ق	ק	...
6 Nasalis	ṅ (ng)	...	...	ङ	{ 𐬢 (ng) / 𐬣 (N) }	...	...	...	...	...
7 Spiritus asper	h	...	...	ह	𐬵 (𐬓 *hv*)	[illegible]	ه	ه	ה	h, hs
8 „ lenis	ʼ	...	...	...	...	...	ا	ا	א	...
9 „ asper faucalis	ʻh	...	...	...	...	...	ح	ح	ח	...
10 „ lenis faucalis	ʼh	...	...	...	...	...	ع	ع	ע	...
11 „ asper fricatus	...	*ʻh*	...	...	...	...	خ	خ	ח	...
12 „ lenis fricatus	...	*ʼh*	...	...	...	...	...	...	...	...
Gutturales modificatae (palatales, &c.)										
13 Tenuis	...	*k*	...	च	𐬗	[illegible]	چ	...	...	*k*
14 „ aspirata	...	*kh*	...	छ	...	...	...	...	...	*kh*
15 Media	...	*g*	...	ज	𐬘	[illegible]	ج	ج	...	...
16 „ aspirata	...	*gh*	...	झ	...	...	غ	غ	...	...
17 „ Nasalis	...	*ñ*	...	ञ	...	...	...	...	...	...

CONSONANTS (*continued*).	MISSIONARY ALPHABET. I Class.	II Class.	III Class.	Sanskrit.	Zend.	Pehlevi.	Persian.	Arabic.	Hebrew.	Chinese.
18 Semivocalis	y	...	....	य	𐬌𐬌, 𐬫 } init.	[illegible]	ي	ي	י	y
19 Spiritus asper	...	($\acute{y}$)	....	...	....	...	...	...	...	...
20 „ lenis	...	($\grave{y}$)	....	...	....	...	...	...	...	...
21 „ asper assibilatus	...	*s*	....	श	𐬱	[illegible]	ش	ش	...	...
22 „ lenis assibilatus	...	*z*	....	...	𐬲	[illegible]	ژ	...	...	*z*
Dentales.										
23 Tenuis	t	...	....	त	𐬙	[illegible]	ت	ت	תּ	t
24 „ aspirata	th	...	....	थ	𐬚	...	...	...	ת	th
25 „ assibilata	...	...	TH	...	....	...	ث	ث	...	...
26 Media	d	...	....	द	𐬛	[illegible]	د	د	דּ	...
27 „ aspirata	dh	...	....	ध	𐬜	...	...	...	ד	...
28 „ assibilata	...	...	DH	...	....	...	ذ	ذ	...	...
29 Nasalis	n	...	....	न	𐬥	[illegible]	ن	ن	נ	n
30 Semivocalis	l	...	....	ल	....	[illegible]	ل	ل	ל	l
31 „ mollis 1	...	*l*	....	ळ	....	...	...	...	...	...
32 „ mollis 2	...	...	L	...	....	...	...	...	...	...
33 Spiritus asper 1	s	...	....	स	𐬯	[illegible]	س(ث)	س	שׂ	s
34 „ asper 2	...	...	s (ʃ)	...	....	...	...	...	ס	...
35 „ lenis	z	...	....	...	𐬰	[illegible]	ز (ذ)	ز	ז	z
36 „ asperrimus 1	...	...	z (ʒ)	...	....	...	ص	ص	צ	ʒ, ʒh
37 „ asperrimus 2	...	...	ẓ (ʒ)	...	....	...	ض	...	...	...

Dentales modificatae (linguales, &c.)										
38 Tenuis	...	*t*	...	ट	...	...	ط	ط	ט	...
39 " aspirata	...	*th*	...	ठ	...	...	ظ	ظ	...	...
40 Media	...	*d*	...	ड	𐬜	𐬛	...	...	...	...
41 " aspirata	...	*dh*	...	ढ	...	...	...	ض	...	...
42 Nasalis	...	*n*	...	ण	𐬧	...	...	...	...	...
43 Semivocalis	r	...	...	र	𐬭	𐭥,ط,ا	ر	ر	ר	...
44 " fricata	...	*r*	...	...	...	...	...	...	...	*r*
45 " diacritica	...	...	R	...	...	...	...	...	...	...
46 Spiritus asper	sh	...	...	ष	𐬴	𐭱	...	...	...	sh
47 " lenis	zh	...	...	...	...	...	...	...	...	...
Labiales.										
48 Tenuis	p	...	...	प	𐬞	𐭯	پ	...	פּ	p
49 " aspirata	ph	...	...	फ	...	...	...	...	פ	ph
50 Media	b	...	...	ब	𐬠	𐭡	ب	ب	בּ	...
51 " aspirata	bh	...	...	भ	...	...	...	...	ב	...
52 Tenuissima	...	*p*	...	...	...	...	...	...	...	...
53 Nasalis	m	...	...	म	𐬨	𐭬	م	م	מ	m
54 Semivocalis	w	...	...	...	𐬎	...	...	...	...	w
55 " aspirata	hw	...	...	...	...	...	...	...	...	...
56 Spiritus asper	f	...	...	...	𐬟	𐭯	ف	ف	...	f
57 " lenis	v	...	...	व	𐬬	ا,𐭥	و	و	ו	...
58 Anusvâra	...	*m*	...	सं	𐬅 ã	...	...	...	...	...
59 Visarga	...	*h*	...	सः	...	...	...	...	...	...

VOWELS.	MISSIONARY ALPHABET. I Class.	II Class.	III Class.	Sanskrit.	Zend.	Pehlevi.	Persian.	Arabic.	Hebrew.	Chinese.
1 Neutralis	0	...	...	...	...	...	...	...	ֲ	ă
2 Laryngo-palatalis	ĕ	...	...	...	...	...	...	...	...	...
3 „ labialis	ŏ	...	...	...	...	׀ fin.	...	...	...	...
4 Gutturalis brevis	a	...	...	अ	𐬀	𐭠 init.	َ	َ	ַ	a
5 „ longa	â	(a)	...	आ	𐬁	𐭠	ـَا	ـَا	ָ	â
6 Palatalis brevis	i	...	...	इ	𐬌	...	ِ	ِ	ִ	i
7 „ longa	î	(i)	...	ई	𐬍	𐭩	ـِي	ـِي	ִי	î
8 Dentalis brevis	li	...	...	ऌ	...	...	...	...	...	...
9 „ longa	lî	...	...	ॡ	...	...	...	...	...	...
10 Lingualis brevis	ri	...	...	ऋ	...	...	...	...	...	...
11 „ longa	rî	...	...	ॠ	...	...	...	...	...	...
12 Labialis brevis	u	...	...	उ	𐬎	...	ُ	ُ	ֻ	u
13 „ longa	û	(u)	...	ऊ	𐬏	𐭥	ـُو	ـُو	וּ	û
14 Gutturo-palatalis brevis	e	...	...	...	𐬆(e) 𐬇(e)	...	...	...	ֶ	e
15 „ longa	ê (ai)	(e)	...	ए	𐬉, 𐬊	𐭩	...	...	ֵ	ê
16 Diphthongus gutturo-palatalis	âi	(ai)	...	ऐ	...	...	ـَيْ	ـَيْ	...	âi
17 „ „	ei (ĕi)	...	...	...	...	...	...	...	...	ei, êi
18 „ „	oi (ŏu)	...	...	...	...	...	...	...	...	...
19 Gutturo-labialis brevis	o	...	...	...	𐬋	...	...	...	ָ	o
20 „ longa	ô (au)	(o)	...	ओ	𐬌	𐭥	...	...	וֹ	...
21 Diphthongus gutturo-labialis	âu	(au)	...	औ	𐬄 (au)	...	ـَوْ	ـَوْ	...	âu
22 „ „	eu (ĕu)	...	...	...	...	...	...	...	...	...
23 „ „	ou (ŏu)	...	...	...	...	...	...	...	...	...
24 Gutturalis fracta	ä	...	...	...	...	...	...	...	...	...
25 Palatalis fracta	ï	...	...	...	...	...	...	...	...	...
26 Labialis fracta	ü	...	...	...	...	...	...	...	...	ü
27 Gutturo-labialis fracta	ö	...	...	...	...	...	...	...	...	...